# Psychodrama in Counselling, Coaching and Education

Volume 4

The series situates psychodrama studies and research in Asia and beyond in a global context. It provides a unique and innovative resource for the latest developments in the field, nurturing a comprehensive and encompassing publication venue for humanistic psychodrama and sociodrama in therapy and coaching. The series publishes peer-reviewed volumes related to therapy, psychotherapy, counselling, coaching, HRD, team development and education including training. The series reflects on cultural creativity and new developments beyond J L Moreno in the second century of the existence of Psychodrama. The editor, with the assistance of distinguished scholars from Asia and elsewhere specializing in a variety of disciplinary and thematic areas, welcomes proposals that are related to the above-mentioned wide-ranging psychodrama studies. The series promotes the understanding of psychodramatic tools which are relevant in education, coaching, and team development. The series will appeal to researchers, clinicians/practitioners, and graduate students in the behavioral, social, medical, psychological and MBA sciences as well as leaders in Education, Corporate world and politics. It accepts monographs, edited volumes, and textbooks.

Reinhard T. Krüger

# Disorder-Specific Psychodrama Therapy in Theory and Practice

Springer

Reinhard T. Krüger
Burgwedel, Niedersachsen, Germany

ISSN 2662-5490 ISSN 2662-5504 (electronic)
Psychodrama in Counselling, Coaching and Education
ISBN 978-981-99-7507-5 ISBN 978-981-99-7508-2 (eBook)
https://doi.org/10.1007/978-981-99-7508-2



This Springer imprint is published by the registered company Springer Nature Singapore Pte Ltd.
The registered company address is: 152 Beach Road, #21-01/04 Gateway East, Singapore 189721, Singapore

Paper in this product is recyclable.

# Series Preface

We are pleased to continue this Springer Nature psychodrama book series titled, *Psychodrama in Counselling, Coaching and Education* founded by Jochen Becker-Ebel, Germany, and acting series editors: Scott Giacomucci, US, and Heloisa Fleury, Brazil.

This volume is the fourth book of the series, *Disorder-specific Psychodrama Therapy in Theory and Practice* by Reinhard T. Krüger, Germany.

After decades of research, practice, and experience as a psychodrama training director at the Moreno Institute in Überlingen, the author has combined his expansive knowledge in this valuable guide for practitioners and justified the psychodramatic method theoretically. The author, Dr. Reinhard T. Krüger, is a German psychotherapist and psychiatrist with an MD.

Shama Parkhe did an extraordinary job translating this book. She is not only a qualified translator, but a CP in psychodrama, therapeutic community practitioner, relational psychotherapist, and group analyst. The translation was organized and supported by Vedadrama India Pvt. Ltd.

The previous three books in this series are:

- *Experiential Therapy from Trauma to Post-traumatic Growth: Therapeutic Spiral Model Psychodrama* by Kate Hudgins and Steven Durost. This volume offers an updated and comprehensive presentation of the Therapeutic Spiral Model of psychodrama for trauma treatment.
- *Psychodrama in Brazil,* edited by Heloisa Junqueira Fleury, Marlene Magnabosco Marra, and Oriana Hadler. The editors and contributing authors articulate the rich practice wisdom of psychodrama in Brazil including content on history, culture, diverse clinical contexts, work with various vulnerable populations, and psychodrama within politics and society.
- The first book in the series, *Social Work, Sociometry, and Psychodrama* by Scott Giacomucci, provides a comprehensive integration of sociometry and psychodrama into the social work field. As an open-access book, it has been accessed 300,000 times already.

We also look forward to introducing future books in this series soon.

The series situates psychodrama practice and research in Asia, the USA, South America, and beyond in a global context. It provides a unique and innovative resource for the latest developments in the field, nurturing a comprehensive and encompassing publication venue for humanistic psychodrama and sociodrama in therapy, coaching, education, and communities. The series publishes peer-reviewed volumes related to therapy, psychotherapy, counselling, coaching, Human Resource Development, organizational dynamics, education, and training. This series will annually publish two monographs, edited volumes, and/or textbooks.

The rich tradition of Dr. Moreno's methods, including sociometry, psychodrama, and sociodrama, has been primarily disseminated through private post-graduate training institutes over the past 100 years of its existence. This academic book series brings the creativity and innovation of these experiential approaches more fully into academia with publications included in academic databases freely accessible to thousands of individual students, researchers, and professors.

The series reflects on cultural creativity and new developments beyond Dr. Jacob L. Moreno in the second century of the existence of Psychodrama. The editors, with the assistance of distinguished scholars from Brazil, Germany, Indonesia, India, Taiwan, Turkey, and USA specializing in a variety of disciplinary and thematic areas, welcome proposals that are related to the above-mentioned wide-ranging psychodrama studies. Books in this series will also emphasize the unique histories and methodologies emerging in international psychodrama communities. The platform created by this series highlights psychodrama practice wisdom from around the world in the English language, making it more accessible to a wide audience. Additionally, this book series includes books that systematically integrate psychodrama philosophy and practice into other established fields of group psychotherapy, social work, counselling, psychology, coaching, trauma theory, education, and organizational development.

The series promotes the understanding of psychodramatic and sociometric tools which are relevant for counsellors, supervisors, trainers, educators, creative arts therapists, group workers, and community or organizational leaders. The series will appeal to researchers, practitioners, and graduate students in the behavioral, social, medical, psychological, and business sciences as well as leaders in education, the corporate world, and politics.

As series editors, we would like to extend our gratitude to Springer Nature, Mrs. Satvinder Kaur, New Delhi, and her team, for believing in the creativity and strength of psychodrama. This series will serve to promote the methods of sociometry and psychodrama in multidisciplinary contexts to ultimately enhance the provision of social services, psychotherapy, education, scholarship, and research throughout the world.

Philadelphia, USA — Scott Giacomucci
Sao Paulo, Brazil — Heloisa Junqueira Fleury
December 2023

# Foreword

During the last half of the century, the use of psychodrama has spread all over the world. A great deal has been done to teach this method and to give people a chance to experience it in action. But since most directors are not committed to the written word, not enough has been done in conceptualizing this practice. Until psychodrama directors start to describe in detail what they do and formulate the theory on which their approach is based, they will not be able to demonstrate its value to the fullest.

Still, there are a lot of fine books about the practice of psychodrama out there. What makes this new book so special? I can think of two reasons. Firstly, this book focuses on the application of psychodramatic techniques to specific mental disorders, and secondly, it emphasizes the importance of creative mentalizing activities within the therapeutic process. These two aspects make this comprehensive book both unique and innovative. It is a long-awaited contribution to the literature on psychodrama that I hope will widen the acceptance of psychodrama as a viable alternative psychotherapy method within psychiatry and psychotherapy.

Even though psychodrama originated as a therapeutic method for alleviating mental suffering, it is not used widely in clinical settings today. One reason for this may be that psychodramatists have committed a relatively small proportion of their scientific literature to the analysis of the mechanisms by which psychodrama therapy achieves its well-known therapeutic effects. Many procedures of psychodrama therapy have been described. Yet these procedures have not yet been embedded in an inherently systematic, comprehensive theory of psychodrama techniques, nor have their specific individual effects been associated with the various mental disorders known to us. That is why it has been difficult for psychodramatists to establish whether patients are suited to psychodrama therapy and to identify the indication for a particular psychodramatic approach. For the same reasons, comparing the outcome of psychodrama therapy with other research and treatment methods has also been challenging. This book now closes this gap in psychodrama literature. It establishes a connection between the diagnostic categorization of patients and specific psychodramatic approaches. By illustrating this connection, this book can help to introduce our knowledge of the unique therapeutic possibilities presented by psychodrama into the science of mental health and the process of knowledge accumulation in cooperation with institutions. At the same time, this book makes it easier for psychodramatists to adopt new knowledge from other fields of psychiatry and psychotherapy and integrate it into their psychodrama therapy work.

The present work makes a tremendous contribution to explaining the therapeutic value of psychodramatic work with the inner relationship images and the mentalizing processes of people. Moreno wrote: "Psychodrama is a way to change the world in the here and now using the fundamental rules of imagination without falling into the abyss of illusion, hallucination, and delusion" (J. L. Moreno "Magic Charter of Psychodrama", 1972). As an image-based method, psychodrama focuses on the ability of human beings to create a symbolic representation of the inner world which is continuously manifested in our dreams and play. The concept of 'as-if' has a central place in the methodology and philosophy of psychodrama. Its use of role-playing, auxiliary egos, the stage, warm-up exercises, props, and deliberate distortion of time and place is based on the mentalization ability of the protagonist. Role-playing encourages participants to re-enact situations from the past 'as-if' these events were happening in the present. Participants relate to inanimate objects 'as-if' these were alive, and they talk to other group members 'as-if' they were old acquaintances or significant persons from their lives. But there is a need to explain how such intentional activities within psychodrama help to move the therapeutic process forward. The present book improves our understanding of how such techniques may be applied to various clients, all of whom may not easily enter the imaginative 'as-if' world.

Ever since my first personal experience of psychodrama, I have been impressed by the quick process in which the initial 'as-if' quality of role-playing is transformed into a genuine sense of emotional relief. But even more powerful was the feeling that such abreaction of pent-up tension was often accompanied by a kind of empowerment, a sense of having uncovered a secret, and a feeling that "now I can be as I am".

When I later observed talented psychodrama therapists at work, I was amazed. Their sensitivity, intuitive skill, and creative use of dramatic art were extraordinary. It looked almost magical, I felt. But they said: "No. It can be learned. You can also learn it!" And so my arduous training began. After many years, however, I still had many questions about how it worked and what each concept meant. I tried to read Moreno's books and discussed the various therapeutic aspects of psychodrama for many hours with Zerka Moreno. Slowly, I wrote about one or the other aspect to clarify what was happening during a psychodramatic session. One of my conclusions was that psychodrama seemed especially effective for people who had experienced a specific trauma. But I also observed that psychodrama might not always help everyone in the same way. While psychodrama may be suitable for many people at various points in their life, some cannot enter into the imaginative world of role-playing or have great difficulties doing so. As a result, I feel there is a need to continue to study and investigate psychodrama.

In this context, the present book is a step in the right direction. It brings a fresh understanding to the art of psychodrama by an author with significant experience in psychodrama therapy. This volume creates a sounder conceptual basis for one's actions in psychodrama therapy and will inspire new discussions of Moreno's contribution to the development process of psychotherapy.

Israel, Amcha Peter Felix Kellermann

# Foreword of the Second Edition German Language

Reinhard T. Krüger's book *Disorder-Specific Psychodrama Therapy: Theory and Practice* by Vandenhoeck & Ruprecht is now in its second edition. This book is a stroke of luck in many ways. It is impressive not only because of the extensive psychotherapeutic experience that the author has gained in more than 40 years of psychiatric practice. This experience is also felt in the psychodramatic case descriptions with which he illustrates his theoretical considerations. A significant new addition is Krüger's integration of the psychoanalytic *mentalization* theory into an understanding of psychodrama. He describes the psychodramatic play as a *process of mentalization*. This process starts from the direct identification of the protagonist with what he experiences in the play through several differentiated intermediate steps in psychodrama to a level of reflection. This process enables a new perspective of reality and new ways of acting. In doing so, this book has given psychodrama, which was mainly based on *Moreno's role theory* up until now, a new theoretical basis. This makes the psychodramatic action methods compatible with other psychotherapeutic approaches.

According to Fonagy, a well-known British psychoanalyst, *mentalization* is the human ability to understand interpersonal behavior in terms of *mental states*. In this way, the individual not only answers the question of *what* the other person or he himself is doing but also *how and why*. This is only possible under the prerequisite that the person concerned distances himself from his actual experience to such an extent that it is eventually possible to *reflect* on his experience. This is not as obvious as it might sound. Up to the age of about 3, children consider their internal experience of the world to be the actual reality. The child's experience, therefore, changes externally from situation to situation without the child being able to establish a connection between the associated internal states of experience. In the further course of development, however, the difference between wishes and reality grows increasingly. As a result, the child's play gains its typical *as-if quality* ('I act as if I am a police officer. But I am not'). At the age of about 4, it finally becomes possible to represent these different experiences psychologically. In a further mentalization step, the child finally thinks about them reflexively.

The psychodrama play is designed on the basis of this same pattern. Here, too, the protagonist is initially fully identified with his inner experience. The processing of the play using psychodramatic methods such as setting up the scene, doubling, role-playing, changing roles, changing scenes, role feedback, identification feedback, and sharing enables the gradual mentalization of what has been experienced. This allows those affected to view the contrived experiences from a different perspective.

But that's not all. The shift in attention from role theory to the mentalization of the patient also makes it possible to understand the patient's structural disorders, which provide information about the extent of the patient's ego integration. Today, one will no longer confront a patient with their inner conflicts in psychoanalytic therapy if they are not yet able to recognize them as belonging to him or herself. Similarly, in psychodramatic play, one wouldn't confront the patient with situations he is not yet able to cope with internally, as the enacted situations would only have a re-traumatizing effect. The *disorder-specific psychodrama therapy* that Reinhard T. Krüger develops in this book considers this requirement. One example of this is the recommended way of dealing with traumatized patients. With the help of the psychodrama play, they must first acquire the necessary inner stability before they can carefully approach the traumatic situation. Another example is the recommended way of dealing with the patient's self-injurious behavior, which can briefly give a pleasurable feeling of liberation in crises, but at the cost of a lasting adverse effect in real life. The symbolization of the dysfunctional inner processes with additional chairs makes it possible for the patient to recognize them as dysfunctional, perhaps for the first time, and to develop an awareness of dysfunctional self-regulation.

I am a psychoanalyst as well as a psychodrama therapist. In addition to my work as a psychoanalyst, I have also worked with psychodramatic groups in the course of my professional career. I did this out of the joy of understanding the latent scene that gets enacted in psychoanalysis in the therapeutic relationship between the analyst and the patient. I wanted to understand it as a psychodramatist through the actual setting up of the scene in the psychodramatic play and not just through the exploration of one's countertransference. The different experiences I gained in this way have enriched me in many ways. And yet, while reading this book, I have learned some things I would not want to miss in my wealth of experience.

I wish that the readers of this book will have a similar experience when they read it.

Hannover, Germany Christa Rohde-Dachser

# Preface

My patients, through our human encounters and their therapeutic processes, have helped me to recognize how healing takes place in psychodrama therapy. For this, I am incredibly grateful to them. In the case studies in this book, stemming from forty years of psychiatric-psychotherapeutic practice, I have changed the names and some of the facts to preserve the patients' anonymity. I have asked many of them for permission to publish my account of their process.

Beginning in 1971, I learned the *intuition-guided*, process-oriented style of directing from Grete Leutz. From Heike Straub I received important impulses for the *therapeutic* application of psychodrama. Karl Peter Kisker taught me, as a psychiatrist, to think and work with the person, not the symptom, in my encounters with patients. Karlfried Graf Dürckheim helped me, with his existential psychological work, to recognize that healing is more than merely the sum of the individual mechanisms that lead to healing (Krüger, 1997, p. 11 f.). Many thoughts about the content of this book arose in discussions with participants and co-directors in training seminars and with psychodrama friends, and in recent years in the training seminars in Budapest that took place as a result of the cooperation with Teodóra Tomcsányi. My 40 years of work with the Moreno-Institut Überlingen and my 25 years of editorial work in both the *Psychodrama* magazine and the *Zeitschrift für Psychodrama und Soziometrie* (Magazine for psychodrama and sociometry), currently being published by Christian Stadler and Sabine Spitzer, have allowed me to pose questions and find answers. Stefan Gunkel collaborated with me on Chaps. 1–3 and 5, and other chapters were contributed to by Gudrun Beckmann, Hans Benzinger, Günter Büchner, Krisztina Czáky-Pallavicini, Birgit Koerdt-Brüning, Annelie Kolbe-Krüger, Volker Kollenbaum, Zsuzsa Marlok, Anne Möhring, Marén Möhring, Cameron Paul, Alfons Rothfeld, Gudrun Runge, Zsófia Sáfrán, Kristina Scheuffgen, Ingrid Sturm, Gábor Török, Gunhild Warbende, Kurt Weber, Stefan Woinoff, and Birgit Zilch-Purucker. I thank Günter Barke for the production of the illustrations.

In the interest of gender equality in the terminology and to preserve the readability of this book, the individual chapters refer either to a female therapist and a male patient or a male therapist and a female patient.

The first edition of this book was published in 2015, and a second revised edition in 2020 by Verlag Vandenhoeck & Ruprecht in Göttingen. I thank Günter Presting and Ulrike Rastin for their immense help with the publication. The book has since been translated into Hungarian (2017, Budapest: L'Harmattan) and Russian (2017, Moscow: KLAAS). The second edition of the German text has been largely updated and supplemented for the English translation. I am very grateful to Shama Parkhe and Jochen Becker for their great help in organizing and translating this book. It was a joint marathon and adventure over five years, where we could only reach the goal together.

Burgwedel, Germany — Dr. Reinhard T. Krüger

## Reference

Krüger, R. T. (1997). *Kreative Interaktion. Tiefenpsychologische Theorie und Methoden des klassischen Psychodramas*. Vandenhoeck & Ruprecht.

# Contents


1 **What is Psychodrama?** ..... 1
References ..... 5

2 **Mentalization-Oriented Metacognitive Theory of Psychodrama** ..... 7
2.1 The Creative Process as the Basis of Life ..... 7
2.1.1 The Structural Aspect of the Process of Self-organization ..... 10
2.1.2 The Process of Energetic Exchange ..... 10
2.1.3 The Aspect of Action in Creative Processes ..... 11
2.1.4 The Functional Aspect ..... 12
2.2 The Creative Process of Mentalizing and Its Management via Intuition ..... 12
2.3 The Interrelationship Circuit Between the Tools of Mentalizing and the Eight Core Psychodrama Techniques ..... 15
2.4 Defenses, Spontaneity, and the Resolution of Different Types of Defenses Using Psychodrama Techniques ..... 19
2.4.1 Disturbances in Internally Representing the Conflict System ..... 20
2.4.2 Disturbances in Inner Interacting ..... 24
2.4.3 Disturbances in Internal Rehearsing ..... 29
2.4.4 Disturbances in Internal Integrating ..... 33
2.5 The Attunement and Agreement Process Between the Patient and the Therapist During Psychodramatic Play ..... 39
2.6 Developing the Modes of Mentalization ..... 42
2.7 The Neurophysiological Foundations of Psychodramatic Play ..... 48
2.8 The Diagnostic Psychodramatic Conversation ..... 52
2.9 Psychodramatic Self-Supervision and Supervision ..... 55

2.10 Disturbances in the Therapeutic Relationship, Transference, Countertransference, and Resistance ........... 65
2.11 Group Dynamics, Transference, Countertransference, and Resistance in Group Psychotherapy .................... 69
2.12 The Implications of Mentalization-Oriented Theory for Psychodramatic Work ................................ 76
2.12.1 Psychodrama is More Than a Method of Group Therapy; It is a Form of Psychotherapy ........... 76
2.12.2 The Interrelationship Circuit Between the Patients' Mentalizing and Their Psychodramatic Play Must not Be Interrupted ....... 77
2.12.3 The Use of Psychodrama Techniques Becomes Easier ........................................ 78
2.12.4 The Therapist Thinks in a Systemic and Process-Oriented Manner .................... 80
2.12.5 The Group is to Be Understood as a Self-organizing System ...................... 81
2.12.6 The Mentalization-Oriented Theory Strengthens the Effects of Psychodrama Therapy and Counseling ........................ 81
2.13 Comparison Between the Self-Image-Focused and System-Focused Style of Directing Groups .............. 83
2.14 Similarities and Differences Between Mentalization-Orientated Theory and Other Theories of Psychodrama Therapy ........................ 83
References ................................................ 94

**3 The Pathogenesis of Mental Illnesses, Diagnostics, and Therapy Planning** .......................................... 101
3.1 Symptom-Based Diagnosis and Process-Based Diagnosis ..... 101
3.2 The Disturbances in Mentalization and the Resulting Conflicts ............................................ 102
3.3 Diagnosis and Planning in Counseling ..................... 104
References ................................................ 108

**4 Personality Disorders, Narcissism and Borderline-Organization** ................................ 111
4.1 What Are Personality Disorders? .......................... 111
4.2 Particularities in the Treatment of People with Personality Disorders ............................................ 112
4.3 Particularities in the Treatment of People with Borderline Personality Disorder .................................. 117
4.4 Structural Disorder as a Fundamental Problem and Additional Diagnosis for People with Personality Disorders ............................................ 120
4.5 An Overview of the Different Steps of Treatment ........... 123

4.6 Doppelganger Technique in a 'Normal' Psychodramatic Play ... 126
4.7 Representing the Working of the Ego-States Using Chairs ... 130
4.8 Psychodramatic Approach to the Dominant Defense Pattern ... 140
4.9 Resolution of Defenses Through Splitting in People with Borderline Personality Disorder ... 149
4.10 Resolving the Fixation in a Whole Defense System ... 154
4.11 What Can Psychodrama Offer to Schema Therapy? ... 160
4.12 Integrating Inner Change into Inner Relationships' Images ... 163
4.13 Self-Development of Therapist and Psychodramatic Responding ... 166
4.14 Disturbances in the Therapeutic Relationship and Negative Therapeutic Reaction ... 174
References ... 178

**5 Trauma-Related Disorders** ... 181
5.1 What is Special About Trauma Therapy? ... 181
5.2 Definitions of a Trauma-Related Disorder and a Traumatizing Situation ... 183
5.3 Symptoms of Trauma-Related Disorders ... 185
5.4 Dissociation as a Central Characteristic of Trauma-Related Disorders ... 186
5.5 The Therapist Witnesses the Traumatization and the Dissociating ... 188
5.6 The Seven Phases of Psychodramatic Trauma Therapy ... 191
5.7 Trauma-Specific Diagnosis ... 192
5.8 The Initiation of Trauma Therapy ... 196
5.9 Self-Stabilization and Associated Techniques ... 202
5.10 Trauma Processing ... 207
5.10.1 Processing Trauma Experience Through Acting into a Coherent Story ... 207
5.10.2 The Four Functional Workspaces for Trauma Processing ... 209
5.10.3 Trauma Processing with the Help of Auxiliary Therapists ... 213
5.10.4 The Information and Control Space ... 214
5.10.5 The Safe Place ... 216
5.10.6 The Observation and Narration Room ... 221
5.10.7 The Interaction Room Between the Victim and the Perpetrator ... 223
5.10.8 Processing the Reaction to the Trauma Processing Session ... 225
5.10.9 The Contraindication of Reversing Roles with the Perpetrator ... 226

5.10.10 Trauma Processing Using the Table Stage in Individual Therapy ... 228
5.10.11 Trauma Processing in Group Therapy ... 230
5.11 Integrating Inner Change into Everyday Relationships ... 231
5.12 Secondary Traumatization ... 234
5.13 The Natural Self-Healing System in Humans ... 238
5.14 Coping Fairy Tales as a Technique for Trauma Processing ... 239
5.15 The Shaping of the Therapeutic Relationship ... 243
5.16 Secondary Trauma and Burnout in Therapists ... 247
5.17 Concepts of Psychodramatic Trauma Therapy by Other Psychodramatists ... 249
5.17.1 Peter Felix Kellermann (2000, pp. 23–40): The Therapeutic Aspects of Psychodrama with Traumatized People ... 250
5.17.2 Marcia Karp (2000, pp. 63–82): Psychodrama of Rape and Torture: A Sixteen-Year Follow-Up Case Study ... 252
5.17.3 Eva Roine (2000, pp. 83–96): The Use of Psychodrama with Trauma Victims ... 253
5.17.4 Anne Bannister (2000, pp. 97–113): Prisoners of the Family: Psychodrama with Abused Children ... 254
5.17.5 Clark Baim (2000, pp. 155–175): Time's Distorted Mirror: Trauma Work with Adult Male Sex Offenders ... 255
5.17.6 Jörg Burmeister (2000, pp. 198–225): Psychodrama with Survivors of Traffic Accidents ... 257
References ... 258

**6 Anxiety Disorders** ... 263
6.1 The Social Conditions of Fear ... 263
6.2 What Are Anxiety Disorders? ... 265
6.3 The Self-Protective Behavior in Patients with Panic Attacks as an Obstacle in Therapy ... 270
6.4 Initiation of Treatment in Patients with Panic Attacks ... 272
6.5 The Different Steps in Metacognitive Therapy for People with Panic Attacks ... 279
6.6 The Disorder-Specific Therapy of a Patient with Social Phobia ... 281
6.7 Crisis Intervention for Performance Anxiety ... 287
6.8 Other Psychodramatic Approaches in the Therapy of Anxiety Disorders ... 288
6.8.1 The Therapy of a Patient with Social Phobia by Moreno ... 288

6.8.2 The Treatment of Specific (Isolated) Phobias ....... 289
6.8.3 Other Psychodrama Therapists' Approaches to Panic Attacks ....... 291
References ....... 293

7 **Obsessive–Compulsive Disorders** ....... 295
7.1 Obsessive Thoughts, Compulsive Acts, and their Psychodynamic Function ....... 295
7.2 The Disorder-Specific Treatment of Compulsive Behaviors ....... 297
7.3 The Treatment of Obsessive Thoughts Without Compulsive Actions ....... 301
7.4 Self-stabilization and Ego-Strengthening Through Role-Playing ....... 304
References ....... 307

8 **Depressive Disorders, Masochism and Suicidale Crises** ....... 309
8.1 What is Depression? ....... 309
8.2 The Different Forms of Depression ....... 311
8.3 Therapy for Depression in Current Conflicts ....... 314
8.4 Therapy for Depression Caused by Neurotic Conflict Processing ....... 317
8.4.1 The Basic Principle of Psychodramatic Therapy for Depressed People with Neurotic Conflict Processing ....... 319
8.4.2 The Seven Steps of Psychodramatic Dialogue in Neurotic Depression ....... 322
8.4.3 The Integration of Improved Self-actualization in Relationship Images from Childhood ....... 332
8.4.4 The Therapist's Participation as a Doppelganger and an Auxiliary Ego in the Psychodramatic Dialogue ....... 335
8.4.5 Psychodramatic Group Therapy for Patients with Depression ....... 337
8.4.6 Therapy for Depression in Separation Conflicts ....... 340
8.4.7 Therapy for Prolonged Grief Reactions ....... 343
8.5 Therapy for Masochism and a Pathological Superego ....... 347
8.6 Therapy for Severe Depression Bordering on Psychosis ....... 358
8.6.1 Vicarious Mentalization in the Therapeutic Relationship ....... 359
8.6.2 The Activation of a Sense of Self-regulation in the Symptom of Suicidal Fantasies ....... 360
8.6.3 Rebuilding the Inner Fantasy Space in Everyday Life ....... 361

8.6.4 Symbolizing in Nocturnal Dreams as an Amplification for Understanding the Patient's Self-regulation in Everyday Life ....... 362
8.6.5 The Doppelganger Technique in Self-injurious Thinking ....... 363
8.6.6 The Integration of Improved Self-actualization into the Inner Relationship Images ....... 366
8.6.7 Limitations in the Therapy of People with Depression ....... 368
8.7 Treatment with Psychopharmacology ....... 370
8.8 Suicidal Crises ....... 371
8.8.1 Fundamentals of Suicidal Crises ....... 371
8.8.2 Constricted Thinking in the Pre-suicidal Syndrome ....... 371
8.8.3 Criteria for Assessing the Risk of Suicide and the Need for Therapy ....... 372
8.8.4 The Encounter with Death as a Wake-Up Call and an Impetus for a New Beginning ....... 375
8.8.5 Therapeutic Interventions in the Event of Risk of Suicide ....... 378
References ....... 382

**9 Psychotic Disorders** ....... 385
9.1 The Historical Development of the Treatment of People with Psychosis ....... 385
9.2 Blockages in the Therapeutic Relationship in Psychiatric Treatment of Psychosis ....... 388
9.3 Mentalization Disorders as the Cause of Delusional Production ....... 390
9.4 The Psychodynamics of Psychotic Decompensation ....... 393
9.5 Moreno's Secret in the Psychotherapy of Psychoses ....... 396
9.6 Moreno's Metacognitive Approach in the Psychotherapy of Psychoses ....... 398
9.7 The Transmodal Relationship with Patients Experiencing Psychosis ....... 401
9.8 Why Metacognitive Psychodrama Therapy Can Causally Stop the Delusional Production ....... 404
9.8.1 The Separation of the 'Dream Ego' from the 'Everyday Ego' Using the Two-Chair Technique ....... 407
9.8.2 The Doppelganger Dialogue in the Initial Psychotherapeutic Consultation ....... 410
9.8.3 The Doppelganger Dialogue for Crisis Intervention in Patients with Acute Psychosis ....... 413

9.8.4 Practical Implementation of the Doppelganger Dialogue ... 415
9.8.5 The Theory of the Therapeutic Effect of Doppelganger Dialogue ... 422
9.8.6 Psychopharmacological Treatment and Personal Emergency Plan ... 426
9.8.7 Collaborative Therapy Planning ... 429
9.8.8 Moreno's Auxiliary World Method in Contemporary Form ... 430
9.8.9 Application of the Auxiliary World Method to Delusions of Grandeur ... 438
9.9 Transforming a Depersonalization Process into a Creative Process of Self-direction ... 439
9.10 Healing Psychotic Disintegration of Self Through Psychodramatic Play with Hand Puppets ... 441
9.11 Moreno and Casson's Theoretical and Practical Insights ... 445
9.12 Group Psychotherapy for People with Psychosis ... 448
References ... 451

**10 Addiction Disorders** ... 455
10.1 Psychotherapy for Addiction Disorders ... 455
10.2 The Definition of Addiction and Dependence ... 457
10.3 Epidemiological Data and Treatment Statistics ... 460
10.4 Diagnosis and Addiction-Specific Symptoms ... 461
10.5 Psychodynamics of Addiction Development ... 472
10.6 The Nine Phases of Addiction Therapy ... 476
10.6.1 Awareness of Addiction, Level of Suffering, and Motivation ... 478
10.6.2 The Decision to Abstain ... 485
10.6.3 Participation in a Self-help Group ... 488
10.6.4 Working Out the Personal Rock Bottom and the Surrender ... 489
10.6.5 Relapse Prevention and the Therapeutic Approach to Relapses ... 493
10.6.6 The First Two Years of Disorder-Specific Psychotherapy ... 498
10.6.7 The Co-treatment of a Comorbid Psychological Illness ... 501
10.7 The Therapeutic Relationship and the Psychodramatic Responding ... 503
10.8 Group Therapy ... 508
10.9 Pill Addiction and Drug Addiction ... 511
10.10 Non-substance-Related Addictions ... 513
10.10.1 Psychodynamic and Therapy ... 513

10.10.2 The Ideal Addiction Scene and the Positive Function of Addictive Behavior in Self-regulation ..... 514
10.10.3 Gambling Addiction and Eating Disorders ..... 516
10.10.4 Sex and Porn Addiction ..... 519
10.10.5 Internet Gaming Disorder ..... 524
10.11 Co-dependency and Secondary Traumatization of Caregivers ..... 527
References ..... 529

**11 Pathological Deviant Behavior** ..... 533
11.1 Peculiarities in the Treatment of Persons with Pathological Deviant Behavior ..... 533
11.2 Case Example of a Patient with Fetishistic Disorder ..... 534
11.3 The Psychodynamics of Patients with Pathologically Deviant Behavior ..... 535
11.4 The Disorder-Specific Therapy of Pathological Deviant Behavior ..... 536
11.5 Developing Deviant Behavior into a Holistic Story ..... 539
11.6 Fetishistic Acts as Masochistic Behavior ..... 541
11.7 Importance of Abstinence from Deviant Behavior for Inner Mental Transformation ..... 543
References ..... 544

**Bibliography** ..... 547

**Author Index** ..... 549

**Subject Index** ..... 553

# Chapter 1
# What is Psychodrama?

Jacob Levy Moreno (1889–1974), who developed Sociometry and psychodrama, emigrated as a psychiatrist from Vienna to the USA in 1925. He is one of the founding fathers of group therapy and has been significant in promoting its development in the USA from 1931 onward. According to Moreno, group therapy is not to be equated with psychodrama (Moreno, 1959, p. 69 f.). Instead, he understood "group therapy" to be "simply" a group process in which "the immediate and sole focus is on the psychological health of the group and its members" (Moreno, 1959, p. 53). With this in mind, Moreno worked with existing groups in social institutions such as schools, dormitories, and prisons from 1932 onward. He supervised the employees there, provided organizational consultation, and worked sociotherapeutically using sociometric methods (Moreno, 1974) and role-plays.

In 1936 he founded a small psychiatric clinic in Beacon/New York. At that time, psychotherapy was still in the early stages of its development worldwide. In his 12-bed sanatorium, Moreno treated his mentally ill patients based on the fundamental principles of a therapeutic community. He integrated into the treatment of his patients his earlier experiences of role-playing with children and improvisational theater with adults in Vienna (Moreno, 1970), as well as his insights from his work in social institutions in the USA.

As a psychotherapist, Moreno treated his patients primarily in an individual setting (Straub, 2010, p. 28) (see Sect. 2.6.1) and used role-plays. He let patients develop their own roles or those of others on stage, initially without any role reversal (Moreno, 1945, p. 11 ff.; 1959, p. 221 ff.). Assisting therapists supported the patients as auxiliary egos in the various complementary roles. It was not until later that Moreno (1959, p. 210) integrated role reversal between the protagonist and an auxiliary into his therapeutic work. That was the birth hour of psychodrama as a psychotherapy method as we know it today.

The psychodrama psychotherapy described in this book is based on the concept of the creative human.



R. T. Krüger, *Disorder-Specific Psychodrama Therapy in Theory and Practice*,
Psychodrama in Counselling, Coaching and Education 4,
https://doi.org/10.1007/978-981-99-7508-2_1

**Important definition**

The *concept of the creative human* is based on understanding humans as living beings who are constantly adapting to external living conditions. However, in doing so, humans have to maintain their own complex structures in order to be not adversely affected. For this purpose, humans use an internal creative process of self-development. This includes the systemic development of internal self-image and internal object image in the current external situation. These development processes control their external behavior in the current situation. Humans perform these processes of self-development through mentalizing. As a result, they become an *actor* in their own internal conflict processing.

This view of the creative human ascribes "great importance to the self-regulating processes on all levels of human living and experience" (Kriz, 2012, p. 318). It sees humans as "systemically organized holistic structures" (Kriz, 2014, p. 128 ff.). Psychodrama accomplishes this mentalizing in the as-if mode of play. In this way, psychodrama therapy proves to be a method of humanistic psychotherapy (Kriz, 2012). Psychodrama therapists do not find *suitable approaches* for their *current practical work* with their patients in books. Instead, they find the appropriate psychodrama technique within themselves *as the patient's implicit doppelganger*. They playfully identify with the patient *as an implicit doppelganger* and want to 'understand *themselves*'. They want to find an appropriate solution in 'their own' conflict on the patient's behalf and therefore use the appropriate psychodrama technique in the patient's play (see Sect. 2.5).

**Central idea**

Psychodrama promotes the *internal* self-development of humans in *external* conflicts. Therefore, a theory of psychodrama is also a theory of self-development of humans applicable across all psychotherapy methods.

*All* psychotherapy methods try to understand persons in psychological distress and to jointly work on finding solutions to their conflicts. Therefore, there are similarities in the thinking and the approaches between various psychotherapy methods. For example, mentalization-oriented psychodrama therapy (see Sect. 2.2) also incorporates depth psychology, behavioral, systemic, and transpersonal therapy.

1. The psychodrama therapist uses, for example, *depth psychological concepts* when she connects and justifies currently inappropriate behavior or an inappropriate affect with difficult childhood experiences through scene change. She uses the concepts of transference, countertransference, and resistance when dealing with disturbances in the therapeutic relationship (see Sect. 2.7). But the psychodrama therapist also thinks systemically in mentalization-oriented psychodrama therapy.
2. The therapist helps the patient to further develop his inner self-image and object image *through role reversal* and, thus, dissolve blockades in internal conflict processing. In doing so, she views the patient's conflicts (see Sects. 8.4.1–8.4.7) and the therapeutic relationship (see Sect. 2.7) *systemically* (see Sect. 2.4.3).
3. Elements of behavioral therapy can also be of value. Once the patient understands his old ways of dysfunctional self-regulation, he practices discarding the old way and looking for new, more appropriate behavioral opportunities depending on

the situation. In the therapy of persons diagnosed with personality disorders, the therapist changes metacognitive processes through psychodramatic chair work, similar to the work in schema therapy (see Sects. 4.7–4.11). For example, she represents the patient's self-censorship with a chair symbolizing his 'inner blind soul killer'. The patient should symbolize it with a hand puppet and lock him up in a cupboard at home. He is supposed to look at it once daily and write down a list of his sadistic superego's statements. *Over time*, this helps him notice the 'soul killer' actions quicker.

4. Many psychodramatists also make use of transpersonal psychological knowledge. For example, the therapist actively recognizes and supports the patient's passage through initiatory experiences (Dürckheim, 1984, p. 39 f.). These are profound inner changes that can occur when passing through one of the primary fears of man: the fear of death, the fear of absolute loneliness, the fear of becoming crazy, or the fear of absolute emptiness (see Sects. 5.9, 5.10.5, 5.13, 5.14, 8.8, 9.5 and 10.7). The passage through these basic fears can evoke a feeling of the specialness of life, the experience of security in extraordinary love, the knowledge of greater meaning, or the experience of the fullness of being.

Depending on the current situation, the therapist in mentalization-oriented psychodrama therapy focuses her practical psychodramatic work on.

1. the patient's cognitive thought content
2. the metacognitive processes of mentalizing
3. the individual identity of the patient
4. his systemic identity
5. his social identity or
6. his transpersonal identity.

Figure 1.1 depicts these different focus areas as the poles of the diagram. In this way, the patient potentially develops his personal and ideal identity further. The focus of the work is not an either-or but a both-and approach. I have therefore illustrated the movements between the different focal points of the work as circles.

Over time, various schools of psychodrama have developed different focus areas in their work. Classical psychodrama, according to Moreno, works metacognitively, without really saying it (see Sect. 2.14). It promotes the concept of spontaneous and creative humans and the progressive development of individual groups and the whole society. It is often determined by transpersonal values. The mentalization-oriented, metacognitive psychodrama presented here follows the overarching concept of mentalizing. It justifies the disorder-specific application of psychodrama techniques against the background of *a holistic systematic theory*.

**Central idea**

The composer Gustav Mahler (1860–1911) once said: "Following tradition is not to preserve the ashes, but to pass on the flame." The mentalization-oriented theory in psychodrama helps preserve Moreno's passion and pass it on. However, mere admiration of Moreno's ashes prevents us, psychodrama therapists, from being spontaneous and creative. The therapist must find and admit Moreno's creativity in herself.

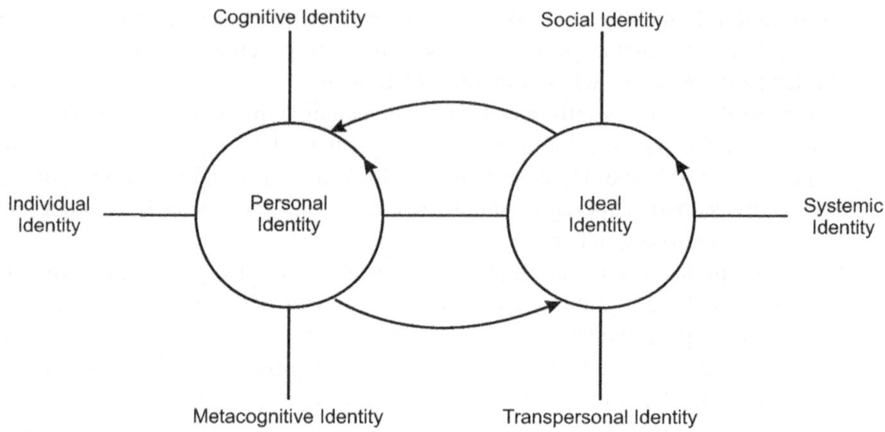


**Fig. 1.1** The focal points of therapeutic work in mentalization-oriented psychodrama

Since my first encounter with psychodrama, I have concerned myself with two questions: "How does psychodrama work?" "How does healing occur?" I came a step closer to answering these questions when I discovered the analogy between the central psychodrama techniques and the mechanisms of nocturnal dreams (Krüger, 1978, see Fig. 3 in Chap. 2, Circle C). I had a creative breakthrough in 1995, which helped me further understand the effects of psychodrama techniques (Krüger, 1997, S. 11 f.). In five months, I developed a cross-sectional theory of *metacognitive processes*. The uniqueness of psychodrama lies in the fact that the psychodrama techniques used in a play implement the internal metacognitive tools of the patient, which produce their thoughts and feelings. They release these tools from their blocked state and further develop conflict processing (see Chap. 2). Psychodramatists work directly metacognitively using psychodrama techniques.

"Metacognition" is thinking about the processes of thinking. In my understanding, the therapist works in a metacognitive manner when she, together with the patient, uses psychodrama techniques to change the metacognitive process, which creates the patient's thought contents. In doing so, she does not focus simply on the content of the patient's thoughts, for example, his feelings, the events, and his memories of his marital conflict. Together with him, she also improves the *functioning of the tools* he uses in creating these thought contents (see Sects. 2.2 and 2.7). In psychoanalysis, metacognition finds application in defense mechanisms, dream analysis, and mentalization theories. In behavioral therapy, firstly, therapists oriented themselves toward the patient's external behavior and then developed cognitive-behavioral therapy. This approach attempts to alter the contents of thinking, detect dysfunctional presuppositions and convictions, and replace them with more appropriate thought contents. In the third wave of behavioral therapy, therapists are now focusing their attention on the metacognitive processes that *create* the dysfunctional content of the client's thinking. It is, for example, the core concept in Schema therapy.

**Central idea**

The mentalization-oriented theory of psychodrama helps us understand 'what we do in Psychodrama when we do what we do' (Marineau, 2011, p. 43). This understanding leads to a flexible, metacognitive disorder-specific therapy (see Sect. 2.14). The encounter between the therapist and patient or the group becomes the starting and end point of therapy.

In this book, I first describe theoretically what we do in psychodrama when we do what we do. Then, I explain disorder-specific psychodrama methods for different illnesses based on this theoretical foundation. The mentalization-oriented theory makes it possible to apply psychodrama in individual as well as in group therapy settings (see Sect. 2.6.1).

## References


Dürckheim, K. G. (1984). *Von der Erfahrung der Transzendenz*. Herder.

Kriz, J. (2014). Einladung zu einer Begegnung. Morenos Werk aus der Sicht der Personenzentrierten Systemtheorie. *Zeitschrift für Psychodrama und Soziometrie, 13*(Suppl. 6), 121–135.

Kriz, J. (2012). Antrag der Arbeitsgemeinschaft Humanistische Psychotherapie (AGHPT) an den wissenschaftlichen Beirat Psychotherapie. *Zeitschrift Für Psychodrama Und Soziometrie, 11*(2), 311–330.

Krüger, R. T. (1978). Die Mechanismen der Traumarbeit und ihre Beziehung zu den heilenden Vorgängen im Psychodrama. *Gruppenpsychotherapie Und Gruppendynamik, 13*(2), 172–208.

Krüger, R. T. (1997). *Kreative Interaktion. Tiefenpsychologische Theorie und Methoden des klassischen Psychodramas*. Vandenhoeck and Ruprecht.

Marineau, R. F. (2011). Die Integration von Morenos Erbe. *Zeitschrift für Psychodrama und Soziometrie, 10*(1) [Supplement 3: »Psychodrama—Empirische Forschung und Wissenschaft«, herausgegeben von C. Stadler, M. Wieser, VS Verlag für Sozialwissenschaften], 35–44.

Moreno, J. L. (1945). Psychodrama and the psychopathology of inter-personal relations. Beacon, N.Y.: Beacon House.

Moreno, J. L. (1959). *Gruppenpsychotherapie und Psychodrama. Einleitung in die Theorie und Praxis*. Thieme.

Moreno, J. L. (1970). *Das Stegreiftheater* (2nd ed.). Beacon House. Original work published 1923, Gustav Kiepenheuer.

Moreno, J. L. (1974). *Die Grundlagen der Soziometrie. Wege zur Neuordnung der Gesellschaft* (3rd ed.). Westdeutscher Verlag.

Straub, H. (2010). Seit fünfzig Jahren arbeite ich mit dieser spannenden Methode. In D. Ensel, & G. Stiegler (Eds.), *Ein Stück im Himmel. Psychodramatikerinnen begegnen sich* (pp. 25–42). *Zeitschrift für Psychodrama und Soziometrie* 9 (Suppl. 2).

# Chapter 2
# Mentalization-Oriented Metacognitive Theory of Psychodrama

## 2.1 The Creative Process as the Basis of Life

All living beings have to be creative and keep making little inventions. Otherwise, they cannot survive in their constantly changing environment. The idea is to find creative solutions that preserve one's own complex structure in the process of adaptation. For example, sexuality, reproduction, culture, and the development of social and political systems are creative solutions for maintaining one's own complex structure, adapting to new environments, and ultimately even overcoming death.

A creative process always includes four consecutive phases (see Fig. 2.1): (1) First, there is a particular order with *dynamic equilibrium.* (2) An internal or external compulsion to adapt causes a conflict in the balance. In the *conflict phase,* the person or the institution concerned attempts to overcome the conflict by applying *old* familiar solutions. When the old solutions prove inadequate for the present conflict, it leads to inner conflicts, resulting in symptoms. Inappropriate old solutions in a new situation are called defenses in psychotherapy. (3) When the inner conflict increases progressively, at some point, it leads to a collapse of the old equilibrium. As a result, the individual or the institution enters a *phase of crisis and chaos* in his conflict processing. He regulates himself temporarily as per the principle of trial and error. In psychodrama, this phase of conflict processing is termed '*status nascendi*' or the '*state of spontaneity*' (Moreno, 1946/1985, p. 104, Schacht, 2009, p. 72). (4) Time and again, *new solutions* emerge spontaneously in this phase. If one of these new solutions is *positively confirmed*, externally and internally, it stabilizes. (5) The individual integrates this new solution as a new pattern in his repertoire of conflict management strategies. He develops a *new dynamic equilibrium and new order* in his mental self-organization. His inner structures thus grow in complexity (see Fig. 2.1) (Schacht, 1992, p. 100, 2003, p. 21).

**Central idea**

The sequence of the four phases of a creative process is present in all development processes, in the process of evolution, and also in natural human conflict resolution. For example, a



R. T. Krüger, *Disorder-Specific Psychodrama Therapy in Theory and Practice*, Psychodrama in Counselling, Coaching and Education 4,
https://doi.org/10.1007/978-981-99-7508-2_2

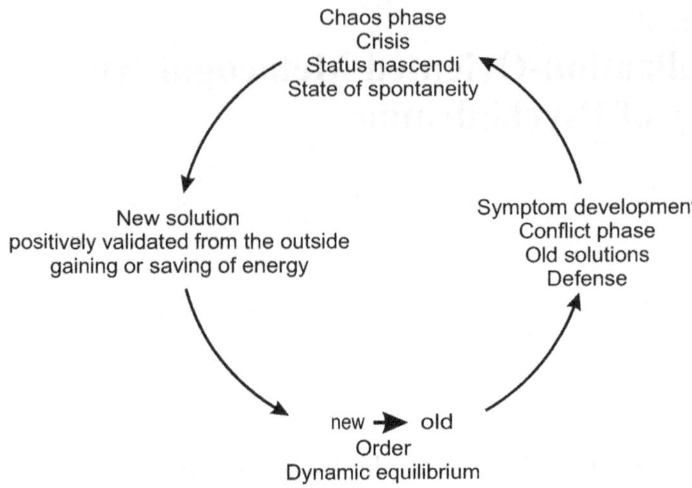


**Fig. 2.1** The four phases of a creative development process

new finch species emerged on the Galapagos Islands within 30 years. In contrast to the other finches, this one had *long* beaks. Apparently, the increasing number of birds with *short* beaks were experiencing food scarcity (conflict phase). As a result, fewer young birds per pair survived (crisis). However, there were some with longer beaks among the bird parents. They could dig deeper into the trees and soil for insects and find more food for their young ones. As a result, they had more offspring. External confirmation of the new solution (*long* beaks) led to the development of the new long-beaked finch species within 30 years. The long-beaked finches extended the dynamic balance of nature in the Galapagos Islands.

A fundamental principle of evolution is to save energy. "In evolution, what consumes less energy in reaching the same goal, survives in the long run." (Ciompi 2021, p. 182). Whoever has an advantage prevails over the others. The evolution of the nervous system was a new solution used by animals and humans to conserve energy. The ability to internally model, process and resolve conflicts in the working memory in the as-if mode replaced the high-energy-consuming method of trial and error. Successful solutions are stored in the brain's memory centers through neuronal interconnections. They are actualized and recalled in a new, similar situation with minimal energy consumption and reapplied to the current situation. We don't need to reinvent the wheel in every new situation. Inner thinking and solving conflicts in the as-if mode is now called mentalizing (see Sect. 2.2). Humans are currently dominating the development of animal and plant life because they have perfected this new solution. Saving energy in resolving conflicts has given humans an evolutionary advantage over other living beings. Humans have multiplied from 1 million to 8 billion in the last 4000 years.

However, the multiplication of humans in a relatively short time and their demand for a good life for themselves and their offspring has turned energy saving upside down compared to earlier times. For fifty years, we have been at a turning point that has never existed on Earth before. Humans are the first beings to consume excessive amounts of energy resulting in the destruction of the basis of life for humans and animals on Earth. The climate is changing rapidly because of us. Many species of living beings are already facing extinction. In the context of climate change, we are currently transitioning from *the conflict phase to the chaos phase*. We have the choice of deciding whether to continue using only *old solutions* at the beginning of the chaos phase of the current climate crisis and inevitably act more and more destructively. We continue to have more and more wants. Our demands keep getting bigger and bigger, whereas our planet's natural resources are increasingly becoming scarce. We, humans, are waging wars over increasingly scarce resources.

**Central idea**

Mere *knowledge* about the impending climate catastrophe is not enough. The pure knowledge content is *not neuronally interconnected with action sequences, physical sensations, and affect* (see Sect. 2.7) in human memory. The impending suffering of people must occur so that *we also experience it psychosomatically*. It is our psychosomatic experiences that make experiences real for us. People who swap roles with their conflict partner in psychodramatic self-supervision (see Sect. 2.9) often say afterward: "I only thought my colleague was afraid of me. But now I felt that too!" The colleague's fear becomes a reality for them only when they have felt their conflict partner's physical sensation and affect in the role reversal *in their own body*.

The increasing suffering is now gradually leading to a change of perspective and a more comprehensive view of one's life as part of humanity. In the context of the climate crisis, we are looking for *new solutions* at all levels of society that consider our planet's limited resources. It's no longer about winning or losing. The new solutions require *cooperation instead of war*. The new solutions must serve not only the interests of individuals but also the interests of the community, one's own country, *and* other countries on Earth. Moreover, they must be *systemically equitable* (see Sect. 8.4.2).

Psychodrama therapy cannot solve the climate crisis. However, it can help to link the *individual symptom formation* of patients with the climate crisis (see Fig. 2.1 above) as well as *with* current social concerns and not just with everyday conflicts and childhood deficits. This is because psychodrama can promote *cooperation* in relationships in a unique way through the instrument of role reversal (see Sects. 2.2, 2.9, and 8.4.2).

The conflict processing of human beings is a *complex* creative process. Therefore it is helpful to *distinguish between the four different aspects* of conflict processing: (1) the perspective of *structural* development, (2) the perspective of the processes of *energy* exchange, (3) the perspective of interaction in the inner structures, and (4) the perspective of the *functional* organization (Krüger, 1997, p. 24 ff.) (Fig. 2.2).

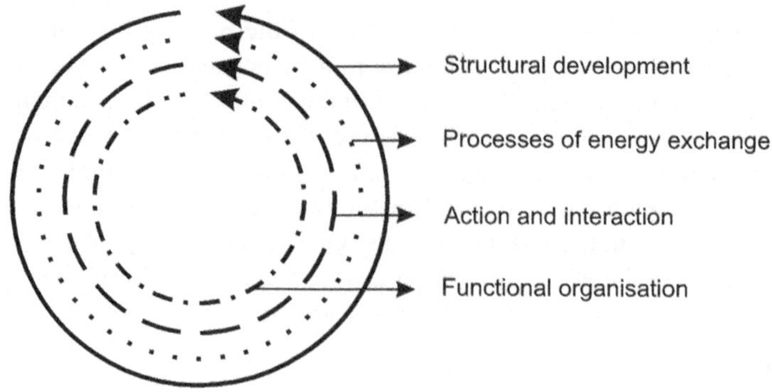


**Fig. 2.2** The four different aspects of creative conflict processing (Krüger, 1997, p. 25)

### *2.1.1 The Structural Aspect of the Process of Self-organization*

**Central idea**

The natural creative process of working through conflict differentiates and expands the internal images involved in the conflict and integrates them to form a comprehensive, meaningful structure. "All therapeutic methods introduce complexity" (Kriz, 2014, p.133).

In disorder-specific psychodrama therapy, patients with psychotic disorders, for example, 'think' through their delusional scene in the as-if mode of play (see Sect. 2.6) to form meaningful stories (see Sects. 9.8.4 and 9.8.8) with the help of dialogues with their doppelganger and the auxiliary world method. In doing so, they develop more complex structures in their conflict processing. The more complex one's inner relationship images or process structures are, the more *capable they are of dealing with conflicts.* This is because the scope and the differentiation of the spontaneous-creative processes in the inner structures grow with an increase in the complexity of the internal systems (Sabelli, 1989, p. 166 f.; Schacht, 1992, p. 127). On the other hand, a person is less capable of coping with conflicts and more likely to decompensate in times of crisis if his internal mental structures are less complex.

### *2.1.2 The Process of Energetic Exchange*

When a person is in a conflict, it causes psychophysical and emotional tensions in his internal representation of the conflict system. His mental energies center themselves on this internal representation. For example, in the event of an impending job loss, his associated thoughts, images, and feelings are energetically so charged that he may have difficulty concentrating on playing with his children at home. High energy potentials in a conflict system activate a person's holistic process of intuition and cause him to seek new solutions through mentalizing (Ciompi, 2019, S. 125). The lower the energy potential, the lower his psychological stress, and therefore the smaller the chances of him overcoming the conflict. Conversely, the 'louder' his symptoms are, the better chances he has of finding a new, more complex solution for his conflict.

In psychodrama, the theory of *energy potential* in conflicts is referred to as 'warming up' (Leutz, 1974, p. 95 ff) and '*catharsis*'. The therapist can help the group members activate the energy potential of their mentalizing *by engaging* in warming-up activities at the beginning of a therapy session. This increases the energy potential in their inner conflict systems. The energy potential in a person's conflict system is therapeutically amplified further through the therapist and the group members: (1) They see him, understand him, and accompany him in the context of *his conflict processing* in a supportive manner. (2) They double him if needed. (3) As auxiliary egos, they stimulate the creative process of his inner conflict processing in their respective complementary roles. The protagonist uses his therapeutically amplified conflict energies to activate, complete, and connect the contents of his different memory centers of acting, feeling, thinking, and perceiving (see Sect. 2.7). This increases the number of neurophysiological process structures involved in his mentalizing. High energy tension in the neuronal circuit of the memory centers can discharge through an integrative catharsis in the form of crying or laughter. Already Moreno (1959, p. 251) established: "Every pathogenic warming up process that affects a small area of the personality can be absorbed and nullified by a warming up process that has a broader scope but includes this smaller part." Moreno defined this principle as the 'warming up rule'.

### 2.1.3 The Aspect of Action in Creative Processes

The lesser a person *acts* in reality and fantasy, the less capable he is of coping with conflicts. Acting and interacting help to create connections in internal images, to understand reality in a conflict system, and differentiate this reality from fantasies and inaccurate interpretations. Schulte-Markwort once reported a longitudinal study (Schulte-Markwort, 2002, a oral communication of the Kauai longitudinal study by Werner & Smith, 2001) in which they had tried to identify criteria, as *early as infanthood*, that would enable therapists to predict how the person's mental health *would be in adulthood*. According to their findings, the *activity level of the children* was the most significant criterion: The higher the activity level of an infant was, the lesser the likelihood of them experiencing psychological difficulties later in life. This correlation can be explained by the simple fact that *one must act internally and externally* to process and overcome conflicts. People with a low activity level are at a greater risk of being traumatized by overwhelmingly stressful situations. A traumatizing situation is defined by the fact that the person concerned is not capable of fighting or fleeing in this situation and, therefore, *cannot act* (see Sect. 5.2).

### 2.1.4 The Functional Aspect

A fourth aspect of the creative process is the point of *functional* process organization. The functional process organization in human conflict processing is fulfilled by the tools of mentalization (see Sect. 2.2).

## 2.2 The Creative Process of Mentalizing and Its Management via Intuition

Living beings need to develop a creative inner process of self-development so that they can adapt to the constant changes in their environment and their own body without their highly complex structure disintegrating.

**Central idea**

The inner process of self-development in the external situation is mediated through the process of inner mentalizing. As a metacognitive process, it produces the thought content in our awareness.

It was a creative leap for me to move from the *cognitively oriented* approach to psychodrama techniques to the *metacognitive* approach (Krüger, 1978, 1997, 2015). I relearned the way conflict resolutions materialize in psychodrama.

**Central idea**

Psychodrama is mentalizing through external play in the as-if mode. It is derived from nature and, in this sense, a biological method of psychotherapy. Psychodrama works on a person's *internal* images and processes them in the as-if mode. The events *on stage* are not to be equated with *external* reality (see Sect. 2.14). Psychodrama has its roots in children's play and the theater (Leutz, 1974, p. 28 ff.). In 1795, Friedrich Schiller (2009, p. 64) said: "Man... is only fully human where he plays." From this, I derive the insight: "Man is only fully human where he mentalizes."

**Important definition**

I define mentalizing as a partly conscious and partly unconscious creative process of constructing internal reality images which helps people (1) internally follow the external interactions in the current situation and, thus, control their own actions, (2) understand themselves and others in a given situation, (3) process conflicts, (4) search for adequate or new solutions to conflicts, as well as (5) plan their actions.

Mentalization is the *result* of mentalizing; mentalizing is a process leading to this result. "Mentalizing is intrinsically linked with the development of the self, with its increasingly differentiated internal organization and its participation in human society" (Fonagy et al., 2004, p. 10 f.). Therefore, psychodramatists have their patients externalize the creative process of their mentalizing *on stage* (Buer, 1980, p. 99; Holmes, 1992; Kellermann, 1996, p. 98; Moreno, 1965, p. 212 and 1959, p. 111; Seidel, 1989, p. 197; von Ameln, 2013, p. 9) to "think" through their conflict with the help of psychodrama techniques in the as-if mode of play (see Sect. 2.4).

It is for this reason that psychodrama belongs to the group of mentalization-based treatment methods (MBT).

Its creators consider mentalizing a crucial point of reference and a concept for improving and refining therapeutic work in all psychotherapy methods (Allen et al., 2008, p. 7 f.). "We mentalize when we become aware of our own or others' mental states—for example when we think about feelings. [...] More specifically, we define mentalizing as an imaginative mental activity that lets us perceive or interpret human behavior in terms of intentional mental states" (Allen et al., 2008, p. xi). "Very often, we mentalize quickly without being aware of it. [...] Mentalizing makes it possible to understand and predict social situations as well as to modulate our own emotions" (Brockmann & Kirsch, 2010, p. 279). "Skillful mentalizing does not alone solve problems or free one from disorders; rather, it increases the concerned person's capacity to do that" (Williams et al., 2006, quoted in Allen et al., 2008, p. 7).

**Central idea**

Mentalizing is a holistic creative process involving representing, interacting, rehearsing, and integrating (see Fig. 2.3). I understand these four steps as metacognitive tools of mentalizing. Human intuition guides the work of their four tools of mentalizing. Therefore, the image of the man is the image of a *creative human* for psychodramatists.

Earlier, I used to refer to the tools of mentalizing as "*organizational functions*" of the self (Krüger, 1997, pp. 84ff). However, I now integrate my theory of organizational functions with the theory of mentalizing by Fonagy et al. (2004). This facilitates the scientific discussion and helps to further develop the mentalizing theory of Fonagy et al.

### Exercise 1

I invite you to familiarize yourself with the metacognitive tools *of your mentalizing*:

1. Think of a conflictual relationship in your private *or* work life.
2. Spend two minutes thinking about this conflict.
3. *What* conflict did you think of?

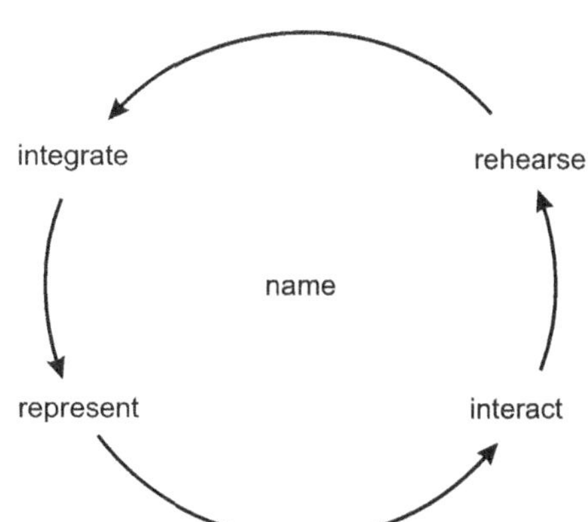


**Fig. 2.3** The four metacognitive tools of mentalizing

4. Now reflect on *how* you thought about this conflict in these two minutes.

The seminar participant, Ms. A., answered these questions: "I was thinking about the conflict with my boss in my counseling center." In doing so, she shares the content of her conflict. However, the fourth question captures the *metacognitive tools* the individual uses in mentalizing their conflict:

1. At the beginning of conflict processing, the person *represents* himself and his conflict partner as an inner image and looks at his conflict partner from his own perspective. His thoughts about the conflict thus contribute to his inner perception. He takes note of who and what belongs to the conflict picture. In the case of patients with severe structural disturbances or patients suffering from psychosis, the inner representation of the conflict is often already distorted. For example, people with psychosis sometimes experience their own affect as a voice from outside. The mere use of *disorder-specific* techniques of scene construction and doubling can therefore have a huge therapeutic effect on these patients (see Sects. 9.2 and 10.5). For example, Ms. A. internally saw her boss in front of her: "She is pregnant and acts as if nothing has changed. But we should plan how things should continue when she goes on maternity leave."
2. The person *interacts* in his inner conflict image, recreating the interactional events from memory, like in a film. In this way, he visualizes the reality of the relationship (Plassmann, 1999). Through inner interaction, the energy in the conflict can be felt as an *affect*. For example, Ms. A. reported: "In my mind, my boss just sat there. That's the problem."
3. One often mentally *rehearses* his inner image. In doing so, he tries to explore the conflict beyond reality *in his imagination* and find a new solution. The *individual* self-actualization in the conflict thus becomes *dialogic-systemic* self-actualization in conflict. He reflects in the as-if mode: "*If* I do this, the other will do the following. *If* the other says so, I will do the following." In his imagination, he makes his wish or will clear to his conflict partner and acts alternately in his and the conflict partner's roles. He differentiates and expands his self-image *and* the image of the conflict partner *in relation to each other* and frees them from their fixations. Through this, he recognizes the conflict partner's *motivation* behind why he behaves the way he does. He takes stock of *his contribution* to the conflict. He gains a systemic understanding of the cause and effect of the conflict. Ms. A. replied: "I've already thought about speaking to my boss. I *could* ask her how the counseling center should continue during her maternity leave. But I'm afraid that she will dismiss me."
4. The person also spontaneously looks for personal experiences from the past and higher-level connections that causally determine the current relationship conflict. In doing this, he links and *integrates* experiences from *other* times and places with current experiences. By integrating a current conflict with an experience from another time, the person concerned creates the process quality of meaning (Plassmann, 1999). For example, Ms. A said: "I'm afraid to ask my boss because my relationship with her is not that good. She's quite authoritarian. Everything has to be according to her rules. But I can't stand the uncertainty. *It's always been*

*like that for me.* I need to know where I am. My boss is similar to my mother in that regard. She doesn't care about my feelings."

Conflicts are accompanied by emotions. The emotions disrupt concentration in accomplishing current everyday tasks. The tension of the conflict and the emotions trigger a process of mentalizing. This process aims to liberate the emotions from the inner conflict and enables the person to act appropriately in the external conflict. Those who can mentalize well live "more economically and are therefore more capable of surviving" (Ciompi, 2021, p. 153). Humans control their inner mentalizing with intuition. Through the holistic process of intuition, one tries to achieve a coherent gestalt closure in his mentalizing process: "Until one's perception merges to form a closed gestalt, the ego continues to be compelled to execute its synthesizing function, requiring a certain quantum of neutralized energy. This quantum is set free once the gestalt has been closed and the expenditure of neutralized energy can be reduced" (Lorenzer, 1970, p. 86). Those who *learn* to mentalize more complexly also *develop* their intuition on and on. Intuition-led mentalizing often requires only a few seconds to reach gestalt closure. But it can also take minutes, hours, or even days to finally get to the end of the process and for the feeling to arise: "That's it!" The intuitive insight, the "aha!" moment, results from successful mentalizing.

**Question**
What is this intuition?

**Important definition**

Humans use their intuition to steer the process of their mentalization toward a subjectively consistent solution (see Fig. 2.1 in Sect. 2.1). According to the emergence principle, the process of intuition is more than the sum of its parts. The holistic process of intuition (see Fig. 2.4) is more than the sum of the work of the individual tools of mentalizing (see Chap. 1). It is precisely this "more" that is the secret of intuition.

With this understanding of the term "intuition", I agree with Allen et al. (2008, p. 27), when they say: "We construe implicit mentalizing as *intuition.*" "Intuition […] forms the basis of our ability to react appropriately to non-verbal communication; many of these reactions occur outside our explicit perception. […] When we mentalize, we constantly move back and forth between the implicit and explicit processes" (Allen et al., 2008, p. 27 f.).

## 2.3 The Interrelationship Circuit Between the Tools of Mentalizing and the Eight Core Psychodrama Techniques

"What psychodramatists do when they do what they do?" (Marineau, 2011, p. 43). *A therapy method* must be able to explain its specific therapeutic interventions against the backdrop of a *self-contained, systematic theory.* All psychodramatists

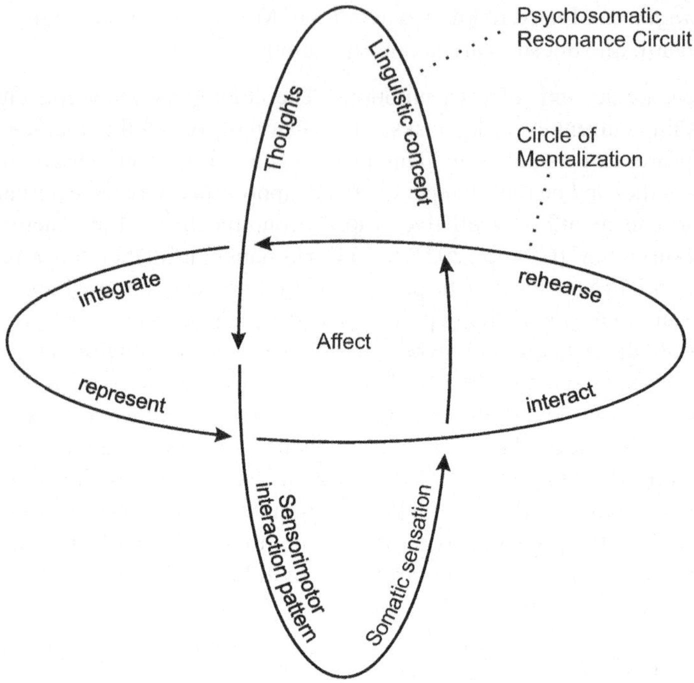


**Fig. 2.4** The holistic process of intuition

have one thing in common—they all employ psychodrama techniques in their work. For many years, it was common in psychodrama literature to describe the different psychodrama techniques one after the other, each with its particular application and effect, *without relating them* to one another. Moreno and Moreno (1975b, p. 239 ff.) described thirteen or rather seventeen techniques (Moreno, 1959, p. 99 ff.). One of his employees, T. Renouvier, described 351 techniques (Moreno, 1959, p. 99), and Schützenberger-Ancelin (1979, p. 79 f.) described 76 techniques. For a long time, doubling, mirroring, and role reversal were the only techniques defined as 'central techniques' (Leutz, 1974, p. 43 ff.) because Moreno had associated these three techniques with the 'most important phases' in child development (Moreno and Moreno, 1975a, p. 135 ff.; Moreno, 1959, p. 85 f.). As a matter of fact, doubling, mirroring, and role reversal do distinguish psychodrama from role play.

In order to develop a systematic theory of psychodrama techniques, it is helpful to look at the function of *each* psychodrama technique *in the overall creative process* of a psychodramatic enactment. Which psychodrama techniques are *necessary* to create and holistically conclude the creative process of a psychodramatic enactment? The answer is: There are *eight central psychodrama techniques* (Krüger, 1997, p. 11 f.): scene construction, doubling, role play, role change, role reversal, mirroring, change of scene, and sharing (see Fig. 2.5). All other psychodrama techniques are merely specific application forms or combinations of these eight central techniques.

**Central idea**

The eight central psychodrama techniques build on each other in their therapeutic effect (see Sect. 2.6). As a whole, they mediate the creative process of conflict processing in a psychodramatic play (Krüger, 2002a). Limiting to the eight central psychodrama techniques makes it possible to develop a psychodramatic play theory and describe the therapeutic effects of psychodramatic plays differently.

Figure 2.5 gives an overview of the different theoretical concepts of metacognitive process work. You will notice a *relationship between* a person's holistic process of intuition, the eight central psychodrama techniques, the eight defense mechanisms of psychoanalysis, the four functions of mentalizing, the four mechanisms of dream work, and the four functional process qualities (Plassmann, 1999).

| | |
|---|---|
| A | The holistic process of intuition |
| B | Functional qualities of a process |
| C | Mechanisms of dream work |
| D | Metacognitive tools of mentalising |
| E | Psychoanalytical defence mechanisms |
| F | Central psychodrama techniques |

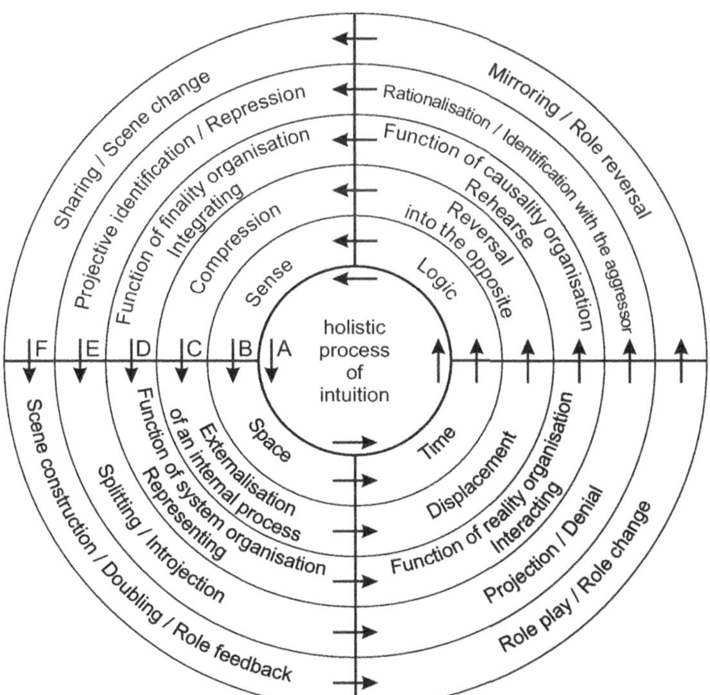


**Fig. 2.5** Functions of the metacognitive process work and its relation to psychodrama techniques (Layout by Sturm, 2009, p. 123, revised)

**Central idea**

The four tools of mentalizing implement the four process qualities of space, time, logic, and sense in the process of inner mentalizing. The function of the four tools of mentalizing is guided by intuition (see Fig. 2.5). They turn into *defense mechanisms* if their work is blocked (see Sect. 2.4). They turn into *mechanisms of dream work* if they are drawn into the whirlpool of self-disintegration in patients with psychosis (see Sect. 9.3) and then produce delusional content.

In Fig. 2.5, you will find for each tool of mentalizing, *in the same quadrant* of the circle, there is a psychodrama technique, defense mechanism, or mechanism of dream work *completing or blocking the same step of mentalizing*. Thus, for example, the disorder-specific application of the psychodrama technique of *scene construction* is indicated when the *defense of splitting* blocks the appropriate *inner representing* of the conflict. Therefore, you'll find *the setting of the scene, representing, and splitting* in the same lower left quadrant. The different structural levels according to the OPD (working group OPD, 2006) are *not included* in the circle model. This is because the structure levels describe deficits, not the metacognitive tools or functions of conflict processing and mentalizing.

**Central idea**

The central psychodrama techniques *are* metacognitive tools of *inner* mentalizing (see Fig. 2.5 in Sect. 2.3) implemented in the as-if mode of the *external* play (Krüger, 1997, p. 84 ff.). The central psychodrama techniques do not change the content of thinking right away. Instead, they implement the *metacognitive processes* we humans constantly use *to produce* our content of thinking (see Chap. 1). This knowledge is key to understanding the therapeutic effects of psychodrama. The *direct metacognitive* work of psychodrama techniques is a *unique selling point of psychodrama*. In other psychotherapy methods, the therapist *cannot directly change* the work of the metacognitive tools of conflict processing (see Sect. 2.6), until they use psychodrama techniques.

During psychodramatic play, an interrelationship circuit exists between the *inner* mentalizing of the protagonist and his drama process on the *outer* stage (see Fig. 2.7 in Sect. 2.5). The patient controls his *outer psychodramatic play* with his *inner mentalizing*. But he differentiates and also expands his *inner* mentalization with the help of the *external* drama process. The psychodrama techniques use this interrelationship circuit to free the patient's metacognitive tools of inner mentalization from his fixations (see Sect. 2.4). As a result, the protagonist experiences himself as self-effective in his internal images in the psychodramatic play.

Psychodrama is a natural healing method. In psychodrama, the therapist connects her own *natural* psychological processes with the patient's *natural* psychological processes. In psychodrama, the therapist, as an implicit doppelganger, lends her soul to the patient (see Sect. 2.5). She mentalizes on behalf of the patient when the patient's tools of mentalizing *are blocked by defenses* and *freely* employs the tools of mentalizing as psychodrama techniques in his psychodramatic play.

**Central idea**

Psychodramatists should not *do* psychodrama; they should allow psychodrama within themselves.

## 2.4 Defenses, Spontaneity, and the Resolution of Different Types of Defenses Using Psychodrama Techniques

**Question**

Why should psychodramatists consider the depth psychology concept of 'defense'?

In the course of evolution, more than any other living being, humans have developed the ability to resolve conflicts *internally simply by thinking* in the as-if mode (see Sect. 2.6). They *no longer* have to search for solutions to *internal* conflict *only* through *external* trial and error. That's why humans have large forebrains. In a new conflict situation, people automatically use the old solutions stored in their memory first. This saves mental and physical energy. However, the problem arises when people are fixated on their *old* solutions and do not notice that they do not fit the *new* situation. They then project the *inner image of the old conflict situation* onto the new situation and do not perceive the difference between the old and the new situation. They, therefore, also *act* according to the *old* situation. Thus, they act *neurotic*. The ability to imagine the *current* situation *appropriately* in the as-if mode is blocked. Their tools of mentalizing no longer work freely. This block in internal conflict processing is called a defense. In role theory, defense is described with the linguistic concepts of 'role fixation' and 'insufficient' role distance (Leutz, 1974, p. 177). The *theory of defense* deals with the same question that Moreno answered with the *theory of spontaneity* more than 60 years ago: According to Moreno (1974, p. 13), they *are spontaneous* who behave in a *new* way in an *old* situation or behave *appropriately* in a *new* situation. In this sense, only those whose tools of mentalization work *freely* in the current situation and are not fixed in an old solution are spontaneous. Moreno (1970, p. 77) described the benefit of *spontaneity in conflict* through psychodrama with the phrase: "Every true second time is a liberation from the first."

**Central idea**

When the tools of mentalizing are blocked in a current situation, they become defense mechanisms. However, psychodramatists *freely* use the tools of mentalization in the as-if mode of play *as psychodrama techniques* (see Sect. 2.3). They thereby dissolve the blocks in the tools of mentalization. The resolution of a specific defense through the *appropriate* psychodrama technique (see below) follows the principle of similarity in medicine (Moreno, 1939, p. 5). As early as 1796, Samuel Hahnemann (1796) said: "Similia Similibus Curentur," which means "Similar subjects have to be treated with a similar approach."

**Exercise 2**

As a training leader, you can let your group members experience spontaneity directly through a spontaneity exercise. In groups of two, the participants tell each other a short episode from their life for 10 min each. But this story should be *a lie* from beginning to end. You will notice: The group members come back to the whole group laughing. *They became spontaneous* as they imagined a *new solution to an old life experience* with the help of a fictional story. "Lies reveal a man's deepest truth. For lies are like the dreams that lend words to the voices of the unseen" (Kamphovener 1975, p. 27).

**Important definition**

Defense mechanisms are *blocked tools* of mentalization that repeatedly produce the same *old* solution in processing conflicts. The *different* defense mechanisms describe *different types of blocked spontaneity*. The *central* defense mechanisms each block a specific mentalizing tool in conflict processing.

Understanding defense mechanisms as *blocked* tools of mentalization prevents a narrow deficit-oriented view of the human being and promotes spontaneity in the therapeutic relationship. In therapy, patients usually resolve the superficial blocks in their mentalization first and only later their *core defense*. The theory of defense mechanisms helps the therapist promote change for the patient in the right direction with a lot of time and patience.

Psychoanalysts are aware of more defense mechanisms than those depicted in Fig. 2.5 (see Sect. 2.3) and described below in Sects. 2.4.1–2.4.4. I have *only* mentioned those defense mechanisms that block a specific *metacognitive tool of mentalizing* (see Sect. 2.2). Some well-known defense mechanisms are a special combination of *several* central defense mechanisms. Somatization, for example, is a combination of defense through introjection, repression, and denial (see Sects. 2.4.1–2.4.4). Regression is a combination of projection and repression. Idealization is a combination of projection and denial.

**Central idea**

The analogy between the tools of mentalizing, psychodrama techniques, and defense mechanisms makes it easier to understand how each defense mechanism changes the way conflict is processed.

## *2.4.1 Disturbances in Internally Representing the Conflict System*

The process of *representing* answers the question "Who with whom?", *interacting* sheds light on the question "How?", the *mental rehearsal* answers the question "Why?" and *integrating* answers the question "What for?" In case of disturbances in internal representing, the affected person *cannot, at least not holistically, internally represent his inner self-image and object image in their external situation.* This leads to a disruption of inner self-development (see Sect. 2.1) in the external situation. The human self is a constant creative process of development including the development of inner self-image and object image in the external situation.

In psychodrama, the *internal* representation is realized by naming the conflict and *external* scene construction. The external representation of the conflict system helps him *also represent the conflict internally* (see Sect. 2.2). The first step of psychodramatic play is the *external* representation of the people or parts of the self interacting in the *conflict system.* They are represented with auxiliary egos or objects. In the case of an *interpersonal conflict*, the conflict system consists of the people involved in the conflict, and in the case of an *intrapsychic conflict*, it consists of the parts of the self or ego states involved. The *natural* ability to internally name and represent the conflict system can be blocked and thus lead to incorrect results: (1) In psychosis, the *patient's process of self-development has disintegrated* (see Chap. 9). For example, the patient experiences his own emotion related to his self-image or his self-reproaches as a voice from outside. In mentalization-oriented therapy, the therapist and the patient use the doppelganger dialogue and the *auxiliary world method* (see Sect. 9.6.5) to construct the patient's delusional scene and interact in the as-if mode of play. In this way, the patient can stop the disintegration of self and his delusional production. (2) *Defense by splitting* manifests as splitting of the inner self-image into two contrary ego states that alternately and seemingly arbitrarily determine the external interaction. (3) *Defense by introjection* blocks the development of self-image in *interpersonal* relationship conflicts.

**Setting the Scene and Splitting**

*Definition of defense by splitting*

(Krüger 2020, p. 137): There are two types of defense through splitting: (1) The inner process of development of self-image in the external situation is divided into *two contrary* inner self-images: "During the course of an interaction, two opposite sides of a conflict dominate the scene *alternately*... with the patient being in blatant denial of the other side" (Kernberg, 1991, p. 49). In his inner reality construction in the current conflict, the patient represents *only one* of the two opposing sides of his self-image without realizing it. His two internal reality constructions are organized around two opposite emotions: sad and angry or needy and pseudo-autonomous. (2) Dissociation in patients with trauma-related disorder separates the observing ego with its thoughts and linguistic concepts from the acting ego with its sensorimotor interaction patterns, physical sensations, and affect. In a traumatizing situation, dissociating is a form of self-protection. However, later, it converts into a clinical symptom known as *a flashback*.

*Where does defense by splitting occur?*

For example, patients with borderline personality disorder unconsciously switch back and forth between a needy, clingy ego state and a pseudo-autonomous, arbitrary ego state (see Sect. 4.3). Patients with trauma disorders alternate between their healthy adult thinking and their trauma film (see Sect. 5.4); those suffering from addiction alternate between the ego state of everyday thinking and their addictive thinking (see Sect. 10.5); patients with psychosis alternate between their healthy adult thinking and their dream ego (see Sect. 9.6.4). Dissociating is an indication of trauma-related disorder (see Sect. 2.5).

*How is splitting resolved?*

Splitting is resolved therapeutically by *naming* and *externally* representing the opposing ego states using the two-chair technique. "The *psychodramatic* splitting of self-representation helps the patient to overcome his *defensive* splitting" (Powell, 1986). The therapist sets up, next to the chair of the patient's self-representation in the external situation, a second empty chair for the patient's currently inactive contrary self-representation. The *temporal succession* of the two contrary inner self-images thus becomes a *spatial juxtaposition.* The two contrary self-images are *concretely visible next to each other on the outside.* This undoes the *denial* of splitting. The two-chair technique is also the basis for the psychodramatic resolution of dissociation (see Sect. 5.10). In psychodramatic trauma processing, the patient switches back and forth between the chairs in the trauma scene, the narration room, and the safe place.

**Important definition**

*Self-representation* is the *process* of internally representing the self-image in the current situation. *Object representation* is the *process* of internally representing the object image in the current situation.

**Central idea**

The *external psychodramatic role change* between the contrary ego states in the as-if mode of play resolves the *internal unconscious switching* between the two contrary ego states. The patient switches from the chair of one ego state to the chair of the other and back again, all the while looking at his conflict partner. Thus, the patient gradually frees his internal process of self-development (see Sect. 2.1) in the external situation from fixation in the defense through splitting.

## Doubling, Role Feedback, and Introjection

In defense through introjection, there is a partial or complete *blockage* of the development of self-image in the external situation. The affected person automatically accepts his conflict partner's one-sided misperception of him and thinks just like this one, for example, that "he is stupid and always wants to fight". He experiences the suffering of another as if it were his own (Ferenczi, 1970, p. 126), or he blindly assumes his conflict partner's expectation.

*Where does defense through introjection occur?*

In people who defend by introjection, the creative inner development of self-image in the external situation is blocked, and so is the appropriate self-actualization during the conflict. It often makes them depressed. Mrs. B.'s husband devalued and accused her in disputes: "You're crazy! I can't stand your emotional talk!" Mrs. B. made his perception her own. Like him, she believed that she was abnormal and conformed to her husband's wishes. Her defenses through introjection blocked her perception of her own emotions of hurt, disappointment, and loneliness.

Through their natural empathy, children who have incurred secondary trauma from their traumatized parents often have *introjected* their parents' traumatic, pathological self-organization as if the trauma were their own. Some others think, feel, and act in *self-injurious and masochistic* ways because they appropriated the inappropriately destructive attributions of their caregivers *during childhood*. For example, as a little girl, a patient with obsessive-compulsive disorder had heard from her mother, "You were aggressive when you were a child. You always wanted to hurt your little brother. That's why I could never leave you alone with your brother." She blindly introjected her mother's inappropriate attribution into her self-image, remained fixed in the biased self-image, and developed a destructive superego. When she wanted to follow her inner impulses, thoughts of death and doom would come to her mind. The patient then had to calm her "sadistic inner tormentor" (see Sect. 7.2) by accepting his incorrect interpretations of the current situation and attempting to override the supposed "danger" through compulsive actions.

*How is defense through introjection resolved?*

The therapist asks the patient about *his affect* in the conflict situation or helps him to consciously perceive the interactional events in the situation and to feel and name his own feelings through *doubling*, *interview*, and *role feedback*. When doubling, the therapist mentalizes the patient's experience *on his behalf* and verbalizes it. The patient tentatively absorbs the sensations, feelings, and thoughts verbalized by the therapist and "introjects" them into his self. Affective resonance is the basis for appropriate doubling (Plassmann 2019, p. 47) between patient and therapist. The therapist activates the current resonance pattern (see Sect. 2.7) in the patient's inner self-image by doubling, and completes it with missing elements such as the impulse to act, the sensorimotor interaction patterns, physical sensations, affect, appropriate linguistic concept, or associated thought (see Sect. 2.7). There are two types of doubling—verbal doubling and the doppelganger technique.

A. *Verbal doubling* (Krüger, 1997, p. 116 ff.): The therapist lets the protagonist engage in a soliloquy (Moreno, 1945b, p. 15). She enters *his* soliloquy internally *with her own* thinking and feeling and verbalizes, on behalf of the protagonist, what she perceives, thinks, and feels toward the "conflict partner": "*He* just doesn't respond. That makes me angry. I hate *him!*" In verbal doubling, the therapist fills gaps in the patient's psychosomatic resonance circle between the memory centers of sensorimotor interaction patterns, physical sensations, affect, linguistic concepts, and thoughts (see Sect. 2.7).
B. *The doppelganger technique* (Krüger, 1997, p. 120 ff.): The therapist *interacts shoulder to shoulder with* the protagonist in psychodramatic play and speaks *directly* with his 'adversary in the conflict': "I am so angry *with you*! Stop it! This is violence!" The doppelganger technique is indicated when the patient has lost ego control over the workings of his mentalizing tools, for example, in the event of loss, rigid fixation in an old adaptive attitude, self-disintegration, or frozen affect. Then, as a doppelganger, the therapist *directly represents the patient's right to life and dignity* to his interaction partner if necessary (see Sects. 4.8 and 9.8.8). Thus, she brings the patient's self to birth in his conflict scene and activates his self-actualization and conflict processing.

**Central idea**

In my understanding, the *interview* and *role feedback* can be assigned to the psychodrama technique of doubling. *In role feedback*, the protagonist *doubles themselves*. During the *interview*, the protagonist gives role feedback for his *immediate* thoughts and feelings.

The therapist uses role feedback during the debriefing of the psychodramatic enactment. She asks the patient: "What did you experience in the play?" The patient then *subsequently* verbalizes his feelings and perceptions during the play. The therapist doubles him verbally if necessary. In doing so, she helps him to differentiate his emotions and explicitly *marks* the patient's sensations, feelings, behavioral impulses, and thoughts that fill in gaps in the mentalization of his conflict. The technique of role feedback is *not* tied to a psychodramatic play. For example, *in the psychodramatic conversation* (see Sect. 2.8), the therapist asks the patient what he experienced during the argument with his wife the day before. In response, the patient gives role feedback for the fight with his wife the day before *without re-enacting the fight psychodramatically.* The therapist can also ask the patient *directly in the play situation or the current encounter*: "What do you feel in your body when you say that and do that?" This technique is called an *interview* in psychodrama.

Healthy people can resolve their defense through introjection when they feel unwell or are in a lousy mood by *internally naming their affect.*

**Exercise 3**

Look inwards when you are feeling bad and *name* your current affect: "I am afraid", "I am sad", "I am helpless", "I am exhausted", "I am angry". Authorize your current feeling *without prejudice.* You will notice: Naming the affect will resolve your discomfort or resentment within 1 to 3 days (Shödrön, 2008, p. 174 f.) because, over the three days, your *feeling intuitively searches for the associated conflict situation that triggers you.* The internal representation of the conflict then promotes your inner conflict processing. Your inner conflict processing dissipates your general discomfort.

**Central idea**

The *psychodramatic* introjection of elements of the psychosomatic resonance pattern (see Sect. 2.7) during doubling helps the patient resolve his *defense* through introjection. The disorder-specific doubling frees the internal development of self-image from fixation in the external situation. Thus, a patient once again becomes spontaneous in the external situation when defending through introjection.

## 2.4.2 *Disturbances in Inner Interacting*

*Inner interacting* with the conflict partner builds on the internal representation of the conflict system. In inner interacting, the person imagines the chronological sequences of interaction in his internal conflict image like in a film from his memory and develops his subjective reality in his conflict. The process of *inner interaction* in the conflict can be blocked in two ways: (1) defense through denial and (2) defense through projection. When *defending through denial,* the affected person filters out unpleasant or guilt-ridden interaction sequences from his perception. When *defending through projection,* he is fixated on a particular *image of his conflict partner.*

**Role Play and Denial**

Definition of denial: A healthy person can adequately retrace the chronological sequence of interactions in a recalled event or a plan. However, when defending through denial, the affected person filters out important interaction sequences from his memory or planning (Mitscherlich, 1967, S. 39). According to Freud, it's like "a visual impression falling on the blind spot of the retina" (Freud, 1975, p. 348). The wish is then the father of the thought. Or the fear or a feeling of guilt determines how reality should be perceived in the inner conflict image (Mitscherlich, 1967, p. 39). The affected person acts according to the motto: "... and so he came to the harsh conclusion that what must not be cannot be" (Christian Morgenstern). I once presented my patient's protagonist-centered psychodramatic play in supervision. He was a physically fit man but drowned while diving in a swimming pool a few days after the group session. I re-enacted the interaction sequences of the treatment. This resulted in a clear causal connection between the psychodramatic play and the patient's 'suicide'. Fortunately, my co-director was also present and said: "But Reinhard, the play was completely different!" She then psychodramatically demonstrated the *entire* protagonist-centered play with *all* interaction sequences. I had hidden important details from the play due to my defense through the introjection of guilt. It became clear that *there was no causal relationship.*

*Where does denial occur?*

Defense through denial is common. For example, it ensures the defense through introjection. Patients with borderline organization *deny* the contradiction between their two alternating, contrary ego states and demand that their conflict partner *also* ignore this contradiction. People who suffered relationship trauma *in their childhood* often assume the role assigned to them in the *current* interaction system and deny the inappropriate behavior of their current interaction partners. Or they develop a *compensatory role*, such as helper syndrome. As a superb helper, the girl, who was lonely in childhood, sees *all* those she cares about as needing help and blocks the exploitative or abusive behavior of her attachment figures from her perception. The outsider humiliated in childhood behaves arrogantly and cool in adulthood.

*How is denial resolved psychodramatically?*

When defending through denial, one unconsciously filters out certain interaction sequences from his perception or memory. Therefore, the therapist lets the protagonist re-enact the temporal sequence of the interactions in his dispute with his conflict partner step-by-step from memory in a *psychodramatic role-play* (see Sects. 2.8, 8.4.2, 8.6.2, 8.6.3, 8.8.5) In doing this, the therapist promotes the *development of appropriate self-image* in his conflict through doubling, interview, and role feedback. For example, she doubles him verbally: "When I look at my brother, I realize that he ... That makes me angry." *Acting* in the as-if mode of play, the protagonist fills gaps in the psychosomatic resonance circuit between his sensorimotor interaction patterns, physical sensations, affect, linguistic concept, and thought (Krüger, 2021). Acting along the red thread of time allows forgotten or repressed interaction sequences to resurface. Understanding the inner construction of reality in role-play resolves the protagonist's fixation on a particular self-image. The patient perceives the reality of his conflict more fully.

***Case example 1***

*A depressive patient was fixated in the role of a helper. Therefore, she automatically felt guilty when a work colleague took her own life. She had been the last person who had spoken with the work colleague. In group therapy, the patient re-enacted the last meeting she had with her work colleague in the parking lot step-by-step. During the play, she remembered: she had noticed that her colleague was not doing well. But she didn't know anything about her colleague's suicidal thoughts. She tried different ways to start a conversation with the "colleague". She even offered to help. But the "colleague" didn't want any help. In the psychodramatic play, the protagonist remembered the colleague's dismissive and rejecting reactions. She perceived anew that, despite her best efforts, there was no chance to reach her colleague emotionally. Her denial of rejection dissolved. The therapist then had the protagonist search for the reason for the colleague's suicide in a fictitious psychodramatic dialogue (see* Sect. 8.4.2*). In the role reversal, the patient realized that the colleague had killed herself because she had been desperate because of the separation from her long-term partner. The patient then said goodbye to her "colleague" in a psychodramatic dialogue (see* Sect. 8.4.7*).*

**Central idea**

A person who defends through denial hides certain interaction sequences from his memory or planning and thus changes his internal perception of reality. Re-enacting the temporal sequence of interactions in the creative *psychodramatic role-play* helps to complete the *defensive* 'false' sequence with missing actions and thus to resolve the defense through denial. The disorder-specific interaction in the role play frees the patient's inner self-development in the conflict situation (see Chap. 1) from its defense through denial and allows the patient to become spontaneous again.

## Role Change and Projection

*Definition of projection*: People constantly construct an internal image of their external reality in life. In doing this, they also *playfully* ascribe certain feelings, actions, and thoughts to their conflict partners. The inner construction of their object images then controls their current outer actions. This attribution becomes a defense through projection when they rigidly hold on to *a specific object image of their conflict partner*. Defense through projection is a *multi-stage process*: (1) A certain external stimulus triggers an affect, which updates an old positive or negative interaction pattern. König (1982) sees a need "for intimacy, for familiarity … in an environment that reproduces familiar inner parts in ourselves" in the defense through projection. (2) The projecting person inappropriately ascribes a motivation to his current conflict partner, allowing him to retain his affect. (3) He, therefore, always reacts to him *in the same inappropriate way*. (4) In doing so, he forces the current conflict partner into a complementary counter-role and fights in him what he fights off in himself. According to Greenson (1975, pp. 197, 137), "When a person projects, he transfers something of his self-representation out into or onto another person."

*Where does projection occur?*

Projection secures other forms of defense. For example, patients with borderline organization often feel manipulated when the therapist comes too close to them with an offer of help. In reacting to the therapist, the patient then automatically shifts from their needy ego state to their autonomous ego state. He does not see that he *himself* is "manipulating" the therapist by alternating between his contrary ego states and acting in equivalence mode. The more disturbed a patient is, the more he has to project to maintain his own psychological balance. But even people with "only" *neurotic* conflict patterns defend through projection in conflicts. For example, they suffer because of their conflict partner, but they inappropriately cling to the fact that their conflict partner means well and is also suffering. Or they project their own rejection onto the conflict partner, although the latter may "only" protect themselves from feelings of chaos through their distanced behavior (see case example 10 in Sect. 2.9).

People often develop inappropriate enemy images during social or economic crises or war. Enemy images develop through a fixation in a certain biased negative object image. Projecting aggression onto enemy images "helps" people find a *simple* explanation for the emergence of the crisis and to see themselves as victims. This fixation of the object image is often determined by old social myths. Those affected then fight, for example, those who flee to their country because they assume they want to conquer their country. Centuries ago, however, they themselves conquered their country and expelled or killed the locals. Projection helps people *in the present* to hide the reality that triggered the current social and economic crisis, for example, corruption, and the unequal distribution of wealth. But the drama is: If one doesn't perceive the problems appropriately, one can't solve them sustainably either. Society is increasingly split into "the good guys" and "the bad guys". For example, the conspiracy theories during the Corona pandemic helped some people see themselves as victims of the "aggressive, authoritarian" rulers. In doing so, they projected their own *egoistic* desires for power onto those in power.

*How is projection resolved?*

In childhood, role change and role-playing with high-energy counter-roles helps to differentiate and realistically develop the inner *object image* in conflict. In doing so, the internal cliché of the 'bad father' *or* 'good father' is turned into a holistic person with good *and* bad sides.

In the case of projection, the therapist lets the protagonist psychosomatically differentiate and expand his *inner object image* in the as-if mode of play through role change and role-playing *in the role of his conflict partner*. She doubles him *in the opposite role* and thus helps him. *In the opposite role*, the protagonist develops a connection between *the conflict partner's* external behavior and internal physical sensations, affect, linguistic concepts, and thoughts. As a result, the inner object image of the conflict partner becomes free from fixation. In group therapy, some patients solely heal as a result of the opportunity to differentiate and expand their fixed inner object images and self-images as auxiliary egos in the protagonist-centered plays of other patients (see case example 66 in Sect. 8.4.5).

At the beginning of his psychodramatic work, Moreno (1945b) did not know about role reversal. However, he had his patients switch to other roles and enact them in role-plays. For example, he had his patient Robert role-play the inner object images of his mother, father, and other authoritarian males. But he did not yet use *role reversal*, where the patient *stands opposite himself* in his antagonist's role *and perceives himself as if he is looking in a mirror*. In the case of *intrapsychic conflicts*, the therapist has the patient switch to the counter-role of another ego state. For example, people with a borderline organization can explore the counter-role of their conflicting pseudo-independent, authoritarian ego state and bring it under their ego's control. Role change also occurs in fairy tale plays, for example, when a patient takes on the opposite role of the "wicked witch" in the fairy tale "Hansel and Gretel".

***Case example 2***

*As a child, 45-year-old Mrs. C did not receive any validation for her feelings, and her mother narcissistically abused her. She survived by taking on the role of helper assigned to her by her mother. She continued to play the role of helper even as an adult in her small family. She was the good, helpful partner and mother, projecting her own needs onto her selfish, degrading husband and selfish, adolescent daughter. The therapist had her re-enact an argument with her teenage daughter and change into her daughter's role. As a daughter, the patient screamed at the mother, devalued her, and "howled like a wolf". She refused any pressure from outside and saw everything in a negative light. In the daughter's role, Mrs. C. expanded her inner object image of her daughter in the conflict. She experienced that the "daughter" did not take the mother seriously with her offers of help and played off her power with relish. As a daughter, the patient did not feel depressed or suicidal, contrary to what she had previously assumed. This expansion of the internal object image dissolved the patient's projection of helplessness. She looked at her daughter's provocative, aggressive behavior with fresh eyes and could name it as such.*

***Case example 3***

*The father of a 10-year-old boy had killed himself. The boy then participated in a psychodramatic child therapy group. During symbolic play, he committed about thirty "suicides" in different ways over eighteen months. In this way, without knowing it, he differentiated his inner object image of the suicidal father in the metaphor of the symbolic play, expanded it into a holistic image with good and bad parts, and thus resolved his traumatic fixation.*

In therapy, children enact their role as well as their counter-roles through role play *in symbolic plays*. Thus, they learn to indirectly free their self-image and object image in conflict from their biased fixations, and to shape their inner self-image and object image in conflict more appropriately (Krüger, 2017a, p. 133ff; 2017b, p. 273ff.).

***Case example 4***

*A 40-year-old woman told: She was betrayed by her partner. She had to unconsciously "play" the opposite roles in the triangular conflict in her real life too. First, she was the betrayed victim. But then, in real life, she unconsciously switched to the role of the lover of a man who was in another relationship. Finally, she also "played" the role of a woman cheating on her steady partner with another man. Only then could she be free and content in a stable partnership. By acting out the object images in her everyday life, she further developed her inner object images in the triangular conflict and liberated them from fixation.*

**Central idea**

The free and creative *psychodramatic* role play in the role of one's conflict partner helps to resolve the *defensive* fixation in a certain object image. Changing roles and acting out the *inner object image* in the role-play frees the *inner* development of the object image from its fixation by projection and allows one to become spontaneous again.

### *2.4.3 Disturbances in Internal Rehearsing*

The patient explores the cause and effect in his conflict through *internal interacting and rehearsing* between his inner self-image and object image and frees them from their fixations. He recognizes his conflict partner's motivation and also his own involvement in the conflict. Thus, he gains a systemic understanding of the relationship. The naturally existing ability to appropriately rehearse mentally (see Sect. 2.2) can be blocked in two different ways and thus lead to incorrect results: 1. Defense through identification with the aggressor and 2. defense through rationalization.

**Role Reversal and Identification with the Aggressor**

*Definition of defense through identification with the aggressor*: Anna Freud (1984, p. 92) defined defense through identification with the aggressor as an "exchange between the aggressor and the attacked". Identification with the aggressor is a combination of introjection and projection (Freud, 1984, p. 88). Introjection and projection are mutually dependent defenses and thereby stabilize each other. Identification with the aggressor secures and strengthens the defense through introjection, denial, and projection. In the end, the patient perceives himself, the victim, as the perpetrator, and the conflict partner, the perpetrator, as the victim. The cause and effect are reversed. As a result, one's perceptions of reality and the cause and effect in the conflict are blocked.

*Where does the defense through identification with the aggressor occur?*

The confusion between cause and effect in relationship conflicts can arise in everyday relationship conflicts, in interpreting relationship conflicts from childhood, in a grief reaction, etc. For example, the husband of the patient in case example 63 (see Sect. 8.4.2) repeatedly devalued her in disputes and accused her: "You're crazy! Always this emotional talk!" The patient blindly accepted her husband's causal construction and projected her own role as a victim onto her husband. She believed: "*He* suffers because *I'm* not normal."

Defense through identification with the aggressor masks more basic forms of defense in the case of *traumatic* identification with a perpetrator introject from the past. The affected person then *masochistically* devalues himself in the present, just as he was devalued in childhood by the damaging caregiver, and thinks about himself: "You are nothing, you are not able to do anything, you're not good for anything" (see Sect. 8.5). In this case, the inner causal construction is blocked by "complicated and multi-stage defense processes" (Thomae, 1985, p. 406), including the defense through splitting. A psychodramatic dialogue with role reversal with a "perpetrator" from the past is contraindicated in such cases (see Sect. 5.10.9). The therapist must first address the splitting and post-traumatic disorder.

*How is the defense through identification with the aggressor resolved psychodramatically?*

The psychodramatic dialogue with role reversal is the indicated method. The therapeutic effect of external role reversal in the as-if mode of play builds on the therapeutic effect of scene construction, doubling, role-playing, and role change (see Fig. 2.6 in Sect. 2.4.3).

*In the psychodramatic dialogue with role reversal*, the protagonist represents his conflict partner with the help of an auxiliary ego or an empty chair. He then explores *the reality* in the inner conflict image by role-playing in *his* role, changing roles, and role-playing in *the role of his conflict partner*. *Additionally*, the protagonist tries, of his own volition, *new behavior* in *his role* in the *old* situation in the as-if mode of play. In a role reversal, the individual actions of the protagonist and the individual reactions of the "conflict partner" should interlock like the links of a zipper in frequent role reversal. For example, he tells the "conflict partner" what he feels and why he feels it. Or he negotiates with the "conflict partner" to achieve a fairer balance between giving and taking in the relationship (see Sect. 8.4.2). In doing this, the protagonist reverses to his conflict partner's role *after each action* and acts the

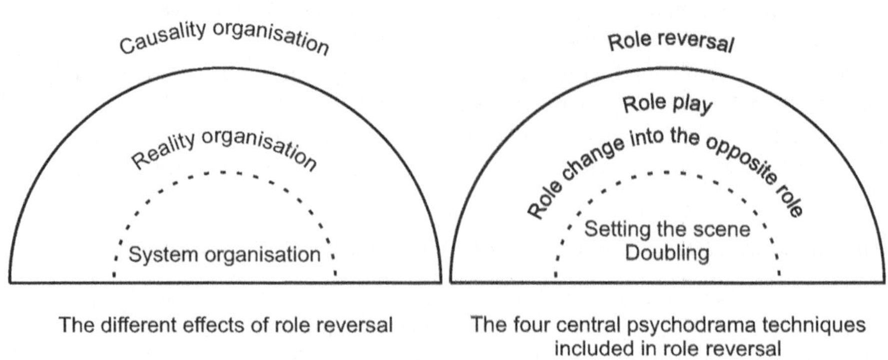


**Fig. 2.6** The complex therapeutic effects of role reversal

way he thinks he would react to his new action. In this way, the protagonist recognizes *which* of his own behavior and that of his conflict partner could *enable* or *prevent* a new solution to the conflict. The external role reversal helps him complete both *psychosomatic resonance patterns* of his inner self-image and object image, separate from each other, into *holistic psychosomatic resonance patterns*. This helps him to psychosomatically experience whether his conflict partner is acting in this way to protect himself internally or to externally reject the other (see case example 10 in Sect. 2.9). He thus learns both his and his conflict partner's true motivations and knows how they both tick in the relationship. Thus, he knows more clearly whether creating a systemically fair relationship balance is *possible*. He knows more about cause and effect in the conflict.

The therapist can resolve the mutual stabilization of defenses through introjection and projection using the seven steps of the psychodramatic dialogue (see Sect. 8.4.2). The first step resolves the defense through projection. This also automatically weakens the defense through introjection (see case example 15 in Sect. 2.14 and case example 63 in Sect. 8.4.2). Steps 3 and 4 resolve the defense through introjection. This also weakens the defense through projection (see Sects. 2.9 and 8.4.2). Steps 6 and 7 weaken the *mutual stabilization* of defenses through projection and introjection.

**Central idea**

In the case of defense through identification with the aggressor, the *external psychodramatic* role reversal helps to overcome the *defensive* inversion of cause and effect in the inner role reversal. Rehearsing with frequent role reversal frees the internal development of self-image and object image in the external situation from its fixation in the defense through identification with the aggressor.

## Mirroring and Rationalization

*Definition of rationalization*: People often identify the causes of a conflict by looking internally at the interaction from a metaperspective and interpreting and assessing the interactions in the situation. However, this internal change into the metaperspective can be blocked by the defense through rationalization. The affected person then secures his inappropriate understanding of cause and effect by providing an inappropriate interpretation or assessment. "Rationalizations are equally used to ward off anxiety and deny instincts: people with neurosis concoct a system of justifications which help them categorize their neurotic feelings and reactions as 'right' or 'necessary', perhaps even 'reasonable' and 'valuable'" (Dührssen, 1972, p. 31, 187).

*Where does defense through rationalization occur?*

In every new situation, people first use old and familiar explanatory models because it takes more psychological energy to form a *new, personal* opinion about the causes of the conflict. However, it is crucial to notice when the old explanation does not fit and to look for a new, more *appropriate* one. After all, if one does not appropriately identify the cause of a conflict, one cannot resolve the conflict appropriately. *Inappropriate explanations* of the situation are primarily based on the individual's affect and protect their special defense. The affect looks for a suitable explanation. For example, a depressed patient often assesses himself with the assumption "Everything I did today was bad. I am a loser." But, the affected person is perhaps simply exhausted at this point and would assess his actions differently at other times. Or he underestimated the dimension of the problem.

*How is rationalization resolved psychodramatically?*

Rationalization can be resolved only if the more basic forms of defense have been resolved beforehand. When rationalizing, the affected person holds on to a *particular* view of the conflict from the metaperspective. The therapist, therefore, uses the psychodramatic technique of *mirroring*. She stands with the patient *outside the interaction scene* acting psychosomatically in the observer position and asks him to look at the conflict from a metaperspective: "How do *you* feel about what you did?" "What happens between you as a boy and your mother?" The protagonist then internally recreates the interaction in his relationship conflict from the outside from a metaperspective. He describes what he sees and names and evaluates the interaction holistically from the yes-but position of the expert: "The mother is not interested in what the boy feels and thinks. She's using him!" *As a cognitive doppelganger*, the therapist supports the patient in mirroring to call a spade a spade and to develop his *own* assessment of cause and effect in his conflict. When mirroring, the patient develops a *systemic understanding* of the relationship conflict.

The mirror technique is often used *unnoticedly* in psychodrama:

1. The therapist engages *in a psychodramatic conversation* with the patient (see Sect. 2.8) *and represents* his self-image and object image with two additional chairs externally in the therapy room (see Fig. 2.9 in Sect. 2.8). The patient then narrates what happened in the argument with his boss. He looks at the two chairs of self-image and object image *from a metaperspective*. The method can strengthen the cognition in the conflict (see Fig. 2.8 in Sect. 2.7).
2. In the role reversal, the patient sees his *self-image* in his conflict *from outside* through the eyes of his conflict partner.
3. The therapist also uses the mirror technique in step 5 of the psychodramatic dialogue (see Sect. 8.4.2). Looking at the symptom scene (see Sect. 2.8), she helps the patient to name his external perceptions of himself and his conflict partner with the appropriate linguistic concepts. The use of other linguistic concepts, such as, 'egoistic and selfish' instead of 'not careful' and 'not mindful', activates other psychosomatic resonance patterns (see Sect. 2.7). The patient then classifies his interaction pattern in his memories under a different linguistic concept.

***Case example 2 (continued)***

*Mrs. B. had re-enacted the argument with her aggressive pubescent daughter. During debrief, the therapist pointed to the two chairs representing the mother and the daughter and asked: "How do you assess your behavior towards your daughter? How would you describe your daughter's behavior?" Mrs. B.: "Friederike is disrespectful." Therapist: "Please don't say what isn't, that she is disrespectful! Please tell me how you perceive your daughter in real!" Suddenly Mrs. B. bursts out: "Friederike is an egomaniac. She pisses me off! I can't stand to be near her!".*

4. When *processing the trauma* (see Sect. 5.10), the patient shall tell his trauma story primarily from a metaperspective, from the narration and observation space. Auxiliary therapists enact the narrated interactions as doppelgangers and auxiliary egos.
5. Even with crisis intervention using the *table stage*, the patient and the therapist look at the development of his crisis together *from a metaperspective* and thus get an overview of his current life situation. This strengthens the patient's cognition.

Viewing a conflict from a *metaperspective* is not the same as *metacognitive therapy* (see Sect. 2.14). When mirroring, the patient looks at *the interactions in his relationship conflict* from the outside. In metacognitive therapy, however, he looks at *his dysfunctional defense pattern* from the outside (see Sect. 4.8). Metacognition is thinking about *the way you think* and not thinking about an interactional event.

**Central idea**

*Psychodramatic* mirroring helps to overcome a 'false' assessment of an external situation. It frees the systemic process of the patient's internal self-development in the external situation from fixation in the defense through rationalization.

## 2.4.4 Disturbances in Internal Integrating

In conflict processing, *current* actions, affect, interaction patterns, and defense patterns do *not* always match the *current* conflict. One, therefore, naturally associates *inappropriate* actions and affect spontaneously with appropriate experiences from the past and gives them a positive meaning in the past context. This association is the result of integrating, the fourth tool of mentalizing (see Sect. 2.2). Integrating helps one understand himself better while thinking, acting, and feeling *in a neurotic manner*. The naturally existing ability to integrate appropriately can be blocked (1) by defense through repression and/or (2) by defense through projective identification.

### Change of Scene and Repression

*Definition of repression*: "In repression, the ego confirms its power in two ways: the instinctual representative feels one side of its power expression, whereas the instinctual impulse feels the other" (Freud, 1931, p. 215; Krüger, 1997, p. 199). In repression, a feeling or an action from the past (the instinctual impulse, according to Freud) is inappropriately attributed to a *present* interaction. One cannot remember the *threatening past conflict* associated with the neurotic feeling or action. It is repressed. The inappropriate thinking, feeling, or acting that made sense in *previous* contexts is acted out *blindly in the present*.

***Case example 5***
*A patient always panicked in the present, even if her husband frowned. She, therefore, repeatedly acted unreasonably in her current marital relationship and withdrew from*

*it. She withdrew the same way she did in childhood when she panicked because her father had a choleric attack. "If you want to explain the hysterical attack, you only have to look for the situation in which the motions in question were part of a justified behavior"* (Freud, 1931, *p. 256).*

*Where does repression occur?*

There are two different types of repression. (1) In repressing a *past interaction pattern* that matches the current *inappropriate* affect, the patient inappropriately acts out *his affect* from the past in the present. (2) In repressing *the past affect that fits the current inappropriate interaction pattern,* the repressed feeling shows up in the present only as a psychosomatic reaction, for example, a racing heart, and the patient *interacts inappropriately* in the present.

*How is repression resolved?*

The therapist helps the patient mentally connect the inappropriate affect or interaction pattern in the present to the appropriate, "true" interactive relationship from the past:

1. The therapist *asks him* if he knows the *inappropriate affect* or interaction pattern from his past.
2. In the psychodramatic play, she has the protagonist switch to an appropriate childhood scene in order to actualize his *repressed affect* or interaction pattern and integrate it into the genetic conflict.

**Central idea**

The external linking of the inappropriate interaction pattern and affect with an interaction pattern from the past helps the protagonist to neuronally classify his current sensorimotor interaction pattern, physical sensation, and the affect in his memory under another descriptive linguistic concept (see Sect. 2.7): "I know this from my mother!" This frees the current interaction pattern with his wife from the old psychosomatic experiences. He can freely develop his inner self-image and object image in the relationship with his wife. On the other hand, the interaction pattern "mother" gets an update. Self-image and object image in his relationship with the mother become from their old fixations through a psychodramatic dialogue with role reversal and develop further (see Sect. 8.4.6).

Goldmann and Morrisson (1988, p. 29ff.) called this procedure "the psychodramatic spiral". The protagonist first plays a *current* conflict and then, by changing scenes, integrates the inappropriate feeling into a relevant *childhood scene.* He subsequently looks for a new appropriate behavior in the psychodramatic encounter with his *current* conflict partner.

3. The therapist connects the patient's *current neurotic interaction pattern* with his childhood experiences and verbally communicates this connection as an *interpretation.* In doing this, the scene change happens *only internally.*
4. The patient writes a *fictional letter* to an attachment figure from childhood (see Sect. 4.12). The patient must *never post the letter*. In the letter, he explains to the attachment figure all that he has now learned about the connection between his *current* problems and his *childhood* experiences.

5. The patient integrates, with the help of the *psychodramatic dialogue and role reversal*, his newly gained self-image into the internal image of a relationship *with a close attachment figure from his childhood* (see Sects. 4.12 and 8.4.2).

***Case example 5 (continued)***
*The patient mentioned above, who reacts with panic to her husband's frown, first re-enacted the scene with her husband psychodramatically. Then, the therapist asked her: "You panic when someone frowns. Where does that stem from?" So he named the interaction pattern. The patient replied: "It was the case with my father. He was very short-tempered and often hit me!" The therapist then had the patient perform an external psychodramatic scene change to the appropriate childhood scene and re-enact the childhood scene, taking into account the boundaries of trauma therapy (see* Sect. 5.10.11*). Acting in this way, the patient appropriately linked (integrated) her present inappropriate affect of panic with the past relationship conflict with her father. Thus, she experienced the original positive meaning of her panic reaction. The patient could separate the real conflict with her husband from the transference conflict with her father because of the new link.*

6. The therapist also uses *integrating through scene change* in fairy tales and impromptu plays in group therapy. In debriefing, the therapist asks the group participants: "Did you behave similarly to how you do in everyday life, even in the play? Or did you do the opposite?" Thus, their experience in the fairy tale play amplifies their experiences from everyday life or childhood conflicts.

***Case example 6***
*A seminar participant spontaneously chose the role of a star box in the impromptu play "A Garden in Spring" and played it. But his star box was "half collapsed". In debriefing, the participant suddenly realized that this image symbolized his current psychological state of mind in his life crisis. As a result, he began engaging in psychotherapy after the seminar.*

**Central idea**

The *psychodramatic linking* of the inappropriate affect or interaction pattern with the *appropriate* conflict from the past through scene change helps to overcome *an inappropriate linking* with a 'false' conflict. The disorder-specific *psychodramatic* scene change frees the internal creative process of self-development (see Sect. 2.1) in an external conflict situation from its fixation in the defense through repression.

### Sharing, Amplification, Projective Identification

*Definition of projective identification*: Defense through projective identification is a complex process that stems from childhood and serves to adapt to difficult family circumstances. (1) The affected person *took on the role* assigned to him *in his family* by the family and split off his sense of self (Parin, 1977): "External adaptation takes place automatically … A necessary ego split is usually not noticed … The adaptation offers a narcissistic satisfaction that one is someone who corresponds to one's role

…". (2) The affected person *identified with the family's explanatory patterns.* He did not distinguish between the systemic role implicitly assigned to him by his family and the self-directed personal role. (3) The affected person also blindly *identified with the values and goals of the family system.* His ego developed the ability to "occasionally or temporarily use external authorities or institutions instead of his internalized superego." Parin speaks of the "externalization of conscience", "clan conscience," and "identification with the group ego". "Extreme living conditions … and … also imposed or highly charged ideologies … favor such ego development".

The defense through projective identification is stabilized *in the present* by the fact that the person concerned and other members of his current relationship system *mutually narcissistically affirm* each other in the splitting of their self. Those affected then reinterpret their own inappropriate thoughts, feelings, and actions through ideological rationalization, for example, submissiveness to Christian humility, violence against immigrants in loyalty to the fatherland, or an attitude characterized by resentment into a socially critical attitude (Dührssen, 1972, p. 31) (Krüger, 1997, p. 217).

People who defend themselves through projective identification are fixed in a defense system in the process of their inner self-development in the therapeutic relationship, for example in defense through grandiosity combined with masochistic self-censorship. *The therapist,* who inwardly accompanies the patient in the process of his self-development in the situation, unconsciously identifies with the patient's defended part of self and inwardly protests against his grandiose claims or his masochistic self-devaluation. The patient's rigid defense pattern and the therapist's vicarious feelings are mutually dependent. In the end, the therapist experiences the patient's split-off affect as her own. According to König, 1991 (quoted from Heigl-Evers et al., 1997, p. 351), the therapist is "unconsciously manipulated" to become similar to a part of the self that the patient has delegated to her.

*Where does projective identification occur?*

Those affected usually suffer from a structural disorder (see Sect. 4.4). They have often experienced childhood relationship trauma in a family shaped by traumatized parents. For example, they grew up as a child in a disintegrated family. Or they have internalized their parents' defense system and thus stabilized the family. However, those affected don't attach any appropriate meaning to these deficient interaction experiences. This is only possible if one has had positive relationship experiences through sufficient resonance from their caregivers in childhood and is, therefore, *able to internally compare* negative and positive experiences.

Affected persons are usually insecure and emotionally unstable. Therefore, they often stabilize themselves by taking on a role in an overtly or latently authoritarian community. A religious sect, a criminal gang, or a right-wing extremist party gives them inner support. However, authoritative organized communities are not flexible in their relationships and prevent further *growth* of the person. A mature step in puberty or midlife can lead to an identity conflict between the systemic *role* in the authoritarian community *and the self* and a breakdown in blind identification with the system. As a result, the affected person loses the inner support that the community gives him and must once again confront his old insecurities surrounding his identity. Sometimes, he experiences existential fear of absolute emptiness, loneliness, going mad, or death. For example, people who decompensate into psychosis have previously stabilized by assuming their ascribed role in a rigid family system (see Sect. 9.4). They identified with the group ego of their family or community. Even severely psychosomatic patients defend themselves through projective identification. Unlike patients with psychosis, however, they have already developed more mature, complex inner structures before the collapse of their psychological balance. As a result, their mental breakdown does not lead to a dissolution of the ego boundaries between internal and external but is "only" dealt with as a conflict between the body and soul.

*How is projective identification resolved?*

When defending himself through projective identification, the affected person is stuck in a rigid defense system. He comes for counseling, coaching, or therapy when the narcissistic gratifications for his adjustment are missing in his relationship system or the current situation requires that one's *emotions* be justified. Perhaps, he may no longer be able or willing to fulfill the systemic role expected by the authoritarian community or institution. He experiences an identity conflict between his systemic role in the community and his own self.

In the case of defense through projective identification, the therapist implements the same approach as in the therapy of people with personality disorders (see Sect. 4. 8). In doing so, she goes back with the patient along the path of defense through projective identification: (1) The therapist internally justifies the disturbance in the relationship caused by the patient's defense. (2) She internally names *her own* affect. (3) She considers the specific defensive behavior with which the patient triggers this affect in her. (4) She attributes this specific behavior to a particular defense pattern of the patient. (5) She names this for the patient and represents it as an ego state with an empty chair and a hand puppet outside in the therapy room. Thus, looking at his externally represented defense pattern, the patient himself feels the emotions that he had delegated to the therapist before. (6) She describes the positive meaning of the patient's defense pattern in the holistic process of his self-regulation. (7) She integrates his defense pattern with his childhood conflicts (see Sects. 4.8 and 4.10).

***Case example 7***

*In the therapy of a patient with panic attacks, the therapist represents the rigid defense pattern of self-protection through perfectionism as a second chair next to her and asks: "When you experience difficult feelings, how long do you pretend as if nothing is wrong and fight those feelings?" The patient replies: "Always!" Therapist: "When was the first time?" The patient then narrates various traumatizing stories from her childhood without any emotional involvement and then cheerfully asks: "Do you want to hear more such stories?" Therapist: "No, this is too much for me because I really internally imagine the events you experienced back then!" The patient begins to cry: "It's too much for me too!" As a child in a broken family, the patient had not learned to perceive and classify her own emotions because of her identification with the systemic role ascribed to her. She had tried to perfectly meet the family's expectations. Therefore, the therapist experienced the patient's loneliness and abandonment on her behalf and shared it with her: "I can't take it anymore. It's too much for me!" In identifying with the therapist, the patient absorbed the therapist's emotion, which was her own suppressed emotion, into her self-image and only now realized: "I can't do it anymore either."*

The therapist can clarify the inadequacy of the patient's defense pattern by amplifying the rigid defense pattern: "American President Gorge W. Bush's grandiosity led him to believe that he had to ward off all evil in the world. He destroyed the society in Iraq through war and thereby causing what he wanted to fight against: the mullah regime of Iran gained great influence in Iraq and the Islamic State terrorist group emerged. The therapist can explain *the distancing from an old rigid defense* pattern by amplification too. For example, the therapist shares about other patients or fairy tale characters who have experienced similar conflicts between a massive pressure to conform and their sense of self and have found a solution, such as Cinderella or the "Girl Without Hands". The patient can identify with the role of the heroine or hero in the fairy tale. He feels seen and validated through the sharing or amplifications. Fairy tales usually have happy endings. Therefore, such amplifications encourage patients to search spontaneously and freely for a self-determined life, like the heroine of the fairy tale.

**Exercise 4**

If you want to experience amplification, you can do so by rehearsing the method of fairy tale association (Krüger, 1992, p. 230 ff.): (1) search for the name of a fairy tale. (2) Choose *a specific* person or character from this fairy tale. (3) How do you see this figure in front of you? What is it doing right now? Pause the inner film and describe the situation you see in front of you. (4) Write down the result of this exercise. Your fairy tale association is an amplification of a core personal conflict of your own with a probability of at least 80%.

During the psychodramatic work on defense through projective identification, the therapist or the group members confirm the patient's attempt to free himself from his old defense system through personal *sharing*. For example, they report how they let go of an old conformist attitude and find themselves. The patient learns that other humans have experienced similar existential fears and identity conflicts and dealt with them differently. *Amplificatory* interpretations are also helpful.

**Central idea**

The *psychodramatic* split between the systemic role and the self helps the patient resolve the *defensive* split between the systemic role and the self through projective identification. The disorder-specific sharing and amplification free the internal creative process of self-development in the external conflict situation from its fixation in the defense through projective identification.

**Recommendation**

Psychodrama techniques specifically free tools of mentalization from their blockages. The therapist should supplement this theoretical knowledge with her intuition in her practical work (see Sect. 2.5). This helps her to appropriately develop the relationship with *this particular patient in this situation*, here and now. The present moment is more true than any theory, technique, or method. The therapist is allowed to *not know* and *does not have to know everything immediately* when directing a psychodrama play. Her apparent ignorance helps her become a midwife in the patient's self-development in the psychodramatic play.

## 2.5 The Attunement and Agreement Process Between the Patient and the Therapist During Psychodramatic Play

Humans develop their inner self in conflict through mentalizing. In Psychodrama, the tools of mentalizing become psychodrama techniques (see Sects. 2.2 to 2.4). Psychodrama therapists promote the patient's internal self-development in external conflicts (1) verbally and by using psychodrama techniques as an *implicit doppelganger* and (2) by participating in the psychodramatic play as an interacting doppelganger.

**Exercise 5**
If you are a psychodramatist, notice what you pay attention to in your practical work as a therapist: direct a psychodrama following only your intuition! When and how do you use which psychodrama technique, and why?

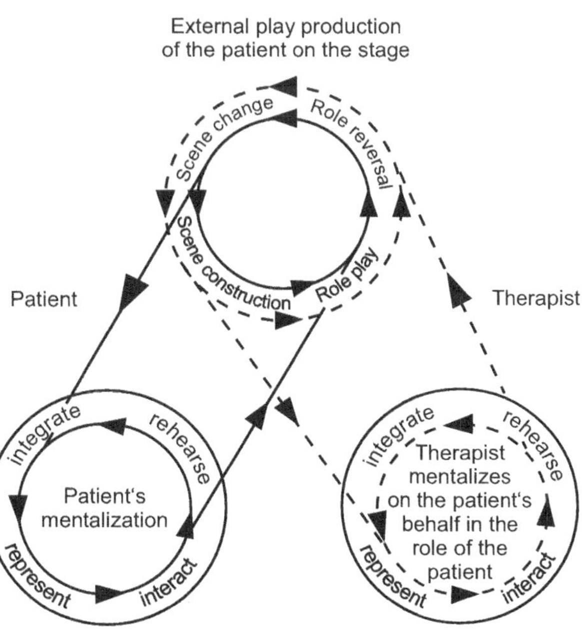


**Fig. 2.7** The Shared Mentalization Process of a Patient and Therapist in a Psychodramatic Play (Krüger, 2012, p. 300, revised)

**Central idea**

The intuitive impulse of the therapist to use a specific psychodrama technique results from an intuitive, semi-conscious, semi-unconscious creative attunement and agreement process with the patient. During the psychodramatic play, the psychodrama therapist and the auxiliary therapists accompany the patient *internally as implicit doppelgangers* in his holistic process of internal self-development in the external situation. This process includes the systemic development of inner self-image and inner object image in the external situation (see Sect. 2.2).

**Important definition**

Every therapist is an *implicit doppelganger* when she tries to understand the patient and promote his self-development. She identifies with the patient's self-development and mentalizes on his behalf. If she does not know how to continue, she verbally asks for the necessary information

She says: "You say you are exhausted. How does your exhaustion affect your everyday life? Since when are you exhausted?" Patient: "Since I lost my job." Therapist: "How did this happen?" The therapist spontaneously tries to internally understand what causes the patient's exhaustion and how it affects him in the present. She searches for the *relevant external conflict* that caused the exhaustion. *But*, she would also like to know how the patient perceived reality in his triggering conflict. She wants to understand what happened in the triggering conflict. She, therefore, asks the patient to *psychodramatically* enact his systemic process of internal self-development in the conflict with his boss. The therapist, as an implicit doppelganger, uses her own tools of mentalizing as psychodrama techniques (see Sect. 2.4) in directing the play. However, she then does not know what the patient's boss answered. She, therefore, asks the patient to change his role and respond to himself from the role of his boss.

**Central idea**

Moreno once said: "I had two teachers, Jesus and Socrates" (Yablonsky, 1986, p. 241). In directing the psychodramatic play, the therapist realizes the Socratic attitude: "I know that I don't know, but I would like to know." But alternately, she also acts *internally as* the patient's *implicit doppelganger* and realizes the Jesus attitude: "Bear one another's burden." The therapist *alternates again and again between* the Socratic and Jesus attitudes.

**Important definition**

In psychodrama play, the therapist and auxiliary therapists of the group take over, as *interacting doppelgangers,* the roles of the patient's self-image *or* object image and help him to shape his inner process of self-development and to free it from his fixations.

In acting psychodramatically, the patient expands his inner conflict images with the help of the therapist and the auxiliary egos to include the *psychosomatic experience*. In the role of his inner self-image and object image, he develops a holistic psychosomatic resonance pattern between sensorimotor interaction patterns, physical sensations, affect, linguistic concepts, and thoughts (see Sect. 2.7). The therapist and the auxiliaries *physically act* and complete his self-development in the as-if mode of play. The patient's conflict is jointly choreographed so to speak. The auxiliary egos assume the same posture as the protagonist in his complementary roles. In terms of content, they say the same thing and intensify the affect through sound modulation. They reverse roles and interact with the protagonist. The therapist also dances along with the protagonist, so to speak. If the protagonist reverses roles, she positions herself on the protagonist's side in his respective role (see Sect. 8.4.4). In doubling verbally, she positions herself diagonally behind him and, thus, gives energy to the patient's mentalization. If she wants to get an overview of the situation, she looks at the scene from a metaperspective. Dancing along with the protagonist's story as implicit and interacting doppelgangers makes it easier for the therapist and the auxiliaries to understand the protagonist's self-development in his conflict and to free him from fixations in defense.

Children sometimes communicate solely through sensorimotor interaction and psychosomatic expression of affect, without saying a word. A three-year-old girl was playing alone in the garden. A boy of the same age walked up to the girl from the street. The girl looked at him skeptically. The little boy danced in front of her for ten seconds. The girl looked at him with interest and repeated his dance movements. Then she hesitated and danced in her own way in front of the boy. The boy looked at her and imitated her dance. Afterward, they both turned around, went to the sandbox, and played together. It seemed like they knew each other well. They hadn't said a word to each other since they met.

**Central idea**

By definition, psychodrama works psychosomatically because the patient physically acts on the stage in the as-if mode of play.

**Recommendation**

In only verbally performed video therapy, the *psychosomatic* encounter level is lacking to a great extent. Therefore, the therapist should let the patient use two chairs in his room to represent his internal self-image and object image in his conflict and, if necessary, a third chair for his dominant defense pattern (see Sect. 4.8). *At least the patient* himself should act psychosomatically *in his room* with role reversal and act out his defense pattern in the as-if mode. This improves the therapeutic effects of video therapy.

Many psychodrama psychotherapists are tempted to look for new and impressive psychodrama techniques when they *encounter disturbances* in attunement and agreement process with the patient during the psychodramatic play. In doing this, they leave the role of implicit doppelganger and treat the patient as an object. But understanding psychodrama as a method of mentalizing through psychodramatic play helps the therapist avoid her own confusion. As an implicit doppelganger, she lets the patient retrace the paths of his mentalizing in psychodramatic play. In the case of disturbances in play, she intuitively slows down the work *at the right point* and uses less complex *psychodrama techniques* to dissolve a less complex defense (see Figs. 2.5 and 2.6).

The therapist can only use a particular psychodrama technique if she, as an implicit doppelganger, can *freely* use the appropriate mentalizing tool *in her own conflict processing*. For example, if she doesn't think of her own conflicts systemically, she will not *use role reversal freely* in the patient's conflict. Likewise, if she has *not processed her own trauma*, she will not have the impulse to represent the patient's flashback with a chair next to him and thus make his unconscious change between his trauma film and his healthy adult thinking the subject of therapeutic communication (see Sects. 4.8 and 5.8).

**Central idea**

If a therapist has a problem using a particular psychodrama technique, it may indicate *a gap in her self-experience*. An increase in her *self-awareness* can then lead to a dissolution of the block in using the respective psychodrama technique appropriately. An increase in *self-awareness*, progress in the application of psychodrama techniques, and the theoretical understanding of her own therapeutic actions are mutually reinforcing.

## 2.6 Developing the Modes of Mentalization

Fonagy et al. (2004) have defined the developmental steps of mentalization as the development of 'modes of mentalization'. In what follows, I integrate the theory of Fonagy et al. with Schacht's theory (2009, p. 22 ff.) of childhood development. In his theory of development, Schacht combined Moreno's (1946/1985, p. 64, p. 74 ff.) theory of role development with the 'psychoanalytic findings of operationalized psychodynamic diagnostics on personality structure (working group OPD, 2006)' (Schacht, 2009, P. 13), the 'psychoanalytic studies on structure-related psychotherapy by Rudolf (1998, 2006)', and the developmental levels of Selman (1984). With this in mind, I have developed a concept of *seven different modes* of mentalization (Table 2.1).

**Central idea**

The process of mentalizing involves the use of seven different modes of mentalizing that build on one another: the dream mode, the equivalence mode, the as-if mode of play, the as-if mode of thinking, the systemic mode, the metaperspective mode, and the narrative mode (Krüger, 2017a, 2017b, p. 135 ff.).

1. When the inner process of self-development disintegrates, one uses the tools of his mentalization in the form of mechanisms of dream work (Krüger, 1978, see Sect. 9.3): (1) The inner *representation* becomes the dream mechanism: *'Inner thoughts are perceived as external reality'*, (2) the inner *interaction* becomes the dream mechanism of *'displacement'*, (3) the inner *rehearsal* and inner role

**Table 2.1** Developing the modes of mentalization

| Modes of mentalization, according to Krüger | Role levels, according to Schacht | Modes of mentalization, according to Fonagy |
|---|---|---|
| Dream mode | | Teleological mode |
| Equivalence mode | Psychosomatic role | Equivalence mode |
| As-if mode of play | Psychodramatic role | As-if mode |
| As-if mode of thinking | Sociodramatic role level 1 | Mentalizing mode or reflective mode |
| Systemic mode | Sociodramatic role level 2 | Reflective mode |
| Metaperspective mode | Sociodramatic role level 3 | Reflective mode |
| Narrative mode | Sociodramatic role level 4 | Reflective mode |

reversal becomes the dream mechanism of *'reversal into the opposite role'* and (4) the inner *integration* becomes the dream mechanism of *'condensation'*. Thinking in the dream mode is similar to thinking in the teleological mode (Brockmann & Kirsch, 2010, p. 280): When thinking in the teleological mode from the 9th month of life "the child can interpret its own and others' actions as goal-oriented, but it cannot yet see the underlying causes and motives. Only what can be observed counts".

*People with psychosis* experience delusions because their mentalizing tools work as mechanisms of dream work (see Sect. 9.3). *Mentally healthy people* become *creative in a unique way* when mentalizing in dream mode because they are able to control their thinking in dream mode when awake. They know that their absurd fantasies are only *inner* fantasies that do not reflect external reality. Their mentalization in the dream mode takes place *in the service of their ego* (Balint, 1970, p. 187 f.). The dream mode extends our perceptions and experiences in an *illogical* manner, thereby leading to freedom of thought, which is necessary for creating new solutions (see Sect. 9.4). In the psychodramatic play, the dream mode is developed through scene construction, doppelganger dialogue (Krüger, 2013b, p. 221 ff.), and auxiliary world technique (see Sects. 9.8.4 and 9.8.8).

2. Children develop the ability to think in equivalence mode from 15 to 18 months of life. They learn to organize their thoughts in space and time. They internally develop a rudimentary inner self-image and object image in the external situation. However, they do not yet distinguish between their inner *reality construction* and their *external perception of the conflict*. Thinking in the equivalence mode is still linked to the external action and therefore depends on the supportive interaction with attachment figures or objects like puppets. According to Schacht (2009, p. 24), small children then mentalize on the *psychosomatic role level*. 'Toddlers behave as if their and others' thoughts reflect the real world in its original form ...What small children believe is, in their opinion, really the way things are' (Fonagy et al., 2004, p. 264).

**Important definition**

*Adult patients* who think in the equivalence mode unconsciously assume that their defensive inner reality construction adequately reflects the *external* reality in the conflict. As stated by Fonagy, Gergely, Jurist, and Target (2004, p. 96 ff.), they confuse 'internal states (such as thoughts, fantasies, and feelings) with outer reality. They experience these thoughts and feelings as reality—not as mere internal representations of reality.' As a result, patients who are fixed in a defense and *inadequate internal* reality construction also act *inappropriately* in *external* reality. But not every person who acts in the equivalence mode is also structurally disturbed. His conflict processing is *only* characterized *by a defense*.

3. From 15 to 18 months, a child also learns to think in the *as-if mode of play*. According to Schacht (2009, p. 24), that is the *psychodramatic role level*. Unlike the more complex modes of mentalization described below, thinking in the as-if mode of play is *still connected to the external interaction with external objects*. It serves the inner differentiation between the self-image and object image in the external situation. The child needs real objects such as a puppet, a stuffed toy,

wooden blocks, or even attachment figures who support him. The child creates his own fantasies by *acting externally in the as-if mode* of play and learns to control them independently *in the play.*

Three-year-old children can differentiate 'between ... thoughts and real things *in play*; they begin to play with as-if games and can easily recognize when somebody is acting "as-if"—for example when daddy is pretending to be a dog' (Fonagy et al., 2004, p. 262). They can reflect on inner states and false, alternative, or changing convictions *in play* and develop their internal ideas. According to Fonagy et al. (2004, p. 268), they are not yet able to *also* do this *outside of* play, only *in their inner thinking*. 'When playing, the child is always ahead of his average age and daily behavior! He appears to be more mature than his age' (Vygotsky, 1978, p. 102, quoted after Fonagy et al., 2004, p. 266). Role-playing has a Surplus-Reality-Effect (see Sect. 2.6). However, the child is still unaware that 'in thinking about events and holding convictions relating to these events, he is merely forming subjective, interpretational constructions of these events' (Schacht, 2009, p. 25). From 15 months to 4 years, a child thinks *either* in equivalence mode *or* in the as-if mode of play (Fonagy et al., 2004, p. 262).

4. From the 4th to the 6th year of life, the child gradually integrates the *as-if mode of play* in his internal thinking and develops the *as-if mode of thinking*. Fonagy et al. (2004, p. 268) have broadly named this function of mentalization as the *'reflective mode' of mentalizing* or the 'mentalizing mode'.

**Important definition**

According to Fonagy et al. (2004, p. 297 f.), in contrast to the state of psychic equivalence, the 'as-if' mode of thinking is 'characterized by an awareness of the representational character of internal states: by separating or 'dissociating' [...] his mental representations from reality, a child can distinguish his thoughts and fantasies from reality.'

The child now uses his existing inner self-images and object images to let them *interact internally*. He develops his self-images and object images into small stories with interaction sequences *in the imagination alone* without the help of *external objects*. He *thinks* in scenes. In free psychodramatic role play, a child playing the role of a mother will seek someone to play the complementary counter-role. The child verbally negotiates his *role expectations* with the other person. For example, as a 'cowboy,' he needs an 'Indian,' and as an 'Indian,' he needs a 'cowboy'. The child recognizes that his views and feelings are *subjective* and that others can hold differing views. According to Schacht (2009, p. 24, 30), this is level 1 of the sociodramatic role level.

By 1946, Moreno (1946/1985, p. 70 ff.) had already developed a theory of the *development of mentalizing in childhood*. He named it 'the theory of role development in children'. In this, he explained the development from mentalizing in the mental equivalence mode to mentalizing in the as-if mode of thinking (Moreno (1946/1985, p. 72). He used different linguistic concepts, but his thoughts were similar to those of Fonagy, Gergely, Jurist, and Target. Instead of the psychic equivalence mode, he spoke of the stage of 'all-identity' (Moreno, 1946/1985, p. 70). According to Moreno (1946/1985, p. 73), reality and fantasy are not separate in the stage of all-identity.

Those who mentalize at this level of development are acting in their 'psychosomatic role'. With the beginning of the 'second universe' in the child's fourth year of life, fantasy and reality become separate (Moreno, 1946/1985, p. 72). 'Two stages of warm-up process emerge, one for action in reality and the other for action in fantasy, and these begin to organize themselves.' Both run parallel to one another. 'The problem is not that one could give up fantasy in favor of reality, or vice-versa' (Moreno, 1946/1985, p. 77). The trick is instead to establish means and ways of overcoming life situations such that one can 'switch back and forth between these different paths'.

**Central idea**

*According to Fonagy*, the *reflective mode* of mentalizing in the *theory I describe* here also includes the systemic mode presented below, the metaperspective mode, and the narrative mode.

5. The *systemic mode of mentalizing* develops from around the age of ten. Children develop the ability to *role reverse internally* and to assume a self-reflective and reciprocal perspective. When interacting with their caregiver in everyday life, they repeatedly change into the role of their associated *inner* object image in external situations and constantly develop them further. They can also see themselves through the eyes of the other in the current situation. Thus, in a relationship, they can think reflexively about themselves and therefore recognize the *mutual conditionality* of their own and their interaction partner's behavior. They learn to assume joint responsibility for the conduct of their conflict opponent. Schacht (2009, p. 25 ff.) states this is the sociodramatic role level. The systemic mode of mentalizing is achieved through *inner* role reversal.
6. Youngsters develop the metaperspective mode of mentalization from around the age of 15 years. They learn to see themselves and their interactions *internally* from a metaperspective and to observe themselves 'from the perspective of an impartial third party'. This helps them assess the conflict using values and norms: "That is fair", "That is unfair". Schacht (2009, p. 33) says they reach the sociodramatic role level 3.
7. At 15–20 years, people develop the ability to think of their conflicts even in the *narrative mode* of mentalization. They reach the sociodramatic role level (Schacht, 2009, p. 33). Usually, people automatically synthesize 'new information with previous knowledge as they take it in. When the event is of personal importance to them, they unconsciously rewrite these feelings into a story' (van der Kolk et al., 1998, p. 72). Thinking in the narrative mode, the person determines how the conflict began and how it ended. They integrate *personal experiences from other times and* places into their history. They give meaning to their own experiences against the background of universal human experiences, the society as a whole, ecological contexts, or spiritual experiences. When processing conflict, they come to a subjectively coherent gestalt closure. They gain clarity on what is important in the conflict. The unimportant information can then be forgotten. Thus their narration becomes *a true personal story that evokes a sense of identity.* The *autobiographical self* emerges (Damasio, 2001,

p. 210), constructing the contents of the conflict processing into a "story of the self…".

The *modes* of mentalizing describe the stages of *psychic development in children*. They must not be equated with the *tools* of mentalization *in adults*. In an acute conflict, *everyone* thinks more or less in equivalence mode (Fonagy, 2021, https://www.youtube.com/watch?v=dheWephlvkg, October 3, 2021) because he is more or less severely fixated on a certain defense. But he is not disturbed in the beginning. He 'only' equates his internal image of the conflict with the external reality of the conflict. A person who projects rejection onto their conflict partner also perceives them as someone who rejects them *and acts accordingly* (see case example 10 in Sect. 2.9).

Psychodrama transforms thinking in equivalence mode into thinking in the as-if-mode. The patient thus gains ego control over his inappropriate thinking, feeling, and acting in the current situation. He becomes spontaneous in Moreno's opinion (1974, p. 13). This is the starting point of psychodrama as a psychotherapy method. Moreno discovered this healing effect of the psychodramatic play in his improvisational theater. He has told the story many times (Marineau, 1989, p. 74).

***Case example 8* (Moreno, 1959, *p. 14 f.*)**

*"We had a young actress who was particularly successful in portraying saints, heroines, and romantic tender creatures". One of her admirers fell in love with her, and they married. One day her new husband came to Moreno, very depressed, and stated that his wife was unbearable in the marriage. "She behaves recklessly, is quarrelsome, uses the most vulgar expressions, and if he reprimands her in anger, she even acts violently." Moreno wanted to help the man and his wife. He asked him to come to the theatre in the evening as usual. However, Moreno suggested that the actress play a completely different role that evening. He offered her the role of a street girl. She enthusiastically took up the suggestion. She "played the role with such genuine vulgarity that she was unrecognizable. The audience was fascinated, it was a huge success. […] From then on, she preferred to perform in similar roles. Her husband understood immediately".*

*The husband went to see Moreno every day. After a few days, he told him: "There has been a change […], she still has her outbursts of anger, but they have lost their intensity. They are also shorter; sometimes, she suddenly smiles because she remembers similar scenes she plays on stage. And I laugh with her for the same reason. […] Sometimes, she starts to laugh even before she has a fit because she knows exactly how it will go. Even now, she gets worked up sometimes, but in a much weaker form than before".*

The actress initially thought, felt, and acted toward her husband in equivalence mode. If she felt angry in his presence, she assumed that her husband was currently making her mad and, therefore, vented out her anger on him. She took it for granted that her internal image of the marital relationship, created through mentalizing, adequately reflected external reality. Thus, as Fonagy et al., (2004, pp. 96ff.) say, she "confused inner states (such as thoughts, fantasies, and feelings) with outer reality and perceived it as reality rather than as mere inner representations of reality". But Moreno then let the actress act out her anger outbursts in the improvisational theater in the roles of offensive women, for example, in the role of a prostitute. Indeed, the actress still had to play out angry scenes with her husband at home. But even before that, she noticed that her angry behavior would correspond to her actions on stage, and thus laughed at the absurdity of the situation. She realized that her anger outbursts were part of her own character. As a result, she became aware of the inappropriate acting out of her anger. This improved their marital relationship.

When used appropriately, psychodrama techniques integrate the as-if mode of play into the equivalence mode of thinking. One thus becomes a director in his internal conflict processing.

***Case example 9***

*A patient with borderline personality disorder, pornography addiction, and major depressive disorder (F33.3, F60.31, and F63.9) was narcissistically abused by his mother as a child and youth. He was also severely humiliated in his school frequently. According to the patient, the mother had aimed to raise him to become the prime minister someday. At the end of therapy, the patient said: "I now have more trust in my intuition. My 'shoulder mother' (the mother who breathes down his neck) is no longer there. Now, I have become the prime minister. But not the way my mother wanted it in the outer world, instead of in my inner world!" At the end of therapy, he could make adequate use of his good intuitive and cognitive abilities. He celebrated his new freedom and spontaneity with friends by throwing a party. He summed up his therapy outcome: "I have found myself!".*

Moreno described the therapeutic effect of psychodramatic play in 1923 in his book '*Das Stegreiftheater*' (Moreno, 1970, p. 77 f.) with the following words: "Every true second time is the liberation from the first. Liberation is an ideal term because total repetition ridicules its object. We gain the aspect of being the creator in our own life, in everything we have done and continue to do—the feeling of true freedom, the freedom from our nature. The second time makes you laugh about the first time. The second time too—people appear to—speak, eat, drink, beget, sleep, wake, write, argue, fight, acquire, lose, and die. But [...] every form of being is lifted by itself in the as-if mode, and being and as-if are lost in a laugh. [...] This as-if is the unleashing of life. [...] Prometheus has grabbed the bonds, not to overcome or kill himself. He brings himself out again and, through as-if, proves that his existence in bondage was the act of his free will".

**Central idea**

In psychodrama, people can gain ego control of their dysfunctional thinking, feeling, and acting and become free to behave differently. They develop (1) the aspect of being a creator in their own *life*, (2) the aspect of being a creator in the *cognitive* processes of their thinking, and (3) the aspect of being a creator in their *metacognitive* processes of thinking.

## 2.7 The Neurophysiological Foundations of Psychodramatic Play

**Important definition**

In the course of life, humans record their physical and psychological experiences and conflict resolutions as neuronal connections between their different memory centers (Ciompi, 2004, p. 215; Roth, 2001). They create *psychosomatic resonance patterns* between individual sensorimotor interaction patterns, physical sensations, affect, linguistic concepts, and thoughts. The *existing* psychosomatic resonance patterns help to react *quickly* in the current situation, thereby saving the brain cells some work and energy. As a result, people don't have to keep reinventing the wheel again and again in similar situations.

*Sensorimotor interaction patterns* emerge when playing the piano, during sexual intercourse, when mountaineering, etc. *Physical sensations* include pain, exhaustion, or tiredness, for example. Political parties and states try to claim and occupy *linguistic concepts* such as 'solidarity' or 'democracy' for themselves. The words 'freedom' or 'god' activate a different psychosomatic resonance pattern shaped by personal experiences in each person. In psychodrama, shared language helps when mirroring (see Sect. 2.4.3) to classify personal perceptions *in the memory stores* under a different linguistic concept: A 'beautiful childhood' then becomes the experience of the 'abandoned inner child'. Some *psychodramatic warm-up exercises* use the activation of sensorimotor interaction patterns through acting to activate inner energetic images and feelings that are then acted out. In contrast to the *inner role reversal* in thinking, the individual develops two different holistic psychosomatic resonance patterns, one of his inner self-image and the other of his inner object image, separate from each other, *in the external role reversal in the as-if mode of play* (see Sects. 2.9 and 8.4.2). In this way, he understands himself and others on a *psychosomatic basis* and *psychosomatically* recognizes the difference of inner self-protection and external

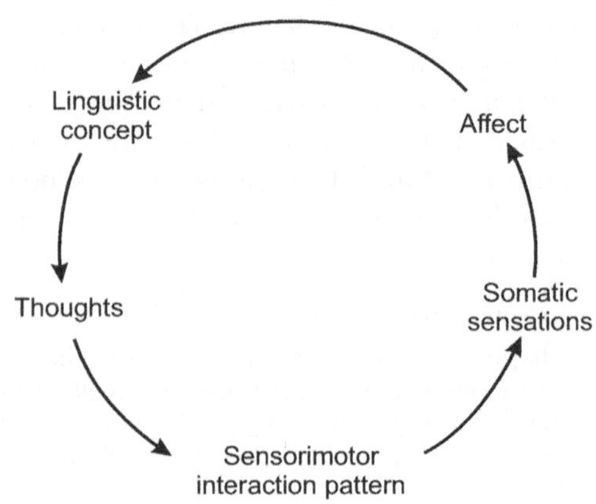


**Fig. 2.8** The psychosomatic resonance circuit between the various human memory centers

affective release or the inner motivation for acting a certain way. He then knows how *he and the opponent* in the conflict tick in the relationship.

**Exercise 6**

You can do this exercise to experience how your psychosomatic resonance circuit works. (1) First, sit upright in your chair with your arms on your knees and close your legs. What does this posture evoke in you emotionally?—You are likely to feel a little fear, be highly alert, full of expectation, and more adaptable. (2) Now sit casually in your chair, half-lying and at an angle, with your arms crossed. What does this attitude evoke in you emotionally?—You probably feel more self-confident, superior to the person you are talking to, and more like someone who waits things out and not wants to go ahead. Through your psychosomatic resonance circuit, you have activated a connection between your physical posture and the associated physical sensations, affect, and thoughts.

Roth (2001, pp. 185 and 187) thinks that "creative people have more favorable features of the neuronal networks" than others and that "a lack of plasticity of the cognitive and executive system is a consequence of a lack of plasticity of the involved neuronal networks." Psychodrama play helps *the five* different memory centers of sensorimotor interaction patterns, physical sensations, affect, linguistic concepts, and thoughts to participate more *comprehensively* in conflict processing: (1) Psychodramatic play activates the *psychosomatic resonance circuits* of the inner self-image *and also* of the inner object image and frees them from their fixation through interaction and role reversal (see Sects. 2.4.2 and 2.4.3). (2) It differentiates and completes the *psychosomatic resonance circuit* of inner self-development in the external conflict situation and loads it with energy. (3) New connections to other *similar* psychosomatic resonance patterns arise spontaneously and autonomously. In this way, people *integrate* current experiences with their past experiences (see Sect. 2.4.3). They spontaneously check whether they can also use the *old solution* in the current situation. (4) Psychodramatic play *increases the complexity* of the neurophysiological processes of conflict resolution. More complex structures achieve the same goal with less energy and, in the long run, become an advantage for survival (Ciompi, 2021, p. 114). (5) It *frees* the psychosomatic resonance circuit from fixations in *obsolete* psychosomatic resonance patterns. This is what Moreno (1959, p. 98) meant when he said: "However important verbal behavior may be, action precedes and encloses the word."

In psychodrama, the therapist works together with the patient on the conflict level at which the dysfunctionality of his conflict processing arises. As an implicit doppelganger (see Sect. 2.5), she repeatedly carries out the inner conflict processing of the patient in herself via *her own* psychosomatic resonance between her five memory centers and thus understands what the patient communicates. If she doesn't understand him, she asks the patient for the missing information: "What are you feeling in the role of your mother right now?" In the case of *blockage* through a defense, she uses the appropriate psychodrama technique (see Sect. 2.4) to free the patient's internal self-development from its fixation in the current situation. In this way, the patient develops new, more suitable, and complex psychosomatic resonance patterns and more appropriate links between them *of his own volition.*

**Important definition**

The *creative ego* is the driving force and the integrating authority in the systemic process of inner self-development of humans in the current situation (see Sect. 2.1). According to Blanck and Blanck (1980, p. 32), this ego is "a metaphor. For it has neither form nor place—only function". It is a "metapsychological construct that serves to facilitate understanding in theory formation and discussion, but which does not exist as such, because one can only speak of the existence of the ego if it functions."

The concept of the psychosomatic resonance circuit is helpful in understanding the *neurophysiological processes* of conflict resolution. However, it still represents these processes in a simplified way. In reality, they are much more complex. The psychodramatic play intervenes in the interplay between the unconscious 'Proto Self', the consciously capable 'Core Self," and the 'Autobiographic Self" (Damasio, 2001, p. 210). This interplay is characterized by 'wide-ranging possibilities for the meta-representation of the information processing processes [...] (for example in the prefrontal cortex): The brain models its own functioning' (Schiepek, 2006, p. 11 f.). There are 'structural and functional loops and recursive interrelated representations' that 'temporally and spatially coordinate the cerebral maps of reciprocal links, integrate sensory and motor events, and connect them to circuits, thereby giving rise to representations and metarepresentations. From a synergetic perspective, this is a result of multiple, parallel-networked, and hierarchically integrated systems that relate their self-organizing dynamic to one another and create synchronization patterns (folders) over widely ramified areas of the brain'. I call these synchronization patterns 'psychosomatic resonance patterns'.

Psychodramatic play promotes *the development of spontaneity and creativity* in the conflict processing of humans and thus enables them to react *adequately* to a new situation and in a *new way* to an old situation (Moreno, 1974, p. 13). The liberating effect of self-determined play is evident *not only* in humans but also in animals. In the Süddeutschen Zeitung (1st/2nd March 2008, No. 52, p. 22), under the heading 'Play is of apparent significance—it helps master life in the complex world,' Breuer wrote: "The impulse to play is innate in most mammals; it is also to be found in some bird species, and sometimes even tortoises will play with a ball to pass the time. [...] The roles of the hunter and the hunted are constantly reversed in the fight performed by young rats, lions, or foxes." However, the play of animals is certainly *not*, as commonly assumed, *a behavioral training* for the seriousness of adult life. Kittens prevented from indulging in any form of play later demonstrated hunting skills equivalent to those allowed to play (Tim Caro, University of California).

On the other hand, Pellis (Sergio Pellis, the University of Lethbridge in Alberta, Canada, 2007) discovered that rats not allowed to play rough and tumble up to the age of puberty had a *significantly underdeveloped medial prefrontal cortex* in comparison to other rats permitted to play. Breuer continues, "This brain area is partly responsible for social competence. Therefore, Pellis believes that these animals would have difficulty dealing with numerous tasks in their lives." Without play, animals are "less adaptable than would normally be the case". Bekoff (Marc Bekoff, University of Colorado) claims to recognize "the evolutionary purpose of playfulness as being training for the unexpected." Instead of simply learning specific patterns of movement for predictable situations, it is more about being able to physically and mentally adapt one's behavior in a new situation quickly and adequately—and this talent is developed only in free play. Everything else could be learned, if need be, in other ways. Several indications support this point of view: Pellegrini & Kato (2002, p. 991 ff.) noticed that "boys who exhibited better skills at games involving fighting and clamor were also socially more competent. Children who were playful at a pre-school age were more adept at dealing with psychologically stressful situations". In many studies, "three-year-old children [...] who enjoyed taking part in make-believe games with others also performed well at tasks that required mind reading and emotional understanding" (Fonagy et al., 2004, p. 55). According to Lillard (1993, quoted by Fonagy et al., 2004, p. 56), "symbolic play can serve as the 'zone of proximal development' for those competencies [...] that underlie the ability to read others' thoughts."

The significance of play in the development of mentalizing also becomes apparent in *psychodrama psychotherapy for children*. Moreno (1985, p. 132 f.) established that role play in spontaneity training made them appear more "intelligent" to others. When children with psychological symptoms participate in non-directive psychodramatic group therapy, they are mostly *unable to play at the beginning of their treatment*. They take on roles only for a short time and often stand outside the stage 'simply' as observers. But once they have learned to play, after sixty group sessions, most of them no longer display any symptoms. In symbolic plays, they developed their metacognitive tools of mentalizing and resolved the blocks in their conflict processing. They have now become freer to understand themselves and their conflict partner suitably in present conflicts and are able to find adequate solutions spontaneously. They have learned to appropriately shape the *inner* systemic process of their self-development as well as the development of their *inner* self-image and *inner* object image *in the external situation*.

**Central idea**

According to Winnicott (1985, p. 63), the ability to play is a central prerequisite for the success of therapy, even in adult psychotherapy: "Those who are not able to play must first learn to play. Interpretations made too early are simply useless or have an unsettling effect. [...] They lead to adaptation." To understand an interpretation, the patient must be able to expand the *verbal* interpretation to include the associated *psychosomatic* resonance pattern and link it to other similar psychosomatic resonance patterns. In doing so, the patient *thinks* in the as-if mode, *internally* moves back and forth between different interaction patterns, and creates meaningful contexts between them. He *plays internally* in this process. The psychoanalyst Winnicott, therefore, let some of his severely disturbed patients, who couldn't play, learn to play in three-hour therapy sessions.

## 2.8 The Diagnostic Psychodramatic Conversation

The diagnostic psychodramatic conversation is a standard psychodrama method employed in individual therapy, counseling, and coaching. It helps a patient to mentalize his conflict (see Fig. 2.9 below). I use this method in almost every individual session, including the first session.

1. *Before your conversation with your patient, place two additional empty chairs* for the symptom scene in your therapy room at a small distance from where you will be sitting with your patient (see Fig. 2.9). The chair next to the patient symbolizes his inner self-image in his recalled conflict, and the other chair opposite this chair symbolizes his inner object image, for example, his internal image of his conflict partner. Both the empty chairs should be placed such that they *directly face each other*. They should *not face the patient and the therapist* because the chairs represent the patient's inner conflict image *in another place and time.*
2. You can start with a standard, *verbal* therapeutic conversation about the patient's argument with his conflict partner. In doing so, the patient shouldn't move to sit on the empty chair as he would in a psychodrama role play. You will intuitively look for a scene that creates or amplifies the patient's symptom or shows how the patient deals with the symptom.

**Central idea**

The two additional chairs in the therapy room represent the patient's inner process of self-development in his everyday conflicts, separate from the therapeutic relationship (see Chap. 1). This process includes the development of the inner self-image and the inner object image. The patient and the therapist thus answer the question of who interacts with whom and how in the patient's conflict.

3. During the conversation, as a therapist, point with your hand to the empty chair that symbolizes your patient's internal *self-image* while discussing his thoughts,

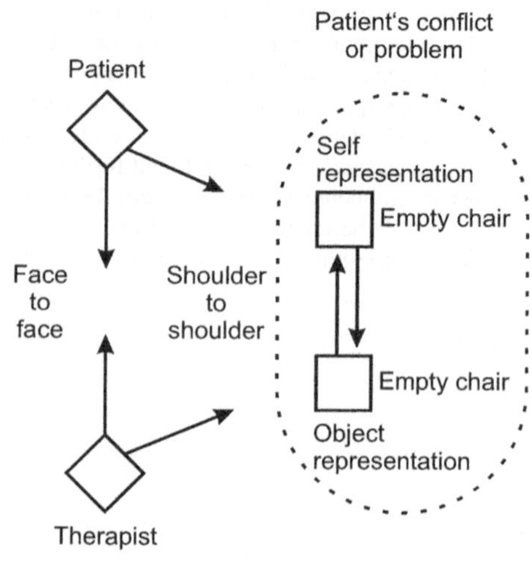


**Fig. 2.9** The external psychosomatic separation of the patient's symptom scene from the therapeutic relationship in the diagnostic psychodramatic conversation

feelings, and actions in his conflict. But please point to the empty chair representing the internal *object image* when you both discuss his *conflict partner's thoughts, feelings, and actions*. Stretch out your arm entirely in doing so. In the event of a mood disorder, create a suitable interaction frame for the patient in the symptom scene for his depressive mood in his everyday life. The chair for the self-image then symbolizes, for example, the depressed, listless patient in his bed. The chair for the object image symbolizes his wife, who takes care of him, or his boss, who waits in vain for him at work.

4. *Look at* the respective chairs when pointing toward them. This is a prerequisite *for the patient* to look at the two chairs in his symptom scene. Imagine the interactive process in the conflict scene internally as if you were watching a movie.
5. During the conversation, let your patient reconstruct the chronological sequence of interaction patterns step by step in his conflict from memory *while looking at* the two empty chairs. Ask him: "How did this conflict with your partner begin? What is the current situation of your conflict? What did you think, feel, and do? What happened next?"
6. Ask the patient step by step: "What did you think? … feel? … do in this situation?" "What do you think your partner felt? What did she think? What did she do?" Thus, the psychodramatic conversation *also includes the technique of circular questioning from systemic therapy*.
7. If necessary, extend the representation of the symptom scene to a full circle of 3–8 empty chairs when counseling a *family* or a *team*. These would then represent all those involved in the conflict.

**Recommendation**

You cannot understand the therapeutic effect of the psychodramatic conversation just by reading. This is because your therapeutic impulses to act also emerge *psychosomatically*. Therefore, try to apply the method of diagnostic psychodramatic conversation in your practical work with patients.

You will notice that your therapeutic work or counseling becomes therapeutically more effective through this *seemingly simple technique* of "psychodramatic conversation". The reasons are:

1. The patient's emotionally meaningful conflict or symptom and its energy shift become *externally* visible *on the other two chairs*. The therapist and the patient can define the conflict to be discussed more efficiently and keep the *focus* of their conversation on *that one* conflict. It is more difficult for the patient to jump from one subject to another.

**Important definition**

But some patients change the subject in the psychodramatic conversation again and again. That indicates a structural disorder in the patient. Changing the subject helps the patient protect himself from emotional conflict energies that arise as a result of him *concentrating on one individual* conflict. Perhaps he might struggle in dealing with the conflict because of insufficient ego strength.

**Central idea**

In the psychodramatic conversation, the patient and the therapist look, from the observer's position, at the patient's everyday conflict on the other chairs and retrace *the interaction sequences* in his inner conflict image *chronologically* in the as-if mode of thinking. They look, from a metaperspective, similar to psychodramatic mirroring. They develop a *joint new assessment* of reality in his everyday conflict. This frees the patient's inner self-development in the everyday conflict from the *defense through rationalization* (see Sect. 2.4.3).

**Recommendation**

The psychodramatic conversation method systematically improves the patient's cognition in his everyday conflict by resolving the defense through rationalization. It could therefore make cognitive behavioral therapy more effective.

## Question

Why do the patient and therapist *feel more free* to relate to each other in the psychodramatic conversation than in a normal verbal conversation *without* the two additional chairs?

2. During the psychodramatic conservation, the therapist and the patient internally project the patient's conflict from his everyday life *externally on the two empty chairs*. In doing so, they separate the patient's psychosomatic resonance pattern (see Sect. 2.7) in the current therapeutic relationship from his psychosomatic resonance pattern in his *everyday conflict then and there* by representing them *externally* with chairs. As a result, the patient can easily speak about emotionally intensive conflicts, panic attacks, or delusions. A psychosomatic resonance pattern connects the sensorimotor interaction pattern, physical sensations, affect, linguistic concept, and thought in the current situation (see Fig. 2.8 in Sect. 2.7).
3. But the therapist also internally projects the patient's psychosomatic resonance pattern from his everyday conflict *onto the other two chairs*. She sees 'two patients': the patient in the current relationship with her and the 'other patient' in conflict with his opponent then and there. This reduces the emotional pressure of conflict in the current therapeutic relationship. The therapist *feels more free and creative*. She can make better use of her therapeutic skills. Transferences and countertransferences occur less quickly.
4. Looking at the two empty chairs in his symptom scene repeatedly, the patient focuses less on whether he is being understood *by the therapist* and what *the therapist* could be thinking of him. This reduces his distrust of the therapist. As a result, he feels more free in dealing *with himself* and his relationship conflict.
5. The patient sees the inner object image of his everyday conflict on the other chair in front of him in the *here and now*. This actualizes his perception of *his feelings* toward his "conflict partner", thereby intensifying the experience of the therapeutic conversation.
6. The patient and therapist stand *shoulder to shoulder* and look at the *external* representation of the patient's conflict. The therapist helps the patient retrace the confrontation in his externally represented relationship conflict from his memory in the as-if mode of thinking. She accompanies him as an implicit doppelganger in

the inner interaction with his conflict partner in his everyday conflict and verbalizes *her* perceptions in *his* conflict on his behalf, if necessary. She may even allow the patient *to rehearse the potential future mentally* and consider *the impact of her new behavior*. The *shared* differentiated mentalizing of the patient's conflict takes time. It enables, differentiates, and expands the patient's inner conflict processing. The psychodramatic conversation improves the patient's cognition in his conflict.

**Central idea**

Shoulder to shoulder means: The therapist implicitly becomes *a doppelganger* for the patient in his inner process of self-development in his everyday conflict. The therapist and patient together look at a third person or an object, shoulder to shoulder,

7. The patient and the therapist focus their joint attention on the inner development of the patient's self-image *and* object image in his everyday conflict. They experience that the development of his self-image and object image are mutually dependent. Thus, they gain *a systemic view* of his everyday conflict. As a result, *the therapist* is less likely to identify unilaterally *either* with the patient *or* his opponent in his conflict situation.

The therapist can also use psychodramatic conversation in *group therapy*. She sits together with the group members in a semicircle. She represents the inner self-image and object image of an individual group member with two empty chairs on the stage (the open side of the semicircle). She alternatingly points to one of the *two empty chairs* when talking about the individual's conflict. The psychodramatic conversation then focuses only on one theme for group discussion and activates the mentalizing of the protagonist as well as of other group members.

## 2.9 Psychodramatic Self-Supervision and Supervision

The effect of the *psychodrama techniques* is not dependent on the *therapist's direction*. You can try it out. Try to solve a relationship conflict from your everyday life *on your own*, with the help of psychodrama techniques, *without any guidance from a psychodramatist*. In doing this, apply the method of *psychodramatic self-supervision* (Krüger, 2011, p. 201 f., Krüger, 2017a, 2017b).

***Case example 10***
*40 years ago, I was working as a doctor in the polyclinic of the Hannover Medical School. I had been suffering increasingly for months due to the conflicts with our chief physician. He seemed to reject me. Our relationship was tense. As a psychodrama trainee, I finally decided to clarify the problematic relationship for myself using psychodrama. In my living room at home, I placed an empty chair in front of me and imagined my chief physician sitting on the empty chair opposite me, as I had learned: What does he look like, sitting there? What is his posture like? What gestures is he*

*making? Then I told my 'chief physician', beyond the boundaries of reality, everything that had been bothering me about him: "I am hard working. I think about what I'm doing. But you keep dismissing me. Am I doing something wrong? I don't even know what you want anymore!" Then I changed to the role of the chief physician. I sat on his chair and assumed his posture: I sat up straight as a rod. I became paternal in my gestures. I suddenly noticed: "Ah, that's what it's like! It feels like I have a walking cane inserted in my back instead of a spine!" In the role of my chief physician, I felt bothered by this spontaneous, lively assistant. I struggled to maintain my composure when faced with him. I was afraid of forgetting myself and losing track of things. Back in my role, my anger at the chief physician had disappeared. I thought: "If the cold shoulder treatment I'm receiving from this man is merely self-protection, and he isn't rejecting me, then I don't have a problem with it. I can leave him to it!" My tensions in the relationship with my chief physician were gone the very next day in the polyclinic. They also never came back later.*

*The enactment process helped me mentalize and think through the conflict to the end. As a result, my internal image of my chief physician expanded to include the knowledge of his "self-protective behavior". I had reenacted the body posture of my senior physician and, in doing so, experienced his psychosomatic sensorimotor blockade (see below and* Sect. 2.7*). My changed inner object image allowed me to see him with fresh eyes in everyday life.*

**Exercise 7**

Please apply the method *with psychosomatic acting*. You can't understand the great therapeutic effect just by reading about it. Engage in a fictional psychodramatic dialogue with your' conflict partner' using role reversal. You can use this exercise even if you are not a psychodramatist. This work requires only 5–20 min. Apply the 12 rules given below when you do psychodramatic self-supervision:

1. Choose a room for your self-supervision in which you will be *alone and undisturbed*.
2. Place an empty chair in front of you for your conflict partner or a problematic patient, and imagine this person is sitting on the chair.
3. Look at *your 'conflict partner'* on the empty chair. First, determine internally what overall impression you have of this person. Notice the object image on the second chair in the *here and now*. Don't imagine a situation from the *past*.
4. *Name the affect* that the sight of your conflict partner triggers in you. This is exhausting because a conflict partner often forbids you to feel what you feel. Communicate this *feeling* verbally to your conflict partner.
5. The ensuing psychodramatic dialogue should be *purely fictional*. Express *everything you think and feel* toward your conflict partner and ask all the questions you would like to ask them. Get everything out! For example, if you are a therapist, do *not* treat your 'patient' *therapeutically*. Instead, speak freely and authentically to him in the psychodramatic dialogue. You cannot hurt him in reality because your conflict partner is not sitting on the other chair in reality. You "only" imagine him.

6. During the dialogue, speak *out loudly* in both roles.
7. After every action, reverse roles and respond from your conflict partner's role as you think they *would* react. In the conflict partner's role, ensure that you always *assume their posture*. It is essential to do this because you enter the subjective role experience of your conflict partner also *psychosomatically*.

**Exercise 8**
You can check this observation with an exercise. Sit on your conflict partner's chair and, as an experiment, *take on a completely different posture*; for example, sit in an extremely relaxed manner or very upright. You will notice that a different posture creates a different *physical and mental* state in you. As a result, another *psychosomatic resonance* circuit is activated in you (see Sect. 2.7).

8. Make sure that you *reverse roles frequently*. This is important because if you say too many things to your 'partner' *at once without reversing roles*, you will not be able to react *to each statement* when you change into his role.
9. Check again and again what you *physically feel in your own role*. Name the *affect* that you are *feeling*. In doing this, be careful not to confuse your *feelings* with your *thoughts*. Tell your' conflict partner' what you feel during the dialogue, openly and often.
10. Try and feel, at least once, exactly what you *feel in the role of your conflict partner, too*. Name *his affect* for yourself also. In doing this, the point is not to learn to *empathize* better with your conflict partner but to *understand how he steers himself in the relationship*.
11. End the dialogue when you intuitively get the feeling: "Now I have understood what it is all about," or after 15 to 20 min if you realize: "I can't go any further right now!"
12. At the end of the psychodramatic dialogue, *immediately* write down the answers to the following questions on a piece of paper: 1. What was *new* for me *in the actual enactment* in my experience in my conflict partner's role *or* my role? 2. What became *clearer* for me during the dialogue? Please write down your experience from the play without *any interpretations*! It is important to note down your answer *immediately*! Otherwise, within a few hours, you will forget your *psychosomatic experiences* in your and your conflict partner's role, along with the new findings. Even seemingly trivial experiences in the play can be significant for your inner conflict processing (see case example 10).

**Central idea**

You can recognize the success of the psychodramatic self-supervision based on three indices:

a. Your internal *state of tension* subsides in your relationship with your conflict partner.
b. Your *negative feelings* toward him *disappear*.

c. You become *curious about the next real encounter* with your conflict partner. The twelve steps of psychodramatic self-supervision correspond to the instructions that a psychodrama leader would give. They are a synthesis of many years of practical experience with psychodramatic dialogue in various fields of work. Therefore, *each of the twelve steps is important*. Psychodramatic self-supervision helps the protagonist extend his *individualistic view* of the conflict to a *systemic view* (see case example 10).

**Recommendation**

In psychodramatic self-supervision, *take* your psychosomatic experience in the role of your conflict partner *seriously*. Indeed, this is "only" *your* inner construction of your object representation. But this experience is much more differentiated and psychosomatically more comprehensive than if you try to solve the conflict just by thinking. For example, during the role reversal in the as-if mode of play, you psychosomatically experience the connections between *his* sensorimotor interaction patterns, physical sensations, affect, linguistic concepts, and thoughts (see Sect. 2.7) when in the role of the conflict partner (unlike in a real encounter). In this way, you differentiate and complete your inner object representation and develop a more complete and coherent inner object image.

Some psychodrama therapists say: "I practice self-supervision *only* in thought. That works too!" Of course, it works. But the result will remain unclear. Therefore, it is better to practice self-supervision *with the help of two chairs*!

**Central idea**

In the psychodramatic self-supervision, you complete the *two* holistic relational psychosomatic resonance patterns of your inner self-image *and also* your inner object image in the relationship through the external role reversal. In doing so, you use your five neurophysiological senses: sensorimotor acting, physical sensations, feeling your affect, searching for linguistic concepts, and developing associated thoughts. And you guide them with your intuition. Completing a *holistic psychosomatic resonance pattern* helps you to *psychosomatically* experience whether your conflict partner is acting a certain way on the outside because he wants to protect himself internally, or whether he really rejects you (see case example 10). You then know his true motivation and how he ticks.

The *frequent external role reversal* realizes the interacting and rehearsing in your conflict processing. You will learn to identify and differentiate the cause and effect and *your* and *your conflict partner's share* in the conflict in your relationship.

Empirical evidence demonstrates that psychodramatic self-supervision when used per the above guidelines, leads to progress in inner conflict processing in 80–90 percent of conflicts. This also applies to long-term conflicts. The reasons for this are:

1. In psychodramatic self-supervision, you use three psychodrama techniques to freely implement three tools of mentalizing in your conflict processing *in the as-if mode of play*, namely representing, interacting, and rehearsing (see Sect. 2.2).
2. In a conflict, the inner role reversal is more or less blocked by the defense through projection and introjection. Otherwise, you would know how to resolve your conflict. In self-supervision, however, you *free* your *inner* role reversal from its fixation through *frequent external role reversal* (see Sect. 2.4.3). In doing this, you will discover the cause and effect of your relationship conflict (see Fig. 2.5 in

Sect. 2.3). In addition, you will recognize *your own part* as well as *your conflict partner's part* in the conflict.

3. In acute conflicts, everyone defends themselves more or less through introjection and projection. Humans defend through *introjection* if they inappropriately internalize an attribution or expectation of the conflict partner in their self-image. In doing this, the conflict partner's statement "*You* are a difficult person" becomes "*I* am a difficult person!" In the fictional dialog, however, the protagonist names *his own true affect* and expresses it *openly* to his "conflict partner": "I am hurt and angry at you." He expands his inner self-image of "I am difficult" to include his affect "I am angry". In doing so, he breaks the taboo imposed by his conflict partner and allows himself to feel what he feels. In this way, he can *freely develop* an appropriate inner self-image again *in a new, real encounter* and reassess whether he is *really* difficult in this situation. His *defense through introjection* is resolved (see Sect. 2.4)."
4. Humans defend through *projection* when they are fixed in a biased inner image of the object, for example: "He only wants to assert his interests." However, in the *external* role reversal, the protagonist enters his conflict partner's *inner world* and *psychosomatically* experiences: "I try very hard to make everything work! I mean well!" In this way, the protagonist supplements his inner object image of "He only wants to assert his interests" with the feeling "I'm trying very hard and mean well!" The development of his inner object image is thus set in motion again. In the next real encounter, the protagonist notices those actions and feelings in the conflict partner which he had previously suppressed. The defense by projection is resolved.

**Central idea**

After the psychodramatic self-supervision, the protagonist usually does *not yet know* how he will behave in a real encounter with his conflict partner. So he checks again in the next real encounter: 'Is my conflict partner who I thought he is? Or is my experience in his role in self-supervision true?' The protagonist *spontaneously* reorients (see case example 10) and tries to deal with himself and his conflict partner in a *new and appropriate* way. This makes the relationship more collaborative.

**Important definition**

Psychodramatic self-supervision frees the internal systemic process of self-development in the current situation (see Sect. 2.1) from its fixation in defense. This process includes the constant further development of internal self-image and object image in the course of external interactions. Humans complete the internal process of self-development through mentalizing: the *inner representing* of self-image and object image in the current *external* situation (see Sect. 2.4.1), *interacting and mentally rehearsing* between self-image and object image, and *integrating*. The further development of the inner self-image also changes the inner object image, and vice versa (see Sect. 8.4.2).

10–20% of people do not progress in their conflict processing by psychodramatic self-supervision because they suffer from deficits in the ability to mentalize (see Sect. 4.4). As a result, they cannot adequately work out the difference between their own and their conflict partner's experience in the external role reversal. In such a case, the affected person should get therapeutic help to re-develop his mentalization tools and the ability to reverse roles.

Most people make remarkable progress in less than 20 min when using psychodramatic self-supervision to process their conflicts internally. And yet, everyone has an inner *resistance to* this work. The reason is: The affected person has to be interested in the needs and motivations *of his opponent when reversing roles*. That provokes displeasure. The displeasure makes one find excuses: "Self-supervision will offer me nothing new. I can manage the conflict by reflecting on it." People usually succeed in doing this. However, the *old way* of processing conflicts usually takes longer and costs more energy overall.

A high degree of psychological strain in the conflict or the desire to learn to think *systemically* in conflicts are good motivating factors to overcome the *natural resistance against* psychodramatic self-supervision. I decided to practice the method of psychodramatic self-supervision at least *once weekly*, always on a Monday. Sometimes I do it two to six times a week. I use it in *private* relationship conflicts, to prepare myself for a difficult conversation, or as self-supervision in relationships *with patients*. It takes only 2–10 min because I am well-trained to do it.

**Central idea**

*Regular psychodramatic self-supervision* makes me braver and more humble in private relationships and therapeutic relationships with patients. I practice it as a spiritual exercise, with the same sincerity I meditate daily. Thus, I try to take responsibility for the development of my inner object images and inner self-image in difficult relationships and to resolve my projection and introjection again and again. The constant liberation of my self-development from its fixations makes me more alive and creative (see Chap. 1).

Try it out for six months! You will become more *spontaneous*, more lively, and more capable of managing your relationships. In doing this, you materialize again and again the *psychodramatic vision of the spontaneous-creative human* (see Sect. 2.1) and develop it further within yourself. I often recommend the exercise for participants of introductory seminars, therapists, or students for their own personality development and their "psycho-hygiene". I also teach the method *to patients*, sometimes at the beginning of a course of therapy but usually within the last third of the therapy process (see Sect. 5.11). When *patients* practice psychodramatic self-supervision at home once a week, they save themselves valuable therapy sessions.

In the last ten years, private and social human conflicts have intensified energetically through the climate crisis, the Ukraine war, and Corona crisis. These crises result in social splits and the development of enemy images. I recommend opposing these destructive developments. Psychodramatic self-supervision helps to resolve enemy images and promotes cooperation instead of confrontation because the protagonist systematically gives the conflict partner the right to exist. The protagonist fully verbalizes her own truth in the relationship beyond reality. But she also explores the truth of the conflict partner in role reversal. Gandhi says: "Truth is God." Realizing the truth in a relationship is the basis for every *sustainable* conflict resolution.

**Central idea**

Regular psychodramatic self-supervision is *peace work*. During the Cuban Missile Crisis, Moreno demanded: Kennedy and Cruschtschow should make role reversal with each other. I think, according to Gandhi, we should only ask of others what we do ourselves.

**Recommendation**

In the case of *purely online therapy*, the therapist should carry out self-supervision with the "patient" in her room after four sessions. This is because the interpersonal psychosomatic resonance between the therapist and the patient is partially blocked in the online encounter via video. Psychodramatic self-supervision helps the therapist close any gaps in her psychosomatic perception of the patient by playing the patient's role (Krüger, 2021).

*Therapists* can use the psychodramatic self-supervision even in the case of *disturbances in the therapeutic relationship*. Thus therapists can solve approximately 40 percent of their supervision cases *without the help of a supervisor*. In a further 50 percent of cases, it may be that they gain a new insight or something becomes evident to them, and they resolve countertransference. But in these cases, their state of internal tension and their primary negative feelings concerning the patient remain unchanged. This can be a diagnostic indicator that the emotional reaction of the therapist is *an appropriate reaction* to splitting processes within her patient's self-regulation: By acting in the therapeutic relationship, *the patient* delegates a split-off part of self to the therapist. The therapist, however, *unconsciously* introjects the patient's split-off part of self into her ego through her empathy for the patient. For example, she vicariously feels the *negative affect* split-off from the patient (see Sect. 4.8). In such cases, the therapist should therefore not respond *inappropriately* to her own *appropriate* negative affect as that would result in the acting out of countertransference. Instead, she should continue the psychodramatic self-supervision with the following five additional steps: (see Sect. 4.8):

13. The therapist makes an internal paradigm shift and focuses her attention *no longer on the patient but on herself.* She acknowledges *her own* disorder in the relationship.
14. Before going through the 12 steps of self-supervision, she felt a *negative emotion* toward the patient. She remembers this negative affect and names it, for example: "I was afraid", "I felt powerless", "I felt confused," or similar. It is difficult to name one's own affect because the patient unconsciously forbids the therapist from perceiving and feeling.
15. The therapist determines *the actual external behavior* of the patient that triggered this negative affect in her. She internally attributes this external behavior to *one of the six* possible dysfunctional ego states (see Sect. 4.7): the patient's self-injurious thinking, his 'self-protective behavior through adaptation or grandiosity', 'his inner traumatized or abandoned child', 'his inner angry child', his 'traumatized self' (see Sect. 5.8) or his 'addictive thinking and feeling' (see Sect. 10.5). In doing so, she grasps, for example, *not the contents* of his self-deprecation ("It's always like that with me! I just take a back seat then. I can't do it any other way! I'm just incapable!"). Instead, she centers her attention on the *dysfunctional metacognitive process,* his 'self-injurious thinking' (see Sects. 4.7 and 4.8) which creates different thought contents of his self-deprecation, and responds: "I call that, what you are doing right now, as self-injurious thinking. You have a self-deprecating voice within you that says to you: 'What? Do you have a will of your own? Shame on you!'"

16. The therapist continues the self-supervision. She represents the patient's dysfunctional ego state with an empty chair externally in the therapy room (see Sect. 4.7). She places the chair for self-injurious thinking *opposite him* or the chair for one of the other ego states *next to him* (see Fig. 4.1 in Sect. 4.2). It may be that the therapist suspects the patient may have a *borderline organization*. She then places a second chair next to the patient for his 'dependent and needy side' when the patient is acting in an authoritarian, independent manner. If he is currently acting in his dependent and needy ego state, she places next to him a second chair for his 'authoritarian, independent side' (see Sect. 4.9).
17. The therapist continues the psychodramatic dialog of self-supervision. In doing so, she integrates the second chair for the dysfunctional ego state of the patient into her outer perception. Perhaps the internal state of tension and the therapist's negative emotion toward her "patient" dissipate through steps 13–17 of the self-supervision. That is a diagnostic indicator that the patient is fixated on a rigid defense system and suffers from a personality disorder. The therapist frees herself from her complementary counter-reaction by naming and representing the patient's dominant rigid defense pattern with a second chair beside him.

**Central idea**

If the internal *state of tension and the therapist's negative affect* in the therapeutic relationship are resolved by going through steps 13–17 of self-supervision, she can also use these steps in the patient's *real therapy* as intervention techniques.

In psychodramatic self-supervision, the therapist often speaks of subjects to which she fears the patient would react allergically *in a real encounter*. In role reversal with the 'patient', she notices that sometimes her intervention positively 'reaches' *her in the role of the 'patient'* and that she, as the patient, is *not* hurt by the intervention and considers terminating therapy. This gives her the courage to also use these interventions *in real encounters.*

You can also use steps 13–17 of the psychodramatic self-supervision to clarify *personal* conflicts, for example, in a professional relationship with a colleague. You will become more spontaneous toward your conflict partner and find new solutions in the relationship. You will also become more tolerant of a difficult trait of your *conflict partner* without betraying yourself. In the encounter with your conflict partner in *everyday* life, always *imagine* the chair for his dysfunctional ego state *next* to him. Your cooperation will improve.

In an experimental effectiveness study, Marlok et al. (2016) proved the efficacy of self-supervision for the practice of counseling. The authors compared psychodramatic self-supervision with a supervision technique based on the writing paradigm by Pennebaker (1997). According to Pennebaker, the consultant writes down all of his thoughts and feelings from a consultation session without any control or censorship. Both techniques contribute 'to a reduction in feelings of emotional strain and blockage… In the case of psychodramatic self-supervision *with role reversal,* however, there was a considerably greater improvement in the ability to care for the client and to counsel him in a truly helpful manner.'

**Recommendation**

As a therapist, practice psychodramatic self-supervision once a week with your "patient" or "client" for just 5–10 minutes. You will notice: (1) You attune yourself to the patient's mood (Johann Braun 2022, only verbal communication!) and *orient yourself* in the therapeutic relationship. (2) You become more brave and humble in the real encounter with your patients. You are more clear in your communication because you are more certain of what you trigger in the other person with your answers. (3) You believed that you didn't have any problems with your patients. But, in choosing a patient, you intuitively and unintendedly will have selected a problematic relationship. (4) Your therapeutic work becomes Encounter-Focused Therapy.

A *qualitative study* that I coordinated confirms the findings of Marlok et al. *even for the field of psychotherapy*: Six therapists carried out psychodramatic self-supervision for three of their patients *after every fourth session*, for 10–20 min over five months. They noted down the results. Finally, they compared the process of these three treatments with *three others* with a similar degree of severity and for which they carried out *no self-supervision.*

The psychodramatic self-supervision changed the therapeutic relationship. But, of course, the changes did not always occur in *all* cases and not in *the same way.* Below, I summarize the therapists' responses:

1. In the therapy sessions *using* psychodramatic self-supervision, the therapists felt *more strongly connected* to their patients in the sense of unconditional acceptance. Their communication and the encounter was deeper. The therapists were *less afraid* of being pulled into the patient's suffering due to their empathy. They could be genuinely compassionate toward the patient due to a secure relationship with their own self.
2. They often resolved their own defense through introjection or projection and their countertransference reaction, sometimes their own transference.
3. As a result of the physical-emotional experience in both roles, the therapists could *diagnostically* understand the inner dynamic processes of the patients better.
4. The therapists did not become latently irritated as quickly. They adhered less to preconceived hypotheses. As a result, the real encounters with the patients became more spontaneous and creative. The therapists were often astonished, more curious, and authentically interested in their patients.
5. The therapists were able to notice their emotional reactions more easily and spoke about them with their patients more frequently. They showed more courage, for example, in empathetically confronting their patients. Their patients felt understood and supported nonetheless.
6. The *patients* became more open and sincere, too. They *also dared* to mention their irritations in the therapeutic relationship. The patients experimented more in their everyday life.
7. The therapists became more patient with their clients and with themselves. One therapist, for example, felt helpless and incompetent in working with a person with trauma and chronic pain. He had seen no progress in therapy. However, self-supervision helped him realize that the patient highly appreciated him and his work nevertheless.

Psychodramatic self-supervision is therapeutically more effective than *self-reflection* (Marlok et al., 2016) because it applies the *metacognitive tools* of mentalizing as psychodrama techniques *in its free form.*

The research findings for psychodramatic self-supervision *without guidance from a professional* are astoundingly similar to those of a qualitative study on the effectiveness of role reversal in one-to-one supervision *directed by a supervisor* (Daniel, 2016). The 17 steps of psychodramatic self-supervision are also a model for psychodramatic supervision *by a supervisor*.

*In supervision*, the therapist or counselor usually presents a case in which a patient's defense and the therapist's countertransference have caused a disturbance in the therapeutic relationship. The patient acts out old, inappropriate solutions, and the therapist responds in a more or less complementary way. Many supervisors let their supervisees *verbally narrate* their cases in supervision with findings, anamnesis, and their therapeutic experiences. Together they search through a wealth of information to find the heart of the patient's and the relationship's disorder. This process is tedious and prone to error.

It is easier and less prone to disruption if the supervisor lets the supervisee conduct a fictional psychodramatic dialogue with her "patient" using the 17 steps similar to psychodramatic self-supervision because the *core disturbance of the patient* is often reflected as a *disturbance in the* current *therapeutic relationship.* The first 12 steps of the *fictional* psychodramatic dialogue systematically liberate the therapist from her defenses through introjection or projection and, thus, from her own countertransference through unconscious *concordant identification with* the patient or *complementary identification* with his conflict partner.

The first 12 steps of self-supervision for *patients with a personality disorder* reveal the heart of the disorder. Indeed, the supervisee becomes empathetic again. But usually, she does not know how to proceed therapeutically. She is trapped between her "patient's" rigid pattern of defenses and her own negative emotional reaction to his defense. Therefore, the supervisor asks the supervisee to go through steps 13–17 of psychodramatic self-supervision. The supervisee thus makes the patient's rigid defense pattern the object of therapeutic communication. In doing this, the supervisee uses mental rehearsal in the psychodramatic dialogue. Thus she finds out which therapeutic interventions can dissolve the patient's personality-specific rigid defense and which interventions leave his defense untouched or even strengthen them. In *individual supervision*, the supervisor as a doppelganger can take on the role of the supervisee and the *supervisee* plays the role of his own patient. In doing so, they testify whether new therapeutic interventions could be helpful or not. In *group supervision*, other group members, as doppelgangers, take on the role of the supervisee, not the supervisor herself.

## 2.10 Disturbances in the Therapeutic Relationship, Transference, Countertransference, and Resistance

The psychodrama techniques implement the tools of inner mentalization in the as-if mode of play. During the play, the therapist *internally* accompanies the protagonist's systemic process of self-development (see Sects. 2.4 and 8.4.2) in his conflict processing as an implicit doppelganger by developing the patient's inner self-image as well as his inner object image in his conflict.

**Central idea**

A prerequisite for appropriate psychodrama techniques is that the therapeutic relationship flows without any fixation. If the relationship between the protagonist and the therapist is disturbed, the therapist's spontaneity is blocked. For example, she 'forgets' to use role reversal if she unconsciously identifies with the protagonist *or* his opponent. Addressing the disturbances in the *therapeutic relationship*, therefore, takes precedence over protagonist-centered plays.

I first used the method of psychodrama in group therapy in 1974. In the beginning, I let the patients present their problems in *long* protagonist-centered plays. But four of my patients discontinued therapy during the first four weeks. Today I think they were right to leave because I overwhelmed the protagonists for my learning. This experience resulted in me engaging with the topics of defense and resistance (Krüger, 1980). I had to learn: that psychotherapy is about *the people* first and only then about the *psychodrama method*. Unlike in psychodrama *training groups*, I have to proceed with small steps in a *therapy group. The souls of the patients do nothing without a purpose.*

*How shall a psychodrama psychotherapist deal with disturbances in the therapeutic relationship?* Moreno was known for having a rather directive leading style as a group leader. He believed that "Resistance simply means that the protagonist does not want to participate in the production. It is, therefore, a challenge for the therapist to overcome this initial resistance" (Moreno, 1946/1985, p. VIII). What Moreno referred to as 'resistance' is called 'defense' in depth psychology. A patient who fixates on a defense in the *current* relationship subconsciously uses an *old* solution pattern learned in childhood, *even though* this pattern does not fit the current situation. In terms of depth psychology, I understand *resistance* as a *combination* of transference from the patient and countertransference from the therapist. The combination of transference and countertransference interferes with therapeutic progress.

There are four different disturbances in a therapeutic relationship, (1) disturbances caused by the patient's *defense*, (2) disturbances caused by the patient's *transference* on the therapist, (3) disturbances that are brought about by *the therapist's* transference on the patient and (4) disturbances caused by the patient's transference *as well as* the therapist's countertransference. By definition, the therapist and patient *always* act out their transference and countertransference *unconsciously*.

If the patient is acting out *transference* in the therapeutic relationship, he subconsciously acts out an *old* interaction pattern that he learned in childhood or its opposite. If the *transference is positive*, he perceives the therapist, for example, as the good mother he did not have. In doing so, he imposes a taboo on the therapist, preventing *her* from developing any negative feelings toward him. In such a case, the therapist is enticed to continue to be loving and caring, even though she no longer wishes to. If she doesn't notice this, she reacts with positive *countertransference*. Her positive *countertransference* interferes with further progress in therapy. She then doesn't justify *her own* feelings and acts out her *countertransference*.

If the patient's *transference is negative*, the patient experiences the therapist similarly to an inadequate caregiver in childhood.

**Recommendation**

The therapist should *first* resolve her countertransference *before* working on the patient's transference. Otherwise, the work on the patient's transference will be distorted by *the therapist's* defense through projection or introjection. When the therapist recognizes her countertransference and dissolves it, she perceives the patient in a different light. As a result, the patient's 'resistance' sometimes disappears *on its own* (Dieckmann, 1981, p. 56; Klüwer, 1983, p. 830 f.).

It is therapeutically not helpful to consider the therapist's *every* emotional reaction to the patient as countertransference. I recommend defining countertransference as the therapist's *unconscious* reaction to the patient. I distinguish three different levels of countertransference: (1) conflict-related countertransference, (2) character-related countertransference, and (3) disintegration-related countertransference.

1. *Conflict-related countertransference*: The therapist accompanies the patient internally as an implicit doppelganger in his inner systemic creative process of self-development. If the patient is stuck in a certain inner object image *or* inner self-image through projection or introjection, the therapist becomes curious about how the patient's conflict partner would react if the patient behaved differently. However, the patient considers it taboo to question his own view of things. This fixes the therapist in the complementary counter-reaction. Therefore, if the patient has *a fixed inner object image*, she defends by projecting it onto the patient, fixes it onto her own biased object image, and hides the patient's unsuitable actions from her perception. Accordingly, when the patient defends through introjection, the therapist is often fixed in her own defense through introjection and adapts to the patient's expectations. The 12 steps of psychodramatic self-supervision (see Sect. 2.9) can help the therapist to resolve an unconscious identification *with the patient or his conflict partner*.
2. *Character-related countertransference*: Patients with personality disorders defend through projective identification (see Sect. 2.4.3). The therapist accompanies the patient in his internal systemic process of self-development in the current situation. But, this process is blocked through a rigid defense. Thus, the therapist automatically identifies with the patient's defended part of self and tries to enforce its right. But, the patient fights it by acting out his defense. The therapist then reacts to the patient's rigid defense with an *appropriate negative affect* (helplessness, anger, resignation) (see Sect. 4.8). When the therapist suppresses her appropriate negative affect, she acts out her character-related countertransference. She then devalues the patient *or* herself: "The patient is too ill." "He's

acting like a kid." Or, "I'm incompetent", "I don't have enough experience." The therapist can resolve the disturbances in the therapeutic relationship through steps 13–17 of psychodramatic self-supervision (see Sect. 2.9).
3. *Disintegration-related Countertransference*: The patient's communication or actions indicate self-disintegration and arouse anxiety in the therapist. She fixes her biased inner object image on the patient's strange communication, stops her empathy process, and ascribes a diagnostic term to the patient's strangeness, for example, the term "psychosis". She blocks out from her perception the communication and actions that do not fit the diagnostic term. The therapist's inner distancing from the patient leads to a vicious cycle between the therapist's projection ('a psychotic') and the patient's projection ('the therapist doesn't like me') in therapy. Disintegration-related countertransference occurs in patients with psychotic disorders. The therapist can free herself from the countertransference through a doppelganger dialogue (see Sect. 9.8.2).

In the case of negative transference, the therapist resolves the transference by *differentiating* between the transference conflict and the real conflict.

***Case example 11 (*Krüger, 1997*, p. 256 f., abridged)***
*In a five-day seminar, the director does not immediately respond to 34-year-old Ralph's wish to be the protagonist, even though the group chose him to be the protagonist through* sociometric *selection. In the following session, Ralph complains to the director: "You are just like my father! He was also never there for me!" The director makes Ralph an offer: "Would you like to show me what your father was like? We can then compare the similarities and differences between your father and me!" This develops into a protagonist-centered play. Ralph enacts a scene from when he was five: the 'father' is sitting in an armchair in the living room and reading a religious book. The five-year-old Ralph is sitting on the floor building a large ship with building blocks. He proudly says to his 'father': "Look, daddy!" The 'father' ignores the boy and continues reading. The boy repeats: "Daddy, look what I have built!" The father reacts dismissively. He looks out the window, becomes very stiff, and has obvious difficulty suppressing an outburst of anger. Ralph is disappointed and goes to his mother in the kitchen. Later, when his younger brother follows him back into the living room, Ralph destroys the ship he had built so carefully as a precautionary measure. The group is emotionally very moved in the follow-up discussion.*

Following the protagonist-centered production of a childhood conflict, the protagonists usually receive so much attention, understanding, and compassion from the director and the group members, that they often forget to return to the original plan of treating *the relationship between the protagonist and the therapist*. In this case, the director must actively remind the group of the original aim of the collaborative work, even if he *subjectively* sees no similarity between himself and the negative transference figure of the patient. During the treatment of the disturbance in the relationship, the director and the group members trace the group interactions sequentially based on what they remember. The therapist *internally* actively looks, from the patient's perspective, for *his external actions that were similar* to those of the transference figure of the patient.

***Case example 11 (continued)***

*During the debriefing of the play, the therapist asks the protagonist, as was agreed: "Where did you find me being similar to your father, and where was I different?" The patient and the therapist agree that the following actions of the director resembled the father's behavior: (1) Just like the father did in his childhood, the director dismissed Ralph when he did not respond to Ralph's wish to be the protagonist. In doing this, his external behavior was very similar to the father's behavior. The director's intention, however, was different from that of the father. He had just joined the group after a change of directors. The group had unconsciously chosen Ralph to find out how the director works. The director wanted to protect Ralph from being used by the group. (2) Like Ralph's father, the director had the habit of looking out the window. However, the director explained: "I can then sense better what is happening within the group more freely". (3) The day before, the director gave a lecture to the seminar participants on the topic "Religiousness in Psychodrama". That was similar to the father reading a religious book. (4) The director remembered that in the previous group session, he was still internally occupied with the content of this lecture. He shared this openly with the group: "Ralph, it is your protagonist play and your request for undivided attention that managed to bring me fully into the group after the strenuous lecture". It wasn't until the comparison with Ralph's father that the director recognized Ralph's transference to him also included a real conflict. He invited Ralph at the end of the group session: "Unlike in your childhood, you are allowed to overreact here. You can freely express how you feel even in the future, especially if you feel rejected. You shouldn't let yourself be treated the same way in the group as you were in your childhood by your father?".*

The therapeutic approach to resolving a patient's negative transference includes the following steps:

1. The therapist openly *names her emotion* toward the patient and specifies the behavior that triggered this emotion in her (see Sect. 4.13).
2. This often changes the patient's positive transference into a negative or strengthens his latent negative transference. As a result, the patient experiences the therapist as an absent caregiver from his childhood, helpless, disoriented, sad, disappointed, dull, or powerless. The patient had had enough of that in childhood.
3. The therapist addresses a *negative* transference as soon as possible.
4. She describes *her own actions* which triggered the patient's negative transference and *his emotional response* to her actions. She then asks him about his past experiences with a similar interaction pattern: "Where do you think it comes from when you feel afraid *when* someone frowns at you?"
5. The therapist places an additional empty chair in the therapy room, three meters away from her, to *represent* the patient's negative transference figure (see Fig. 4.4 in Sect. 4.13).

6. The therapist helps the patient describe the recalled interaction with his transference figure. Then, if necessary, she encourages him to show this interaction in a *protagonist-centered play* (see case examples 11).
7. The therapist and the patient work together in delineating the similarities and differences between her and the transference figure (see case example 11). The therapist may have *behaved similarly* to the negative transference figure, but mostly her *motivation behind this behavior* was quite different. For example, she wanted to be honest with him and take him seriously (see Sects. 4.13 and 4.14). She *did not* want to offend the patient and *doesn't* leave him alone.
8. The therapist and the patient deliberate actively: "Which of your actions would be an *old* behavior, and what would be a *new* and progressive behavior in the therapeutic relationship?" The mutual understanding and agreement result in a tele-relationship between the two (Krüger, 2010c, S 231ff.).
9. The therapist concludes a contract with the patient: The patient may feel sensitive about his neurotic wound. However, unlike in his childhood, *he should try to tell the therapist if his wound is activated* in the therapeutic relationship in the future. The therapist then promises to honestly share with him *how* she feels and the motivation behind her actions in *that* situation.

**Central idea**

Every conflict resulting from a transference also includes an actual conflict (Blatner, 2010, p. 7; Holmes, 1992, p. 45 f.; Kellermann, 1996, p. 104). Resolving transference in the therapeutic relationship can only be considered successful (Krüger, 2010c, p. 228) when the therapist and the patient can, in the end, agree on what they understand *as the real conflict* and the *product of transference* in the disturbance in the therapeutic relationship. The confirmation of reality in the conflict has an *ego-strengthening* effect on the patient and promotes their autonomy development.

**Recommendation**

Psychodrama therapists should know a range of therapeutic options that can help to resolve a patient's transference, their own countertransference, and resistance in the case of disturbance in the therapy process. Without such options, they will actively try to deny disturbances in the therapeutic relationship and often act out their countertransference. Thus, they will no longer remain spontaneous in the therapeutic relationship and cannot fully utilize their therapeutic abilities.

## 2.11 Group Dynamics, Transference, Countertransference, and Resistance in Group Psychotherapy

The participants in a group develop a "socio-dynamic distribution of function" (Heigl-Evers, 1968, p. 290) within the first five to eight sessions. "For a group to be able to optimally use its possibilities and personal resources to achieve the (self) set goals, it needs someone who takes the initiative and demands new concepts. It needs people who participate, show allegiance, and support the initiatives loyally and with commitment. And it needs someone to stand up against it, to oppose competently and to get the drivers to review their concepts" (König & Schattenhofer, 2006, p. 53).

Raoul Schindler (1973, p. 30 ff.) has divided the sociodynamic functions of the group into the omega position, the alpha position, the beta position, and the gamma position.

1. A group member in the omega position protests against the group's current goal *"based on inferiority and weakness"* (Heigl-Evers, 1968, p. 283). The Omega is recognizable *by his actions*: He eventually wants to stop group therapy, often comes too late, or misses the group. He almost falls asleep during the session, clowns around, or is the most silent group member.
2. The group member in the *alpha position* leads the group action overtly or latently. He represents the group against external opponents and expresses through his actions "Follow me! This is how we achieve success!"
3. A group member in the *beta position* observes what is happening in the group from a reasonable distance and intervenes as an expert in an integrating manner. The beta position is, therefore, also the *default position of the therapist*: "Taking up the beta position enables the therapist to adopt the attitude of benevolent neutrality desirable for every treatment ... The beta is the representative of Yes-but! He is someone who doubts from a largely neutral position, expresses concerns, and gives appropriate advice and pointers" (Heigl-Evers, 1967, p. 95).
4. According to Schindler (1957/1958, p. 311), in the *gamma position,* one is "without one's own responsibility, lives in the alpha's affectivity, and occupies the place that the unconscious of the alpha demands. As gamma, one's experience of group events is based on identification with the alpha." As followers, the gammas support the alpha, protect him, give him emotional strength through their like-minded will, and control him.

**Central idea**

The ideal protagonist in a psychodrama group is the group member in the alpha position or the gamma position.

The group participants in the alpha or gamma position promote the current group topic with their protagonist-centered plays and benefit from each other through similar conflict dynamics. At some point, however, a group topic will be exhausted. The group then searches for a new group topic by trial and error. This leads to group conflicts, in which a new group topic is constellated. With the new group topic, those group members who are most sensitive to it because of their own problems then take on the alpha and the omega position. Group conflicts are just as important for the development of the group as protagonist-centered plays (see Sect. 8.4.5). The director also allows group conflicts to be dealt with *psychodramatically* (see case example 12). Group conflicts help to work out the *latent group topic* negotiated in the conflicts. The group members in the Alpha and Gamma positions can then further advance the group action in protagonist-centered plays.

***Case example 12***

*In the 28th session of group therapy, Dora berates the group moodily and loudly: "It's all pointless here, the group doesn't help anyone." The group members respond to her and report small successes that have already occurred. Waltraud gets involved and accuses Dora of "unreasonably high expectations". But Dora protests: "I hate this cuddling!" From the inferior omega position, she draws the group members' attention to the fact that they treat each other kindly. As the alpha, Waltraud defends the way relationships are formed in the group.*

*The director does not ascribe Dora's criticism of the group to himself. Instead, he suggests that Dora and Waltraud clarify their relationship with one another: "Waltraud, please take a close look at the posture Dora is sitting in. And you, Dora, please note Waltraud's posture!—Now, please switch roles and sit on the other chair in the posture you just saw the other one hold. —Now, reenact your discussion from the other role, just as you experienced it!—After that, play the roles a little beyond reality!".*

*In the debrief, Waltraud says, "It was a strange experience playing Dora. I was afraid. I had to yell and be aggressive so as not to let the others get to me." In the role of Waltraud, Dora felt: "I didn't feel comfortable as Waltraud, I always had to be satisfied, I wasn't allowed to criticize anything!" The therapist asks Dora as an omega (mirror question): "How did you experience yourself from Waltraud's role?" Dora says thoughtfully: "Yes, she actually seemed helpless.—That's right, sometimes I feel that elsewhere too. I yell so that others don't get too close to me." The therapist turns to Waltraud as an alpha: "And how did you perceive yourself from the other role?" Waltraud: "Waltraud seemed to me as if she could not harm a fly!" The therapist asks Waltraud the transference question: "Do you recognize this about yourself from other relationships, that you cannot harm a fly?" Waltraud immediately remembers her workplace problems. As a social worker with disabled children, she had completely overburdened herself: "I never fought my superiors. I finally quit to save myself." The group members report who can identify more with Dora or with Waltraud. The therapist requests Dora to tell how someone made her helpless and aggressive by getting close to her. He recommends that Waltraud deal with her workplace conflict psychodramatically in the next group session.*

The relationship between alpha and omega is characterized by *reciprocal complementarity* (Heigl-Evers, 1967, p. 88 f., 1968, p. 289): The patient in the alpha position *represses* what the patient in the omega position expresses openly. However, the patient in the omega position represses what the patient in the alpha position expresses openly. In the case example, Dora, as the omega, played out her mistrust of "cuddling" in the group, while Waltraud, as the alpha, suppressed this skepticism. However, as alpha, Waltraud acted out her willingness to be content irrespective of the group circumstances, which Dora, as an omega, repressed in herself. The latent group theme was the conflict between the two polarities "I want to live in harmony forever, and I don't fight back" and "I always want to be honest, even if that makes me an outsider."

When choosing the protagonist, the director supports those group members who want to work on a problem as alpha or gamma. In the case example, these were the people who brought up the problem of always desiring to live in harmony and being there for others even if they fail, are overwhelmed, or let themselves be taken advantage of. The director *can also participate* in choosing the right protagonist. If he has little or no desire in leading a particular protagonist's play, it is an indication that this play is not suitable in the context of current group dynamics. In choosing the protagonist, the director looks for the latent group theme: (1) He first determines the group member in the omega position. It is easier to recognize the omega than the alpha because he protests against the goal or the setting of the group *through his actions*. (2) The director internally grasps the *positive sense* in the helpless acting of the omega. (3) He formulates the complementary counterposition to the omega and looks for the group member who is most likely to represent this counterposition. (4) He supports the group members in the alpha or gamma position in their desire to play in the following sessions because they further the development of the group. (5) Or the director lets one of the two conflict partners work out the difference between the real and the transference conflict in their relationship (see case example 11 in Sect. 2.10). Differentiating between transference and reality in a relationship helps the group members to define their old neurotic behavior as 'their old behavior' and look for new behaviors.

The protagonist-centered plays of group members in the alpha and gamma positions are *also helpful for the omega* because the omega's protest is indirectly represented by the protagonist's *conflict partners* in their play. The omega is thus integrated into the group with his protest. He indirectly learns and develops his own identity in the group's plays. The group participants should get to know the consequences of their own actions in a psychotherapy group. They have to experience these consequences directly in the group as a reality. When choosing the protagonist, for example, the approval of the group members matters. But it is just as important that the protagonist himself feels the suffering and has enough courage and energy to play the game. Only then there is a chance that he will process his conflict in his play. If a patient is reluctant to embark on a journey, there is a reason. The director, therefore, asks him with interest: "What makes it difficult for you to play here today?" The patient's anxiety may be due to a neurotic defense. But it may also be *realistic*. Perhaps the patient realistically feels that he *cannot* work on his problem successfully *at this point in this group situation*. The therapist then works on the relationship conflicts in the group first (see case example 12). Many psychodramatists let the group members *select* the protagonist for the current session *sociometrically*. They believe then they act abstinent.

**Central idea**

A director is *always* part of the group dynamic and changes it through his actions, personality, therapeutic interventions, feedback, and the rules and values he represents. So the question is not whether he has a sociodynamic function in the group but *how* he deals with it and whether he is *aware* of the group position he occupies. His default position is the beta position, both in conflicts between the group members and in the protagonist-centered play in the conflict between protagonist and antagonist.

If the director unilaterally favors self-assertion in the group, over time, he will push anxious group members into the omega position. On the other hand, a director with a helper attitude pushes those group members into the omega position in particular, who no longer feel like empathizing with the suffering of others. A director with a biased value system ends up in the alpha position of the group over time. The more biased he is, the more likely it is. He should then integrate the omega's protest as a *complementary truth* in his understanding of cause and effect in the group. Otherwise, the group and the director will get stuck in a shared group resistance.

The sociometric selection of the protagonist is problematic *in the case of group resistance* because the group members act out their conflicts in their relationship with the therapist. In such a case, they often choose the patient in the omega position to be the protagonist. But he protests helplessly against the group's resistance. Leading his play, the group director then tries to free the protagonist from his helplessness. That usually doesn't work. He thus finds *himself* in the omega position (Krüger, 2011, p. 198f.). He feels overwhelmed and powerless when directing. In such a case, the therapist continues as follows: (1) He makes a paradigm shift and justifies his own feeling of being overwhelmed and powerless in the context of the group situation. (2) He stops the protagonist's play at an appropriate point and does a normal debriefing. (3) He centers his attention on the current *relationships between* the group members and actively promotes the interactions *between* the group members and the protagonist in the omega position. The alpha is the one who most strongly defends the omega's protests through their attitude or actions. (4) The director asks the group members in the alpha and the omega positions to resolve their relationship difficulties psychodramatically.

As a psychiatrist, Moreno was an ingenious psychotherapist, healer, artist, and prophet. However, as is well known, he had a *directive leadership style*. Directors with a directive leadership style take the alpha position in group dynamics. They pay too little attention to disruptive reactions from group members and tend to defend through projection (see Sect. 2.4.2). A director in the alpha position can "use the great opportunity to support the development of the super-ego of group members, as would be the case with abandoned people" (Schindler, 1957/1958, p. 311). However, patients in group therapy are usually *not abandoned*. A director in the alpha position tends to overlook his *subconscious contribution* to the disturbances in the group's relationships. As a result, the disturbances cannot be resolved. This will hinder the further development of the group members. "When the director finds himself in the alpha position, the group presents itself as his unconscious, and he is only able to analyze himself in the group" (Schindler, 1957/1958, p. 311). A director in the alpha position is at risk of narcissistically abusing the group members. The longer the group runs, the more the risk. He's the star of the group, his followers in the gamma position dazzle in his glow. The group members more or less openly develop a hierarchy among themselves. The director uses the group members who adopt his goals to support him. However, he will dump them if they develop desires or beliefs that differ from his own.

Moreno, who developed psychodrama, was trapped in this alpha trap. He did not conduct long-term group psychotherapy himself (Leutz, 2013, verbal communication). However, he often came to a training group and took over the group's leadership *for this one session*. He would even call participants from a training group to his office *individually* (Marcia Karp, 2002, only oral communication) and tell them: "You are a genius!" Each of the chosen ones believed they had a very special relationship with Moreno. But Moreno often dumped his students again. In the introduction to his book "Das Stegreiftheater" (Moreno, 1970, p. XIV), he writes: "The task of the psychodrama academy is … to discover and train directors of the highest culture. Unfortunately, not all directors we have trained have the same quality. We, therefore, have to remove many directors from the practice." Moreno's son (Moreno, 1995, p. 6f.) stated: "Moreno saw himself as the *father* of therapeutic action methods. However, his demands for loyalty often jeopardized relationships with promising students." Moreno's son removed many accounts of Moreno's "incredibly active love life" from Moreno's extensive autobiography for publication (Moreno, 1995, pp. 12f., p. 33). In a MeToo debate today, Moreno would not get away unscathed (Moreno, 1995, p. 22 and p. 33).

In a directive leadership style in a group, the director projects his own blocked impulses into the group member in the omega position.

***Case example 13***

*In a training seminar in Budapest, a psychodrama director demonstrated the seven steps of psychodramatic dialogue with role reversal using the example of a participant's marital conflict (see* Sect. 8.4.2*). In the debrief, three participants said: "It would have been important also to explore the protagonist's childhood. She could have explored why she is adjusting in her marriage in such a way." Another group member, Mr. A., added: "It makes me angry when you, as the director, are also discussing the whole play theoretically now!".*

*Mr. A. had repeatedly irritated the director with critical remarks before. The director felt increasingly annoyed with Mr. A. He noticed that he can no longer pay attention to the other group members sufficiently. That's why he practiced psychodramatic self-supervision by conducting a fictional conversation with "Mr. A" in his hotel in the evening (see* Sect. 2.9*). In the psychodramatic dialogue, he shared with "Mr. A.": "I'm angry with you. You always have something to criticize. I find you arrogant!" The director switched roles and responded as Mr. A: "I find you arrogant too!" The director switched back to his own role. He wondered what Mr. A. could see as arrogant about him. But he understood: "I am enthused by the effectiveness of the psychodramatic dialogue. When it comes to marital conflicts, in particular, it is important to always look for solutions directly in the current relationship. But the group participants are experienced therapists! After all, they might have some success exploring childhood events in protagonist-centered plays of marital conflicts. If I present my way of working as the only way, I'm actually arrogant!".*

*The director suddenly became curious: "What would have been different in the approach practiced here in Hungary in exploring childhood?" He thus went from the alpha to the beta position and adopted the "Yes-but" attitude with the help of the psychodramatic self-supervision. The following day he suggested that the protagonist replay her marital conflict and go back to her childhood: "Perhaps one of you group members would like to direct the play. Then we can compare the advantages and disadvantages of the two approaches." The protagonist was ready for the alternative play. But no group member wanted to direct it. The director was a little disappointed.*

*However, the relationship problems in the group were resolved by his offer. In the following sessions, the group members continued to work with interest on the given seminar topics.*

In the training group, the director had, without realizing it, found himself in the alpha position of the group. Mr. A. protested against the director because he perceived that he was using the group members for his own purposes. He was the action leader of the *group's resistance* against the director's goals. If a director is involved in group conflict, he should attempt to resolve the group conflict on his own *after the group session* through psychodramatic self-supervision (see Sect. 2.9). In doing so, he chooses the group member that *disturbed him the most in the group*, the action leader of the group resistance. He then looks for the positive meaning in the action leader's thinking and feeling in the group resistance in self-supervision *with role reversal*. The contents of the disruptive group member's protest are often the *complementary truth* that the director himself suppresses in his perception of the situation. In the case example, the director realized that he himself had also behaved arrogantly without realizing it. He incorporated the group's complementary truth, "You're not being mindful of us!" in his perception of the group situation. He thus internally reached the therapeutically *favorable* beta position of Yes-but again (see Sect. 2.9.5, Krüger, 2011, p. 310 ff.; Schindler, 1957/1958, p. 310 ff.): Yes, he wanted to convey the agreed content of the seminar, *but* he was *also* curious about the group members' contrary experiences. He offered to clarify these other experiences in a protagonist-centered play exploring childhood too.

Directors can also capture and work on the latent group theme with the help of fairy tale plays. The group participants sociometrically choose a fairy tale, look for a role in it, and act out the fairy tale together. Experience shows that in groups that have existed for some time, the hero or heroine of the fairy tale usually represents the truth suppressed by the group. For example, a group that works sensibly and effectively enacts the "Hans in Luck" tale, in which the hero lives in the moment and enjoys life, contrary to social norms. A director *in the alpha position* of the group can see the complementary truth repressed by himself in the action impulses of the hero of the fairy tale. His own truth and the truth of the hero in the fairy tale often stand in a reciprocally complementary relationship. This brings the director back into the therapeutically favorable beta position of the group. He understands and spells out the latent group theme. He then asks the group participants how they each deal with the latent group issue. For example, this can be the conflict between the position "I always act purposefully" and "I like to live in the moment". Next, the director asks the group members to make a sociometric constellation on the latent group theme. He symbolizes the two opposing positions of group dynamics, each with a chair in two opposite corners of the group room. He then asks the group members to find their place *on the line between* these two opposite poles. This place is intended to symbolize the respective intrapsychic balance between the two poles of the conflict. Each group member justifies their choice of position on the line *between* the two extreme positions.

**Central idea**

Resolving disturbances in group relationships requires the director to be willing to consistently *review his self-image* in the mirror of the group members' reactions, examine his attitude, and learn something new about himself. The *reality* in group relationships is always *inter-subjective.*

## 2.12 The Implications of Mentalization-Oriented Theory for Psychodramatic Work

**Central idea**

The mentalization-oriented understanding of psychodrama psychotherapy differentiates and expands the theory and practice of psychodrama *and changes it.*

### *2.12.1 Psychodrama is More Than a Method of Group Therapy; It is a Form of Psychotherapy*

Many therapists understand psychodrama psychotherapy as a psychotherapy method *dependent* on the *group therapy format* for its therapeutic efficacy. Moreno (1959) himself once said: "Psychodrama is depth therapy in and of a group." But psychodrama is a *psychotherapy method* that can be applied to *various formats.* A format (Buer, 2005, p. 289) is a setting such as group therapy, individual therapy, supervision, coaching, or team development. But, *different methods* can be applied to the group therapy format, for example, psychodrama, psychoanalysis, theme-centered interaction, behavioral therapy, group dynamics, and others. Psychodrama therapists who bind the *psychodrama psychotherapy method* to the *group therapy format,* unnecessarily limit their options for therapeutic action. It is not 'the group' but the *direct work on the metacognitive* processes which is the hallmark of psychodrama.

**Central idea**

Patients are fixated on defense patterns *in individual therapy sessions* in the same way *as* in group therapy sessions. The therapist can, therefore, dissolve the patient's defense with the help of psychodrama techniques, *even in individual therapy* (see Sect. 2.4). Psychodramatists, who understand the *metacognitive* effects of psychodrama techniques, use them in 50–80% of their individual therapy sessions.

*Moreno* mainly used psychodrama *in the individual therapy format* to treat his severely ill inpatients. Straub (2010, p. 28) reported that she worked for eight months as an intern in Moreno's sanatorium in Beacon in 1954. Of the twelve patients in the clinic, approximately eight were diagnosed with psychotic disorders at a time. While Straub worked there, Moreno *did not once put these patients together in a therapy group.* The only psychodrama case examples in Moreno's standard works (Moreno, 1959; Moreno & Moreno, 1975a, 1975b; Moreno, 1946/1985) are those in which Moreno worked *in an individual therapeutic setting.* Indeed, according to Leutz (2013, only oral communication), Moreno often participated in group therapy sessions *led by his students*, but only ever for one sitting. He would take over the directorship of the group in this one session, and then the psychodrama psychotherapists led the group on their own *in the following sessions.*

The definition of psychodrama as a group therapy method has had negative consequences: (1) It blocked the development of theory. (2) Psychotherapists and counselors who work *with outpatients* treat 95 percent of their patients in an *individual setting*. Therefore, Psychodrama *as a group therapy method* is attractive only to a few therapists. (3) Many psychodrama training institutes teach psychodrama primarily *as a group therapy method*. Therefore, future psychodrama therapists learn too little about the use of psychodrama in individual therapy.

**Recommendation**

The more severe the patient's difficulty in mentalizing, the stronger the indication to use psychodrama *as individual therapy*. The therapist should decide on the setting of psychodrama therapy after considering the patient's ability to mentalize.

Patients with severe deficits in their mentalizing will only benefit from psychodramatic group psychotherapy *after* they have developed an awareness of their dysfunctional conflict management in disorder-specific individual therapy (see Sect. 4.8). *But in a hospital setting,* the therapist can offer *disorder-specific* group psychotherapy. For example, Sáfrán and Czáky-Pallavicini (2013) developed a structured method for the group psychotherapy of patients suffering from post-traumatic stress disorder. Waldheim-Auer (2013, p. 196) and Waniczek et al. (2005) worked with a group of people suffering from addiction disorders.

### 2.12.2 The Interrelationship Circuit Between the Patients' Mentalizing and Their Psychodramatic Play Must not Be Interrupted

It is important that, at the end of the therapy session, the patient's *internal* conflict images have been enhanced by *external* psychodramatic play. But if the connection between the patient's internal mentalizing and external play *is interrupted, the inner images remain unchanged.* This can happen, for example, when a patient enacts a traumatic scene on the stage. The therapist often doesn't notice that the patient has dissociated (see Sect. 5.10). In such a situation, his conflict processing during the play is blocked by a state of shock.

***Case example 14***

*A psychodrama psychotherapist complains in supervision: "I have psychodramatically worked with a traumatized patient and addressed her experience of being physically abused by her mother for two hours in a group. I let her do everything, including a fictional conversation with her mother through role reversal. But then, in the follow-up discussion, the patient said: 'That was nothing new for me. I already knew it all!'" The therapist felt devalued and helpless. She did not notice that the protagonist had dissociated during the psychodrama play and was, therefore, unaware of her emotions. As a result, she was emotionally absent for the duration of the play. She performed the play only at a cognitive level. In such a case, the therapist herself experiences a lot during the enactment of the trauma experience, but the patient does not feel anything. While dissociating, she simply adapts and conforms to the therapist's instructions. The supervisor recommended that a disorder-specific approach would help resolve dissociation when working through trauma (see* Sect. 5.10*).*

### 2.12.3 The Use of Psychodrama Techniques Becomes Easier

Psychodramatists who use mentalization-oriented thinking in psychodrama (see Sect. 2.2) *closely follow the path of natural internal conflict processing* in their practical work. They thus make fewer detours. Psychodrama is highly complex, even if it appears simple from the outside. A psychodrama therapist needs the courage to work with the patient along the path of his dysfunctional conflict processing in the as-if mode of play.

The mutual creative process of a psychodramatic play is sometimes akin to a shared trip during white water rafting. This is why many psychodrama psychotherapists protect themselves from the play's undercurrent and gather as much information as possible from the protagonist about the conflict *before the enactment*. When constructing the scene, for example, they let the protagonist "*double the auxiliary ego*" by playing the role of his conflict partner. The protagonist stands *behind* the auxiliary ego representing his wife, and the therapist asks him: "How old are you as your wife?" "How do you feel standing here opposite your husband?" "How long have you two been married?" "Are you employed?" 'Doubling the auxiliary ego' interrupts the patient's internal warm-up process for his protagonist play. This is because, when 'doubling' in this manner, the patient shifts internally from *his* role into that of *his conflict partner*. In doing so, he opposes his own impulse to act and blocks it internally. Then, when the protagonist begins playing *his role*, he must first reactivate his *own* feelings and desires.

If the therapist gets too much information beforehand, she is tempted to develop some hypotheses *before* the play has begun and decide in advance what the content of the patient's enactment could be. Such assumptions can easily block *the therapist's* free creative process of mentalizing on behalf of the patient, thereby leading to disturbances in the creative process of attunement and agreement with the patient during psychodramatic play.

**Recommendation**

The therapist should *not* have the patient relate the events of his conflict *before the play*. She is thus better able to remain spontaneous and curious and to assume the Socratic attitude, which will help her employ the right psychodrama techniques (see Sect. 2.5).

Before the actual play, the therapist can limit herself to four questions and instructions (see Sects. 2.9 and 8.4.2): (1) She asks the protagonist when constructing the scene: "Who is or was involved in the conflict?" Then, she lets the protagonist choose a group member to take on the opponent's role *or* represent it with an empty chair. (2) She addresses him in his role and asks: "How old is your wife?" (3) "What is your general intuitive impression of her?" (4) "What posture is she in?" The auxiliary ego who is playing the protagonist's "wife" should then use this limited information to intuitively develop an idea for the formation of the wife's role. In doing so, the auxiliary ego does not always get the reality of the role *right the first time*. Therefore, the therapist asks the patient, if required, to reverse roles with the auxiliary ego, enact parts of the scene, and 'show' how his wife is, how she reacted, or how she would reply.

Some therapists restrict the spontaneity and creativity of the psychodramatic work by practicing other habits. When doubling, for example, they *always* lay their hand on the shoulder of the patient. In exceptional cases, this can be an important gesture that testifies to the closeness of the therapist. However, one should avoid laying hands on the shoulders *regularly* when doubling.

**Exercise 9**

If you are a psychodramatist, work with a colleague to explore the similarities and differences between doubling *with* a hand on the protagonist's shoulder and doubling *without physical contact with the protagonist*. Check whether you experience a difference between the two types of verbal doubling, both as a director and in the role of the protagonist. You will notice that when you are *in the role of the protagonist*, the physical contact caused by the therapist's hand distracts you *from being yourself* and *your spontaneous inner mentalizing*. It shifts your attention from yourself *to the therapist's words*. Doubling without laying on of hands, on the other hand, activates your own inner mentalizing.

Similarly, the *regular 'de-rolling'* of auxiliaries after a psychodrama is also questionable. Leutz (2013, oral communication) introduced this technique in her practical work with psychodrama. De-rolling is necessary when a group member has had to remain in a *challenging* auxiliary ego role for an extended period. In all other cases, however, the group members *spontaneously* find their way out of the auxiliary ego roles and go back to being themselves as they formulate their role feedback in the *past tense*: "In the play, I *felt* annoyed when in the role of your wife." The sharing also helps them find their way back to themselves as they report some of *their own* similar experiences and thus gain distance from the protagonist's experience.

Some therapists ask the protagonist to 'de-role' their auxiliary egos by 'brushing off the roles' with their hands, from the shoulders down along the body. This is supposed to 'prevent the development of transferences'. However, this is a naïve assumption because transferences are always *unconscious*. A transference will continue to exist after the protagonist de-roles his auxiliary.

**Central idea**

Psychodramatic work is highly complex, even if it appears simple from the outside. Psychodramatists who introduce *too many* rules and an extensive, complicated repertoire of techniques in their practical work impress their audience and themselves. But, they don't follow the patients' inner mentalizing processes. In mentalization-oriented psychodrama psychotherapy, the therapist does not attempt to 'do good'. Rather, she intuitively lets go of 'doing wrong' and omits the superfluous.

### *2.12.4 The Therapist Thinks in a Systemic and Process-Oriented Manner*

In mentalizing, conflicts are naturally 'structured as dyads or dialogues' (Dornes, 2013, p. 79). They must therefore be *systemically* understood as a *relationship conflict* between the patient's inner self-representation and corresponding object representation (Sect. 2.2) or as an intrapsychic conflict between two parts of the self or two ego states (see Sects. 4.3, 4.10, and 10.5). The psychodrama therapist intuitively pays attention to the interplay of energetic forces and counterforces in the patient´s conflict management in her practical work. She constantly conceives this as an action and reaction in the conflict system of the patient. In group therapy, the focus of the conflict processing can be on the *interaction in* (1) the systemic self-organization process of the individual patient, (2) the relationship between the therapist and the patient during their *real encounter*, (3) the relationship between the therapist and the protagonist *during the psychodramatic play*, or (4) the systemic self-organization of the group.

**Central idea**

The human self is a self-organizing system. If the patient progressively changes *his self-image* in a conflict, he will distance himself further from his conflict partner or assert himself better against him. The change in his self-image automatically *changes the conflict partner's behavior*. Conversely, if the patient changes *his inner image of the conflict partner*, it automatically changes the patient's *own behavior* (see Sect. 8.4.2).

The therapist also understands the therapeutic relationship with her patient as a self-organizing system. Changing her self-image will automatically also change her patient's behavior. Likewise, a change in her internal image of the patient automatically changes her own behavior.

**Central idea**

The therapeutic relationship succeeds when the therapist does justice to her patient and to herself. *The soul of the patient does not do anything for free.* But the soul of the therapist doesn't do anything for free, either. Therefore, in practical work, the therapist always pays attention to her emotions.

*Disturbances in the therapeutic relationship* hinder spontaneity and creativity *in a psychodramatic play*. In such a case, the therapist *cannot freely follow* the patient's mentalization process in the play (see Sect. 2.10).

### 2.12.5 The Group is to Be Understood as a Self-organizing System

**Central idea**

In psychodrama group therapy, the idea of the creative human transforms into the concept of the *creative group* as a self-organizing system. The therapist sees herself as part of this system.

With a systemic and process-oriented style of direction, the therapist avoids determining the course of a group session through methodological guidelines. She understands the group *as a living, self-organizing system* (Krüger, 2011). She applies the psychodrama techniques *only when* they are indicated and follows her intuition in doing so. For example, the group members shall learn to offer their sharings *spontaneously*. The therapist asks the group to offer their sharings *only when* she feels that the protagonist needs to be reintegrated, as an equal among equals, into the human community of the group. The therapist asks the protagonist and his auxiliary egos *for role feedback only* when she observes that the protagonist has not yet adequately mentalized his experience of the *external* drama. The psychodrama techniques should be indicated in the actual process of conflict processing. If they are not, the therapist should try to hold back. She then lets group members learn from the consequences of their actions or inaction in the group. In doing so, the therapist remains in the therapeutically valuable beta position (Heigl-Evers, 1967, p. 95). This is the position of the specialist who intervenes with a systemic orientation and actively mediates between the interpersonal interactions in a group from a yes-but attitude.

Rules can help create a sense of safety for the participants *at the beginning of a closed group*. Consequently, the participants find it easier to overcome their neurotic withdrawal while getting to know each other and establish trust more readily. However, these rules become *problematic at a later stage*, when the issues of inferiority, power, and rivalry actualize or when the issues of autonomy and detachment finally rise to the surface. The leader then *finds herself in the alpha position*. Over time, a therapist in the alpha position will hinder and *not encourage the development* of the group members. She would deny *her subconscious contribution* to the disturbances in the therapeutic relationship. Sooner or later, these disturbances will block the patient's and *therapist's* mentalizing processes, thereby hindering the group's therapeutic progress and giving rise to group resistance (see Sect. 2.11).

### 2.12.6 The Mentalization-Oriented Theory Strengthens the Effects of Psychodrama Therapy and Counseling

Grawe (1995) has identified four general mechanisms of change that are the basis for the efficacy of *all psychotherapy methods*: problem actualization, resource activation, clarification of motivation, and problem-solving. These mechanisms are valid for every psychotherapy method, regardless of the therapeutic techniques used. However, these general mechanisms of change in each psychotherapy method are repeatedly blocked in the therapy of patients experiencing mental health difficulties. Different psychotherapy methods have developed a variety of therapeutic interventions *to prevent or resolve* such disturbances in the therapeutic relationship.

Psychodrama is particularly well suited for this because, when *adequately used*, psychodrama techniques follow the path of the patient's *natural* mentalization process *in the as-if mode of play* (see Fig. 2.3 in Sect. 2.2). Thus, psychodrama can implement the *general mechanisms* of change even in psychotherapy of severe mental disorders:

1. Problem actualization: Through psychodramatic play, the patients realize the *inner* process work of their conflict *outside* on the stage of the therapy room or the desk in the as-if mode of play. The therapist uses the three-stage model (see Fig. 4.1 in Sect. 4.2), where interpersonal conflicts, intrapsychic conflicts, and conflicts in the therapeutic relationship *are present* side by side. The processing of conflicts is *updated experientially.* The conflicts become tangible *in the here and now* and change for the better.
2. Resource activation: The therapist focuses on the person's capacity to be creative. She activates the natural tools of mentalization using psychodrama techniques. The therapist's basic attitude is, "Why not? A person's soul does nothing for free." This also applies to therapy in the context of people with psychotic disorders (see Chap. 9). If necessary, the therapist works with the patient to radically work out the positive meaning of old defensive behaviors and integrate it into the appropriate framework. She recognizes and names the patient's positive abilities, appropriate coping strategies in the present and as a child, possible transpersonal experiences, and positive stabilizing factors in childhood and his current relationship network. She gives them all appropriate meanings.
3. Clarification of motivation: The patient gains the ego's control over its unconscious defense processes *in the as-if mode of play.* He thus clarifies his motivation for his conflict resolutions in his inner conflict images. He works out the subjectively *positive sense* of his *deviant* thoughts, feelings, and behavior. In doing so, he understands himself better. He learns to distinguish between old and new solutions to his conflicts and to actively influence what happens to him.
4. Problem solving: The patient doesn't just *re-enact* his conflict in the psychodramatic play. The therapist accompanies the patient in processing the conflict, mentalizes on his behalf if necessary, dissolves his fixations in old solution patterns in his conflict image, intervenes as a doppelganger if the patient loses himself, introduces a fictional supportive doppelganger into the interaction or encourages him to rewrite traumatic events as coping stories. In this way, she creates a *surplus reality.* An example of this is the seven steps of the psychodramatic dialogue in the treatment of people struggling with depression (see Sect. 8.4.2). The play progressively changes the patient's inner conflict image. As a result, he perceives the reality of his conflict in his everyday life in a new way. According to Moreno, he becomes *spontaneous* and automatically finds a new, more appropriate solution to his old conflict (see Sect. 2.6).

## 2.13 Comparison Between the Self-Image-Focused and System-Focused Style of Directing Groups

In my understanding, the self is a systemic process. It includes the development of the inner self-image and the inner object image in the current situation (see Sects. 2.1, 2.9, and 8.4.2). In psychodramatic play, many therapists focus their attention solely on the development of self-image. This can lead to a cognitively oriented leadership style that does not fully exploit the direct metacognitive effect of psychodrama techniques (see Sect. 2.14) (Table 2.2).

## 2.14 Similarities and Differences Between Mentalization-Orientated Theory and Other Theories of Psychodrama Therapy

**Question**
How do you explain the therapeutic effect of psychodrama therapy?

The following problems arise in the theoretical explanation of the practical work in psychodrama: (1) the spontaneity trap, (2) the before-after trap, (3) the diffusivity trap, (4) the cognition trap, (5) the equivalence trap, (6) the self-image trap, and (7) the technique trap.

1. **The Spontaneity Trap**

Psychodrama is effective even without theory. One can experience psychodrama in a seminar and then apply the psychodrama techniques in their own work. This is because psychodrama techniques are metacognitive tools of the *natural inner* conflict processing and they realize the holistic process of intuition in the *as-if mode of play* (see Sect. 2.2). Psychodrama is effective *even when* the explanations for its effects are inadequate. A psychodrama training teacher said 20 years ago: "I gave up trying to explain what I do in psychodrama. I just apply it. That's fine!" But, the application of psychodrama techniques *without theory* means that the therapist cannot adequately justify her own effective practical procedures with psychodrama to other therapists. As a result, she may even have doubts about the efficacy of her own method.

This textbook justifies the practical approach in psychodrama with the *multidisciplinary theories* of self-development (see Chap. 1 and Sect. 9.3), mentalizing (see Sects. 2.2 to 2.4), play (see Sects. 2.4 and 2.6), metacognitive processes (see Sect. 2.4 and Chap. 4), and psychosomatic resonance (see Sect. 2.7). These theories help to systematize the therapeutic experiences of Moreno and other psychodramatists and to compare them with the experiences and theories of other psychotherapy methods.

For example, the mentalization-oriented theory of psychodrama makes it possible to justify the method-specific therapeutic interventions of psychodrama against the

**Table 2.2** Different styles of direction

| Self-image-focused style of direction | System-focused style of direction |
|---|---|
| In the case of *disturbances in group relations*, the director focuses her psychodramatic work on helping *individuals*. Her psychodrama work is predominantly centered on the protagonist | In the case of *disturbances in group relations*, the director focuses her psychodramatic work on the *system* of group relationships |
| The director tries to avoid feeling insecure. Instead, she takes a more directive approach to *conflicts in therapeutic relationships* or *groups* | The director acknowledges her own feelings of insecurity, reluctance, or discomfort and tries, when necessary, to reorient herself openly. She trusts her intuition and takes a systemic and process-oriented approach in her actions |
| The director *interprets* the behavior of others. She assigns roles from the family model to help describe the behavior, for example, "She wants me as a good mother" or "She is behaving like a child." | The director centers her attention on *the relationship between* herself and others. She engages in psychodramatic self-supervision outside the therapy sessions (see Sect. 2.9). She tries to be fair to others as she would to herself |
| She interprets her patients' refusal to agree with her recommendations as resistance | She defines resistance as a joint fixation of the patient *and the therapist* on a transference and countertransference relationship that hinders progress in therapy |
| In case of disturbances in the therapeutic relationship, she thinks: *Either* the patient has a problem, *or I* have a problem | In case of disturbances in the therapeutic relationship, she thinks that *both* the patient or the group *and I* have a problem. We, therefore, *share* a *common* problem |
| She thinks in accordance with the principle of right or wrong | She adheres to the principle that "The mind of a patient does nothing without reason, *and* neither does mine." Therefore, she acknowledges her feelings *as well as* the feelings of others |
| She thinks hierarchically. In the case of disturbances in the therapeutic relationship, she assumes the attitude of the knowledgable one and feels tempted to think of the patient as ignorant, incapable, or unmotivated | *Even when there are disturbances in the therapeutic relationship*, she makes an effort to see the other person as an equal. She is prepared to adopt a contrary perspective temporarily. She assumes the position of a healthy, naïve child or that of Socrates: "I know that I do not know. But I would like to know." In group dynamics, this is the beta position (see Sect. 2.11) |
| When using psychodrama techniques, she assures herself by collecting a wealth of information before initiating a psychodramatic play | The therapist follows her intuition in applying psychodrama techniques such that the patient implements the metacognitive tools of his inner mentalizing during the play on the stage (see Sect. 2.5). The psychodramatic work thus appears to be quite 'simple'. The memories and fantasies are immediately enacted on stage instead of first being narrated |

(continued)

**Table 2.2** (continued)

| Self-image-focused style of direction | System-focused style of direction |
|---|---|
| In a relationship conflict, the therapist justifies her approach in accordance with the method: "This is how it's done in psychodrama" | In the case of relational conflicts, the therapist justifies her actions in accordance with the relationship. She actively attempts to differentiate the mutual transference elements *from the fundamental aspects* of the relationship conflict (see Sect. 2.10) |
| The therapist attempts to protect her patients *and* herself from 'mistakes', 'unnecessary suffering', and disturbances in the relationship by establishing a set of boundaries for the group process | The therapist follows her intuition when directing the group. She is prepared to live with the *consequences* of her actions but also *questions her actions* when necessary. She *also lets the patient* live with the consequences of *his* actions. She knows that she cannot prevent the occurrence of transference relationships and that these can even contribute to the therapeutic progress (see Sect. 2.10) |
| The therapist experiences conflicts in the therapeutic relationship and the group as disruptive. She struggles in dealing with relationship conflicts *psychodramatically* | She considers conflicts in the therapeutic relationship and the group to be courageous. She has learned a range of *psychodramatic* possibilities to deal with relationship conflicts (see Sect. 2.11) |
| As a leader, she perceives her position outside the group dynamics. Therefore, when clarifying issues concerning group dynamics, she applies sociometric methods *without including herself* in the selection process | She understands the group as a self-organizing system and *considers herself a part of the group system*. Therefore, when analyzing group dynamics, she applies Schindler's systemic concept of the group positions—alpha, beta, gamma, and omega (Schindler, 1957/58) (see Sect. 2.11), thereby identifying the latent, underlying group issue. Subsequently, she develops this further with the group members using sociometric methods (Krüger, 2011, p. 203 f.) |
| When relationship conflicts arise in the group, the director unconsciously shifts from the neutral beta position to the *directive* alpha position (see Sect. 2.11) | When relationship conflicts arise in the group, the director attempts to remain in the beta position (see Sect. 2.11). However, when necessary, she *consciously and playfully* shifts into positions unoccupied by the group members in current group dynamics |
| *In group conflicts*, the director unconsciously pushes that patient, *who, when acting out her repressed wishes, has the most decisive influence on others, into the omega position*. In group dramas, the group members often reversely reflect the intrapsychic conflicts of the director | In a conflict, the director understands the *protest behind* the actions of the omega as the *complementary truth* to the alpha's fact. If she had been in the alpha position up to that point, she now shifts back into the beta position |

background of *a holistic systematic theory.* The mentalization-oriented, metacognitive psychodrama, therefore, fulfills an essential condition for being recognized as an independent psychotherapy method.

**Central idea**

Psychodrama has a unique feature when compared to other psychotherapy methods: Psychodrama techniques *freely* implement the naturally existing *metacognitive* tools of the human inner conflict processing in the as-if mode of play (see Sect. 2.3). Psychodramatists oriented to role theory cannot describe this unique feature of psychodrama.

## 2. The Before-After Trap

Many psychodramatists following the Moreno tradition (Moreno, 1946/1985, p. II ff., 153 ff.) explained their practical approaches using various role theories (Hochreiter, 2004, p. 128 ff.; Leutz, 1974, p. 36 ff. 153 ff.; Petzold & Mathias, 1982; Schacht, 2009; Stelzig, 2004, and others).

**Important definition**

Moreno (1985, P. IV) defined "role" as "the functioning form the individual assumes in the precise moment in which he reacts to a specific situation in which other persons or objects are involved." Moreno thus described the externally visible role.

Moreno's definition of role describes the externally perceptible role in a situation at a given point in time. This 'role' is *the result* of the metacognitive process producing this functioning form of the role (see Fig. 2.10). But, psychodrama techniques don't work *on the result of a metacognitive process.* They work on the metacognitive *process itself* that *produces* the externally perceptible 'role'. Therefore, one cannot use the linguistic concept of 'role' to explain what psychodramatists do when they use psychodrama techniques.

This is evident in Moreno's theoretical concept of *role pathologies.* A person's *external role exercise* can be disturbed by a 'role deficit', an 'insufficient role repertoire', a 'role deficiency syndrome', a 'role confusion', an 'intra-role conflict', an 'inter-role conflict', or a 'lack of role flexibility' (Leutz, 1974, p. 153 ff., Stelzig, 2004). When the therapist uses terms of role pathology, she describes *deficits* in the patient's thinking, feeling, and acting in the current situation in a person-centered

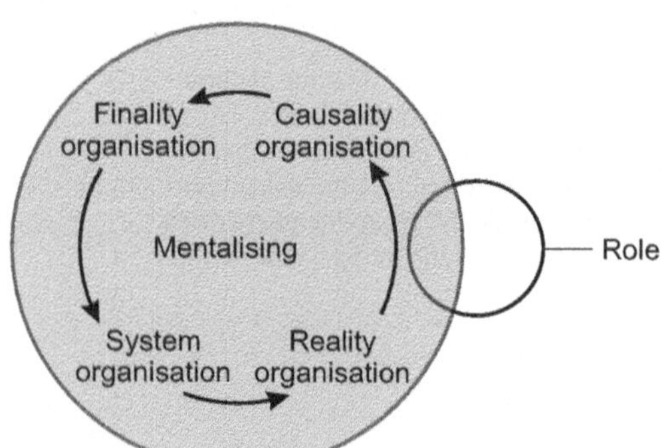


**Fig. 2.10** The process of mentalizing and the role as the externally perceptible *result of mentalizing*

manner from the outside. The concepts of role pathology are useful in formats in which all the conflict partners *are present*, such as in team supervision, or organizational consulting. In doing so, the psychodramatist and her clients deliberate on how the clients could feel, think, and act more appropriately *in the current real situation*. They may practice that in role training, if necessary.

**Central idea**

A psychodrama director, who *directly* tries to change the *role pathology* of a patient using psychodrama techniques, automatically converts the psychodrama into cognitive-oriented psychodrama therapy. *Unfavorable* thought content should be replaced with *favorable* content. A therapist who allows the psychodramatic play to unfold freely despite a role pathology *also* achieves metacognitive changes in the protagonist. This is because the psychodrama techniques he uses are metacognitive tools.

3. **The Diffusivity Trap**
   Many psychodramatists who explain their actions with role theories, act purely intuitively in their practical work and use individual theoretical concepts from depth psychology, behavioral therapy, or systemic therapy. For example, some psychodramatists in training only use the role theories *after the play* so that they conform to the rules of the psychodramatic training institutions when in discussion with other psychodramatists. Moreno's quotations or personal anecdotes about the effect of psychodrama help the psychodramatists bond with one another. For example, Burge (2000, p. 307); Karp (2000, p. 70); Leutz (2000, pp. 190, 195) and Roine (2000, pp. 95f.) consider role reversal to be an 'important technique' when working with traumatized people. But none of them asked any of their traumatized patients to swap roles with their perpetrators (see Sect. 5. 10.9). The more psychodrama therapists *base their practical work directly on role theories*, the less they rely on their intuition and the metacognitive effect of psychodrama techniques (see Sect. 2.2), and the more likely it is that they work only with a cognitive orientation.
4. **The Cognition Trap**
   In the therapy of *people with trauma disorders,* Hudgins (2000, p. 240 f.) interprets the *metacognitive process* of dissociating (see Sect. 5.10.2) as an unconscious splitting of parts of self. She looks at the patient *as an object* and not as an *implicit doppelganger*. She treats the consequences of dissociating, not the cause. The dissociating patient must learn, with help from an interacting doppelganger, to collect his split-off parts of self so that they are available to him again. She illustrates her approach using the example of a *fictitious patient* named 'Greta'. The therapist has the group members take on *eleven* stabilizing *roles* in the patient's trauma processing. When 'Greta' dissociates nonetheless, the therapist "asks a trained auxiliary to take on the role of the one containing the dissociation. Collette […] took up the role and started drifting around the room with a white scarf. She swished it in the air and said: 'I can pick up and hold all the dissociations in the room. Greta, help me gather it together so I can keep it here. You can have it back if you need it, but I think it's safe now to see what´s happening.' The director … said: 'Yes, Greta, pick up the pieces of

fuzziness that are floating around the room and put them concretely in the white scarf there. Tell the collector what to do with them.'" Hudgins let the fictitious Greta respond: 'I am not dizzy or dazed right now, but you can stand over there in the corner with your scarf just in case I get too scared.'

The traumatized patient should reduce the consequences of dissociation in this way. Hudgins doesn't treat the cause of dissociation. Dissociating is an inner dysfunctional *metacognitive* process that results in the symptom of dissociation. This process comprises three steps (Wurmser, 1998, p. 425 f.) (see Sect. 5.10.2): (1) When dissociating, the patient's ego *splits into an observing and an acting ego* (Wurmser, 1998, p. 425 f.). The therapist, as an implicit doppelganger, therefore, sets up a second chair *next* to the patient for 'her traumatized 'ego' when beginning to process trauma in the therapy room. In doing so, she externally separates the psychosomatic resonance pattern (see Sect. 2.7) of the *trauma experience* from the patient's psychosomatic resonance pattern in the *current therapeutic relationship.* The therapist and the patient stand shoulder to shoulder, look at this traumatized part of the patient's self *from an observer position* (see Sect. 5.10.6), and, thus, identify with the patient's cognition. The split between an observing and acting ego is thus *psychodramatically* realized externally in the therapy room. (2) Dissociation also includes the defensive process of *denying* this split (Wurmser, 1998, p. 425 f.). The therapist resolves the *denial* of the trauma by representing the patient's 'traumatized ego' with an empty chair. The result is that the patient *consciously perceives his "traumatized ego"*. His denial of the splitting is thereby resolved. (3) Dissociating also includes a positive counterfantasy protecting the denial of splitting (Wurmser, 1998, p. 425 f.). Therefore, the therapist helps the dissociating patient to stabilize herself through a *positive counterfantasy.* For this purpose, she and the patient develop a 'safe place' together (see Sect. 5.10.5). In *trauma processing*, the patient alternates between his psychosomatic 'acting ego' in the trauma scene, the 'cognitive ego' in the observation and narrative room, and the supportive 'safe place'. Thus, he gains ego control over his dissociation in the as-if mode of play (see Sects. 4.8 and 5.10). He becomes the creator of his life (Moreno, 1970, S. 78) in his dissociation.

Similarly, Schwehm (2004, p. 139, 146 ff.) uses a cognitive approach in the therapy of patients with alcohol dependency. Schwehm interprets the inability of persons with addiction to control themselves as a 'role deficit' for the 'role of a director'. He, therefore, suggests training in the 'role of a director' to improve the patient's ability to control his thinking, feeling, and acting. For this purpose, the therapist goes with the patient into a 'control room' which is separate from the stage. He then invites the patient to view his problematic addictive acting from a metaperspective. As a 'director,' the patient is now required to suggest to himself how he can think, feel, and act more appropriately in a given situation. This approach resolves the defense through rationalization (see Sect. 2.4.3) and confronts the patient with the reality of his own actions. In this way, it strengthens the patient's cognition.

But, in people with addiction disorders (see Sect. 10.5), the deficit in self-regulation is a result of *a metacognitive disorder*, namely the result of defense through splitting. In a conflict, these patients *unconsciously* alternate repeatedly between the ego state of healthy adult thinking and the contrary state of addictive thinking, feeling, and acting. In the addictive ego state, their *addictive inner reality construction* determines their perception of external reality: "My wife is grumbling again. But I have only had one beer. Living with such a bossy woman certainly forces me to drink! So now I will go to the pub and drink properly with my friends!" The next day, the patient feels guilty about drinking. He has returned to the ego state of healthy adult thinking.

Therefore, the therapist works *explicitly metacognitively* in mentalization-oriented psychodrama therapy for people with addiction disorders (see Sect. 10.6.1). She lets the patient realize his *unconscious* alternation between healthy adult thinking and addictive thinking *in the as-if mode of play*: (1) The therapist represents the patient's addictive ego state with an empty chair placed *next to him* in the therapy room. (2) She names the chair he is sitting on as the chair for his healthy adult thinking. (3) When the patient internally moves to his addictive thinking, she gestures to the second chair. In this way, she draws his attention to *the change in his addictive ego state*. (4) If necessary, she lets him perform the *inner movement* into his respectively contrary ego state by changing to the other chair and *enacting it externally* in the as-if mode of play.

In this way, the patient learns also to internally separate his addictive thinking and feeling from his healthy adult thinking, to internally recognize his addictive thinking in the as-if mode as 'dry drinking', and to visualize the negative consequences of any addictive acting. That makes it easier for him not to drink again. The patient develops ego control of his alternation between his contrary ego states. He thus *really* becomes a 'director' of his conflict between his healthy adult thinking and his addictive thinking (see Sects. 10.6.1 and 10.6.4) (Fig. 2.11).

5. **The Equivalence Trap**

70 years ago, Moreno (1947, p. 9; Schwehm, 2004, p. 140) assumed that the human memory contains 'inner roles' and 'role clusters'. In a *psychodramatic play*, these would go from the inner world to the stage and are therapeutically modified by the psychodramatic play in a meaningful way. The roles could then be retrieved *in this therapeutically modified form* in real everyday life. The 'inner roles' theory equates

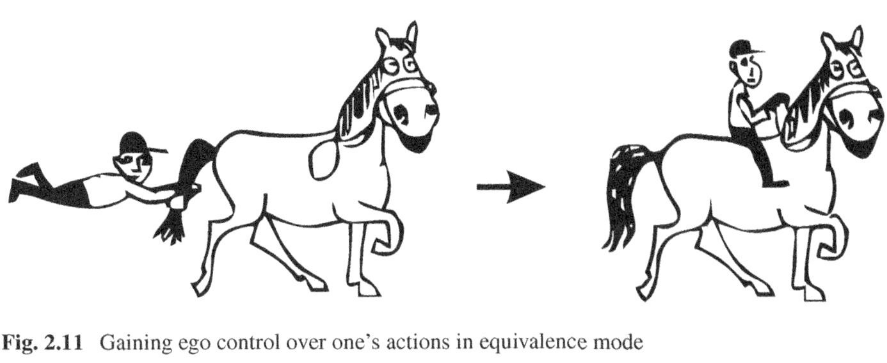

**Fig. 2.11** Gaining ego control over one's actions in equivalence mode

the patient's role in *his real everyday life* with his *inner* symbolic images in the *psychodramatic play* and assumes that when a protagonist enacts his marital conflict psychodramatically, he shows how he behaved toward his wife and how his wife reacted in reality.

However, one should be careful not to confuse "*internal* roles" with *external* roles. Neurophysiologically, "it makes no sense [...] to compare the brain with a serial computer or the memory with a process by which data is stored and retrieved" (Schiepek, 2006, p. 5). People change their memories of a conflict through the half-conscious, *half-unconscious* inner conflict processing sometimes even within one day. The longer the recalled event, the more the *recalled* conflict will deviate from *the original reality of the conflict*. As a result, the conflict *depicted* in the psychodramatic play is less likely to reflect the reality of the conflict in the past. This is why, for example, teachers always ask pupils involved in violent actions in school to relate and write down their experience of the events *immediately*. The ability to process memories in such a way that we see ourselves as the hero of the story or as a victim of evil has been advantageous in human evolution. In addition, the ability *to act internally* is a prerequisite for any further internal conflict processing.

**Central idea**

In the psychodramatic play, we work systemically on the inner self-image and the inner object image in an *inner* conflict image, i.e. on *inner representations* of reality, and not on *external reality* itself (see Sects. 2.9 and 8.4.2). If we free our *inner* self-image *or inner object image* from its fixations, we perceive reality differently in the next *real external encounter* with the conflict partner and spontaneously behave in a new way. What appears as reality to the patient in the play is "only" the current state of processing the *reality* he remembers.

Many psychodramatists let their patients or clients represent *parts of the self* with objects or chairs and deal with them psychodramatically. The linguistic concept *'parts of self'* is used very vaguely. Therapists use it to describe negative affect, symptoms, resources, or character traits, i.e. what Moreno called "inner roles". For example, the therapist asks the patient to represent their "grandiosity" (see Sect. 4.8) with an empty chair or an object. The patient should then engage with this part of the self in a psychodramatic dialogue with role reversal. In addition, he should also put the negative parts of his self in their place, and with the help of the therapist, recognize the positive value of other parts of his self and interpret them as helpful (see Sect. 6.8.3). The evaluation of the parts of one's self is dependent on the benefit of those parts for the patient. This method of psychodrama therapy is oriented toward the cognitions of the patient and the therapist. It is therapeutically successful in situations requiring cognitive psychodrama therapy. However, it is rather unsuitable for the treatment of metacognitive disorders.

6. **The Self-Image Trap**

**Central idea**

In mentalization-oriented therapy, the therapist focuses her attention on the systemic creative process of self-development in the current situation. This process includes the *inner representing* of inner self-image and inner object image and its appropriate development through *inner interacting* and *mental rehearsing* (see Sects. 2.9 and 8.4.2).

***Case example 15***
*Mrs. Castle, a patient with neurotic depression, feels resigned and tells her fellow group therapy members: "My husband forbids me from meeting with my girlfriend and going to an Italian restaurant with her!" The group members object: "You can't let him do this to you!" The therapist invites Mrs. Castle to enact her marital conflict and to psychodramatically show how her husband forbids her. But Mrs. Castle declines: "No, I cannot do that!" The therapist is disappointed because he can't internally imagine the scene where the husband forbids the wife. Therefore, he invites group members with the strongest objections to representatively enact the conflict between Mrs. Castle and her husband on the stage. The group members oblige. Two group members set up the scene in Mrs. Castle's living room as they imagined. One group member acts as the patient's doppelganger, while another group member plays the role of her husband. During the play, Mrs. Castle offers corrections from the outside. When the second group member acts 'incorrectly' in the husband's role, Mrs. Castle objects: "My husband doesn't behave like this!". Thus, the therapist invites Mrs. Castle to take on her husband's role. Without being aware of it, Mrs. C. explores what her husband feels towards her and thinks about her and how he would react to her changed behavior. When her doppelganger articulates her wish clearly and distinctly, she, as her husband, reacts in a disgruntled and indignant manner. Nevertheless, she, in the role of her husband, allows her doppelganger to go out to dinner with her friend.*

*Fourteen days later, Mrs. Castle reports that she went out to dinner with her friend at an Italian restaurant. The therapist is surprised: "How did that happen!" Mrs. Castle answers: "But I still knew he would agree with my wish." When she presented her wish to him, indeed, her husband made a sullen face. But he hadn't forbidden her from going out with her friend.*

**Question**
How do you theoretically explain this patient's change in behavior *without* her enacting and developing *her own role* in the psychodramatic play? Try explaining this therapeutic progress with role theories!

Two psychodrama training leaders speculated: "She saw the successful behavior of her doppelganger and then *imitated* it in reality." However, this speculation disregards the fact that the intelligent patient *cognitively* knew how to behave more courageously *before* the play. But she was afraid because of her defense through identification with the aggressor. So what was the reason she suddenly did it anyway? The patient expanded her inner object image of her husband during the play. In the role of her husband, she psychosomatically experienced that he would agree to her wish if she stood her ground. This new knowledge resolved her unconscious identification with the aggressor (see Sect. 8.4.2). The resolution of her defense through projection ("he forbids me") also weakened her defense through introjection. Thus, she dared to translate her wish into action. *The change in her internal object representation automatically changed her behavior as well. She did not need to rehearse a new behavior in a role play.* Psychodramatists often don't fully utilize the therapeutic power of role reversal. A psychodrama training leader even strongly objected to this theory: “In psychodrama, we work with the person who comes, not with the antagonist!”.

**Central idea**

In fifty percent of cases, the therapeutic effect of the psychodramatic dialogue in relationship conflicts is based on the change in the *internal object image* by role reversal.

Role theories change the practical psychodramatic approach more or less strongly toward a more cognitively oriented psychodrama. For example, Schacht developed a theory of role development in children (see Sect. 2.6), from which he derived a development-oriented approach to psychodrama therapy. *In the psychodrama play*, the patient shall *go through the next step in his role development*. The therapist helps him to do this. She mirrors the patient verbally, as a good mother would do. In doing so, she playfully engages with the patient’s structural level in her thinking and feeling (Schacht, 2009, p. 319), adapts her facial expression and gestures to the patient’s suffering, and answers verbally as a supportive interaction partner would (Schacht, 2009, p. 270 f.). This practice leads to individual “renourishing” (Wicher, 2014, p. 56 f, 85) of the patient in his play and the interaction with the therapist.

Schacht is not interested in the *direct metacognitive* effect of psychodrama techniques and therefore does not use this effect *consciously*. He *does not* distinguish the patient’s external role behavior in everyday life from the patient’s role play in his inner conflict image. He only looks at the development of *the self-image in the play*, but not at the development of *the inner object image*. The *systemic approach* of psychodrama, which is naturally present in the form of role reversal, is lost. For example, in a psychodramatic confrontation with a conflict opponent, Schacht *doesn’t* resolve the projection and introjection through rehearsing *during role reversal* (see Sects. 2.9 and 8.4.2). Instead, he repeatedly asks his patients *in their role of self-image* if they believe to ‘have the upper hand’. He explains to them that they “should only try to pursue a goal contrary to the interests of others if this is the case” (Schacht, 2009, p. 325). In this approach, the direct *promotion of inner role reversal* during the enactment replaces the *outer role reversal* in the as-if mode of psychodramatic play. The more a psychodrama therapist conforms to the role development-oriented psychodrama theory in her practical work, the less she allows the *direct metacognitive* effect of the psychodramatic role reversal. For this reason, even psychodramatists who do not justify their actions theoretically are more likely to use a metacognitive approach than the role theory.

Psychodrama therapists *with orientation in role development* are not concerned with the direct metacognitive effects of psychodrama techniques (see Sect. 2.4). As a result, when treating people with personality disorders, they do not take into account the *positive function* of a rigid defense as part of the holistic process of self-regulation. They look *at the deficit in role development* and try to remedy it *cognitively* in the play. Thus, the therapist becomes the enlightened one, while the patient becomes the one who does not know. However, *metacognitive* disorders should be treated *metacognitively*. In metacognitive therapy, the therapist explicitly makes the patient’s rigid defensive behavior the subject of therapeutic communication:

1. The therapist grasps the patient's dominant defense pattern as an ego state (see Sect. 4.7–4.11).
2. She names it, represents it with an empty chair on stage, and explains the positive function of his rigid defense in the holistic process of the patient's self-regulation.
3. The patient moves into the chair of this other ego state and *psychodramatically plays* the dysfunctional work of this ego state in the as-if mode.
4. He moves back to the chair of his healthy adult thinking.
5. In this way, he gains the ego control over his dysfunctional self-development in the current situation. As a result, he no longer needs to act it out in the equivalence mode.

***Case example 16***
*In the first therapy session, a 20-year-old patient, Mr. Banks, reported excruciating compulsive thoughts. When driving, he would be stricken by the fear that he had run over a pedestrian at every bump on the road. He would check the road in his rear-view mirror but also often turn around and drive back to make sure he was mistaken. He did this even though he "knew that running over a pedestrian would feel very different and that he would have seen the person". The therapist uses empty chairs to represent the patient's rigid defense system, which metacognitively controls the patient's obsessive thoughts and actions: He positions a "sadistic tormentor spirit who infused him with the threatening thoughts" opposite Mr. Banks. He places a hand puppet of an aggressive-looking devil on the chair symbolizing the 'sadistic tormentor spirit'. The therapist then places a second chair for his compulsive actions next to the patient and reinterprets these positively as self-protective behaviors: "These actions help you to actively check whether you have done what the tormentor spirit states. By doing this, you protect yourself from the accusation of failing to stop after causing an accident and losing your driver's license." The therapist then points to Mr. Banks: "Moreover, there is you who engages in healthy adult thinking. As you said, you know that running someone over would feel different; you knew these frightening thoughts are unrealistic." Mr. Banks is astonished by this interpretation of his internal psychic processes and feels relieved. Before setting up the constellation with the chairs, driving back with the car would have seemed senseless because he knew he couldn't have run anyone over. The arrangement gave meaning to each of his contradicting ego states in the overall context of the creative process of his conflict processing. The patient gained access to himself as a director in his dysfunctional metacognitive processing. He acquired "the perspective of the Creator of his own life" (*Moreno, 1970, *p. 78). During his further therapy, Mr. B recognized that the "blind tormentor" was a result of his childhood traumatic experience caused by his sister. The compulsive thoughts and actions of the patient proved to be the masochistic actions of a trauma film in the guise of a substitute fantasy (continued in* Sect. 7.2*).*

7. **The Technique Trap**

The *belief* in the method of psychodrama cannot replace the *knowledge* of what we do in psychodrama when we do what we do. Without theoretical knowledge, the therapist's understanding of psychodrama is limited to what can be achieved with the psychodrama techniques, and nothing else. If she fails to treat psychosis with *the usual psychodrama method*, she believes:"Psychodrama is not a suitable method for this purpose." Moreno's amazing successes in treating psychosis can then be attributed only to his special personality (see Sect. 9.6). When a psychiatrist succeeds in stopping a patient's delusions in a single session with disorder-specific, metacognitive psychodrama therapy (see Chap. 9), he is not surprised, but simply delighted (see Sect. 9.8.5). He couldn't have justified his actions meaningfully without a proper theoretical explanation.

**Central idea**

By understanding psychodrama techniques as mentalization-oriented metacognitive therapeutic interventions, we psychodramatists regain and retain the sovereignty of defining and interpreting our psychodrama intervention techniques. Psychodrama is no longer just a toolbox that serves to improve other psychotherapy methods in their practical work.

Therapists from *other schools of psychotherapy often intuitively* recognize that there is something special about psychodrama. They may even integrate individual psychodrama techniques into their own methods. They then interpret their *psychodramatic* approach within the frame of the conventional theories *from their own schools*. As a result, they understand psychodrama techniques as therapeutic interventions that are *part of their own methods*. This happens, for example, in systemic therapy (Bleckwedel, 2008; Klein, 2010; Lauterbach, 2007; Liebel-Fryzer, 2010), integrative therapy (Petzold, 2004), Pesso therapy (Pesso 1999) or drama therapy (Jennings et al., 1994). Half of the therapeutic interventions in schema therapy (Arntz & van Genderen, 2010) are psychodrama techniques. I consider the integration of psychodrama techniques in other psychotherapy methods to be desirable because it eases their direct work on metacognitive processes.

## References

Allen, J. G., Fonagy, P., & Bateman, A. W. (Eds.). (2008). *Mentalizing in clinical practice*. American Psychiatric Publishing Inc.

Arntz, A., & van Genderen, H. (2010). *Schematherapie bei Borderline-Persönlichkeitsstörung*. Beltz.

Balint, M. (1970). *Therapeutische Aspekte der Regression*. Klett-Cotta.

Blanck, G., Weller, H., & Blanck, R. (1980). *Ich-Psychologie II: Psychoanalytische Entwicklungspsychologie*. Klett-Cotta.

Blatner, A. (2010). Tele: The dynamics of rapport. www.blatner.com/adam/pdntbk/tele.htm. 14 June 2023.

Bleckwedel, J. (2008). *Systemische Therapie in Aktion. Kreative Methoden in der Arbeit mit Familien und Paaren*. Vandenhoeck & Ruprecht.

Brockmann, J., & Kirsch, H. (2010). Konzept der Mentalisierung. *Psychotherapeut, 55*, 279–290. https://doi.org/10.1007/s00278-010-0751-x

Buer, F. (1980). Vorüberlegungen zu einer Theorie psychodramatischer Praxis. *Gruppendynamik, 2*(2), 85–109.

Buer, F. (2005). Aufstellungsarbeit nach Moreno in Formaten der Personalarbeit in Organisationen. *Zeitschrift für Psychodrama und Soziometrie, 4*(2), 285–310.
Burge, M. (2000). Psychodrama with Vietnam veterans and their families: Both victims of traumatic stress. In P. F. Kellermann, & M. K. Hudgins (Eds.), *Psychodrama with trauma survivors. Acting out your pain* (pp. 299–316). Jessica Kingsley Publishers.
Ciompi, L. (2004). *Die emotionalen Grundlagen des Denkens*, (3rd ed.). Vandenhoeck & Ruprecht.
Ciompi, L. (2021). *Ciompi reflektiert. Wissenschaftliches, Persönliches und Weltanschauliches aus der Altersperspektive.* Göttingen: Vandenhoeck & Ruprecht.
Daniel, S. (2016). The usefulness of role reversal in one-to-one supervision: A qualitative research project using heuristic enquiry. *Zeitschrift für Psychodrama und Soziometrie, 15*(Suppl. 7), 235–253.
Dieckmann, H. (1981). Der Anstoß zur Individuation. *Analytische Psychologie, 12*, 42–64.
Dornes, M. (2013). *Die Seele des Kindes. Entstehung und Entwicklung* (4. Aufl.). Fischer Taschenbuch Verlag.
Dührssen, A. (1972). *Analytische Psychotherapie in Theorie, Praxis und Ergebnissen.* Göttingen.
Ferenczi, S. (1970). *Schriften zur Psychoanalyse I.* Fischer.
Fonagy, P., Gergeley, G., Jurist, E. L., & Target, M. (2004). *Affektregulierung, Mentalisierung und die Entwicklung des Selbst.* Klett-Cotta.
Freud. S. (1931). *Schriften zur Neurosenlehre und zur Psychoanalytischen Technik. (1913–1926).* Internationaler Psychoanalytischer Verlag.
Freud, S. (1975). *Psychologie des Unbewussten.* Studienausgabe Bd. 3. Fischer-Verlag.
Freud, A. (1984). *Das Ich und die Abwehrmechanismen.* Fischer Taschenbuch Verlag.
Goldmann, E.E. & Morrison, D. S. (1988). Die Psychodrama-Spirale. *Psychodrama, 1*, 29–37.
Grawe, K. (1995). Grundriss einer allgemeinen Psychotherapie. *Psychotherapeut, 40*, 130–145.
Hahnemann, S. (1796). *Versuch über ein neues Prinzip zur Auffindung der Heilkräfte der Arzneisubstanzen, nebst einigen Blicken auf die bisherigen*, 212–250.
Heigl-Evers, A. (1967). Gruppendynamik und die Position des Therapeuten. In K. Höck (Ed.), *Gruppenpsychotherapie in Klinik und Praxis* (S. 87–101). GFU.
Heigl-Evers, A. (1968). Einige technische Prinzipien der analytischen Gruppenpsychotherapie. *Zeitschrift für Psycho-Somatische Medizin, 14*, 282–291.
Heigl-Evers, A., Heigl, F., Ott, J., & Rüger, U. (1997). *Lehrbuch der Psychotherapie* (3rd ed.). Gustav Fischer.
Hochreiter, K. (2004). Rollentheorie nach J. L. Moreno. In F. Fürst, K. Ottomeyer, & H. Pruckner (Eds.), *Psychodrama-Therapie. Ein Handbuch* (pp. 128–146). Facultas.
Holmes, P. (1992). *The inner world outside. Object relations theory and psychodrama.* Routledge.
Hudgins, M. K. (2000). The therapeutic spiral model: Treating PTSD in action. In P. F. Kellermann, & K. Hudgins (Eds.), *Psychodrama with trauma survivors. Acting out your pain* (pp. 229–254). Jessica Kingsley Publishers.
Jennings, S., Cattanach, A., Mitchell, S., Chesner, A., & Meldrum, B. (1994). *The handbook of dramatherapy.* Routledge.
Kamphoevener, E. S. (1975). *An den Nachtfeuern der Karawan-Serail. Märchen und Geschichten alttürkischer Nomaden.* Rowohlt.
Karp, M. (2000). Psychodrama of rape and torture: A sixteen-year follow-up case study. In P. F. Kellermann, & M. K. Hudgins (Eds.), *Psychodrama with trauma survivors. Acting out your pain* (pp. 63–82). Jessica Kingsley Publishers.
Kellermann, P. F. (1996). *Focus on psychodrama. The therapeutic aspects of psychodrama* (2nd ed., pp. 229–254). Jessica Kingsley Publishers.
Kernberg, O. F. (1991). *Borderline-Störungen und pathologischer Narzissmus* (6th ed.). Suhrkamp.

Klein, U. (2010). Das Spiel mit der Komplexität. zu den systemischen Grundlagen szenischer Arbeitsformen. *Familiendynamik, 15*, 196–211.
Klüver, R. (1983). Agieren und Mitagieren. *Psyche: Zeitschrift für Psychoanalyse und ihre Anwendung, 37*, 828–840.
Kriz, J. (2014). Einladung zu einer Begegnung. Morenos Werk aus der Sicht der Personenzentrierten Systemtheorie. *Zeitschrift für Psychodrama und Soziometrie 13*(Suppl. 6), 121–135.
König, O. & Schattenhofer, K. (2006). Einführung in die Gruppendynamik. Carl-Auer-Verlag
Krüger, R. T. (1978). Die Mechanismen der Traumarbeit und ihre Beziehung zu den heilenden Vorgängen im Psychodrama. *Gruppenpsychotherapie und Gruppendynamik, 13*(2), 172–208.
Krüger, R. T. (1980). Gruppendynamik und Widerstandsbearbeitung im Psychodrama. *Gruppenpsychotherapie und Gruppendynamik, 15*(3), 243–270.
Krüger, R. T. (1992). Der Märchen-Assoziationstest. *Psychodrama, 5*(2), 229–238.
Krüger, R. T. (1997). *Kreative Interaktion. Tiefenpsychologische Theorie und Methoden des klassischen Psychodramas*. Vandenhoeck & Ruprecht.
Krüger, R. T. (2002a). Wie wirkt Psychodrama? Der kreative Prozess als übergeordnetes theoretisches Konzept des Psychodramas. *Zeitschrift für Psychodrama und Soziometrie, 1*(2), 273–316. https://doi.org/10.1007/s11620-002-0023-z
Krüger, R. T. (2010). Was ist Tele? Eine Erklärung und Weiterentwicklung des Telekonzeptes von Moreno. *Zeitschrift für Psychodrama und Soziometrie, 9*(2), 225–238.
Krüger, R. T. (2011). Die Gruppe als sich selbst organisierendes System. Konsequenzen für die psychodramatische Arbeit mit Gruppen. *Zeitschrift für Psychodrama und Soziometrie, 10*(2), 191–208.
Krüger, R. T. (2012). Kreativität als Mittel der Heilung in der störungsspezifischen Einzeltherapie einer schwer depressiven Patientin. *Zeitschrift für Psychodrama und Soziometrie, 11*(2), 297–310.
Krüger, R. T. (2013). Die therapeutischen Funktionen und Indikationen des Doppelns. *Zeitschrift für Psychodrama und Soziometrie, 12*(2), 217–232. https://doi.org/10.1007/s11620-013-0196-7
Krüger, R. T. (2017a). Psychodramatische Selbstsupervision in Praxis und Theorie. *Zeitschrift für Psychodrama und Soziometrie, 16*(2), 273–285. https://doi.org/10.1007/s11620-017-0396-7
Krüger, R. T. (2017). Mentalisieren durch psychodramatisches Spiel in der Kindertherapie. *Zeitschrift für Psychodrama und Soziometrie, 16*(1), 133–149. https://doi.org/10.1007/s11620-017-0388-7
Krüger, R. T. (2021). Der psychosomatische Resonanzkreis. Wie man die wichtigsten Methoden des Psychodramas auch in der Online-Begegnung nutzen kann. *Zeitschrift für Psychodrama und Soziometrie, 20*(2), 253–266. https://doi.org/10.1007/s11620-021-00594-0
Lauterbach, M. (2007). *Wie Salz in der Suppe. Aktionsmethoden für den beraterischen Alltag*. Carl-Auer.
Leutz, G. A. (1974). *Das klassische Psychodrama nach J. L. Moreno*. Springer.
Leutz, G. A. (2000). Appearance and treatment of dissociative states of consciousness in psychodrama. In P. F. Kellermann, & M. K. Hudgins (Eds.), *Psychodrama with trauma survivors. Acting out your pain* (pp. 187–197). Jessica Kingsley Publishers.
Liebel-Fryzer, I. (2010). Systemische Aktionsmethoden in der Einzelpsychotherapie. Kleine Interventionen für den Praxisalltag. *Familiendynamik, 15*, 210–219.
Lillard, A. S. (1993). Pretend play skills and the child's theory of mind. *Child Development, 64*, 348–371.
Lorenzer, A. (1970). *Sprachzerstörung und Rekonstruktion*. Suhrkamp Taschenbuch Wissenschaft.
Marineau, R. F. (1989). *Jacob levy moreno, 1889–1974, Father of psychodrama, sociometry and group psychotherapy*. Tavistock & Routledge.
Marineau, R. F. (2011). Die Integration von Morenos Erbe. *Zeitschrift für Psychodrama und Soziometrie, 10* (1) [Supplement 3: Psychodrama—Empirische Forschung und Wissenschaft, herausgegeben von C. Stadler, M. Wieser, VS Verlag für Sozialwissenschaften], 35–44.

Marlok, Z., Török, G., Martos, T., & Czigány, L. (2016). Wirksamkeitsuntersuchung zur Selbstsupervision mit Rollentausch unter Angehörigen helfender Berufe. *Zeitschrift Für Psychodrama und Soziometrie, 15*(Suppl), 217–233.

Mitscherlich, A. (1967). Die Unfähigkeit zu trauern. *Grundlagen kollektiven Verhaltens*. Piper-Verlag.

Moreno, J. L. (1939). Psychodramatic shock therapy. A sociometric approach to the problem of mental disorders. *Sociometry, 2*(1), 1–30.

Moreno, J. L. (1945b). *Psychodrama and the psychopathology of inter-personal relations*. Beacon House.

Moreno, J. L. (1946/1985). *Psychodrama, volume I* (7th ed.). Beacon House.

Moreno, J. L. (1947). *The future of man's world*. Beacon House.

Moreno, J. L. (1970). *Das Stegreiftheater* (2nd ed.). Beacon House. Original work published 1923. Gustav Kiepenheuer.

Moreno, J. L., & Moreno, Z. T. (1975a). *Psychodrama, volume II. Foundations of psychotherapy* (2nd ed.). Beacon House.

Moreno, J. L., & Moreno, Z. T. (1975b). *Psychodrama, volume III. Action therapy and principles of practice* (2nd ed.). Beacon House.

Moreno, J. L. (1995). *Auszüge aus der Autobiographie*. inScenario Verlag.

Moreno, J. L. (1959). *Gruppenpsychotherapie und Psychodrama. Einleitung in die Theorie und Praxis*. Thieme.

Moreno, J. L. (1965). Therapeutic vehicles and the concept of surplus reality. *Group Psychotherapy and Psychodrama, 18*, 211–216.

Moreno, J. L. (1974). *Die Grundlagen der Soziometrie. Wege zur Neuordnung der Gesellschaft* (3rd ed.). Westdeutscher Verlag.

OPD. (2006). *Operationalisierte Psychodynamische Diagnostik OPD-2. Das Manual für Diagnostik und Therapieplanung*. Hans Huber.

Parin, P. (1977). Das Ich und die Anpassungsmechanismen. *Psyche—Zeitschrift für Psychoanalyse und ihre Anwendung, 35*, 481–515.

Pellegrini, A. D., & Kato, K. (2002). A short-term longitudinal study of children's playground games across the first year of school: Implications for social competence and adjustment to school. *American Educational Research Journal, 39*, 991–1015.

Pennebaker, J. W. (1997). *The healing power of expressing emotions*. Guilford Press.

Pesso, A. (1999). Werden, wer wir wirklich sind. In: *Pesso-Bulletin 2004* (10), 3–17.

Petzold, H., Mathias U. (1982). *Rollenentwicklung und Identität*. Junfermann.

Petzold, H. (2004). *Integrative Therapie. Modelle, Theorien und Methoden einer schulenübergreifenden Psychotherapie (3 Bände* (2nd ed.). Junfermann.

Plassmann, R. (1999). Körperpsychologie und Deutungstechnik—Die Praxis der Prozessdeutung. In W. Kämmerer (Ed.), *Körpersymptom und Psychotherapie. Der Umgang mit dem Symptom: Zur Spannung zwischen krankem Körper und Person*. VAS.

Plassmann, R. (2019). *Psychotherapie der Emotionen. Die Bedeutung für die Entstehung und Behandlung von Krankheiten*. Psychosozial-Verlag.

Powell, A. (1986). Object relations in the psychodramatic group. *Group Analysis, 19*, 125–138.

Roine, E. (2000). The use of psychodrama with trauma victims. In P. F. Kellermann, & M. K. Hudgins (Eds.), *Psychodrama with trauma survivors. Acting out your pain* (2nd ed.), (pp. 83–96). Jessica Kingsley Publishers.

Roth, G. (2001). *Fühlen, Denken, Handeln: Wie das Gehirn unser Verhalten steuert*. Suhrkamp.

Rudolf, G. (1998). Der Prozess der depressiven Somatisierung. In G. Rudolf & P. Hennigsen (Eds.), *Somatoforme Störungen* (pp. 171–184). Schattauer.

Rudolf, G. (2006). *Strukturbezogene Psychotherapie. Leitfaden zur psychodynamischen Therapie struktureller Störungen* (2nd ed.). Schattauer.

Sabelli, H. (1989). *Union of opposites. A comprehensive theory of natural and human processes*. Brunswick.

Sáfrán, Z., & Czáky-Pallavicini, K. (2013). Das Bewältigungsmärchen in der Gruppentherapie von Menschen mit Traumafolgestörungen—zusammen in der Not sein. *Zeitschrift für Psychodrama und Soziometrie, 12*(2), 269–282. https://doi.org/10.1007/s11620-013-0201-1

Schacht, M. (1992). Zwischen Ordnung und Chaos. Neue Aspekte zur theoretischen und praktischen Fundierung der Konzeption von Spontaneität und Kreativität. *Psychodrama, 5*(1), 95–130.

Schacht, M. (2003). *Spontaneität und Begegnung*. inScenario.

Schacht, M. (2009). *Das Ziel ist im Weg. Störungsverständnis und Therapieprozess im Psychodrama*. VS-Verlag. https://doi.org/10.1007/978-3-531-91462-6

Schiepek, G. (2006). Psyche und Soma: Erklärt die Selbstorganisation des Gehirns die Emergenz mentaler Phänomene? In F. Resch, & M. Schulte-Markwort (Eds.), *Kursbuch für integrative Kinder- und Jugendpsychotherapie. Schwerpunkt: Psyche und Soma* (pp. 5–22). Beltz.

Schiller, F. (2009). *Über die ästhetische Erziehung des Menschen. Kommentar von Stefan Matuschek*. Suhrkamp.

Schindler, R. (1957/1958). Grundprinzipien der Psychodynamik in der Gruppe. *Psyche—Zeitschrift für Psychoanalyse und ihre Anwendung, 11*, 308–314.

Schindler, R. (1973). Das Verhältnis von Soziometrie und Rangordnungsdynamik. *In: Heigl- Evers, A. (Hrsg.): Gruppendynamik*. Vandenhoeck & Ruprecht.

Schützenberger-Ancelin, A. (1979). *Psychodrama—Ein Abriß. Erläuterung der Methoden*. Hippokrates.

Schwehm, H. (2004). Wirkfaktoren des Psychodramas bei der Behandlung Abhängiger. *Zeitschrift für Psychodrama Und Soziometrie, 3*(2), 133–159.

Seidel, U. (1989). Psychodrama ohne Gruppe. Basistechniken in der Einzelarbeit. *Psychodrama, 12*, 193–205.

Selman, R. L. (1984). *Die Entwicklung des sozialen Verstehens*. Suhrkamp.

Shödrön, P. (2008). *The Pocket Pema Shödrön. Edited by Eden Steinberg*. Boulder: Shambala Publications.

Stelzig, M. (2004). Rollenpathologie. In F. Fürst, K. Ottomeyer, & H. Pruckner (Eds.), *Psychodrama- Therapie. Ein Handbuch* (pp. 147–160). Facultas.

Straub, H. (2010). Seit fünfzig Jahren arbeite ich mit dieser spannenden Methode. In D. Ensel, & G. Stiegler (Eds.), *Ein Stück im Himmel. Psychodramatikerinnen begegnen sich* (pp. 25–42); *Zeitschrift für Psychodrama und Soziometrie, 9*(Suppl. 2).

Sturm, I. (2009). Elisabeth—Drehbuch für die Präsentation einer Kasuistik. Zur Anerkennung des psychodramas in der Schweiz. *Zeitschrift für Psychodrama und Soziometrie, 8*(1), 120–140.

Thomä, H.; Kaechele, H. (1985). Lehrbuch der psychoanalytischen Therapie. Springer-Verlag.

von Ameln, F. (2013). Surplus Reality—der vergessene Kern des Psychodramas. *Zeitschrift für Psychodrama und Soziometrie, 12*(1), 5–19. https://doi.org/10.1007/s11620-012-0178-1

van der Kolk, B. A., Burbridge, J. A., & Suzuki, J. (1998). Die Psychobiologie traumatischer Erinnerungen. Klinische Folgerungen aus Untersuchungen mit bildgebenden Verfahren bei Patienten mit posttraumatischen Belastungsstörungen. In A. Streek-Fischer (Ed.), *Adoleszenz und trauma* (pp. 57–78). Vandenhoeck & Ruprecht.

Vygotsky, L. S. (1978). *Mind in Society: The Development of Higher Psychological Processes*. Harvard University Press.

Waldheim-Auer, B. (2013). Leben mit Konsum und Rückfällen. *Zeitschrift für Psychodrama und Soziometrie, 11*(Suppl. 1), 195–207. https://doi.org/10.1007/s11620-012-0176-3

Waniczek, S., Harter, K. E., & Wieser, M. (2005). Evaluation von Psychodramatherapie bei Abhängigkeitsstörungen. *Psychotherapie Forum, 13*, 12–16. https://doi.org/10.1007/s00729-005-0073-6

Werner, E. W., & Smith, R. S. (2001). *Journeys from childhood to midlife*. Cornell University Press.

Williams, L. L., et al. (2006). Training psychiatry residents in mentalization-based therapy. In J. G. Allen & P. Fonagy (Eds.), *Handbook of mentalization-based treatment (Chapter 11)* (pp. 223–231). Wiley.

Winnicott, D. W. (1985). *Vom Spiel zur Kreativität* (3rd ed.). Klett Cotta. (Original work published 1971: Playing and reality, Tavistock)

Wicher, M. (2014), Psychodramatherapie mit Kindern. In: *M. Wicher (Hrsg.). Psychodrama-Psychotherapie mit Kindern und Jugendlichen. Ein Handbuch*, 39–85. Facultas.

Wurmser, L. (1998). *Das Rätsel des Masochismus. Psychoanalytische Untersuchungen von Gewissenszwang und Leidenssucht* (2nd ed.). Springer.

Yablonsky, L. (1986). *Psychodrama. Die Lösung emotionaler Probleme durch das Rollenspiel.* Klett-Cotta.

# Chapter 3
# The Pathogenesis of Mental Illnesses, Diagnostics, and Therapy Planning

## 3.1 Symptom-Based Diagnosis and Process-Based Diagnosis

Most psychotherapists in Germany refer to the ICD 10 (2004)—the "International Statistical Classification of Diseases and Related Health Problems"—when diagnosing and classifying mental illnesses. The ICD divides psychological disorders primarily according to the type and severity of the *symptoms* of the disorders. The diagnostic terminology of the ICD is useful to define what is understood as a disorder, for scientific communication, and to clarify costs for treatment for health insurance providers.

Symptoms are the *outcome* of disturbances or blocks in the patient's creative processes of mentalizing and conflict processing. Under sufficiently favorable conditions, a human being's self-regulating processes "constantly take place in the form of assimilation and accommodation. [...] It is a matter of giving up inadequate process structures in favor of new, less painful process structures. [...] Under less favorable developmental conditions, individual process levels can develop patterns that serve as emergency or partial solutions for overcoming challenges but are dysfunctional to other process levels and/or are not adaptive for further developments. In this way, the structures of the understanding of self (i.e., reflective consciousness), for example, less symbolize the organismic experience or the felt needs and more the *interpretation and understanding of the social environment* ('introjects') [...]. Actualizing such dysfunctional (partial) solutions can thus lead to the development of symptoms" (Kriz, 2012, p. 319).

Mentalization-oriented metacognitive psychodrama therapy works on the dysfunctional self-regulatory processes that produce the symptoms and not on the symptoms directly. The therapist understands that "mental disorders, even the most severe disorders, [...] are not mere deficits and dysfunctionalities; in a certain sense, they are also active, even if [...] they are processes with defensive and/or



R. T. Krüger, *Disorder-Specific Psychodrama Therapy in Theory and Practice*, Psychodrama in Counselling, Coaching and Education 4,
https://doi.org/10.1007/978-981-99-7508-2_3

compensatory functions. Therefore, they can also be considered functional dynamic constructs" (Mentzos, 2011, p. 283).

In practical psychotherapeutic work, psychodrama therapists implement the idea of the spontaneous-creative human *as a process*. In their work, they focus on the blocked *processes* that lead to the *development* of symptoms. In psychodrama therapy, these processes turn out in:

1. the space of creative *inner conflict processing*
2. the space of creative *psychodramatic play*,
3. the space of creative *attunement and agreement between* the psychodrama therapist and the protagonist *in the psychodramatic play*, and
4. the space of creative *real relationship between* the patient and his therapist and other group members.

## 3.2 The Disturbances in Mentalization and the Resulting Conflicts

The severity of a mental disorder is determined by the severity of blockades in the inner process of self-development. These appear as disturbances in the mentalization process. Mentalizing is the half-conscious, half-unconscious, creative inner mental process that helps people understand themselves and others in a given context. It also helps people process their conflicts, search for appropriate or new conflict solutions, and plan their actions. Nowadays, many psychotherapists offer *two qualitatively different diagnoses*, one based on *symptoms* according to the ICD-10, and an additional *structural* diagnosis, indicating the extent of blockades in the inner processes of self-development. The extent of these blockades determines the degree of *structural disturbance* (see Sect. 4.4). The structural diagnosis directs the therapist's attention *not* to the patient's symptoms but to the 'specific mental functions or dysfunctions' which *produce* the symptoms (Rudolf, 2006, p. 3).

I differentiate between five different severities of blockades in self-development in a current situation. These are expressed in different degrees of disturbances in mentalization. They are based on the different levels of integration in Operationalized Psychodynamic Diagnosis (OPD-2).

**Central idea**

The therapist records the degree of disturbance in mentalization through a diagnosis of the patient's quality of conflict (see Table 3.1 in Sect. 3.3). The quality of conflict indicates the level of mentalization at which the patient's conflict processing is blocked or deficient. It determines which psychodramatic approaches are to be used.

1. *Actual conflicts without a neurotic solution pattern*: The patient's mentalization process is blocked due to an acute relationship conflict or event. It can be triggered by *current* stressful situations or transition phases, such as a marital conflict, the death of a caregiver, or a workplace conflict. The patient perceives the conflict appropriately but cannot cope with it *and/or* does not appreciate himself

enough for what he does in coping with the conflict (see Sect. 8.3). The patient is *structurally well-integrated*. The therapist obtains a diagnostic overview of the patient's conflicts through the symbol work on the table stage (see Sect. 8.3). She addresses an acute relational conflict with a psychodramatic conversation (see Sect. 2.8) and/or with the *first four* steps of the psychodramatic dialogue with role reversal (see Sect. 8.4.2). In doing so, she resolves the blocks in mentalizing the acute conflict. The therapist works out with the patient the *actual* extent and *consequences* of the conflict. She records the patient's existing coping methods and appreciates them adequately, thereby therapeutically activating the patient's healthy adult conflict resolution skills.
2. *Relationship conflicts with a neurotic solution pattern*: The patient's mentalization process is blocked in all relationships by an old *neurotic solution pattern*. The old neurotic solution pattern prevents the patient from resolving this conflict appropriately. He cannot adequately differentiate or assert himself in relationships. He does not strike a fair balance between the 'give and take' in relationships (see Sect. 8.4.2). However, the patient is *well-integrated* structurally. The therapist centers the therapeutic work on the relationship conflict that triggered the patient's suffering. She helps the patient cope with the conflict using the *seven steps* of psychodramatic dialogue with role reversal (see Sect. 8.4.2), which resolves the block in mentalization that has *existed since childhood*.
3. *A slight deficit in mentalization* occurs in patients who protect the inner blockades in their process of self-development with a rigid defense pattern. Such a deficit in mentalization can be found, for example, in people with personality disorders, post-traumatic disorders, or addiction disorders. The patient is then structurally *moderately integrated*. The therapist uses the psychodramatic techniques of neurotic solution patterns. But *additionally*, she also makes the patient's dominant rigid defense pattern the subject of therapeutic communication. She defines it and represents it with an empty chair as an ego state on the stage (see Sect. 4.8). The patient develops awareness of his rigid defensive pattern (see Sect. 4.8) through this *explicit metacognitive therapy*.
4. *A severe deficit in mentalization* leads to serious intrapsychic conflicts in relation to one's self in all relationships. The patient is only *slightly integrated* structurally. His metacognitive processes of self-development are fragmented and do not work in tandem with each other (see Sect. 4.10). The therapist, therefore, sets up the entire system of the patient's metacognitive dysfunctional ego states by symbolizing them with chairs (see Sect. 4.7) and promotes cooperation between them through psychodramatic dialogues with role reversal. It liberates the patient's healthy adult thinking from his fixations.
5. The *disintegration of the process of self-development* occurs during the decompensation into a nearly psychotic condition or psychosis. The patient is *structurally disintegrated*. The patient's ego works only on coping with the symptoms and not on the conflicts that cause the symptoms (see Sect. 9.2). Therefore, any therapeutic intervention focused on the triggering conflicts would increase the disintegration of the patient. Therefore, as a doppelganger, the therapist firstly *mentalizes, on behalf of the patient*, his thoughts, feelings, and wants that are in

his symptom's control (see Sects. 8.6 and 9.3). For people with *psychotic disorders*, for example, the tools of mentalizing work as mechanisms of dream work caused by the disintegration of the inner process of self-development. Therefore, the therapist must enter the delusion using the doppelganger dialogue (see Sects. 8.6 and 9.6.2) and the auxiliary world technique (see Sect. 9.6.5) in order to convert the mechanisms of dream work back into tools of mentalization thereby interrupting delusional thinking. In doing so, the patient learns to once again differentiate between reality and fantasy.

## 3.3 Diagnosis and Planning in Counseling

Many social pedagogues, teachers, and pastors work as counselors in schools, church institutions, family and educational counseling centers, pastoral care, or *coaching*. They have received further training, for example, in psychodrama or *systemic* counseling. Some universities offer training in *counseling*, for example, the Institute of Mental Health at Semmelweiss University in Budapest. In Germany, Psychodrama Institutes offer a two-year training with the title "Psychodrama Practitioner". It comprises a total of 464 h of lectures and seminars.

The tasks and goals of counseling are varied. Counselors are employed to work in areas of crisis intervention, child or marriage counseling, or addiction counseling. They support the client in the event of a chronic illness and offer them special assistance (see Table 3.1, right vertical column). Counseling usually lasts only for a short period of one to ten sessions. However, it may increase to twenty sessions and more in exceptional circumstances. Counselors can also practice psychotherapy when focused on resolving *one specific conflict*. However, they refer their clients to psychotherapists in case of severe mental health difficulties.

**Central idea**

This is because 10–20 sessions are certainly not enough to achieve what psychotherapists achieve in 50–100 sessions. On the other hand, counselors work in places where people's problems arise, for example, in schools, and try to solve them immediately before they become chronic.

Counselors are often under a lot of pressure to perform. But sometimes, patients prefer counseling over psychotherapy because of the following reasons:

1. In many countries, people have to pay for psychotherapy themselves. But it is not always affordable. Counseling, however, may be free or cheaper.
2. Usually, the number of psychotherapists in the country is relatively small.
3. Or the psychotherapists have a waiting period of one year.
4. Psychiatrists often limit themselves to giving a diagnosis and prescribing psychotropic drugs. Therefore, their patients need additional help to understand themselves and their conflicts.

Nevertheless, some psychotherapists insist that counselors need to be familiar with the diagnosis of mental disorders. I think that is inappropriate because the

**Table 3.1** Qualities of conflict and the corresponding psychodrama intervention techniques

| Disturbances in mentalization | Conflict processing qualities | Interventions | *Counseling and coaching:* No. of sessions, referrals |
|---|---|---|---|
| 1. Different types of disturbance | Social problems (e.g., debts, crime, migration, homelessness) | Specific help on the actual social stage (e.g., when submitting applications, with job placement) | 1–10, referral to relevant offices, persons, and aid associations |
| 2. Miscellaneous | Acute psychological crisis (e.g., suicidal ideation, breakdown of the family) | Table stage with stones, psychodramatic responses | 2–10, weekly, possibly inpatient therapy |
| 3. Temporary blockage in mentalization, structurally well integrated | Acute conflict *without* a neurotic solution pattern (marriage, grief, separation, job) | Psychodramatic conversation, psychodramatic dialogue step 2–5, psychodramatic self-supervision of the client, the technique of the self-control circuit (see Sect. 5.7) | 2–10, weekly |
| 4. Permanent blockage in mentalization, structurally well integrated | Conflicts in several relationships with a neurotic solution pattern | Psychodramatic dialogue steps 1–7, dialogue with the inner child, systemic family constellation, establishment of the dominant dysfunctional ego state | Up to 20, weekly or even fortnightly, possibly referral to psychotherapy |
| 5. Slight deficits in mentalization, structurally moderately integrated | Slight intrapsychic conflict provoking interpersonal conflicts (personality disorder, borderline, trauma, addiction, cancer) | Two-chairs-technique establishing the dominant dysfunctional ego state, if required trauma therapy or addiction therapy | Up to 20, weekly or even fortnightly, possibly referral to psychotherapy |

(continued)

**Table 3.1** (continued)

| Disturbances in mentalization | Conflict processing qualities | Interventions | *Counseling and coaching:* No. of sessions, referrals |
|---|---|---|---|
| 6. Severe deficits in mentalization, structurally poorly integrated | Severe intrapsychic conflict provoking intense interpersonal conflicts (personality disorder, borderline, trauma, addiction, cancer) | Setting up the whole system of ego states, disorder-specific psychotherapy | up to 10, fortnightly, supportive work only, referral to psychotherapy, also inpatient |
| 7. The disintegration of mentalization, structurally disintegrated | Confusion of identity (severe addiction, psychosis) | Mentalizing on behalf in steering the symptoms, dialogue as a doppelganger, auxiliary world technique | Supportive counseling every 2 to 4 weeks, parallel treatment by psychiatrists and others |

diagnostic approach used in ICD 10, referred to by many psychotherapists, is somewhat confusing for counselors and doesn't guide their psychodramatic actions. The *symptom-oriented* diagnostic system does not provide enough guidance for appropriate therapeutic action. Counselors are not "small therapists". They should develop their own professional identity and ways of working. It includes *planning* the goal and scope of counseling with the client *in the first* session. One can do this through the following steps:

1. The counselor focuses on addressing the core of the client's disorder. She captures the essence of the disorder by diagnosing the quality of her client's conflict (see Table 3.1).
2. The counselor uses psychodramatic intervention techniques that match her client's conflict qualities (see columns 2 and 3 in Table 3.1).
3. The counselor discusses the expected number of consultation hours and the overall duration of the counseling process *with the client in the initial session.* Experience has shown that having greater clarity in this agreement positively influences the success of the counseling process.
4. The counselor uses as many sessions as are required for the specific conflict quality of her client (see column 4 in Table 3.1).
5. The counselor limits her interventions to the client's *current conflicts* and their *current state of self-regulation.*
6. In the case of clients with personality disorder, trauma disorder, or addiction disorder, she always sets up *only one chair* to represent the *dominant* defense

of the client, in addition to the chair representing healthy adult thinking (see Sect. 4.7). The client should 'only' learn to question the *dominant* dysfunctional metacognitive process in his conflict processing, for example, his defense through grandiosity. This then changes his behavior *in all his relationship conflicts*. The chairwork *with one ego state* requires at least 10–20 sessions. The chairwork *with several ego states* (see conflict quality 6 in the table) is suited for a psychotherapy process of 50–100 sessions.

The psychodramatic intervention techniques mentioned in column 3 of Table 3.1 build on one another from top to bottom. The more disturbed the client's mentalization (column 1 in Table 3.1), the greater the number of intervention techniques (see column 3) used by the consultant in succession. An example: A 39-year-old client seeks counseling to address her big fears. She is panicking because she doesn't know *if she wants* to marry her boyfriend or not. It appears to be an "acute conflict without a neurotic solution pattern". However, the client is *generally* a bit inhibited. She is afraid of having to take care of her dominant father-in-law at some point after marriage. In the first session, the counselor works with the table stage. In the second session, however, she also uses psychodramatic conversation (see Sect. 2. 8). She asks the client to portray a *memory* of an argument with her boyfriend. In the *following sessions*, the counselor applies step 3 of the psychodramatic dialogue *with role reversal*. In doing this, the client tells her 'partner' what she feels, thinks, and wants *in her role* and responds to herself by reversing into *her partner's role*. In the debriefing (step 4 of the psychodramatic dialogue, see Sect. 8.4.2), the client considers *what was new* for her in this play or what *became clearer*. It turns out that the 39-year-old client is blocked *by a neurotic pattern* in the argument with her 'partner'. Therefore, steps 6 and 7 are also necessary for the psychodramatic dialogue (see Sect. 8.4.2): The counselor assumes the role of the client as a *doppelganger*, and *the client* plays the role of her partner. In step 6, the counselor speaks to the 'partner' *on behalf of the client* about what she thinks and feels in her role. In step 7, she negotiates appropriate conditions for marriage with the 'partner' on behalf of the client. For example, she tells the 'partner' that she does *not* want to look after her father-in-law in old age. *In the role of her partner*, the *client herself* checks the extent to which the partner would accept this condition.

Counselors with little professional training should limit their engagement to clients with conflict processing qualities 1, 2, 3, and 7, as mentioned in Table 3.1. Counselors who have completed professional training to become psychodrama practitioners can also apply the intervention techniques mentioned for conflict levels 4 and 5. A counselor can use psychodramatic self-supervision to diagnose a client's quality of conflict (see Sect. 2.9). If the counselor understands the client with the help of steps 1–12 of psychodramatic self-supervision and becomes curious about the following conversation, it is indicative of 'relationship conflict with or without *a neurotic* solution pattern'. In contrast, *clients with intrapsychic conflicts* in relation to one's self often operate from a rigid defense system. Their actions *also* lead to *disturbances in the relationship with the counselor*. The counselor can diagnose an 'intrapsychic conflict provoking interpersonal conflicts' (see Table 3.1) as follows (see Sect. 2.9): (1) She validates her feeling of disturbance in the relationship with the client. (2) She checks *which* dysfunctional ego state of the client triggers her negative affect. (3) She *symbolizes* the client's dominant dysfunctional ego state with an empty chair and places it on the stage (see Fig. 4.1 and Sect. 4.2). (4) If this dissolves her negative affect, it is an important indication that the client has an intrapsychic conflict in all relationships. The client is probably only moderately or poorly structurally integrated (OPD, 2006).

*Building a relationship* with clients often by itself forms the basis for their growth and stabilization in therapy. In an acute crisis, the counselor should always schedule a second consultation with the client after the first meeting. It stabilizes the success of the first meeting. After referring the client to a psychotherapist, the counselor meets with the client for further counseling sessions *until* the client tells her that the first interview with the psychotherapist *really* did take place. This is because clients often do not reach the psychotherapist they have been referred to. The counselor should engage in psychodramatic self-supervision at least once during a *counseling process requiring more than two sessions* (see Sect. 2.9). Self-supervision improves their ability to care for the client appropriately and provide them with helpful counsel (Marlok et al. 2016).

## References


ICD-10-GM. (2004). *Systematisches Verzeichnis. Internationale statistische Klassifikation der Krankheiten und verwandten Gesundheitsprobleme.* 10. Revision—German Modification. Version 2004–Stand 15. August 2003. Köln: Deutscher Ärzte-Verlag.

Kriz, J. (2012). Antrag der Arbeitsgemeinschaft Humanistische Psychotherapie (AGHPT) an den wissenschaftlichen Beirat Psychotherapie. *Zeitschrift für Psychodrama und Soziometrie, 11*(2), 311–330.

Marlok, Z., Török, G., Martos, T., & Czigány, L. (2016). Wirksamkeistuntersuchen zur Selbstsupervision mit Rollentausch unter Angehörigen helfender Berufe. *Zeitschrift für Psychodrama und Soziometrie, 15*(Suppl), 217–233.

Mentzos, S. (2011). *Lehrbuch der Psychodynamik. Die Funktion der Dysfunktionalität psychischer Störungen* (5th ed.). Vandenhoeck & Ruprecht.

OPD. (2006). *Operationalisierte Psychodynamische Diagnostik OPD-2. Das Manual für Diagnostik und Therapieplanung.* Hans Huber.

Rudolf, G. (2006). *Strukturbezogene Psychotherapie. Leitfaden zur psychodynamischen Therapie struktureller Störungen* (2nd ed.). Schattauer.

# Chapter 4
# Personality Disorders, Narcissism and Borderline-Organization

## 4.1 What Are Personality Disorders?

The diagnostic category of 'personality disorders' (ICD-10 F60–F62) includes patterns of pathology that belong neither to the group of the psychoses nor to that of the neuroses. They are *not defined by symptoms* or combinations of symptoms. Instead, they present "lasting patterns of experience and behavior that [...] deviate from the socio-cultural expectations and [...] are defined more based on character traits and less by functional impairments" (Mentzos, 2011, p. 149). According to the DSM-IV, such lasting patterns manifest in at least two of the following four areas: cognition, affectivity, formation of interpersonal emotional reactions, and impulse control [...]. The patterns are stable and long-lasting and begin during adolescence at the latest (Mentzos, 2011, p. 151 f.). According to Mentzos (2011, p. 150), the clinical patterns that are termed "personality disorders" today include what was known as "borderline states", "psychopathy", "abnormal personalities," and "character neuroses" in the past. In the case of personality disorders, Mentzos (2011, p. 157 ff.) differentiates between the paranoid personality disorder, the schizoid, the schizotypal, the dissocial, the narcissistic, the hyperthymic, the dependent, the histrionic, the avoidant, the depressive, the compulsive, and the borderline personality disorder. The most common form is reportedly borderline personality disorder. The ICD-10 describes borderline personality disorder (F 60.31) as follows: in addition to emotional instability and lack of impulse control, the individual also experiences disturbances in self-image, aims, and inner preferences, as well as a chronic feeling of emptiness, intensive but unstable relationships and a tendency toward self-destructive behavior with parasuicidal actions and suicide attempts. Research shows that 30%–90% of people with borderline personality disorder are traumatized (Gunkel, 1999, p. 54 ff.). It is, therefore, always important to ask about relationship traumas in childhood and/or trauma experiences in adulthood during the diagnostic phase. One can then include trauma therapy elements (see Chapter 5) in the treatment, if necessary. The therapist should also actively ask her patients about alcohol abuse or other



R. T. Krüger, *Disorder-Specific Psychodrama Therapy in Theory and Practice*, Psychodrama in Counselling, Coaching and Education 4,
https://doi.org/10.1007/978-981-99-7508-2_4

addictions, or abnormal behaviors (ICD F10–F19, F63, and F65). These are present in approximately 30% of patients with personality disorders. In the case of patients with addiction disorders, the treatment plan must also include addiction therapy right from the beginning (see Sect. 10.6.6), for, if left untreated, they impair the success of the therapy process.

## 4.2 Particularities in the Treatment of People with Personality Disorders

People with personality disorders suffer from a long-term fixation of their inner process of self-development in a defense system. Thus, the development of their inner self-image and object image is also inadequate in the conflict situation. *The defense system* usually develops in childhood. It repeatedly produces the same *dysfunctional thought content* in the patient's inner reality construction. It helps patients to cover up or compensate for the deficits in the development of their mentalizing tools (see Sect. 2.2) and their trauma experiences. With time, they start identifying with their different ways of being and experience their dysfunctional inner reality construction as part of their identity and personality. Their defense system serves the function of concealing an *identity problem*, a problem of self-worth, or serious relationship problems (Mentzos, 2011, p. 154). Psychodynamically speaking, the dysfunctional character traits of people with personality disorders are "pseudo-solutions to fundamental conflicts which are sensible in some respects and were probably necessary at the time of their genesis. However, they are not only faulty but also cause suffering in the long run" (Mentzos, 2011, p. 152 f.).

**Central idea**

Patients with *personality disorders* have no awareness of their rigid defensive patterns. They do, indeed, experience that they are different from others. However, they only know *their* defensive inner reality construction. Their otherness is part of their self-image.

This results in limited flexibility of the afflicted person (Young et al., 2008, p. 32 f.): "They often express that they have no hope of finding any possibility to change themselves. Their trait problems are ego-syntonic. For example, their self-injurious patterns are such fixed components of their being that they cannot imagine changing them. Because their problems are central to their sense of identity, giving them up feels like death to them—the death of a part of themselves. If you try to confront them with the problem, they cling vehemently, almost as a reflex, sometimes even aggressively, to what they already hold to be true about themselves and the world around them. [...] As difficulties in interpersonal contact are often the central problem, the therapeutic relationship is one of the most important aspects, both for the initial assessment of these patients and their treatment process [...]."

The defense system of people with personality disorders is a form of self-protection that stabilizes their precarious psychological balance. While their dysfunctional character traits cause varying degrees of suffering in *their social environment*, they usually seek therapy only when the problem has secondarily led to a "clinically significant illness or impairment in the social, or professional, and other important functional areas of their lives" (Mentzos, 2011, p. 152). Often they 'only' report *these secondary problems* to the therapist in the beginning. They would like the psychotherapist to support them in their inappropriate perception of reality (see Sect. 4.13). When the therapist fails to fulfill this expectation, it results in a more or less open power struggle in the therapeutic relationship. For example, patients with depressive personality disorder (see Sect. 8.5) act out masochistic, self-injurious thinking, and self-protection through adaption. They constantly devalue themselves. The therapist often responds spontaneously: "Yes, alright. *But if you* were as inefficient as you say, you wouldn't be able to cope with your demanding work! And you wouldn't have received your performance bonus." In doing so, the therapist resists the patient's defense and gets entangled in his dysfunctional self-organization.

Patients with personality disorders must be treated differently than those with neurotic disorders (Rudolf, 2006, p. 2). This means *not just* "being supportive, promoting emotional experience and interpreting unconscious conflicts and resistance". Otherwise, psychotherapists run the risk of realizing "towards the end of the available treatment period" that "while their patients have managed to make some changes, they are still entwined in many intractable difficulties on the whole, including those originating from an increasingly entangled and unresolved transference relationship" (Rudolf, 2006, p. 2).

**Central idea**

It isn´t enough if the therapist focuses *only on the patient's cognitive thought content. Because in doing so,* she will continue to follow the changing subjects of his conflicts, from one crisis intervention to the next. Even though she can moderate the effect of the patient's crises in doing so, there will hardly be any change in the fundamental *metacognitive problem* by the end of therapy.

***Case example 17***

*A 42-year-old administration employee with intermittent thoughts of suicide and a schizoid personality disorder (ICD F60.1) was repeatedly 'bullied' by his superiors due to his arrogant behavior. In the ensuing conflict situations, he managed to resist the degrading hostilities, completely undeterred, like no one else could. In the therapeutic relationship, he usually demanded purely functional "concrete perspectives and help" without any emotional involvement. The therapist accompanied the patient through his recurring crises. They repeatedly worked out solutions that were socially acceptable in his 'bullying situations'.*

*The psychotherapy contract was planned to last for a total of fifty sessions. At the end of therapy, the patient was dismissed from his job and then again from his next position. The patient decompensated into a major depressive episode. It was not until the event of the unsatisfactory result at the end of the therapy that the therapist had the idea to link the patient's manifold relationship problems with his early childhood experiences: a one-and-a-half year-older sister drowned shortly before his birth. The traumatized mother had wanted to retreat to a convent at that time. But a priest prevented her from doing this. The patient, who was conceived shortly after this, was presumably the 'wrong child' for his mother. The patient was latently unwanted. As an infant, he probably couldn't connect emotionally to his mother, who was in shock. The patient did not learn to read his emotions and regulate them. Now he reacts to fearful situations with outwardly arrogant, self-protective behavior (see* Sect. 4.7*). This has helped him avoid feeling the underlying panic reaction of the 'small, unwanted child'.*

In the therapy of people with personality disorders, it is not enough to work only *on the resulting effects* of metacognitive fixation in the patient's relationship conflicts (see Sect. 8.4.2). The therapist must also *explicitly metacognitively* make the patient's internal process of self-development and thereby the patient's defense system, which causes the patient's relationship conflicts, the subject of joint therapeutic communication. Otherwise, the therapist becomes entangled in the patient's dysfunctional self-regulation in relationship conflicts. For example, a masochistic acting patient says: "I can't do anything." The therapist replies: "But you have studied and worked as an engineer!" The patient: "But the others in the company are much better." The therapist: "But your boss has not had any complaints about you. So it is likely that you are doing well after all!" The patient: "But I am always so insecure and feel worthless." The therapist: "But you are there for your children. Your wife also stands by you." It is therapeutically not enough *to replace* the unfavorable thought contents with more favorable ones *in every conflict*.

In *explicit metacognitive therapy*, the therapist also makes the *general principle* which causes the patient to produce inappropriate thought content in the external situation and obstructs his internal self-development (see Sect. 4.1), the subject of therapeutic communication. The dominant defense pattern in each case is stabilized through other defense patterns. The therapist initially represents *the dominant defense pattern* externally with an additional chair and a matching hand puppet (see Sect. 4.8). The patient sits in the chair for his healthy adult thinking. The chair for realistic, healthy adult thinking and the chair for his dominant defense pattern are placed next to each other *on the outside*. Thus, the internal *metacognitive confusion* between the dominant defense pattern and healthy adult thinking is resolved. In case example 17, this is the confusion between healthy adult thinking and his metacognitive process of "self-injurious thinking". "Metacognitive therapy focuses … shifts the examination of cognitive contents to the metacognitive level … Metacognitive therapy deals with the metacognitive factors that lead to persevering metacognitive processes and misguided coping strategies" (Wells 2011, p. 18) (see Sect. 4.8).

**Important definition**

Other people perceive the dominant defense pattern of persons with personality disorders as their *character trait*. The defense system results in biased thinking, feeling, and acting in conflicts and is also actualized in the therapeutic relationship. I refer to the metacognitive defense patterns of a person with a personality disorder as "dysfunctional metacognitive ego states".

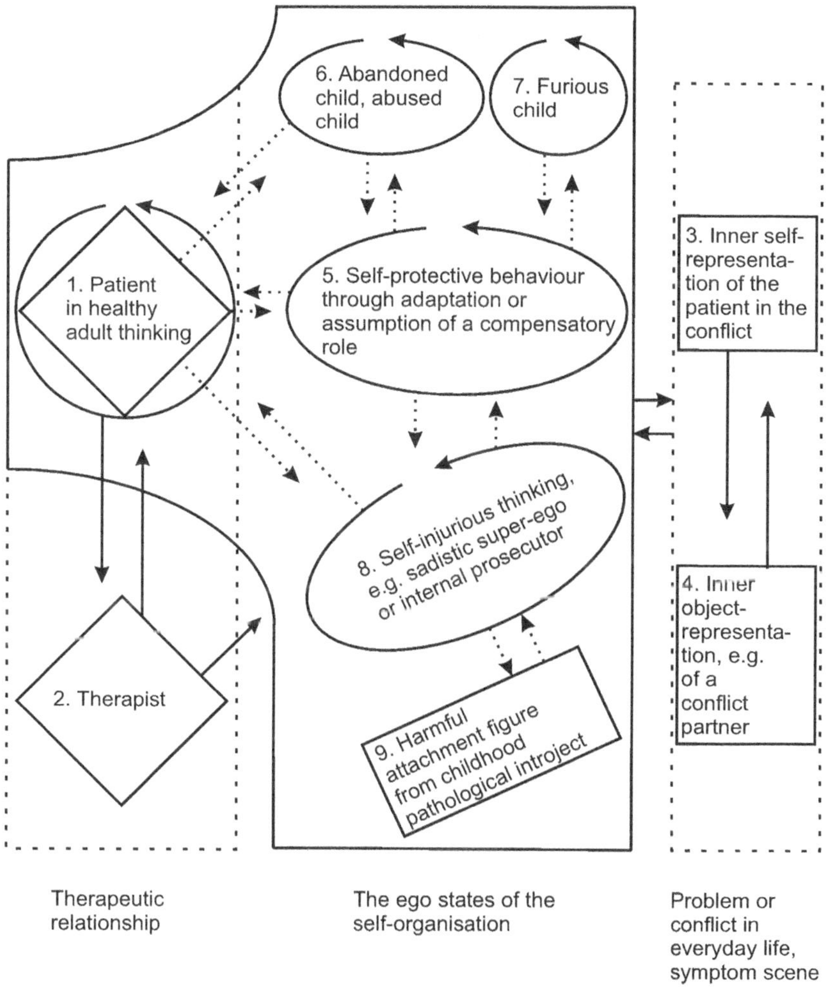


**Fig. 4.1** The three stages of internal self-development of patients with personality disorders in the therapeutic relationship and their representation using empty chairs in the therapy room

**Important Definition**

Watkins and Watkins (2003, p. 45) define an ego state as "an organized system of behavior and experience whose elements are bound together by some common principle, and which is separated from other ego states by boundaries that are more or less permeable". Putnam (1988, p. 24 ff.) speaks of states of individual consciousness that center around specific emotions, body images, forms of cognition, and perception, as well as memories and behaviors that are dependent on particular states, which occur repeatedly and appear to be relatively stable. These are self-organizing and self-stabilizing structures. I attribute individual *defense patterns* to the 'common principle' of an ego state (see Sect. 4.10). Each metacognitive ego state has a specific psychosomatic resonance pattern in the neural connections between the memory centers of sensorimotor interaction patterns, somatic sensations, affects, linguistic concepts, and thoughts (see Sect. 2.7).

**Exercise 10**
The following exercise will help you learn what a metacognitive ego state is and work with it constructively: (1) Identify a character trait or a reaction in yourself that you dislike or find problematic. (2) Project this quality, internally, onto a strange fictional figure, a person who, definitely and quite naturally, lives out your trait in their context, perhaps just in hard times. For example, you can attribute your instinctive helper and rescuer behavior to a fictional hero figure. (3) Choose an object, such as a doll or a puppet, to symbolize this fictional character. (4) Give this figure a suitable name, for example: "This is the white knight in me" or "This is my inner Mother Teresa". (5) Let the hand puppet tell an episode from their life: "Once when I …". The narration of an experience always includes a beginning, a minor conflict or something astonishing, and an end. Write the story on paper. (6) Over the next ten weeks, make up another ten stories from the life of your fictional figure and write them down.

This exercise helps you capture your unpopular way of reacting and acting as a *metacognitive ego state*. Through these stories, you give your unpopular character trait a coherently *different* frame in a *different* world where its acting gets a positive meaning. You differentiate and expand your knowledge of the *metacognitive* functioning of your undesirable trait. You learn to integrate the as-if mode into the equivalence mode in acting your trait. Perhaps, you befriend the trait you rejected and recognize its *positive* sides (see Sect. 7.3). You become free to act out *or to omit* your character trait *in control.*

Everyone has more or less strong, individual *traits*. A peculiar character trait does not make someone have a personality disorder. Traits are only considered *pathological* if the affected person (1) causes damage to others and/or himself due to the peculiarity of his inner reality construction and (2) he or she is unable to learn from the damage. The defensive, *inadequate* internal reality construction in patients with personality disorders *repeatedly* lands them in the same *biased* interpretation of the world.

For example, people with *narcissistic personality disorder* tend to abuse their interaction partners narcissistically. This helps them to stabilize their defense through grandiosity. Their defense through grandiosity is stabilized through a more or less sadistic superego. The grandiosity helps them to split off and deny feelings of inferiority, loneliness, shame, and emptiness. There is *overt, autonomous grandiosity* and *covert, dependent grandiosity.*

1. With open grandiosity, the patient must always be cool, the best, a great guy, and a hero. He tries to push the boundaries of human capacity. He is not interested in the *normal* problems of everyday life. A person with problems is a weakling for him, and he believes they are responsible for their own problems. President Donald Trump once said: "Anyone who lets themselves be captured in war is a loser."
2. People with *hidden, dependent grandiosity* are less likely to be noticed as individuals with narcissistic personality disturbances and are more difficult to recognize as such (see case example 21 in Sect. 4.6). They are followers of apparent heroes

or charismatic leaders in authoritarian systems. They are fans of their stars and bask in their glamor. They adapt to their idol. They allow their star to assign them a role in their institutional system, passively take over the explanatory method of the star or the hero, and allow themselves to be exploited and corrupted. In doing so, they try to realize their inner grandiose self-image in everyday life. They deny everything disturbing in their perception. It's all about the common illusionary goal. If the goal is not achieved and they risk failing, there is a *self-injurious, blindly accusing authority* in them that says: "You are nothing! You can do nothing! You are a loser! You have to make more of an effort! Then it will work!" In this way, people with hidden grandiosity deny their inner emptiness, feelings of inferiority, and meaninglessness and split them off.

## 4.3 Particularities in the Treatment of People with Borderline Personality Disorder

**Important Definition**

*Inconsistency* in thoughts and feelings is characteristic of people with Borderline Personality Disorder. According to Mentzos (2011, p. 167), in contrast to other personality disorders, borderline personality disorder is characterized "by definition, by unstable states and structures. [...] The changeability [...] represents its most important characteristic". The changeability is *in itself constant*. It is the alternation of two contrary ego states, as a result of the defense of splitting, that is the most prominent characteristic of this disorder (see Fig. 4.2 below). One speaks, therefore, of a "stable instability of the borderline" (Mentzos, 2011, p. 167).

I once asked therapists in a workshop: "What makes the therapy of people with borderline personality disorder so difficult?" They answered: (1) These patients demand help in their battle with their adversaries and expect that the therapist provides this help *unconditionally*. (2) They idealize the therapist *blindly* from the first encounter. (3) They terminate the therapy *abruptly*. (4) They accuse the therapist *out of the blue* and debase them. (5) They think in black-and-white patterns. There can be *no two differing truths* alongside each other. For example, the patient interprets help that is *attached to a condition* as a *refusal* to help. (6) The patients constantly *override the rules* of the setting. For example, they break the rules of the group setting. (7) Negative transferences suddenly appear without warning. (8) They often act apparently without any awareness of the problem. (9) The therapist feels she has to start from scratch in every session, although the therapist and the patient were in agreement in the previous session. (10) The therapist feels trapped in the black-and-white thinking of the patient. She does not know what she should believe. She suspects that the patient is lying because he constantly contradicts himself. (11) The patients react to supposed rejection with anger or indifference and are no longer emotionally available to the therapist. (12) The therapist oscillates between compassion and anger. It is not seldom that she feels helpless and incapable as a professional.

Kernberg (1981) made significant developments in the psychotherapy of people with borderline syndrome. For this, it was important to understand the 'stable instability' of these patients as 'temporally sequential activation between two contrary ego states' (Kernberg, 1981, p. 14) (see Fig. 4.2 below). The patients oscillate between the dependent, needy ego state and the pseudo-autonomous authoritarian ego state.

**Central idea**

In patients with borderline personality organization, the process of *inner reality construction* is disturbed due to the defense through splitting. The patients alternate more or less quickly between two *contrary emotions*. They randomly feel angry and then sad and distressed again. There is no healthy adult thinking.

Their *oscillation* between the two contrary ego states helps with self-stabilization. The defense through splitting helps to protect a *defense system* of self-protection through denial and a sadistic superego. Therefore, the oscillation shouldn't be understood as an attempt to manipulate the therapist. The oscillation between the contrary emotions helps the patients to get rid of the internal tensions that occur when their early experiences of deprivation, loss, or trauma are triggered *in the present*. These patients begin to feel helpless, unable to act, and dependent when they allow their neediness and sadness in relationships to prevail for some time. Therefore they react to closeness in relationships with anger, indiscriminate behavior, and pseudo-independence *as a precautionary measure,* acting on the belief "Help yourself, otherwise, nobody will help you!" They have learned '*not* to trust' from their childhood

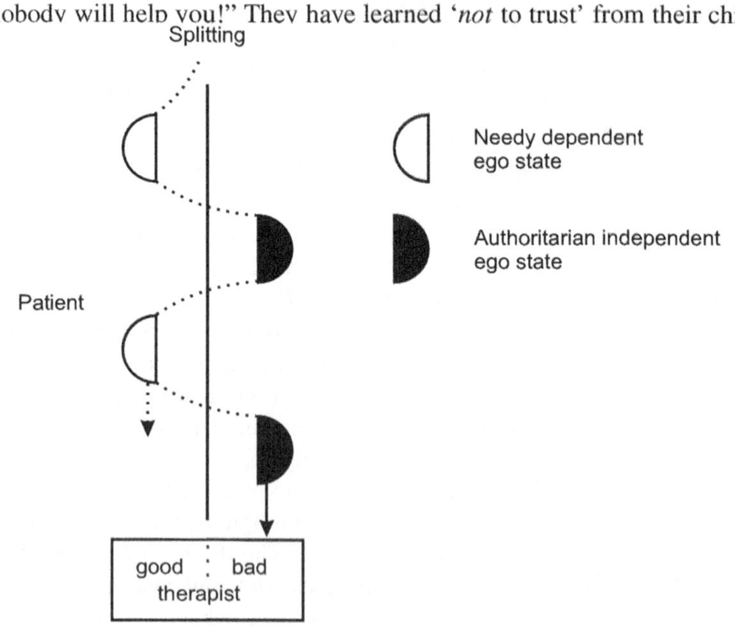


**Fig. 4.2** The sequential oscillation between the two contrary ego states in the defense through splitting

experiences. In doing so, they drive their attachment figures away from themselves. As a result, they find themselves alone. Once again, they feel needy and *act this out*.

Patients with borderline personality disorder explain the rapid changes in their feelings with *external* actions toward their current attachment figures. This means they think in *equivalence mode* (see Sect. 2.6) during a conflict: When they feel needy, they idealize their attachment figure and see them as a helper in their battle against the evil in the world. When their illusory expectations are unfulfilled, they react with anger. In an angry state of mind, they conclude that *their attachment figure* has done something to make them angry. Therefore they start to fight with them. After acting out their emotions, their anger can return seamlessly to the dependent, needy ego state. As a consequence of this instability, they experience people *either* as a friend *or* as a foe. They find themselves either in a good *or* an evil world. For these patients, their suffering "results [...] less from the blocked beginnings of their action (as in a neurotic conflict) and more from the actions of others, which is difficult to bear. It is the failure of fulfillment by others, the denied approval, the withdrawn attention, and the demand made that causes the suffering. The suffering is experienced as unbearable tension with fearful or angry feelings. It is an intolerable suffering and thus demands *immediate* action" (Rudolf, 2006, p. 50).

Kernberg (1991, p. 49) understands the defense of splitting as "the active separation of contrary introjections and identifications." The patient acts out his sadness and despair in the needy, dependent ego state. These emotions include the thinking, feeling, and acting of the 'abandoned or abused child' (see Sect. 4.7). In the pseudo-autonomous, authoritarian ego state, the patient acts out his anger and fury. This ego-state fuses the ego states of the 'angry child', the 'self-protective behavior', and the 'pathological introject' (see Fig. 4.1 in Sect. 4.2). This can go to the extent where patients who were traumatized in their childhood engage in an unconscious role reversal and *sequentially re-enact* the drama of their trauma experience without even noticing it. First, they act out the role of their pathological aggressor introject. After that, they are "beaten" *by the reaction of their social environment* to their dysfunctional behavior and feel rejected and devalued, as they did in their childhood. They are once again the 'traumatized child' they had been.

**Important Definition**

According to Kernberg (1991, p. 49), the defense of splitting manifests clinically "in the way that [...] contrary sides of a conflict dominate the scene alternately whereby the patient demonstrates a flat denial of the other side and appears completely unaffected by the contradictory nature of their behavior and experience".

The therapist often reacts to the patient's contradictory behavior with the feeling that the patient is manipulating her. She believes he is 'lying' and *consciously* telling her only half of the story.

***Case example 18***

*A psychotherapist reports in supervision: "The in-patient therapy with my 35-year-old patient, Mrs. E., is getting nowhere! I like the woman. But she leaves me baffled and helpless. Whenever she makes some progress in her therapy and can finally admit her feelings of loneliness and neediness, she suddenly flips out again. She throws tantrums and smashes things in the ward. Afterward, she behaves as if she wasn´t the person who acted!" The patient's acting out had left the therapist helpless and caused her to doubt herself. However, the patient had probably not experienced herself as being contradictory at all. The supervisor let the therapist re-enact a typical encounter with the patient psychodramatically. It then became clear: So far, the therapist had treated this patient as a neurotic person. She had interpreted the patient's suffering only as the suffering of the 'abandoned child', which the patient was in her childhood.*

**Central idea**

Persons with borderline personality disorder unconsciously defend against the perception of their *contradictory nature* through denial (Rohde-Dachser, 1979, p. 70). They actively hide their inconsistency, true to the motto: "For, he reasons pointedly, that which *must not, cannot* be." This quote is from the poem *The Impossible Fact* by Christian Morgenstern. When the therapist tries to address the *contradictions* in the therapeutic relationship and to clarify the causes of 'misunderstandings', the patient experiences this attempt *as an attack* and denies his inconsistency. The patient imposes a 'Double Bind' on the therapist.

**Important definition**

A *double bind* exists when a person in a relationship places an inherently contradictory demand on the other person, either implicitly or explicitly, and *also* refuses the other's attempt to discuss the *contradiction* with them.

The therapist feels helpless when caught in the double bind of a borderline patient. She gets angry, projects her rejection and devaluation on the patient, and acts out character-related countertransference (see Sect. 2.10). Or she attempts to make sense of her patient's contradictions, and herself goes 'crazy'. This can go so far that, in the end, she begins to doubt her abilities as a therapist and seriously considers whether she should give up her profession. According to Rohde-Dachser (1975, only verbal communicated), such a reaction is a diagnostic criterion indicating that the patient is suffering from borderline personality disorder. The patient's mood swings *cannot* be explained causally by the *real* events in the therapeutic relationship. The patient's oscillation between his contrary ego states only helps him vent *his inner tension* and stabilize his volatile *intrapsychic* balance. In such a situation, the therapist has to consciously accept the patients' contradictions as they are and confront them by setting up the contrary ego states *externally* on stage (see Sect. 4.9).

## 4.4 Structural Disorder as a Fundamental Problem and Additional Diagnosis for People with Personality Disorders

**Recommendation**

In the psychotherapy of people with personality disorders, the secondary diagnosis of 'Structural Disorder' should always be made after the descriptive diagnosis of 'Personality Disorder'. This is because "personality disorder" refers to a group of interrelated symptoms.

But, the structural diagnosis describes the level of mentalizing in internal conflict processing and the gravity of the deficits in the ability to mentalize (see Sect. 3.2).

Mentalizing is the internal process of reality construction that helps us understand ourselves and others in the context of a situation, process conflicts, search for new or adequate conflict solutions, and plan our actions (see Chap. 1). The literal sense of the term 'structural disorder' (Rudolf, 2006, p. 48ff.) emphasizes the *structural* deficits in the self-organizational processes of the patient (see Sect. 3.2). However, these deficits arise through metacognitive blocks in the internal process of self-development and result in *functional* deficits of mentalization. Rudolf states (2006, p. 50) that "structure refers [...] not to content [...], but to the level of organization of the mental functions that regulate one's sense of self and behavior in relationships." "The diagnostic question is not: 'What occupies this person in terms of *content*?' but 'How does his personality *function* in particular situations?'".

**Important definition**

Rudolf (2006, p. 49) defines the term '*structural disorder*' as "the limited availability of functions required for regulating the self and its relationships. The structural functions affect the ability to cognitively differentiate between oneself and others, to control one's actions, feelings, and self-value, to understand oneself and others emotionally, to make emotional contact with others, to maintain emotionally important relationships internally, to keep oneself in balance, and to find orientation."

The basis of every structural disorder is the block in the inner process of self-development through a defense system. The splitting results from traumatization or severe deficit experiences in childhood (see Sect. 5.2). People with structural disorders have lacked sufficient positive experiences of supportive *and* flexible relationships in their initial years of life. Their inner process of self-development remains unstable. They experience enormous tension when emotionally aroused. But their unstable self-development is protected through a defense system of self-protection through adaption or grandiosity and self-injurious thinking. *Neurotic patients* 'only' defend through blocks in inner interacting, rehearsing, and integrating in their relationship conflicts (see Sects. 2.2–2.4). They *are able to remember* their childhood conflicts *and, therefore, represent* their current conflicts *appropriately*. However, patients with severe structural disorders cannot adequately remember the events in their past relationship conflicts because they didn't even notice them due to their complex defenses. According to Rudolf (2006, p. 22), in cases of *severe disorders* in mentalizing, it is futile to ask the patients about their *negative memories* from childhood. The patients could *not perceive* the negative relationship experiences in their childhood *as negative* because nobody mirrored their negative emotions adequately. Their negative relationship experiences from childhood are 'only' indirectly 'stored' as blocks and mentalization deficits in the inner process of self-development. The patients experience their rigid defense patterns as part of their identity. Indeed, they suffer from the resulting relationship conflicts. But they don't suffer from their *dysfunctional character trait or* the *metacognitive disorder* that produces relationship conflicts because they are not aware of the blocks in their inner self-development.

**Recommendation**

In the disorder-specific therapy of patients with personality disorders, the therapist lets the patients work out their relationship conflicts also with psychodramatic dialogue and role reversal (see Sect. 8.4.2). But she *also* focuses her attention on the more or less pronounced metacognitive blocks in the patient's inner process of self-development and tries to resolve their rigid defense (see Sect. 2.2).

Persons with severe structural disorders are less able to play and feel quickly overwhelmed when processing current conflicts *psychodramatically* because of blocks in their inner process of self-development. It is not unusual for the connection between their *internal* mentalizing and their *external* psychodramatic play to be interrupted during a 'normal' psychodramatic play (see Sect. 2.12.2). In a psychodramatic play, they are often *not* able to fill their own role or that of their adversary and are *not* capable of role reversal. The patients are used to thinking in black-and-white patterns according to the belief: "Either I am right or my opponent". The as-well-as attitude in role reversal would challenge their stable defense and identity. The incapability to reverse roles is, therefore, a diagnostic indicator of a structural disorder.

***Case example 19***

*Mr. A., a 48-year-old patient, suffers from a borderline personality disorder, chronic alcohol abuse up until ten months ago, and a major structural disorder (ICD F60.31, F10.2). During a period in which he was feeling relatively well, Mr. A. reported having feelings of guilt toward his 23-year-old son: "He no longer speaks to me. At present, he is taking his final examinations at school. But I'm worried that he may not be able to cope with his life. I try to be good to him. I do everything for him. I tidy his room, cook food, and bring it up to him. I try to pamper him." The therapist asks Mr. A.: "Would you like to try telling your son, in a role-play, that you are concerned about him and that you have feelings of guilt towards him?" Mr. A. heeds the request reluctantly. During the role reversal, he answers his own question while in his son's role: "But I have made it through my apprenticeship and managed to do shift work after that. And now I'm in night school with an average grade of three!" Mr. A. is confused and notices: "I don't know what my son expects of me!" The therapist: "Then why don't you just ask your son here in the role-play!" Mr. A. is surprised: "That is true! Can I do that?" The therapist: "Why not! You have already told me that you grew up in a children's home and that no one took any interest in you. If you ask your son now, he will realize that you are interested in him as a father. That is what children experience as love!".*

*Mr. A. overcomes his hesitation and asks his "son": "What do you expect from me?" In the following repeated role reversal, the therapist takes on the role of the protagonist. Going beyond the boundaries of reality, he asks the "son", played by Mr. A.: "What do you need from me? Do you notice that I am making an effort?" In his son's role, Mr. A. takes the time to experientially "search" for what his son feels toward him, thinks of him, and wants from him. Thus, the patient completes the external role reversal in the as-if mode of play (see* Sect. 2.6*) also internally. He develops a theory of mind about the inner reality of his son. At the end of the session, he groans: "This is hard work here! This is not what I was expecting!" He smiles at* *the therapist, half despairing: "I work up a sweat here!" (Continued in* Sects. 4.6, 4.13, *and* 4.14*).*

Persons with structural disorders think and act out the blocks in their inner process of self-development in the equivalence mode (see Sect. 2.6). They equate their inner, defensive construction of reality with the outer reality. In disorder-specific therapy, patients must therefore resolve the blocks in their process of self-development caused by the rigid defense. To do this, the patient must understand the positive function of his unconscious defenses in the holistic process of self-regulation in the as-if mode of play and integrate the rigid defense pattern into relevant experiences from childhood (see Sects. 4.8 and 8.5). They thus gain ego control over their defenses and 'the Creator aspect of their lives' (Moreno, 1970, p. 78). They recognize that their image of reality is 'only' their own inner representation of reality and not a realistic image of external reality.

## 4.5 An Overview of the Different Steps of Treatment

**Central idea**

In therapy, persons with personality disorders should recognize the fixation of their inner self-development process in their respective dominant defense pattern and gain ego control over this defense. The patient's defenses are actualized in his present relationships and must therefore be dealt with *in his present conflicts*.

Disorder-specific therapy requires a great deal of *support and time in the therapeutic relationship* due to the complexity of the transformation processes. The therapy takes place in an individual setting, if possible, because the therapy of metacognitive disturbances is technically complex. The *therapist* must be able to recognize her own character traits and metacognitive processes. When learning the method, she often takes a developmental step in her own self-experience.

1. The therapist *diagnoses* the personality disorder based on the patient's symptoms and the consistent dysfunctional character traits in his everyday life and the therapeutic relationship. She experiments working with the patient using the *table stage* or the *psychodramatic dialogue*. Indications of a structural disorder are: The patient cannot give symbolic meaning to objects on the table stage. Or he is unable to engage in a role reversal (see Sect. 4.4). The therapist actively asks about concomitant addictions and trauma experiences. She includes these in the treatment if necessary.
2. Psychotropic drugs should be prescribed to people with personality disorders during their psychotherapy process *only if necessary* because there is "evidence that psychotropic drugs interfere with emotional and cognitive change processes and slow down the healing process" (Giesen-Bloo et al., 2006, quoted in Arntz & van Genderen, 2010, p. 116). Furthermore, it is essential to ensure close cooperation when the patient is being treated with medication by a psychiatrist because

psychiatrists often prescribe very *high dosages* fearing decompensation in the patients.

3. In a psychodramatic dialogue, the psychotherapist progresses slowly but steadily, often making varying use of the doppelganger technique (see case example 19 in Sect. 4.6). In doing this, the therapist acts as an auxiliary and mentalizes the patient's experience of his conflict vicariously.
4. Due to the specific metacognitive block of their inner self-development process in the therapeutic relationship, patients with personality disorders evoke a complementary negative affect in the therapist, for example, helplessness, anger, or powerlessness. In psychodramatic self-supervision (see Sect. 2.9), the therapist defines this appropriate negative affect, grasps the patient's dominant defense pattern, which evokes her negative feeling (see Sect. 4.8), names this, and represents it in the therapy room with an empty chair. For example, when she suspects borderline personality disorder (see case example 24 in Sect. 4.9), she places *two* empty chairs for the "patient", one for his pseudo-independent-authoritarian ego state and another for his clingy needy ego state.

**Central idea**

The *disorder-specific* psychodramatic treatment transforms the unsuccessful therapeutic relationship encounter into a successful one. This psychotherapy can therefore be called "Encounter Focused Therapy" (EFT).

5. In the therapy session, the therapist works *explicitly* metacognitively on the patient's *dominant* defense pattern (see Sect. 4.2). *In explicit metacognitive therapy,* the patient learns to recognize his dominant defense pattern and gain ego control over his defense pattern. In doing so, the patient has to take the following steps of mentalizing: naming the ego-state, representing it, acting it in the as-if mode of play, rehearsing dialogues with other defense patterns, and integrating the ego-state with childhood experiences (see Sect. 2.2).
    - 5.1 The therapist marks the patient's dominant defense pattern as an ego state by *explicitly naming* it *when the patient is acting it out.*
    - 5.2 She *represents* the dominant defense pattern with an empty chair in the room. In doing so, she *explicitly* makes it the subject of joint therapeutic communication (see Sect. 4.8). For example, a patient acts masochistically and says to the therapist: "In any case, no one wants me! I always make mistakes! I'm a loser!" The therapist then does not empathically share the *individual contents* of his statements. She does not even contradict him *in terms of the content*. Instead, she captures the *general underlying principle* that creates his many different dysfunctional thought contents. She names this principle for the patient: "You think in a self-injurious manner". She then uses an empty chair to symbolize his 'self-injurious thinking' as an ego state in the therapy room (see Sect. 8.5). In doing so, the therapist characterizes his masochistic thinking, feeling, and behavior *outwardly as deviating* from his healthy adult thinking.

5.3 The therapist lets the patient switch to the chair representing his dominant dysfunctional ego-state and *enact* it in the as-if mode. Thus, the patient *actively* differentiates it and completes the associated psychosomatic resonance pattern into a *holistic* resonance pattern (see Sect. 2.7). He *psychosomatically* feels the difference between the *dysfunctional* inner reality construction and '*healthy adult* thinking' (see Sect. 4.8). In the course of therapy, the patient learns to *think* in his dominant defense pattern *in the as-if mode* (see Sect. 2.6). In this way, he gains control of the ego over his *dysfunctional* thinking, feeling, and acting. He no longer has to act out his defense in everyday life with the same duration and intensity. His self-image changes in the *equivalence mode* (see Sect. 2.6). A patient needs to engage in 10 to 20 therapy sessions *before* he can think in his dominant defense pattern *in the as-if mode* (see Sect. 3.3).

6. If necessary, in addition to the *dominant* defense pattern, the therapist also represents, with empty chairs, *other defense patterns of the patient* that stabilize the *dominant* defense pattern (see Sect. 4.7). The higher the severity of a patient's *structural* disturbance, the sooner (see case example 21 in Sect. 4.7). Sometimes this happens in one of the first sessions (see case example 21 in Sect. 4.7).

**Central idea**

The various defense patterns of the patient's defense system stabilize and mutually reinforce each other's dysfunction (see Fig. 4.1 in Sect. 4.2 and Sect. 4.10). The therapist works on all of a patient's defense patterns only in long-term therapy. At the end of therapy, the patient should be able to think in *each* of the four qualitatively different metacognitive ego-states in the *as-if mode* (see Sect. 2.6).

7. The therapist lets the patient *interact* with his own defense patterns, represented as ego states, *using the psychodramatic dialogue* in the as-if mode of play (see Sect. 4.10). The role reversal between them clarifies the mutual relation of their work in the overall process of internal conflict processing. The dialogue helps to compensate for deficits in the development of mentalizing. The resolution of a defense system and learning to develop one's self in the current situations can take one to three years.
8. The therapist combines the work on the patient's defense system with elements of trauma therapy if necessary (see Sect. 4.5). For example, she lets the patient develop a 'safe place' (see Sect. 5.10.5) and a coping fairytale (see Sect. 5.14). Or she processes, together with the patient, his old traumas from childhood (see Sect. 5.10.10).
9. The patient *integrates* the progress of his development into his family and social relationships. The therapist supports him with the help of psychodramatic dialogue and other methods (see Sect. 4.10).

## 4.6 Doppelganger Technique in a 'Normal' Psychodramatic Play

In patients with severe structural disorders, the inner process of self-development in external situations is blocked through a defense. The patient often thinks in equivalence mode (see Sect. 2.6) and is unable to distinguish between the real and the imaginary. He, therefore, perceives, for example, the therapist's *verbal doubling* (see Sect. 2.1) not as an offer but as a demand to think and feel like the therapist. However, the therapist can still use the psychodramatic dialogue with role reversal *for crisis intervention* (see Sects. 2.14 and 8.4.2). Then, she must adapt her method to suit the patient's low mentalization capacity (see case example 19 in Sect. 4.4).

**Central idea**

The lesser a patient's capacity to engage in the play, the more often the therapist must enter *as a doppelganger* (see Sect. 2.4.1) in the psychodramatic play of his conflict situation (Krüger, 1997, p. 117 ff.). As a doppelganger, she *verbalizes* the experience *she* has *in his role* and *interacts with his 'conflict partner'* on his behalf. Thus, she processes the conflict with the patient in the as-if mode of play.

***Case example 19 (1st continuation, see*** Sect. 4.4***):***

*Mr. A. has significant problems with his manager during his reintegration into the work process after one year of invalidity: "It's been three weeks since I am back at work, and I am being asked to sign a performance review. The performance stated that I have a backlog in my casework and lack elementary knowledge. I refused to sign it. My boss wants to get rid of me! I've got severe stomach pain again." The therapist tries in vain to point out the reality of the workplace situation to the visibly agitated man: "You're a civil servant! You manage to do 95% of the required work! Your boss has got nothing on you!" The words fall on deaf ears. Mr. A. reacts to the rejection at work with panic and anger, like the unwanted child from his childhood. He is thinking in the equivalence mode and is angry with the therapist because he doesn't seem to recognize his distress. The therapist is concerned that Mr. A's attitude of denial could cost him his position as a civil servant. But, Mr. A. needs this job to stabilize his mental state.*

*The therapist, therefore, moves the conversation about the conflict to crisis intervention in the as-if mode of play. He places two empty chairs facing each other on the stage: "Please come and have a fictional discussion with your boss and tell him about your anger and resentment. Maybe that will give you some emotional relief." Mr. A. obliges to this invitation feeling embarrassed and awkward. Surprisingly, he behaves rather humbly and is not as angry toward his boss in the play. When Mr. A. moves into the role of his boss, the therapist takes on the role of the patient as a doppelganger. He repeats what Mr. A. had said to his boss. But he also verbalizes on behalf of the patient what he, the therapist, feels, thinks, and wants in his role. In doing so, he integrates the information given by the patient earlier in the conversation: "I am disappointed and angry. It takes time to present each of my cases to one of the five team leaders! I am losing my time at work in this process. If you consider the meeting time, I'm pretty good at my work performance! Besides: I am not asking the team leaders because I lack basic knowledge. First, you insist I ask them if anything is unclear, and then you interpret that as a lack of knowledge. That is unfair! You are treating me badly!" In the play, Mr. A. doesn´t fully embody the role of his young, ambitious boss. He answers awkwardly and often slips back into his own role. However, he listens to the therapist in the role of his doppelganger with great interest. He corrects the statements where necessary. Sometimes he coaches him as a trainer would his apprentice. At the end of the psychodramatic enactment, he spontaneously says: "Oh, I'm feeling better already: my stomach doesn't pain anymore!" In the follow-up discussion, the patient and the therapist summarize the possible courses of action worked out in the psychodramatic scene for dealing with the conflict with his boss. Therapist: "Just keep doing what has to be done, and don't let yourself be misled. The important thing is that you learn to stand your ground in the conflict. This is difficult for you. But it will also give you a lot, for example, self-confidence and money. You will receive €1000 less in your monthly salary if you take early retirement" (continued in* Sects. 4.13 *and* 4.14*).*

There are three different forms of *mentalizing on behalf* using the doppelganger technique:

1. Fuhr (1991, only verbally communicated) recommends in general: "The higher the severity of a patient's illness, the greater the need for the therapist to act out the patient's conflicts *on his behalf* in his presence at the beginning of therapy." This can go as far as the therapist having to perform the psychodramatic enactment *alone* using role reversal at the beginning of the therapy. While doing so, the patient will usually *spontaneously* correct and coach the therapist (see case example 15 ion Sect. 2.14).
2. The therapist takes on the role of the patient *in his psychodramatic enactment* and expresses, as a doppelganger, what she perceives, thinks, feels, and wants *in his role.* At the same time, the patient plays the role of his adversary (see Sect. 8.4.2).
3. Scharnhorst (Ursula Scharnhorst 1987, only verbal communication) suggested, as a therapist, if necessary, one can change into the role of the patient *directly in the real relationship* and mentalize on his behalf. The therapist thus *psychosomatically* explores what it's like to be the patient by imitating him (see case example 20). This approach is indicated when the therapist, despite their concerted mutual efforts, does not understand the patient but would like to understand him. This procedure is also possible in a group setting.

***Case example 20* (Krüger, 1997, p.144 f.)**

*The 22-year-old Mrs. B. is diagnosed with borderline personality disorder (ICD F60.31). She informs the group in their tenth group session that she wants to end group therapy: "The group doesn't help me, I'm feeling worse." Mrs. B gets angry and devalues anyone who speaks to her. Initially, the group members react helpfully but then become increasingly aggressive. Any attempts to clarify relationships make the patient more uncertain. Mrs. B. withdraws in the end. She appears extremely tense. The therapist is helpless. He does not understand what is happening inside*

*Mrs. B. He asks her: "May I reverse roles with you? I would like to understand how it is to be you and how I would feel in your role." Mrs. B. is surprised. But she agrees. She sits on the therapist's chair without taking on his role. The therapist sits on the patient's chair and, as a doppelganger, assumes her posture: He crosses his legs, moves his right hand around his mouth playfully, and repeats: "Everything is so tense here. – Nobody is concerned about the other. Nothing is happening. I'm feeling worse!" As the therapist models the patient, he concentrates closely on what he is feeling in her role. He notices that he is feeling increasingly paralyzed. He verbalizes what he experiences: "I notice that I am feeling numb. I'm drifting off completely. It's a vague feeling. I don't want this!" With great internal effort, he pulls himself out of the non-verbal state of paralysis and becomes angry: "I've had enough of this here! I want out of here! This is pissing me off! It's not helping me! I want to go to a clinic! Everyone is just sitting around, all uptight! I'm just getting worse!".*

*Mrs. B. openly watches the therapist with interest. She occasionally confirms his further elaboration of her role with a nod. In the end, the therapist exchanges places with the patient again. In the follow-up discussion, the therapist shares what he experienced in her role: "To begin with, I was just sitting there normally and said that I wanted to leave the group. I didn't feel that very deeply. But then, when I was criticized, I noticed how I started feeling increasingly numb. I fell away into some abyss of darkness behind me. That scared me. I didn't want it, and I started to fight it. I didn't see who I was attacking at all. They all looked the same to me, man, woman, or therapist. I just wanted to escape my paralysis. Fighting it gave me strength. The paralysis went away." Mrs. B. recognizes herself in the pictures the therapist describes. Her emotional numbness has disappeared: "That's just how it is!" She begins to cry: "I was not feeling good in the past week. Since Thursday, when I was here in the group. It started right in the beginning, I couldn't feel my body anymore. It was as if everything beneath me had disappeared. I didn't know if there was any ground below me or not. I thought I was falling. The only thing I knew was that I couldn't feel myself. As if there were kilometers of nothingness below me." Mrs. B. continues to cry. After some time passes, she begins to breathe more gently and slowly relaxes.*

In working together *with symbols on the table stage* (Krüger, 2005, p. 266 f.), the therapist and the patient symbolize all that is significant in their therapeutic consultation, using stones and wooden blocks: the patient's ego, his conflict partners, *but also all his feelings*, his qualities, and other relevant objects. The therapist empathizes playfully with the inner process work of the patient. She helps him, implicitly as a doppelganger and an auxiliary, to name the things on the stage, differentiate them, and 'read' his emotions. Thus, the patient creates *a symbolic landscape of the system of his conflicts on the table stage,* using stones and blocks, in the as-if mode of play and further develops the truth of his soul in the play.

***Case example 21***

*The 41-year-old Mr. D. is diagnosed with narcissistic personality disorder, major depressive episode, and internet gaming disorder (ICD F60.8, F32.2, F63.8) with a moderate structural disorder. After a lengthy hospital stay, he felt suicidal when he came for outpatient therapy. He hated himself and had masochistic thoughts. The disorder-specific treatment of his internet addiction and his decision to remain abstinent relieved him of his shame and guilt. He had made good progress over two years. In this process, the image of his 'own magic box' symbolized his free will. The patient's mother had abused him narcissistically as a child. His progress in therapy, however, brought him into an intrapsychic conflict with his pathological mother introject, such that he decompensated into depression once again.*

*In the therapy session, Mr. D. states without emotion: "I no longer have a magic box. I have no right to it." He notices, with the help of the therapist, that his inner 'shoulder mother', the ego state of his self-injurious thinking (see* Sect. 4.7*), is once more blindly denying him any right to his own wishes, as it had done in the past: "You are an idiot, you are bad! You are egotistical! Your illness is simply your weakness! The others don't find it easy either!" In discussing his newly lost willpower, Mr. D. tells of his interest in dollhouses: "I remember it as clear as a bell. I was about eight years old and was visiting another family when I saw a dollhouse for the first time: I just marveled at it. There were tiny chairs and plates, lamps, and cupboards, all just like in real life but miniature. I couldn't believe it. My hands just seemed to want to reach for the things of their own will. I was fascinated and thrilled. But the daughter of the family was standing in front of the dollhouse and wouldn't let me play with it. Then my mother came in and took me out of the room under some pretext. I believed her!".*

*The therapist would like to free the patient from his identification with his mother. Therefore, he asks the patient to set the scene of his childhood memory on the table stage, with the help of stones and blocks for himself, his feelings, the girl, his mother, and the dollhouse. Mr. D. replays the childhood memory with the stones. The therapist wants the patient to get in touch with his 'self' in the play differently from his experience in childhood. Therefore he takes the symbol for the mother, a large, round stone, off the table and places it two meters away on a chair: "What would you have instead needed in this situation as a child? What should a good mother have done, in your opinion? I am replacing the stone for your mother with another green stone on the table to represent another fictional good mother!" Mr. D. hesitates: "She would have come and admired the dollhouse. Perhaps she would have persuaded the girl to let me play with the dollhouse!" The therapist mentalizes as an implicit doppelganger in the ideal world of the patient, where wishes come true: "Yes. And before that, the good mother would have looked at you, noticed your shining eyes, and maybe said: 'Oh Daniel, the dollhouse is so beautiful, don't you think? Can you believe your eyes?' Then the good mother would have turned to the girl and said: 'Christine, could Daniel perhaps take the little chair in his hand?'" Mr. D. is very moved: "Yes, the good mother would have taken an interest in me!" Therapist: "Yes, she would have seen your shining eyes, shared your enthusiasm, and empathetically mirrored your enthusiasm in words." Mr. D. feels deeply understood. The therapist and Mr. D. agree that his real mother 'stole' his own willpower and his ability to wish during his childhood: "A good mother would have affirmed and shared your wishes with you and not used some trick to estrange you from your wishes!".*

*In the next therapy session, Mr. D. shares: "Since the last session, I have once again felt that everything is meaningless as if I am in a slump. On the day after our session, I had the feeling: I should work now. But at the same time, there was the impulse: 'Don't do it!' I just let all my tasks slide." The therapist places two chairs in the room, one for the 'self-protection through adaptation' and one for the 'abused* child *from childhood' (see* Sect. 4.7*). He points to the second chair of the 'abused child': "I believe the feeling of meaninglessness still belongs in your story with the dollhouse from last time. Your sense of meaninglessness is probably the feeling that you felt as a child when your mother took you away from the dollhouse under some pretext and had no interest in what you wanted! You now dare to feel that meaninglessness so clearly. That is progress!" Mr. D. physically experiences the feeling of meaninglessness 'in his upper belly, poisonous green, like a liquid that seeps into all areas of his life.' The therapist: "You feel the meaninglessness spread within you when your mother negates all that you yearn for and wish for."*

*It is only now that Mr. D. tells, for the first time, the story of how he made a dollhouse out of matchboxes and egg cartons at the age of fourteen: "I even baked little loaves of bread to go with it. But one day, the dollhouse simply disappeared! So when I was eighteen, I bought myself some dollhouse furniture. I hid it under my coat and smuggled it back into the house. I understand it better now that my mother and the feeling of meaninglessness are so happy with each other!".*

*In the next therapy session, Mr. D spontaneously says: "Today I'm somehow feeling constantly angry! Angry with other drivers who cut me off on the motorway. And with a woman on the telephone who was harsh to me. I'm going to tell her tomorrow she shouldn't be so stern! I feel confident again! I have access to my dollhouse again! That is my magic box. Instead of sadness, I now associate joy with my dollhouse!" Therapist: "Your sense of meaninglessness and your anger belong together! We carried out some archaeological excavations together in the last session and went in search of your willpower." Together, the therapist and the patient formulate the focus of therapy (*Kämmerer, 1989, *only verbal communication): "My depression helps me to feel my sense of meaninglessness. My sense of meaninglessness always arises when I dare to give permission to my desires. Or when I wish for empathy and compassion from someone. This will continue to happen until I associate my feeling of meaninglessness with my relationship with my mother and take my dollhouse back from my mother's hands.*

## 4.7 Representing the Working of the Ego-States Using Chairs

Patients with personality disorders get into relationship conflicts due to metacognitive blocks in their inner process of self-development (see Sect. 4.1) in the current external situation. These blocks lead to inadequate inner reality construction. The dominant defense pattern also blocks the attunement and agreement process *in the therapeutic relationship* relatively quickly. As a result, *the present* therapeutic relationship *itself* becomes the stage for the patient's inner self-development. The more disturbed the patient is, the sooner and stronger the attunement process gets blocked. "The neurotic mode is that of internalizing. [...] The structural mode is that of externalizing, for the tensions are ascribed to the outside and are fought there. [...] Here, the tension takes effect predominantly in action and the interpersonal space" (Rudolf, 2006, p. 50).

The patient's internal process of self-development (see Sect. 4.1) comprises three different areas of the inner reality construction represented *with chairs outside* in the therapy room (see Fig. 4.1 in Sect. 4.2):

1. The patient sits opposite the therapist on the *stage of the present therapeutic relationship* (Krüger, 1997, p. 250 ff.; Pruckner, 2002, p. 151) and thinks more or less as a healthy adult (chair 1 in Fig. 4.1).
2. The therapist represents the patient's internal self-image and object image in his everyday conflict *externally as the symptom scene with two chairs on the stage* (see Fig. 2.9 in Sect. 2.8 and Fig. 4.1 in Sect. 4.2, chairs 3 and 4). In a marital conflict, for example, one chair will be for the 'patient' himself and the other for his 'wife' (see Fig. 2.9 in Sect.2.8), both facing each other.
3. The therapist represents the *various defense patterns of the patient's defense system as metacognitive ego-states* on the *stage of metacognitive processes* (Fig. 4.1 in Sect. 4.2, chairs 5–9).

**Central idea**

Explicit metacognitive therapy of the blocks in the *inner* self-development process in the *external* situation should always be *related* to the patient's *current* conflict, which is represented in the symptom scene, *or* to the work on the relationship between the patient and the therapist in the here and now. Otherwise, the work on his metacognition is lost in space and time and becomes diffuse.

The explicit metacognitive psychodrama therapy looks relatively simple from the outside. However, in doing so, the therapist is performing a complex task *internally*. Her work is guided *by her emotional reactions* to the patient's concrete actions in the therapeutic relationship (see Sect. 4.8).

**Recommendation**

If you wish to integrate the therapeutic work on metacognitive ego-states in treating one of your patients, you can photocopy Fig. 4.1 from Sect. 4.2 as a template. Lay this copy on the table in front of you as you continue to work. The map of the patient's *ego-states* will help you to orient yourself to the various blocks in your patient's self-development and to remain internally flexible.

The different metacognitive ego-states of the patient are defined as follows:

1. The *'self-protective behavior'* is the generic term for the metacognitive ego-states of patients whose dysfunctionality is based on defense through denial. The patient acts as if it is nothing. He unconsciously refuses to perceive his own disturbing feelings or the disturbing behavior of the conflict partner. The metacognitive ego-states belonging to the category of self-protective behavior include: (1) The

patient protects himself from feeling his own emotions *by adapting* to the expectations of his interaction partner. (2) In *protecting himself through grandiosity*, the patient subconsciously has to play the role of a hero or a great guy. Nothing can harm him. A hero shows no weakness. Feelings of insecurity or failure are taboo. (3) The patient *protects himself* from retraumatization *by controlling* the external situation and other persons. Controlling the situation helps to protect oneself and others from disaster and feelings of helplessness. (4) Patients with post-traumatic stress disorder have to split off and deny their trauma experience to themselves and others. They develop *self-stabilization techniques* that help them deny their instability. For example, patients with post-traumatic stress disorder tend to distract themselves by working 80 h weekly. Or they control the actual situation unreasonably. They thus try to avoid situations that would make them or their interaction partner helpless and powerless and would trigger a flashback (see Sect. 5.4). (5) Patients with trauma-related disorders often automatically assume the systemic role assigned to them by their current relationship system (see Sect. 8.5). Patients functionally fulfill the tasks of the assigned systemic role. They split off their sense of self because their sense of self would activate old trauma experiences. For example, the patient takes on a *role in an authoritarian political or religious system* and also represents this role externally (Parin, 1977). The authoritarian system gratifies his role assumption with narcissistic appreciation. That helps him to suppress feelings of self-doubt, fear, insecurity, disorientation, or powerlessness and to deny internal conflicts. The therapist actively interprets, for the patient, *each* self-protective behavior through denial as 'one of many possible solutions' for dealing with himself and with others.

In schema therapy, the dysfunctional ego state of self-protective behavior is called the 'avoidant protective mode' (Arntz & van Genderen, 2010, p. 12): the patient "appears relatively mature and calm. The therapist could assume that the patient feels good. The patient applies this protective mode so that she doesn't have to feel or show her feelings of fear (an abandoned child), inferiority (punishment), or anger (an impulsive child). […] It is dangerous to show feelings, express wishes, and state one's opinion. The patient is afraid to lose control over her feelings. […] This becomes particularly clear when she commits to relationships with other people. The self-protective mode keeps others at a distance."

2. The therapist immediately names *every appropriate* thought, feeling, and action of the patient in his conflict as '*healthy adult thinking*' (chair 1 in Fig. 4.1 in Sect. 4.2). The chair on which the patient sits opposite the therapist during the consultation represents the 'healthy adult thinking' of the patient. Healthy adult thinking is the state of spontaneity (Moreno, 1974, p. 13): "Spontaneity drives the person to have an *appropriate* response to a *new* situation *or* a *new* response to an *old* situation." When in a conflict, a patient with 'healthy adult thinking' can internally represent reality *appropriately without any defense* and deal with his conflicts appropriately.

**Important definition**

In every external situation, people construct an internal image of the current external reality. They interact *externally* according to this *internal* image. They think as healthy adults if their inner reality construction has not been altered by a defense.

The development of healthy adult thinking includes the development of *new psychosomatic resonance patterns.* A 30-year-old man with a major structural disorder presented with recurrent major depressive episodes (F33.2). Together, the therapist and the patient understood the metacognitive triggers of his depression. In the meantime, the patient has not decompensated into depression again in two triggering situations. Nevertheless, in the 18th therapy session, he says with a naive friendly smile: "The therapy has not helped me so far. I only feel that something is changing here inside me," *he puts his hand on his chest*: "But I can't describe what it is." The therapist is happy: "You don't need to be able to describe it either!"

In schema therapy, the healthy adult mode is "precisely the mode the patient should cultivate and ultimately retain. [...] It is seldom highly developed in the early phase of therapy [...] The lag in the patient's development in areas such as relationship formation, independence, the ability to express himself, or the sense of self-worth, and a lack of experience in dealing with realistic boundaries make it necessary for the therapist to act as a representative for the 'healthy side'. This [...] is particularly true at the beginning of therapy. [...] During later phases, this mode helps [...] to reach healthy goals" (Arntz & van Genderen, 2010, p. 17).

3. The dysfunctional ego state of the *'inner traumatized or abandoned child'* is a special type of the patient's 'inner child'. This *'inner child'* is the child the patient was in childhood. The therapist can also give the "traumatized child" a personal name: the 'inner ashamed child' or 'inner unseen child'. Perhaps the patient *remembers that, as a child,* he was beaten by his father. His father wanted him to be different from how he was. His crying would have only angered his father even more. Or he heroically endured the bad treatment of his grandparents and didn't tell his parents anything about it as he didn't want to cause them even more worry. The therapist represents one such painful childhood memory of the patient in the therapy room with an additional empty chair for the 'abandoned child' or the 'traumatized child' (chair 6 in Fig. 4.1in Sect. 4.2). This chair represents the patient's denied feelings. The 'inner traumatized child" should develop into the 'inner healthy child' in the course of therapy.

In such a case, the therapist names the pathogenic quality of the painful childhood experience and speaks in plain language. She names, for example, the traumatizing situations explicitly as 'trauma experiences' (see Sect. 5.5). When the therapist represents the inner 'traumatized child' with a doll on an empty chair placed next to the patient, patients who were traumatized in childhood often feel threatened in the here and now. The presence of the 'traumatized child' acts like exposure to trauma. The therapist, therefore, always asks the patient immediately: "What does it trigger in you when you look at your traumatized child there?" If the patient has negative feelings, she places the chair with the doll far away in the corner of the room or the front of the door (see Sect. 5.8).

Understanding the *biographical* origin of the patient's self-protection makes it easier for the therapist to no longer be disturbed by the patient's self-protective behavior *in the present*. The patient also understands himself better by connecting his self-protective behavior with his childhood.

**Central idea**

The metacognitive ego state of the '*abused or abandoned* child' shall develop further into the ego state of the '*healthy* inner child' during psychotherapy. It then becomes a symbol for the 'self' of the patient.

I have adopted the term 'the abused or abandoned child' from schema therapy. In this mode, the patient is "sad, despairing, inconsolable and often panic-stricken, [...] her voice often changes to that of a small child. Her thoughts and behavior become like that of a four to six-year-old. She feels alone in the world. [...] Everyone will take advantage of her and leave her in the lurch. The world is a scary, dangerous place. Little Nora divides the world into black and white. She demands immediate and constant validation and solution to her problems [...]" (Arntz & van Genderen, 2010, p. 14).

4. The metacognitive ego state of the 'inner angry child' usually is an *expression of internal maturation* and *development* of the 'traumatized or abandoned child' into a 'healthy inner child' in the course of therapy (see case examples 16 in Sect. 2.14, 48 in Sect. 5.12, and 54 in Sect. 6.4). But, it may also surface when the patient with borderline personality disorder blindly defends the painful feelings and passive desires from his childhood through angry behavior. In such a situation, the therapist places the empty chair for the patient's 'angry inner child' (chair 7) next to the chair of the 'abandoned or traumatized child'. She understands the patient's destructive anger as justified in the sense of defense against the negative feelings of the 'traumatized or abandoned child'. Patients diagnosed with borderline personality disorder oscillate relatively arbitrarily between fury and despair, i.e., the 'clingy needy ego state' and the contrary 'pseudo-autonomous, authoritarian ego state'. The 'clingy needy ego state' contains, among other things, the 'traumatized inner child', and the pseudo-autonomous, authoritarian ego state contains the 'angry inner child' (see Sects. 4.3 and 4.9).

In schema therapy, Arntz and van Genderen (2010, p. 15) name the *dysfunctional* ego state of the 'angry child' as the 'angry, impulsive child': "The 'enraged Nora' behaves like an angry, frustrated and impatient little child (approximately four years old), who doesn't spare a single thought for others. [...] The patient is verbally and sometimes also physically aggressive and makes vicious remarks toward others, including her therapist. She is upset because her needs are not being met and her rights remain ignored. [...] Not only is she bad-tempered, but she also wants everyone to notice how badly she is being treated. She achieves this by attacking others [...], injuring herself, and trying to kill herself or even others out of revenge [...]. In a mild form, Nora will [...] show her anger by missing sessions or terminating therapy altogether. [...]."

5. The dysfunctional ego state of 'self-injurious thinking' is the umbrella term for a patient's masochistic thinking, feeling, and acting. This is triggered by the demands of a sadistic superego in the present. It is based on the identification with the aggressor developed in childhood. Patients devalue themselves *masochistically* in their relationship to others and feel inferior and guilty *even before* they have been criticized or attacked by others. According to Rohde-Dachser (1976, only verbal communicated), "masochism is the cry for empathy". What she means is that patients who act masochistically in *current* relationships act out their old self-censorship that was appropriate *in childhood*. This self-censorship helped them to protect themselves from additional harm in difficult relationships in their childhood (see Sect. 8.5).

**Important definition**

*Internal 'self-injurious thinking'* should not be confused with *external self-harming behavior* in trauma patients. The 'scratching' of the forearm is *a clinical symptom*. Traumatized patients use *external self-harm* as a self-stabilization technique to end a flashback. The physical pain of 'scratching' terminates the mental numbness of the dissociative state.

In the encounter with a masochistic patient, the therapist responds by placing another empty chair *opposite the patient* to represent the patient's 'self-injurious thinking and behavior' (chair 8). The category of 'self-injurious thinking' is symbolically named with personally appropriate terms depending on the extent of self-destructiveness: the 'sadistic superego', the 'blind sadistic critic', the 'blind inner prosecutor', the 'blind inner governess', the 'inner soul killer', or the 'tormentor who gives him bad thoughts' (see Sect. 7.2).

**Central idea**

The 'self-injurious thinking' of patients with personality disorders may 'die' during therapy. *Back when* they were a child, it helped them in censoring themselves to prevent being hurt or disappointed in interaction with aggressive or neglecting attachment figures. However, the 'self-injurious thinking' has lost its *historical* protective function in the present. In therapy, the patient shall learn in the here and now *not to treat themselves* self-injuriously like they had to in the past (see Sect. 8.5).

The 'ego state of self-injurious thinking or acting' is referred to as the 'punitive or over-critical mode' in schema therapy (Arntz & van Genderen, 2010, p. 16). The patient is "scornful, disapproving and humiliating" toward himself. [...]. This mode calls Nora a big mouth. If she fails to achieve something, it is only because she did not try hard enough. The punitive mode has little interest in feelings. [...] When something goes wrong, it is her fault. In her mind, her success is dependent exclusively on her will to succeed. If she fails or something does not work, she obviously does not want it. [...] She provokes punishment everywhere, even from her therapist. She refuses to cooperate with her treatment. This often leads to premature termination of therapy."

6. If necessary, the therapist places another empty chair behind the chair for the 'self-injurious thinking' to represent the *inner object image of the patient's attachment figure from his childhood* (chair 9) who had *harmed* him through abuse or neglect.

In the case of traumatized patients, this chair can also represent a *pathological introject* (see Sect. 5.12).

In Fig. 4.1 (see Sect. 4.2), the positions of the metacognitive ego states in the therapy room and the direction of the arrows for the different 'viewing directions' are not random. The direction of the chairs informs whether the defense pattern in question is changing the patient's internal self-image or *his internal object image*. The self-protective behavior, the 'abandoned child', and the 'angry child' are placed next to each other, looking in the same direction as the patient's 'healthy adult thinking'. In this way, the patient connects them internally with his self-image. The chairs for self-injurious thinking (chair 8) and the internal object image of the harmful attachment figure from his childhood (chair 9) are always placed *face to face opposite the patient*. They distort the patient's *internal* object images in *external* conflicts.

**Central idea**

The therapist *confronts* the patient harshly when she names his dominant defense pattern and represents it with a chair on the stage in the therapy room. During this confrontation, however, she looks *at the second chair on the stage in the therapy room*, which symbolizes the patient's defense pattern. In this way, *together with the patient*, she delegates his defense pattern to the *other* chair. Thus, the patient experiences: "The therapist is bothered by *my character trait*, but she does *not* challenge me *as a person*." This makes it easier for the therapist to confront the patient (see Sect. 4.8).

**Exercise 11**

You cannot understand this experience just by reading and thinking about it. Experience it for *yourself* through psychosomatic acting in an exercise. To do this, try out *two types of confrontational interpretation* in a role play with a colleague: Confront the "patient" in a *purely verbal* manner in the first round. *Look at him* and name his dysfunctional metacognitive ego state and its positive function in his self-regulation when facing him. In a second round, please also verbally name the dysfunctional ego state acted by the patient. For the dysfunctional ego state, however, place *an additional chair* next to or in front of the patient and *look at the chair*.

***Case example 22***

*The 26-year-old tile layer Mr. C. suffers from recurrent depressive episodes, internet gaming addiction disorder, a narcissistic personality disorder (ICD-10 F33.2, F63.8, F60.8), and a medium grad structural disorder. He has been in individual therapy for half a year now. He pretentiously asserts that with his one-man company, he can "land any contract he wants". In the course of the therapy, the therapist learns that the patient only manages to do this because he always offers his customers the lowest price. His calculations result in lower prices because he devotes far too little time to his work. At the same time, his fear of criticism from his customers pushes him to be a perfectionist in his work. For this reason, he seldom keeps to his time plan. When his plan fails, however, he suffers significant self-esteem crises, sometimes even reaching the point of suicidal thoughts. This is because Mr. C gets caught in a flashback from his childhood. He came from a broken family. As a little boy between the ages of four and ten, Mr. C. often sat alone in the hallway on the step, crying and waiting for his parents. His neighbors would often take pity on him and take him into their apartment. As a child, despite his intelligence, Mr. C spent three years in a special needs school due to his family's negligence and a neurotic learning disorder. At present, the patient is, as an adult, almost incapacitated for work due to his symptoms. He has frequent conflicts with his wife as a result of financial concerns. His wife wishes to separate from him soon.*

*In the therapy session, Mr. C. seems despairing and once again at risk of suicide. The therapist cannot reach Mr. C. with verbal communication alone. It is as if there is a glass wall between the therapist and the patient. The therapist decides to carry out a crisis intervention with psychodramatic metacognitive therapy in this therapeutic situation. Together with the patient, he maps out the patient's dysfunctional self-regulation. The relationship conflict with his wife is represented as the symptom scene using two chairs (see* Fig. 4.1 in Sect. 4.2, *chairs 3 and 4). The therapist places a chair next to Mr. C. to represent his self-protective behavior through grandiosity (chair 5): "Mr. C., when planning your working hours, you heroically try to push others' limits. You calculate far too little time for the work at hand. You are then proud to have received all contracts. Then you want to execute the work perfectly within the planned time. Furthermore, you are a white knight who cares about justice in others' conflicts." Mr. C.: "Yes, that is something I am good at, I can give my all for the good of others! And it works out well! I dragged my step-daughter out of the drug scene. However, I just can't manage to do it for myself!" Therapist: "When someone else is mistreated, you feel angry inside. I'm going to place this other chair next to you for the angry child in you (chair 7). But you cannot get angry when someone criticizes you, for example, a client or your wife. Instead, you revert to being the abandoned and shamed child from your childhood (chair 6). I'm going to place this chair over here for the abandoned child you were. Please, take a seat on this chair!" Mr. C. follows the therapist's instructions. The therapist now points to the empty chair where the patient had been sitting: "This is the chair for your healthy adult thinking (chair 1). Sitting on this chair of healthy adult thinking, you are currently feeling: 'I would like to be able to do everything better, but I can't!'".*

*The therapist positions another chair opposite Mr. C. for his 'self-injurious thinking and feeling' (chair 8). The therapist stands behind this chair and verbalizes as an auxiliary ego the workings of this dysfunctional ego state: "And at the same time, you say to yourself as your inner humiliating censor: 'You say that you can't? You make things easy for yourself! Sooner or later, it has to be possible once only! You are quite a weakling!'" The therapist asks the patient to move back to the chair for his healthy adult thinking (chair 1) and doubles him verbally: "But I really can't do it. I want to. But I just sit there; it's like I'm standing on the brakes. Is that right?!" Mr. C.: "Yes, I want to do it, but when I want it, it's as if my brain just freezes up. All of a sudden, nothing works anymore!" The therapist moves to stand next to the chair for the sadistic superego (chair 8): "Then this part of you pops up and says: 'Well obviously that's the way it is, you are a loser!'" Mr. C.: "Exactly. Then I think: You're not made for this. You went to a special needs school; you can't even write properly! The last time I heard that was from my father in 2001: 'You're never going to manage that!' At that time, I wanted to become a drug representative because I worked through all of my wife's written questions of examination 50 times with her and could answer all of the questions!" The therapist places another chair behind the chair of the 'inner critic' (chair 9), symbolizing the patient's father: "I think that you devalue yourself today just as your father devalued you in the past! Perhaps in time, you can learn to let go of this self-censorship! You actually can't need it!" By the end of the therapy session, the glass wall in the therapeutic relationship has disappeared. And it didn't reappear in the following therapy sessions. Setting up the constellation of the dominant self-injurious ego state and the other metacognitive ego states with empty chairs helped the patient and the therapist to re-orient and understand the self-regulation of the patient.*

**Recommendation**

I recommend adhering to the following rules when setting up the metacognitive ego states: (1) The therapist initially sets up *only the dominant defense pattern* and describes *its positive function* in the patient's self-regulation. This opens the door to the other defense patterns involved in the patient's defense system (see Sect. 4.8). (2) The more severely a patient is structurally disturbed, *the longer he needs* to orient in his dysfunctional process of self-development. (3) Using too many chairs at once tends to confuse the patient. The therapist may have to work *only with the dominant metacognitive* ego state for many sessions. (4) The more acute the patient's plight, *the more active* the therapist acts as an implicit or interacting doppelganger (see Sect. 2.5) in the constellation work (see case example 22).

**Central idea**

Every person is aware that he is thinking about conflicts. However, he does not have a thinking model to grasp and understand the *metacognitive blocks* in his inner process of self-development (Sattelberger, 2013, only verbal communication!). Therefore, the therapist must actively help the patient combine his *own* experience with the described thought model of *the metacognitive ego states.*

The therapist helps the patient *integrate metacognitive thinking* into his own mentalization with the following methods:

1. She names the patient's respective dominant defense pattern as a dysfunctional ego state. She describes his characteristic pattern of thinking, feeling, and acting *if and when* he acts it out *in the present.* In addition, she also names its positive function in the holistic process of his self-regulation.
2. Together, the therapist and the patient retrace his internal process of self-development within the framework of a *current* conflict. For example, during the conversation about his marital crisis, the patient tells the therapist: "I hate being sad." The therapist then reformulates his statement and points to the chair symbolizing his self-image and object image in the symptom scene: "You despise yourself because your wife has separated from you. You pull yourself together". The patient replies: "But nobody wants to hear anything about my sadness!" The therapist: "In your experience, no one in your family cares about what you are feeling." She points to the chair for his "self-injurious thinking": "And now you forbid yourself from feeling your sadness and think: 'Sadness is nonsense!' I am representing your inner self-injurious voice with this chair opposite you." The therapist adds: "But when you feel sad, is there also that unseen sad child

in you, the child you used to be? I will place this other chair over here for your abandoned inner child."

3. The therapist symbolizes the ego states with hand puppets. The puppets should have a *special characteristic* to demonstrate each metacognitive ego state. For example, the chair representing self-injurious thinking will have a grinning devil, a witch, a scowling robber, or a bureaucrat. Or the therapist symbolizes the traumatized child by placing a doll on the corresponding chair. In this way, the patient experiences his metacognitive ego state *externally as an interaction partner on the object level*. The *external space between* the patient's self and the hand puppet invites the patient to interact with this ego state *externally* in the as-if mode of play (see Sect. 4.10).
4. The therapist and the patient jointly *name* the metacognitive ego state that the patient just acted out with *appropriate individual* names. Thus, self-injurious thinking becomes the 'blind child destroyer' or the 'blind governess'.
5. Whenever the patient again switches into another ego state in the moment, the therapist points to the chair of this other ego state. She names it and says, for example: "Now you are feeling and talking from the role of your self-protection!" Or: "You then adapt your behavior and act as if nothing is wrong." Or: "Your inner blind soul killer is telling you again: 'You are nothing, you can't do anything, you are good for nothing.'"
6. Often the patient acts out his dominant defense pattern also *in the present therapeutic relationship* in the equivalence mode, *even when* the ego state is represented as a chair next to him. In such a case, the therapist lets the patient switch to the other chair of the dominant ego state *externally* and act out this ego state in the as-if mode of play (see Sect. 4.8).

If the therapy room is very small, the therapist can symbolize the various metacognitive ego states *with stones and wooden blocks on the table stage*, instead of chairs on the big stage. However, then the patient will *not* experience the work of his defense patterns with all the senses *psychosomatically*. On the other hand, when working on the miniature table stage, the patient symbolizes his ego states with stones of *different sizes, shapes, and colors*, and he can use these personalized symbols once again in the next therapy session (Zilch-Purucker, 2012, only verbal communication!). *In group therapy*, the therapist should only ever represent the one *dominant dysfunctional* ego state with a chair, which the patient acts out *in the here and now* (see Sect. 4.8). Too many chairs will confuse the patient and the group.

Therapists should work *on their own character traits* for at least ten sessions in an individual setting with the help of psychodramatic chair work. This will help them gain ego control over their traits (see exercise 7) and deal with their peculiarities much better. Internally, they will become more flexible and creative.

Constellation work is a long-known method of action in psychodrama. For example, when setting up the 'cultural atom', the therapist represents the patient's fear with a stone outside on the table stage or places a chair next to him for his 'anxious inner child'. However, the therapist works 'only' on the patient's *cognitive thought content* that has been named by the patient *himself* when setting up the cultural atom. In *explicit metacognitive therapy*, however, the therapist focuses her attention on the *metacognitive* blocks in the patient's internal process of self-development. The therapist's character-related countertransference (see Sect. 2.10) to the patient's dominant rigid defense pattern (see Sect. 4.8) is the starting point for the therapeutic work on the metacognitive ego states.

## 4.8 Psychodramatic Approach to the Dominant Defense Pattern

**Important definition**

A defense pattern is a dysfunctional tool of mentalizing. The creative process of inner self-development, inner self-image, and inner object image in the external situation is blocked, leading to inappropriate results and also an inappropriate perception of the current external reality.

**Central idea**

The *dominant* defense pattern in the patient's defense system is different for different personality disorders. For example, *self-injurious thoughts* are dominant in those with *depressive personality disorder*. Self-protective behavior, in the form of *grandiosity*, is dominant in those with *narcissistic* personality disorder. On the other hand, people with *borderline personality disorder* alternate between the 'clingy needy ego state' and the contrary 'pseudo-autonomous, authoritarian ego state' (see Sect. 4.9).

***Case example 22***

*Mr. E. suffers from a social phobia and anxious-avoidant personality disorder (ICD-10 F60.6). He is "always exhausted" because of his work. He devalues himself in all relationships. He thus anticipates criticism from his respective attachment figure when in conflict. He is trapped in a helplessness syndrome. He acts out his helplessness masochistically, even in his relationship with the therapist. The therapist initiates a therapeutic communication about the patient's masochistic behavior: "I see that you devalue yourself instinctively. I'll place a chair over here, opposite you, to represent your 'self-injurious thinking'". Mr. E.: "But I think that's true. I have no reason to be exhausted." The therapist: "Please shift to this other chair, which represents your self-devaluation! What do you think of Mr. E. here? What can he not do?" Mr. E. sits on the "chair of self-devaluation" and answers while looking at his own chair: "Actually, it's amazing how he still manages to do his job! But he will certainly not last for a long time. Others are much better than him!" The therapist: "It sounds as if you despise yourself!" Mr. E.: "Yes, that's right!" Therapist: "Please shift back to your first chair. I will name it the chair for your healthy adult thinking. I see that your inner self-critic, here in the other chair, does not even notice what exactly you do. He knows in advance that you are mediocre. He's blind!" The therapist sets up two other empty chairs to represent the patient's symptom scene (see* Fig. 2.9 *in* Sect. 2.8*). He points to the chair that represents the patient's internal self-image: "Please describe what Mr. E. is doing over there at his job. What is he doing and* *what is he experiencing?" At the end of the session, Mr. E. says, "I did not know the weight I am constantly lugging around with me. I think I am depressed." The patient has at first developed an awareness of his self-injurious thinking through this disorder-specific method of treatment. His self-injurious thinking suppressed his healthy adult thinking.*

***Case example 23***
*The 52-year-old Ms. F. suffers from borderline personality disorder (ICD-10 F60.31, F33.2). Her employer has fired her without prior notice. After a short stay in the hospital, she is sitting in front of the therapist without any self-reflection, feeling agitated and furious. She rants about her former boss. However, she does not tell what has happened at her workplace. She has an unspoken demand for a complete understanding of her anger from the therapist. At first, the therapist identifies with the patient's boss spontaneously. However, he avoids criticizing the patient due to her lack of self-reflection. Instead, he grasps the general metacognitive principle of her acting out and represents it as an ego state externally in the therapy room: "I am placing a chair beside you to represent the 'angry child' in you, as you are just now. Would you please sit on this chair once?" Ms. F. follows the request and spontaneously says. "That's right! I feel like a child too! My boss behaved quite badly!" All of a sudden, as if she is a changed person, the patient calmly describes the events that preceded her dismissal. It turns out to be a bizarre story of bullying. The therapist now has a much better understanding of the patient's emotional reaction. He develops compassion for her and can provide her with the needed support (continued in* Sect. 4.13*). The patient's ego state of the "angry inner child" had suppressed her healthy adult thinking. (Continuation in* Sect. 4.14*)*

In the therapy of people with personality disorders, initially, the therapist naturally identifies with the patient's inner process of self-development and accompanies him in it as an implicit doppelganger (see Sect. 2.5). At some point, however, patients with a personality disorder defend themselves with projective identification (see Sect. 2.4.4). They act out their defense in the therapeutic relationship. The therapist then automatically identifies with the patient's *defended* part of self and wants to help her get justice. But, the patient fights this defended part of the self. As a result, the therapist's identification with the patient's *defended* part becomes stronger and stronger. Thus, she unconsciously opposes his dominant defense pattern. For example, she identifies with the patient's self because she feels tormented by his masochistic self-censorship (see case example 22 above).

**Central idea**

When patients defend with projective identification, the therapist's negative affect is an *appropriate* response to the dominant defense pattern acted out by the patient in the *current* therapeutic relationship. Therefore, in therapy, the therapist focuses on the disturbance in the *current* therapeutic relationship.

However, the therapist often defends her own appropriate negative feelings and restricts herself from feeling what she feels. For example, she defends herself through *introjection and rationalization*: "I'm ashamed to feel so angry. As a therapist, I'm not allowed to feel this way." In doing so, she personalizes her feelings of powerlessness or anger and *devalues herself*. She may even link her appropriate negative affect to a problem from *her own* childhood and consider that as an indication of her own need for therapy. Or she may respond to her negative affect with a *projection*. She *then devalues the patient* by *interpreting* his disruptive behavior as "the behavior of a stubborn child." Or she suspects: "The patient is too severely disturbed for psychotherapy".

A patient with *narcissistic personality disorder*, for example, is firmly fixated in the self-protective behavior through grandiosity. He expects a grandiose therapist to help him get better in a few sessions. The therapist first tries to meet the patient's grandiose expectations. But her helpful offers make the patient aware of his neediness. Thus, he runs the risk of slipping into a trauma film from his childhood. He, therefore, rejects the therapist's offers of help in order to stabilize himself. The therapist then feels helpless and inferior on his behalf. The more she tries to help, the more strongly the patient rejects her. The therapist then internally devalues the patient and acts out character-related countertransference (see Sect. 2.10).

**Central idea**

The therapist must undergo a paradigm shift in the therapy of people with personality disorders. She must let go of the helper attitude. She must interpret her *own negative affect* as an *appropriate* reaction to the patient's dominant defense pattern and try to make her negative affect useful in the patient's therapy process.

This can be done with the following procedure (see Sect. 2.9):

1. The therapist validates the disturbance in the therapeutic relationship.
2. The therapist differentiates and names the affect triggered in her by the patient. In doing so, she consciously gives herself permission and space to feel what she feels. She thus dissolves her own secondary defense through introjection.
3. She asks herself: "*Which of the patient's concrete actions* trigger this negative feeling in me?" She describes the patient's external defensive actions in a way that is close to the experience.

**Central idea**

In this step, a relatively large number of therapists confuse the patient's *external defensive actions* with their *own interpretation* of the patient's actions. For example, they act out the helper attitude. They then unconsciously identify with the patient's abandoned or traumatized inner child and represent it externally. But, in doing so, they represent the *suppressed* metacognitive ego state, but not the defense pattern with which the patient *suppresses his inner child*. For example, in the case of defense through grandiosity, they set up a chair behind the patient for his ego state of the 'unseen, abandoned child'. But, they do not talk about the patient's *dominant defense through grandiosity*.

**Recommendation**

The therapist should work with the patient *on the current conflict* triggered by the patient's dominant defense pattern in the therapeutic relationship or his everyday life. She should not switch her focus to the patient's trauma or deficit experiences from childhood. For the initial 10–15 sessions, the therapist should use an empty chair to represent only the patient's *dominant* defense pattern which triggers her negative affect in the encounter with the patient. She represents a *second ego state* for a short time, for example, the traumatized child, only if she wants to clarify the *positive function* of his rigid defense pattern in the holistic process of his self-regulation.

4. The therapist grasps the patient's external defense behavior and assigns it *internally to one of the metacognitive ego states* (see Fig. 4.1 in Sects. 4.2 and 4.7). There are seven possibilities to do so: (1) the 'self-protective behavior', (2) the 'self-injurious thinking and behavior', (3) the 'angry' child ", (4) the 'abandoned or traumatized child', (5) the traumatized ego (see Sect. 5.2), (6) the exchange between a pseudo independent, angry ego state and a dependent, needy ego state (see Sect. 4.9), or (7) the ego state of addictive thinking (see Sect. 10.6). The habitual self-devaluation of the patient thus becomes the ego state of 'self-injurious thinking' (chair 8 in Fig. 4.1), his exaggerated perfectionism becomes the ego state of 'self-protective behavior through adaptation' (chair 5), neediness becomes the ego state of the 'abandoned or traumatized child' (chair 6), angry allegations become the ego state of the 'angry child' (chair 7), and downplaying of consumption of alcohol becomes the ego state of the 'addicted ego' (see Sect. 10.6).
5. If the patient acts out his dominant defense pattern in the current therapy session, the therapist *names* it verbally. In doing so, she appreciates, *as a metacognitive doppelganger*, its *positive function* in the holistic process of his self-regulation and *describes* it: "(1) You always have to be a great guy (defense pattern). (2) This is because you have to protect yourself from negative feelings (specific negative feelings). Or: "If you are not a great guy then you will develop negative feelings. (3) The therapist, acting as an implicit doppelganger, names the presumed negative feelings: "You would then feel insecure or helpless." (4) Then the sentences follow: "You couldn't handle these feelings. (5) That's why you believe that it's good for you if you make an effort to always be a great guy! It's not the best solution, but it's a solution." The therapist creatively paints the positive meaning of his rigid defenses until the patient himself says: "Yes... but..." (see Sects. 9.8.2–9.8.5).

**Central idea**

First, the patient acts out his defense pattern in *equivalence mode* and justifies it with external reality. But he should now recognize the *positive sense* of his defense in the process of self-regulation. So he can learn to think of his defense in the *as-if mode*. He understands it as an internal representation of an old solution, and no longer as an appropriate solution *for the current external situation* (see Sect. 2.6). Thus, the patient gains *ego control* over his unconscious defense. He becomes free to choose. He *can* consciously act out the old behavior in the current situation or he *can* also seek for a new behavior. Thinking in the as-if mode is achieved through four different steps: (1) Describing the positive function of the defense pattern in self-regulation. (2) External distancing from the defense pattern by setting up the associated chair, (3) Questioning the age of the defense pattern and its integration into childhood experiences, (4) Playing out the role of the defense pattern in the as-if mode of play (see Fig. 4.1 in Sect. 4.2).

In the *psychodramatic* implementation of the as-if mode into the equivalence mode, the therapist follows the central principle of healing in psychodrama therapy: The patient should become "the creator of his own life." "The as-if mode unleashes life... Prometheus gives birth to himself in the as-if mode and thus proves that his existence in shackles was the result of his own free will" (Moreno, 1970, p. 78). In describing the *positive function* of self-regulation ("You must do this otherwise you will develop negative feelings which you would struggle to deal with"), the therapist *indirectly* links the patient's dominant defense pattern with the biographical context in which the defense arose (see Sect. 2.4.4). For example, in defense through grandiosity, the splitting off of feelings of loneliness and excessive demand was necessary to cope psychologically at one point in time.

6. In naming the defense pattern, the therapist *immediately represents* it externally *with an empty chair* on the room stage: "I notice that you think and behave in a self-injurious manner in the relationship with your wife. I am placing this chair over here for your self-injurious thinking. The chair symbolizes your inner sadistic critic. It says: You are an incapable husband!" The patient experiences a purely verbal confrontation *without any external representation of the defense* pattern as a criticism because he acts his defense in the equivalence mode (see Sect. 2.6). But, the therapist names *and represents* his defense pattern *externally* with a chair in the as-if mode of play. *The patient* thus gains *external distance from* his dysfunctional thinking, feeling, and acting. Over time, that helps him to gain awareness of his problem. He considers: "Perhaps I *am* thinking in a self-injurious manner and it is not true that my wife despises me. I have to examine my feelings once more." *The therapist* now sees the patient externally in his own role, thinking as a healthy adult, separated from the second chair of his defense pattern. Together with the patient, she looks at his defense from a metaperspective, shoulder to shoulder, and makes it the subject of therapeutic communication. This resolves the therapist's negative affect.

**Exercise 12**

Learn about the metacognitive constellation work by acting psychosomatically. You cannot understand it just by reading about it. You can only understand the effect of therapeutic action by experiencing it in your body. Look for a personal character trait that you don't particularly love. Talk about it *purely verbally* with a colleague for three minutes. Then start the conversation all over again, but represent your character trait externally with a second chair next to you. You will notice: You quickly feel ashamed and criticized in the *purely verbal* conversation. However, when you represent your character trait *as a chair* next to *you,* you feel less guilty and hurt because you physically distance yourself from your character trait in the as-if mode. You are free to decide whether or not you want to switch to the chair next to you in the *as-if mode of play* and act out your disliked character trait.

7. When working with the metacognitive ego states, the therapist simply makes statements and does not ask any questions *in the subjunctive*: "Could it be that you are thinking in a self-injurious way?" This is important because the patient thinks in the equivalence mode. He can't distinguish between the therapist's mere consideration and a real opinion. Therefore, the therapist acts in the as-if mode

of play and says: "I understand that your angry inner child has surfaced. I'm placing this chair over here for your angry inner child." She *doesn't ask* the patient *if she may* set up an ego state. The therapist's statements and actions give the patient the opportunity to directly reject the second chair in the as-if mode of play. If necessary, the therapist simply removes the chair for the patient's 'angry inner child': "Yes, I can see that you see it differently. I'll put the chair for your 'angry inner child' back along with the other chairs in the circle! Sometimes I try something out and think out loud to make something clear to myself."

**Central idea**

Using the two-chair technique, the therapist *externally separates* the patient's defense pattern from his healthy adult thinking. Thus, as a metacognitive doppelganger, *the therapist can alternately* identify with the patient's dominant defense pattern, symbolized as the second chair externally, *or* with the patient's healthy adult thinking. She empathizes with the patient's *two opposing ego states* as a doppelganger and develops sympathy for each of them one after the other. This reduces the therapist's negative affect and her internal tension toward the patient.

8. The therapist represents the patient's dominant metacognitive defense pattern with a suitable hand or finger puppet and places it on the chair of the ego state. She symbolizes, for example, the ego state of his 'sadistic superego' with the hand puppet of a bureaucrat, devil, or witch: "That is your inner critic. He believes that everything you think, feel, and do is wrong. But this critic is *blind* and doesn't even consider *your situatio*n!" As a therapist, you can try the chair work once *without* puppets and then *with* puppets. You will notice: symbolizing the ego state with a hand puppet turns the ego state into an interaction partner in an external symbolic play. The patient in case example 23 (see above) responded to the representation of her dominant dysfunctional ego state with a hand puppet, saying, "You have always said that. But this figure makes it all so clear to me now!".
9. As a doppelganger, the therapist gives the patient's dominant dysfunctional ego state a voice and mentalizes *on his behalf* in his ego state *in the as-if mode of play*. For example, she points with her hand at the *externally* represented ego state of the 'sadistic inner critic' and says: "Your inner critic is blind and doesn't see your reality. He says to you: 'You are nothing, you can do nothing, and you are no good!'".
10. In further discussion with the therapist, the patient often falls back into his rigid defense pattern. He thinks, for example, in a self-injurious manner and says: "Of course, I still know far too little..." In such a case, the therapist immediately ascribes this statement to the appropriate dysfunctional ego state and points *with her hand to the chair* of his 'self-injurious thinking': "Your self-injurious thinking is once again saying: 'Exactly! The others are much better informed than you! They are also much more intelligent than you!'" In this way, the therapist immediately marks the patient's *inner* role change in his *dysfunctional* ego state, enabling him to experience the shift between his ego states externally in the as-if mode of play.

11. Together, the therapist and the patient think of a *personally suited symbolic name* for the patient's dominant dysfunctional ego state. In this way, for example, his 'self-injurious thinking' becomes his 'blind inner critic', his 'governess', his 'blind sadistic inner prosecutor', or his 'inner soul killer.
12. If the patient inappropriately values his defensive behavior directly in the therapeutic relationship and defends it in equivalence mode, he cannot yet think of his defensive pattern in the as-if mode, even though it is represented externally as a different chair. Therefore, the therapist asks him to externally change into the role of his defense pattern: "You are thinking in a self-injurious manner. So please switch to the chair of your blind, sadistic inner critic and *devalue yourself* actively with statements! What do you say to depressed Michael?" This *external* role change lets the patient *externally differentiate* between his defense pattern and his healthy adult thinking in the as-if mode of play.
13. Together, the patient and the therapist, as a metacognitive doppelganger, act out his dominant defense pattern in the as-if mode of play.

**Central idea**

The patient should *psychosomatically* act out his metacognitive defense pattern that creates his dysfunctional thoughts. Thus, he internally activates and creates neural links between the memory centers of his sensorimotor interaction patterns, affect, physical sensations, linguistic concepts, and thoughts (see Sect. 2.7), which are part of his metacognitive defense pattern. He completes the neural connections to form a holistic psychosomatic resonance pattern. However, the *new linguistic concept* of the defense pattern in memory causes it to be neuronally connected *differently*, for example, the resonance pattern of the term 'beautiful childhood', is *now* classified under the term 'abandoned child' (see Sect. 2.7).

14. After that, the therapist points with her hand at the empty chair on which the patient had *initially* sat: "This is the chair for your healthy adult thinking. Look, the chair is empty at the moment!".
15. She lets the patient switch back to the chair of his 'healthy adult thinking' and helps him, as an implicit doppelganger, to expand his *healthy adult thinking* in the as-if mode.
16. The therapist's work becomes increasingly encounter-focused as the therapy progresses. She names the patient's dominant defensive pattern but additionally also verbalizes *her negative affect* triggered by the patient's defensive behavior: "I feel small and powerless in the here and now because you have to be the great guy again." Thus, the therapy becomes Encounter-Focused Therapy (EFN).
17. The therapist's verbalization of negative feelings may trigger a negative transference in the patient. In such a case, the therapist provides an additional chair for the transference figure and, together with the patient, differentiates between the real conflict and transference conflict in the therapeutic relationship (see Sect. 2.10).
18. Patients with personality disorders mostly need 10–15 sessions to learn to delegate their dominant defensive pattern to *another chair* in the as-if mode of play and to *feel the difference* between their defensive thinking and '*healthy adult thinking*' in the therapy session. The therapist can help the patients by

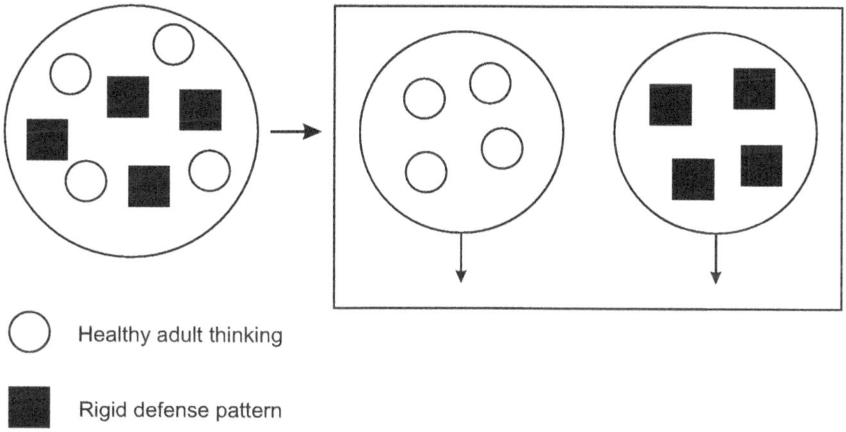


**Fig. 4.3** Resolving metacognitive confusion using the two-chair technique

asking them: "Please get an appropriate puppet for your 'sadistic inner critic' or print out a suitable picture from the computer Keep this puppet anywhere in your home. Look at the puppet for two minutes every day! After that, lock the puppet in the cupboard again. In doing so, you will learn to distance yourself internally from your self-injurious thinking." The symbolic act helps the patient to neuronally wire the *distance* from his self-injurious thinking.

The therapist also helps herself by symbolizing the patient's dominant rigid defense pattern because she resolves her character-related countertransference (see Sect. 2.10) or does not get drawn into countertransference at all (Fig. 4.3).

**Central idea**

In metacognitive therapy of patients with personality disorder, the therapist concentrates on what's important, true to the motto: first things first. The therapist thus develops a focus for further treatment.

### Exercise 13

Try to represent the dominant dysfunctional ego state during the treatment of a patient with personality disorder and use the method described above. You will notice: It reduces your negative affect and has a liberating effect on the therapeutic relationship when you represent your patient's rigid defensive behavior as a metacognitive ego state *externally with a chair* in the therapy room and, as a metacognitive doppelganger, also explain to him *the positive function* of the rigid defense pattern in the holistic process of his self-regulation.

**Recommendation**

The therapist should not let herself be irritated by the patient's initial resistance to working with ego states. She has to lovingly introduce the patient to the concept of working with the ego states. Many therapists are not consistent enough with the chair work at the beginning (see Sect. 8.5). As a therapist, use your intuition when working with the chairs! The patient is happy to experience you *trying to* understand him.

In the therapy of people with personality disorders, I differentiate between cognitively oriented constellation work and metacognitively oriented constellation work. *Cognitively oriented constellation work* is similar to working with the cultural atom or social atom. When setting up the patient's rigid defense pattern, the therapist speaks of the patient's 'ego parts' or 'parts of self' or 'working with parts'. For example, she says to the patient: "You have a grandiose part in you." Together, the therapist and the patient work out the differences between his healthy adult thinking and thinking in the defense pattern and try to *replace* unfavorable thoughts with more favorable thoughts ones. They consider the situations in which it is helpful to strive for grandiosity, and those in which it would be disadvantageous. Some therapists invite the patient to engage in a *psychodramatic dialogue with their symptoms* and have them reverse roles with a symptom, for example, with their anxiety, sleep disorder, or exhaustion. The therapist then helps him to recognize the positive meaning of his symptom (see Sect. 6.8.3) or to distance himself from the unwanted part of himself. In this approach, the therapist works on the patient's unfavorable *thought content* and not on the *metacognitive* processes that produce the unfavorable thought content. The therapist and the patient *do not try to understand* the positive function of his defense pattern in his dysfunctional self-regulation or the genesis of his defense. However, patients with a personality disorder suffer from a *metacognitive* disorder and it must be treated *metacognitively*. Cognitive therapy does *not treat the cause* of the metacognitive disorder (see Sect. 4.2). The therapist gets caught up in the cognition trap (see Sect. 2.14).

Explicit metacognitive therapy is more specific and has a lasting therapeutic effect in treating metacognitive blocks in the inner process of self-development than purely cognitive therapy centered on the patient's thinking content (see Sects. 2.14, 4.9, 5.8, 6.8.3, and 7.2). This is because the patient's new awareness of his rigid defense pattern changes his feeling and thinking *in all relationships*. If a patient with narcissistic personality disorder is 'only' 20% less grandiose and cool *in all relationships*, he may not be fired from his job, or his marriage may not break.

The therapist can also apply the explicit metacognitive procedure described above *in group therapy*: In doing so, she will only represent the patient's *dominant* defense pattern as a metacognitive ego state. For example, she will represent his *self-protective* behavior through adaptation with an empty chair *next to him in the circle*. Or she will represent his *self-injurious* thinking with a chair *opposite him*.

## 4.9 Resolution of Defenses Through Splitting in People with Borderline Personality Disorder

The dominant defense pattern in patients with borderline personality disorder (see Sect. 4.3) is the oscillation *between two contrary dysfunctional ego states*. This oscillation suppresses healthy adult thinking. Patients defend through a mechanism known as splitting. They actualize the two inner contradicting psychosomatic resonance patterns *alternately in their current relationships*. They *subconsciously* switch back and forth between their needy, dependent ego state and the contrary pseudo-autonomous, authoritarian ego state (see Fig. 4.2 in Sect. 4.3). This change is secured *secondarily* by the defense through *denial*.

**Central idea**

Patients with borderline personality disorder suffer from *metacognitive* disorder. Their defense through splitting prevents them from coherently *representing* their relationship conflicts internally because they oscillate between the contrary ego states of authoritarian anger and clingy sadness. This also results in the *dysfunctional* functioning of the *more complex* steps of mentalizing: interact, rehearse, and integrate (see Sect. 2.2).

In metacognitive therapy, the therapist *names* the two oscillating contrary ego states, *represents* them with chairs, and makes the *oscillation* the subject of therapeutic communication (see Sect. 4.8).

***Case example 24***

*A 35-year-old physiotherapist, Ms. M., suffered from serious relationship problems due to a borderline personality disorder. She was up to twenty minutes late for almost every group therapy session. She often 'had' to go home as she was a single parent to her daughter. When the group participants were asked to think of a 'safe place' at home (see* Sect. 5.10.5*), she 'did not take the time' to do so. When asked, she reacted superficially guilty. But she did not change her behavior. The other group participants resigned and would crack some jokes whenever she was late again. They were afraid of Ms. M.'s latent arbitrariness and aggressiveness. They were increasingly accommodating of Ms. M's provocative behavior in the group. Ms. M. finally got used to no longer justifying the violations of the group setting.*

*On the first evening of an intensive weekend announced a year earlier, Ms. M. informed the therapist, "Unfortunately, I will not be there all morning tomorrow". When asked why, she added: "I have to work". The therapist felt helpless and angry with the patient. He was increasingly unable to concentrate on the other group members. He practiced self-supervision at home with the help of a fictional psychodramatic dialogue (see* Sect. 2.9*) to reduce his inner tension and to be able to sleep better. The first 12 steps of self-supervision did not lead to a new finding that would have resolved the disturbance in his relationship with Ms. M. It then occurred to him that perhaps Ms. M. is switching between two contrary ego states. Therefore he placed a second chair next to 'her' in self-supervision.*

*The first chair now represented the 'clingy, needy Ms. M., who likes to come to the group and wants to make serious progress'. For her, the director was 'the good therapist she wants to learn from'. Her second chair represented 'the radically autonomous, authoritarian Ms. M'. In self-supervision, the therapist switched to her authoritarian role and played it out. He experienced that in this role, he was internally triggered by the friction and the argument with the group members. As Ms. M, he perceived the director as 'a ridiculous nitpicker who wants to enforce arbitrary rules that he has read or learned!' The therapist changed into the role of 'the clingy, needy Ms. M'. He noticed that he was mentally blocking out the previous provocative behavior in the other role. Back in the role of authoritarian Ms. M., he experienced his neediness and 'yesterday's news' and his arbitrariness as a mere reaction to the therapist's actions: "Your criticism is ridiculous! I have paid for the weekend. I can therefore decide what I want to do and what not! This is exactly what we should learn here!" The therapist switches back to his role and responds in the fictional psychodramatic dialogue: "I find this arbitrary! You are so clever and behave in such a way that none of your actions is bad on their own. Nevertheless, if you really want to learn something here, I need a certain degree of reliability from you. I am therefore asking you to try and follow the group rules!".*

*After self-supervision, the therapist felt more free in the group the next day. He was interested in the other group members again. His sense of chaos was gone. He no longer felt unsettled by Ms. M's actions and could remain at an acceptable distance from her. He thought: "She simply lives out what she is currently feeling and thinking authentically and honestly, without being bothered by her own contradictions." Amazingly Ms. M. came to the following sessions on time without the therapist informing her of his new findings. However, she did not stand the therapist's benevolent distance for long. Four weeks later, in the group session, she addressed the disorder in the relationship with the therapist herself. The therapist took the opportunity to clarify the relationship with her. He told her: "I have decided to fully believe that you are looking for trust here and want to work on yourself. But there is also an independent, authoritarian side in you, with which you hinder yourself! I am placing a second empty chair next to you for this side." The therapist and Ms. M. concluded that her arbitrary behavior was an expression of her 'inner angry child'. Anger had always helped her push her feelings of hurt and sadness away.*

The work on the metacognitive disturbance of patients with borderline personality organization comprises the following steps:

1. The *patient* violates the therapy setting or provokes, although he also exudes need. This creates a disturbance in the therapeutic relationship or group relationships.
2. The *therapist* feels increasingly confused and helpless by the patient's conflicting expectations and his emotional acting out.
3. The *therapist* justifies her feelings of helplessness and bewilderment. She proves the borderline personality organization by psychodramatic self-supervision (see Sect. 2.9). In doing so, she sets up *a second chair* next to the patient, either for his needy, dependent ego state *or* his pseudo-autonomous, authoritarian ego state. If the therapist's bewilderment *dissolves,* she concludes that her diagnosis of borderline personality disorder is correct. Establishing the second contrary

ego state of the patient frees the therapist from the *double bind* imposed by the patient (see Sect. 4.3).

**Central idea**

The therapist perceives the two contrary ego states by setting up two chairs *spatially separated from each other*. This makes it easier for her to *empathize with each of the two* opposing ego states internally *as a metacognitive doppelganger, separate from one another*, without getting caught up in the contradiction. She internally develops *two contradicting psychosomatic resonance patterns* as a response to the patient's contradicting behavior: In the as-if mode of play, she is the *metacognitive doppelganger* who, together with the patient, feels sad and needy, *and* also the metacognitive doppelganger who feels happy about the patient's autonomy and likes to provoke. When the patient switches to his contrary emotion, the therapist *also* switches to *her own contrary* psychosomatic resonance pattern. Switching to the as-if mode of play resolves her disorientation and helplessness and she can therapeutically act again.

4. In direct therapy with the patient, the therapist initially works *'only' in her imagination* with the image of two chairs for the patient.
5. She waits for a suitable opportunity to represent the contrary ego state *also directly* in the therapy situation. The indications to represent the contrary ego state are: (1) The patient's action in the here and now disrupts the therapeutic relationship. (2) *The patient himself* addresses a disruption in the therapeutic relationship. For example, some patients are irritated because the therapist no longer has an adverse reaction to her contradictory acting out (see case example 24 above). (3) The patient behaves needy in therapy but acts *dissocial* in everyday life without any awareness of the problem.
6. The therapist names the patient's oscillation between the two contradictory metacognitive ego states *as it happens in the here and now* in therapy: "You just switched between your needy ego state and your autonomous ego state". The therapist immediately represents his contrary ego state externally, next to him, with the help of a second chair: When the patient acts in a pseudo-autonomous, authoritarian manner, she places next to him 'the chair for his needy side, which is not satisfied here'. When he is in need, she places the "chair for his angry, independent ego state" next to him. A *purely verbal* procedure would hurt the patient because he thinks in equivalence mode. He would think: "She insinuates that I am needy. But I'm angry!" Or: "She insinuates that I am angry. But I am needy!".
7. Whenever the patient shifts back to his *contrary* ego state again, the therapist points to the chair of this other ego state: "I think you are now thinking and feeling from your needy ego state" or "… from your angry, arbitrary ego state".
8. In her practical work, the therapist *names* the "pseudo-autonomous, authoritarian ego state" and the "needy, dependent ego state" of the patient with a *personal* name that matches the patient's thoughts and feelings in the current situation. The contrary ego states are then called "the authoritarian Karl" and "the dependent Karl", "the independent side," and "the needy side," or "the headstrong Maria" and "the loving Maria".

9. The therapist lets the patient switch from one chair to the contradictory chair *externally* in the as-if mode of play at least once when the patient *internally* switches to the other ego state (see case example 25 below). For example, she invites him: "You are angry right now. Then sit down on the angry chair and be angry!" The patient performs the *external* role change in the *as-if mode of play, acting psychosomatically* (see Sect. 2.6). This helps him to notice the role change between his contrary ego states in everyday life more easily and to carry it out over time *in the as-if mode of thinking*. Thus, he consciously experiences his inner instability. But, the patient feels like he is taken seriously and his core suffering is understood.
10. As a metacognitive doppelganger, the therapist recognizes and appreciates the *positive function* of his defense through splitting in the holistic process of his self-regulation (see Sect. 4.8) and explains it to the patient: "You are angry right now because you are getting a raw deal for your needy side here. You are not experiencing the security you need here!" Or: "You are currently feeling sad and empty. But if someone comes close to you, you have an allergic reaction. You don't want to be dependent. You have had bad experiences with dependence." Over time, the patient must understand *why it is the best solution for him* to switch *back* to the opposite ego state *in the current situation*.

**Central idea**

Defense through splitting is ingeniously simple self-protection in emotional instability. The patient voluntarily switches to the pseudo-independent position if he can't stand the closeness and is afraid of becoming dependent. However, he will arbitrarily switch back to the sad needy position when he has hurt and driven away everyone and feels alone. The patient should *psychosomatically* experience the *positive function* of his switching in the holistic process of his self-regulation in the *as-if mode of play*. He thus learns to notice it more easily when he again switches to the contrary position in everyday life. He gradually gains some control over his oscillation. Gaining ego control means: He acts out his oscillation less frequently in the equivalence mode because he understands it as an internal representation of an old solution in his self-regulation and can think of it *in the as-if mode*. He becomes free to examine the impact of his oscillation *in the actual* conflict situation and to decide whether he wants this effect or not. The patient no longer has to deny his contradictions to himself. Over time, the patient learns to realize that he is oscillating. His dysfunctional acting out becomes shorter and weaker. He may even laugh sometimes before acting destructively again (see case example 8 in Sect. 2.6).

**Central Idea**

"The new split, caused *psychodramatically*, makes it possible to overcome the earlier *defensive* splitting" (Powell, 1986).

Some patients with borderline personality disorder experience severe mood swings, seemingly for *no external reason*. They alternate seemingly arbitrarily between "sadness" and "anger".

### *Case Example 25* (Powell, 1986, Quoted from Krüger, 1997, p. 101)

*'Jane tells the director that she feels confused. She cannot describe what it is because 'it's messed up'. But she knows: it's about her family. Her face is flushed with agitation. She looks angry and is close to tears at the same time. The director suggests*

*that she look at her feelings one by one. This encouragement, put forward kindly, makes Jane cry. She thinks she needs to be sad. The director places a "sad chair" for her and asks her to sit on the chair. He takes a few steps away from her. Jane sits down. She squeezes her handkerchief and realizes: 'It is not good. I'm too angry.' The director lets her sit on an 'angry chair' and says: 'Allow yourself to express all that belongs to this chair. Be as angry as needed!' Jane suddenly thinks of what she wants to say and where she wants to say it: her family has bought Christmas presents, and she is standing in front of Selfridges. The street is full of people. Jane chooses some group members to fill the roles of her family members. The rest of the group takes on the role of the crowd. Then Jane accuses the family publicly (this is important because her family always claims to get on well) of repeatedly being pretentious and dishonest. Jane exchanges roles with her father, mother, and so on. It turns out that none of them regrets their behavior in any way. Rather, they are ashamed of Jane's outburst and try to calm her down. This time, Jane screams back. She explains why she is happy not to be like her father, not to be like her mother, and so on. She bravely defends her individuality. But then she shows the therapist that she wants to leave the chair. She is overwhelmed with sadness and starts to cry. Now, sitting on the "sad chair," Jane reveals her longing for love and intimacy with her family. Again she comes up with a scene that reflects her needs. She doesn't want to be hugged physically, that would suffocate and devour her. Instead, she chooses a Christmas scene. The family sits around the Christmas tree. Jane sees herself as part of the whole family, but also has her independence.'*

11. The therapist represents the patient's *other* defense patterns as ego states with chairs. In patients with borderline personality disorder, *healthy adult thinking* is initially not easily accessible during the external conflict. The contradictory ego states are also always trapped in a defense system. This consists of self-protection through denial and self-injurious thinking in acting out a sadistic superego. Both stabilize each other and are additionally protected by the defense through splitting.

At some point in the course of therapy, the therapist symbolizes the patient's difficult childhood experiences as his 'inner traumatized abandoned child' with an additional empty chair next to him in the therapy room. In addition, she occasionally places an empty chair next to the chair of his 'pseudo-autonomous authoritarian ego state' to represent the 'distancing self-protective behavior' that developed in his childhood, and later other chairs representing his 'inner angry child' and his 'self-injurious thinking'. The patient can buy hand puppets for his 'distancing self-protective behavior' and his 'inner angry child' and give them a place in his apartment. He should look at the 'knight in shining armor' and the 'angry little boy' once a day and maybe even talk to them. This helps him to justify his anger and understand the anger as a personal allergic reaction to negative traumatic feelings. In this way, the patient *integrates* his defense system with his life experiences from childhood. The therapist and the patient are better able to understand the distress hidden in the acting of the contrary ego states. Subsequent therapy follows the treatment process used in the therapy of people with other personality and trauma disorders (see Sects. 4.8, 4.10, 4.12, and 4.5).

Patients with severe borderline organization create chaos in the therapeutic relationship. In such a case, the therapist also uses the technique of psychodramatic responding (see Sect. 4.13). If the patient's transference is negative, she also differentiates the real conflict from the transference conflict (see Sect. 2.10). Some patients act destructively in their pseudo-autonomous, authoritarian ego state. In such a case, the therapist sticks to her metacognitive understanding of the disorder, makes I statements, and acts consistently in a disorder-specific manner. I call this 'disorder-specific psychotherapy' for people with borderline organization 'Encounter-Focused Therapy' (EFT).

## 4.10 Resolving the Fixation in a Whole Defense System

Metacognitive defense processes are internal processes of reality construction used by humans to generate thought content and to process conflicts. They fixate one's internal process of self-development, self-image, and object image on old solutions from the past that are inappropriate in the current external situation. The defense processes in people with personality disorders are trapped *in a system of defense mechanisms*. The defense mechanisms include splitting, projective identification, denial, introjection, projection, and rationalization.

**Central idea**

Psychodramatic metacognitive therapy liberates the metacognitive processes from their fixation. It is a *systemic therapy* of the holistic process of metacognition.

1. The work on the respective *dominant* defensive pattern also opens access to the patient's *other defense patterns.*

**Central idea**

In a defense system, the rigid defense patterns mutually stabilize each other in their dysfunction. For example, patients who act masochistically are often fixed in defense through grandiosity. Grandiosity helps them silence the voice of their inner soul killer. Naming and representing defense patterns with chairs help them psychosomatically experience the relationships *between the defense patterns.*

If *counseling* or therapy is limited to 10–20 sessions, the therapist should *only* work *on the dominant* defense pattern (see Sect. 3.3). But, in *long-term therapy,* the therapist also works on the *other* defense patterns.

2. The therapist also names and represents the patient's *other* defense patterns with empty chairs, if they *currently block* the patient's inner process of self-development (see Fig. 4.1 in Sect. 4.2).
3. The therapist lets the patient repeatedly switch over to the chair of the defense pattern *he is currently experiencing* and play it out psychosomatically. In this way, the patient completes the psychosomatic resonance pattern between the

memory centers of sensorimotor interaction patterns, physical sensations, affect, linguistic concepts, and thoughts in this ego state into a holistic psychosomatic resonance pattern (see Sect. 2.7). The more the patient is structurally disturbed, the more important it is to act out the defense pattern in therapy. For example, after a patient had creatively played the role of his 'inner soul killer as a hand puppet, he said: "It is good that the soul-killer has so many facets. That makes it clearer for me! Before, I couldn't fight him back so well because I didn't know when he would appear!" Another patient, a fifty-year-old artisan, often thought in a masochistic self-injurious manner during his psychotherapy. At the beginning of the therapy session, he would always pick out the hand puppet of the grinning red devil from the closet. He would position it on the chair of the 'self-injurious thinking' and inform the therapist that he had 'slipped' into his trauma film again.

4. The therapist asks the patient *about the age of the dominant dysfunctional ego state*, for example, of his *self-protective behavior*: "For how long have you been adapting in conflict situations, in a way that you push your emotions away and only focus on being functional?".

**Central idea**

In thinking about the genesis of his defense pattern, the patient links and integrates his defense pattern with appropriate difficult childhood experiences. Thus, he recognizes the original positive meaning of his defense (see Sects. 2.4.4 and 6.4).

Self-protection through adaptation was *a creative solution* for the child to pretend nothing was wrong. This helped the child avoid attracting any attention when his father screamed again under the influence of alcohol. Some patients boost the process of their inner change by working on it *daily*. They buy themselves a hand puppet or a suitable Playmobil for their 'abandoned child', their 'self-injurious thinking', or their 'self-protection through grandiosity'. They put them up *at home* and talk to them. Sometimes they keep their 'child ego-state' in a small 'bed' at home and cover it with a pillow. One patient would let the doll for her 'traumatized inner child' sleep next to her in bed at home. Whenever she felt bad for herself, she would complain about her suffering to her doll. Thus she would justify her feelings and ascribe them to her traumatic experience as a child. Then she would hug the doll and comfort her. Comforting the traumatized inner child helped the patient feel better again (see Sect. 5.8).

5. Patients diagnosed with personality disorders switch back and forth between the different defense patterns of their defense system relatively quickly when thinking. This change *happens* unconsciously.

**Central idea**

By naming, representing, and interacting, the patient completes the psychosomatic resonance patterns of each involved ego state with missing elements (see Sect. 2.7). Each ego state gets its own right to exist in self-regulation.

The psychodramatic work on the *intrapsychic* conflicts of the patient shows (1) The 'self-protective behavior' and the 'self-injurious thinking' usually work well together (see case example 26 below). They stabilize each other as a defense system in the fight *against* the 'healthy adult thinking' and the 'angry child'. (2) The 'self-injurious thinking' suppresses the 'angry child'. The 'blind inner critic' and the 'angry inner child' *cannot coexist. Either* the 'inner critic' *or* the 'angry child' is in charge. (3) The 'Self-injurious thinking' and 'the abandoned or traumatized child' often live together in a pathological symbiosis. (4) Even the 'self-protective behavior' suppresses the 'abandoned or traumatized inner child'. (5) The 'angry child' can suppress healthy adult thinking. (6) The 'abandoned child' and the 'angry child' appear *alternatingly* in patients with borderline organization and paralyze the 'healthy adult thinking'. However, they can learn to help each other in therapy.

If necessary, the therapist lets the patient conduct psychodramatic dialogues between his healthy adult thinking and his suppressed ego state. In doing so, she herself joins as a doppelganger and an auxiliary ego. Every now and then, she takes a small step beyond the given reality. For example, the patient works out what his adult ego state and inner child have to *tell each other* in the dialogue between his inner 'abandoned child' and his 'healthy adult thinking'. As an auxiliary ego, the therapist accentuates the *childlike logic* in the role of the child and the *adult logic* of thinking in the role of the adult. The 'child ego state' wants to be seen by the 'adult ego state' and wants to have his needs met *immediately*. When in the role of his 'adult ego state', the patient allows space for the feelings and wishes of his 'child ego state'. But, as a person with life experience, he also has an overview of the life situation. He, therefore, explains the world to the 'abandoned child' and helps him take everyday life's necessities seriously. Out of consideration for the 'traumatized child', the 'adult ego state' *should not* 'chicken out' and avoid all conflicts.

In disorder-specific therapy, the 'abandoned child' or the 'traumatized child' should be integrated into the patient's inner process of self-development in the external situation. Thus, the traumatized child can develop into a 'healthy inner child' and eventually become a *consultant for* the adult ego state. For example, a 60-year-old patient noticed that he was 'feeling bad' when he was at his workstation at 4 p.m. He took his 'inner little John' out of his backpack and asked him: "Do you know why I feel so bad?". His 'child ego state' replied: "Isn't that clear! You have worked *continuously* from 8 a.m. to now 4 p.m. today. You haven't taken a single break and haven't eaten anything yet!" The patient immediately left everything behind and went for a walk in the nearby park. His child ego state had helped him to get out of his blind self-protection by adapting to the expectations of others.

The *dominant* defending ego state is different in *different* personality disorders. In people with narcissistic personality disorder (see Sect. 4.2) or panic attacks (see Sects. 6.4 and 6.5), self-protection through grandiosity or perfectionism is dominant. This helps ward off feelings of failure, humiliation, or insecurity. In people with depressive personality disorder and masochism (see Sect. 8.5) and with obsessive–compulsive neuroses (see Sect. 7), self-injurious thinking plays a dominant role and blocks the patient's self-actualization. In people with borderline organization (see Sects. 4.3 and 4.9), the unconscious oscillation between the needy and the pseudo-autonomous ego helps the patient stabilize himself. 'Inner maturing is the ability *to realize* in an increasingly shorter amount of time that I am on the wrong path' (Dürckheim 1985, only oral communication).

**Central idea**

Process-oriented metacognitive therapeutic work on the defense patterns helps the patient to learn to psychosomatically recognize the "wrong path" of his rigid defenses in increasingly shorter periods, to integrate the defense pattern into the genesis, and thus to gain ego control over his defense pattern.

At the end of therapy, patients can *also* often *resolve new blocks* in their metacognitive work *by themselves*. This helps them to orient themselves, if necessary. A patient reported: "My four ego states help me a lot. If I feel bad, I examine which ego state I am in internally. Then I find my inner balance again." The patient's four ego states included his 'inner child', his 'inner soul slayer', his 'self-protection through adaptation', and his 'healthy adult thinking'. In such autonomous orientation work, the patient first *recognizes* and *names* the *dominant dysfunctional* ego state he is currently living in. He then reflects on the *other* ways of thinking and feeling he is neglecting in the here and now. Internally, he establishes a relationship with these possible alternatives, brings them to life within himself, and thus frees himself from his fixation in his *dominant defense.*

***Case example 26***

*A 38-year-old patient diagnosed with an emotionally unstable personality disorder (F60.31) learned that "she should pay more attention to herself and her feelings" in her eight-week of inpatient psychotherapy. After being reintegrated into her professional life, she found herself in a high psychophysical state of excitement during a conflict in the workplace. In the therapy session, she complained: "Again, I did not pay sufficient attention to myself and my inner child in the argument with my colleague. I'm annoyed with myself!" The patient attributed sole responsibility for the problems at work to herself. The therapist and the patient together elaborated on the dysfunctional ego states in her self-regulation during the said conflict. The patient represented her 'self-injurious thinking' with the hand puppet of a 'demeaning, blindly acting bureaucrat' and her 'self-protective behavior through adaptation' with the hand puppet of a 'nerd'. The therapist: 'Your blindly demeaning bureaucrat and your inner nerd work wonderfully together!" The patient: "Yes, I always notice it from my states of excitement that my 'inner bureaucrat' and my 'nerd' are already at work again".*

*The patient found it difficult to look at the hand puppets of her inner 'nerd' and her inner 'bureaucrat' from the outside: "Mr. Krüger, tell me how to resolve this!" In the next therapy session, however, she had already found a solution on her own: "I created some distance internally and looked at the conflict situation with my colleague again from the outside. Then I noticed: 'What is the problem if I miss my bus and reach home only an hour later because of her? Nothing at all! Nothing would happen!' Having considered that, I nevertheless requested my colleague again to end her work on time. I was then able to lock the office in peace and still got my bus on time!'" The therapist: "So you created some internal distance and looked at the conflict from a different perspective from the outside. You found a solution to your conflict on your own and thought like a healthy adult. I congratulate you!".*

Patients with personality disorders often have *transpersonal experiences.* The affected patients are mostly not aware of this. They often even devalue the special transpersonal quality of their self-regulation. One patient, for example, complained: "I am too sensitive for the world. In my relationship with people I meet, I blindly give out everything positive I have in me. Afterward, I am completely exhausted. My husband thinks I'm too good for this world!".

**Central Idea**

The therapist should not misunderstand a transpersonal experience as *a defense pattern.* A *transpersonal* character trait must be recognized and named according to its *transpersonal* quality. Only then can the patient also gain control over his thinking, feeling, and behavior in his *transpersonal* identity (see Chap. 1) and think about it in the as-if mode.

The patient's fixation on a *transpersonal quality* is an attempt to remain true to his *transpersonal* experience. Initially, the therapist and the patient work out the positive value of this quality. For instance, in case example 26 (see above), the therapist asked the patient (see Sect. 7.3): "Please attribute this special character trait you experience as stressful to a fictional person. 'Be too good for the world' should be natural and make sense within the context of their living environment. Afterward, please tell me an episode from this person's life." The patient found the figure of a nun in a monastery: "This is only a soul, almost something like a saint. Her name is Clare". The patient continues: "The nun cares for an old woman in the hospital ward and delights her with her mere presence. When she is exhausted, she spreads her arms as she stands in her herb garden and lets the light of heaven flow into her body." The patient burst into tears during this therapeutic work. With the therapist's help, she understood her crying as sadness about the world not being as good as it should be. The therapist asked the patient to think of ten more episodes from the life of 'St. Clare' in the following weeks and write them down. The transpersonal interpretation and the symbolization of her special character trait as 'holy Clare' helped the patient gain more control over the external behavior of her transpersonal identity. This put the patient in the yes-but position with regard to her special character trait, and she was free to think as a healthy adult.

An inner transpersonal identity is an expression of a *transpersonal conscience* (see Sect. 8.8.4).

**Central idea**

A patient with a personality disorder thinks like a healthy adult when he orients himself in his self-regulation in the as-if mode and identifies the metacognitive ego state he is possibly stuck in with his thinking, feeling, and behavior in the current situation. Thus, he is free to choose whether to act out his old defensive pattern or to think, feel and act in a new and more appropriate way.

If necessary, the therapist can promote the development of 'healthy adult thinking' with *amplifications* (see Sect. 2.4.4) or with the technique of the *fictitious supportive doppelganger*: for example, she explains how *other patients* have found themselves in their therapy. Or she places a second chair next to the patient's chair. She invites the patient to assign this chair to a good friend or a wise old man and asks him to switch to the role of 'friend': "What would your friend advise you in this situation?" The patient then starts a psychodramatic dialogue with his 'friend'. During role reversal, he steps into the role of the friend, playfully brings *the ideas of the 'friend'* to life, and gives himself some advice (Leutz, 1980, pp. 17 ff.). The therapist can also ask the patient to find a *fairy tale character* to support his 'healthy adult thinking': "Imagine this fairy tale character sitting on the chair next to you". The fairy tale character is said to have already experienced the patient's suffering. However, unlike the patient's tales of woe, fairy tales usually end well. 'Cinderella', for example, can be a *role model* for the patient. She never gave up on herself and hoped that something would change, even when she had to sleep in the ashes. She complained about her suffering to the doves. And despite the humiliation by her sisters, she planted the branch brought by her father into the earth at her mother's grave.

Relapses into old behavior can indicate that the therapist did not pay enough attention to the stabilization of the dominant defense pattern through other defense patterns. The following three case examples demonstrate this:

1. A patient came into the therapy session in an intense state of excitement. She reported having massive conflicts with her daughter-in-law. She was no longer speaking to her. As a result, the patient entered her childhood trauma film. In this state of mind, she had put her baby doll, which symbolized her 'inner traumatized child', *in her own bed*: "I wanted to 'protect' my 'inner child'." The therapist strongly recommended that she take her 'child ego state' to another room and make her a 'cozy bed' there. Thus, the patient stabilized her self-protection through this external distancing (see Sect. 5.8).
2. Another patient informed the therapist without any awareness of the problem: "My inner child is dumb. It doesn't talk!" The therapist wanted to know the reason behind it. He changed into the role of her inner traumatized child externally in the therapy room and held a soliloquy in this role (see Sect. 4.6). In this role, he *vicariously* figured out why it was the best solution for the patient's 'inner traumatized child' not to speak. Thus, he justified the patient's self-protection from the complaints of her inner child. In the next therapy session, the patient's 'inner child' had started talking. Over time, it developed into a 'healthy inner child'.
3. In another case, shortly before the end of the long-term therapy, the therapist noticed that the patient had not yet specified the *private* name for his self-injurious thinking (see Sect. 4.7). Thus, the patient had adapted to the demands of his sadistic superego. It took the patient and the therapist, together, a total of thirty minutes to name the patient's self-injurious thinking with the *personal* name 'child breaker'. This name gave the patient a new feeling of power over his inner self-injurious thinking.

*Therapists* need to have a good relationship between their *own* inner child and their adult ego state when working with people with personality disorders. This is because the therapist must be able to *instantly feel* her *own* emotions in the relationship and be curious, just like a child. The access to the therapist's own inner child is repeatedly blocked by adaptation, grandiosity, or self-injurious thinking. In such a case, the therapist should name *her own* dominant defense pattern and symbolize it as an ego state with a hand puppet. For example, she can represent her great sense of duty with a 'blind inner slave'. She places her 'inner slave' in her study and examines it every once in a while if and when she may have obeyed him again in her everyday life. Thus, the therapist gains ego control over her masochistic submission to her 'blind inner slave'. She becomes more flexible and creative. Therapists should have experience in dealing with their metacognitive processes if they want to do metacognitive therapy.

## 4.11 What Can Psychodrama Offer to Schema Therapy?

*Psychodramatists* introduced constellation work into the world of psychotherapy. They developed techniques such as the setting up of roles in the '*social atom*' or the inner roles in the '*cultural atom*'. They help the patients symbolize their own negative feelings, aching parts of the body, or inner attitudes with the help of hand puppets, objects, or other players (Krüger, 2007) and led psychodramatic dialogues between them. For example, the therapist symbolizes the patient's fear (see Sect. 6.8.3) or his 'fearful inner child' by placing a chair next to him.

Schema therapists (Young et al., 2008) have systematized the constellation work against the background of psychoanalytic and behavioral theories and made them useful for the *metacognitive* therapy of people with personality disorders. They say: Schema therapy "is an innovative, integrative therapy. [...] It combines elements of cognitive behavior therapy, attachment theory, gestalt therapy, object relations theory, constructivist psychotherapy, and the psychoanalytic schools to form a multi-faceted, holistic concept and treatment model" (Young et al., 2008, p. 29). Half of the schema therapy techniques are known as psychodrama techniques: chair work with the patient's ego states, psychodramatic dialogue with role reversal with *childhood* attachment figures, psychodramatic dialogue with *current* conflict partners, and the doppelganger technique.

**Central idea**

Psychotherapy methods that aim to *directly* change the patient's *metacognitive* processes *have to* use psychodramatic techniques. Because the psychodrama techniques directly implement the *naturally existing metacognitive* tools of inner conflict processing (see Sect. 2. 4).

Unlike in the past (Krüger, 2007), I have relied on the *terms used in schema therapy* when naming the metacognitive ego states in this book (Arntz & van Genderen, 2010, pp. 10 ff., Young et al., 2008). The names are closely associated with a patient's ego. This makes it easier to communicate with patients about their *metacognitive* processes. However, the *psychodramatic metacognitive therapy* (described in Sects. 4.7–4.10) for the dysfunctional metacognitive ego states and defense patterns of patients differs from the schema therapy work in the following ways:

1. The *psychodrama therapist* expands the constellation of metacognitive ego states (see Sect. 4.7) to include the two chairs for the *patient's symptom scene* (see Sect. 2.8 and Fig. 2.9). The symptom scene includes the patient's inner self-image and object image in everyday conflict. The creative development of the inner self in an external conflict also includes the development of the inner self-image and object image. Therefore, metacognitive psychodramatic work on defense patterns should always be *related to* the patient's externally represented conflict in his everyday life *or* the interaction between the patient and the therapist in the here and now. Otherwise, it becomes blurred in space and time.
2. In the *psychodramatic* metacognitive work, the therapist sets up *two different* chairs for the 'self-injurious thinking' of the patient (chair 8 in Fig. 4.1 in Sect. 4.2) *and* the inner object image of the harmful caregiver from his childhood (chair 9). The chair for the harmful caregiver is placed *behind* the chair for his self-injurious thinking. The patient developed self-injurious thinking in childhood as self-censorship (see Sect. 8.5) to avoid being beaten, devalued, or left out of the relationship and to not make life even more difficult for his parents. The old masochistic *self-censorship* is superfluous, and it can 'die'. The patient remains a moral person even without it. But, the inner object image of the *attachment figure* survives forever. Authors who wrote about their parents' war trauma or crimes during the National Socialist era did so only after the death of their father or brother. The self-censorship against their own self-development in their relationship with their father was then no longer necessary to maintain the psychological balance of the damaging attachment figures. Writing became a liberation from self-censorship.
3. The schema therapists distinguish between ten (Young et al., 2008) or even eighteen different *equivalent* dysfunctional modes of internal conflict management (Jacob & Arntz, 2011, p. 44 ff.; Roediger, 2011, p. 110 ff.). I divide the metacognitive ego states qualitatively into *four categories:* self-protection behavior, self-injurious thinking, abandoned child, and angry child. The number of categories of metacognitive ego states is limited by the number of possible defense patterns (see Sect. 4.10). Therefore, in psychodramatic metacognitive therapy, the therapist sets up *only a maximum of four dysfunctional ego states* for each patient. These should have personal names.
4. The psychodrama therapist *responds psychodramatically* (see Sect. 4.13 and Krüger, 2007) in the therapy of persons with a personality disorder, if necessary. She *also* names *her* metacognitive ego states from which she thinks, feels, and acts in the therapeutic relationship and symbolizes them as *parts of her self-image* externally with chairs. I distinguish between three task-related self-images: the 'therapist as an encountering human being', the 'grandiose therapist', and the 'therapist as a competent expert'. The therapist *responds psychodramatically to the patient* by externally switching back and forth between these three self-images in the therapeutic conversation in the as-if mode of play. This releases the therapist's internal process of self-development (see Sect. 4.1) in the therapeutic relationship from its fixation in a biased self-image.

5. A few years ago, schema therapists Arntz and van Genderen (2010, p. 67 ff.) had their patients psychodramatically re-enact *traumatic* childhood experiences. After an interim discussion, the patients had to enact their childhood scenes a second time but behave *more courageously as a child in the scene*. The therapist took on the role of the harmful caregiver from childhood in this 'revision of the situation'. But, she enacts the role *differently* in the repeated scene *from how it was before*. As a mother, for example, she was sufficiently attentive and loving. *Psychodramatists* never ask a protagonist to act more boldly *as a child* in their *own* childhood scene. Patients with personality disorders often misunderstand such instructions and conclude that the therapist believes that they *behaved incorrectly as a child* at the time. Additionally, the improved self-actualization in the inner relationship images of attachment figures from childhood can also lead to an increase in pathological symptoms because of the actualization of the sadistic superego. Patients often struggle with guilt after such work (Arntz & van Genderen, 2010, p. 70 f.), "because they did not react adequately in the situation at the time". Psychodrama therapists, therefore, always let their patients *change* their old inner images of childhood relationships in a psychodramatic dialogue *while in their current role as adults* (see Sect. 4.12). Or they introduce supporting fictional doppelgangers in the childhood scenes, for example, *other fictional good parents* (see Sect. 5.14). Even schema therapists are doing this sometimes. They call this method "imaginative rewriting by an assistant" (Jacob & Arntz, 2011, p. 134 ff.).

**Question**

What can psychodrama offer to schema therapists?

1. Schema therapists *can* use psychodramatic self-supervision (see Sect. 2.9) as a diagnostic instrument. If steps 1–12 of self-supervision do not resolve the disruption in the therapeutic relationship and the countertransference, the patient likely suffers from a personality disorder.
2. Steps 13–17 of psychodramatic self-supervision help to find the dominant defense pattern and open the door to the patient's defense system.
3. Simultaneously, they help to rehearse an appropriate therapeutic approach.
4. The metacognitive doppelganger technique (see Sect. 2.5) helps the patient to gain ego control over his defensive actions (see Sect. 4.8) so that he can think about it in the as-if mode.
5. The understanding of the self as a dual process helps to free not only the inner self-image but *also the inner object image* in the external situation from its fixations and to break down the defenses through projection in old relationship images. This then indirectly promotes the patient's self-actualization in relationships (see Sects. 2.9, 4.12, and 8.4.2).

## 4.12 Integrating Inner Change into Inner Relationships' Images

The defense system of patients with personality disorders blocks their internal process of self-development in relationship conflicts. Therefore, from the very beginning, the therapist repeatedly works on the patient's fixation in the development of inner self-image and object image (see Sect. 8.4.2) in their current conflicts. The patient thereby releases his healthy adult thinking from his fixations and gains awareness of his rigid defense.

During the last third of therapy, the therapist helps the patient, with the help of psychodramatic dialogues and role reversal, to integrate his new understanding of himself into his *old internal relationship images* (see Sect. 8.4.2). As a result, they get updated, so to speak. The following options have proven successful in this integration work:

1. The patient writes a *fictional letter* to an attachment figure from childhood while he is at home in a stress-free environment. The attachment figure should *not* be a perpetrator who had abused the patient because that would be equivalent to exposure to trauma. The patient must *never post the letter*. In the letter, he explains to the attachment figure all that he has now learned about the connection between his *current* problems and his *childhood* experiences. He mentions things by name (see case example 55 in Sect. 6.6). He specifies how *he wants* to understand the development of his symptoms and their causes.

The patient gives the letter to the therapist to read. The therapist uses the content to diagnose the patient's progress and recognize possible gaps in therapy. The patient himself can retrieve the letter in *later crises* and read the reasons for his earlier decompensation once again. In reading the letter, he will also become aware of the constructive steps that led him out of his illness. In writing such a letter, the patient appropriately integrates his current inappropriate interaction patterns and affect with his childhood experiences. This helps him to act them out less often in his current conflicts. One patient was moved to tears when her therapist asked her to write such a letter. She immediately noticed that the letter would give her the opportunity and permission to accept her own feelings and insights. In writing the letter, she allowed herself to *oppose* the recurring devaluations of her family *internally*.

2. When *writing a fictional letter* to attachment figures from the past, the patient often remembers *traumatic experiences* from his childhood that have *not yet* been discussed in therapy. The therapist uses this opportunity to help the patient process the hurtful experiences from his childhood by applying techniques of trauma therapy (see Sect. 5.10).

**Recommendation**

For example, the therapist and the patient, together, reflect on (see case example 21 in Sect. 4.6) what the patient *would have needed* to help with their traumatic experience in the past (Sáfrán & Czáky-Pallavicini, 2013, p.274 ff.). If necessary, they look for a *fictional helper* who comforts the child in imagination and, as a fictional doppelganger, protects and supports him in his traumatizing situation (Kellermann, 2000, p. 31; Arntz & van Genderen, 2010, p. 29 ff.; Grimmer, 2013). They use the table stage to determine how the *fictional* helper should have acted and what the patient would have felt as a child (see Sect. 5.10.10).

3. The therapist can also ask the patient to write a *fairytale of coping* (Krüger, 2013; Sáfrán & Czáky-Pallavicini, 2013). This technique is described in detail in Sect. 5.14. In it, the patient tells the story of a childhood incident that caused him suffering and transforms it into a fairytale in the *second* part. In the *third* part, his needs and wishes are to be fulfilled. In doing so, the patient expands his tale of childhood trauma with supportive fantasies to resolve the blocks in the internal process of self-development in relationship images from childhood. It is advisable to work with the fairytale of coping when the patient has little access to his needs and desires (see case example 40 in Sect. 5.14). Working with the fairytale of coping, the therapist can diagnostically notice the patient's therapeutic progress or any gaps in his development (see Sect. 5.14).

**Central idea**

Patients with structural disorders often accept difficult living conditions without any complaint. Life happens to them. They didn't learn anything different in their childhood. They have no idea about what is 'normal'. They often consider 'normal' an illusionary wish. Experiencing the *'normal'* at least in fantasy, frees the internal process of self-development from its fixations and promotes self-actualization in conflicts.

4. The patient integrates, with the help of the *psychodramatic dialogue and role reversal*, his newly gained self-image into the internal image of a relationship *with a close attachment figure from his childhood*. In his *fictional* dialogue with this person, he speaks *as the adult he is now* (see Sect. 4.11). He chooses an attachment figure who witnessed his fate in childhood, for example, a brother or a grandmother. Under no circumstances should this person be the perpetrator who traumatized the patient (see Sect. 5.11). The patient verbally shares his new knowledge about himself and his childhood with this attachment figure in the as-if mode of play. In the psychodramatic dialogue with *role reversal*, he examines why they were unable to support him sufficiently in childhood by stepping into the role of his attachment figure. This helps him to reconcile with them *in the present*. In this process, the patient also focuses on developing his old inner object images of attachment figures from childhood through mental rehearsal and role reversal, thereby dissolving the defense through projection. He achieves this by reversing roles and further developing the inner object images in the play into a holistic psychosomatic resonance pattern (see Sect. 2.7). He psychosomatically learns the motivations behind his unconscious self-protection and conscious action. Resolving projection makes it easier to resolve the defenses through introjection in the old relationship images (see Sects. 2.9 and 8.4.2) and liberates one's inner self-development in current relationships from old interaction patterns.
5. The patient integrates his newly acquired healthy adult thinking *into relationships with his current conflict partners* using psychodramatic dialogues (see Sect. 8.4.2). In doing so, he verbalizes his own experience and inner truth in

the relationship with his conflict partner. In the role reversal, he also recognizes the inner truth of *the 'conflict partner'*. Patients who have been trapped in their defense systems are often amazed at how differently other people 'tick' internally.

6. The therapist teaches the patient the method of *psychodramatic self-supervision* (see Sect. 2.9) (Krüger, 2011, p. 201 f.). Patients can use it to work independently on their current relationship conflicts at home and reduce their defenses through introjection and projection. This will also help them reduce their therapy sessions. In addition, they will recognize themselves and others more clearly in the conflicts in their everyday life.

***Case example 27***

*A woman who was traumatized in childhood felt dizzy whenever she did not sufficiently define her boundaries in relationships. She learned psychodramatic self-supervision in therapy (see* Sect. 2.9*) and used it regularly. After four weeks, she reported: "The chair work is great! I use it to clarify my position. My dizziness has reduced a lot by now. I have noticed: 'Sometimes people are not against me at all, they only focus their attention on themselves!' I always thought that I was narrow-minded when I wasn't generous. But when I work with the empty chair, I learn to justify my feelings. Additionally, when I am in the role of the other, I often do not understand what I want. I have to make my position clearer in relationships!".*

7. Patients with personality disorders often struggle to *stabilize* their *internal changes over time.* Their anger or the wishes of their 'inner child' are paralyzed by their 'self-protection' and their 'self-injurious thinking'. In such a case, the therapist helps the patient symbolize their anger as an 'anger stone'. The patient should *put it in his pocket.* When in conflict, he can touch the 'anger stone' and in doing so, justify his anger internally. Or the patient can buy a *finger puppet* for his 'inner child' and put it in his handbag. He pulls it out when necessary and talks aloud to his 'little John'. The concrete *external* presence of his 'anger stone' or his 'inner child' stabilizes the patient's internal process of self-development in external conflict. Thus, he justifies his own feeling and thinking.

The temporal stabilization of new knowledge through external symbolization promotes the development of new neuronal circuits in the brain's memory centers. Patients with psychosomatic complaints like to avoid arguments with their conflict partners. They say, for example: "My wife can talk better than me anyway!" However, if the patient refrains from arguing with his wife, he switches back to his old psychosomatic resonance pattern in which he was afraid instead of being angry. His defense through identification with the aggressor (see Sects. 2.4.3 and 8.4.2) and the resulting confusion between the roles of the perpetrator and the victim then lead to psychosomatic complaints. In such a situation, the 'anger stone' or the puppet for his 'angry inner child' helps the patient regain *internal* access to his feelings of anger. That opens the door to other solutions in his brain. The patient does *not* have to 'let out' the anger.

## 4.13 Self-Development of Therapist and Psychodramatic Responding

Patients with personality disorders often draw the therapist or the counselor into their defensive behavior through projective identification and their actions in the equivalence mode.

A biased adaptation to the patient's expectations blocks the therapist's internal process of development of their self-image in the therapeutic relationship: (1) The more hopeless a person with personality disorder feels, the more the therapist is fixated in the ego state of *empathically compassionate people.* (2) The more demanding and grandiose a patient appears, the more the therapist tries to grandiosely expand her boundaries as a human being during therapy and to make the impossible possible. (3) The more factual and unemotional the patient is in describing his problems, the more likely it is that the therapist will react *as a competent expert* with premature explanations and factual information. (4) The more a patient oscillates between two contrary metacognitive ego states (see Sect. 4.3), the more the therapist feels torn between compassion and anger.

In such a case, the therapist can free herself of her fixation through psychodramatic responding. In doing this, she alternatingly realizes her three task-related self-images (see below) directly in the encounter with the patient. Psychodramatic responding is indicated when *two* of the following *five* criteria are met: (1) The patient has moderate or low structural disorder. He thinks and acts in black-and-white patterns and equivalence mode. (2) He is not mentally open to engaging in chair work with his metacognitive ego states. He quickly moves from one subject to another. (3) He makes contradicting demands on the therapist without developing awareness of the contradiction. (4) The patient violates the therapy setting or does not agree to the appropriate therapy conditions. (5) The therapist has compassion for the patient who acts in equivalence mode but also wants to say difficult things and state reality clearly.

**Important definition**

The psychotherapist has *three tasks* in therapy: She thinks and speaks as *an encountering person, a competent expert*, and a *healer*. She understands these three tasks as her *three* inner self-images (see Fig. 4.4) and represents them with chairs in the therapy room. Thus, each of the three self-images develops its own psychosomatic resonance pattern between the memory centers of sensorimotor interaction patterns, physical sensations, affect, linguistic concepts, and thought (see Sect. 2.7).

The therapist uses the following three steps in using the technique of 'psychodramatic responding: (1) She *names* the chair she is currently sitting on as the chair for her as the *encountering human being*—the person the patient meets (see Fig. 4.4). As the 'encountering human being', she steps out of her systemic role as therapist and allows herself to express her thoughts and feelings *freely*. She justifies her feelings in the relationship and verbalizes them. (2) The therapist *sets up* a chair to her *right* for herself as a *'professionally competent expert'*. As a *'competent therapist'*, the therapist informs the patient factually about the conditions of therapy and general therapeutic experiences. She asks diagnostic questions and offers interpretations. (3)

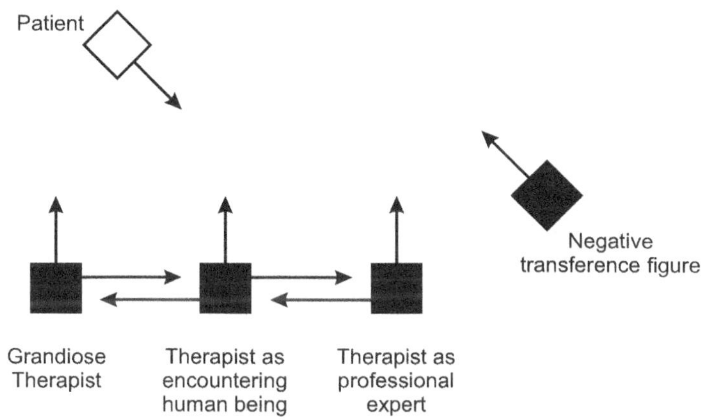


**Fig. 4.4** The therapist's three task-related inner self-images and the chair for the negative transference figure

The therapist places another chair to her *left* for herself as a *'grandiose therapist'*. As a *'grandiose therapist'*, she behaves true to the motto 'Why not?' She follows her ideals as a healer and helper. She creatively searches for a way of healing for the patient, even if she has little hope, and fails in doing so in the end.

When talking to the patient, the therapist pays attention and notices which of her task-related self-images is active in her thinking, feeling, and acting *in the moment*. If she spontaneously switches to another task-related self-image *internally*, she communicates this with the patient by physically moving to the respective chair. She verbalizes this shift: "As a professional, competent therapist, I mean…" (Krüger, 2007). Thus, the therapist frees herself from a biased fixation in only one of the three task-related self-images.

***Case example 19 (2nd continuation, see* Sects. 4.4 *and* 4.6*)***
*At the age of 39, Mr. A. received outpatient psychiatric treatment for severe depression and suicidal ideas. The therapist diagnosed him with borderline personality disorder (ICD F60.31) and chronic alcohol abuse (ICD F10.2) with severe structural disorder. In the first year of his life, Mr. A. was placed in a Catholic children's home by his mother. He was raised by nuns. His caregivers forcibly excluded him from the children's home at the age of 17 because of a sexual love affair with an intern. Mr. A. had already physically injured his wife several times in aggressive breakthroughs. In the first interview, Mr. A. replies to the question about his therapy goal: "I'm coming here somewhat scared. I cannot be treated at all!" In the therapeutic relationship, he sees himself 'as a Playmobil dwarf', but the therapist 'as a ten-meter-tall giant'. The patient expects from the therapist: "You should totally see through me. Then you can fix me quickly! I want to work through my childhood!" The therapist is startled. He feels overwhelmed by the patient's expectations.*

*(Due to lack of space, some of the patient's reactions are missing in the following text.) The therapist responds to the patient from the middle chair of the 'encountering*

*human being': "I think it is very kind of you that you trust me so much." The therapist places a second chair to his right and sits on it: "That is the chair for me as a professionally competent therapist. As a competent therapist, I say: Working through your childhood will not help you deal with your depression. On the contrary, it is more likely to harm you. Because in doing so, your past experiences of feeling deprived will come to life again. That will probably make you more unstable." The therapist places a third empty chair to his left (see* Fig. 4.4 *above) and sits on it: "This is the chair for me as a great therapist. As a grandiose therapist, I would like to fulfill your wish to come to terms with your childhood. Why not! Where there is a will, there is a way!" The therapist sits back on the middle chair: "But this task scares me as a human being. Because in my experience: 'If I have wanted too much as a therapist, I have failed. I started as a tiger and ended up as a bedside rug!'" The therapist switches to the chair on the right: "I see myself as a professional, competent therapist! And I mean: 'Please let us tackle your problems one by one!'" Mr. A. is irritated: "I feel a real depressive surge, there is again pressure in my stomach, my head, my legs! I feel left alone. I'm not getting the help I wanted. I can already see: I am too complicated for you, I cannot be treated!".*

*The therapist interprets this statement by the patient as jumping in for a negative transference. He sets up an additional empty chair a little further away. This symbolizes the patient's negative transference figure: "This is the chair for your mother who gave you away to the children's home. And I also see your teacher sitting there, the one who did not want to accept you as a foster child. As a therapist, I am not meeting your expectations either! But unlike your mother, I am not pushing you away. I will not leave you alone! I want to work with you. But I want to work with you on the problems you have in the present. I would like to walk with you step by step and look at one problem at a time!".*

*The therapist speaks to the patient about his alcohol problem in the last twenty minutes of the therapy session. He symbolizes this with the help of an empty chair next to the patient (see* Sect. 10.5*): "I'll put another chair here, next to you, for you as someone who drinks too much alcohol. Maybe your depression is also related to your drinking. You drink a lot more than you want and cannot fulfill your resolutions of changing it. That makes you feel guilty and inferior. This makes you depressed!" The therapist has the patient fill out Jellinek's 30-item questionnaire (see* Sect. 10.4*). Mr. A. ticks 17 of the 30 questions with 'Yes'. Five affirmations are enough to assume that one is 'probably an alcoholic'. Mr. A. is shocked: "My father was an alcoholic and perished from it." Mr. A. joins a therapy group for addiction disorder (3rd continuation in* Sect. 2.14*).*

**Exercise 12**

You cannot understand the therapeutic effect of 'psychodramatic responding' just by reading about it. Experience it through a role-play with *psychosomatic acting:* Place an empty chair in front of you in your therapy room. Imagine one of your patients with a personality disorder is sitting on it. Talk to the 'patient' *as the 'encountering human being'*. In doing so, express authentically and share the feelings triggered by the patient. Now place an empty chair to your right for you as a *'professional, competent therapist'*. Touch the chair and confirm your *own competence.* Feel the relationship with your 'patient'. Now remove this second therapist's chair again. Talk to the 'patient'. Notice how you feel as the 'encountering human being' *without* having the 'competent chair' next to you, representing your theoretical knowledge and practical expertise. Once again, place the chair of the 'competent therapist' next to you and check whether this changes anything for you in the given situation. If so, what is the difference?

You will notice: It relaxes you when you, as the therapist, verbalize your own feelings as the 'encountering person' *and when* the chair for the 'competent therapist' is placed next to you in *real*. As a result, you stop adapting to the systemically expected role. You feel more spontaneous, sociable, curious, and compassionate as a therapist. You give yourself more permission to be helpless and *not know everything*. But you are still able to act appropriately.

**Exercise 12 (continued)**

In the next step, please sit on the chair of the 'professional, competent therapist'. Now remove the chair for the 'encountering therapist' for a while. Give the 'patient' some factual information from the role of the competent therapist. Notice what it is like for you *without* the chair for the 'encountering human being'. Once again, place the chair of the 'encountering therapist' next to you. Focus on how you feel internally again. Do the same experiment with the chair of the 'grandiose therapist'. First, place it next to you. Then sit down on the 'grandiose therapist's chair'. Feel the relationship with the 'patient'. Then sit back on the chair as the 'encountering person' and *remove* the chair for the 'grandiose therapist'.

You will notice: If you are *just grandiose without* having the chair for the 'encountering human therapist' on the right and the chair for the 'professional, competent therapist' further to the right, it feels like a hike on a narrow line in the high mountains. You don't exist as a *normal* human being. But if you sit on the chair for the 'encountering person' and the chair for the 'grandiose therapist' is *not* there, it feels like you are missing something important. You lose your therapeutic vision and the reason why you became a therapist. You lose your spiritual identity and your inner fire. The ego state of the 'grandiose therapist' stands for the conscious, playful identification with the healer god (Hillmann, 1980, p. 107), that is, for the dream of being an *ideal* therapist. Also, limitless empathic compassion for the patient, even to the point of burnout, is an expression of the ego state of the 'grandiose therapist'. Some *therapists* find the chair for the 'grandiose therapist' to be superfluous. But if you switch to the role of the patient, you will notice: *For the 'patient'* it is important that the therapist, like a good mother in need, *at least tries* to make the impossible possible, *even if she fails.* The therapist's grandiose fantasies make the patient feel that *his wishes* are being taken seriously.

The therapist follows her intuition (see Sect. 2.2) in 'psychodramatic responding'. In doing so, she takes the following steps:

1. While sitting on the middle chair of the 'encountering human being' opposite the patient, she verbalizes how she *feels in the current interaction*, for example: "I feel

sad if you say this", "I feel helpless listening to you", or "I feel overwhelmed if I identify with you". The therapist's *negative* affect often is an *appropriate* response to the *dysfunctional* acting out of the patient in the equivalence mode (see Sect. 2.9).

2. The therapist captures the patient's unconscious expectations from her while he is acting and thinking in equivalence mode. She searches for *the inner task-related self-image* which would *fulfill* the patient's expectations. She places the respective chair next to her for this desired ego state. She moves to this chair and acts it out in the as-if mode of play. For example, when working with a patient diagnosed with narcissistic personality disorder, she moves to the chair of the 'grandiose therapist'. She verbally assures the patient that she 'as a grandiose therapist' *would like* to try to fulfill his wishes. She thinks out loud about how that might be possible and what the consequences would look like. In doing this, she paradoxically exaggerates her grandiosity and, for example, gives him advice on how to bring out inner change *immediately*.
3. But then she changes to the *chair of the contrary task-related self-image*. This is the chair of the 'encountering human being'. She acts out this ego state of being herself in the as-if mode. She tells the patient: "As a human being, I have to tell you: I have often tried to accomplish the impossible. But then I mostly failed!" For example, in the case of a patient with *masochistic behavior*, the therapist *first* breaks out of her adaption and, as an 'encountering human being', protests against the patient's self-injurious thinking: "I feel some pressure on my chest. If you devalue and criticize yourself repeatedly, I feel helpless and powerless." But then she moves to the chair of the 'therapist as a competent expert' desired by the patient and directly contradicts the 'encountering therapist' next to her: "As a competent therapist, I think: Renate, it doesn't work that way! You are the therapist! You can't be helpless and powerless toward Mr. B! You must help him!"
4. In the case of an *internal shift* to another task-related self-image, the therapist does not have to *physically* move to the other chair *every time*. She can also *point with her hand* to the other chair: "As a grandiose therapist, which I am, I mean…".
5. When the therapist authentically communicates her personal feelings and thoughts to the patient as the 'encountering human', it occasionally triggers some *negative transference* in the patient. In such a case, the therapist immediately symbolizes such a negative transference with a *fourth* chair and names the *negative transference figure* (see case example 19 above 2nd continuation). She places this chair three meters away from her, facing the patient (see Fig. 4.4 above). Then, together with the patient, she works out how, as a therapist, she acted *similarly* to the transference figure and *also* how she is *different* (see Sects. 2.10 and 4.14 and above case example 19, 2nd continuation).
6. The therapist often faces a dilemma in *crisis interventions* with patients in severe distress. As a professional, she wants and needs to give the patient a clear opinion, but she knows that the patient will react with negative transference, break off the relationship or have an angry outburst. In such a case, the therapist can

explain her dilemma to the patient *through a psychodramatic dialogue with role reversal between* her various task-related self-images in the as-if mode of play. For example, she moves to the chair of the 'grandiose therapist', looks at the chair of the 'encountering human', and says: "You could still try harder and let go of your rules for once. You can see: Mr. A. is not doing too well! He is suffering!" The therapist now reverses roles with the 'encountering human therapist' and addresses the 'grandiose therapist': "I would like to remind you, Renate, as a human being, that you have often tried to make the impossible possible. And then you have failed. Please remember that you cannot work 24 h a day. If you end up burning yourself out, it is of no help to Mr. A.!" Or the therapist moves to the chair of the *'professional competent therapist'* and responds to the 'grandiose therapist': "But, as a competent therapist, I am telling you: Don't fool the patient. I know from experience that you won't be able to do that in five or ten sessions. Mr. A. needs long-term therapy of at least 100 sessions."

**Recommendation**

In psychodramatic responding, the therapist shares essential factual information with emotionally unstable patients, *without saying it directly to them.* For this purpose, she acts out her *internal* reflections *in the form of an external psychodramatic dialogue between the two patient-related ego states* of 'encountering ' and 'competent therapist' in the as-if mode of play. The patient, who is thinking in the equivalence mode, feels that his expectations are being taken seriously because the therapist allows her inner self-image, which *matches* his expectations, *to exist externally* as a chair. However, he *also* unwillingly hears factual information from the "competent therapist" on *the other* chair.

**Central idea**

In the therapy of patients with severe structural disturbances, who think and act in equivalence mode, 'psychodramatic responding' *helps the therapist* free the development of her inner self-image in the therapeutic relationship from fixation and prevent *secondary* countertransference. She experiences the three *externally* represented inner self-images as *three different possibilities* of acting in the encounter with the patient. She thus gains ego control over the *cooperation between her three task-related self-images* and can use all three of them freely and appropriately.

*The patient* experiences the therapist's contradicting inner self-images externally as chairs *in the therapy room.* His inner *object image of the therapist* is thus differentiated into three images side by side. This also leads to a *differentiation of his inner self-image* in the therapeutic relationship. The patient usually does not want to let go of any of the "three therapists". He realizes that he needs authentic personal encounters in order to learn to trust again. He realizes that despite all reservations, he wants to feel secure in therapy with a supportive and competent therapist. He realizes that he can have high expectations of therapy, which only a great therapist can fulfill, but that he has to lower his expectations because of his need for stability in the therapeutic relationship. Even if the patient thinks in the equivalence mode, he can also internally perceive and understand the co-existence of the therapist's three different tasks *through the external representation* of the three self-images *with three chairs.* Psychodramatic responding is an important method of encounter-focused therapy (EFT) (see Sects. 2.9, 4.5, and 4.14).

You can take on the *role of the patient* in exercise 12 (see above) and notice how you feel in the interaction when the 'therapist' moves back and forth between her three internal self-images. You will notice: As a patient, you would like to experience your 'therapist' *not only* as an empathetic person. You would also want them to prove to be a professional, competent specialist. The 'grandiose therapist' should not be missing either. When the 'therapist' sometimes dares to wish for crazy things as a 'grandiose therapist', you, as a patient, feel free and can laugh.

Heigl-Evers, Heigl, Ott, and Rüger (1997, p. 176 ff.) have already recommended the '*principle of response instead of interpretation*' in the therapy of people with personality disorders. This is similar to the technique of psychodramatic responding.

**Central idea**

In using the psychoanalytic principle of 'response instead of interpretation' the therapist names her affect and describes the specific behavior of the patient which triggered her feelings: "When I listen to you, it feels a lot for me, and I can't take it anymore! I'm starting to feel some chaos internally." She can also add: "I'm confused when I listen to you. I think I feel something that you feel too." Thus, the therapist helps the patient to represent his *inner object image of the therapist* with a lot more complexity and to free it from projections. The patient perceives the therapist's inner mental state more clearly and realizes that he can influence it. In 'response instead of interpretation', the therapist often names the feelings that the patient defends, on his behalf (see Sect. 4.6).

***Case example 28***

*A 45-year-old female patient with social phobia and relational trauma in childhood reports in the initial interview, smilingly without any emotional involvement, of difficult childhood experiences. One is more terrifying than the other. Suddenly she interrupts her flow of speech and asks cheerfully: "I can tell you a lot more stories like this, Mr. Krüger, should I?" The therapist doesn't draw the patient's attention to the emotionless nature of her communication. He consciously identifies himself with her ego state of the 'abandoned, not seen child', and makes his inner experience available as an I statement: "No, please don't, I can no longer stand it because I can truly imagine what you are saying and I sympathize with your suffering as a child!" Only now does the patient begin to cry herself: "This is getting too much for me too!" The therapist's response helped the patient feel her split-off emotions.*

**Central idea**

In 'psychodramatic responding', the therapist names *her three therapeutic tasks*, represents them externally with chairs, and acts them out alternatingly in the as-if mode of play. Thus, she expands the psychoanalytic principle of 'response instead of interpretation' and acts not only *as an encountering human being*.

Therapists can also use the technique of 'psychodramatic responding' in group therapy or other group settings. The external differentiation between the therapist as an 'encountering human being' and the therapist as a 'professional competent expert' has proven particularly useful.

***Case example 29***

*A school psychologist worked in a crisis intervention team. After a school rampage, she cared for the children mentally. Afterward, she comes to supervision. She reports:*

*"I often feel the need to cry when I encounter the children and the young people. That bothers me!" Unlike the therapist herself, the supervisor experiences this reaction of the therapist in identifying with the children as appropriate and valuable. He would like to check whether his assessment of the situation can help the psychologist. He lets the supervisee re-enact her encounter with a grade 10 class: the therapist listens to the students. She is close to tears. The supervisor asks her to verbalize her feelings beyond reality here and now in the reenactment of the crisis intervention. The school psychologist tells the 'children' in the psychodramatic play: "I am so sorry that you had to experience this. You are still far too young to experience violence, terror, and death!" The supervisee is unsettled during the debriefing of the play and says: "But I can't just act as a human in the situation! I was called to give the children psychological support!".*

*The supervisor: "May I test an alternative and try to deal with your shock differently in your place?" The psychologist switches to the role of a 16-year-old student. The supervisor plays the role of the psychologist. He repeats: "It makes me very sad that you had to experience such violence. When I see you sitting there, you are so young, just starting your life. And then this terror and this violence! That just wears me down!" Like the psychologist, the supervisor allows himself to be shaken internally in the play. But then he places a second empty chair to his right and touches it: "But I also came here as a professional expert to intervene in the crisis. I want to help you where you need me." The supervisor sits down on this other chair: "As a professional expert, I would like to know how you have dealt with this dire experience so far. Some of you have surely already found a way to calm yourself down and distance yourself from yesterday's horrific events. How did you spend the afternoon yesterday? We can collect all the possibilities of self-stabilization you have already found and used. After that, I can show you other ways of looking after yourself after such an experience of violence.*

*In the debriefing, the supervisee says: "If you do it like that, crying isn't that bad. As a student, I was amazed to see you, as a psychologist, so shaken. But that did me good. I didn't find that strange because you did your job as a consultant with the second chair!" The supervisor: "I am sure that your crying is the most precious thing you can give the students. If you verbalize and name your feelings authentically, you are also doing it on behalf of the boys and girls who have to act cool. But it is precisely through your emotional reaction that you are a role model. You help the students find themselves again and emotionally regulate their inner chaos."*

*In another role-play, the psychologist explores how she feels in the role of the counselor when she places the second chair next to her for the 'competent therapist'. Afterward, she puts away the chair for the 'professional competent expert' and notices how she experiences the situation without this second chair. In the end, she says in astonishment: "I never thought this would be so easy!" The supervisor: "It just seems simple on the outside. However, it's a very complex method. By placing your two metacognitive ego states side by side, represented with two chairs, you show the children: One can have two sides, a sensitive, injured side, and a competent, cool side. These two sides are not mutually exclusive. In doing so, you will become a role model for the children. The next time you have to intervene in a crisis, try to put this second chair next to you as a 'professional, competent expert'. See whether it changes something for you!".*

**Recommendation**

The method of 'psychodramatic responding' can also be used in many ways *outside of psychotherapy*, for example, in job-related communication training for educators, medical students, psychology students, teachers, or geriatric nurses. This technique helps people, who work with people, to develop their professional identity.

**Central idea**

With the help of this technique of 'psychodramatic responding', therapists and counselors learn that they *codetermine* the patient's or client's external reaction *with their inner attitude* in counseling.

***Case example 30***

*In a course for psychotherapists, the leader demonstrated the method of 'psychodramatic responding'. A participant played the role of a patient with addiction from their own patient group. When treating the 'patient', the leader moved back and forth multiple times between his own three patient-related ego states represented by the three chairs. He said while on the 'grandiose chair': "As a therapist, I can tell you: We'll manage it. I have twenty-five years of experience as an addiction therapist. So where do you want to start?" In the role of the patient with addiction, the course participant felt that the self-confident therapist's behavior disempowered her as a woman and made her adopt a passive stance: "As a patient, I suddenly felt small and was afraid!" In the second demonstration, another therapist played the role of a man with addiction. The same intervention by the leader encouraged the 'patient' to spontaneously move to the chair of his 'self-protective behavior through grandiosity' and immediately compete with the therapist: "Well, not bad! Try it! Nobody has managed to crack me so far!".*

## 4.14 Disturbances in the Therapeutic Relationship and Negative Therapeutic Reaction

**Recommendation**

In the therapy of people with personality disorders, disturbances in the therapeutic relationship are a result of the person's fixation in a defense system. In metacognitive therapy, the therapist understands these disturbances as the patient's *unconscious* desire to resolve his fixation. Disturbances in the therapeutic relationship should therefore be dealt with as a priority. The patient makes greater progress in therapy when the therapeutic relationship flows freely.

For this purpose, the therapist uses encounter-focused therapy (EFT) when working with patients diagnosed with personality disorders (see Sects. 2.9, 4.5, and 4.13): (1) She works on the patient's defense system (see Sects. 4.7–4.10). (2) She practices psychodramatic self-supervision including steps 13–17 (see Sect. 2.9). (3)

She responds psychodramatically (see Sect. 4.13). Ultimately, there is no right or wrong in the therapeutic relationship. Instead, only the *reality in the relationship* matters. The *patient's* soul doesn't do anything without a purpose, nor does the *therapist's*. In the beginning, some patients are overtly or covertly reluctant in working with the empty chairs. In such situations, the therapist should explain to the patient that she needs the chair work to orient *herself* to his problems and questions. In doing this, the therapist can and should believe her intuition. Even a patient with reservations usually ends up feeling taken seriously because he understands himself for the first time. The patient feels often deeply touched by the therapist's consequent empathy. The therapist feels relieved and happy with such outcomes.

Patients with *severe structural disturbance* often tempt the therapist, with their acting out and overwhelming symptoms, to focus their attention *on the thought contents* in their conflict processing (see case example 14 in Sect. 2.12.2). As a result, despite her knowledge of the disorder-specific methods in the therapy of patients with personality disorders, the therapist 'forgets' to use the psychodramatic metacognitive chair work *consistently* (see Sects. 4.8 and 8.5).

***Case example 23 (continued from* Sect. 4.8*)***

*The 52-year-old Ms. F. had been dismissed by her employer without notice. That had retraumatized her. She decompensated again into a severe depression. She had to be on sick leave for a long time. The therapist worked on her dysfunctional metacognitive processes with the help of chair work. However, due to the lack of resonance from the patient, he did not pursue it consistently enough. It was only when the patient attempted suicide that the therapist noticed that he had pursued her only with empathy and compassion in her conflicts.*

*During a free hour, he once again tried to understand her inner process work with the help of psychodramatic self-supervision (see* Sect. 2.9*). This helped him to work consistently and explicitly metacognitively in the subsequent therapy sessions. He set up the following ego states with chairs next to her in each session: (1) To the patient's right was the chair for her self-protection. Throughout her life, the patient had always tried to meet the expectations placed on her perfectly, for example, the expectations of her as a social worker, as a mother, and as a wife. The therapist symbolized her self-protection with the hand puppet of a pretty woman. (2) In addition, the therapist used another chair to represent the patient's recurring 'preverbal panic state'. He placed it far away in the corner of the room and symbolized it with the hand puppet of a sensitive girl in a tattered dress. (3) He set up a third chair opposite the patient with a hand puppet of a wolf with large, sharp teeth. The wolf symbolized her feeling of a 'vague threat'. The external representation of her dysfunctional defense patterns helped the patient to work her way out of the traumatized child's ego state. She named her inner panic states as 'very vague fear' and assigned it to her childhood: "The wolf keeps slipping into the present with me and threatens me again and again!" The therapist felt that he understood the patient's true distress for the first time.*

Patients *with borderline personality disorder* often develop a sudden negative transference to the therapist during therapy. This can lead to the termination of therapy. The therapist understands this negative transference as an 'allergic reaction' to one of her *real* actions. She must internally adopt the patient's perspective to recognize the specific action that triggered an allergic reaction in the patient. In a negative transference, the patient's blocked self-development is portrayed as a latent or overt conflict in the therapeutic relationship. The therapist should address this conflict *before all other topics* because the patient's emotional energy in the therapeutic relationship is tangled in it (see case example 19, 2nd continuation in Sect. 4.13 and 3rd continuation below). A *negative transference* can be resolved in the following way:

(1) The therapist addresses the disturbance in the therapeutic relationship on her own. (2) In doing so, she immediately sets up an empty chair a little away from herself for the *negative transference figure* that the patient projects onto her (see Fig. 4.4 in Sect. 4.13 and case example 19, 3rd continuation below): "*You have had enough of this in your childhood* when you were left alone. *You don't need to experience this again!*" (3) The therapist describes the *real part* of the conflict in the therapeutic relationship and her actions which were *externally quite similar* to the behavior of the harmful caregiver in the patient's childhood. (4) However, she then informs the patient that her *motivation* to act in this way was different from that of the harmful attachment figure from his childhood: "I have been critical of you. But, I wanted to be honest with you". "I want to take you seriously!" "I don't want to overwork myself. Otherwise, I'll get sick, and I would end up leaving you alone just as your parents did." In addition, the therapist tells the patient explicitly: "We have a problem in our relationship. But I won't leave you alone. I promise you. We are in the same boat in therapy. We're going through rough waves together and trying to get along." (5) In *differentiating the real part of the relational conflict from the transference part* (see Sect. 2.10), the therapist alternatingly points to the chair for the transference figure from childhood *or* to her own self at another time. In doing this, she allows the patient to feel his feelings. Differentiating between the transference conflict and the real conflict in the therapeutic relationship is an important element of encounter-focused therapy (EFT).

***Case example 19 (3rd continuation, see* Sects. 4.4, 4.6, *and* 4.13*)***

*Five years after having undergone 50 h of therapy, Mr. A. started therapy for the second time with the same therapist. He had relapsed as an alcoholic. He had been temporarily retired. However, he returned to his old office six months ago after undergoing rehabilitation therapy. Now Mr. A. wants to end the second phase of therapy also after fifty hours: "It doesn't help me anymore. The long journey is uncomfortable. And I don't want to become dependent on you either." But, the therapist offers Mr. A. an extension of therapy to work with him on his severe structural relationship disturbances: "I think that you want to end therapy because the end of your relationship with me lies ahead of us." The therapist points with his hand to the empty chair representing the patient's 'self-injurious thinking' (chair 8 in* Fig. 4.1*): "You feel this is your own free decision. But I see this as self-harming, masochistic behavior. You want to protect yourself from once again being the unwanted child you were in childhood." The therapist points with his hand to the chair of the "harmful caregiver in childhood" (chair 9 in* Fig. 4.1 *in Sect. 4.2): "Back then, as a child, you were* *given to the children's home by your mother!" The therapist points to himself: "In your relationship with me, you are now doing the same as was previously done to you." The patient begins to cry, he is very touched: "Oh, it is going to be tough to continue further! I don't know how I would deal with my feelings of being alone!" Therapist: "That is exactly what continuation of therapy would be about. You will recognize that you have these feelings and then learn to deal with them. Think about whether you want to learn that!" The patient did not extend the therapy. However, the dissolution of the negative transference helped the patient and the therapist to part with dignity.*

Patients with borderline organization and relationship trauma from childhood sometimes react paradoxically to the benevolent empathy and help of the therapist. Sometimes they even decompensate into a psychotic episode (see case example 31 below).

**Recommendation**

Even if the therapist feels that she has made every reasonable effort in therapy, she should always look for the cause of a *negative therapeutic reaction* from the patient *in the therapeutic relationship*. Again, the principle applies: "The patient's soul does nothing for free".

***Case example 31* (Krüger, 1997, pp. 97 f., 103 f.)**

*A 32-year-old housewife, Mrs. L., is diagnosed with emotionally unstable personality disorder (F60.31). Before starting psychotherapy, she had already been in inpatient psychiatric treatment twice, for a short duration 'because of a psychosis'. Getting in touch with her is difficult. She appears artificial and puppet-like in her behavior. Mrs. L. plays a protagonist-centered play for the first time in her group therapy. She works on the conflict with her mother-in-law. The mother-in-law lives with the patient's family in her house. The conflict is an ordinary family conflict without any brisance. In the debriefing session, some group members encourage Mrs. L to be less subordinate to her mother-in-law. But other group members also understand the mother-in-law's needs.*

*Three days later, Mrs. L. is brought to the practice by her husband in an emergency. She is highly psychotic and in a completely fragmented state of mind. She fluctuates between gaining some insight into being ill and having absolute mistrust. She looks like a troubled child. What was the reason for the patient's psychotic decompensation? Before the psychodramatic argument with her mother-in-law, Mrs. L. had stabilized herself with the help of the defense of splitting. In the earlier psychotic episodes, she had aggressively devalued her husband. However, once she became 'healthy' again, she idealized her husband based on the inner belief: "Frank would be an ideal husband if my mother-in-law wasn't there." In this way, Mrs. L. could maintain her 'good' self-image in her relationship with her husband: she was the good-hearted victim of the 'bad' mother-in-law. She received narcissistic appreciation from her husband for her efforts to adjust and was able to deny her 'evil' side to herself. However, the psychodramatic confrontation with the mother-in-law brought Mrs. L's split-off anger and her wishes for separation to the surface. Her anger internally evoked the pathological introject of her abusive father. In her psychosis, she acted as if her father were present. There were many breakups in relationships, alcohol abuse, and violence in her family of origin.*

*In retrospect, the therapist interpreted his empathy for the patient and the sympathy of the group participants in the psychodramatic play as well-intentioned, but 'also bad'. He replied to the patient: "For other people, such support would be fine. But as a child, you experienced a lot of abandonment and violence. You have learned to put aside your longing for understanding. I'll place a second chair here, next to you, to represent your longing. If your longing is suddenly fulfilled in the group, then it is dangerous for you because the fulfillment of longing lets you feel your abandonment as a child again. The feelings of abandonment flood you. The group members and I meant well in the therapy session. But we have acted badly with you." The therapist also places a second chair next to himself: "This chair represents me as a therapist who has overwhelmed you with his affection and understanding."*

*The patient was able to use the representation of her inner splitting with chairs in her favor. She recognized her inner dilemma. After a short neuroleptic drug treatment for only one week, Mrs. L.'s psychotic disintegration had disappeared. When she returned to the group fourteen days after having been on vacation, the therapist was amazed: Mrs. L. had changed noticeably. She seemed softer, more authentic, and more in agreement with her feelings. The puppet-like, distant aura had disappeared and did not return in the further course of therapy.*

## References

Arntz, A., & van Genderen, H. (2010). *Schematherapie bei Borderline-Persönlichkeitsstörung*. Beltz.

Giesen-Bloo, J., et al. (2006). Outpatient psychotherapy for borderline personality disorder: randomized trial of schema-focused therapy vs. transference-focused psychotherapy. *Archives of General Psychiatry, 63*, 649–658.

Grimmer, K. (2013). Die psychodramatische Doppelgängertechnik und die Entwicklung von Sicherheit gebenden, inneren elterlichen Rollen', guten Elterintrojektien' – bei Angststörungen. *Zeitschrift für Psychodrama und Soziometrie12*(2), 189–199.

Gunkel, S. (1999). Die Häufigkeit posttraumatischer Belastungsstörungen: Epidemiologische Befunde. In G. Kruse & S. Gunkel (Eds.), *Trauma und Konflikt. Zugangswege zu einer traumaorientierten Psychotherapie* (pp. 48–83). Hannoversche Ärzte-Verlags-Union.

Heigl-Evers, A., Heigl, F., Ott, J., & Rüger, U. (1997). *Lehrbuch der Psychotherapie* (3rd ed.). Gustav Fischer.

Hillmann, J. (1980). *Selbstmord und seelische Wandlung* (2nd ed.). Rascher.

Jacob, G., & Arntz, A. (2011). *Schematherapie in der Praxis*. Beltz Verlag.

Kellermann, P. F. (2000). The therapeutic aspects of psychodrama with traumatized people. In P. F. Kellermann & M. K. Hudgins (Eds.), *Psychodrama with trauma survivors. Acting out your pain* (pp. 23–40). Jessica Kingsley Publishers.

Kernberg, O. F. (1981). *Objektbeziehung und Praxis der Psychoanalyse*. Klett-Cotta.

Kernberg, O. F. (1991). *Borderline-Störungen und pathologischer Narzissmus* (6th ed.). Suhrkamp.

Krüger, R. T. (1997). *Kreative Interaktion. Tiefenpsychologische Theorie und Methoden des klassischen Psychodramas*. Vandenhoeck & Ruprecht.

Krüger, R. T. (2005). Szenenaufbau und Aufstellungsarbeit, Praxis und Theorie, Variationen und Indikationen im Gruppensetting und in der Einzelarbeit. *Zeitschrift für Psychodrama und Soziometrie, 4*(2), 249–274. https://doi.org/10.1007/s11620-005-0091-y

Krüger, R. T. (2007). Psychodramatische Aufstellungsarbeit und Beziehungsklärung in chaotisierenden therapeutischen Beziehungen. *Balint Journal, 8*, 23–30.

Krüger, R. T. (2011). Die Gruppe als sich selbst organisierendes System. Konsequenzen für die psychodramatische Arbeit mit Gruppen. *Zeitschrift für Psychodrama und Soziometrie, 10*(2), 191–208.

Krüger, R. T. (2013). Wo das Wünschen noch geholfen hat. Die Arbeit mit dem Bewältigungsmärchen. *Zeitschrift für Psychodrama und Soziometrie, 12*(1), 103–112.

Leutz, G. A. (1980). Das psychodramatisch-kollegiale Bündnis. *Gruppenpsychotherapie Und Gruppendynamik, 16*, 176–187.

Mentzos, S. (2011). *Lehrbuch der Psychodynamik. Die Funktion der Dysfunktionalität psychischer Störungen* (5th ed.). Vandenhoeck & Ruprecht.

Moreno, J. L. (1974). *Die Grundlagen der Soziometrie. Wege zur Neuordnung der Gesellschaft* (3rd ed.). Westdeutscher Verlag.

Moreno, J. L. (1970). *Das Stegreiftheater* (2nd ed.). Beacon, N. Y.: Beacon House. Original work published 1923. Gustav Kiepenheuer.

Parin, P. (1977). Das Ich und die Anpassungsmechanismen. *Psyche – Zeitschrift für Psychoanalyse und ihre Anwendung, 35*, 481–515.

Powell, A. (1986). Object relations in the psychodramatic group. *Group Analysis, 19*, 125–138.

Pruckner, H. (2002). "Du sollst nicht fragen, das Kind will nicht reden." Psychodramatherapie mit traumatisierten Kindern. *Zeitschrift für Psychodrama und Soziometrie, 1*(2), 147–176.

Putnam, F. W. (1988). The switch process in multiple personality disorder and other state-change disorders. *Dissociation, 1*(1), 24–32.

Roediger, E. (2011). *Praxis der Schematherapie. Lehrbuch zu Grundlagen, Modell und Anwendung* (2nd ed.). Schattauer.

Rohde-Dachser, C. (1979). *Das Borderline-Syndrom.* Wien.

Rudolf, G. (2006). *Strukturbezogene Psychotherapie. Leitfaden zur psychodynamischen Therapie struktureller Störungen* (2nd ed.). Schattauer.

Sáfrán, Z., & Czáky-Pallavicini, K. (2013). Das Bewältigungsmärchen in der Gruppentherapie von Menschen mit Traumafolgestörungen—Zusammen in der Not sein. *Zeitschrift Für Psychodrama und Soziometrie, 12*(2), 269–282. https://doi.org/10.1007/s11620-013-0201-1

Watkins, J. G., & Watkins, H. (2003). *Ego-States, Theorie und Therapie.* Carl-Auer-Systeme.

Young, J. E., Klosko, J. S., & Weishaar, M. E. (2008). *Schematherapie. Ein praxisorientiertes Handbuch.* Junfermann Verlag.

# Chapter 5
# Trauma-Related Disorders

## 5.1 What is Special About Trauma Therapy?

Psychological trauma can result in *different* clinical disorders: post-traumatic stress disorders, anxiety disorders, obsessive–compulsive disorders, depression, personality disorders, psychosomatic complaints, addiction disorders, and psychotic episodes (see Sect. 5.2). Therefore, in such cases, the therapist should also use trauma therapy elements in psychotherapy, if necessary.

**Recommendation**

Therefore, *a causal treatment* of these disorders includes methods of trauma therapy described in this chapter. The more experienced a therapist is, the more courageous she becomes to perceive and process the trauma.

**Central idea**

"All professionals in the field of trauma therapy agree that we must adapt conventional psychotherapeutic methods to meet the needs that arise from traumatic stress. This means that conventional psychoanalytic or behavioral therapy does not meet the needs, but neither does conventional family therapy, gestalt therapy, body therapy, etc." (Reddemann & Dehner-Rau, 2004, p. 77). The reason is the defense of dissociation in the case of trauma-related disorders (see Sect. 5.10.2).

Special experiences in the treatment of people with trauma-related disorders are:

(1) Those affected dissociate as soon as their trauma experiences are 'triggered' by external events. As a result, they experience the current situation in the equivalence mode as if they are being traumatized in the *present*. (2) The flashbacks repeatedly lead to crises in the therapeutic relationship, thereby collapsing the therapeutic progress. (3) *Unrecognized flashbacks* discourage both the therapist and the patient, resulting in negative transference and countertransference reactions. (4) Patients with trauma-related disorders suffer from the impact of their trauma. However, often they do *not give* their trauma *any meaning*. (5) Some of the behaviors and ways of thinking in trauma patients appear to be neurotic at first. However, in truth, they are useful and helpful for the patient. They are self-stabilization techniques that protect him from



R. T. Krüger, *Disorder-Specific Psychodrama Therapy in Theory and Practice*, Psychodrama in Counselling, Coaching and Education 4,
https://doi.org/10.1007/978-981-99-7508-2_5

slipping into a flashback and feeling like he is losing his dignity or being scared to death. (6) Flashbacks are often triggered by *very small* scenic stimuli. These stimuli resemble memory fragments from the trauma situation. For example, a specific smell or the sight of a man in a white coat triggers a flashback sometimes.

***Case example 32***

*The 67-year-old Mr. A. sought outpatient psychotherapy to treat his recurrent moderate depressive episodes (F33.1). Five years ago, his thyroid had been removed because of cancer. He decompensated into depression once again four weeks ago. This was triggered by a regular check-up concerning his cancer. He groans in agony in the psychotherapy session: "It was good all summer! I could really enjoy the time! But now I am again powerless, resigned, and helpless. I'm afraid!" The therapist understands the patient's depression as the result of retraumatization: the patient contracted polio meningitis when he was a four-year-old little boy. He had to spend eight months alone in an isolation room in the hospital. His family was not allowed to visit him. Doctors and nurses clothed in white 'attacked' him at regular intervals. They held him with physical force and stabbed him with a syringe in the back to withdraw nerve fluid from his spinal canal. At age 67, if Mr. A. sees a man in a white coat, he again experiences a flashback. The therapist recognizes the flashback through the significant negative effect of a small specific scenic trigger. His flashback does not occur if he sees a woman in a white coat or a man in a green coat.*

*Mr. A. hates himself in his depression because of his 'weakness'. He comments sarcastically: "I am obedient again." The therapist feels helpless in the face of the patient's depression. In the beginning, he interprets his behavior as a neurotic adaptation. He asks why Mr. A. is still doing the follow-up examinations for cancer more than five years after his operation: "Your cancer never metastasized. If the doctors offer you check-ups, you blindly obey them! Your depression is telling you that you are going in the wrong direction!".*

*Two weeks later, Mr. A reports: "I canceled the last follow-up. But I did it because of the flu. My wife encouraged me to do this. I felt as helpless and dependent as a child! I needed someone who would allow me to do that!" Only now does the therapist realize that the patient felt and behaved like the little four-year-old boy in the hospital during the last therapy session. In his flashback, he had been unable to engage in healthy adult thinking (see* Sect. 4.7*). The therapist apologizes: "I'm sorry! It was unfair of me to get angry and ask you to be less conformist. You couldn't help it! When you are having a flashback, you have no choice. It is as if you are sleepwalking under hypnosis." The therapist places an empty chair next to the patient. He places the hand puppet of a little boy on it and points with his hand to this second chair: "The chair represents the little four-year-old boy in you who is traumatized." The patient looks at the doll and is visibly annoyed. The therapist: "I notice that the chair for the little traumatized boy is too close to you. I'll put it here in the corner of the room." The therapist and the patient work together to find indications for the flashback. The patient writes them down: (1) "When I feel like a child again." (2) "When I feel lethargic again." (3) "When I internally feel: You must be nice!" (Continuation in* Sects. 5.5 *and* 5.9*).*

## 5.2 Definitions of a Trauma-Related Disorder and a Traumatizing Situation

According to the ICD-10 (2004, p. 187), post-traumatic stress disorder (ICD-10 F43.1) (PTSD) arises "as a delayed or protracted reaction to a stressful event or a situation of shorter or longer duration with an extraordinary threat or catastrophic magnitude that would cause deep despair in almost anyone. [...] The beginning follows the trauma with a latency lasting from a few weeks to months. [...] In a few cases, the disorder takes a chronic course over many years and then turns into a permanent personality change (F62.0)."

There are two main forms of *coping* with psychological trauma–internalization and dissociation. Analogous to this, one can differentiate between two forms of trauma-related disorders, (1) relationship trauma in childhood and (2) post-traumatic stress disorder caused by trauma in adulthood. Patients who were *traumatized in childhood* often suffer from borderline personality disorder (Mentzos, 2011, p. 170), another personality disorder, depression, or anxiety disorder. These patients are fixed in a mutually stabilizing defense system of *masochistic self-censorship and compensatory mechanisms* (Mentzos, 2011, p. 39) that they developed as children in response to their childhood trauma. The defense system helped them avoid giving meaning to the traumatic experiences. Self-protective behavior (see Sect. 4.7) includes defense through grandiosity, perfectionism, or functioning in the role assigned from the outside (see Sect. 4.7). Patients with post-traumatic stress disorder because of *trauma in adulthood* have *not yet* developed a rigid defense system.

1. *Direct traumatization* in childhood occurs through sexual abuse, violence, or severe experiences of loss. These events mostly take place in the family context. *Indirect traumatization* in childhood occurs when a child is physically and emotionally neglected by traumatized or severely mentally ill parents. The child then experiences his wishes and needs as 'wrong' and thus develops reactive masochistic self-censorship and defense through grandiosity and perfectionism to avoid rejection by emotionally unstable caregivers. In adulthood, this leads to masochistic thinking and acting (see Sect. 8.5). The unseen, *"abandoned child"* could not sufficiently develop the tools of his inner conflict processing in interacting with his childhood caregivers.

   Traumatized children cope with the trauma through internalization (Hirsch, 2004, p. 2). "A traumatic introject persists, threatening like a dreadful hostile, archaic superego (causing symptoms and pathological behavior), which is only partially held in check by various forms of identification with the aggressor (primarily fusing and secondarily identification)" (Hirsch, 2004, p. 1). Those affected internalize their trauma experience in the form of a perpetrator-victim complex.
2. Patients with adult-onset *post-traumatic stress disorder* (PTSD) suffer from flashbacks in response to even minor external triggers. They cope with their trauma

through dissociation. A sudden, extreme impact of violence had initially overwhelmed their psychic apparatus. They split off their observing ego (their cognitive processes) from their acting ego (the perception of affect, physical sensations, and sensorimotor interaction patterns) when dissociating (see Sect. 5.4). This helps patients survive mentally, *at least in the beginning* (Hirsch, 2004, p. 2). However, dissociation persists as a response and becomes a permanent *pathological defense* if the trauma is *not processed*. As a result, the clinical picture of post-traumatic stress disorder develops with recurring flashbacks.

**Important**

Three conditions define a traumatizing situation: (1) The person concerned is emotionally overwhelmed by the situation. (2) He cannot fight and (3) He cannot flee. He, therefore, *cannot physically act* to protect himself.

***Case example 33***

*Kurt Lewin (Hans-Ulrich Wolf, 1999, oral communication) reported on school children locked in a cave while visiting the cave. The teacher was outside the cave when the entrance to the cave collapsed. All children suffered from post-traumatic stress disorder after their rescue. Only one boy was not affected. They investigated why this child had processed the event differently than the other children. It turned out: this boy had not been overwhelmed with panic like the others and had not just waited passively. Instead, he continued to look for an exit from the cave. Eventually, he found an exit and led the other children out of the cave. A short while later, the cave collapsed completely. So the boy wasn't frozen in shock. He had acted and tried to change the threatening situation.*

*The same happened to a cashier and his colleague in a bank robbery. The cashier kept negotiating with the perpetrator about handing over the money. But, his colleague hid under a table in panic and feared the perpetrator might discover her at any moment and shoot her. Unlike his colleague, the cashier did not develop any post-traumatic stress disorder afterward.*

**Recommendation**

Therapists should know *which* events *can potentially* traumatize a person.

Gunkel (1999, p. 54 ff.) has made a list based on international literature: 46–78% of Holocaust victims are traumatized. 30% of soldiers who experienced combat missions and 12% of soldiers without any experience of combat mission suffer in retrospect from a trauma disorder, 16–35% of Vietnam veterans, 10–20% of Canadian UN soldiers, 25–50% of refugees, 31% of victims of state repression or violence, 90% of political prisoners from Vietnam who have experienced torture. Three months after sexual abuse or rape, 48–80% of those affected have a trauma-related disorder, four times as often in *sexually* abused children as in *physically* abused children. 10–23% of the bus drivers who were attacked while driving suffer from a trauma-related disorder. 7–34% of police officers develop trauma-related disorders after rescue missions or violent experiences, for example, 31% after the collapse of a grandstand. 16% of those affected develop post-traumatic stress disorder after a cardiac infarction, 13%

after heart transplants, and around 10% after blood cancer treatment. Between 30 and 40% of parents suffer from trauma-related disorders after treating a child with cancer, between 18 and 23% after traffic accidents, 22% after a plane crash, 5–42% after natural disasters such as earthquakes, and 14% after losing a close reference person. There is also a high trauma potential if one was unwanted as a child, had to experience cancer themselves, or had to provide long-term care for a seriously ill family member. Patients with post-traumatic stress disorder (PTSD) have often experienced not just one but multiple traumas in their life.

**Central idea**

PTSD can be a result of accidents or natural disasters. Trauma experiences caused by *violence by people* are more likely to result in PTSD because those affected also lose their basic trust in relationships.

Not *everyone* is traumatized by a *potentially* traumatizing event. The percentages in the list above show this. The consequences of traumatizing events depend on (1) the age at which the traumatizing event occurs, (2) the severity and duration of the traumatizing events, and (3) the number of traumatic events the individual had to experience. A history of mental illness can lower the threshold for developing a trauma-related disorder. The patient's psychological resilience is an important protective factor. Sensitive people are more easily traumatized.

***Case example 34***

*A student who was repeatedly depressed for months sought help in an esoterically oriented group that offered 'guided regressions'. The group members searched for their own experiences of violence in their 'past lives' under the guidance of a 'guru woman' who seemed to be traumatized herself. Anyone who did not participate in the 'regression' or left the group was considered 'evil and devilish'. After spending six months in this community, the student decompensated into paranoid psychosis. The sensitive young woman had not been able to endure the tension of the conflict with the idealized 'master' and had collapsed mentally. She was convinced that the sect's leader had become influenced by extraterrestrials and became 'evil'. That was a true symbolic image of the actions of the 'master'. But, the student experienced this symbolic image as an external reality in the equivalence mode (see* Sect. 2.6*).*

## 5.3 Symptoms of Trauma-Related Disorders

According to Gunkel's review of the literature (1999, pp. 54 ff.), around 5% of male and 10% of all female Americans develop post-traumatic stress disorder as a result of a traumatic event at some point in their lives. Around 26% of bulimia patients have experienced sexual assault or rape and suffer from trauma-related disorders, as do 68% of prostitutes and 52% of patients with eating disorders. Around 35–52% of persons with psychotic disorders suffer from trauma-related disorders four to eleven months after an acute phase of illness, as well as from 'invasive psychiatric treatments'. According to the study, 30–90% of people with borderline personality disorder are traumatized. According to a more recent review (over 53 studies) by Simpson and Miller (2002) (quoted from Schäfer & Reddemann, 2005), 27–67% of women and 9–29% of men with addictions were sexually abused in childhood. 33% of women and 24–33% of men with addictions were physically abused in childhood. A Dutch study of patients with alcoholism demonstrated that 28% of men and 46% of women experienced physical *or* sexual violence or physical *and* sexual violence in childhood.

According to Reddemann (1999, p. 88), traumatized people suffer from constant agitation (DSM-IV criterion D: 'hyperarousal') and sleep disorders. They are easily vulnerable, excessively nervous, and find it difficult to calm down. They are constantly in fear, are easily insulted, and are less capable of dealing with conflict, especially when the topics of conflict are related to their traumatic experience. "The repeated experience of the trauma in the form of intrusive memories (DSM-IV criterion B: intrusions) [...] against the background of a constant feeling of numbness is characteristic of people with traumatic experiences" (ICD-10). 'The Broca speech area is not activated or not sufficiently activated during a flashback. In other words, speech and language are not or hardly accessible" (van der Kolk & Fisher, 1995). People with traumatic experiences exhibit one or more of the following symptoms: acute anxiety states, depression, multiple psychosomatic symptoms, somatization disorders, phobic or compulsive behavior, a constant feeling of numbness and emotional dullness, recurring nightmares and flashbacks, outbursts of anger, indifference in interpersonal relationships and the inability to love, mysterious behavior, drug or alcohol abuse, distracting, 'sensation-seeking' lifestyle and/or dissociative states with depersonalization and derealization through to mini-psychoses. Avoidance (DSM-IV criterion C) of activities and situations that could trigger memories of the trauma is also pronounced. Thoughts of suicide are not uncommon. Often there is an unconscious wish to control everything to avoid being helpless at the mercy of a threatening or chaotic situation again.

## 5.4 Dissociation as a Central Characteristic of Trauma-Related Disorders

**Important definition**

According to van der Kolk and Fisher (1995), the 'nature of trauma is to be dissociative'. People with relationship trauma in their childhood *also* dissociate when their trauma experience is triggered (see case example 32 in Sect. 5.1).

**Central idea**

For people with traumatic experiences, dissociating is "like everything that we can later describe as pathology [...], a normal way of coping with the trauma" (Reddemann, 1999, p. 87). It helped those affected *by the original traumatizing situation* to detach themselves from the overwhelming and destructive feelings and to experience the trauma as if it happened to someone else (Putnam, 1988, p. 53).

"When the physiological mechanisms of fight and flight no longer work, the only thing left for humans is dissociation as a quasi-psychological flight mechanism. [...] Traumatized people often describe these experiences by reporting that they left their bodies in the traumatic situation" (Reddemann, 1999, p. 87). "Dissociation leads to the trauma memories [...] being organized as sensory fragments and intense emotional states [...]" (van der Kolk et al. 1996). Dissociation in the traumatizing situation can help those affected *still function externally* and, for example, save their lives (see case example in Sect. 5.17.2). The consequence, however, is that later the trauma experience is not processed like other experiences because the patient immediately dissociates when attempting to deal with the trauma. His ability to process conflict freezes. In the case of post-traumatic stress disorder, the traumatic memories often only become conscious in a new, protected environment. By definition, however, they are then *unprocessed*. Those affected get caught in the vortex of their unprocessed trauma memories and are tormented by their trauma images. Even small triggers evoke the dissociation again. Dissociating becomes a *symptom*.

**Central idea**

According to Reddemann (1999, p. 89), the agonizing thing about flashbacks is "that they are experienced as if they were happening now, which means the reliving of traumatic states is not remembrance, but retraumatization." "Triggered by a memory, the past can come alive with sudden sensory and emotional intensity such that the victim feels as if the entire event is happening again in the present. Patients with PTSD seem trapped in their trauma and cannot distinguish it from the present" (van der Kolk, Burbridge, and Suzuki, 1998, p. 58 f.). They experience their flashback in equivalence mode (see Sect. 2.6).

Dissociating is a "complex psycho-physiological process involving the disintegration and fragmentation of the consciousness and [...] the memory, the identity and the perception of oneself and the world around" (Gast, 2000, p. 170). According to Gast, there is a distinction between five main dissociative symptoms: amnesia, depersonalization, derealization, identity insecurity, and identity change.

A flashback with dissociating leads to an uncontrollable full-blown stress reaction. If the fear is uncontrollable, the hippocampus in the human brain begins to pull in the extensions of its nerve cells (Hüther, 2002, *only* from oral communication). In people with severe post-traumatic stress disorder, the hippocampus volume can decrease by 8–22% (van der Kolk et al., 1998, p. 69). This leads to hyperexcitability and disinhibition of behavior because it is more difficult to bear and process *emotionally arousing information* with a reduced hippocampus volume. Those affected often estimate new stimuli as a general threat and react immediately with aggression or withdrawal (van der Kolk, Burbridge, and Suzuki, 1998, p. 72).

**Important definition**

Wurmser (1998, p. 425 f.) has developed a definition of dissociating that captures *several metacognitive processes*. He understood dissociating as 'a *form of a split between the observing and acting egos* with depersonalization as an important event. This split or dissociating involves a massive denial of inner reality, namely overwhelming emotions (blockade of emotions). Other forms of defense also play a role but pale in comparison to the defense through denial/blockade of emotions. This also includes a *counter-fantasy* that supports denial and is intended to invalidate the perception of reality'.

**Central idea**

When dissociating, those affected split the current psychosomatic resonance circuit (see Sect. 2.7) in the *internal* process of self-development in the *external* situation into (1) the cognitive process of thinking and naming and (2) the psychosomatic process of sensorimotor interaction, physical sensation, and emotional experience (see Sect. 2.7).

## 5.5 The Therapist Witnesses the Traumatization and the Dissociating

Many patients with trauma-related disorders ascribe *no meaning* to the traumatic events in their mental development. They defend through denial and don't talk about it either. Because if they did, they would potentially activate the associated psychosomatic resonance pattern and with it their *unprocessed* panic, horror, and alienation of the traumatizing situation and have a flashback. Traumatized patients thus feel defenseless in response to the trauma-related symptoms. They aren't able to do anything which further intensifies the symptoms. They are afraid of going crazy when they have a flashback. But they 'don't want to burden other people with their problems'. They are *ashamed* of their 'abnormal' thoughts and feelings. They notice that they are different from others and fear being excluded from the community. Only 2.9% of the soldiers in the German Armed Forces allegedly suffered from post-traumatic stress disorder after a deployment in Afghanistan (Schulte-Herbrüggen & Heinz, 2012, p. 557). But 9–20% of American soldiers developed depression or post-traumatic stress disorder after deployments in Afghanistan (Wittchen et al., 2012, p. 559), 14% of them even became seriously ill (Süddeutsche Zeitung, December 20, 2011, p. 9). Many US employers are reluctant to hire veterans from the Iraq wars because of the reputation of emotional instability that precedes them. Presumably, German veterans *only rarely talk about* their trauma experience because they rightly fear the hindrances in their promotion in the Armed forces.

**Central idea**

Patients with PTSD develop masochistic self-esteem issues or compensatory behaviors in response to their flashbacks. The therapist *must not* interpret and treat a traumatized patient's self-esteem issues or depressive inhibition *as neurotic* because that often *intensifies* the patient's depression.

**Recommendation**

The therapist informs the patient as early as possible that his depression results from a traumatic experience and puts a second chair next to him for his traumatized ego (see Sect. 5.8): "The chair symbolizes your traumatized ego and your trauma film. You don't understand yourself because you experience flashbacks even with small triggers. This causes you to devalue yourself in addition to your traumatic experience."

The patient needs at least five therapy sessions to integrate the terms "trauma" and "flashback" with his own life experiences. But then he *feels relieved*, re-interpreting his symptoms. He no longer feels defenseless in response to the trauma-related symptoms because *he can act.* The therapist and the patient develop a plan for trauma therapy. The masochistic vicious circle disintegrates gradually. The patient understands himself for the first time. He develops a new motivation for therapy. The new self-knowledge opens therapeutic access to the patient's psychodynamically important conflicts.

***Case example 32 (1st continuation, see* Sect. 5.1*)***

*In the first interview, Mr. A massively devalued himself because of his internal depressive paralysis: "Actually, I just want some peace! But my wife always criticizes me for being so withdrawn. I should play some sports and pursue some hobbies. I want that, but it doesn't work! We quarrel quite often." While taking the case history, the therapist discovered the trauma the patient experienced when he was four. He placed a second chair next to him and placed the puppet of a little boy on it: "Mr. A., that's the little boy in you who, at the age of four, had to spend eight months alone in an isolation room in the children's hospital. I suspect that you were traumatized by this dire experience as a child! How do you feel when you see the little boy you were, sitting over there on the chair?" Mr. A: "Not so good." The therapist places the chair of the 'traumatized child' in the other corner of the room behind the window curtain: "I think it is better for you this way! Otherwise, the old memories will flood back to you." The therapist places a second empty chair next to him and places the hand puppet of a knight on it: "This other chair represents your self-protection through adaptation and grandiosity. You learned in childhood not to give meaning to your trauma experience. You were a brave hero who could do anything and take anything." The therapist points his hand to the 'traumatized child' behind the curtain: "But now, if you go to the clinic for a follow-up examination and see the doctors' white coats, you slip into your old trauma film. You feel and think like you did when you were four years old! Please, just read about trauma and flashback on Wikipedia!" Mr. A. initially reacted skeptically. But he then gave more details about his experiences at the age of four. He came home after the hospital stay and longed for safety and security as a four-year-old boy. But his mother immediately sent him with his grandmother to the Black Forest for a cure. He was supposed to learn to walk again after polio. The patient's parents were rigidly fixated on the old norms and values from World War II. It was only his performance that mattered to them. His father had been a hero in the war.*

*After two years of individual therapy, the patient finally saw himself as 'traumatized.' The patient's 'depressive phases' had disappeared except for the week he went for a medical follow-up. Mr. A. enjoyed his life and, for example, played creatively with his grandchildren. His wife, a former nurse, understood him better now. She allowed him to be different from others and to withdraw when necessary. The patient no longer devalued himself masochistically. He had developed a good relationship with his inner traumatized little boy. Mr. A. also informed the hospital doctors about his trauma disorder. He negotiated special conditions for himself. For example, he ensured he did not have to wait five hours for the examination in the outpatient clinic as he usually did. He had always met a lot of men in white coats there. But now, he would be the doctor's first patient to be examined at eight o'clock in the morning. The doctor spontaneously offered that he would take off his white coat.*

*During his follow-up, the patient remained in the hospital alone in an isolation room for three days because he was injected with radioactive substances as a precaution to combat possible metastases. But he got a hospital room on a higher floor with a better view. And he was allowed to go for a walk in the park on the third day but could not approach other people that day because of his radioactive radiation. The patient thus experienced that, unlike in childhood, he could change his unbearable situation in the hospital of his own free will. He had gained some control over the retraumatizing situation. (continued in* Sect. 5.9*).*

**Central idea**

In metacognitive psychodramatic trauma therapy, the therapist symbolizes the patient's traumatized ego with a second chair next to him. In this way she separates his psychosomatic resonance pattern *in the traumatizing situation* there and then from his psychosomatic resonance pattern *here and now in the therapeutic relationship.* A psychosomatic resonance pattern includes the *inner* sensorimotor interaction pattern, the physical sensation, the affect, linguistic concepts, and the thoughts in the *external* situation (see Sect. 2.7). In the two-chair technique, the patient and therapist stand shoulder to shoulder and look at the patient's traumatic experience *from a meta-perspective.* This strengthens his cognition. He can talk and think more freely about the traumatic event. *Without* the second chair, the two psychosomatic resonance patterns would mix and most likely cause a flashback.

By naming and externally representing the 'traumatized ego' with a chair, the therapist becomes *a witness to the truth* of the patient's *existential* need. She acts *retrospectively* in the present as the patient's close caregivers *should have* acted in the past. Often a witness to the truth is *missing* during or after the traumatic event. The caregivers looked away. They were comfortable or fearful of aggression. But the therapist, as the witness, pays attention to what happens. She calls a spade a spade. She stands by the victim's side. Experience shows that this reduces the secondary self-devaluation after a traumatizing experience (Mentzos, 2011, p. 38 f.). Self-doubt arises, for example, when a mother actively looks the other way as the father sexually abuses their daughter. Everyday life in the family goes on as if nothing had happened. The abused girl then secondarily begins to doubt whether the crime actually took place. Or the girl believes the perpetrator that she *herself* 'wanted' or 'provoked' the sexual assault. In such a case, the victim develops a false self-image. The traumatized child needs a witness to the truth, who *validates* their feelings of betrayal, fear, and shame as a victim and counteracts *unjustified* feelings of guilt.

**Central idea**

In metacognitive trauma therapy, the therapist is an implicit doppelganger in the patient's inner process of self-development in the external situation (see Sect. 2.5). She must actively decide whether or not she wants to understand the patient's adverse experiences from adulthood or childhood as traumatic experiences. If she decides to do so, as a witness of the truth in her interaction with the patient, she calls the spade 'a spade'. This, *at least retrospectively,* removes the secondary insecurity of the patient caused by the flashback.

***Case example 35***

*A 42-year-old patient gave the therapist feedback in the final therapy session: "In the beginning, the work on the relationship with my partner was actually a skirmish.*

*However, there was a turning point for me in therapy. This was when you told me that my experiences with my father in childhood were a trauma. That's when my experiences became real for me. That gave me the right to feel what I feel. I believed that my fear of death was a real fear of death from the physical abuse by my father. That it was true! Before, I thought: 'You have to pray! Others have it worse!' By naming it as 'Trauma', you took me by the hand and walked with me for a while. It hurt me! But it was a crucial moment. I got to the core of it myself. I opened the door to my inner child, who was sitting behind the door: I opened the first door first. The child wasn't there. Then I opened the second door. She wasn't there either. She wasn't behind the third door either. But then there she was, behind the fourth door, sitting fully wet and feeling afraid!" (Continued in* Sect. 5.15*).*

Some therapists avoid openly naming a patient's trauma and flashback directly in front of the patient. They fear that it will retraumatize the patient. In doing so, they unconsciously identify with the patient's defense through denial and act out counter-transference. But in patients with trauma-related disorders, *dissociating* contributes to the development of symptoms. Therefore, it is essential to treat *dissociation* in psychotherapy.

## 5.6 The Seven Phases of Psychodramatic Trauma Therapy

**Recommendation**

"Trauma is chaos, and chaos needs structure" (Reddemann, 2007, *only* oral communication). The patient had no influence on the traumatizing event *in the traumatic situation* itself. *In therapy*, he should therefore have control over what happens to him. The individual steps of trauma therapy are to be discussed openly and clearly with him.

The therapeutic approach can ideally be divided into seven *consecutive* phases (see Fig. 5.1): (1) The *preliminary phase* of trauma therapy addressing the patient's defense system (see Sect. 4.10), (2) *Trauma-specific diagnosis*, (3) *Trauma-specific crisis intervention*, (4) Learning *self-stabilization* techniques, (5) The *processing of trauma with exposure to trauma*, (6) the *phase of integrating the inner change* into childhood and current relationships, and (7) The therapist and the patient work on the defense system developed in childhood (see Sect. 4.10) in order to free the self-development from its fixation.

Many patients with trauma-related disorders come to therapy with a diagnosis of personality disorder, anxiety disorder, depression, or addiction disorder. Often the therapist only notices it *first during the treatment* that the patient is suffering from a *trauma-related* disorder. A trauma-specific diagnosis (see Sect. 5.7) and learning the self-stabilization techniques require at least ten individual sessions. This work can also be done by consultants from the helping professions. But, one should proceed with *processing the trauma* (see Sect. 5.10) only during *long-term therapy* of more than 30 sessions. It requires further training as a psychodrama therapist.

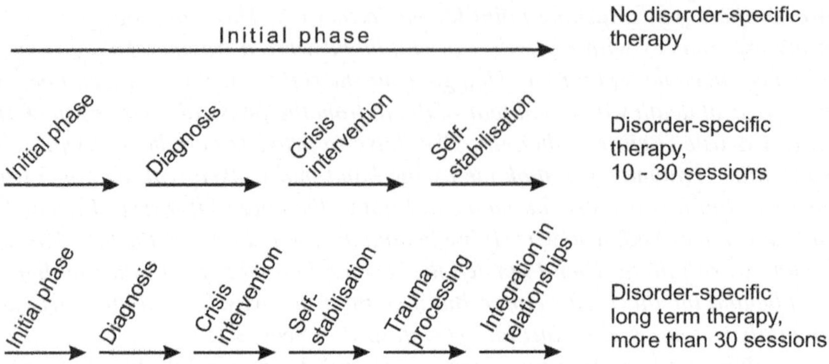


**Fig. 5.1** The six phases of psychodramatic trauma therapy

**Central idea**

In the mentalization-oriented psychodrama therapy of trauma-related disorders, the therapist always works also metacognitively. She lets the patient realize the *metacognitive processes* of his dissociating in the as-if mode of play and focuses on them in her therapeutic communication (see Sects. 2.14 and 5.10).

Patients who suffered relationship trauma in their *childhood* developed permanent mutually stabilizing compensatory mechanisms and masochistic self-censorship (see Sect. 8.5) to help them cope with their lives to some extent. Their rigid defense patterns often lead to severe relational disorders, depression, or anxiety disorders. But, the patients experience their defense through perfectionism and grandiosity and their self-censorship as parts of their character and identity (see Sect. 4.2). They couldn't internally develop a concept of appreciation in relationships in childhood. They, therefore, give no meaning to their traumatic childhood experiences. For example, they often see their traumatizing parents as 'loving parents'. They also perceive their unfortunate living conditions in the present as 'normal' and their 'personal fate'.

**Central idea**

In the *preliminary phase* of trauma therapy, patients with trauma-related disorders must often first work on their defense through grandiosity, perfectionism, and masochistic self-censorship. This is the only way they gain access to their childhood traumatic experiences (see Sects. 4.8 and 4.10).

## 5.7 Trauma-Specific Diagnosis

Patients with childhood relationship trauma often come with presenting complaints of anxiety, depression, severe relationship disorders, or an addiction. Mostly they do not know that they are suffering from a trauma-related disorder. The therapist may recognize the traumatic quality of the patient's childhood experiences, perhaps while taking the case history. But if she works with the patient *empathically* during therapy, she often unknowingly takes over the patient's defenses and 'forgets' to give his trauma experiences sufficient attention.

**Central idea**

Only when the symptoms persist for a considerable period, and there are noticeable disruptions in the therapeutic relationship, the therapist becomes aware of something essential still missing in the therapy process. In such a case, the therapist can use steps 13–17 of psychodramatic self-supervision (see Sects. 2.9 and 4.8) to identify the patient's dominant defense pattern.

**Recommendation**

If during therapy, the therapist suspects that the patient's symptoms, for example, his depressive episodes, *may* reflect a trauma-related disorder, she *re-examines* the patient's diagnosis.

The following therapeutic experiences indicate a trauma-related disorder: (1) The patient *repeatedly* decompensates psychologically. (2) The *extent* of the psychological breakdowns is difficult for the therapist to empathize with and does not match the seemingly harmless triggering circumstances. (3) The patient exhibits *symptoms* of a trauma-related disorder (see Sect. 5.3). (4) He is unusually *distant* in verbal communication or cannot be reached emotionally. (5) The *therapist feels incapable*, helpless, strange, or mystified in the therapeutic relationship. (6) If the therapist represents the 'inner child' of a patient with childhood trauma with a second empty chair (see Sect. 4.7), the patient *rejects his 'inner child'* instead of addressing him (see Sect. 5.8).

**Recommendation**

The therapist must not *depend on the patient's consent* when diagnosing a 'trauma-related disorder' because many patients ascribe no meaning to their trauma experience. If they did that, they would get caught in their flashback or activate their inner 'blind sadistic prosecutor' (see Sect. 4.7). Therefore, the therapist first decides *on her own* whether she perceives the patient as traumatized.

Some conspicuous, apparently pathological behaviors of the patient are to be understood as *necessary* self-protection through self-stabilizing actions. The therapist may reinterpret them in a radically positive way. For example, the therapist *spontaneously* sees a 90-h workweek in a person with *neurosis* as problematic and questions it. In the case of a *patient with trauma*, however, she interprets it as a 'self-discovered technique of self-stabilization in the case of a trauma illness'.

*Working with the table stage* (see Sect. 5.10.10) helps to gain an overview of the interaction between the existing conflicts when making a diagnosis. The *technique of the self-regulation circle* (Krüger, 2010a and see below) is indicated to retrace the patient's self-regulation in *recurring conflicts* and recognize any flashbacks that occur in the process. The *chair work* (see Sect. 4.7) helps to increase the patient's awareness of his defense through adaptation, grandiosity, and masochistic self-censorship.

The therapist works as follows when working with the *self-regulation circle*:

(1) She puts an A3 size sheet of paper on the table and draws a large circle on it. (2) She marks the crisis with a minus sign on the *right* side of the circle and the

patient's well-being with a plus sign on the *left*. She marks the conflict process with an arrow, from the positive pole to the negative and vice versa. (3) The patient then notes his thoughts, feelings, actions as well as the events, step by step, along the circumference on the right side indicating the way *into* and on the left side indicating the way *out of* the crisis: "What did I do? What did I feel? What did I think? What did I want then? Then what happened? Then again what did I do? … feel? … think? … etc." The patient uses the self-regulation circle to understand his recurring conflicts: What is his contribution to causing the crisis? But also, what is his contribution to becoming well again?

***Case example 36***

*The 28-year-old Mrs. A seeks* crisis intervention *because she is 'feeling bad again'. She has had several traumatic experiences in her childhood and youth. She struggles with borderline syndrome with reactive psychotic episodes (F60.31). The small, pretty woman looks exhausted and depressed. She reports: "I have hardly slept in the last 14 days. Therefore, I had to go home yesterday while working in the supermarket. I messed everything up. Everyone points their fingers at me. They want to test me!" The therapist makes an offer: "Together, we could examine and make a note of what happens when you have mood swings." The patient creates a self-regulation circle. At the end of their collaborative work, the following is written on the paper along the circumference from well-being to crisis: (1) "We are going to my grandma's home unannounced. (2) She is happy. (In her childhood, the grandmother was the only one who gave the patient support and security in the broken family.) (3) My husband is nice. Grandma is doing fine. I am fine. (4) The vacation is over. We are driving home. (5) I'm afraid that people at work won't want me. (6) I have trouble sleeping, have stomach cramps, and I panic. (7) I am afraid of failure and being a bad mother to my son. I have diarrhea. (8) I am afraid of being considered lazy. (9) I am constantly afraid that other people will see what is happening to me and laugh at me. (10) I play something for everyone. They shouldn't notice anything. (11) Nothing works at home anymore. (12) Nothing is fine at work. (13) I think other people are testing me."*

*On the way from crisis to well-being, the patient notes: (14) "Shame motivates me to perform. (15) I am afraid of being considered evil. That's why I try to be a good person. (16) I work a lot and work overtime without pay. I am good at home and a good mother. (17) My self-esteem increases. I'm doing fine. (18). But I feel bad when I have nothing to do." The therapist positively interprets the patient's imperfect solutions as 'self-discovered self-stabilization techniques'. This stabilizes the patient. She feels understood and gains distance from her dysfunctional actions and feelings during the crisis. She even smiles a little at the end of the session. She takes home the paper with the self-regulation circle.*

*Five days later, Mrs. A. reports spontaneously in the following therapy session: "I have discovered something. Something is still missing in the circle: When my husband and I returned from our vacation, the laminate floor in the hallway of our apartment had swollen. My husband accused me of pouring water on it while cleaning it. I knew very well that it was not true. I even told him that. But he didn't believe me.*

*Afterward, it turned out that a water pipe had burst during our vacation. I often have to justify myself for things I am not responsible for." The therapist and the patient add four additional steps to the 'self-regulation circle' between steps 4 and 5: 4 A. "My husband or others, like my father in childhood, do not believe me. My thoughts and feelings don't matter. 4 B. My trauma film takes over: I feel I am nothing, and I am no good. 4 C. I become insecure and devalue myself. 4 D. I feel that I am being manipulated." The patient knows the feeling of manipulation from her childhood. Her alcoholic father and mother had abused her narcissistically.*

When working on the self-regulation circle, the therapist avoids any evaluation and strictly adheres to the conviction: 'The patient's soul does nothing for free'. The more inappropriate the patient's thinking and feeling in the described conflict, the more likely it is an *expression of a flashback*. The therapist names the trauma as 'trauma' where applicable. He explores, together with the patient, the external stimulus that triggered the flashback. But then he does *not* continue exploring the trauma experience so as not to destabilize the patient further. Instead, he reinterprets the patient's self-protective behavior and denial in a consistently positive way. He refers to it as a 'solution' or 'self-stabilization technique' she has found herself, even if the solution seems ludicrous initially (see steps 17, 18, and 19 in case example 36 above). Working with the self-regulation circle strengthens the patient's *cognition*. It helps her observe and describe the content of her conflict from a meta-perspective, as well as internally assign her psychosomatic experiences on the table stage. The therapist, as an implicit doppelganger (see Sect. 2.5), stands *shoulder to shoulder* with the patient during the elaboration and mentalizes on her behalf if necessary. He helps her to name and differentiate her feelings. In doing so, he activates the patient's inner mentalization in her recurring conflict and facilitates her inner conflict processing. With the therapist's help, the patient learns to think of her recurring conflict in the as-if mode. This method helps patients feel more courageous when dealing with their recurrent conflict, more hopeful, and lively in their encounters. The mutual psychosomatic resonance warms the therapist's heart.

**Exercise 13**

Create a self-regulation circle *for one of your own recurring conflicts*. Underline the *personally* meaningful statements and mark in red the actions for which you think: "But it can't stay that way!" You will notice: Until now, you have understood your problem in such a way that you are swaying between *two opposing poles*: "I'm not feeling well, now I'm fine again, now I'm not well again". But the image of your self-regulation circle changes the internal development of your self-image in your conflict (see Sect. 2.4.1). You can see your participation *in the emergence* of your conflict and also *in coping with it* with greater clarity.

## 5.8 The Initiation of Trauma Therapy

### Question

Why Moreno's statement 'Acting heals more than talking' is important in psychodramatic trauma therapy?

The trauma-specific *diagnosis*, the *crisis intervention*, and the *initiation of trauma therapy* merge into one another. Trauma therapy is usually initiated due to a disruption or crisis in the therapeutic relationship (see Sect. 5.7) or in the patient's everyday life. Even a therapeutic conversation about a *traumatic* experience can exacerbate a patient's symptoms or trigger a flashback. This also applies to trauma-related disorders caused by trauma in childhood. For example, a 36-year-old patient in a psychosomatic clinic had a pseudo-epileptic seizure in the initial interview as he narrated his childhood experiences. He went into a trance state in which he 'acted out' his rape as a child in the children's home.

**Central idea**

The therapist struggles with a *dilemma* in trauma therapy. The patient asks her to treat his trauma-related disorder. However, as soon as the patient remembers his traumatic experience and talks about it, he often feels bad and slips into his flashback. His conflict processing freezes. Therefore, he cannot process his trauma experience *through talking*.

The therapist resolves the therapeutic dilemma in mentalization-oriented trauma therapy by letting the patient retrace the three metacognitive steps of dissociation in therapy in the as-if mode of play. Over time, the patient develops ego control over his dissociating (see Sect. 2.14). The therapist thus works also on his dysfunctional metacognitive processes that produce his dysfunctional cognition and makes them the subject of therapeutic communication.

1. She decides that she wants to understand the patient's symptoms as trauma-related.
2. As an implicit doppelganger and witness to the truth, she explains to the patient (see Sect. 5.5) that his symptoms are caused by a 'trauma experience'.
3. In naming a *relationship trauma from childhood*, the therapist immediately places a second chair next to the patient representing his self-protection: "This chair represents your self-protection through self-stabilizing actions. As a child, you experienced that it is good to suppress your trauma memories and distract yourself."
4. Then, the therapist places the third chair behind the chair for self-protection to represent the patient's 'traumatized child'. She places the puppet of a female or male child on this chair: "I understand that your depression is the *symptom of* a trauma-related disorder. You were traumatized as a child when you were hospitalized in an isolation room for eight months. The chair with the little puppet symbolizes you as the four-year-old child".
5. The sight of his 'inner traumatized ego' or 'traumatized child' can trigger a flashback in the patient. The therapist, therefore, always asks the patient *immediately* after setting up the third chair: "When you see the emotionally hurt little boy on

the chair over there, what emotions does it trigger in you?" The more severe the trauma and the stronger the patient's structural disturbance, the more likely he is to seek help from the therapist: "That scares me!" or: "I don't like the child. I'm disgusted with him!" Such a reaction is a *diagnostically* valuable indication that the patient has a trauma-related disorder. Non-traumatized patients are more likely to answer: "The child makes me sad." "I feel sorry for him."

6. If the patient reacts with panic or disgust to his inner child, the therapist *immediately* grabs the chair representing the patient's 'traumatized child' and moves it to another place far away in the room.

**Central idea**

In this distancing technique, the therapist acts *as a metacognitive doppelganger on the patient's behalf* (see Sect. 4.8) and follows her *own* inner impulses. This is because the patient has learned, as a child, to endure all events and pretend as if nothing happened. The inner masochistic self-censorship developed in childhood prevents him from willingly *distancing himself* from his traumatized ego. He doesn't even know he can do that because he didn't have enough help with his self-development as a child.

In doing this, the therapist informs the patient: "I'm going to place this chair at the other end of the room between the plants. You can see the little boy there. Is that ok?" The therapist makes *a small bed* with two towels for the 'little boy' on the chair and gently strokes his head once: "So, now he's well looked after".

7. The therapist asks the patient how he is feeling now. The patient mostly doesn't understand this approach and is amazed. However, he feels physically 'better again'.
8. The therapist sits down in her chair again. She checks whether, as the patient's implicit doppelganger, *she herself still* feels paralyzed by the presence of his 'traumatized child' in the back of the room. If the therapist continues to feel blocked in her relationship with the patient, she carries the trauma chair out of the therapy room and through the door all the way out into the hallway and explains: "The chair for your traumatized self is still paralyzing me". Afterward, she sits down in her chair again and observes whether *her* paralysis has now disappeared: "I feel better this way!"
9. Often the patient then takes a deep breath. It is *only now* that he notices the presence of his 'traumatized child' has *paralyzed him* too.
10. The therapist talks to the patient about how he felt when the third chair of his 'traumatized child' was still in the room.
11. She interprets the patient's bodily reactions at the sight of his 'traumatized child' as the 'beginning of a flashback'. She *informs* the patient about the definitions of psychological trauma and flashback: "You *want* to think, feel and act differently in the flashback. But you *can't* because you feel existentially threatened."
12. The therapist practices a self-stabilization technique with the patient if necessary.
13. She plans the subsequent steps in trauma therapy together with the patient.

The patient sometimes understands the statement, "You are traumatized", in equivalence mode: "The therapist cannot tolerate me being insecure or weak." Therefore, the therapist does not ask the patient: "*Could* it be that you are traumatized". Instead, she marks it as a real finding: "*You are* traumatized." And *immediately* represents the patient's "traumatized ego" *with a chair next to him.* As a result, the patient also represents his 'traumatized ego' *internally* separately from his self-image in the relationship with the therapist. The *external* distance to the second chair for his 'traumatized ego' helps him to distance himself from it *internally* as well.

Patients who were only traumatized in adulthood usually do not have a developed defense system against the intrusion of their trauma film. They dissociate even with the smallest of external triggers or feelings of insecurity, feelings of being at someone's mercy, and helplessness (see Sect. 5.2).

**Central idea**

According to Wurmser (1998, p. 425 f.), dissociating is a form of "split between the observing ego and the acting ego... This split includes a massive denial of the overwhelming feelings." Psychodramatic dissociating helps the patient retrace his *defensive* dissociating as a creative process in the as-if mode of play and bring it under his ego's control.

The therapist's approach to *adult* post-traumatic stress disorder is slightly different than to childhood relationship trauma. It is similar to the therapy approach used for *anxiety disorder* with real justified fear (see Sect. 6.2):

1. She addresses the trauma as a witness to the truth. However, she does not represent a defense system because this is not yet developed.
2. The therapist immediately places a second chair next to him for his 'bad feelings', 'trauma', or 'traumatized ego'. She thus carries out the inner '*split* between the observing ego and the acting ego' outside on the stage in the as-if mode of play.
3. The patient usually perceives his 'traumatized ego' as much too close. He is drawn into the trauma experience. Therefore, the therapist takes the second chair representing his 'traumatized ego' and places it far away in the corner of the therapy room or in front of the door. It is good for the patient when he can no longer see his 'traumatized self'. Putting away the trauma chair is a distancing technique similar to the safe vault technique. It dissolves the patient's panic a little and stabilizes his soul.
4. The therapist asks the patient what works well for them at home if they are troubled by trauma memories. Then, she asks him to make a written list of these actions and refers to them as 'self-discovered self-stabilization techniques'. If necessary, she adds to this list and practices further self-stabilization techniques with him (see Sects. 5.9 and 6.2).

**Exercise 14**

You cannot understand metacognitive therapy just by reading about it. Therefore, try acting psychosomatically in *a role-play* with a colleague. Explore how it feels to confront a patient with a diagnosis of 'trauma-related disorder'. Use *two different versions*: In the first part of the exercise, you inform the 'patient' about his trauma-related disorder and his recurrent flashback, *face to face, without using the second chair*. You will find out: *In his role as the patient without* the second chair, your colleague feels devalued and like he has become an object of observation. In the second part of the exercise, when confronting him, you place a second chair next to him to represent the 'traumatized ego' of the 'patient'. You look at this chair shoulder to shoulder *with your 'patient'*. Then, as described above, you act as a metacognitive doppelganger and move the second chair further away on his behalf.

You will notice: When confronted with his trauma, your colleague feels more comfortable in his role as the 'patient' *with the trauma chair next to him* because he looks at his 'traumatized ego' as a chair *from the meta-perspective*. But, the two-chair technique is also good for you as a therapist. In the interaction with the patient, as an implicit doppelganger, you internally develop two different empathy processes *alongside one another*. On the one hand, you identify with the patient's 'traumatized ego' and feel his fear yourself. On the other hand, you identify with the "patient" in the role of his observer and stabilize him as a doppelganger *in the meta-position*.

The therapist uses the two-chair technique *in group therapy* as well.

***Case example 37***

*At the end of a group therapy session, a 45-year-old distressed woman shares: "Somehow, I'm standing by my side. Today I wanted to practice not feeling ashamed anymore when I have to show myself. But now I feel bad!" The therapist senses a latent panic in the patient. He takes an empty chair and places it next to her: "You say you're standing by your side. So you are standing next to Margrit, who thinks as a healthy adult, that you are otherwise. I am therefore placing this chair next to you to represent the healthy adult Margrit. I suspect you got caught in a trauma film when you forced yourself to confront your shame. Please move to this other chair of your healthy adult thinking!" The patient sits down on the other chair. The therapist: "If you don't want to show yourself, it's not your neurotic inhibition. I believe hiding your inner world from others is an old form of self-protection. It has helped you avoid existential threats in the past." The patient confirms the existential quality of her fear. She feels relieved. The radically positive revaluation of fear as a form of self-protection in a trauma experience stabilized her.*

The therapist can also use the *table stage* for an *initial trauma-specific consultation*. As with crisis intervention (see Sect. 8.8), the therapist symbolizes the *temporal* sequence of the patient's crisis *as a timeline,* with one stone for the beginning and another for the present. Then, together with the patient, she represents his ego *with three stones* on the table, one for his 'competent ego', one for his 'traumatized ego', and one for his 'self-protection through adaptation or grandiosity'. Furthermore, they represent the people involved, the patient's feelings and ideas, the institutions involved, and the relevant objects with stones and wooden blocks. In doing so, the therapist helps the patient create his *soul landscape*.

The therapist explains to the patient the definition of dissociating in a psychodramatic symbolic act: She touches the stone for his 'competent ego' with one finger: "This stone represents your healthy adult thinking." She takes this stone from the table stage and puts it *under the table* on the floor: "If you have a flashback, you internally change from your healthy adult thinking into your traumatized ego." The therapist points her hand to the other stone representing his 'traumatized ego' on the table: "You only feel inferior in the trauma film. Your thinking is blocked. Nothing works anymore. In psychotherapy, we call this a flashback! Both your traumatized ego and competent ego appear in you one after the other. In therapy, you can learn to notice when you have a flashback and when you think as a healthy adult in therapy." The therapist touches the third ego stone on the table: "This stone represents your self-protection through hiding and your self-stabilizing actions."

**Recommendation**

The therapist can give *ego-strong* patients the stones for their 'competent ego' and 'traumatized ego' to take home with them: "Put these stones in your pocket or put them on your desk at home. Look at these stones once a day. If you can't tolerate the sight of your 'traumatized ego', take the stone to the cellar and lock it in a cupboard!" In this way, the patient represents the external separation of his trauma-related psychosomatic resonance pattern from his inner self-image here and now in his memory centers. The patient needs 6–12 months to neuronally rewire this disconnect in memory. The trauma experience is no longer stored under the term "I am inferior", but under the new term "I am traumatized".

***Case example 38***

*The 38-year-old Ms. C., traumatized* in child*hood, travels 300 km for a crisis discussion with the therapist. She complains: "For the first time, I feel I am in the right place at my job. But my employment contract is limited to one year. It expires in four weeks. I should speak to my boss. But I'm scared because my boss is very insecure and unreliable. If I tell him I want a new employment contract, he'll terminate me immediately!" The therapist invites Ms. C. to present her concerns to the 'boss' through role reversal in a fictional psychodramatic dialogue. It turns out that her boss does seem to be a problematic person. In the fictional dialogue, Ms. C. reacts increasingly insecurely and aggressively toward her boss's behavior and 'forgets' what she wants. The therapist asks her: "Do you notice this in other relationships that you become so chaotic and aggressive when someone behaves in an unreliable manner toward you?" Ms. C.: "My boss is exactly like my mother. With her, what is right today was wrong the next day! If the wooden board is supposed to be in the sink in the evening, it shouldn't be in the sink in the morning. Whenever I reminded her of her task, she simply denied everything: 'I never said you must have been imaging things.'".*

*The therapist fetches two finger* puppets *from a cupboard and suggests: "Please choose two finger puppets or two Playmobil toys. The puppets should be small enough for you to hold them in your hand. One puppet should symbolize you as an adult, and the other should represent your child ego. You say you want to meet your boss about your employment contract. Then put the child puppet in your right and the adult puppet in your left pocket. As you stand on your boss's doorstep, speak to your child puppet internally as the adult you are: 'Yes, I know that you are scared and confused. You're right, the boss is stupid! But now the point is that, as an adult, I must preserve my interests and achieve my goal! Otherwise, we will soon have no more money to buy food. I'll comfort you when the conversation is over!' Then go into your boss's room and tell him what you want to say as an adult!" Ms. C. goes home after the therapy session.*

*Six months later, Ms. C. gratefully told the therapist: "I was able to talk to my boss then, and it went well! I even had the puppet in my hand. That helped me a lot! But it was good that I also had the puppet for my competent ego with me! At one point, the puppet representing my traumatized child threatened me. But then I was able to hold on to the puppet for my competent ego." The external presence of the finger puppets allowed the patient to internally delegate her flashback to the finger puppet of her 'traumatized child'. This enabled her to think and act as a healthy adult in a situation that would otherwise have triggered a flashback.*

**Central idea**

The 'inner traumatized child' should potentially develop into a '*healthy inner child*'. Then, it can advise the patient if they are needy. The 'inner child' thus becomes a symbol of the patient's true self. The therapist supports this development with a psychodramatic dialogue (see Sect. 8.4.2) between the adult ego and the child ego (see Sect. 4.10). At the end of the therapy, the therapist can *diagnose* the extent of the treatment's success from the quality of the patient's interactions with his 'inner child'.

The external representation of the flashback as a stone or a puppet is a *distancing technique*. Traumatized patients can use this technique if they feel agitated at night or have severe sleep disorders. They carry the puppet, which represents their traumatized child, from their bedroom into their living room at night. They make a small bed for the puppet in a closet and tuck it in. They go back to their bedroom and try to sleep there. Distancing techniques are techniques for self-stabilization. For example, the patient can symbolize his trauma with an object and lock it in a cupboard in the basement or bury it in the ground in the garden or the forest. This method is similar to the *safe vault technique*. The therapist asks the patient *to imagine* a safe vault in a place *only accessible to him*. Only the patient has a key to the safe. In his *inner imagination*, he goes to the safe with the 'trauma' symbolized as an object. He opens it with his key and puts his 'trauma' inside. He locks the safe again and hides the key in a place only he knows. Then he returns from his imagination to reality. Distancing techniques improve one's mental state in a crisis. However, the relief usually only lasts for a few hours or days. Psychodramatists help their patients perform the distancing techniques not only in their imagination but *also in a sensorimotor way*. *External physical* distancing in the as-if mode of play actualizes other internal images via the psychosomatic resonance circuit between the memory centers of sensorimotor interaction patterns, physical sensations, affect, linguistic concepts, and thoughts (see Sect. 2.7). The patient *internally* feels more confident when the 'trauma' has been distanced *externally*.

## 5.9 Self-Stabilization and Associated Techniques

Reddemann (1999, oral communication) says: "Trauma therapy is self-stabilization, self-stabilization, and nothing but self-stabilization! Many trauma patients do *not* go beyond the self-stabilization phase in their psychotherapy. But they still benefit from their therapy." The following *trauma processing* (see Sect. 5.10) requires that the patient has previously learned techniques of self-stabilization and can apply them.

**Important definition**

In a flashback, patients think in equivalence mode and experience the current situation as if the trauma happened in the here and now. Self-stabilization techniques help the patient to activate helpful psychosomatic resonance patterns within themselves. Unlike in a flashback, these techniques *enable the patient to internally think and act* in the as-if mode in the current situation. The ability to act internally in the as-if mode is crucial in mastering life. It is also the prerequisite for trauma processing (see Sect. 5.10).

The self-stabilization work should always be related to the "traumatized ego" symbolized by another chair. Over time, many traumatized people *autonomously* find specific techniques to stabilize themselves. "In fact, it was through our patients that we first came across these possibilities of creating an inner safe place or helpful beings" (Reddemann, 1999, p. 90). In the flashback, the patient once again experiences the existential distress of the traumatizing event. Therefore, anything that helps patients get out of the dissociative state of consciousness is good. Some signs that would be a symptom in *people with neurotic disorders* can be positively reevaluated as 'a self-discovered self-stabilization technique' *in traumatized patients.*

**Central idea**

Burge (2000, p. 315) believes that sometimes even *antisocial* behavior has to be interpreted as a measure for self-stabilization in trauma therapy, for example, withdrawal from relationships. Exaggerated fearfulness and a great need for control can be understood as an attempt to act differently as compared to during the trauma event *as a precaution.* In doing so, the affected person tries not to lose track of things, at least in the current situation. The patient protects himself and others from feelings of helplessness and the threat that reminds him of his trauma.

Many patients simply distract themselves when they feel bad. For example, they play games on the computer or sit in front of the television. The therapist might see this as critical *for other patients* doing the same. Reading books can also stabilize the soul. A patient with relationship trauma *in childhood* was terrorized by her traumatized father. But in the evening, she always read novels about the daughter of a forester named 'Pukki' in bed. She stabilized herself through her identification with 'Pukki´s experiences. The good always triumphed over the bad in these novels. Many patients with trauma-related disorders play sports, which is sometimes even addictive. Sports activities are essential to trauma therapy because *physical activities* also stabilize the soul. Working is also a self-stabilizing technique because the patient has to concentrate on the subject of his work, which distracts him. He forges social relationships at his workplace. He knows what is wrong and what is right *in his work*. He receives recognition, thereby improving his self-esteem. The money he earns makes him independent.

***Case example 39***
*A 55-year-old teacher sought therapy because of exhaustion and migraines. In her childhood, she was 'not wanted' by her parents and grew up in a broken family. When she was seven, she saw her teacher mistreating other students at school. She then decided, "One day, I'll be a good teacher!" And she did. In old age, however, she lost the strength to live up to her own grandiose ideals in her work. She couldn't tolerate being just a 'normal' teacher for her students. She got engulfed in a grave trauma-related identity crisis.*

People *traumatized in childhood* often develop trauma-related anxiety and depression *after the end of their professional life*. Because excessive work protects traumatized people from allowing their feelings to surface and becoming dependent on others. In 2004, Radebold (2004, pp. 33, 41) found that 20% of those over 60 years old in Germany suffered from depression and anxiety. In other countries, however, it was 'only' 10% of those over 60 years. These older adults were traumatized as children by experiences during the Second World War, for example, when they were fleeing, during a bombing, or when they lost close relatives. "They had 'no noticeable symptoms' in their working life before the age of 60 [...]; all through their life they *functioned* inconspicuously and some even well enough due to the specification of the tasks delegated to them" (Radebold, 2004, p. 12). However, if these people were to lose a close caregiver to death in old age or if they *themselves* became sick, helpless, and dependent, it would easily trigger their traumatic experiences from childhood, and they will be *retraumatized* (Kellermann, 2009, p. 30f.)

**Central idea**

*Some* people can process a traumatizing experience adequately well (see Sect. 5.13). They get to a deeper, *transpersonal* level of feeling and thinking *without therapy*. After encountering death or the absurd, those affected feel unexpectedly at home in something super-personal and experience a new transpersonal connection with something larger.

For example, they are 'wonderfully protected by good forces [...]' (Bonhoeffer 1944). This experience does not occur on the level of well-being and wellness. It opens the door to something new, essential, a new *expanded* identity, one's own 'inner being' (Dürckheim, 1984, p. 39 f., 168, 1985, only oral communicated). Such a step in development makes some affected people human and wise in new ways. The potentially traumatic experience leads to 'post-traumatic growth' (Fooken, 2009, p. 65 ff.).

**Central idea**

Traumatizing experiences lead those affected into basic human fears (Dürckheim, 1995, only oral communicated). They open the existential level. Going through a basic fear can become a transpersonal experience.

Going through the *fear of death* can give rise to a feeling of a great, comprehensive life. Going through *absolute loneliness* can give rise to all-embracing love in the affected person. Going through the *fear of madness* can result in an experience of all-encompassing sense. Going through the *fear of absolute emptiness* may eventually result in one experiencing the abundance of being. According to Dürckheim (1995, oral communication), transpersonal experiences can occur in the areas of nature, art, love, or religion. If possible, *trauma therapy* should *also* include *the existential or spiritual* level of the soul. Trauma patients would often search autonomously for *transpersonal* experiences to self-stabilize themselves. But they seldom gave them the appropriate meaning. The therapist must, therefore, *actively* seek such a transpersonal experience in her patient's life. She acknowledges this experience as 'existential' or 'in the broader sense as spiritual'. The patient should learn to use such an experience as a resource for his soul. That improves his chances of recovery.

***Case example 32 (2nd continuation, see* Sects. 5.1 and 5.2*)***
*Mr. A., traumatized in the hospital at the age of four, withdrew from all relationships throughout his childhood and adolescence. He built treehouses in the forest with the wood waste from a nearby carpentry company. The treehouses were a shelter and, at the same time, a 'safe place' for him (see* Sect. 5.10.5*). As a child and adolescent, he often wandered alone through the fields and the forests and observed the animals. He often sat alone by a small lake surrounded by forest all around. He was just there, becoming one with nature. Nobody wanted anything from him.*

***Case example 40***
*A 40-year-old patient grew up in a family characterized by physical and sexual violence. Even as a child, he often fled secretly into the forest at night. He screamed in the dark, just like the ravens he heard in the forest. He became so one with nature. As part of his therapy, he wrote a fairy tale of coping (see* Sect. 5.14*): In it, the teacher noticed during his primary school days that "little Karl was always unfocused at school. So she visited his family at home. There she discovered his mother's bruises. His father had abused his mother. The teacher informed the youth welfare office. In the fairy tale of coping, little Karl was placed into a caring foster family with his sister." Unfortunately, this tale's healing effect disappeared again after a few weeks. The patient felt: "Over time, the little boy in the fairy tale of coping became suspicious of his foster parents. He couldn't believe that the foster parents really loved him." Therefore, the patient had to expand his coping fairy tale: "The little boy would leave the foster parent's house at night if necessary and go into the woods to a raven tree. He would climb the tree and enter a hallway through a door inside the tree. When the ravens came flying in, they would go in through the door and turn into people. When the little boy came, the Ravens would always greet him warmly as a member of their clan. There were six doors in the large hallway in the raven tree. These led to different rooms, one to play in, another to sleep in, and another to eat in,* etc. *The boy always went into the room he needed. He would return to his foster family during the day." For several years, the patient kept inventing new episodes in his fictional life with the foster family, if necessary. The world of ravens would help stabilize himself. He experienced: "I can reach into the depths. My soul comes alive. I am no longer dependent on others" (continued in* Sect. 5.14*).*

***Case example 41***
*A woman with relationship trauma was 'not wanted' by her parents as a child and did not get a good enough response to her own existence from her family. She found the desired response in religious contexts: As a five-year-old girl, she often went to church alone. She sat down in front of the altar and prayed to God. As an adult, she explained to the therapist: "I had someone to talk to there".*

***Case example 21 (see* Sect. 4.6*, continued)***
*A patient whose mother had narcissistically abused him had built a dollhouse in his childhood against massive opposition from his mother. At the end of therapy, he used this creation for self-stabilization. Whenever he found himself drowning in his feelings of senselessness again, he would put the dollhouse on his lap and play with it. He regained access to his internal feelings and desires through external acting and playing with his dollhouse. The patient described his dollhouse as his 'magic box'.*

In the phase of self-stabilization, the therapist and the patient first look for existing actions the patient has developed *autonomously* to make him feel better. The patient himself often evaluates these behaviors as "crazy, you shouldn't act like that". However, the therapist re-evaluates these neurotic actions radically positively and explicitly names them "self-stabilization techniques". She represents each of these actions with a rock or block of wood on a second chair symbolizing the patient's self-protection. These actions result from the defense through grandiosity, perfectionism, control, or adaptation to the expectations of the community (see Sects. 4.7 and 4.8). In this way, the therapist gives the patient's "existing self-stabilization techniques" appropriate meaning. The patient should write down the self-stabilization techniques on a piece of paper and number them. He can read this list at home when needed. Even reading the list is a self-stabilizing technique. This clears up the fog in the patient's head as he realizes he *can do something* about suffering a flashback.

**Central idea**

The patient acts out his autonomously developed self-stabilizing actions in equivalence mode because he cannot but do so. However, he now makes neuronal links between the sensorimotor interaction patterns, physical sensations, affect, and thoughts of these actions, and the linguistic concept of 'self-stabilization' in his memory. Thus, they are available to him in the as-if mode of thinking. The patient can consciously use them when needed.

The therapist also teaches patients other self-stabilization techniques as needed:

1. When patients dissociate, they often involuntarily revert to the posture, facial expressions, and gestures they had *during the original trauma event*. The therapist, therefore, encourages the patient: "Please concentrate on what you see in the room here and now! What do you feel in your body right now? What do you smell? What do you hear? Stretch your limbs, and now change your breathing. Correct your posture. Assume a posture that is familiar to you in situations *of wellbeing*, joy, or sporty competitions" (Christine Rost, 2013, only oral communicated). The *sensorimotor* activity involved in this exercise often helps the patient astonishingly quickly to return to healthy adult thinking.

2. The 'safe place' self-stabilization technique is described in Sect. 5.10.5. It leads the patient into a complex, individually designed, fictional experiential space where he can stabilize himself *by acting*. Some elements of the 'safe place' technique are *also* known *individually* as self-stabilization techniques, for example, the introduction of inner helpers or fictional, good parents (Grimmer, 2013, p. 194 f.).
3. A helpful fictional interacting doppelganger enters the protagonist's play of the traumatizing situation and helps the patient to protect himself from disintegration through surplus reality. He banishes the perpetrator, creates a shelter, or helps the protagonist escape. In this way, he gives support to the protagonist's self. Integrating such a stabilizing experience into the trauma memory in the as-if mode of play differentiates and expands the capacity to cope with the trauma (Kellermann, 2000, p. 31). It helps the patient to reassure himself emotionally that his trauma has and is allowed to have great significance for him and that he is allowed to feel what he is feeling (Kellermann, 2000, p. 27 f.). The doppelganger technique has been part of the standard repertoire of therapy for people with trauma-related disorders in psychodrama *since Moreno*.

***Case example 42***

*A 26-year-old student, Ms. E., was traumatized by a hospital stay in her second year of life. She repeatedly shared with fear in group therapy: "I do not want to imagine that my mother or father will die one day. I can't even think about it!" The therapist offers the patient: "Would you like to tell your mother through a protagonist-centered play that you are terribly afraid of her death?" Ms. E. engages in a fictional psychodramatic dialogue with her 'mother'. In doing this, she steps into the role of the mother through role reversal and replies as the mother: "But I too will die at some point. That's the way it is!" This sentence triggers panic in Ms. E. again. At first, she understands her fear 'only' as panic about the inevitability of death.*

*The therapist: "What scares you most about your mother's statement?" Ms. E., in a low voice: "Then I'll be alone!" The therapist: "You are afraid of being alone!" Ms. E: "Yes!" The therapist wonders: "And it doesn't help you feel less scared if you think about your boyfriend and getting married soon!" Ms. E.: "No." The therapist: "Was there a time when you felt lonely as a child, and your mother and father were not available to you?" Ms. E. ponders: "Not really!" But then she remembers: "My mother once told me I had to be in the hospital for three weeks due to pneumonia when I was two years old. It was a matter of life and death for me. My mother said: 'When I visited you in the hospital, you always turned your face away from me and looked at the wall.' As a result, my mother felt very insecure. She no longer knew whether I even loved her as a child."*

*The adult student plays the story told by the mother. As a one-and-a-half-year-old girl, she is seriously ill 'in the hospital bed'. When the 'mother' visits, she turns away and turns her back on her. Two group members play the roles of the 'mother' and the 'father'. However, they spontaneously act differently than the mother in the original story. They speak to little Sabine and caress her back. They don't stop showing her their gentle love and affection. Until the end of the play, the protagonist lies motionless in her 'bed' with her face to the wall, without crying. After the play, the therapist asks the patient for role feedback. Ms. E. is happy and relieved: "That was so nice! Although I didn't turn around, I felt your love and affection as my parents! But the most important thing was: I noticed how much I love my mother. I love her a lot! My mother told me this story so differently. That's why I've always doubted whether I love her. But that's not true at all!" Tragically, the patient's mother fell ill with cancer six months later and died. But Ms. E could accompany her in a good way as she died without decompensating again because she was now sure that she had always loved her mother.*

4. The patient can also use *imaginative techniques* for self-stabilization. For example, he writes a fairy tale of coping (Krüger, 2013). Or he alleviates his nightmares with Imagery Rehearsal Therapy (Krakow, Kellner, Pathak, Lambert, 1995). Or he consciously develops a positive counter-image to his negative emotions (Reddemann, 1999, p. 90). I describe these techniques in Sect. 5.14.

## 5.10 Trauma Processing

### *5.10.1 Processing Trauma Experience Through Acting into a Coherent Story*

Usually, "when people absorb information [...], they automatically synthesize it [...] with their prior knowledge. If the event has personal significance, then they rewrite these feelings into a story without being aware of this process of rewriting [...]" (van der Kolk et al., 1998, p. 72). The story's logic and meaning then determine the significance of the individual elements of the story *for conflict resolution.* The unimportant elements can get lost in the neuronal interconnections of the memory. This saves memory space in the brain. The core pathology in people with trauma, however, is dissociating.

**Central idea**

Dissociating results in the trauma event remaining "stored in the form of isolated images, somatic sensations, smells, and sounds [...]. [...] Apparently, the integrative functions fail, such that the spatial and temporal allocation of incoming information is disturbed" (van der Kolk et al., 1998, p. 72). Traumatized people cannot synthesize their trauma memories with previous knowledge or categorize them and rewrite them in a personal story that integrates the memory fragments and gives them meaning in the larger context.

In the case of trauma, for example, *unfinished movements* are frozen in the body's memory. If the patient had stepped on the brakes before his car accident, the panic from back then resurfaces with the same leg movement in similar situations. Sometimes the affected person also experiences *intense feelings* but cannot remember the associated event. In the event of a trauma, the individual sensorimotor interaction pattern, physical sensations, and affect remain *unaltered* in memory as fragments.

The shock freezes one's conflict processing ability. The fragments are not integrated into a story. However, because of their high energy potential, they re-enter the present experience even with small triggers. The affected person then experiences the traumatizing event in the equivalence mode (see Sect. 2.6) as if it happened in the here and now. Naming linguistic terms and thinking is hardly or not at all available during a flashback. The language center in the left hemisphere is not or not sufficiently activated. The patient cannot understand his seemingly meaningless psychosomatic reaction. He is insecure and has doubts about himself. As a consequence, he secondarily suffers from masochistic low self-esteem and depression. The incoherent feelings and physical reactions make it difficult to cope with everyday life and trap one's energy. Therefore, *trauma processing* begins with patients narrating the trauma event repeatedly (Kellermann, 2000, p. 28). "A person must integrate the cognition, emotions, bodily experience, and actions of a traumatic experience for processing or synthesizing it" (Reddemann, 1997, p. 666).

**Central idea**

In trauma processing, the patient should further develop his trauma memory into a holistic trauma history. To do this, the patient must integrate his sensorimotor interaction patterns, physical sensations, and affect in his trauma experience with appropriate linguistic concepts, and thoughts (see Sect. 2.7) into a holistic psychosomatic resonance pattern and link this appropriately with other memories.

The indication for the type of trauma processing depends on the therapy goal. If a patient only remembers a few parts of his trauma story, the therapist can have the patient use the *screen or video* technique to develop the existing puzzle pieces into a coherent *fictional story*. In doing so, the patient takes on the role of his 'observing ego' and sees his 'acting ego' in action from outside 'on a screen in a film'. He thus integrates *all his memory fragments* into a subjectively coherent, holistic story. The story gives the individual memory fragments an appropriate meaning in a superordinate context. The feeling of meaninglessness disappears.

***Case example 43***

*A 48-year-old patient with bulimia (F50.2) kept talking about an event from when she was five years old. At the time, she had come home from shopping and was completely confused for three days. Her concerned parents asked her about it. As a five-year-old, she could only tell her parents something about a 'red car'. It was unclear what had happened to her then. The therapist made an appointment with the patient to develop the event into a coherent, holistic story. He sat down with the patient in front of a fictional screen. The therapist and the patient let the events from when the patient was five unfold in front of them as a film per the video technique. The patient held the remote control for the 'video player' in her hand and let the imaginary 'film' begin. She let it run forward or pressed rewind in some places. With the therapist's help, she determined what had happened back then: the five-year-old girl goes through the village on her way to the butcher. A red car stops next to her on the road. The driver is a middle-aged man. He offers to give her a lift to the city center. She doesn't want to go at first. But then she gets in hesitantly. The man doesn't stop the car at the butcher's. He drives her out of town on a country road. He pulls the girl out of the car and pushes her down onto the embankment. He strips in front of her and forces her to give him oral pleasure. He then threatens the girl: "Don't you dare tell anyone about this. If you do, I'll come and hurt you!" Then he drives away and leaves her stranded. The girl goes home completely distraught. The parents notice that something is amiss with the girl. They ask her very affectionately and treat her with care. But the girl can't tell the parents anything. According to the imaginary story, the perpetrator represents the vacuum cleaners. He drives away to a city 40 km away. He lives there as a family man with his wife and two children.*

In other patients with trauma-related disorders, talking and imagining alone is *not* enough.

**Central idea**

Van der Kolk et al. (1996, p.195) think: "With their propensity to act and their lack of words, these patients can often express their inner states more clearly through physical movements or images. Painting *and psychodrama* can help them develop a language essential for effective communication and the symbolization that occurs in psychotherapy."

Traumatized patients, in particular, affirm Moreno's sentence, which is otherwise only valid with restrictions (Krüger, 1997, p. 71): "Acting is more healing than talking" (Pörtner, 1972, quoted from Leutz, 1974, p. 145). For example, the patient Jill reports in the case example by Karp (2000, p. 77 f.): "In the hospital, I had two sessions per week, but it… was a recitation with more pills. The reality was not there. It was like telling a story, whereas, in psychodrama, you relive it.… In reliving it, you go through the emotions; otherwise, it's just like reading out of a book. It doesn't have the same impact.… But when you are re-enacting it, you have to be in control because you have to say: 'All right, if I had a choice, this is what I would have done'". Patient Maria in the case example by Roine (2000, p. 86) has similar views: "I… went to a psychologist for many years. I talked and talked but never got behind the words and into my feelings, not because I didn't want to, but because, as a child, I had learned well how to escape from my feelings and how to disappear inside myself to avoid facing reality".

### 5.10.2 The Four Functional Workspaces for Trauma Processing

According to van der Kolk (1995), it is the 'nature of trauma' to be dissociative. The dilemma in trauma therapy is that: trauma patients must go through dissociating to process their trauma. If the patient goes through dissociating, however, his conflict processing freezes.

**Central idea**

A patient experienced 'nothing new' during a two-hour psychodramatic re-enactment of the trauma event (see case example 14 in Sect. 2.12.2). This was because she dissociated and split off his sensorimotor interaction patterns, physical sensations, and affect. The usual psychodramatic re-enactment of a traumatic event is often not therapeutically sufficient.

Dissociation (see Sect. 5.4) is a dysfunctional metacognitive process involving four consecutive steps:

1. When a patient dissociates, he unconsciously *splits* his ego into *observing ego* and *acting ego*. He goes inwards into his observing ego, and functions externally at the level of words and thought, but stops the inner perception of his physical sensations and the panic in his acting ego. This creates the feeling of depersonalization. He then stands beside himself. He experiences everything as 'unreal' or 'like in a film'.
2. The patient stabilizes himself by *denying* his traumatic experience. He *pretends nothing has happened*: "What's in the past is past. I'm looking ahead!" In this way, he remains more or less able to act in his current life.
3. The patient stabilizes the denial of his traumatic experience with a *compensatory counter-fantasy* (Mentzos, 2011, p. 39). In the case of childhood trauma, this develops into compensatory reaction formation over time. For example, the patient gives meaning to his life by taking on a role as a helper or member of a sect-like community.
4. Reaction formation is secured by a precautionary or exaggerated *need for control* and by ideological rationalizations (see Sect. 4.7). Excessive control helps the patient avoid situations of helplessness that could trigger his flashback. For example, as a 40-year-old mother, a patient would control her eight- and twelve-year-old children with excessive anxiety and constraint. She herself was traumatized as a young political prisoner in Poland. Any *possible* danger to her children triggered a flashback in her. She couldn't bear to imagine that her children might be at the mercy of a threat.

**Central idea**

A traumatized patient, when dissociating, perceives his external world in the equivalence mode (see Sect. 2.6), as if the traumatizing situation from the past *was happening now*. He does *not* differentiate between the internal flashback and the present external reality. He is in a state of ego confusion.

**Recommendation**

In metacognitive trauma processing, the therapist represents the four steps of the dissociation process as different workspaces with chairs *externally* in the therapy room and names them (Krüger, 2002, p. 133 ff.). The patient thus perceives the four metacognitive workspaces in the as-if mode of play. He learns to represent them *internally* in the as-if mode of thinking and to distinguish between them consciously. The *defensive* dissociation is resolved by *the psychodramatic* re-enacting of the dissociation process.

The therapist takes the following steps in doing so:

1. The split between the acting and observing ego is realized by setting up a second chair for the '*traumatized ego*'. The patient then sits on the chair of his healthy adult thinking and looks at the second chair representing his "acting ego". The chair of the 'acting ego' symbolizes the *interaction space between himself as the victim and the perpetrator* (see Fig. 5.2).

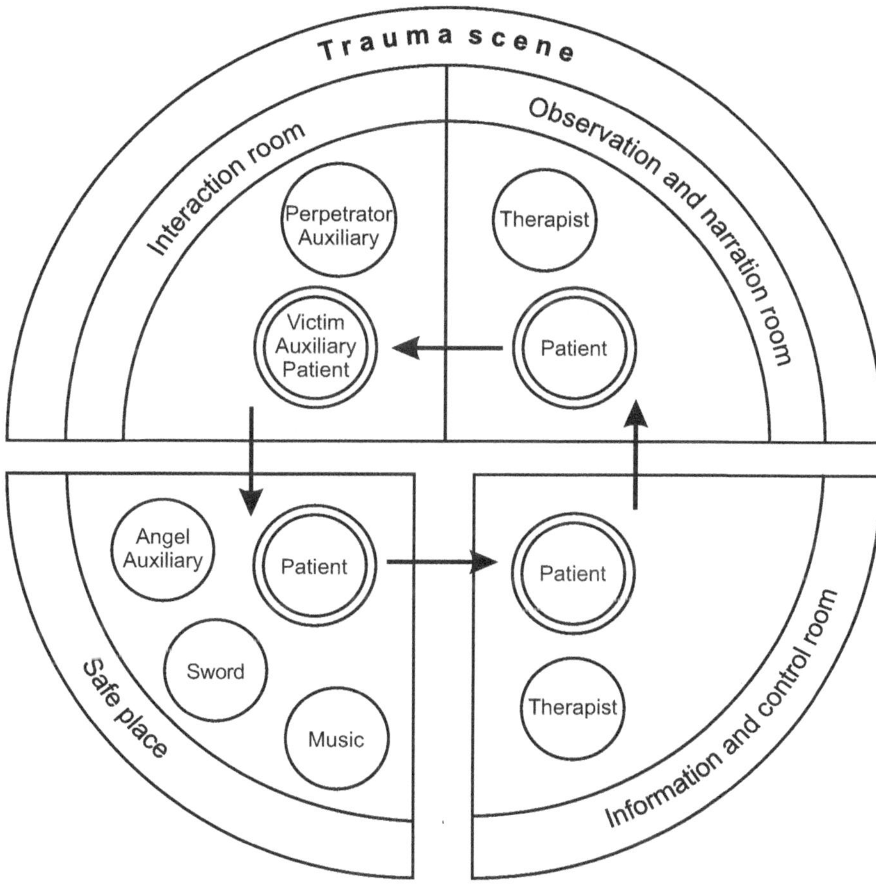


**Fig. 5.2** The four work rooms for disorder-specific psychodramatic trauma therapy

2. The chair for healthy adult thinking represents the patient's *observing ego* and the *narration and observation space*. The patient looks, from the observation room, at his 'acting ego' in the interaction space and sees himself as a 'victim' in interaction with the 'perpetrator'. In this way, he forms a relationship with his 'acting ego' and resolves his defense through denial. He no longer pretends as if nothing has happened.
3. In the case of childhood trauma, the therapist places the third chair next to the patient for *self-protection* through grandiosity, perfectionism, or adaption. This realizes the compensatory counter-fantasies and self-stabilization techniques spontaneously developed by the child to master his life. Together with the patient, the therapist records his distinct ways of denial and explicitly *names them* 'self-stabilization techniques'. In doing so, the patient develops ego control over his defense through denial. He learns to use his denial in the service of the ego. If

needed, the therapist supplements the patient's compensatory counter-fantasy, for example, by setting up the 'safe place' (see Sect. 5.10.5).

4. The therapist psychodramatically transforms the patient's need for control into an *information and control space*. The therapist and the patient define the terms 'traumatizing situation' and 'flashback' from the meta-position of his trauma scene (see Fig. 5.2). Traumatized patients had no opportunity to influence and change their traumatizing situation. The therapist, therefore, informs the patient in detail about her therapy plan. She asks for his consent on how to process the therapy, for example, how the traumatizing situation should be rewritten and completed in the re-enactment.

Psychologically healthy people are internally flexible and consistent in switching back and forth between these four inner metacognitive workspaces when processing their conflicts. In this way, they maintain coherence in their *internal* process of self-development in the *external* situation. However, when dissociating, traumatized people are stuck *in one* of the metacognitive processes and live it out in the equivalence mode. Therefore, during trauma processing, the therapist lets the patient move to the various *metacognitive* working spaces and re-enact them in the as-if mode. In doing so, the patient further differentiates each working process *in relation to the traumatizing situation* in the as-if mode of play. In doing so, the patient develops a *holistic* psychosomatic resonance pattern for his trauma event (see Fig. 2.9 in Sect. 2.8) and *gains ego control over his dissociation* during trauma processing.

**Exercise 15**

You can understand the meaning of the four workspaces of trauma therapy only when you psychosomatically act in them in the as-if mode of play. As an implicit doppelganger, accompany one of your traumatized patients in the as-if mode of play through the four different trauma therapy workspaces (see Fig. 5.2 above) in your therapy room: (1) To do this, divide your room into four work rooms with a rope, as shown in Fig. 5.2. (2) Place two empty chairs facing each other in the *interaction room*, one for the patient and one for their perpetrator or the traumatizing event. (3) Set up another chair for your patient in the *narration and observation room* with a view of their trauma event. (4) In the third quadrant of the circle, set up a chair for the patient's role in their *safe place.* (5) Then, sit down in the *information and control room.* Place a second chair in front of you. Imagine that your 'patient' is sitting across from you in that chair. Let your 'patient' move back and forth between these four work rooms in your imagination. What would your patient do in each of these rooms?

**Central idea**

The concept of the four work spaces gives the therapist support and orientation in her *practical* work with traumatized people. She notices in which 'work room' she is currently *present* with her patient. She realizes which therapeutic options she may have neglected *so far*.

The therapist can use the concept of four work rooms for trauma processing in *three different settings*: (1) in psychodramatic trauma processing *with the help of auxiliary therapists* in individual therapy (see Sect. 5.10.3), (2) in psychodramatic trauma processing with the help of the *table stage* in the individual therapy (see Sect. 5.10.10) and (3) in psychodramatic trauma processing *in group therapy* (see Sect. 5.10.11).

### *5.10.3 Trauma Processing with the Help of Auxiliary Therapists*

The psychodramatic trauma processing *with the help of auxiliary therapists* takes place *as follows*:

1. Traumatized patients, by definition, had no control over the traumatizing situation. They are, therefore, afraid of processing the trauma, even if they have decided to do so. Therefore, the therapist and the patient *collaborate* and plan the trauma processing approach step by step: Together, they choose *a specific trauma event*. They agree on what should and should not be done when processing the trauma. During the planning phase, the therapist informs the patient about the four work spaces for trauma processing. She defines the chairs on which they both sit as the 'information and control room'. She also sets up three other chairs on the stage, one for each of the three other work spaces. She moves with the patient from one work room to the other and explains how the patient can use the respective work room during trauma processing. Then the therapist and the patient sit back on the chairs in the information and control room.
2. In three to six individual sessions, the patient learns the self-stabilization techniques required for processing trauma in any situation, including the patient's 'safe place' (see Sect. 5.10.5).
3. The therapist and the patient determine what the patient needs when re-enacting the trauma situation so that what *did not* happen then *happens now* or what happened *then* does *not happen now*.
4. They plan the *timing* of the actual trauma exposure session and determine which auxiliary egos and objects will be required.
5. The therapist engages the necessary auxiliary therapists for the trauma exposure session.
6. The patient asks a trusted family member or a friend to accompany them home from the therapist's office after the trauma exposure session and to stay overnight in their apartment.
7. The trauma processing session with auxiliary therapists lasts two to four hours. There is no time limit for the end. The session takes place as follows:

    a. The patient and the auxiliary therapists get to know each other.
    b. The leading therapist divides the stage and, together with the patient, sets up the control room, the safe place, the observation and narration room, and the interaction room between the perpetrator and victim as planned.

c. The other players take on the roles assigned to them by the patient in these work rooms.
d. The patient and the therapist sit on two chairs in the narration and observation room. The patient narrates his memories *of the trauma situation* chronologically in individual sections. In doing so, the patient pauses at regular intervals so that the auxiliary therapists can enact the respective events.
e. The auxiliary therapists replay the individual sections of his trauma memory in the action room in the playback format. An auxiliary therapist takes on the role of the patient as a doppelganger.
f. Every now and then, the therapist lets the patient move from the narrative room to his 'safe place' to resolve any existing dissociating (see Sect. 5.10.5). She knows that as a therapist, one often *doesn't notice* that the patient is dissociating.
g. The patient should *himself* go into the action room of his trauma scene at least once. Sometimes just 20 s are enough for this. The patient takes on his own role *at the place and time* of his trauma experience and *acts* in his role. This helps him to connect his thoughts and linguistic concepts in the traumatizing situation with the split-off sensorimotor interaction patterns, physical sensations, and affect and thus resolve the dissociation. He *never* changes roles with the perpetrator (see Sect. 5.10.9).
h. In any case, the events in the trauma scene *should be expanded to include the patient's corrective fantasy*. As a result, the patient internally gains the ability to act in the traumatizing situation. The cave has an exit after all. The patient and the therapist have defined this together in the preparatory sessions.
i. At the end of the trauma exposure session, the patient goes to his 'safe place'. He stays there until he is entirely calm again.
j. During debriefing, those involved in the trauma processing session give role feedback and possibly a sharing. The therapist draws attention to *new insights* that the patient or the other players have gained during the trauma processing.

8. The patient is picked up by his caregiver. This person then accompanies him home as planned. The patient should feel safe on the way home and also have someone to talk to at night if necessary.
9. The patient and the therapist process the patient's *later reactions* to his trauma exposure session in two to three further individual sessions (see Sect. 5.10.8).

The process of trauma processing with auxiliary therapists requires 7 to 15 therapy sessions in total. Therapeutically, the *preparatory* sessions are just as important as the trauma exposure session.

### *5.10.4 The Information and Control Space*

People with trauma-related disorders are prone to assessing arousal stimuli *as a general threat* and reacting immediately with aggression or withdrawal, because of the neurophysiological changes in their brain processes and some hormonal changes (van der Kolk, 1998, p. 72). But careful planning of the trauma exposure session reduces the patient's level of anxiety. The therapist and the patient agree on, for example, how long the patient should take on his role in the interaction room of the trauma scene. *During the trauma processing session*, the therapist ensures that all the agreements made between her and the patient are fulfilled. Sixteen years after her successful psychodramatic trauma processing, the trauma survivor Jill in the case example by Karp (2000, p. 82), said: "Being in control was the key because when it happened, I was not in control of anything". Dayton (2000, p. 120) says: "Psychodrama can help an individual... gain mastery and control over their environment." Roine (2000, p. 94) experienced: "By constructing the traumatic events in psychodrama, the protagonist is encouraged to control the situation in a new manner." Burmeister (2000, p. 212) justifies his approach in trauma work with traffic victims in a similar way: "The protagonist should control and maintain empowerment over the re-exposure of the trauma as the main goal of this stage. Otherwise, retraumatization might rupture the therapeutic and healing effect of the work." During the trauma exposure session, if a patient moves from the information and control room to one of the other work rooms, the chairs remain where they are. This makes it easier for the patient and the therapist to return to the control room if necessary and to plan the *further* course of the session together.

**Recommendation**

"The director should make every effort to prepare for the session by explaining what will happen at each stage of the process and get the protagonist's consent to participate in each part of the work." (Kellermann, 2000, p. 35).

***Case example 44***

*A 35-year-old teacher was traumatized by being hospitalized when she was five years old. She had an emergency operation to remove her appendix. For a year before, her parents had interpreted her nocturnal abdominal pain only as a desire for attention. Her parents did not visit her in the hospital. The nurses forbade her to cry. They said, 'Otherwise, you can't go home.' The little girl had not been informed about what was going to happen to her. She, therefore, seriously believed that she 'had been sold'. When planning the trauma exposure session, the therapist and the patient agreed that a doppelganger and other auxiliary egos should act out her trauma memories.*

*However, the therapist and the patient agreed to change the trauma situation. A 'good mother' should stay with her throughout her hospital stay. A good mother should inform her of everything that is going to happen. She should comfort her, protect her, and check in with the doctor if necessary. In the* trauma *exposure session, the auxiliary therapists began by enacting the hospital scenes as the patient remembered them. A doppelganger took on the role of the patient. The patient herself took on her role in the action room of the trauma scene only in the planned desirable scene. After the play, the patient was astonished: "That's strange: I had thought that my wish that my mother would stay with me was completely exaggerated and unreal. But now I've noticed in the play: What I wanted is now standard practice in hospitals as rooming-in. Today it is normal for mothers to spend the night in the hospital with their children!"(Continued in* Sect. 5.11*). The patient's family had been dominated by a traumatized father. She was probably a 'difficult kid' after being hospitalized as a result of her own trauma. In identifying with the defenses of the family, she developed a masochistic self-censorship. Even as an adult, she automatically blocked the emergence of wishful thinking in herself (continued in* Sect. 5.11*).*

## *5.10.5 The Safe Place*

Traumatized people often *spontaneously* develop a compensatory counter-fantasy of a world in which the violence and horror of the trauma event do not exist. These counter-fantasies help them to get out of their dissociative states, feelings of powerlessness, confusion, or loss of a relationship. For example, neglected children often imagine that their parents are not their birth parents and that their birth parents will eventually come and take them home. This *makes it a little easier* for the children to endure violence or neglect from their *present* parents. Or they read books in which the good triumphs over the evil. Such counter-fantasies invalidate the perception of current reality (Wurmser, 1998, p. 425 f.). It enables those affected *to act* in their *internal* conflict processing. In psychodramatic trauma therapy, the patient realizes such a compensatory counter-fantasy with the help of the 'safe place' technique and sets it up *externally* in the therapy room.

**Important definition**

The safe place is a *fictional* fantasy room on the stage *or* in the inner imagination. It should provide *absolute* support and security to the process of self-development in the fictional situation. The patient should experience what he needs as a counter-image to his trauma experience. This place *should not be accessible* to the patient's real present or past caregivers because *real* caregivers from the present or the past always have a negative side. For example, they had limited power to change the trauma situation or because they died.

***Case example 45***

*Ms. D. was a middle-aged patient with post-traumatic stress disorder (F43.1). She suffered from severe sleep disorders, panic attacks with palpitations, and death fantasies. These symptoms were to be understood as flashbacks from the experience of an attempted rape twenty years ago. The perpetrator broke into her car at the time, pressed a knife to her neck, and verbally threatened to kill her. Before her trauma exposure session, the therapist works out, together with her, her 'safe place' on the stage. To do this, he separates an area in the group room with a rope: "This is the area for your safe place. Imagine a different world in this room where you feel safe and secure." The therapist and Ms. D. look for all the elements she needs in the* safe place. *In the end, Ms. D. installed a CD player in it. She can turn it on, and her favorite Kantate by Bach plays in the room. The patient also imagines a guardian angel there. The angel is supposed to cover her protectively with his wings when she flees to her 'safe place' during trauma processing.*

*Three weeks later, during trauma exposure, Ms. D. once again moves to this protected work room at the end of the session. An auxiliary therapist plays the role of the guardian angel and gives her a compassionate and protective hug. Ms. D. begins to twitch uncontrollably all over her body. Her twitching is gradually becoming more frequent and violent. Finally, she cries cathartically from the bottom of her soul. Her horror, frozen for over 20 years, dissolves in the process. It's like Easter when spring comes. The patient's self emerges out of the depth. (Continued in* Sects. 5.10.6, 5.10.7, 5.10.8, *and* 5.16*).*

When *traumatized* in *adulthood*, patients often choose a 'safe place' in nature *without human beings*. They make friends with animals and establish relationships with trees or streams. This place is only accessible to them through a magic word or a hand signal. In the case of *relationship trauma in childhood*, the 'safe place' should *also have a fictional figure or person* who gives the patient the needed support and security. The therapist takes the following steps in working together with the patient to develop their personal 'safe place':

1. She sits with the patient in the information and control room. She uses a rope to draw a boundary around the 'world of the safe place' and sets up an empty chair for the patient in this area: "This is a world in which you are absolutely safe and secure."
2. She asks the patient about a *painful past situation* where he would have needed safety and security.
3. Together with him, she senses his emotions in the difficult situation and names them: "You felt totally powerless" and "… totally abandoned". "You could no longer feel anything". "You stood next to you …".
4. Together with the patient, she looks for a *fictitious* situation that would *trigger the opposite emotions* in him: "In this other world, you feel absolutely safe and secure. You can feel something again, and you become yourself."
5. The therapist points to the separate room of the 'safe place': "There in the other part of the room is a place where you can find everything that you would have needed in this situation. What should happen in this other world so your wish can really come true? What all should be there?"
6. The therapist asks the patient: "Have you ever truly experienced *trust, support, and security* in your life?" She also asks about transpersonal experiences in nature, music or art, religion or love (see case examples 32, 40, 41, and 42).
7. The therapist lets the patient go in a separate room of the 'safe place'. But she *herself* remains standing on the border between the two worlds. She thereby attests through *action* to the *existential quality* of the 'safe place'. The 'safe place' should return to the patient his dignity as a person in his feelings, thoughts, and actions, and his physical and mental integrity.
8. Together with the patient, the therapist symbolizes, with objects, the experiences of security *he has already mentioned* (see 6.). The patient places these symbols in the 'safe place'.
9. In the second step, the therapist and the patient *add missing ele*ments to the construction of the 'safe place'. For example, they look for a person or a figure

from a fairy tale or from literature who would accept the patient as he is in his safe place and support him consistently. If auxiliary therapists or group members are present, they can take on the role of auxiliary egos in the safe place. For example, they play the role of a tree or a guardian angel.

10. The patient explores the situation in his 'safe place' in his own role in the as-if mode of play *by acting*. For example, he *hears* the imagined sea birds. He is able to *see* the sea and *smell* it. He *feels* the comforting or protective gesture of the wise old woman physically and mentally. In individual therapy, the therapist replaces the wise old woman's embrace by giving the patient a blanket 'to warm himself'.
11. The patient should *not* move into the counter-role of the supporting fictional figure or a living being in his 'safe place', not even to 'show how they should behave'. This could trigger a flashback or a pathological regression because the protagonist sees himself, from the role of the good fictional figure, as in a mirror with his neediness, absolute loneliness, or confusion. This triggers intense compassion in him and he may be overwhelmed by the victim's feelings in identifying with him. *In his own role*, however, the patient has control over the extent to which he allows his feelings to surface. He can lean against the person giving protection, 'just' sit next to them or simply walk away again.

**Central idea**

The patient regains access to his split-off sensorimotor interaction patterns, physical sensations, and the affect of his trauma experience *by acting* in his "safe place". Self-stabilization is a stabilization of inner self-development in an external situation that provides support.

12. Often patients are timid and modest in their wishes when building their 'safe place'. The therapist then feels the patient's pain and longing as a doppelganger *on his behalf*. In such a case, the therapist draws the patient's attention to the additional possibilities in the 'safe place': "Your safe place is a fantasy world. You can actually make your wishes come true in this fantasy world! You said the wise old woman comforts you. Does she really *just sit next to you* and listen to you? Or is she perhaps *caressing your back* as well?"
13. Sometimes the patients may masochistically feel guilty in response to their desires. The therapist symbolizes these with building blocks, if necessary, but places them *outside the 'safe place'* in the 'real world' separated by the rope. The 'safe place' should be where wishes are still helpful.
14. When the safe place is completely set up, the therapist prompts the patient: "Please walk around the room of your safe place again. Make contact *with each* of the existing elements. Feel yourself as you do it!"
15. The therapist asks the patient to return to the 'real world' by stepping over the rope.
16. She discusses with him his experience in his 'safe place'. Together with him, she also names what he physically felt and experienced in the 'safe place'.

17. She asks him: "In the next two hours, please write down everything that belongs to your safe place and what happens there. Otherwise, you might forget important elements or actions".
18. She recommends to the patient: "Visualize the experience of your safe place at home in your mind. Or play out the encounters from your safe place at home in your living room, just as you *acted* here in therapy. You are allowed to beautify and positively expand the events in the safe place. Practice the safe place technique as a self-stabilization technique at home! Use the technique when dissociating." The diverse actions and perceptions produced in the external 'safe place' *in the as-if mode of play* activate the experience of security and safety *even at the sensorimotor level.*

**Recommendation**

If you want to develop a 'safe place' with a patient, photocopy the following list of elements of a 'safe place' beforehand. You can then use this list as a guide *during* your work.

1. Elements that stabilize *the inner self-image* in the patient's inner thinking:
   a. The therapist specifies the patient's *positive abilities and strengths* individually with stones or wooden blocks and places them in a corner of the safe place on the floor. Many patients struggle to ascribe *positive* abilities to themselves. In such a case, the therapist asks: "What does your friend, daughter, or colleague like about you?" The patient sits in the safe place on the floor during this work. He takes every one of his 'abilities' in hand and actively assures himself of this ability. This self-stabilization technique *is a resource work*. It can also be practiced as an independent self-stabilizing technique without the 'safe place' technique.
   b. If necessary, the patient represents his own *healthy inner child*, which he may have been *before* his trauma, in his 'safe place' with the help of an auxiliary therapist or a puppet. He interacts with him in the as-if mode of play and forms a relationship with him.
   c. Some patients have discovered the ability to stabilize themselves through manual or artistic activities. In doing so, they experience themselves as self-effective and creative. In such a case, the patient should also place the appropriate tool, for example, the saw, the violin, or the painting board, in his 'safe place', thereby giving his self-efficacy some space in his soul.

**Case example 46**

*A 52-year-old patient remembers his ability to develop new solutions in model airplane construction while developing his 'safe place'. He brings one of his model airplanes with him for his psychodramatic trauma exposure session and a television with a video recording of his model airplane flying. Furthermore, the therapist and the patient seek a memory symbolizing a feeling of absolute security. The patient remembers: As a four-year-old, he sat on the steps of his parent's house and listened to the 'competition' between two church bells: "One was much more melodic, and it always won in the end. It was also slower, but it rang longer than the others." The patient smiles at this memory, relieved: "I used to remember that a lot in the past. But I haven't thought about it for three years until now". Three weeks later, the patient brings a tape recording of the church bells from his childhood for the session of his trauma exposure. The week before, he had gone to his hometown, 200 km away. He recorded the ringing of the church bells that are still there with his tape recorder: "I tried that first at 10 o'clock in the morning. But there were too many cars that disturbed the ringing. I then waited an hour. I could successfully finish recording at 11 o'clock" (Continued in* Sect. 5.10.8*).*

2. Fictional persons, living beings, and symbols that give the patient *support as a relational object* in his safe place:

   a. These can be *transpersonal roles* from nature, trees, forests, or rivers. Or figures from religion, for example, a guardian angel. Or a figure from literature, mythological stories, or fairy tales, such as the seven dwarfs from 'Snow White' or the magician Gandalf. Or people from a movie, Master Yoda or E.T., or symbolic people from history, Martin Luther King, Gandhi, or similar.
   b. The patient can also record a piece of *music* he loves on a DVD. He can then let it play on repeat in his 'safe place' (see case example 45 above).
   c. In the 'safe place', '*animals*' can wait for the patient. These help him, just like the doves in the fairy tale of Cinderella or the seven animals in the grim fairy tale of 'Two Brothers'.
   d. The patient can place a fictional *wise old woman* or a wise old man on a chair in the 'safe place'. Or he can represent his role model there: This person should have survived a similar emotional trauma. But they have processed their fate well and become wise as a result.
   e. The patient can free himself from his flashback in a sensorimotor way by dancing to his music or engaging in other *physical activities* in his 'safe place'.

3. Elements that represent a *healing, existential experience* of the patient: Some patients have had a profound healing experience in art, nature, religion, or love. The therapist lets the patient symbolize such an experience with an object or an auxiliary ego in the safe place. For example, this can be a tree, a forest, a river, or a guardian angel.

The therapist helps the patient *shoulder to shoulder as an implicit* doppelganger in developing his 'safe place'. She is also allowed to express *her own* ideas in the process. The therapist's proposals do not seem directive when expressed *shoulder to shoulder*. Instead, they open up the potential space for the patient's imagination. They activate his mentalization and stimulate him to find *his own* ideas for his 'safe place'. The 'safe place' technique presented here includes *several* self-stabilization techniques.

**Central idea**

Some patients find it difficult to develop their 'safe place' because of their masochistic self-censorship. This technique is *particularly beneficial for those patients*. But, the therapist takes very small steps. *Disorder-specific* trauma therapy is *patient work in the right place*.

**Recommendation**

Participants *in group therapy or an advanced psychodrama training group* should each develop their own 'safe place'. Thus, disorder-specific trauma processing is possible in a group (see Sect. 5.10.11).

## *5.10.6 The Observation and Narration Room*

In the case of *unprocessed* trauma, the original coping through dissociating solidifies "more and more into symptoms. [...] The life-saving function of dissociation becomes the symptom of dissociative disorder. Since the organism has tried to heal itself with these coping strategies, we assume that these coping strategies are useful" (Reddemann, 1999, p. 89). The disorder-specific psychodramatic *trauma processing* helps the patient to dissolve *the split between* the cognitive and the psychosomatic process of conflict processing by *acting in the as-if mode of play* (see Sect. 2.6) and to bring it under the control of his ego (see Sect. 5.10.2).

During trauma processing, the patient thinks and talks *predominantly* in the narrative and observation room and tells his trauma story from there. The external distance helps the patient also gain an internal distance from the trauma scene. A doppelganger and the auxiliary therapists re-enact individual interactions from the patient's traumatic history in the *interaction room* using the playback method. The patient usually goes into the interaction room of the trauma scene just once for a short time. The patient perceives himself from a meta-perspective and gives instructions to the playback actors. Karp (2000, p. 79) reports about her patient Jill: "The distance provided safety. The protagonist instructed and watched group members play out her scenes, occasionally entering the scene to correct the action. For example, ...because a broken bottle held to her neck, ... was held in the wrong place.... It had to be represented exactly as it happened and with her in control of the information." The *meta-position* helps the patient develop self-empathy for her traumatized acting ego.

*Acutely traumatized patients* should narrate their trauma story from the narration and observation room, and direct the interactions of their auxiliary therapists from there. The goal is that they "... see what had happened... without becoming overwhelmed... and... start to process the perceived information cognitively... Such cognitive re-processing of traumatic events... enables traumatized people to make sense of a world that has momentarily lost structure and meaning" (Kellermann, 2000, p. 29; Karp 2000, p. 68 ff.). For example, an acutely traumatized patient had witnessed a terrorist bomb attack with many fatalities (Kellermann, 2000, p. 29). He came to the therapist in a dissociative state of consciousness. He complained: "Everything seems so unreal as if I am in a dream or a movie." He had split off his emotions and sensorimotor experience and was acting from his observing ego (see Sect. 5.10.2). The therapist set up a chair next to him for his observing ego. He let the patient change roles from his acting ego into the role of his observing ego. The patient then narrated his trauma story from that role. A doppelganger and some auxiliaries re-enacted his trauma story *on his behalf* in the interaction room. In this way, the patient connected his cognitions to his split-off emotions. He dissolved his dissociative state of derealization by crying cathartically.

During trauma processing, the therapist sits or stands *shoulder to shoulder* as an implicit doppelganger (see Sect. 2.5) next to the patient in the observation room. Together with him, she looks at the interaction room of the trauma scene and, *as a doppelganger*, helps him to name things appropriately. For example, she describes violence in the trauma scene as 'violence' and abuse as 'abuse'. Collaboratively naming and thinking about his trauma experience activates and expands the patient's *cognition*. In this way, the patient *integrates* forgotten or denied interaction sequences (see Sect. 2.4.2) into his trauma memory. He captures the cause and effects and further develops his traumatic experience into a *coherent* story.

**Central idea**

Trauma patients often falsify the logic in their trauma memories *retrospectively* through masochistic self-censorship (see Sect. 8.5) and *forget* their own brave actions in the traumatizing situation. However, the auxiliary therapists replay the trauma story step by step during trauma processing. This helps the patient, looking at this process from the meta-perspective, to reveal contradictions between his *remembered actions* and his subsequent *interpretation* of these actions.

In the case example by Karp (2000, p. 63 ff.), patient Jill *knew cognitively, even before* the trauma exposure session, that her daughter and husband had *actually* survived the attack and rape in Africa because the family was living together again in England. Despite this fact, she could also *really feel this* only after the psychodramatic trauma processing. The patient in case example 40 (see Sect. 5.9) reported two years after his trauma processing session: "Before the trauma processing session, I always felt and thought: 'I am wrong' and 'You didn't manage anything'. In the trauma processing session, I learned how smart and clever I actually was as a child. The little boy in me is precious!" Because of her mental paralysis *in her nightmares*, the patient in case example 45 believed *wrongly* that she had not resisted the rape attempt.

***Case example 45 (1st continuation, see* Sect. 5.10.5*)***

*During the trauma exposure, Ms. D. narrates the story of the attempted rape from the observation room. She reports what she did as the victim and what the perpetrator said and did. As the victim, she tried to move the rapist's knife away from her neck and grabbed the sharp edge in the process. She wrestled with the perpetrator for a long time and suffered cuts on her neck and hands. The auxiliary therapist, who takes on the role of the patient as a doppelganger, re-enacts the described interaction sequence in the action room. In this case, the perpetrator is represented only by a chair. The doppelganger defends herself in the role of the patient on stage, just as the patient had reported in the narrative room. She screams for help in fear of death. Her scream is so loud that everyone involved feels the fear of death.*

*At this time, the therapist stands shoulder to shoulder next to the patient in the observation room and actively verbalizes what he sees as a doppelganger: "You fought! And how! You fought and wrestled with the man for three-quarters of an hour and even grabbed the knife! Where did you get so much strength from!" During the debriefing, Ms. D. said in astonishment: "I didn't remember that I fought so hard because I am always completely frozen in my nightmares and cannot defend myself!" She continues to share that after 45 min of fighting with the perpetrator, she was so exhausted sitting in the car seat behind the wheel that she stopped resisting: "I then asked him: 'What should I do? What is going to happen now?'" The therapist interprets even this behavior of the patient as quite courageous and appropriate: "When you couldn't go on, you still didn't give up. You kept looking for a solution!".*

*Eight weeks after the trauma processing, the patient stated: "I had always thought that the perpetrator could do whatever he wanted with me, that I was a plaything for him. Now I know that I fought back. I was, in fact, brave and courageous! I am now aware of this at night too. I can defend myself! Feeling paralyzed was the worst!" By re-enacting it in the play the patient expanded her memory into a holistic psychosomatic experience and re-established a relationship with her creative ego. That made her even more courageous in her everyday life: "I have finally opened up and told a long-time friend that his presumptuous overconfidence bothers me. But after the phone call, I wasn't feeling well at all. I have to be careful not to overreact" (continued in Sects. 5.10.7, 5.10.8 and 5.16).*

## *5.10.7 The Interaction Room Between the Victim and the Perpetrator*

In my experience, many psychodramatists are willing to be part of a trauma processing session as a doppelganger and an auxiliary for a low hourly wage because they are often fascinated by the existential dimension of work. *Before the actual trauma processing session*, the therapist takes the patient's consent and shares the trauma story with the auxiliary therapists. Together with them, she decides which of the usual complex roles they will enact.

**Recommendation**

Trauma processing is like *collaborative* white water rafting. One cannot get out of the boat while canoeing in white water. When processing trauma, everyone involved must go *through the heart* of the trauma together with the patient. If the therapist avoids this, the patient intuitively feels that *even the therapist cannot* endure the horror of his traumatic experience. This confirms his conviction that he is 'a burden' on the world. Therefore, trauma processing requires the therapist to make a clear decision on whether she wants to go white water rafting with her patient.

**Central idea**

By definition, trauma *processing* results in the patient dissociating. Therapists often do not notice this because the patient is able to *talk* about his trauma *cognitively*. Therefore, in debriefing, the patient can honestly say (see case example 14 in Sect. 2.12.2): "That was not new for me. I already knew all that." Only the therapist feels the threat and horror of the patient's trauma experience vicariously. Trauma processing requires the patient to dissociate *and then resolve* his dissociation through immediate self-stabilization. Because otherwise, the split between the cognitive and psychosomatic memories does not resolve. For this purpose, the patient must *appropriately* switch back and forth between the four work rooms of self-development in trauma therapy (see Fig. 5.2 in Sect. 5.10.2).

During trauma processing, the patient enters the interaction space of the trauma scene at least once for twenty seconds. In doing this, he does not necessarily have *to meet the 'perpetrator'* in the trauma scene. For example, Karp (2000, p. 71 f.) only asked her patient Jill to psychodramatically enter the spatially separated *space* of her experience of violence *when* her family members *had all been saved* in the re-enacted trauma story. The 'violent perpetrators' had already left the place of attack and rape. In the play, she was supposed to 'only say goodbye to her servants before moving from the African city to England'. 'Protected by the safe environment of the group', the protagonist entered the action room of her trauma scene. She immediately started trembling. All her emotions pent up for years discharged into an hour-long cathartic cry. The patient then slept for thirty hours without a break. She had previously suffered from severe insomnia for years.

***Case example 45 (3rd continuation, see* Sects. *5.10.5 and 5.10.6)***

*Ms. D.'s trauma was processed more than twenty years after the attempted rape. When telling her trauma story in the narration and observation room, Ms. D. had not yet entered into the affective and sensorimotor experience of her trauma memory. Even in this case, the therapist let the patient change into her role in the action room of the* trauma *scene when 'the perpetrator' had already fled. Soon after taking a few steps into the action room of the trauma scene, Ms. D. noticed that she was beginning to panic. Nevertheless, she took a seat in her 'car', represented by two chairs, in which the rape attempt occurred. At that moment, she was 'dizzy'. Her heart started racing, and she was gripped by an intense fear of death, much like in her nightmares. The therapist immediately asked the patient to return to her 'safe place'. There the 'guardian angel' held her in his arms. An auxiliary therapist played this role. Her favorite music, a special Bach cantata, played in the background. Ms. D's twenty years long pent-up emotions dissolved into an intensive integrative catharsis.*

*In the following weeks, her panic and the subsequent cathartic state repeated three more times when she was home. However, this time 'she knew that unlike before, things would end well'. The flashbacks that had tormented the patient every night for twenty years had disappeared for eight weeks. They then came back for a few days. Appropriate processing of the conflicts that had triggered the flashback ended this 'relapse' immediately. (Continued in* Sects. 5.10.7, 5.10.8 *and* 5.16*).*

**Central idea**

When one remembers a traumatic experience, the associated emotions, actions, and sensations remain disconnected due to the dissociation that sets in. As dissociation prevents all access to one's self-awareness and emotions, the corresponding information is stored as *expert knowledge* in the left hemisphere and not integrated into the right-brain procedural memory and the autobiographical-episodic or context-related memory (Markowitsch, 2001, pp. 75, 84 f.). Without *trauma processing*, the gaps in trauma memory often exist for the long term. These gaps are eventually filled with self-destructive assumptions to make sense of the fragmented experience.

### *5.10.8 Processing the Reaction to the Trauma Processing Session*

The therapist continues to support the patient for at least eight weeks *after his trauma exposure session*. She helps him to process the new experiences and integrate them into his self-image. In this way, she prevents the risk of the patient inappropriately questioning his new experiences during the trauma exposure session in the event of a new flashback.

***Case example 45 (4th continuation, see* Sects. 5.10.5, 5.10.6, *and* 5.10.7*)***
*One week after her trauma processing session, Ms. D. considered ending the therapy: "I feel like I'm in heaven, and I want to preserve this feeling". As a result, she was all the more shocked when her flashbacks reappeared at night eight weeks after the trauma exposure. These were triggered by a trip with friends with overnight stays out of the house. Ms. D. felt like a failure. The therapist worked with her to find the cause: the patient had told her friends about her trauma processing session. Her friends were quite inquisitive. But they could not really appreciate the existential depth of the patient's experience. Their superficial reaction made the patient feel different from others again. She felt marked by an adverse fate and feared she would stay that way forever.*

*The patient had to learn that the existential dimension of her experience truly made her a unique personality in a positive sense. The therapist: "You mustn't overwhelm other people! Your girlfriends did not experience your trauma processing. In my experience, only 10–20% of people have had similar existential experiences as you did when you came to terms with your trauma. Only one in five people can understand what you are talking about! Other people are unable to feel the existential dimension of such an experience. In the future, please check whether the person you share your experience with only reacts superficially or really understands you!" The patient's flashbacks disappeared after this clarification.*

*On the advice of the therapist, Ms. D. also symbolized her successful trauma processing concretely. She found a small, pretty box and placed in it a symbol of the precious experience of the trauma exposure session. She tied this box with a woolen ribbon and placed it on her desk: "Before the trauma session, I felt very alone. I don't usually have that feeling anymore, although I notice that I'm getting lonelier"(continuation in* Sect. 5.16*).*

**Central idea**

Trauma survivors live with the scar of Harry Potter on their foreheads all their lives. Successful trauma processing is both a win and a burden. It often leads to *post-traumatic growth*. However, because of the *hidden transpersonal* truth, a part of the survivor's soul feels alienated, and they also alienate other people.

Sometimes, in the case of childhood trauma, the patient is so firmly fixed in his defense that individual fragments of the trauma memory only surface *a few days after* the trauma processing session. It is then important to *recognize them as elements of the trauma experience* and to actively link them to the patient's trauma story.

***Case example 46 (1st continuation, see* Sect. 5.10.5*)***
*40-year-old Mr. B. suffered from dysthymia (F34.1), migraines, and narcissistic personality disorder (F60.8). His trauma exposure session lasted three hours. His trauma memory was about the surgical excision of an eye because of suspected cancer when he was five years old. As a grown man, the patient was still convinced that the operation had been 'performed without anesthesia'. After the trauma exposure session, Mr. B. doubted whether the intensive work had helped him in any way because he did not get the expected cathartic reaction.*

*However, three days after the trauma processing session, the patient had anxiety attacks when relaxing at home. His attacks suddenly shot up 'from the back and constricted his neck' for a minute each time. The therapist had the patient re-enact one of his anxiety attacks psychodramatically. In doing so, he asked the patient to think of a symbolic image that would go well with his feelings of fear. Mr. B. imagined a long hallway in a hospital. He is alone. He is five years old. The walls on the right and left are bare. The corridor is covered with a beige linoleum floor. The hallway is dark, and one can only see a light window at the end of the hallway. As a child, he feels lost, helpless, and alone. He doesn't know what happened to him or what might still be planned for him. The therapist then interpreted the patient's anxiety attacks as flashbacks. This connection between his anxiety attacks and his childhood trauma experience liberated the patient from self-doubt. In the following therapy session, he reported: "I have started cleaning up my neglected apartment. It looked just like me inside." The patient appeared alive and optimistic for the first time in months. He wasn't depressed anymore.*

**Recommendation**

Psychodrama therapists should participate in a patient's trauma processing session *as auxiliary therapists at least once*. The playful use of the four work spaces for psychodramatic trauma processing (see Fig. 5.2 in Sect. 5.10.2) improves one's intuitive sense of dissociation in traumatized people. In addition, the internal imagination of the four involved work spaces makes it easier *not* to get caught up in countertransference reactions in practical work.

### *5.10.9 The Contraindication of Reversing Roles with the Perpetrator*

None of the nineteen authors of the book 'Psychodrama with Trauma Survivors' (Kellermann and Hudgins, 2000) wrote about a role reversal with a perpetrator *in any of their forty case studies*. Many psychodrama therapists even consider the role reversal with the perpetrator to be explicitly *contraindicated* (Burmeister, 2000, p. 213; Kellermann, 2000, p. 37; Pruckner, 2002, p. 106 f.). There are two reasons for this:

1. The direct encounter with the perpetrator in a play is, *by definition, equivalent to trauma exposure*. It makes the patient dissociate. Often the therapist doesn't really notice it. The patient splits off his sensorimotor interaction patterns, physical sensations, and affect from his perception and is mentally absent in the play (see case example 14 in Sect. 2.12.2).
2. Trauma patients often misunderstand the therapist's instruction to reverse roles with the perpetrator as a subtle message. They interpret it as they should learn to understand and accept the perpetrator's motives (Kellermann, 2000, p. 37). However, this increases their auto aggression, their shame, as well as their feelings of guilt.

Some of the authors of the book 'Psychodrama with Trauma Survivors' (Burge, 2000, p. 307; Karp, 2000, p. 70; Leutz, 2000, p. 190, 195; Roine, 2000, p. 95f.), fall into the diffusion trap in their theoretical considerations (see Sect. 2.14) and, still consider role reversal to be an 'important technique' in working with traumatized people. Burge (2000, p. 307), for example, hypothesizes that reversing roles with the perpetrator allows a protagonist to regain access to his *own* anger because, in doing so, he experiences *the perpetrator's* sadism and anger physically and mentally. However, his assumption is *a theoretical assertion that cannot be proven in practice* (see Sect. 8.4). Burge did *not* use *role reversal with the perpetrator* in his case examples. He did not even let the respective 'perpetrator' appear in the two plays *he described*. Karp and Leutz do not describe the role reversal *with the perpetrator*, but 'only' *with a third person present in the trauma event*, a fellow victim. Roine (2000, p. 95 f.) also, *in theory*, hypothesizes that traumatized people with a small repertoire of roles "experience an augmented reality when they reverse roles with the perpetrator and are better able to reclaim their own authentic selves". However, this theoretical assumption is misleading. In doing so, the patient succeeds only in relationships with *authoritarian attachment figures*, and not in the relationship *with a real perpetrator*. In these cases, the patient gains access to his self because he *resolves his defense through identification with the aggressor* through role reversal (see Sect. 2.4.3).

Lesemann (1993, pp. 83, 95) is the only author I know who describes the role reversal with the perpetrator *in his own case study*. He completed a long, overall successful therapy process under supervision. The supervisor advised him that it was necessary to reverse roles with the perpetrator 'to bring the therapy process to an end *successfully*'. Lesemann tried to put this suggestion into practice twice. His traumatized patient entered the interaction room of the trauma scene during the first attempt to meet her perpetrator but immediately stopped the play and ran in panic out of the group room into the hallway. A few weeks later, during the second attempt, she obediently followed the therapist's instructions and reversed roles with her 'perpetrator'. However, if you read Lesemann's article carefully, it becomes apparent that the role reversal *did not have any additional positive therapeutic effect* on the patient. Fortunately, it didn't harm the patient either.

### 5.10.10 *Trauma Processing Using the Table Stage in Individual Therapy*

In individual therapy, the therapist uses the table stage to process trauma. Auxiliary therapists are not involved as doppelgangers and auxiliaries. *After* the trauma-specific diagnosis and crisis intervention, the traumatized patient first learns the necessary self-stabilization techniques (see Sects. 5.7 and 5.9). In doing this, the patient should also develop their own 'safe place'. Thereafter, the therapist and the patient plan the actual trauma processing with all the associated steps. The therapist informs the patient about the four work rooms for trauma processing by externally symbolizing them in the therapy room. Together, the therapist and the patient determine how the events in the trauma processing session should go on in time. They work out what the patient *would have needed in the traumatizing situation* and what *shouldn't* have happened. During trauma processing, the patient should sit on his chair in the narration and observation room and tell his trauma story. As a doppelganger, the therapist enacts all that the patient shares, *on his behalf,* with stones and wooden blocks using the playback method on the table stage (see Sect. 5.7).

**Recommendation**

When processing trauma with the table stage, the therapist always limits the work to *only one traumatic event in a session.* This reduces the risk of pathological regression for the patient. The patient can process *other* traumatic events in *other* sessions.

In the actual trauma processing session, the therapist lets the patient move back and forth between the different workrooms, just like when working with auxiliary therapists (see Sect. 5.10.3–5.10.8). Together, they perform the following steps:

1. In the beginning, the patient sets up his 'safe place' *on the room stage,* three meters away from the table stage.
2. The therapist places two empty chairs beside each other, far from the table. They represent the 'narration and observation room'. The first chair is for the patient as the narrator of his story (Fuhr, 1995, only orally communicated) and symbolizes his 'observing ego'. The second chair is a chair for the therapist as an implicit doppelganger: "This is me as a therapist. I will help you tell your story from this position".
3. The interaction room of the trauma memory is located on the table. The therapist sits at the table and places an 'ego stone' on it for the patient. The patient sits in his chair in the narrative room three meters away. The therapist asks him: "Can you see *the stone on the table* from there? This stone represents *your 'ego' in the traumatic situation*".
4. The therapist stands up and sits shoulder-to-shoulder *next to the patient in the narrative room.* She asks, "How do you feel when you look at yourself there on the table? Please, have a soliloquy here *in the observer position*!"
5. The therapist: "'When I see what was going on in your school from here, I see the nine-year-old Rolf, who …' Please narrate your trauma story in the third person and not in the first person!" The patient talks to the therapist about 'little

Rolf who …', about 'the man who …', 'the child who …', 'the little girl who …' or 'the woman who …'. "This helps the patient *and* the therapist to distance themselves internally from the pull of the trauma experience.

6. The patient talks about who was *present* in the traumatizing situation from his chair in the observation room.
7. The therapist sits down at the table again. She represents the elements of his trauma story *on the table* with stones, wooden blocks, or even small dolls: (1) the patient's acting ego, (2) his feelings, (3) the people involved, and (4) the important objects.
8. Together, the therapist and the patient should go through the heart of the patient's trauma memory. Therefore, the therapist asks him: "What was *the worst feeling* for you in the traumatizing situation?"

**Central idea**

Therapists often misjudge the worst part of the patient's experience of the traumatizing situation. For example, they believe that when a patient was hit in childhood, *the pain* was the worst experience for the patient. However, the patient may respond: "It was the feeling of *humiliation and shame*." This is because, as a child, the patient would sometimes dissociate and thus, didn't feel any physical pain.

9. While sitting on his chair three meters away, the patient narrates from the beginning to the end step by step what happened to the little boy in the traumatizing situation, as well as what he felt, thought, and did in the situation at the time.
10. As a doppelganger and an auxiliary, the therapist replays the interactive events in the traumatizing situation with empathy and fantasy using the symbols on the table. She acts as if she is *playing with a doll's house*.
11. As a doppelganger, she expresses what the little boy on the table in the trauma scene *feels and senses physically*. She screams and cries on his behalf.
12. The therapist occasionally *interrupts her play* on the table stage and goes to the patient in the narration room. From there, *she and the patient together* look at the table stage shoulder to shoulder. As a doppelganger, she names and comments on what is going on at the table stage from the observer position: "This is violence! This is why we have programs for violence prevention in schools *today*." "This is nasty and devious."
13. Time and again, the patient moves to his 'safe place' in the therapy room to resolve a possible dissociation.

**Central idea**

The therapist often *cannot* perceive that the patient is dissociating. Therefore, she *follows not only her intuition but also her experience* when she asks the patient to go to his 'safe place'.

14. The patient should go to the table stage at least once and touch the *stone representing his 'acting self' in the trauma scene* on the table stage. In this role, he soliloquizes with the help of the therapist. The therapist asks him about the worst feeling in his trauma event and, as a doppelganger helps him to name it: "You feel betrayed", "humiliated", and "as if you are nothing".

15. But, after a short time, the therapist lets the patient move back to the 'safe place' set up in the room. He should be able to rest there and resolve any possible dissociation.
16. The therapist creates the desired coping scene on the table stage. In doing so, she follows the *previously* agreed plan. She represents *the helpers and rescuers* with stones or wooden blocks on the table and plays these roles on the patient's behalf thereby changing the traumatizing scene as desired.
17. As an interacting doppelganger of the patient, she follows her own creative impulses in playing on the table stage. In the role of the patient, she mentalizes the patient's feelings on his behalf. In the other roles, she yells and scares the 'perpetrator'. She plays out the *positively changed* interaction sequences of the trauma scene and exaggerates a little bit. She repeatedly asks the patient: "Is that okay for you? Or is it too much?"
18. In the positively changed trauma scene, the patient sits down at the table stage for the second time. He touches his ego stone and plays out the interactions in the coping scene together with the therapist. He experiences the positive *outcome* of his trauma story closely in the role of his acting ego. In doing this, he links his thinking and talking with his split-off sensorimotor interaction patterns, physical sensations, and affect in his trauma memory.
19. *After* enacting the coping scene together, the patient once again goes back to his 'safe place' to relax completely.
20. The joint debriefing follows.

***Case example 47***
*Other children repeatedly beat up Mrs. D. as a child in school. The therapist re-enacts, on the patient's behalf, the hurtful incident from school with stones and wooden blocks on the table stage: The girl is eight years old. Other students tease and beat her. When planning the trauma processing, the patient had wished that two elderly students would come and defend her in the desired scene. The therapist lays out the stones for the older students in the desired scene on the table stage. The two older 'students' protect the 'girl' so that what had happened does not happen again, and what did not happen does happen now.*

Trauma processing on the room stage *with auxiliary therapists* is time-consuming and, therefore, indicated in the case of a *single severe* trauma experience in a specific place at a specific time. Trauma processing with the help of the *table stage* is recommended for people who have suffered long-term sexual, physical, or narcissistic abuse. The therapist lets the patient process two or three of their traumatic memories using the table stage, including their worst experience, too.

## *5.10.11 Trauma Processing in Group Therapy*

Participants in therapy groups, self-awareness groups, or training groups often *unexpectedly* play out one's own trauma experiences when they act out childhood scenes.

But in doing this, the protagonists often dissociate, making the protagonist-centered play therapeutically useless (see case example 14 in Sect. 2.12.2).

**Central idea**

Traumatized people are world champions in 'pretending as if nothing happened'. The therapist often does not notice when the patient is dissociating because the patient does not notice it *himself* and functions perfectly on the outside.

All members in psychodrama groups should develop their own personal 'safe place' early on. The leader can help a single participant define his 'safe place' *in the group* (see Sect. 5.10.5). The other participants think of a 'safe place' *for themselves at home*. In the following session, they present their results *to the group* and add missing elements to their 'safe place' if necessary.

If a traumatizing situation occurs *unexpectedly* in a protagonist-centered play, the therapist proceeds similarly to individual therapy with auxiliary therapists (see Sects. 5.10.3–5.10.8 and Fig. 5.2 in Sect. 5.10.2), but only in one group session.

## 5.11 Integrating Inner Change into Everyday Relationships

People with trauma-related disorders are psychologically injured and often behave differently from other people in everyday life. They feel ashamed, introject (see Sect. 2.4.1) the criticism of their attachment figures, and masochistically use it against themselves. They often struggle with understanding their otherness. They, therefore, readily accept the way in which *significant others* interpret their behavior. For instance, the patient in case example 32 (see Sects. 5.1, 5.5 and 5.9) identified with his parents' norms and values after an eight-month stay in the children's clinic. His parents were only concerned with achievement and success in life. Thus, the patient learned to taboo his desires for comfort and security and perceive them as weaknesses. He learned to invalidate his feelings in a masochistic self-destructive manner. As a result, he tried to conform to a perfectionist performance ideal even in adulthood. He could never enjoy his successes. For example, he needlessly sold his beloved holiday home in Denmark after years of laborious restoration. In the event of threatening relationship conflicts at work, he often withdrew in anticipatory obedience *even before* his opponents attacked him. As a result, he was an outsider at his workplace for a long time and then became self-employed as a specialist.

Traumatized patients quickly feel threatened in relationship conflicts (van der Kolk et al., 1998, p. 72) because conflicts trigger their traumatic sensorimotor interaction patterns, and affect. For example, they *subjectively* experience criticism as violent blows. Or they masochistically confuse their *external* conflict partner with their *internal* soul killer (see Sect. 8.5). They tend to avoid relationship conflicts, adapt to the expectations of their respective social environment, and function well in terms of the expectations of their relationship systems. They then interpret their own *reasonable intentions and desires* as 'evil' (see Sect. 8.5).

**Central idea**

Trauma processing helps loosen the fixation of self-development in the defense system of self-protection through denial and masochistic self-censorship. The patient's self-actualization and self-esteem in dealing with everyday conflicts improve. When therapy is advanced, the patients learn to say 'no' and no longer overwhelm themselves as much. This leads to *new* relationship conflicts at work and in the private sphere.

Progressive changes must be explicitly appreciated as 'new' and positively confirmed by the therapist for them to stabilize (see Sect. 2.1). The patient's new actions *in a situation that would previously have triggered a flashback* are particularly valuable. Traumatized patients often do not notice the *new quality* of their behavior *themselves*. The therapist, however, calls it 'the patient's journeyman's piece'.

***Case example 44 (1st continuation, see* Sect. 5.10.4*)***
*At the end of her therapy, the 35-year-old Ms. F. spoke to her colleague about the distribution of work at their joint workplace. The colleague looked 'angry'. This led to an internal state of agitation in the patient, but not to a flashback as before. Ms. F. could speak to the colleague on her own the following day. The colleague reacted differently than the patient's father, who was traumatized by the war, was even 'relieved' and said: "I was also hoping to talk to you. I misunderstood something yesterday. I'm sorry". The women then intensively discussed their experiences by being vulnerable with each other. The following night, Ms. F. was feeling agitated again. But she was able to resolve her agitation differently than before: she actively visualized the difference between her colleague and her war-traumatized father several times. Ms. F. told the therapist: "I then sent my father back into the past to another place and time". (2nd continuation, see below).*

Another patient was forcibly abused by his older brother. At the end of therapy, he was internally highly agitated as he was humiliated as a craftsman by a customer. However, *unlike before*, he did not regress into his old self-injurious thinking and acting. Instead, he imagined 'all the trigger boys, who torment him in the present, standing next to each other'. He cried with anger for half an hour and justified his sadness. But he didn't get lost in self-pity. He mourned that his life was so difficult because of his childhood trauma. After this inner work, the patient went to an older maternal friend and talked to her about the difficult customer. The friend knew the customer and confirmed his perception that this man was very difficult. She positively affirmed the patient's new behavior. The therapist appreciated the patient's various new solutions in the potentially retraumatizing situation and confirmed that he had created his journeyman's piece in therapy. At the end of his therapy, the patient in case example 35 (see Sect. 5.5) was also able to actively change his trigger situations in the hospital in such a way that he no longer had a flashback when he saw a man in a white coat.

**Central idea**

If a traumatized patient positively influences and changes a situation that is externally similar to his trauma scene, it indicates that he has processed his trauma sufficiently. This is because he has developed the capacity *to act* in this special situation. As a result, by definition, the situation is no longer a *retraumatizing* situation (see Sect. 5.2).

The therapist supports the patient in integrating their inner transformation into the *relationships in the present* with the help of psychodramatic dialogue with role reversal (see Sect. 8.4.2), if necessary.

***Case example 44 (2nd continuation, see* Sect. 5.10.4*)***
*The 35-year-old Ms. F. became more capable of dealing with conflicts in all her relationships after processing her* trauma. *This was the first time she really got to know the people in her social environment. People related to her had three different reactions: (1) The women from her women's group were grateful and relieved that she now openly expressed her wishes. In response to her coy request, it was the first time they joyfully took part in hosting the meetings in her house and even brought small gifts for her later. (2) Some work colleagues were 'only' pragmatic and searched for a solution to the conflict on the factual level. (3) However, Ms. F. had now recognized that three individual women were mostly selfish and inappropriately just asserting their own interests.*

*The therapist showed Ms. F. the technique of psychodramatic self-supervision (see* Sect. 2.9*): "You can save on some therapeutic sessions if you use this method at home alone!" The patient actually engaged in fictional psychodramatic dialogues with her 'conflict partners' at home. In doing so, she realized how different they thought and felt. For example, "sometimes they just hadn't thought about it". At another time, their distancing from the other was 'just self-protection'. However, Ms. F. also noticed that when she reversed roles and was in the role of the conflict partner, she often did not understand herself at all. She concluded: "I think I am not expressing my wishes clearly to others".*

Traumatized patients should *also* integrate their new understanding of themselves and their renewed self-worth into their *relationship images concerning people from the past*. This is because the development of the self is still blocked by defenses *in old* relationship images.

**Central idea**

The traumatized patient must dissolve his defense *in the old relationships* images from the past and free the development of his self-image and object-image in his inner relationship images from their fixation. Otherwise, if the old inner images are actualized in present-day conflicts, he will fall back into his old defensive patterns (Dieckmann, 1991, p. 25).

Therefore, the therapist leaves the patient as the adult he is now, to freely explore how he wants to understand himself and the partner in the relationship: "How did our relationship develop in our life? What do we mean to each other?" In this way, he gets to know his partner anew, as it were.

The integration of the new self-image into the old contents of the memory centers takes place in the following way: To begin with, the patient writes a fictitious letter to a person from his past (see Sect. 4.12 and case example 55 in Sect. 6.6). As an adult, the patient then shares with this person, in a psychodramatic dialogue with role reversal, how he now understands his childhood experiences differently. He says everything he always wanted to say and asks what he always wanted to ask.

**Central idea**

In the psychodramatic dialogue, the patient shares his inner subjective truth about his childhood with a significant person from childhood. But, by reversing roles, he also explores the reaction of 'his conflict partner' in the as-if mode of play and completes the internal psychosomatic resonance pattern *in the conflict partner's role* (see Sect. 8.4.2). As a result, he knows how this person ticks. For example, by reversing roles with his sister's role, he notices that *she* doesn't want to know anything about *his* new truth. Instead, she distances herself from him so as not to breakdown herself. This experience helps the patient to perceive the sister realistically in the *real encounter* and to be mindful of her.

As a result, the patient develops additional interpersonal skills in *real relationships* with family members. For example, during role reversal, he notices that his "aunt" is interested in him and his thoughts. This motivates him to get in touch with his aunt again in *real* life. He may then speak to her about his childhood experiences and search for some family secrets. Even though in retrospect, at least *now* the patient receives compassion from this relative from childhood, along with some new information. These expand his self-image and his knowledge about the perpetrator from childhood. This strengthens his own position toward the perpetrator. It becomes easier for him to break free from destructive relationships with family members.

At the end of the therapy, trauma patients should also integrate their inner change into their *relationship with their current partner or spouse*. In long-term relationships, the first phase of love is usually followed by a phase of the 'struggle for resources'. This also triggers some negative transferences. If the bond is strong enough, both partners can resolve these conflicts. However, this *no longer* succeeds once the couple has entered the stage of *mutual neurotic allergy* (Krüger, 2010b, see Sect. 8.4.3).

The only solution to a mutual neurotic allergy is that both partners inform each other about their own neurotic or traumatic wound in a calm way. Love then means developing compassion for the weakness of the other over time. Both partners should practice being mindful of the other's weaknesses *without betraying their own inner child*. The therapist can promote this development in the couple's relationship with the help of steps 6 and 7 of the psychodramatic dialogue (see Sect. 8.4.2). If an existing mutual neurotic allergy *cannot be spoken of*, this often leads to a separation or divorce (see case example 49 in Sect. 5.12).

## 5.12 Secondary Traumatization

Secondary traumatization occurs *in childhood* in relationships with traumatized parents or *in the present* in relationships with people with post-traumatic stress disorder. Psychotherapists *can also* experience secondary trauma by working with their trauma patients (see Sect. 5.16). Patients with relationship trauma in childhood have often been emotionally hurt by parents who *themselves* suffered from trauma-related disorders and, therefore, could not love their children, for example. These patients deal with their childhood conflicts through *internalization* (Hirsch, 2004, p. 1 f.). The traumatized parent remains present in the patient's soul as 'a traumatic introject that floats around like a hostile, archaic superego', causing symptoms, and pathological behavior.

***Case example 48***

*Ms. G's good therapeutic progress in her trauma therapy led to a dilemma: Her nocturnal psychosomatic complaints, fears, and sleep disturbances intensified when she allowed herself to be inappropriately controlled by her partner as before. Unfortunately, the patient reacted similarly with intensified symptoms when she newly asserted herself during the day and tried to make her relationships more equitable. Together, the therapist and the patient recognized that this was caused by the existence of an internal persistent pathological father introject. The patient's father, traumatized as a soldier in the war, had been unable to allow closeness in family relationships. But he had determined the family relationships through his need for control and his sensitivity to conflicts in an authoritarian manner. Due to his inability to confront conflicts, he always appeared archaically threatening, even if he had never been physically violent. Her pathological father introject hindered the patient's emotional development in her adulthood as an internal hostile archaic superego.*

*The therapist and the patient together looked for ways in which the patient could regain the ability to act in the face of her threatening father introject. The therapist: "It is important that you allow each other a right to life. Your inner father should not want you, as his daughter, to break into pieces! And your inner father also has a right to life. Perhaps you have to use some transpersonal elements which are even more powerful than your father to appease your father". Ms. G. invented the following procedure: In her imagination, she created a safe place by the sea for the nature-loving 'father', a place where he finds peace and quiet and gets what he needs: "The father should set up a home for himself in his safe place. But he is not allowed to enter my world. There is a hut for him in his safe place. Not far from the hut lives a wise older woman, a healer. The father can visit her in her house if he needs help". Three days after this work, the patient could sleep through the night for the first time in a long time. She wrote a fictional letter to her long-dead father. In the letter, she 'gifted' her father the safe place by the sea as described. She announced that she wanted to give him back his suffering. She wanted to represent this symbolically by placing a small stone on his grave.*

*A fortnight later, a nocturnal dream helped the patient realize: "There are two ways I feel about my father now. I have a father who is threatening, but also someone else who is human and has his own story of life and suffering!" The patient slept well with some good and some bad nights over the next few weeks: "Sometimes I am overwhelmed with fear at night, and I have to fight through it again! It makes me angry that I am suffering! But the anger then helps me. The night before yesterday, I sent my real father away. But I imagined his threatening part was sitting on a chair in front of me. I then took a file folder and hit the chair with all my might. I killed the threatening part of my father. This got me out of my trauma film. I find that the negative image of my father is a ghost. I created the ghost myself as a child!" Afterward, the patient actually went to her father's grave. She had never been there after his funeral. As mentioned, she placed the stone of suffering on his grave. Half a year after this intense work, she was generally able to sleep well. Whenever she felt anxious at night, she imagined a new little episode of her 'father's experience' in his safe place by the sea. In doing so, she moved him back to the other world and freed herself from him.*

**Central idea**

People who were secondarily traumatized in childhood have often developed masochistic self-censorship through their spontaneous compassion for their father or mother. As a result, they cannot be angry with their inadequate parents. *Empathy* is a great human ability. Patients with secondary trauma, however, absorb the inner 'ghosts' of their traumatized parents *into their own souls* through their empathy. Because the family does not talk about the parents' traumas, they cannot attribute the latent horror *to the traumatized parent*. They then consider *themselves* to be in the wrong and feel guilty. In such a case, the therapist and the patient work together to find solutions to *appease the traumatized inner parent figure* and return the suffering from their 'ghosts' back to them.

Another patient with secondary traumatization re-enacted a memory from childhood in her therapy group: *As a child*, she stood in the dark, full of fear, with her teddy bear in her arms in front of her parent's bedroom door. She hears her war-traumatized father scream wildly. The mother tries to calm him down. In conversation with the therapist, the patient felt distressed and said: "He needs something from me to feel my love. But that can't be me! I can't and don't want to do that anymore!" *To appease her father's pathological introject*, the patient came up with the following solution: She decided to buy a teddy bear and let it participate in her life at home for several months. Along with her friend, she then wanted to bury him in her father's grave at night secretly.

To the therapist's surprise, another patient wrote a coping fairy tale *for her mother* instead of her own coping tale (see Sect. 5.14): In this fictional story, the mother marries her childhood love in her young adulthood and is happy: "I had to let *her* be fine first. Before that, I couldn't find the way to my own wishful fantasies". The pathological introject cannot be appeased therapeutically in a single session. It sometimes takes patients a few weeks before they find a coherent solution.

*Secondary traumas also occur in current relationships with* close people with post-traumatic stress disorder. This is the experience of women, for example, whose husbands were soldiers in the war or who suffered a serious illness and then developed PTSD. In the case of patients with *secondary trauma*, an ego split occurs between a loving ego state and a resigned, latently hating ego state. The two contrary ego states alternate with each other with a time delay in the relationship. The irresolvable contrast between love and fear or resignation is usually processed masochistically in a self-deprecating way.

In such a case, the therapist proceeds as follows: She lets the patient with secondary trauma engage in a fictitious psychodramatic dialogue with her traumatized 'conflict partner'. However, the patient is caught between the desire to love and *the need not to betray herself*. Therefore, the therapist lets the patient represent *her own internal self-image with two chairs*, one for her 'loving ego' and one for her 'resigned or hating ego'. The patient then initiates a psychodramatic dialogue *between her two contrary self-images* using role reversal. In doing so, the patient seeks a compromise between her two contrary ego states in the relationship with the traumatized conflict partner for the *current situation.*

***Case example 49***

*A 35-year-old patient sought therapy because she had experienced violence in her childhood. Her partner treated her in an authoritarian and devaluing way as a result of his own childhood relationship trauma. The patient gave her partner a lot of chances. For example, she wrote him a 'red letter' asking him to discuss their relationship problems with her: "It's enough for me if we simply try to work this out together!" In response, the partner accused her of being 'self-centered'. He never questioned his own actions. He never apologized. He never sought psychotherapeutic counseling himself. A year later, the patient secretly left their apartment for fear of his aggressiveness. She moved in with friends. But there, she suffered from severe sleep disturbances: "I'm brooding. I blame myself that maybe I haven't tried everything after all!".*

*The therapist set up two chairs next to each other in the therapy room, one for the 'loving Christa' and one for the 'resigned Christa'. He let the patient engage in a psychodramatic dialogue between these two ego states in the presence of the third empty chair for the partner. The therapist played the opposite role in each case. The patient accused 'resigned Christa' from the role of 'loving Christa': "You have failed! You should have adapted and remained content with what Uwe can give!" As an auxiliary ego in the role of 'loving Christa', the therapist experienced 'a pull toward the partner like an addiction'. As 'resigned Christa', the patient explained to her 'loving self' the separation from her partner with the following arguments: "I can't stand it. I'm important too". In identifying with the patient, the therapist sensed her inner distress. He gave role feedback and stated: "In my experience of you, it's not just about pleasure or displeasure. I am experiencing an existential need!" It is only now that the patient remembered the day on which she had first thought of separation. She had been massively debased by her partner in an argument. On her way back home, she seriously considered jumping onto the tracks before the next train when she was at the train station: "My partner has often behaved cruelly toward me. In doing so, he knew that his aggression triggers old fears from my childhood in me." The therapist replied to the patient: "According to the United Nations Charter for Human Rights, you have the right to physical and mental integrity and your dignity as a person! These are absolute values. You can't put that into perspective! Existential values are different from arguments for wellness. Your suicidal fantasies indicate that: You must not ignore them! By the way, if you take your own life, the loving Christa would also be dead and no longer there for her husband!" At the end of the session, the patient in the role of 'loving Christa' gave herself permission to separate and said: "Otherwise the price is too high" (see continuation in* Sect. 5.15*).*

## 5.13 The Natural Self-Healing System in Humans

*Not everyone* develops post-traumatic stress disorder after a potentially traumatic event. Hartmann (1996) substantiates this with an unconscious natural self-healing system in humans. He examined a series of nocturnal dreams of *healthy people* who had suffered acute trauma. He found that *healthy people* can process their psychological trauma with the help of their nocturnal dreams.

The natural self-healing system causes the *dream work* to go through the following steps *when dreaming at night*: (1) The traumatic event first appears in the dream images as it *happened in real life*. (2) The dream work shifts the emotion, for example, panic, through a change of scene into *other images* with emotionally *related* material. These can also be things that happened to *other people* in their childhood, for example, their brothers, sisters, or friends. Or they dream stories of animals or people from books. (3) A few weeks later, a woman who had been raped changed to the *observer position* witnessing another rape where she saw the victim being hurt in a dream: "I was walking down the street with a friend and her four-year-old daughter. Then a gang of male youths dressed in black leather came and began to attack the child. My friend ran away. I tried to free the child. But I noticed that my clothes were being torn off. I woke up in horror" (Hartmann, 1996, p. 3). The dream work let the real raped woman change from the victim role *into a rescuer role* in a situation that was similar to her own traumatic experience. That enabled her *to act again and* actively *process* the conflict in her dream in her internal image of the rape. (4) The dream work *symbolizes* the traumatic affect and event in an appropriate image. The feeling of being existentially threatened is depicted in the dream, for example, in the form of enormous, storm-lashed waves that flood the dreamer in a storm surge. Or the feeling of mental breakdown is symbolized in the dream by a house that collapses over the dreamer. (5) The patient's guilt is also assigned to others in a dream.

The action in the dream results in the dreamer's panic being linked to the *various* memory centers and developed into a holistic psychosomatic resonance pattern and then integrated with similar psychosomatic resonance patterns (see Sect. 2.7). Thus, according to Hartmann, the emotion gradually becomes less intense and changes its character. After a few weeks or months, the trauma plays an "increasingly [...] smaller role in the nocturnal dreams of healthy people, and the dreams return to the pre-traumatic state" (Hartmann 1996, p. 5).

Many religious and social rituals *activate* people's natural internal self-healing system in crises. They improve the *internal* ability to *act* in frightening or potentially traumatizing situations through positive self-affirmation. For example, rituals at funerals, weddings, the baptism of children, when entering adulthood, after a master's examination, or after a state examination. Rituals embed fears and internal changes in the larger framework of human culture. The *artistic* creation of narratives, myths, literature, music, or the painting of pictures also invigorates the natural self-healing system and helps to process trauma. Mario Vargas Llosa, who in 2010 received the Nobel Prize for Literature as a Spanish-Peruvian writer, answered a relevant question: "Writing helped me face my life, all my disappointments, and failures. I think that's wonderful for an artist: you can use everything that goes wrong in your life and turn it into fiction. This is a great liberation" (Die Zeit, supplement, October 2011). The 12 steps of Alcoholics Anonymous also activate the unconscious natural self-healing system (see Sect. 10.7, Krüger, 2004, p. 184 f.). In the second of the twelve steps, they posit that there exists a healing system. But, they name this with the socially known and accepted symbol of 'God'. In the next four steps, members establish a relationship with 'God', i.e., with their inner self-healing system that has not yet been sufficiently developed, and shape the relationship increasingly constructively. For example, they confess their faults to 'God' and ask him for help in their healing. Then comes the ingenious 11th step toward the end. Members ask 'God' to enable *them* to *themselves do* all that *'God'* has done for them up to then. Thus, they ask him to make them capable of taking responsibility for their own healing. In doing so, they integrate 'God' or the inner natural self-healing system into their own soul. From the perspective of self-loss, self-empowerment, and self-healing, the 12 steps of Alcoholics Anonymous are an ingenious invention. They help people to activate and develop their natural self-healing system (see Sect. 10.7).

## 5.14 Coping Fairy Tales as a Technique for Trauma Processing

See Fig. 5.3.

**Central idea**

In trauma therapy, the *therapeutic relationship* and the doppelganger technique are, as it were, a holding container in which the traumatized patient re-develops his damaged or *underdeveloped* natural self-healing system (see Fig. 5.3).

As an implicit doppelganger, the therapist promotes the patient's ability to *switch* back and forth between the trauma memory and self-stabilization autonomously. For this purpose, she uses (1) the method of *coping fairy tales* (Krüger 2013, Sáfrán and Csáky-Pallavicini, 2013) or (2) the *Imagery Rehearsal Therapy* (Krakow, Kellner, Pathak, Lambert, 1995). (3) According to Reddemann (1999, p. 90), the therapist lets the patient *develop positive counter-images* for negative emotional states. (4) The

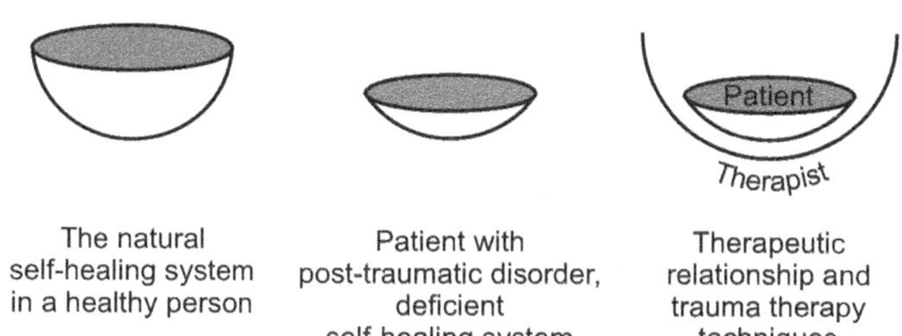


**Fig. 5.3** The Development of the Natural Self-Healing System through Trauma Therapy

patient thinks of a *concrete wishful scene* that clarifies what he would have needed from the other person in the traumatizing situation instead.

*Writing a coping fairy tale* is a method of processing trauma. It helps to rewrite the trauma memory internally and to expand it with a healing fantasy of coping. A coping fairy tale has three sections, (1) the description of *a traumatic event*, (2) the *fairytale-like transformation,* and (3) the *fulfillment of the wish* or the actual longing. The fulfillment of the wish is described in concrete interaction sequences. In them, the large should become clear in the small.

The therapist proceeds with the practical work in the coping fairy tale as follows:

1. She recommends that the patient write a coping fairy tale for a *single* traumatic event.
2. She explains the concept to him by marking *the three sections of the fairy tale* with a stone each *on the table stage*: the traumatic event, the fairytale-like transformation, and the fulfillment of his longing.
3. She places an additional stone on the table for the patient's ego. She encourages him to *always talk about himself in the third person* when talking in the session and when writing the fairy tale at home, for example, 'little Manfred who …' or 'little Renate who …' (see case example 40 below).
4. The therapist and the patient determine the contrast between the *actual* feeling of suffering during the trauma experience and the fulfillment of the *actual* longing in the fairy tale: "What was the worst feeling? What would you have needed instead?"
5. Together with the therapist, the patient defines individual courses of action in his story. The therapist may play out the actions with symbols on the table stage, like playing with a doll's house. Together, the patient and the therapist look at the 'coping fairy tale' timeline on the table.
6. If necessary, the patient can *begin* the coping fairy tale *by thinking of the wishful fantasy.* That is all the more important in the case of a patient with a severe post-traumatic illness.
7. The therapist ensures that the patient does not harm himself by telling *one story of suffering after another* and regressing pathologically. She stops him if necessary: "Stop, let's look at this *one* traumatic event, please. More than one story will be too much for me."
8. The patients develop the *second part* of the coping fairy tale, the fairytale-like transformation, usually only after the first and third parts of the fairy tale.
9. In the second part of the fairy tale, the little boy should not wait *passively* for his wish to be fulfilled. He should at least draw the attention of the 'fairy godmother' or other helpers or rescuers to himself *with a small sign* (Sáfrán & Csáky-Pallavicini, 2013, p. 276), for example, by crying. The patient learns through play that other people *can* react to him in a helpful way *only when* he no longer pretends as if nothing is wrong.
10. The patient writes the fairy tale little by little at home. This often takes him several weeks.

11. The therapist lets the patient show the *final version* of the fairy tale. She reads the text and suggests changes if necessary (see case example 40 below). The patient incorporates the suggestions into his coping fairy tale if necessary. The patient is not allowed to modify the fairy tale *after* the therapist has seen it for the last time. Otherwise, there is a risk that self-destructive patients may later change the coping part of their fairy tale into the opposite.
12. The patient reads the finished coping fairy tale again when he is in crisis *in the future*. The coping fairy tale then serves as a map for inner orientation. The first part of the fairy tale helps him recognize all that he has had enough of in his life and therefore does not need again. Then, while reading the third part of the fairy tale, he remembers what he *actually longs* for or *needs* in life.

***Case example 40 (1st continuation, see* Sect. 5.9*)***
*A 40-year-old patient experienced a lot of violence in his family as a child. Toward the end of his therapy, he wrote a coping fairy tale. The fulfillment of his longing in the third part of the fairy tale involves him moving out of his violent parental home when he was 19. The therapist intervened: "But that is not a wish-fulfillment in the sense of a fairy tale! When did you leave home in reality?" The patient: "At 19 years of age". The therapist encouraged the patient to look for a different solution for the fairy tale: "A wish-fulfillment at the age of 19 is too late. The little boy needs sufficient protection and love by the seventh or eighth year at the latest. Otherwise, it won't help him enough." The patient rewrote the fairy tale. In the new fantasy story, "the teacher in his primary school class makes a home visit to his family. She recognizes the violence and notifies the youth welfare office. The youth welfare office brings the patient and his sister into a nice foster family." Despite being a psychotherapist himself, the patient was amazed at the tremendous therapeutic effect this change had in his story: "I discovered something completely new for me. I didn't even know the as-if mode before. Now I know what people mean when they talk about making a wish!".*

In traumatized patients, the fulfillment of a wish in the coping fairy tale strengthens the process of self-development in traumatizing situations and frees it from fixation. The patient sometimes feels this change directly in his present life. One patient, for example, turned his abusive parents into ravens in his coping fairy tale. In the next group session, he said: "I have suddenly become more grippy in my everyday life. Earlier I used to think twice before saying anything. Now I notice that I respond to people quite spontaneously *without thinking beforehand*. I didn't know I could do this myself." Writing a coping fairy tale helps the patient develop self-empathy and justify their own feelings. *In the coping fantasy*, the patient allows himself to *feel what he is feeling*: When a child is sad, he is allowed to cry and is comforted. If he is afraid, he is hugged and experiences safety and security. If he is exposed to a chronically threatening, violent, or degrading situation, a *good enough mother* enters the threatening situation and fights to protect the child against the perpetrator. Or the mother and the child flee the violent situation and go to a safe place.

The lesser access a patient has to their own desires, the more difficult it is for them to write a coping fairy tale. In this case, the therapist must support him in small steps, which take 20 min each in several therapy sessions. The more a patient struggles, the more they learn. Working with the coping fairy tale is also *diagnostically* valuable. Patients who have *not yet sufficiently processed* their trauma usually do *not complete* the tasks when writing their coping fairy tale. For example, they put off writing their fairy tale for a long time or forget about it completely. Or they leave out a part of the fairy tale. A 50-year-old social worker, for example, 'never got around' to writing his coping fairy tale for more than a year. He then brought his 'coping fairy tale' with him in writing. The therapist read through it and was surprised. His fairy tale *only* consisted of the second part of the fairytale-like transformation. The patient explained to the therapist: "If I had written down a traumatic event from my childhood or the fulfillment of my longing, I would not have been able to work!" The patient wanted to move to another city three months later. The therapist discussed with him how he could stabilize himself in his new job and which retraumatizing situations he should avoid.

Sáfrán and Csáky-Pallavicini (2013) have successfully used the coping fairy tale method even *in group therapy* for patients with *borderline personality organization*. The method made it possible to proceed in a structured and disorder-specific manner. This stimulated the patient's introspection and self-empathy.

Trauma patients often suffer from nightmares. The sleep researchers Krakow et al. (1995) developed Imagery Rehearsal Therapy (IRT) for *the treatment of chronic nightmares*. The patients begin by writing down their nightmares. With the help of the therapist, they then complement the areas that trigger fear or stress with new, non-stressful content. The authors describe this procedure in a case example: The therapist gave the patient the task of keeping a dream diary for four weeks. The patient then had to find a new and *positive* turning point in each of her nightmares. She read these new, *positive progressions* for a quarter of an hour daily for a month and internalized them. "The occurrence of the nightmares reduced significantly after that, and so did the trauma symptoms such as depression or anxiety" (Die Zeit, No. 32, p. 28, August 4th, 2011). By *rewriting their nightmares*, the patients free their self-development from its traumatic fixation in their nightmares. They regain the ability to act in their fantasy. This generally promotes their ability to deal with internal conflicts.

Reddemann (1999, p. 90) activates the natural self-healing system by letting her traumatized patients develop *positive counter-images to negative emotions*: "It has become [...] important for us to stimulate patients—if they are not doing it anyway—to find pictorial descriptions for their emotional states and sensitivities and then also their counter-images. For example, a patient might say that she feels 'like she is in prison'. We would then suggest to her to see what a counter-image would look like and then invite her to let this counter-image work on her. In particular, to let it work on her body and to notice how her body is dealing with it. A counter-image could be, for example, 'I feel like a bird', and we could invite the patient to feel this, particularly in her body, and perhaps even move accordingly. Then we would recommend that every time she felt like she was in prison—and we would point out that this could be the case—she could evoke the counter-image, and we would explain to her that it is possible to oscillate back and forth between these two images and make it like a dance. [...] Numerous interventions in everyday life, in dealing with everyday images and feelings, aim to create this pendulum movement, to create a feeling of counterbalance." In this technique, the patient uses *his negative feeling* to develop a *symbolic image*. Then he looks for a *positive counter-image* for this *negative* image. After that, he notices how this positive counter-image changes his *body perception*. The patient can also represent the *negative* image and the *positive* counter-image with two chairs *next to each other* in the room and then change from his negative image to his positive counter-image *externally*. That makes the *internal* change easier.

Many traumatized patients complain about their attachment figures or their life situation without making any changes. Their masochistic self-censorship *prevents* them from developing *concrete inner wishful thinking* when in a conflict. In such a situation, the therapist proceeds as follows:

(1) She asks the patient: "How do you feel about your relationship with your wife in this situation? Why do you feel that?" (2) She continues: "What would you *need* in this situation *instead*?" (3) The patient thinks of a specific desired scene and describes what will happen in it step by step. (4) The therapist asks the patient: "And if your wish came true now, what would you feel?" A concrete inner wishful thought helps *the patient* orient himself internally in a conflict situation in everyday life. He knows *what he needs* and, therefore, remains capable of *acting in his imagination* in the current conflict situation in everyday life. This promotes his ability to *deal* with the conflict *in reality* and, for example, to say what he would like. Perhaps his inner wishful thinking is only fulfilled to ten percent in reality. However, this is more satisfying for the patient than if he just blindly acts out his *masochistic* inner images in relation to his conflict partner.

The therapist keeps working with the patient *until the end of the therapy,* to loosen the patient's rigid defenses through grandiosity and masochistic self-censorship (see Sects. 4.10 and 8.5). This promotes the patient's process of self-development in current conflicts. The therapist can point to the two chairs of the patient's symptom scene in his everyday life (see Fig. 2.8 in Sect. 2.9) and invites him: "Just try to become a normal person." The patient is usually baffled because he doesn't even know what it's like to be *a normal* person, *a normal* father, *a normal* husband, or *a normal* co-worker.

## 5.15 The Shaping of the Therapeutic Relationship

Patients with trauma-related disorders repeatedly pull their therapists into their defense processes. In this case, as an implicit doppelganger, the therapist unconsciously identifies with the patient's self-protection through grandiosity and becomes a grandiose helper or savior herself. Or she identifies with his masochistic self-censorship and latently devalues the patient because of his self-debasement.

***Case example 35 (continued, see* Sect. 5.5*)***
*A 42-year-old patient was violently abused by her father up to the age of 16. After inpatient treatment, she returns to outpatient psychotherapy and complains with tears in her eyes: "Before the treatment, I fought for survival every day. Now I'm even more exhausted." She reports: "During the inpatient treatment, I felt unencumbered, free, and satisfied. I felt feminine and beautiful. There were 'some sacred moments'. I re-enacted my key experience from when I was seven years old: I'm lying in bed, and there is thunder and lightning outside. I am afraid that Jesus will come and take my parents and sister with him. And then I'll be all alone. Our family belonged to a sect. My therapist let me act out this memory. In doing so, he let my 'healthy adult' perform. She should see what I need and then give it to me! However, besides me as a child, my 'healthy adult' herself was scared on the long way from my room to my parent's bedroom. Therefore, I needed the therapist to knock on my parent's bedroom door. As a child, I wanted to say to my parents: 'Mom, Dad, it doesn't work like that. I need to talk to you.' I had to force myself to open the door. I then switched to my 'healthy adult' role and said to my parents: 'You mustn't continue to talk your daughter into believing that she is a bad child!' After that, I was very proud of the 'adult' in me. The confrontation with my parents was important. In the role of the small child, I noticed: I no longer needed my parents! The little child preferred to return to his room with his 'adult'. My parents didn't do anything in the play. As always, my mother was just a gray mouse! I felt quite alive after saying that aloud for once. I had the feeling: Yes, the 'adult' in me can protect me! I don't need my parents anymore!" Contrary to this statement, the patient is now sitting in front of her therapist in outpatient therapy in her hometown and is exhausted and depressed.*

In this case example, the therapist in the clinic acted as a great helper and healer. He combined three different methods of trauma therapy *in a single session*, (1) the separation of the traumatized child from healthy adult thinking (see Sect. 4.7), (2) the *trauma exposure* through direct encounter with the perpetrator, the father (see Sect. 5.10.7), and (3) the integration of the inner change into the relationships with childhood caregivers (see Sect. 5.11).

**Recommendation**

Some patients had already been in *trauma therapy once* before they came to therapy. In such a case, the therapist assesses which of the seven phases of trauma therapy (see Sect. 5.6) the patient is in and proceeds with him *to the next step* in treatment.

The therapist let the patient in case example 35 act out her childhood trauma directly in the as-if mode of play without using self-stabilization techniques. In the traumatizing situation, she even had to think as a healthy adult and confront her parents as the perpetrators. However, she failed and panicked. The therapist, therefore, had to support the patient as a doppelganger. Thus, as a doppelganger, he created an emotionally corrective experience in the play and involved the patient in doing so. But, he *didn't resolve her defense* through masochistic self-censorship. The patient wanted to preserve her new positive emotional experience after the hospital stay. But, she could only do it in the relationship with her therapist. Unfortunately, she could not take her therapist home with her. *The loss* of the helpful relationship with her therapist in the clinic triggered her old traumatic experience of abandonment from childhood and she decompensated into depression.

Trauma experiences have an existential quality due to encounters with basic human fears (see Sect. 5.9). The therapist, therefore, meets the traumatized patient also as a human (see Sect. 4.13). She makes statements and rarely asks questions. She also justifies *her own feelings* in the here and now. As an implicit doppelganger, she identifies with the patient's inner self-development in the current situation. But then, without noticing it, she gets caught up in the patient's split-off affect and physical sensations. In psychoanalysis, this phenomenon is described as defense through '*projective identification*' (see Sects. 2.4.4 and 4.15). According to König (1984, quoted from Heigl-Evers, Heigl, et al., 1997, p. 351), the therapist becomes similar to the parts of the self transferred from the patient through 'unconscious manipulation'.

**Central idea**

When interacting with a traumatized patient, the therapist often feels helpless, powerless, overworked, angry, nauseous, dizzy, or fearful. These feelings mostly *do not express their therapeutic inexperience*. For example, their anger is often *not anger toward the patient* but rather *the patient's split-off anger*. Likewise, their fear is often not the *fear of the patient* but *the fear split off from the patient*. In identifying with the patient's self-development in the therapeutic relationship, the therapist senses *in herself*, without consciously noticing it, what the patient does *not allow himself* to feel through his defense.

***Case example 49 (see Sect. 5.12, continued)***

*A 40-year-old, self-confident patient was physically abused in childhood. She worked on her* coping *fairy tale in her eighth therapy session (see* Sect. 5.14*). She narrated a traumatic event reflecting her suffering: Little Brigitte was supposed to nap in her room. Suddenly she urgently needed to go to the toilet. But she was not allowed to do this because she would have had to disturb her mother in her afternoon rest. Otherwise, her mother threatened to hit her and not talk to her anymore. The little girl tried very hard not to get wet for one hour. The therapist: "What would the little girl actually have needed in this situation?" This gave rise to a little fantasy story with a 'good enough mother'.*

*In the further course of the session, the patient then narrated other traumatizing experiences from her childhood. She described how she had been beaten by her father, her classmates, as well as her grandfather and said with resignation: "Everyone was allowed to hit me!" The therapist realized too late that he was being drawn into the patient's states of affliction through his empathy. He found himself feeling sick. He was already acquainted with this sickness. Nausea always made him aware that he took on too much in the relationship with a traumatized patient.*

*The therapist, therefore, mindfully interrupted the patient and said: "This is too much for me. I feel a bit sick. It is unbelievable how strong you had to be. You endured and survived everything in your childhood and youth. As a child, you had to turn off your feelings. You simply had to focus on functioning. Otherwise, you would have upset your father and mother even more". The therapist got up and grabbed an empty chair: "I'll place a chair over here next to you for your perfect functioning as a child, for your self-protection behavior". He took a second empty chair and positioned it in the far corner of the therapy room: "This other chair here is for the traumatized child in you who experienced the traumatizing events". The therapist sat down on his own chair again: "Now let's first look for a positive counter-fantasy, for a 'safe place'. I need this for myself so that I can feel better again. The 'safe place' technique is a self-stabilizing technique. It will help you to leave the therapy room in good shape after the session!".*

**Central idea**

In trauma therapy, the therapist unconsciously becomes a metacognitive doppelganger in the patient's self-development. She needs to develop ego control over her work as a metacognitive doppelganger and harness her own feelings and physical sensations for therapy.

Gabi Tarda (only orally communicated 2019) summed up her experience *in the role of the patient* in a trauma seminar with the following words: "As a patient if I experience that the therapist does not want *to help*, but becomes my doppelganger, in some sense I remain alone, but I am not really. The accompaniment of the therapist as a doppelganger increases my own feeling of competence".

As a *metacognitive doppelganger*, the therapist uses the following methods:

1. If she thinks her emotion is part of the patient's trauma experience, she tells the patient how she feels as an encountering human being (see Sect. 4.13). Patients with trauma-related disorders need *a person* who can testify as a witness to the truth of their 'trauma' (see Sect. 5.5). They need the compassion of a person who senses the *existential quality* of their emotional injury. This is an essential impact factor in trauma therapy.
2. **Central idea**
   The therapist and patient retrace the path of the patient's defense through projective identification. The therapist makes his dominant defense pattern, which triggers her affect and body awareness, the object of therapeutic communication and represents it externally as a chair in the room. Thus, the patient *himself* goes into the opposite role of his defense pattern and feels what the therapist felt. The interpersonal acting out of the conflict becomes the patient's intrapsychic conflict again. The therapist proceeds by using chair work with the patient's metacognitive ego states (see Sect. 4.8).
3. The therapist uses psychodramatic responding, if necessary (see Sect. 4.13). For example, she will set up an empty chair next to her for herself as an 'expert therapist'. This makes her and the patient feel internally secure. It stabilizes her in her role as the 'encountering human being'.

The appropriate *management of the therapeutic relationship* is critical in the therapy of *acutely traumatized people*, for example, in the relationship with refugees with post-traumatic stress disorder. The therapist first helps such a patient to resolve his acute dissociation and to attenuate his overactivity. This is the prerequisite for regaining interest in his environment and himself and being able to act again in his own life (Bakhit, 2006, p. 304). Therapeutic work with refugees must take place in a protected setting where the patient has control over what is happening. In refugee shelters, the destruction of the patient's *internal ego structures* must first be compensated for by a secure *external framework*. The therapist informs the patient that she will respect her confidentiality. She adheres to the agreed working hours. The door of the counseling room must not be opened again and again. Victims of torture, need a *stable*, safe social environment as *a prerequisite for effective* trauma therapy. In such a case, the therapist intervenes *as a real doppelganger in the patient's real social environment*. For example, she accompanies him on his visits to the public authorities.

In the therapy of traumatized refugees, the therapist shapes the therapeutic relationship (Bakhit, 2006, p. 310). Together with the patient, she develops a 'safe place' with the help of stones, wooden blocks, or other objects that the therapist has brought along (see Sect. 5.10.5). Among other things, she also represents the patient's abilities and resources. The actual *trauma processing* takes place with the help of the table stage (see Sect. 5.10.10). The therapist is a kind of container for the relationship throughout therapy. She creates trust through attention, appreciation, interest, and *active* relationship building. Thus, she becomes a catalyst for the thawing and integration of the frozen internal emotional processes of the patient. In doing so, the therapist, as a metacognitive doppelganger, *vicariously* experiences his split-off emotions and physical sensations and has to endure them: bewilderment, shame, powerlessness, feelings of guilt, helplessness, feelings of loss, loneliness, numbness, or emotional rigidity. She names the feelings keeping in line with 'the principle of response instead of interpretation' (Heigl-Evers, Heigl, Ott and Rüger, 1997, p. 176ff., see Sect. 4.13): "I notice how I freeze internally and feel paralyzed when I imagine the horror you have had to experience. I think I'm feeling something of what you have felt!" Bakhit (2006, p. 315) recommends: The therapist must "endure and withstand the feelings". She should *refrain from* appealing for encouragement. Instead, she appreciates the existential quality of his traumatic experiences. After some time, the patient's life-affirming ideas will set in again *as if by themselves*.

## 5.16 Secondary Trauma and Burnout in Therapists

**Central idea**

Therapists should be careful with their own resilience when conducting trauma therapy. Time and again, they should activate their own physical, psychological, and social resources *through appropriate exercises*. In doing so, they resolve the blocks in their internal self-development adopted from the patient. This is a prerequisite for their therapeutic abilities to be freely and entirely available to them.

***Case example 45 (4th continuation, see* Sects. 5.10.5, 5.10.6, 5.10.7, *and* 5.10.8*)***
*Ms. D.'s trauma exposure session lasted more than three hours. It was about a life-threatening rape attempt. After leaving his practice in the evening, the therapist*

*noticed that he was looking down the street in both directions when he locked the door. He was afraid that a violent criminal might suddenly attack him. The therapist wondered about this himself. He didn't know himself to be so cautious and afraid. He realized: He had the same fear of darkness that the patient had suffered from before in her trauma exposure session. He was worried. The next morning he remembered: During her trauma exposure session, Ms. D. had given 'Saint George' a wooden sword in hand when in her 'safe place'. The assistant therapist who had played the saint's role had not used the sword. The therapist used this idea for himself. In a second new trauma exposure session, he imagined the protagonist would represent the perpetrator on a chair using a large vertical foam cushion. The patient would then pierce the 'perpetrator' with her sword in a state of rage. The therapist wanted to check with his sword whether the patient's stab was strong enough for the sword to come out of the pillow on the other side. The therapist noticed with astonishment: This fantasy act transformed his internal image of the perpetrator. Until then, the perpetrator had been a terrifying ghost to him. But stabbing made him a living person made of flesh and blood, capable of suffering. The therapist's fear of darkness disappeared after this inner work. It never reappeared.*

**Central idea**

Some of the therapist's own physical or emotional reactions may be feelings or sensations that *the patient* has not yet dealt with sufficiently in trauma processing. In such a case, the therapist, as an implicit doppelganger, tries to *vicariously* integrate the affect delegated to her by the patient into his trauma processing and to think through it *to the end in as-if mode*. In doing so, she gives herself every freedom in her fantasy. She may later communicate the result of this *vicarious trauma processing* to the patient as a sharing in a digested form.

The following methods protect the therapist from secondary traumatization:

1. The therapist also develops a 'safe place' *for herself* and visits it when necessary.
2. In therapy sessions, she internally names *even her own feelings* for herself. In doing so, she internally *separates herself* from her patient and resolves her defense through introjection (see Sects. 2.4.1 and 2.4.4).
3. She works 'only' with a limited number of patients with trauma-related disorders so that she herself does not 'break down'. This is because trauma therapy work exhausts and triggers therapists' *own* conflicts and traumas.
4. Supervision or intervision relieves the therapist's soul and gives her a new perspective on the therapeutic relationship if needed.
5. The therapist's own conflicts being activated in therapy should be an impetus to develop *herself* further internally and, for example, to look for answers to existential questions. For this reason, many therapists withdraw once a year to a place where *they* can develop new internal images and skills together with others. They open up to transpersonal experiences through meditation or get help if necessary to deal with their own conflicts. Again, it's about staying *true to their own self* in motion internally. Otherwise, there is a risk of developing a rigid defense system over time.
6. If necessary, therapists also seek therapy themselves.

Too much compassion can lead to *secondary trauma* or burnout in therapists. On the other hand, therapists who have experienced trauma and have been able to process them adequately in their own therapy, know precisely what their patient is talking about and are a good resonance body for the *existential quality* of trauma experiences. However, there is also a risk that they will overwhelm themselves as helpers and rescuers.

***Case example 50***

*A 40-year-old patient was treated in a hospital for a long time in her third year of life. Her behavior afterward became 'difficult' for her family. As an adult woman, she worked as a psychotherapist in a psychosomatic clinic. There she was known for her big heart for patients with severe relational difficulties and destructive tendencies. Because she consistently protested against disciplinary measures imposed on them. She then skillfully explained to her colleagues the psychodynamic reasons for the cross-border behavior of these patients. However, the consequence of her justified protests was that she often had to treat the most challenging patients herself. And she regularly had more patients to look after than her colleagues. Three years later, she left the clinic because of impending burnout.*

**Central idea**

Therapists who have experienced trauma themselves consider their own compassion for the traumatized patient to be 'normal'. In group dynamics, however, they end up in the omega position of their team (see Sect. 2.11) if they unilaterally insist on pushing through their existential truth. The team members develop an opaque mix of negative transferences and countertransferences. This results in destructive team conflicts.

The clinical team should always recognize the protests of therapists with *traumatic experiences* as *complementary truths*. However, the high demands of therapists with trauma experiences must not overburden the team and the clinic. They need to be integrated into the reality of the clinic.

## 5.17 Concepts of Psychodramatic Trauma Therapy by Other Psychodramatists

Nineteen psychodrama therapists from nine countries have described their own experiences with psychodramatic trauma therapy in the book 'Psychodrama with Trauma Survivors' (Kellermann & Hudgins, 2000). I summarize the most important contributions below.

In the case examples mentioned in the book, *after* the end of their therapy, *patients* repeatedly emphasized that *acting was more healing than talking*. *Previous purely verbal therapies* had not helped them (Kellermann & Hudgins, 2000, pp. 78, 86, 221). Kellermann (2000, p. 14) points out that *trauma processing* often requires *more than just a single* psychodrama play: "As most clinicians and researchers believe these days, for full healing to occur, the core trauma must often be revisited to release dissociated emotions and change trauma-based cognitions". The setting of *group therapy* has a special meaning in psychodramatic trauma therapy (Karp, 2000, p. 69 ff.; Kellermann, 2000, p. 33; Roine, 2000, pp. 83–91; Baim, 2000, pp. 165 ff.; Hudgins, 2000, p. 236 ff.; Burmeister, 2000, p. 218 ff.). Because the other group members witness the protagonist's trauma as 'Trauma' (Dayton, 2000, p. 119 f.). They offer intensive care through their sharing (Kellermann & Hudgins, 2000, pp. 67, 177, 194, 196, 218) and thus help to reduce guilt and shame. *On behalf of all other people*, they take the protagonist back into the human community through their testimony, participation in the protagonist-centered play, and sharing. Nevertheless, many psychodrama therapists *also work individually* (Burge, 2000, pp. 299–316; Burmeister, 2000, pp. 198–223; Roine, 2000, pp. 90, 92). Bannister (2000, p. 101) initially uses individual therapy in the therapy of severely abused children and only later used group therapy.

## 5.17.1 Peter Felix Kellermann (2000, pp. 23–40): The Therapeutic Aspects of Psychodrama with Traumatized People

As an experienced trauma therapist, Kellermann (2000, p. 26) emphasizes: (1) Trauma therapy requires the re-enactment of the trauma scene. (2) But unprofessional re-enactment of the trauma scene poses the risk of retraumatization. (3) Traumatized people easily mislead inexperienced therapists into *evading the crucial traumatizing situation*. Because traumatized patients have a 'strong need for gentleness'. (4) Trauma work needs reliability, support, and safety (see Roine, 2000, pp. 88, 93, 95). (5) The therapist should prepare the patient very well. Before starting with the play, he must discuss every step of the process with the patient and obtain his consent.

Kellermann (2000, p. 26f.) divides psychodramatic trauma processing into six steps. Each step is therapeutically effective even when practiced on its own:

1. *The re-enactment of trauma in a safe environment*: A young girl (Kellermann, 2000, p. 27 f.) had lost her mother in a tragic car accident. She re-enacted the traumatizing scene over and over again. Kellermann thinks that protagonists sometimes *have to repeat* a trauma scene *seemingly endlessly*. This is because when the group participates and echos their feelings, it helps them confirm that they are feeling what they feel. "Getting the traumatic experiences out into the open is in itself a liberation from the earlier tendency to repress the emotional impact of the event." Showing the traumatic experience in public can help the protagonist reduce the event's emotional impact and gain control over the emotional response to the trauma.
2. *The cognitive processing*: A man complained of recurrent flashbacks from the terrible scene of terrorist bomb attacks (Kellermann, 2000, p. 29 f.). His everyday life seemed like a dream or a movie to him. Kellermann asked the group members to translate the terrorist attack into a role play. The director asked the protagonist

to look at what was happening in the play *from a meta-perspective*. This helps *acutely traumatized patients* to develop their linguistic concepts and thinking in the psychosomatic resonance circuit of trauma memory (see Sect. 2.7) into a holistic 'personal history' of what happened. As a result, they resolve their dissociation in conflict processing.

3. *The emotional catharsis*: Kellermann (2000, p. 30) narrates a case example: As a child, "a patient overheard his alcoholic father fight with his mother during the night'. He had asked his parents to be quiet, but he had been hit and reprimanded in a humiliating manner. He had then been sent to bed". The patient re-enacted the childhood scene. When he was 'alone in his bed', he began to sob. The director urged him to 'let go and let his body do what it needed to do'. The patient cried harder. His crying didn't seem to end. Ultimately the tears stopped, but his body went into spasms, convulsing with the hiccupy gasps and shudders that are the aftermath of heavy crying. 'I am going to throw up', he whispered. Someone brought a bucket to let him cleanse his stomach of the disgust that he had kept within him for so long. He lay still for a while and then expressed his feelings toward his parents in words. As a closure, a different father held him until he calmed down sufficiently to return to the group. Kellermann says: "… the symptoms of trauma are the result of a highly activated incomplete biological response to threat, frozen in time. Trauma can be healed by enabling this frozen response to thaw and then complete itself." According to Kellermann, it is crucial that "catharsis is neither induced, nor inhibited, but allowed to emerge in its own time and form."
4. *Elements of Surplus Reality*: A Vietnam veteran was obsessed with guilt for killing his friend (Kellermann, 2000, p. 31 f.). He had watched, from a hiding place, as a wounded friend was captured and later shot. The patient wished that he had the courage 'to do to himself what he had done to his friend'. Following this re-enactment of what had happened in the past, the director suggested that the protagonist enact *what had never happened* but what he would *have liked to happen*. A group member took on the friend role, and the protagonist then saved his 'friend' in the play. He did this against all orders and all reason. "He put him in a safe place. When holding his friend, … he started to cry for his friend as if for the first time." When the protagonist had calmed down, *the group member in the role of his friend* spontaneously said: "It was not your fault that I died. You were my friend. I know that you did the right thing. If you had tried to rescue me, we both would have died. I desire that you will now live for both of us". Kellermann (2000, p. 31) says: If the protagonist experiences shame and guilt, it is important to let him rehearse the better and alternate possibilities of action in the trauma event using surplus reality in the play. This helps with trauma processing. In trauma therapy, the therapist should also always let the protagonist 'undo what was done and do what needs to be done' in the psychodramatic play.
5. *Repairing old relationship experiences through group therapy* (Kellermann, 2000, p. 32f.): The therapist encouraged 'an obese and unhappy woman, who had been abused and neglected as a child,' to stage some specific scenes of her childhood abuse in group therapy. At the end of the play, 'she suddenly became

very likable and attractive' as a lost child in a chaotic universe. The group noticed her new inner beauty. A ray of sunlight accidentally shone on her through the window of the group room. The group *celebrated* this change with a ritual: 'It was as if the patient were born again.' "Adults who have survived abuse as children are especially amenable to some kind of corrective interpersonal learning experience to counteract their impaired sense of trust, security and 'belonging to the human race'. They experience a new sense of safety and intimacy." They are re-integrated into the human community, thereby improving their self-esteem.

6. *Therapeutic rituals* (Kellermann, 2000, p. 35 f.): Traumatic events sometimes affect a whole community. In such a situation, the therapist invites the group members to participate in a crisis intervention session with collective sociodrama. For example, Kellermann worked therapeutically with the surviving employees of an institution six months after multiple murders. He used an old Indian ritual called the 'talking stick'. This stick "is passed around the group, allowing each person holding the object to say whatever they want. Other group members remain quiet but may say 'Hau!' if they agree with what has been said." Using such universal principles of 'Mother Nature' as well as symbols and stories from mythology helps in thawing the frozen emotions. The stories make it easier for the therapist to grasp the group topic and then continue working in a protagonist-centered manner. In the case example, one of the employees, as the protagonist on stage, expressed her feelings of grief and yearning for one of the 'victims'. She also did this on behalf of the other employees without intending to do so. As a result, the other group members could share their own experiences and thus dissolve their *own* emotional blockages.

### *5.17.2 Marcia Karp (2000, pp. 63–82): Psychodrama of Rape and Torture: A Sixteen-Year Follow-Up Case Study*

Karp describes in detail the treatment of a 48-year-old woman with trauma. The patient Jill, along with her husband and daughter, was attacked and raped by eight men in Africa. Jill was an independent woman with a strong personality. After the traumatic event, she organized the necessary medical care for the family as well as their return trip from Africa to England, all on her own. However, she fell into a chronic dissociative state for two years afterward. She was being 'completely submissive like she is a nobody' (Karp, 2000, p. 75). She received outpatient and inpatient psychiatric treatment and was prescribed strong psychotropic drugs. Despite the treatment, she remained depressed and could not leave the house.

Karp successfully treated the patient in just one preparatory individual session and two group weekends four weeks apart. The group members began by re-enacting the patient's fictional ruminations and self-accusations in the playback process: "If I had done that, it would have turned out differently." "If I had hidden my daughter, my husband, or the dogs shot by the perpetrators, then [...]". The enactment of the many 'ifs' made the protagonist realize that the retrospectively devised alternative courses of action would have been in vain: "Implicit but not verbalized, it became clear that if Jill had resisted in any scene, she would have been killed on the spot." Subsequently, the group members enacted the patient's trauma on the stage by following the instructions of the therapist and the protagonist. The protagonist unraveled the events and the sequence of the entire trauma event for the first time in the three-hour trauma exposure session. She directed the play from the narrative and observation space and completed her fragmented memories. She took on *only the role of another family member* in the trauma scene. That was the role of her 17-year-old daughter. *In this role*, she discovered that the most important thing for her 'daughter' was that her mother did not endanger herself through her behavior and die. The 'daughter' didn't expect anything else, even though she had been raped. It was *only in the role of her daughter* that the protagonist realized that as a mother, she had saved her daughter's and her own life with her presence of mind. When the 'perpetrators' left the room for a short time, she and her daughter immediately fled.

During the trauma exposure session, the protagonist moved only once from the narrative room *to her own role* in the interaction room of the trauma event. The 'perpetrators had already left'. Unlike in the real past, she said goodbye to her 'employees' in Africa in the play. In doing this, she began to tremble uncontrollably. The patient's state of dissociative shock resolved. The therapist and the group ensured a safe and stable environment. The husband had accompanied the patient to therapy. He was there for her after the trauma exposure session at their shared hotel. The patient had experienced severe sleep disturbances before the psychodramatic trauma processing. However, after releasing her sensorimotor blocks, she slept for 30 h straight.

*During the violent attack*, the perpetrators told the patient that her daughter and husband were dead. In the traumatizing situation, the patient had split off her sensorimotor interaction patterns, physical sensations, and affect through dissociation. As a result, she couldn't feel the presence of her attachment figures. It was only after processing her trauma that she felt *emotionally reassured* that her husband and daughter *had* survived. She also realized that she had 'been out of control' during the trauma event but had *not remained passive*. In fact, she had acted extremely wisely and appropriately. The group members and the therapist attested to this fact. As a result, her feelings of shame and guilt had now disappeared. According to Karp, shame and guilt are often heavy burdens for rape victims.

### *5.17.3 Eva Roine (2000, pp. 83–96): The Use of Psychodrama with Trauma Victims*

Roine describes four case examples: (1) the therapy of a woman whose uncle sexually abused her as a girl, (2) the treatment of a man whose uncle raped him as a 10-year-old boy, (3) the treatment of a traumatized pedophile man, and (4) the therapy of a torture victim. Roine believes that freedom from trauma must be *through action*. "By reconstructing the traumatic events in psychodrama, the protagonist is encouraged to control the situation in a new manner." The protagonist can only gain the necessary control over the situation *through acting* (Roine, 2000, pp. 86, 94). The energy frozen in the state of helplessness becomes accessible *through action.* If the protagonist is at risk of getting stuck halfway, the therapist should lead him directly to the 'heart of trauma'. Roine quotes Ildri Ginn, the director of the Boston Psychodrama Institute, who said: "When treating such patients, it is more dangerous to stop halfway than to go the whole way" (Roine, 2000, p. 88). "The director must have the courage to touch the emotional core of the subject" (Roine, 2000, p. 95). "Unsuccessful attempts can fixate the protagonist in trauma" (Roine, 2000, p. 93). Roine (2000, p. 88) emphasizes: "If *the therapists* have not understood and experienced the traumas of their own lives, they will not dare to descend into the depths of the patient's pain either."

### 5.17.4 Anne Bannister (2000, pp. 97–113): Prisoners of the Family: Psychodrama with Abused Children

Bannister describes the psychodrama work with severely sexually abused eight to nine-year-old boys and girls based on twenty years of experience. Traumatic events destroy a child's ability to relate. Therefore, before the beginning of the six-month group therapy, traumatized children remain in individual therapy 'until they 'have had the opportunity to form an attachment with at least *one non-abusing adult*' (Bannister, 2000, p. 101). The therapist promotes the development of the children through symbolic games or direct re-enactment of trauma experiences (Bannister, 2000, p. 102). In doing this, Bannister integrates psychodrama therapy, puppetry, working with sound, painting, and music into creative play therapy. These media help the children gain *spontaneous access* to elements of their trauma history and develop new solutions that promote their self-confidence and self-control. Children find it particularly difficult to ascribe appropriate meaning to their experiences of abuse. Therefore, they must directly learn the meaning of their traumatization in a safe environment through symbolic games.

Bannister (2000, p. 105 ff.) structures individual group sessions as follows: (1) At the beginning of each session, the children play the warm-up game, the 'wolf' tries to catch the 'sheep', with hand puppets. The game varies over time. They define specific rules, such as the rule that there are specific 'safe places' which cannot be invaded by the wolf. (2) Children were invited to tell how the puppets from the previous game felt in the here and now. (3) A break for refreshment follows. (4) Then comes the actual play phase. The children work with clay, paint, play with hand puppets, or dress up and do a role play. (5) All of them together speak the group slogan the therapist gave and act on it: "I'm a good person, I'm proud of me, I've been through a lot, look how strong I've got!" (6) During debrief, the children throw a ball to another group member. They thank that person for something they had appreciated during the session.

There are some peculiarities in Bannister's approach: The therapist-patient interaction is one-to-one, *even in the group*. The therapist works with a variety of materials. She also lets the children play *a lot with hand puppets in group therapy*. According to Bannister (2000, p. 103), "the use of puppets is often recommended with children… It may be that this form of projection helps to distance the action". Children with severe abuse also tend to attribute magical powers to perpetrators. The diminished size of the characters as hand puppets makes the play easier for the children to control. The group therapy developed by Bannister is a laborious and time-consuming process. However, scientific studies prove that severely disturbed children develop positively in therapy. Their self-confidence increases, and their self-control improves.

### 5.17.5 *Clark Baim (2000, pp. 155–175): Time's Distorted Mirror: Trauma Work with Adult Male Sex Offenders*

Baim reports on trauma therapy for adult sex offenders. His work is based on the conviction that in most cases, sexual violence is *a symptom of illness*, a symptom of the perpetrator's maladaptive thinking, feeling, and behavior patterns developed largely in response to *their own* earlier trauma (Baim, 2000, p 157). Various studies have shown: 18–93% of violent sexual offenders were *themselves* sexually abused in childhood or were beaten or neglected in an extremely brutal way. But that was never addressed in childhood or later. Therefore, the patients themselves never attached any importance to the trauma. The trauma experiences of these patients remain unprocessed in the memory through dissociation and are stored on the sensorimotor level. The limbic system, which is responsible for emotional regulation and the ability to bond, is 20–30% smaller in children with a history of abuse as compared to other children (Baim, 2000, p. 160). This is why even the slightest stress leads to overreactions and loss of self-control in people with trauma. For this reason, many trauma survivors get used to avoiding feelings *altogether*. However, this makes them emotionally numb.

According to Baim, most offenders do understand *on a cognitive level*, even at the time of their offending, that what they are doing is wrong. However, they cannot control their *emotions* because of their altered brain functions. It is, therefore, superfluous to *cognitively* teach perpetrators of violence why sexual violence is wrong because it does not change their psychophysical dysregulation. At present, the treatment of sex offenders is dominated by the cognitive behavioral approach. However, according to Baim (2000, p. 163), "they have been compliant in treatment, learned to 'talk the talk' … and managed to show improvements in psychometric tests—only to go on to later re-offend". Based on these considerations, Baim concludes: Some of the perpetrators commit the act of violence *in equivalence mode* in a kind of trance state. The victims are fixed in their perception of the act of violence in a perpetrator-victim schema. Feelings of helplessness or powerlessness trigger a kind of suction in them, resulting in a flashback. For this, it is enough that the affected person meets a fearful, powerless person who is just the way he used to be. That is unbearable for him. He hates himself in the other because of his weakness. When he can no longer stand being a victim, his only choice is to become an offender. He reverses the victim-perpetrator roles and acts out his hatred in the role of the powerful perpetrator. The trance state dissolves as soon as the act is finished. At some point, he thinks as a healthy adult again and realizes on his own that he has been violent and hurt another person.

According to Baim (2000, p. 164), one is guilty of malpractice if one does not treat a disease causally after knowing the root cause of the disease. He suggests supplementing cognitive behavioral therapy with trauma therapy. Trauma therapy should reduce the energetic potential of the cycle of violence. Patients have to *emotionally* process their own trauma experiences from their childhood. This is because, as perpetrators, they can only develop the desired empathy for their victims by gaining *empathy for themselves as trauma victims* in therapy. They should learn to stop hating the child they once were.

Baim likes to work with *contrasting* images. For example, he lets the patients set up two sculptures as a warm-up exercise: one of a family where anger and fear are always present and another with images of a hypothetical family that communicates well and supports each other. The group members can intervene in the symbol work and change it. In doing so, they learn what is helpful and harmful for children. They recognize connections to their own behavior as an adult *and also as a child.*

In any case, patients should go through the following steps in psychodrama therapy (Baim, 2000, p. 166): (1) A conversation between me as *a victim of abuse* and those who perpetrated against me; (2) A conversation between me *as a perpetrator of abuse*, and those who perpetrated against me; (3) A conversation between me *as a victim of abuse*, and the victims I have perpetrated against; (4) A conversation between me *as a perpetrator* and the victims I have abused.

In Baim's experience, the most powerful key to the underlying childhood trauma lies *in the role of the perpetrator*. Therefore, he first lets the patient therapeutically process his own act of violence as the perpetrator. The patient should *cognitively* grasp *his role as a perpetrator*. Next, the therapist works out a 'violence circle' with him in writing. The perpetrator develops an idea of how to break this circle. Baim consequently structures the psychodramatic work that follows. Thus, he wants to prevent the patient from dissociating when enacting his *own perpetrator role.* (1) The patient symbolically represents his intrapsychic strengths and a *transpersonal* contact person with whom he can interact on stage. (2) A supportive doppelganger accompanies the patient throughout the entire play. (3) An auxiliary ego takes on the role of the perpetrator in the scene as a doppelganger. (4) The protagonist shares his thoughts, feelings, and behavior during the act of violence *from the observation and narrative room* (5) He *describes* the place where the act of violence took place and defines his own position and actions in this place. (6) The protagonist uses a symbol for 'the scene of the crime' to mark where he was during his crime. (7) He repeats the words he used then but *still* stands *outside the scene.* (8) It is only after that, that he takes on *his own role in the trauma scene* and re-enacts it. (9) In doing so, he repeatedly swaps roles with his previously defined internal and external stabilizing auxiliary ego as well as with his victim. According to Baim, this reduces the emotional dynamic in the perpetrator role and stabilizes the patient internally. (10) Baim lets the perpetrator play the role of a fictional 'Mr. Self-Aware'. This is the role of a *fictional* ex-offender who has successfully completed the therapy program. This *"ex-offender"* is now able to abide by the law and has not relapsed.

Baim's approach to *coping with the offender's childhood trauma* is very similar to that of coping with his crime. He describes this using a case example: His patient Adrian had continuously sexually abused a girl who was related to him between the ages of 9 and 11. To process his childhood trauma, Baim asks his patient to symbolically represent on stage: (1) His ability to care for others, his ability to listen, and so on. (2) A *good* mother. Unlike his mother, the good mother actively intervenes and protects him as a child from his father. His father had previously abused him brutally. (3) A group member plays the role of the transpersonal protective figure Martin Luther King. (4) A doppelganger accompanies the patient till the very end. (5) *Two auxiliary therapists* re-enact the father's abuse. The therapist, the client, as well as the group members, observe the actions of the brutal father *from the narrative room.* They name the incident as 'unbelievable violence'. (6) The protagonist then meets his *fictional helpful, good mother*. This results in an emotional catharsis. (7) The patient also takes on *his own role as a victim* once in the interaction space of the trauma scene. This brings the abuse to life even in his sensorimotor system. However, unlike before, this happens in a new 'holding way'. In the middle of the scene of violence, the new, strong, and just mother saves the 8-year-old boy. The patient reacts with another intense emotional catharsis. Baim followed his patient Adrian's career for more than a year after his release on probation. During this time, the patient continued to develop positively, made further progress, and did not relapse.

### 5.17.6 Jörg Burmeister (2000, pp. 198–225): Psychodrama with Survivors of Traffic Accidents

According to Burmeister, 500,000 people are injured in traffic accidents in Germany every year, 100,000 of them with severe injuries. 10–30% of them develop a chronic post-traumatic stress disorder (PTSD) regardless of the severity of the physical injury (Burmeister, 2000, p. 202 f.). Action methods such as psychodrama involve the motor, sensory, and affective parts of the brain in treatment (Burmeister, 2000, pp. 200, 206). This also activates the trauma memory in the left brain. Burmeister primarily works in an individual setting. He adopts the therapeutic attitude of a doppelganger and a midwife when working with trauma victims. This promotes the self-determined, spontaneously creative action of the patient.

Burmeister divides his integrative therapeutic approach to PTSD into four phases: (1) Those affected react secondarily *to their symptoms* with feelings of shame, guilt, anxiety, and depression (Burmeister, 2000, p. 207). Therefore, the therapist informs the patient in detail about the clinical disease pattern of PTSD in the preparation phase. (2) He engages the protagonists in imagination processes. They should search for memories or scenes from myths, fairy tales, or fantasies, 'which promote the ability to choose, to decide [...] and to be effective again' (Burmeister, 2000, p. 209). In doing this, the therapist helps them as a doppelganger. (3) He lets the protagonist *psychodramatically* set up psychologically stabilizing memories and fantasy scenes as a 'safe place' in the therapy room (Burmeister, 2000, p. 210 ff.). (4) The patient relives her trauma story through re-enactment. However, in doing so, she should modify it (Burmeister, 2000, p. 212 ff.). The patient must *not* stop at the moment of great shock. Instead, she should *courageously end the story differently*. In doing this, the therapist encourages her to use *her own impulses* as a starting point. (5) Unlike in the past, the whole event now takes place in the protective framework of the therapeutic relationship. Burmeister repeatedly uses various self-stabilization techniques, for example, the 'safe place', breathing exercises, or the teddy bears from childhood (Burmeister, 2000, p. 214). (6) The phase of reintegration into the social environment follows. For this purpose, Burmeister (2000, p. 215) uses, among other things, the technique of the 'social network inventory'.

## References


Baim, C. (2000). Time's distorted mirror: Trauma work with adult male sex offenders. In P. F. Kellermann & M. K. Hudgins (Eds.), *Psychodrama with trauma survivors. Acting out your pain* (pp. 155–175). Jessica Kingsley Publishers.

Bakhit, C. (2006). "Es freut uns, dass jemand an uns glaubt". Gruppenanalytische Gespräche mit traumatisierten Flüchtlingen. *Gruppenpsychotherapie Und Gruppendynamik, 42*, 303–318.

Bannister, A. (2000). Prisoners of the family: Psychodrama with abused children. In P. F. Kellermann, M. K. Hudgins (Eds.), Psychodrama with trauma survivors. Acting out your pain (pp. 97–113). London: Jessica Kingsley Publishers.

Bonhoeffer, D. [1944], equoted by Bethgen, E. (Hrsg.) (1951). Widerstand und Ergebung . Gütersloher Verlagshaus, S. 607.

Burge, M. (2000). Psychodrama with Vietnam veterans and their families: Both victims of traumatic stress. In P. F. Kellermann & M. K. Hudgins (Eds.), *Psychodrama with trauma survivors. Acting out your pain* (pp. 299–316). Jessica Kingsley Publishers.

Burmeister, J. (2000). Psychodrama with survivors of traffic accidents. In P. F. Kellermann & M. K. Hudgins (Eds.), *Psychodrama with trauma survivors. Acting out your pain* (pp. 198–228). Jessica Kingsley Publishers.

Dayton, T. (2000). The use of psychodrama in the treatment of trauma and addiction. In P. F. Kellermann & M. K. Hudgins (Eds.), *Psychodrama with trauma survivors. Acting out your pain* (pp. 114–136). Jessica Kingsley Publishers.

Dieckmann, H. (1991). *Komplexe. Diagnostik und Therapie in der Analytischen Psychologie*. Springer.

Dürckheim, K. G. (1984). *Von der Erfahrung der Transzendenz*. Herder.

Fooken, I. (2009). Resilienz und posttraumatische Reifung. In A. Maercker (Ed.), *Posttraumatische Belastungsstörungen* (3rd ed., pp. 65–85). Springer.

Gast, U. (2000). Diagnostik und Behandlung dissoziativer Störungen. In F. Lamprecht (Ed.), *Praxis der Traumatherapie* (pp. 164–211). Pfeiffer bei Klett-Cotta.

Grimmer, K. (2013). Die psychodramatische Doppelgängertechnik und die Entwicklung von Sicherheit gebenden, inneren elterlichen Rollen', guten Elterintrojektien' – bei Angststörungen. *Zeitschrift für Psychodrama und Soziometrie12*(2), 189–199.

Gunkel, S. (1999). Die Häufigkeit posttraumatischer Belastungsstörungen: Epidemiologische Befunde. In G. Kruse & S. Gunkel (Eds.), Trauma und Konflikt. *Zugangswege zu einer traumaorientierten Psychotherapie* (pp. 48–83). Hannoversche Ärzte-Verlags-Union.

Hartmann, E. (1996). Outline for a theory on the nature and functions of dreaming. *Dreaming, 6*(2), 147–170

Heigl-Evers, A., Heigl, F., Ott, J., & Rüger, U. (1997). *Lehrbuch der Psychotherapie* (3rd ed.). Gustav Fischer.

Hirsch, M. (2004). *Psychoanalytische Traumatologie–Das Trauma in der Familie. Psychoanalytische Theorie und Therapie schwerer Persönlichkeitsstörungen.* Schattauer.

Hudgins, M. K. (2000). The therapeutic spiral model: Treating PTSD in action. In P. F. Kellermann & K. Hudgins (Eds.), *Psychodrama with trauma survivors. Acting out your pain* (pp. 229–254). Jessica Kingsley Publishers.

ICD-10-GM. (2004). *Systematisches Verzeichnis. Internationale statistische Klassifikation der Krankheiten und verwandten Gesundheitsprobleme.* 10. Revision–German Modification. Version 2004–Stand 15. August 2003. Deutscher Ärzte-Verlag.

Karp, M. (2000). Psychodrama of rape and torture: A sixteen-year follow-up case study. In P. F. Kellermann & M. K. Hudgins (Eds.), *Psychodrama with trauma survivors. Acting out your pain* (pp. 63–82). Kingsley Publishers.

Kellermann, P. F. (2000). The therapeutic aspects of psychodrama with traumatized people. In P. F. Kellermann & M. K. Hudgins (Eds.), *Psychodrama with trauma survivors. Acting out your pain* (pp. 23–40). Jessica Kingsley Publishers.

Kellermann, N. P. F. (2009). *Holocaust trauma. Psychological effects and treatment.* iUniverse.

Kellermann, P. F., & Hudgins, M. K. (Eds.). (2000). *Psychodrama with trauma survivors. Acting out your pain.* Jessica Kingsley Publishers.

König, K. (1984). Unbewusste Manipulationen in der Psychotherapie und im Alltag. *Georgia Augusta, 40*, 10–16.

Krakow, B., Kellner, R., Pathak, D., & Lambert, L. (1995). Imagery rehearsal treatment for chronic nightmares. *Behaviour Research and Therapy, 33*, 837–843.

Krüger, R. T. (1997). *Kreative Interaktion. Tiefenpsychologische Theorie und Methoden des klassischen Psychodramas.* Vandenhoeck & Ruprecht.

Krüger, R. T. (2002). Psychodrama als Aktionsmethode in der Traumatherapie und ihre Begründung mit der Rollentheorie und der Kreativitätstheorie. *Zeitschrift für Psychodrama und Soziometrie, 1*(2), 117–146.

Krüger, R. T. (2004). Zwei Seelen in der Brust haben–Theorie und Praxis der störungsspezifischen Psychodramatherapie mit suchtkranken Menschen. *Zeitschrift für Psychodrama und Soziometrie, 3*(2), 161–194. https://doi.org/10.1007/s11620-004-0017-0

Krüger, R. T. (2010a). Der Selbststeuerungskreis. In Wiederholungskonflikten vom Objekt des Geschehens zum Subjekt des eigenen Handelns werden. *Zeitschrift für Psychodrama und Soziometrie, 9*(1), 149–160.

Krüger, R. T. (2010b). Der Durchgang durch die gegenseitige neurotische Allergie in längeren Paarbeziehungen. *Zeitschrift für Psychodrama und Soziometrie, 9*(1), 83–92.

Krüger, R. T. (2013). Wo das Wünschen noch geholfen hat. Die Arbeit mit dem Bewältigungsmärchen. *Zeitschrift für Psychodrama und Soziometrie, 12*(1), 103–112.

Lesemann, K. (1993). Mut zum Rollentausch–Stationäre Psychodramatherapie bei sexuellem Missbrauch. *Psychodrama, 7*, 75–96.

Leutz, G. A. (1974). *Das klassische Psychodrama nach J. L. Moreno.* Springer.

Leutz, G. A. (2000). Appearance and treatment of dissociative states of consciousness in psychodrama. in P. F. Kellermann & M. K. Hudgins (Eds.), *Psychodrama with trauma survivors. Acting out your pain* (pp. 187–197). Jessica Kingsley Publishers.

Markowitsch, H. J. (2001). Stressbezogene Gedächtnisstörungen und ihre möglichen Hirnkorrelate. In A. Streeck-Fischer, U. Sachsse, & I. Özkan (Eds.), *Körper, Seele, Trauma. Biologie, Klinik und Praxis* (pp. 72–93). Vandenhoeck & Ruprecht.

Mentzos, S. (2011). *Lehrbuch der Psychodynamik. Die Funktion der Dysfunktionalität psychischer Störungen* (5th ed.). Vandenhoeck & Ruprecht.

Pruckner, H. (2002). »Du sollst nicht fragen, das Kind will nicht reden.« Psychodramatherapie mit traumatisierten Kindern. *Zeitschrift für Psychodrama und Soziometrie, 1*(2), 147–176.

Putnam, F. W. (1988). The switch process in multiple personality disorder and other state-change disorders. *Dissociation, 1*(1), 24–32.

Radebold, H. (Ed.). (2004). *Kindheit im II. Weltkrieg und ihre Folgen*. Psychosozial-Verlag.

Reddemann, L. (1999). Trauma und Imagination. In G. Kruse, & S. Gunkel (Eds.), *Trauma und Konflikt. Zugangswege einer traumaorientierten Psychotherapie* (pp. 84–93). Hannoversche Verlags-Union.

Reddemann, L., & Dehner-Rau, C. (2004). *Trauma. Folgen erkennen, überwinden und an ihnen wachsen. Eine Übung für Körper und Seele*. Trias.

Reddemann, L. (1997). Psychosomatisch-psychotherapeutische Behandlung nach sexueller Traumatisierung. *Psycho, 23*, 665–669.

Roine, E. (2000). The use of psychodrama with trauma victims. In P. F. Kellermann, M. K. Hudgins (Eds.), *Psychodrama with trauma survivors. Acting out your pain* (2nd ed.), (pp. 83–96). London: Jessica Kingsley Publishers.

Sáfrán, Z., & Czáky-Pallavicini, K. (2013). Das Bewältigungsmärchen in der Gruppentherapie von Menschen mit Traumafolgestörungen – Zusammen in der Not sein. *Zeitschrift für Psychodrama und Soziometrie, 12*(2), 269–282. https://doi.org/10.1007/s11620-013-0201-1

Schäfer, I., & Reddemann, L. (2005). Traumatisierung und Sucht – eine Literaturübersicht. *Zeitschrift für Psychotraumatologie und Psychologische Medizin, 3*(3), 9–18.

Schulte-Herbrüggen, O., & Heinz, A. (2012). Psychische Traumatisierung bei Soldaten: Herausforderung für die Bundeswehr. *Deutsches Ärzteblatt, 109*, 557–558.

Simpson, T. L., & Miller, W. R. (2002). Concomitance between childhood sexual and physical abuse and substance use problems: A review. *Clinical Psychology Review, 22*, 27–77.

van der Kolk, B. A., Burbridge, J. A., & Suzuki, J. (1998). Die Psychobiologie traumatischer Erinnerungen. Klinische Folgerungen aus Untersuchungen mit bildgebenden Verfahren bei Patienten mit posttraumatischen Belastungsstörungen. In A. Streek-Fischer (Ed.), *Adoleszenz und Trauma* (pp. 57–78). Vandenhoeck & Ruprecht.

van der Kolk, B. A., & Fisher, R. E. (1995). Dissociation and fragmentary nature of traumatic memories: Overview and exploratory study. *Journal of Traumatic Stress, 9*, 505–525.

van der Kolk, B. A., McFarlane, A. C., & Weisaeth, L. (Eds.). (1996). *Traumatic stress: The effects of overwhelming experience in mind, body, and society*. Guilford.

van der Kolk, B. A., van der Hart, O., & Burbridge, J. (1995). The treatment of post traumatic stress disorder. In S. Hobfoll, & M. de Vries (Eds.), *Extreme stress and communities: Impact and intervention* (pp.421–444). https://doi.org/10.1007/978-94-015-8486-9_19

Wittchen, H.-U., et al. (2012). Traumatische Ereignisse und posttraumatische Belastungsstörungen bei im Ausland eingesetzten Soldaten. Wie hoch ist die Dunkelziffer? *Deutsches Ärzteblatt, 109*, 559–568.

Wurmser, L. (1998). *Das Rätsel des Masochismus. Psychoanalytische Untersuchungen von Gewissenszwang und Leidenssucht* (2nd ed.). Springer.

# Chapter 6
# Anxiety Disorders

## 6.1 The Social Conditions of Fear

People in our modern societies are increasingly becoming anxious, even though prosperity continues to grow and people appear more self-confident on the outside. Twenge (quoted from Wilkinson & Picket, 2010, p. 48 ff.) determines in a summary of 269 studies: "Whether the interviewees were students or children, the result was always the same. At the end of the survey, a student had 85% more anxiety than the population average at the beginning. And the fears in children were higher in the late 1980s than in psychiatric patients in the 1950s. [...] A similar trend is also found in related areas, such as depression. [...] In Great Britain [...], people born in 1970 are twice as likely to experience depression in their mid-twenties compared to an earlier survey of people in this age group born in 1958. [...] In young people, this phenomenon is accompanied by increasing behavioral disturbances such as criminal offenses and alcohol and drug abuse. It affects both young men and women." The youth, however, hide their increasing anxieties by portraying a self-confident compensatory attitude on the outside. This is supported by the fact that "in the 1950s, 12% of teenagers agreed with the statement: 'I am an important person'. At the end of the 1980s, 80% answered in the affirmative" (Wilkinson & Picket, 2010, p. 51 f.). "This kind of self-confidence was (and is) fragile and rejects any criticism–like whistling in the dark. [...] These characteristics are also summed up in terms such as 'pathological egoism', 'insecure self-confidence', or 'narcissism'. [...] In 2006, two-thirds of American college students were reported to have scored above the 1982 average on the narcissism index."

**Central idea**

Wilkinson and Picket determined that increasing income inequality in society reinforces the trend toward more anxiety (Wilkinson & Picket, 2010, p. 50). They attribute this to the fact that psychosocial stress factors are more significant in societies with high-income disparities.



R. T. Krüger, *Disorder-Specific Psychodrama Therapy in Theory and Practice*,
Psychodrama in Counselling, Coaching and Education 4,
https://doi.org/10.1007/978-981-99-7508-2_6

People worry about their social status. The number of social relationships is considerably less. Children are more likely to experience stress in early childhood. "The key realization is that mortality and health in society depend a lot less on its overall wealth than on the distribution of wealth. The more evenly the wealth is distributed, the better the public health" (Wilkinson & Picket, 2010, p. 101). A decrease in income inequality is directly reflected in better public health. This is apparent in the example of Great Britain *in both the world wars* (Wilkinson & Picket, 2010, p. 104) and in the example of Japan *after* the Second World War (Wilkinson & Picket, 2010, p. 107). It is noteworthy that if income inequality increases in wealthy industrialized countries, the health risks increase *even among rich people, decreasing* their life expectancy (Wilkinson & Picket, 2010, p. 95). For example, "in the USA, where the social gap between the rich and the poor is huge, the incidence of serious mental disorders across all income groups is five times higher [...] than in the Scandinavian countries [...]. [...] The allegedly comfortable existence of a millionaire does not protect one against one's anxieties. [...] The rich wall themselves, which perhaps creates an illusion of security. But people don't notice that their social environment is no longer functioning. The stress comes back in through the back door, so to speak. It's the fear of losing something. [...] The USA, Singapore, Portugal, and Great Britain are at the bottom of the rank order. In these states, the top 20% earn seven, eight, or even nine times the income available to the 20% at the bottom. [...] In Japan and Sweden, [...] those at the top earn only up to two to three times the average earnings of their poor fellow citizens. [...] These countries occupy the top position in terms of life expectancy and general health" (Süddeutsche Zeitung from November 2nd, 2009). In line with these findings, "the risk of anxiety disorders in cities is 21% [...] higher than in rural areas" (Christian Weber, SZ, a report from June 24, 2011, on a study by the Mannheim Central Institute for Mental Health by Florian Lederbogen and Andreas Meyer-Lindenberg).

*Other threats also* further the general fearfulness of people: Countries are falling apart. The number of refugees is increasing worldwide. Terrorism and its defense have reached industrialized countries. Climate change is progressing rapidly without adequate countermeasures from the international community. The indebtedness of the industrialized countries is increasing steadily and reaching astronomical heights. The governments of the industrialized countries, responsible for balancing the tensions between the rich and the poor, have primarily surrendered politically to the financial markets. They have handed over the responsibility of finding solutions to existing problems to future generations. At the same time, the psychologically stabilizing factors in societies are also weakening: The relationships between people and the relationship with nature are strained due to increasing urbanization and cyber technologies. Religious values and norms are increasingly being replaced by the values of the capitalist market economy.

## 6.2 What Are Anxiety Disorders?

The term 'anxiety' is used in common parlance to refer to *different types of fear*. Not everyone who feels afraid has an anxiety disorder. In the ICD-10, anxiety disorders are listed under F40 and F41. Nevertheless, fear is a common *emotion* in people with anxiety disorders. It is essential to differentiate between real justified and pathological fears in a *practical therapy approach* (see Fig. 6.1).

**Central idea**

The respective psychodynamic cause of fear determines the disorder-specific therapeutic approach. Therefore, I differentiate diagnostically between real justified fears, exaggerated fears, object-related fears, self-referential panic attacks, and the *secondary* fear of panic attacks (see Fig. 6.1).

1. A *real justified* fear is a signal and warns of *real* danger in an *actual conflict* (see Fig. 6.1). It occurs, for example, in the event of an impending job loss, an examination, cancer, the corona pandemic, or a real threat of loss of a loved one. In such a case, the patient doesn't express fear. Instead, he talks about a current external conflict that frightens him. The therapist then diagnoses acute stress reaction (F43.0) but not an anxiety disorder (F40). An acute stress reaction is a potentially traumatizing situation. For example, in the case of cancer, the patient thinks as a healthy adult in the as-if mode: "I have cancer, I am afraid. But *if I* get adequate treatment, I will *probably* survive the disease." However, she thinks in the equivalence mode when in panic: "I have cancer. So I'm dying."

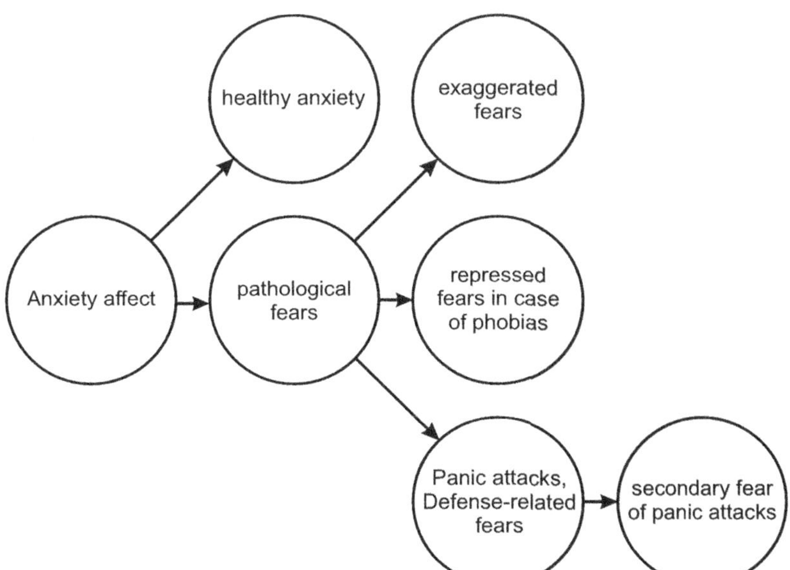


**Fig. 6.1** The diagnostic differentiation of anxiety

In the case of real anxiety, the therapist orients herself through the following procedure (Krüger 2020):

i. He represents the patient's panicked self, her 'fearful ego', with a *second empty chair* next to the chair on which she is sitting: "This is your fearful ego, your stressed self. You are currently sitting in the chair of the coping ego. However, you keep slipping into thinking and feeling as your frightened ego again and again, especially at night when you cannot sleep."
ii. The therapist asks the patient to name *all* of their different fears. He then uses various building blocks to symbolize *each* of the patient's fears on the chair of her 'frightened ego', for example, the fear of dying, the fear of losing control of one's own life, the fear of financial hardship, and/or the fear of becoming needy and dependent. The therapist accompanies the patient as she grasps her various fears as a doppelganger.
iii. He asks her to rate the extent of each of her fears on a scale of 0–10.
iv. He replaces the symbol for her *strongest individual fear* with a *large* object, for example, a waste paper basket. In doing so, he appreciates the magnitude of this particular fear.
v. The therapist lets the patient switch to the chair of her fearful ego and asks her: "Please allow yourself to get in touch with your worst fear. What do you feel and think?" As a doppelganger, he paradoxically sharpens her fearful thinking a little. The patient talks to herself in this role and differentiates her fear in the *as-if mode of play*. In doing so, she completes the psychosomatic resonance in her worst fear of missing parts to a holistic psychosomatic resonance pattern. This neuronally connects the five memory centers of her sensorimotor interaction patterns, physical sensations, affect, linguistic concepts, and thoughts (see Sect. 2.7).
vi. The therapist lets the patient switch back to the chair of her healthy adult thinking and asks about actions that help the patient to deal with her fear: "How do you cope when you feel your worst fear? What is good for you? How do you manage to reduce your anxiety?" The therapist names these actions as 'self-stabilization techniques'. These can be, for example, (1) Becoming aware of the specific kind of threat, (2) Physical movement, (3) Writing a letter to trustworthy people, (4) Pursuing a creative hobby, or (5) Talking to someone else.
vii. The patient writes the discovered self-stabilization techniques on a piece of paper and places this paper on the table in front of her.

**Central idea**

The therapist verbally *appreciates* every self-stabilization technique the patient has already discovered. This is especially indicated if the patient is in a very stressful situation because it has an ego-strengthening effect.

viii. If necessary, the therapist teaches the patient additional self-stabilization techniques (see Sect. 5.9).

ix. The therapist and the patient get an overview of the extent of the *real threat* to the patient in their current conflict.
x. They process potential relationship conflicts with a significant person or an employer using the seven steps of the psychodramatic dialogue (see Sect. 8.4.2).
xi. If necessary, the therapist and the patient work together in a future play to grasp the consequences that would *occur* if the patient did *nothing* about her fear and just *waited*.

The ego confusion between the patient's fearful and coping ego is resolved by *externally representing* the fear with a second chair in the therapy room *next to the patient*. This is because the patient *internally* delegates the various psychosomatic resonance patterns (see Sect. 2.7) of current anxiety-provoking situations *externally* to the second chair. In doing so, she *psychosomatically* frees the development of her inner self-image in the current therapeutic relationship from their fears. *The therapist* sees the patient's two contrary self-images separately as chairs in front of him. This helps him develop compassion *not only* for the patient's coping ego but also for her frightened ego.

**Exercise 16**

You can not understand the two-chair technique just by reading it. You have to try acting psychosomatically. Talk to a friend for five minutes and tell them about your fears concerning the corona pandemic. Then start the conversation all over again and put a second chair *next to you* for your fearful self. Use this second chair to place symbols for your various individual fears. What is the difference in your experience *with* and *without* the second chair? You will notice that if you place the chair for the frightened ego next to you, you will distance yourself from your fears *internally* because they're next to you *on the other chair*. Regardless, you justify your various fears internally.

**Central idea**

*Real justified fears* diminish if the patient informs herself well about the *real* impending threat. This is because the patient must know the reality of the threat to be able *to act appropriately*. Even small, appropriate actions can diminish the real fear of the real threat.

**Important definition**

Fears are *pathological* if they are *inappropriately intense* or *cannot be justified* in a given situation.

1. *Exaggerated fears* arise when an external actual conflict *further* triggers self-referential anxiety in the patient because of fixation in a defense system (see Fig. 6.1 above). As a result, the patient cannot adequately cope with the *real* threat due to self-esteem problems, self-injurious thinking, or dependent thinking. Patients with exaggerated fears often experience a dependent personality disorder (F60.7), fear of failure (F41.2), or depression (see Sect. 8.2). In such a case, the therapist *first* treats the patient's real, justified fear (see above). If the exaggerated fears *persist*, he continues to treat the patient like he would a patient with a personality disorder (see Sects. 4.7 and 4.8).

2. Object-related *fears in isolated phobias* (F40.2) are an expression of a *neurotic conflict*. The patient unconsciously suppresses a *relationship conflict* that has generated fear in the past. He shifts *the emotion of fear*, however, to another relatively insignificant external object (Mentzos, 2011, p. 110), for example, the fear of the choleric father to the dogs that bark. The result is a dog phobia. In such a case, the therapist offers the following steps of therapy: (1) He lets the patient engage in a psychodramatic dialogue in the relationship conflict with the dog using role reversal, (2) And then switch to the analogous conflict in childhood through an external change of scene, and enact the conflict. Thus, the patient integrates her fear into the childhood conflict. In doing so, the patient converts her fear into anger. (3) She integrates this new feeling into her inner relationship image with her father using psychodramatic dialogue with role reversal (see Sect. 6.8.2). Sometimes, an object-related fear is part of a flashback in trauma disorder. For example, a 65-year-old man suffered from a phobia of men wearing white coats, resulting from a hospital admission when he was 4 years old (see case example 32 in Sects.5.1, 5.5 and 5.9).
3. Self-referential anxiety in panic attacks.

**Important definition**

*Panic attacks* are a symptom of *self-referential anxieties*. They are a reaction to an old defense. The defense can be a relational neurotic defense (see Sect. 8.4.2) or an entire defense system in the case of a structural disorder. Patients with a neurotic disorder defend through denial because of their fixation on perfectionism and adaption. Patients with structural disorder panic because they lose control of themselves due to a destabilized defense system. "It's about the unconscious, intrapsychic threat" caused by the impending collapse of the patient's old, rigid defense system (Mentzos, 2011, p.117) (see Sect. 6.3).

**Central idea**

The *dominant* defense pattern of people with panic attacks is defense through denial: "And so he concluded in a razor-sharp manner that what cannot be cannot be." The therapist represents this defense with a chair next to the patient and names it as her 'self-protection behavior'. Together with the patient, he searches for a personally suitable name for the patient's unique way of self-protection. In doing this, he works *explicitly metacognitively* (see Sect. 2.14).

According to the ICD-10, panic attacks are severe anxiety states "that are not limited to a specific situation [...] and are therefore not predictable". They are accompanied by "sudden palpitations, chest pain, feelings of suffocation, dizziness, and alienation. [...] The fear of dying, losing control, or going insane often arises secondarily". For patients with panic attacks, there is an intrapsychic need to blindly maintain their old defense against negative emotions and their perfect goals (Schacht, 2009, p. 92 ff.) *even in the face of real latent threats* (see case examples 52 and 53 in Sect. 6.3, 54 in Sect.6.4 and 55 in Sect.6.6). They often experience the impending collapse of their psychological defense system *physically* in the form of reactions from their parasympathetic system. They then look for a rational explanation for their psychosomatic complaints. In the case of cardiophobia, for example, the diffuse fear is psychosomatically accompanied by tachycardia and shortness of breath. The patient rationalizes her psychosomatic symptoms as a result of an incipient heart attack. The healing principle of 'anger instead of fear' applies to anxious patients with panic attacks because of *neurotic disorders*. In patients with *a structural disorder*, the defense through perfectionism or grandiosity is additionally secured by masochistic self-censorship provoked by a self-destructive superego. Enhanced self-actualization in external conflicts updates the self-destructive superego. According to Mentzos (2011, p. 117), these patients are not afraid of the *actual physical* death, "but rather of the psychological death, [...] fear of losing self or, in other cases, fear of losing control over their impulses". Panic disorder (F41.0) can present as a comorbid condition with trauma-related disorder (see Sect. 5.2), or with personality disorder as borderline personality disorder (see Sect. 4.3).

4. The *secondary fear of panic attacks*. In response to the feeling of existential threat from panic attacks, patients mainly develop a *secondary fear of panic attacks*. As a result, they often try to avoid the situations that trigger their panic attacks.

**Central idea**

The diagnosis of *anxiety affect* provides information on the disorder-specific therapeutic approach. The various anxiety disorders listed in the ICD only describe symptom complexes. They *do not* give any indication of the indicated approach.

1. According to the ICD-10, people with *agoraphobia* (F40.0) are "afraid of leaving the house, entering shops, being in crowds and public places, traveling alone by train, bus or plane". They often experience panic disorder and depressive or obsessive–compulsive symptoms.
2. Patients with *social phobia* (F40.1) are "afraid of being examined and observed by other people. This leads to the avoidance of social situations", low self-esteem, and fear of criticism. "Some common symptoms include blushing, hand tremors, nausea, or the urge to urinate."
3. In people with isolated phobias (F40.2), the phobia "is limited to narrowly defined situations such as proximity to certain animals, heights, darkness, flying, closed rooms, urinating [...] in public toilets, [...] or the sight of blood [...]".
4. Panic disorders (F41.0) are characterized by "recurring, severe anxiety attacks [...] that are not limited to a specific situation".
5. In the case of a *generalized anxiety disorder* (F41.1), the fear is "persistent and not limited to certain environmental conditions, [...] it is rather 'free floating'. The [...] symptoms are variable, [...] such as constant nervousness, tremors, muscle tension, sweating, drowsiness, palpitations, dizziness, or upper abdominal discomfort". A patient may also be afraid of themselves falling sick or "[...] that a relative might soon fall ill or have an accident".

"Around *25% of all people* develop an anxiety disorder in the course of their lives: 6% suffer from agoraphobia, 3% from panic disorder, 5% from generalized anxiety disorder, 11% from a specific phobia, and 13% from a social phobia" (Morschitzky, 1998, p. 130).

## 6.3 The Self-Protective Behavior in Patients with Panic Attacks as an Obstacle in Therapy

In patients with panic attacks self-protection through denial blocks access to the psychodynamic conflicts. Thus, they defend negative feelings.

***Case example 51***
*During the intake interview, a 32-year-old patient said his panic attacks (F40.0) started at the age of 23. That was when he decided to live by the motto: "There is no such thing as impossible!" The panic attacks occurred in situations in which he would have to be kind to himself despite his mistakes.*

***Case example 52***
*An engineer, Mr. C., sought psychotherapy because of massive panic attacks (ICD F41.0). The therapist and the patient together searched for genuine reasons for his fears. It turned out that the patient had just opened the fourth store in a nearby town and wished to open six more. He wanted to 'get rich'. Together the therapist and the patient realized: Mr. C. had always taken loans to open a store. In doing so, he had mortgaged the existing stores. If even one of the stores failed, the others would also become insolvent. The patient realized that his very existence was in real financial danger. He decided not to rent another shop for the time being. However, his panic attacks continued to occur. Two years later, Mr. C. came into the therapist's practice and reported that his panic attacks had disappeared. He was unemployed and divorced. Despite his engineering degree, he now worked as an unskilled worker for 5 euros an hour and was 35,000 euros in debt. Instead of panic attacks, he now had a real existential fear.*

*What had happened? Mr. C. had appointed his wife as the manager of all his stores. But, since they got married, he had noticed that his wife would secretly stash away thousands of euros every now and then. His panic attacks, therefore, had a justified reason. His stores went bankrupt. He had to pay off his debt. He changed employers because he was getting 1,000 euros more monthly in the new company. He took his customer base with him to the new company. However, he was let go from there after six months. He was now in real financial danger. The fear had become a reality. Mr. C. did everything he could to counter this real justified threat; he worked for wages as an unskilled worker. That's why he didn't have panic attacks anymore. After the reunification of Germany, he built a new professional life for himself in the new federal states.*

***Case example 53***
*A 35-year-old businessman had agoraphobia (ICD F40.0) and panic attacks for three years. These typically occurred on the bus, on the train, at the hairdresser's, or in the car on the highway. These different situations had one thing in common: the patient had to adapt to the current situation and pretend it was nothing. He could not leave the situation without others wondering about him and perhaps laughing*

*at him. After a year of group therapy, the therapist and the patient realized that a latent real justified fear had initially triggered his anxiety states. He and his wife had consulted an orthopedic surgeon. In his presence, the doctor said to his wife: "If you do nothing about your back pain, you will be in a wheelchair in ten years!" This real threat had retraumatized the patient. He had had a difficult childhood and an even more difficult youth. His parents divorced when he was thirteen years old. He had slept with his suicidal father for years and was constantly on guard. It was only through his marriage and two children that he led a free and happier life. He could catch up on all he had missed as a child with his supportive, warm-hearted wife. But when his wife became chronically ill, his self-protection through adaptation was at risk of breaking down, and he reacted with panic attacks.*

"The probability of developing an [...] anxiety disorder is high when a benign internalized object offering security (that is the sum of the precipitates of positive relationship experiences in childhood) could not be formed in the course of the patient's development" (Mentzos, 2011, p. 118; Grimmer, 2007, 2013, p. 190 f.).

Patients with structural disorders (see Sect. 4.4) built up *a rigid defense system* in response to narcissistic insults, situations of shame, lack of support, the threatened loss of caregivers, a reaction to devaluation, or as a reaction to physical or sexual violence. As a child, they learned to give no power to their negative emotions and protect themselves by adapting, splitting off their feelings, or defending them through grandiosity. They have, therefore, not been able to learn to deal appropriately with feelings of shame, insecurity, despair, and loneliness. Instead, they play the role assigned to them by their caregivers. The more strongly anxious patients defend their negative emotions, the more likely it is that the anxiety disorder results from a structural disorder or part of a trauma-related disorder.

Panic attacks *typically* occur when the patient fails to cope with a current conflict using the *old* solution of adaptation, perfectionism, or compensation through grandiosity.

**Central idea**

Patients with panic attacks are trapped in a conflict; the *old* defense through denial does not lead to the desired success. But a *new adequate solution* would bring up feelings of shame, insecurity, real fear, devaluation, or abandonment. These negative emotions would trigger panic attacks in the patient.

The inner compulsion to deny negative emotions often suppresses a *real* threat in patients with panic attacks (see case examples 51, 52, and 53 above). For example, a patient with a visual defect had only 15% vision. But he still worked on the computer all day. As his eyesight continued to deteriorate, he developed panic attacks. Another man had been in group psychotherapy for three years because of panic attacks. His panic attacks only disappeared when he told the therapist about his alcohol problem, visited a group for people with addiction disorders, and became abstinent (see case example 110 in Sects. 10.6.2 and 10.9). A teacher developed panic attacks after developing visual problems due to progressive multiple sclerosis. But she continued to drive bravely in the dark at night. An advertising clerk feared she would have panic attacks at work and lose her job. She and her employed husband organized such a tight schedule for the care of their toddler that the slightest disturbance was not allowed to occur at her place of work. Of course, that didn't always work. A year later, she separated from her husband, reduced her pressure to adapt, and her panic attacks disappeared.

**Central idea**

Therapists experience a dilemma when treating anxious patients. They look for "the conflicts behind the panic attacks". They then find out, for example, that their patient cannot assert or distance herself *in her conflicts* due to fixations in childhood. Promoting self-actualization in conflicts then actualizes the *particular negative emotion, which threatens the patient's defense and triggers her panic attacks*. She latently develops a negative transference toward the therapist. The therapist often responds with negative countertransference. In the end, a hidden power struggle impedes progress in therapy.

## 6.4 Initiation of Treatment in Patients with Panic Attacks

**Recommendation**

In disorder-specific psychodrama therapy for people with panic attacks, the therapist begins by making the patient's *dominant* dysfunctional defense pattern—self-protection through adaptation, perfectionism, or grandiosity—the object of therapeutic communication. In doing so, he works explicitly metacognitively (see Sect. 2.14).

The patient should develop a problem awareness of her denial in dealing with her negative feelings. It can be done as follows:

1. The patient and the therapist sit on two chairs facing each other during a therapeutic conversation.
2. The patient describes her anxiety states. In the 'psychodramatic conversation' (see Sect. 2.8 and Fig. 2.9), the therapist symbolizes the scene from her everyday life that triggered the panic attack using two additional empty chairs in the therapy room. One chair represents the patient as the one affected by the anxiety attack. The opposite chair symbolizes the element that makes the situation restrictive, for example, the queue in the supermarket, the tram, or a threatening object, for example, a dog. By *externally* representing the symptom scene with chairs, the patient develops *internal* distance to her psychosomatic resonance pattern in the situation causing panic. She gets into the *observer's position* to her inner process of developing self-image and object image in this situation.
3. The therapist asks the patient about her internal self-regulation during her last anxiety attack: "How did you deal with your panic attack?" The patient usually tries to be brave and strong during a panic attack. She doesn't let on anything. The need to be strong, however, increases the fear of breakdown. The therapist: "You are pretending as if nothing happened and fighting bravely against your fear! Nobody should notice that you are struggling! I call this self-protective behavior. I am *placing this chair* next to you *to represent your self-protective behavior*!"

4. The therapist and the patient identify the particular type of self-protective behavior and name it individually as self-protection through adaptation', 'self-protection through perfectionism', or 'self-protection through grandiosity'. They immediately work out the *positive function* of the defense pattern in the holistic process of the patient's self-regulation (see Sect. 4.8) patient's dysfunctional metacognitive behavioral pattern: In self-protection *through adaptation*, the patient automatically turns the supposed expectations of *other* people from her surroundings *into her* expectations of herself. She tries to fulfill them, does not allow herself to show any 'weaknesses', and continues functioning *as if nothing is happening*, even when overwhelmed. In defense *through grandiosity*, the patient must always be fabulous and someone who can and does everything. Weaknesses and mistakes are not allowed. The defense helps to suppress negative feelings such as helplessness, anger, failure, or loneliness. The therapist confirms *the self-stabilizing function of the patient's defense*: "You put on a brave face and pretend as if nothing has happened, even when you suffer from existential fear! You are a courageous fighter against negative feelings".
5. The therapist repeatedly points to the chair for her self-protection when the patient is talking about her pathological fears *in everyday life* or when she is behaving in a self-protective manner *in the therapeutic relationship* and suggests: "Now you think, feel, and act again from your self-protection." Thus, the patient *internally* links the *abstract* term 'self-protective behavior' with her psychosomatic resonance pattern in the *external* conflict situation that triggers her panic attack.
6. The therapist lets the patient move to the chair for self-protection when she acts out her defense in the therapeutic relationship. While in the chair of the self-protective behavior, she should re-enact the psychosomatic resonance pattern in self-protection in the as-if mode of play and complete it into a holistic psychosomatic resonance pattern (see Sect. 2.7). The therapist helps her in this process as a metacognitive doppelganger (see Sect. 4.8). He then lets her move back to the chair of healthy adult thinking.
7. Together with the patient, the therapist explores the genesis of her self-protective behavior: "*How old is your self-protective behavior?* Where did you learn to continue functioning by pretending in front of people as if nothing happened? And to try with all your might *not* to reveal your inner distress and *not* to attract negative attention?" In doing this, the therapist describes the *patient's interaction pattern* in her defense system. The patient links her interaction pattern of old defense with *appropriate* memories from childhood. The patient often replies: "I've always done it this way." The therapist: "And when was that the first time?" The patient then narrates a matching memory from her childhood. This shows that her self-protective behavior was a *sensible and appropriate* solution *in childhood* so that she would not lose any caregivers and survive mentally. By linking her current defensive behavior with the appropriate childhood memories, the patient gains inner access to her internal process of self-development in her current external situation and to her creative ego (see Sect. 6.1).

**Central idea**

The connection with the genesis shows that the negative affect of the patient in her conflicts in childhood was fear only in the case of *a neurotic disorder*. Whereas in the case of *a structural disorder*, it was often the feeling of shame, loneliness, powerlessness, betrayal, abandonment, helplessness, or confusion. The way through the dominant defense pattern of denial opens the therapist's path to the patient's underlying psychodynamic processes.

8. When *asked about the age* of the self-protective behavior, the patient visualizes painful memories of her past internally. In such a case, the therapist places an additional empty chair for the *abandoned, abused, or ashamed* child *behind the chair for self-protective behavior*. He symbolizes the 'child' by placing a doll on this chair. But he immediately asks the patient: "When you look at your inner child over there on the chair, what does that trigger in you emotionally?" It is not uncommon for the patient to answer: "I don't even want to look!" In this case, the therapist takes the chair for the child-ego and places it in the farthest corner of the room (see Sect. 5.8): "Is it better that way?" In this way, he acknowledges the *retraumatizing quality* of the patient's childhood memories and stabilizes the patient's inner distancing, and justifies it: "I suspect that the break down of relationships traumatized you as a child".
9. The therapist expressly explains to the patient that her secondary fear of panic attacks is justified: "You feel that your existence is threatened. Because you know that if you let your negative feelings surface, you will lose control of yourself".
10. The therapist and the patient work together to find *solutions for dealing with panic attacks*. The therapist sees everything that helps the patient to be in control as a solution. For example, many patients avoid situations that might trigger their panic attacks. In such a case, the therapist *also* appreciates *the avoidance behavior* as a solution and explains: "This solution is certainly not the best, but it is currently the best possible solution *for you*. Because your fear is a fear of annihilation". The therapist asks the patient whether she has developed *other ways* of coping with anxiety. Perhaps, during a panic attack, the patient told *another person* that she was experiencing an attack at that moment. The therapist immediately says to the patient: "Your panic then became weaker! Because you no longer had to hide your negative feelings. You told the other about it. This is a new healthy adult behavior compared to the self-protection behavior you learned in your childhood". The therapist symbolizes each solution of the patient with a building block and places it on the table in front of the patient externally.
11. The therapist informs the patient, if necessary, of *additional solutions* that have helped *other* patients suffering from panic attacks in the battle against their fears.
12. In the case of structural disorders, the therapist interprets the patient's internal conflict with the help of *amplifications* (see Sect. 2.4.4). Together with the patient, he looks for a heroic figure from fairy tales, mythologies, or social contexts, who has experienced and overcome similar difficulties. For example,

the therapist narrates the Grimm fairy tale 'Of the one who set out to learn to be afraid' to patients who *fear intimacy* and panic when they think of committing to a life partner in a long-term relationship. The hero in the fairy tale does *not* shudder during his many gruesome encounters with monsters, ghosts, and those executed. He only feels the fear he has longed for when he lies in bed with the princess at the end of the fairy tale. The hero apparently could not allow closeness and love (Horst Eberhard Richter, oral communication 1992). However, he was at least aware of his self-protection behavior and faced his problem. In doing so, he acted differently from the Wild West Heroes, who always ride off with unmoved faces after conquering the love of a woman. Patients who learned to adapt to almost anything out of compassion for a traumatized parent recognize themselves again in the Grimm fairy tale 'The girl without hands'. This girl *sacrifices her hands* to save her father from the devil. But then she leaves home and marries a king. So she is honored for her noble sacrifice. However, when she has a child with this king, the appreciation from outside brings her inner self to life, and conflicts arise at the royal court. The mother-in-law, the self-destructive superego, wants to kill the young queen. She flees into the forest with her child. She sojourns in the woods for seven years. During this time, her hands grow back. The young woman thus learns, through better self-actualization, to take with her hands what she needs *without self-punishment*. Then she returns to the king healed. Such a fairy tale character can become a supportive fictional doppelganger for the patient. The therapist sets up another empty chair next to the patient for such a fairy tale character. He asks her to enter into a psychodramatic dialogue with this character to consult with her.

13. When narrating stories from childhood, the patient sometimes has a flashback. The therapist stops such a *pathological regression* by telling her what her story triggers *in him* emotionally based on the '*principle of response instead of interpretation*' (Heigl-Evers, Heigl, Ott and Rüger, 1997, p. 176 ff., see Sect. 4.13).

***Case example 54***

*During the initial interview, a 45-year-old patient with agoraphobia (F40.0), Ms. A., reports that she has been suffering from panic attacks for about twenty-five years: "I will probably never get rid of them!" Two years ago, she suffered two attacks of palpitations, sweating, and hyperventilation at her workplace and has been unemployed since then. Her panic attacks start in situations where it would be noticed if she behaved differently than the people around her, for example, at the checkout counter in the supermarket: "I then feel more restless. My heart is racing. I can't do anything when it's my turn and standing in front of the cash register. In the past, I've given my wallet to total strangers so they can pay for me. I then am no longer in control of myself. That has been the case with me for a long time. My anxiety attacks are now almost like a good friend you want to be around. Then I'm out of control."*

*The therapist sets up two chairs a little away from the patient for the symptom scene (Step 2 of the 13 steps described above) and points to the first chair: "One of the chairs is to represent you when you panic in the queue in the supermarket. The other is for the people standing in a queue, in front of whom you don't want to embarrass yourself!" The therapist places an empty chair next to Ms. A., the chair for her self-protective behavior (Step 3): "And then, like a brave heroine, you try with all your might to adjust to the expectations of others. You don't reveal any sign of struggle and withstand it all". Ms. A.: "Yes, that requires so much strength, and I lack it!" (She cries).*

*Therapist (Step 10): "What solutions have you found so far to deal with an anxiety attack?" Ms. A.: "Nowadays, I am telling the others. When I had an attack in the waiting room at the employment office, and they wanted to get an ambulance, I told them: 'I am familiar with such anxiety attacks. You don't need to call for an ambulance.' I know that it'll pass at some point! Even if I'm afraid of having a heart attack." The therapist: "And was it better when you told the others?" Ms. A.: "Yes, then it became easier for me." The therapist: "If you share your fear instead of hiding it from others, your fear will decrease. You have discovered a solution that, in my experience, also helps other patients to reduce their anxiety." (Step 9) He points to the patient: "The solution comes from your healthy adult thinking. That's what the chair you're sitting on stands for". Ms. A.: "But I'm incredibly embarrassed to say that I'm having a panic attack. I always try to behave normally, as one behaves in our society. I don't want to attract any attention." Therapist (Step 3): "You then pretend as if nothing is happening and don't want to annoy other people." He points to the chair representing the strict superego: "You obey your superego again, your inner governess! She says: 'Don't do that!'" Therapist (Step 10): "So you have already found three solutions for dealing with your anxiety attacks. Sometimes you are the heroine and pretend that you are not afraid." The therapist grabs a few brightly colored building blocks and places a building block for each solution on the table in front of the patient: "But then you also avoid situations that cause you panic attacks. This is also a solution if you have existential fear. In addition, you sometimes express your need to other people. This will reduce your anxiety, and you won't have to go to the hospital!".*

*The therapist points to the chair representing 'self-protective behavior' (Step 7): "For how long have you been protecting yourself by adapting to the expectations of others? When did you find this solution for yourself" Ms. A.: "I never wanted to attract any attention, even as a child. That has always been the case with strangers. When I was a child, I had knock knees. But my mother wanted me to go to ballet class. Then I threw myself on the floor and screamed. I felt like I was being brought to the executioner for having knock knees. I was petrified. I didn't have to go because of my screams! It was always difficult for me when I had to leave my protective home as a child. My mother didn't have much time. She spanked me when I scored a five on several dictations at school."*

*The therapist positions two more empty chairs behind the chair for self-protective behavior (Step 8): "The first chair here represents you as the child who was not seen by the mother, was hit, and the second chair is for the angry child who threw herself on the floor when she didn't want to go to ballet class." Ms. A.: "Of course, the hitting wasn't of any help. Even today, I feel insecure when I write and tend to look in the dictionary. Everything has to be perfect when I write something!" Ms. A. continues: "My mother worked thirty hours a week. Since I turned 11, she started seeking treatment every two years. She had ulcerative colitis. I haven't had any contact with her for eight years now. My mother cut contact when I asked if she could pick up my eight-year-old son from school every now and then. I was working part-time back then. But she refused to offer any help. I said to her: 'But I was always with Grandma too. That wasn't a problem for her at the time at all!' But my mother didn't want that." On asking, the patient added: "I liked being with my grandma. She gave me a sense of security and stability. I didn't feel so comfortable with my mother. I was insecure about the relationship. She just was busy with her psychoanalysis. She always claimed that Grandma had tied her and her siblings too tightly. Or her father was guilty of her suffering. Everyone else was always to blame, just not herself! My mother suffered from severe depression and often said she wanted to kill herself. She even threatened to poison us children. I was always suspicious and afraid when I ate the soup!" The patient laughs as she shares these memories.*

*The therapist points to the chair of the 'unseen child' (Step 5): "As a child, you were physically beaten and emotionally abused. This is called psychological trauma!" The therapist does not want the patient to regress too much into her traumatic experience. He, therefore, turns his attention to her self-protective behavior and interprets it positively as a self-stabilization technique developed by the patient in childhood: "Back then, in your childhood, it was important not to reveal your feelings. Otherwise, your mother would have only become angrier". Ms. A.: "I sometimes think of my childhood when I read news about a mother who killed herself and her children." Ms. A. smiles and asks almost cheerfully: "Shall I tell you more? I have even more horror stories!" The therapist replies seriously (Step 13): "No, that will be too much for me!" The patient starts to cry. It is only through this feedback that she recognizes how overwhelmed she feels. Ms. A.: "Yes, I realize I always had to be brave, always grit my teeth and push through!".*

*Therapist: "That's right, that helped you back then. But it must be challenging for you today when you tell other people you are having a panic attack. It is a great achievement for you if you do it anyway!" Ms. A.: "My mother always praised me a lot when I was reticent and good: 'Oh, Sabine was perfect, I didn't hear her at all.'" Ms. A. cries: "The child in me doesn't like it at all! After that, it was always my goal to be as quiet as possible because she praised me: the quieter I was, the better!" Ms. A. cries cathartically: "It's excruciating to talk about it. I was always completely distraught when my mother was upset, and I decided: 'I'll never do that again! I have to try to be even better.'" The therapist reassures the patient in her healthy adult thinking (Steps 4 and 8): "As a child, you learned always to pretend as if nothing had happened and be brave. But do you realize that you have found a new solution in the meantime? You now tell people around you about your fears and experience: When you communicate with others, you get help, which is very different from what your mother gave you in your childhood!" A deep, rich silence develops in the therapeutic relationship.*

*The therapist: "I feel we have worked out a lot today." Ms. A.: "Today, at some point during the session, I was quite nervous again in my tummy when I told you about my mother! I have already thought I'd write it all down!" Therapist: "Yes, but please write it down in the third person. And write down only one traumatic event from little Sabine's life [...] and then immediately write what the child would have needed in the situation instead! If you like, you can bring these little stories and share them with me next time." The therapist and the patient agree to meet for three more sessions to plan and initiate therapy.*

**Exercise 17**

You can not understand the chair work in working with anxious patients just by reading. Therefore, practice the suggested method by acting psychosomatically. Have one of your colleagues role-play an anxious patient. In the first exercise, confront the 'patient' *only verbally* when you are talking to her about her *defenses through conformity, perfectionism, or grandiosity*. You will notice: Your colleague feels criticized and devalued in the role of the patient. *In the second exercise, represent* the patient's self-protection *externally with an empty chair* next to the 'patient'. Say the same sentences to the patient while pointing your hand at the chair of self-protection. You will notice: The 'patient' *does not feel criticized*. As a therapist, you feel free to communicate with her more openly about her defenses. *In the third exercise*, choose another patient and try using a *different defense pattern* at first (see Fig. 4.1 and Sect. 4.2) to loosen the fixation of the patient's inner process of self-development. You will notice: the 'patient's' anxiety level rises immediately. The joint therapeutic work becomes muddles.

It usually takes 10–15 sessions before the steps of metacognitive therapy described above positively affect *patients* suffering from panic attacks. This is because the patient has to connect the names and functions of the ego states with her own emotional experience (see Sects. 4.7 and 4.8).

The chair work has a therapeutically positive effect on people with panic attacks for the following reasons:

1. Patients with panic attacks experience ego confusion between healthy adult thinking and self-protection through adaptation or grandiosity. The patient acts out her defense pattern in the equivalence mode: "The world is what it is. No one in this world wants to know anything about my feelings." The *external* distance to her self-protective behavior represented by the other chair allows the patient to distance herself also *internally* from her defense through denial. This helps her become aware of her rigid defense.
2. The patient and the therapist look at her self-protective behavior from the outside and *give it a name*. In doing so, she connects the psychosomatic resonance pattern of the defense in her memory to the name 'self-protection', and not to the name 'panic attack'. Thus, the new psychosomatic resonance pattern links *differently* with *other* resonance patterns in memory centers.
3. If necessary, the patient acts out her *self-protective behavior* in the as-if mode when changing roles (see Sect. 2.6). In this way, *acting out her defense pattern*, she completes the *neural connections between* the memory centers of her sensorimotor interaction patterns, physical sensations, affect, linguistic concepts, and

thoughts into a *holistic* psychosomatic resonance pattern. This helps her to gain ego control over her self-protection and defense through denial (see Sects. 4.8 and 4.9). She learns to think of her defense *in the as-if mode.* She understands her defensive behavior as an *internal representation* and no longer as a real reaction caused by the external situation. She gets into a yes-but position about her self-protective behavior: "Yes, I protect myself through grandiosity, but I have to be careful not to overwhelm myself with it."

4. The patient learns *to notice it even sooner* when she is thinking in her self-protection mode again in everyday situations. If necessary, she can look for new, more appropriate ways of perceiving and behaving in her everyday life.

## 6.5 The Different Steps in Metacognitive Therapy for People with Panic Attacks

The metacognitive disorder in anxiety patients with structural disorder (see Sect. 4.4) must be *treated explicitly metacognitively*. The procedure is similar to the treatment of patients with personality disorder and comprises the following steps (see case example 55 in Sect. 6.6).

**Central idea**

The defense in patients with anxiety actualizes in the *current* therapeutic relationship or *current* everyday conflicts. Therefore, the therapist must focus their work on the patient's *self-regulation* in the present. He *initially does not work* on the patient's trauma or deficit experiences *from childhood.*

1. The therapist makes the patient's *dominant* defense, her self-protection through adaptation or grandiosity, the focus of therapeutic communication and *represents* it *externally* with an empty chair (see Sect. 4.8).
2. In the following therapy sessions, the therapist repeatedly makes the patient's aware when they act out their old self-protection through adaptation or grandiosity in their everyday life or the therapeutic relationship.
3. The therapist asks about the age of self-protection. Then, he represents the defended experience of the child with an empty chair *and* puts a hand puppet or finger puppet for the inner 'abandoned or ashamed child of the patient' on top of it (see case example 55 in Sect. 6.6). He always asks the patient immediately: "Just look at the child that you were! What emotions does the little girl trigger in you?" If the patient *cannot tolerate* the sight of her inner child, it is a sign that the patient was traumatized in her childhood. The sight of her inner 'child' then corresponds to trauma exposure. In such a case, the therapist places the chair for the inner child *far away* in the corner of the room (see Sect. 5.8) and integrates trauma-therapeutic elements into the treatment.

**Central idea**

In more than a third of patients, the defense through denial enables self-stabilization in a trauma-related disorder. In such cases, the therapist reinterprets it positively and names the patient's defensive actions in everyday life as 'self-stabilization actions'. If necessary, the therapist integrates techniques of trauma therapy into his work.

4. But often, patients with anxiety also feel 'compassion' or 'sadness' when they look at their inner child. In such a case, the therapist asks the patient to engage in a psychodramatic dialogue *using* role reversal: "Please tell this to your inner child!" In this process, the therapist, as an auxiliary ego, takes on each of the opposite roles. While enacting these roles, the therapist integrates all the relevant information he has *already* received from the patient into the play. The patient's adult ego and the inner child are supposed to communicate *their own* wishes and life experiences with one another in the psychodramatic dialogue. In doing so, the 'inner child' and the 'self-protective behavior' learn to grant each other a right to exist.
5. During debrief, the therapist appreciatively confirms any *new* steps the patient may take in dealing with herself: "I am very touched by the fact that you felt sad looking at your inner child. You are now developing new compassion for yourself! You did not have a good enough mother or a good enough father. Therefore, you must now learn to treat *yourself* with sufficient love and care!"
6. The therapist recommends that the patient buy a doll for her inner child and *regularly practice* the dialogue between her adult self and the inner child even *at home*: "Talk to your inner child at home every day for five minutes. Ask how she is doing!" With the help of this exercise, the patient can establish a relationship with the little girl she was in childhood and develop new self-empathy.

**Central idea**

The patient has to *improve the relationship between* herself as an adult and her 'inner child'. Her inner child should develop in therapy. The adult should become a good inner authority for the inner child, similar to good enough parents. The inner child becomes a symbol *for the true self*. Both can advise and help each other. This also applies to the time *after* the end of the treatment.

7. In patients with structural disorders, self-protection through perfectionism or grandiosity is stabilized by a self-injurious superego. The therapist represents *the patient's self-injurious thinking externally* with another chair opposite the patient (see Fig. 4.1 in Sect. 4.2). He gives it a personal name along with the patient, for example 'blind accuser' or 'soul killer'. Both then continue to work consistently in a disorder-specific manner on dissolving the masochistic defenses (see Sects. 4.8, 4.10, 6.7, and 8.5). This loosens up the old masochistic self-censorship. This made sense *in childhood* to avert even greater damage (see Sect. 8.5). Therapeutic work on self-injurious thinking *indirectly loosens* the patient's defense of self-protection through perfectionism or grandiosity.
8. The therapist works with the patient to find out what support and stability would she have needed as a child during each of her traumatizing experiences and lets her write a coping fairy tale for that situation (see Sect. 5.14). This approach incorporates Moreno's idea of *surplus reality* with the help of good objects. It implements Grimmer's concept (2007, pp. 25, 37) of developing 'good inner

parents' in patients with anxiety and is similar to an essential step in Pesso therapy (Schrenker, 2008, pp. 143, 204 f.).

9. The patient writes a *fictional letter to a significant person from childhood* (see Sect. 5.11 and case example 55 in Sect. 6.6). The patient, *as the adult she is now*, communicates the contents of the letter to the caregiver from childhood in a fictional psychodramatic dialogue *with role reversal*. In this way, the patient integrates her old defense pattern and her new self-image into her old internal image of the relationship with this person and renews it (see case example 55 and Sect. 6.6).
10. The patient integrates her improved self-actualization in external conflicts into her internal relationship images *with people in the present* with the help of psychodramatic dialogues using role reversal. Thus, she resolves her defense through projection and introjection in these relationships (see Sect. 8.4.2). This is how she gets to know the people in her life in new ways.

## 6.6 The Disorder-Specific Therapy of a Patient with Social Phobia

In patients with a social phobia (F40.1), according to the ICD-10, "the fear of being examined by other people [...] leads to the *avoidance of social situations*" (see Sect. 6.2). Their masochistic relationship fears result in trying to master all situations perfectly. Any sign of insecurity destabilizes their defense system, including self-protection behavior and self-injurious thinking. Therefore, patients with a social phobia should be treated as described in Sect. 6.5. They should first undergo 10–15 sessions of individual therapy because of the masochistic fear of relationships (see Sect. 6.5).

***Case example 55***

*After his state examination, Mr. B. had not applied for a job for a whole year. He seeks therapy "to find out why he is avoiding it". In the initial interview, the therapist discovers that he experiences social phobia (F40.1) that encompasses all areas of his life. When encountering any new situation, Mr. B is 'addicted to safety' and thinks of how he can avoid being embarrassed beforehand. He, therefore, avoids even the most minor social challenges. For example, he panics when he imagines having to ask for a room in a hotel in French while on holiday in France. He lives with his girlfriend, who is a working doctor. Supposedly, this does not put him under any pressure.*

*During the first therapy session, the therapist sets up two empty chairs in the therapy room for the everyday situations that trigger fear in the patient (see Fig. 2.9 in Sect. 2.8). He also positions a third chair next to him for his self-protection behavior (1st therapy step in* Sect. 6.5*). This helps Mr. B. to understand his avoidance behavior as a self-discovered solution to the fight against his anxiety states. Mr. B. reads about 'social phobias' on the Internet at home. He accumulates knowledge and* *analyzes himself. But this knowledge does not change his avoidance behavior. When his girlfriend becomes pregnant, he decides, with the therapist's help, to propose to her for marriage. Mr. B. had previously rated this action as 'very difficult' on a list of anxiety-inducing situations. His partner is thrilled. They get married. Mr. B. shares his experience: "Once I have promised something, everything works out well for me as it does for other people. It's always been that way. So then I have to!".*

*In the fifteenth therapy session, Mr. B. reports with satisfaction: "My wife is in the last weeks of pregnancy. I am now coping with many situations on my list of problems. It is working well. My fears are like a ball of wool. I have to pull out one thread after the other and work on it!" The therapist hears this plan but feels uneasy. Because, in his experience, Mr. B's general avoidance behavior changes little when he successfully masters individual situations. He, therefore, asks the patient: "How old is your self-protection behavior? How long have you been pretending as if it's nothing when you're scared?" Mr. B.: "It was always like that, even as a child!" The therapist places a fourth empty chair behind the chair for the self-protection behavior, 'for the little boy' who was the patient in his childhood. Mr. B. shares humiliation experiences from childhood: "My older brother and my mother were very close to each other. They are quite similar! My mother is also a doer and tackles everything." Therapist: "As 'the sensitive one,' you were the black sheep in the family!" Mr. B: "That's right, my brother always had to be the greatest. He capped me all the time. Once, when I had six firsts in my school report in elementary school, he wrote a one next to my grades in pencil in all the places where he had already had a first in the last five years. That was more than my six firsts. But my brother had never had six firsts on one report simultaneously!".*

*The therapist places the fifth chair opposite the patient 'for the dominant brother'. As a doppelganger, he speaks directly to his brother's chair: "Karl, I think that you could have given your little brother Rolf the privilege of being better than you at least once! Yeah, don't look like that! I don't think it's okay that you mess up the six firsts he got back then!" The therapist asks Mr. B: "What would your brother Karl answer now?" Mr. B: "Well, he would disagree and say: 'But that's true, he shouldn't act like that here.' The therapist gets angry as a doppelganger: "Karl, leave Rolf alone now!" The therapist gets up and turns his brother's chair: "Get out of this room now or just turn around! It's enough!" Mr. B.: "He won't go. He will come to me, point at me, and grin." The therapist turns angrily to the 'brother': "Well then, I'll get you out of the room now!" He takes the chair representing the brother and places it outside in front of the door. Mr. B. laughs: "He's going, but he's shouting stupid things from outside!" The therapist: "I suppose you were traumatized by your brother in your childhood. Your brother kept confusing you. Now, whenever you feel insecure in a relationship, your trauma film gets triggered, the shaming by your brother!".*

*In the next therapy session, Mr. B reports: "I noticed that I was being avoidant again when I found myself in a problematic situation. But then I was able to catch myself. In another situation, however, I failed. I was annoyed with myself at a hardware store that I avoided everything again." The therapist and the patient explore his defense behavior in this situation by setting up an empty chair for his self-protection behavior. Mr. B. felt insecure at the hardware store because his idea for constructing a changing table was probably not perfect. A vicious cycle developed: his feelings of insecurity were appropriate. However, he reacted to this feeling of insecurity with self-injurious thinking: "I am totally incapable!" He was internally paralyzed. As a result, he could not ask the seller about the 'right kind of wood'. So he left the shop empty-handed. At the end of the therapy session, Mr. B. says sarcastically: "I aim to be infallible. Only then will I not be ashamed." The therapist sets up another chair opposite the 'brother's' chair: "This chair represents your self-injurious thinking, for your inner sadistic critic. The therapist doubles the sadistic critic: "I always say that! You are nothing! And you can't do anything!" He turns to the patient: "Your insecurity about the changing table was appropriate. But your problem is: Whenever you feel insecure, you immediately slip into your trauma film and your self-injurious thinking and feeling." Mr. B.: "I face the same challenge in my job search. I believe I have to be infallible even there!".*

*After seven more sessions of chair work, the therapist suggests: "Perhaps you could write a letter to your brother without mailing it. Tell him how you have discovered the connection between your anxiety disorder and your childhood" (9th therapy step in* Sect. 6.5*). In the following therapy session, the patient reports with satisfaction right from the start: "It was good for me to write the letter. In the first part, I wrote a concise and clear summary of what I learned here. I also made a clear decision in favor of the diagnosis of 'social phobia'. In the second part, I included my brother. That was more difficult. I still feel uncomfortable about blaming him!" The therapist: "Once again, I'm placing the chair for your self-injurious thinking opposite you. You obviously don't need your brother anymore to devalue yourself today! You are doing it yourself!" Mr. B: "Yes, but with the letter, I had to do exactly the opposite of what I learned in my life! When writing the letter, I was downright skeptical about how it all fits together, my childhood, my family, and my current situation!".*

*The letter from Mr. B. to his brother reads as follows: "In exploring the roots of my anxiety disorder and its development, I went back to my childhood as much as possible. My fears have been around for as long as I can remember. As you know, we were always competing against each other as little children, even if it was simply to get mom's attention. As a young man, I certainly did not have an easy time surpassing you in something. You did everything to prevent it. You defined the 'social norm'. You surpassed my successes, ridiculed them, or reinterpreted them as something completely normal. If I achieved something you couldn't, you expressed your dissatisfaction openly. You either disrupted the family peace or just pissed me off. You taught me quite early on that I can never manage to be successful. And if I did, then it would only have painful consequences. These experiences taught me how to behave to receive praise and recognition. Instead of starting an already lost battle, it was better to submit to you and support your position. It was better to wait for what you were doing and then submit than go ahead myself. As a compass for my behavior in the respective situation, I acquired the finely tuned social anxiety that now causes me problems. In this way, I could avoid shameful defeats against you, secure peace in the family, and receive praise for it. However, I paid a huge price for this. I never learned autonomy. I never learned to develop my own will and wishes and to enforce them against resistance. One cannot lead an adult life like this."*

*The therapist asks the patient: "What did you experience while writing your letter?" Mr. B: "In the letter, I left out all comments connected to the roles of my parents!" Therapist: "What do these comments sound like?" Mr. B.: "They were mostly about the duty to intervene! I loved my father, but he wasn't around enough in my childhood. My father always woke up in the morning after we had already left for school. I'm not really disappointed with him. Because he didn't do anything bad, he 'just' did nothing! I was already shy when I was in kindergarten. Once I dared to play on the carpet that was lying there. I then told this to my parents, and my father was delighted! He spontaneously gave me one euro! My brother was standing beside me, and he didn't understand what had happened. He had no problems in kindergarten! It would have been good if my father had encouraged me more often! My father was rarely present, physically and mentally. And so, my mother was at home all day. But my brother was so captivating that he had my mother completely in his pocket. As a small child, he would immediately scream if she stopped the stroller, even for two seconds. That was always so. It's amazing how much influence my brother has on my mother, even today. If my brother has a different opinion, she just changes her own mind." In order to appreciate the patient's inner progress, the therapist places a new empty chair next to his chair for the humiliated child (therapy step 3): "Today is the first time you are expressing serious reservations about your parents and sharing that, as a young son, they have let you down. I think your angry inner child is surfacing! This new chair represents this inner child." Mr. B: "Yes, but I am having self-injurious thoughts again: 'I haven't learned to be self-sufficient. I cannot define success. I don't feel angry if my position is thwarted.' It is shameful that I have to learn the tasks of a three-year-old now at my age!".*

*The therapist: "It's true, you have to learn this. But if you sink into shame now, you are obeying your inner blind sadistic critic again!" The therapist asks the patient (therapy step 4): "Can you please look at the humiliated child you used to be? How do you feel about the child?" Mr. B: "I am ashamed I was a coward as a child!" The therapist (therapy step 5): "Please tell your child this!" Mr. B follows the request. Then he switches to the role of the 'humiliated child'. The therapist takes on the role of the adult patient: "It is shameful that I have to learn the tasks of a three-year-old now!" Mr. B. in the role of the child: "Is it necessary to clarify this with the brother?" Mr. B. switches back to the adult role: "Yes, that's the turn!" Mr. B. in the role of the child: "Do you think we can do it?" Mr. B. in the adult role: "Yes, of course! It isn't easy, but we can do it. You will see!" Therapist to Mr. B: "After your difficult childhood, now is the time to become a good father to yourself!" Mr. B: "Yes, I needed more than I received! Unfortunately, I was in a family that is so different: They don't have soft tones; they don't even need them! My brother and mother do their thing and put all problems aside!".*

*Therapist: "Do you notice that today is the first time you define yourself positively in relation to your family? It is new that you see yourself as 'the one with the low-tone voice!'" The therapist switches to the role of the patient's adult self and repeats the patient's last sentences. Mr. B. in the role of the humiliated child: "I feel very sad, I feel scared of being excluded! I don't even want to hear it! What matters is that I belong! I prefer to pretend and ignore things like the others!" Therapist (2nd therapy step): "Now you are in your trauma film! You realize that you were lonely and abandoned when you were a child! Why don't you step into the role of the angry child and tell me what you feel there?" Mr. B. blossoms in the role of the angry child (therapy step 5). He spontaneously interrupts the therapist, who has taken on his adult role, and vehemently demands of his adult self: "For heaven's sake, fight back!" During the debriefing, Mr. B says: "As an angry child, I realized that I didn't have to wait for you to finish my role. It was amusing to be able to act in this way!" The therapist and the patient agree that he should add critical comments about his parents to the letter he wrote for his brother at home.*

*In the therapy session that follows, the therapist asks right at the beginning: "What did you experience when you included your criticism of your parents in the letter to your brother?" Mr. B.: "That was difficult. For example, I asked myself why my father stopped paying attention to me. Did he have too little empathy, or was he simply not interested in me?" Mr. B.'s father died ten years ago. The therapist seizes the opportunity for a fictional clarification of Mr.B's relationship with the father (therapy step 9): "You could ask him this in a role-play!" Finally, Mr. B. is ready to do so. He sets up two empty chairs in the room, one for himself and one for his father. He then explains to the "father": "I have thought a lot about my anxiety disorder and realized that the reasons for it are connected to my childhood too. Why didn't you pay attention to me more often? Why weren't you there for me?" During role reversal, Mr. B. does not understand what the son means in his father's role: "I love you and your brother Karl. Really, I love you too!" Again in his own role, Mr. B. says uncertainly: "Yes, that's true. But I needed more love!" Mr. B. looks confused and turns to the therapist: "Perhaps all of this is not as true as I thought it would be!".*

*The therapist: "I believe that is your self-injurious thinking again, the voice of your blind inner critic who says to you: 'Rolf, you are just imagining it!' Mr. B., can you go back to the chair of your adult thinking and counsel yourself from there in the conversation with your father? Coach yourself! Rolf knows that he needs more support from his father. But that part of him is blocked. It is taboo for him to think and say it openly!" Mr. B. switches to the chair of his healthy adult thinking and turns to Rolf: "Rolf should express more of what he feels!" The therapist, as an implicit doppelganger: "Yes, and perhaps use an example to clarify what he means!" Mr. B: "Yes, that's good, the example with the chocolate!" Therapist: "Tell that to Rolf!" Mr. B encourages 'Rolf', who is having a fictitious conversation with his father: "Talk more about your feelings and explain it to him using an example!" Mr. B. switches back to his role as the protagonist on stage and says to his father: "You don't understand me. The point is that you should have stepped in! For example, when we were driving around once. Karl and I each got half a bar of chocolate. I was afraid Karl would start an argument because he only had as much chocolate as I did. So I gave him a piece of my chocolate as a precaution so that he would have more. Mom praised me back then for my generosity! You should have intervened at that point!" Mr. B. switches to the role of father. The therapist asks: "Could I just try something different?" He takes on the protagonist's role and verbalizes, as a doppelganger, the patient's thinking, feeling, and sensing while rehearsing in the as-if mode of play (see* Sects. 2.4.3 *and* 8.4.2, *6.6th step of psychodramatic dialogue): "Yes, but in reality, I wasn't generous at all. Because I only did that out of fear of an argument with Karl. I was afraid that Karl would humiliate me again and that I would then be all alone!" Mr. B. as the father: "Yes, that wasn't fair! You should have defended yourself!" The therapist laughs sarcastically while in the role of Rolf: "That's fantastic! But I just couldn't do that! Mom wanted me to act like that too! I had no chance against Karl! He always made me feel small! And that too with mom's support! Mom still does what he wants even today!" Mr. B. as the father: "Yes, I'm sorry!" The therapist as Rolf: "But why didn't you say anything! Were you a coward?" Mr. B. as the father: "Well, in the end, I separated from your mother. Before that, there were a lot of arguments between us. But you are right, for the first fifteen years of our marriage, I was always submissive, maybe for far too long. And I should have supported you so that both you brothers were treated fairly." The therapist as Rolf: "Then you are a bit like me, always evading conflict!".*

*During the debriefing, Mr. B. said: "What was most important to me in the play was that, in my father's role, I felt unconditional affection for my sons and the will to take them seriously. But as a father, I was awkward and didn't know how to do it. My father set out to be different from his father. My grandfather returned from the war late. My father had always argued with him. His father, my grandfather always made authoritarian decisions. My father didn't want to let me down. But he simply didn't stand up to my mother. Something similar happened between him and my mother as it did between my brother and me. My father never got a say in matters at home and thus turned to work. He was a workaholic and, in addition to his job, worked for the Red Cross all the time." During role reversal in the fictional psychodramatic dialogue with his father, the patient expanded his internal object image of his father and, thus, resolved his defense through the projection of rejection.*

*After the birth of his first child, Mr. B. took over the care of his son as well as the role of housekeeper and ended the treatment. His wife started full-time work as a teacher. Mr. B. declined the offer to continue therapy in a group format.*

In the end, the patient did not achieve his original goal of being able to take up a job after completing his studies. But, he faced the challenges of marriage with his long-term girlfriend, had a son with her, and decided to look after the child as a househusband. The therapist graded this solution as a therapeutic success because the patient violated all norms and values of his family of origin by implementing this new life plan. His family had been organized as a narcissistic system. Growing up also means that one sins against the norms and values of the family of origin at least once (Klaus Stangier, 1991, verbal communication).

## 6.7 Crisis Intervention for Performance Anxiety

The therapy model described in Sect. 6.5 can also be used to address distress caused by exam nerves:

***Case example 56***

*In supervision, a therapist reports on the crisis intervention with a 48-year-old woman with long-term examination anxiety (ICD F40.2) and a structural disorder (see* Sects. 4.4 *and* 6.2*). In the first interview, the patient mentioned that she had to take a pedagogical exam a week later. It would need her to demonstrate her practical skills in front of other people. She was feeling terrified at the thought of having to do so. The therapist uses the therapy model described above and reports: "The patient had been in treatment with other therapists for twenty years. However, after only one hour of therapy, this was the first time in her life that she had passed an exam. She was quite afraid during the exam. But unlike before, she went to the exam and didn't run away from the exam room! I think the chair work helped her structure her thoughts and feelings. It was important that I symbolized her self-protection with a chair and saw her as a heroine in the fight against her mental collapse. I then coached the heroine. The structured image of her ego states during the chair work demystified her fear! It was important to organize her inner world: 'That belongs here, that goes there!' As a therapist, I always pointed with my hand at the chairs in doing so. The patient shared all of her previous therapy experiences with me. She bundled them together and coached herself. The positive revaluation was extremely important. I appreciated her perseverance as a heroine and didn't just look at her deficiencies. Eventually, she held on to her self-coaching skills in the real test."*

*The therapist continues: "It was healing for the patient to have felt understood during the session! But it was also good for me as the therapist to have a positive understanding of the patient's defenses. As a result, I had a range of intervention options. This also relieved my internal tension as a therapist. I was pleased and honored that I was allowed to participate in the patient's deep and intimate internal process! As a therapist, I wasn't only empathetic as usual. That was liberating." Supervisor: "Yes, otherwise, as therapists, we tend to identify with the patient's suffering ego and store all of the patient's information and fears in our body. In metacognitive work, however, all fears and information are represented externally in the therapy room with chairs, and the patient's defensive behavior is assigned a positive function within the framework of the patient's self-regulation. The therapist and the patient stand shoulder to shoulder and look from the metaposition at the disturbing defense pattern. In doing so, you, as a therapist, remain open and curious about what is happening."*

**Central idea**

In metacognitive therapy, the therapist symbolizes the patient's defense patterns *externally* with chairs *in the therapy room* and addresses them in conversation with the patient. The therapist develops empathy, both for the patient's self-protection and for the patient's healthy adult thinking. The therapist no longer responds to her defenses with negative countertransference. His dual compassion helps the patient develop empathy for herself like a *good enough mother*.

## 6.8 Other Psychodramatic Approaches in the Therapy of Anxiety Disorders

### *6.8.1 The Therapy of a Patient with Social Phobia by Moreno*

In 1936, Moreno (1945, p. 11 ff., 1959, p. 221 ff.) described the treatment of 'anxiety neurosis' in a 27-page case report. His patient, Robert, suffered from work disturbances, a constant urge to urinate, pain in the cardiac region, and the constant fear of being unable to accomplish his goals. In addition, he was obsessively afraid of attracting attention in his social circle. He feared that he would be late, his shoes would not have been cleaned, his tie would be outdated, and his car might stop working because it had not been checked at the gas station, among other things. The symptoms reported by Moreno meet the criteria of a social phobia (ICD F40.1). At the beginning of psychodrama therapy, Moreno centered his work entirely on the 'Psychopathology of Interpersonal Relationships'. This is the title of his case description. Moreno hypothesized that the patient's disturbance stems from his unconscious identification with his father *and* mother. But they hated each other. They had argued constantly and were finally separated (Moreno 1945, p. 14f.): "Obviously he tried to adapt himself to his father and mother in an original way by internalizing each of their idiosyncracies into a part of his self, thus proving that they did not have to separate, and could live in harmony within him" (Moreno 1945, p. 22). Moreno didn't know anything about defenses. Nevertheless, there was a profound truth in his interpretation. His patient Robert had identified *with the defense patterns* of his mother and his father and had to resolve them.

*Back then*, Moreno was *not yet* familiar with the *role reversal* between the protagonist and his opponent, played by an auxiliary ego. He had his patient Robert 'portray' himself in role-plays. In *other* sessions, he also let him play the roles of his father and mother. In his parents' roles, the patient quickly recognized: "That is not my father, that is me… Oh, that is me, not my mother. When he enacted his father, he discovered that he felt just like his father about his mother, and when he enacted his mother, he discovered that in some respects he felt just as his mother did" (Moreno, 1945, p. 13 ff.).

Moreno (1959, p. 238) had the patient play the roles of fictional *restrictive* authority figures even in *fantasy play*. For example, the patient Robert played the role of a judge against a shoplifter, the role of a prosecutor against a criminal, and the role of a Mephisto. At the time, Moreno (1945, p. 27) was amazed that the patient played the dominant male roles with such enthusiasm. He suspected that his patient Robert "…discloses selective affinity for roles which place him in a position to torture others, … The therapeutic theater gives him a creative excuse to let himself go, and perhaps the enjoyment he has in performing and the completion of detail with which he enacts roles through gestures and words indicate the role he would like to play in life." Presumably, unlike Moreno supposed, enacting the roles of strict authority figures had a positive therapeutic effect on the patient. Because the patient possibly gained specific control over the stringent demands of his superego and was thus able to put them into perspective.

Moreno also let the patient 'Robert' re-enact conflict scenes from his everyday work life and marriage *without reversing roles*. In doing so, he invented the technique of *soliloquy*: he interrupted the patient while enacting his conflict situations and asked him to say out loud what he thought and felt when he acted and reacted in the situation. Moreno let him mentalize out loud (see Sect. 2.2) in the role of his inner self-image in the play. In this way, the patient completed his relational psychosomatic resonance pattern in play into a holistic resonance pattern comprising sensorimotor interaction patterns, physical sensations, affect, linguistic concepts, and thoughts (see Sect. 2.7). Moreno (1959, p. 231) noted: "Soliloquy makes the experience much clearer than it was at the time of the actual event." Here, too, Moreno met his patient Robert's playfulness with unjustified skepticism. But, he didn't appropriately appreciate the patient's internal process of self-development, the development of internal self-image, and internal object image in the as-if mode of play (see Sect. 2.5). Instead, he complained: In psychodrama, "the others [...] have to adapt to Robert at *his* will, [...] the switch from one state to the other, his change in *his* position in the room, his twists and turns in dialogue, and *his* impulse to stop when *he* finds it desirable". At the end of the therapy, Moreno worked behaviorally with a kind of desensitization technique: he built more and more complications into the patient's fantasy play and adapted the *play scenes* to resemble the patient's *everyday* situations: "Objects, events, and people were carefully put in the way of his unlimited urge to explain and display himself" (Moreno, 1959, p. 347). *In this case study*, unlike in other case studies, Moreno did not report whether the patient's symptoms had improved due to the therapy.

### 6.8.2 The Treatment of Specific (Isolated) Phobias

Patients with specific (isolated) phobias (ICD F40.2) have repressed the *original conflict* that generated fear in the past. They have shifted *the emotion of fear to another relatively insignificant external object* (Mentzos, 2011, p. 110). The longer an isolated phobia persists, the more the affected people avoid the fearful situation as a preventive measure (Mentzos, 2011, p. 110). The fears then often lead to *general* avoidance behavior. A secondary fear of anxiety attacks arises in patients with panic attacks.

Chronic anxiety is treated according to the method described in Sect. 6.5. If the phobic symptoms have only existed for a short time, the avoidance behavior is not yet burned into the patient's self-regulation. In such a case, the therapist can apply the approach used in treating *neurotic* behavior. He resolves the defense through repression with the help of psychodramatic dialogue (see Sect. 8.4.2) and changing to the scene of the origin of the patient's chronic anxiety (see Sect. 2.4.4): (1) He lets the patient re-enact the situation that triggered her anxiety in the present in a completely 'normal' psychodramatic manner. (2) He asks the patient, '*How old is your fear of not meeting the expectations of those around you?'* (3) By changing the scene, he lets the patient return to *the origin of the fear* and enact the conflict situation at that time. Thus, the patient links her sensorimotor interaction pattern and affect in the scene of phobia to a frightening childhood experience. According to Leutz (1974, p. 147), the therapist should resolve the 'causes of the anxiety disorder' in this way.

Some psychodramatists also take a behavior-oriented approach in the *psychodramatic treatment* of specific (isolated) phobias. Straub, for example (Straub, 1972, pp. 72, 178 ff.), integrated the concepts of desensitization and conditioning from behavior therapy into psychodrama therapy: (1) The patients with a phobia choose someone (a relative or a caregiver) they know, who would have *no* difficulties in the frightening situation. For example, a woman with a phobia of cats chose her son. (2) The patient observed *her son* closely in *his* interaction with cats and memorized his behavior. (3) She practiced *his* facial expressions and gestures for herself in the role play, initially *without* imagining a cat. (4) In the next step, the patient imagined encountering a cat *in a role play*, but in doing so, she played the role of her *son*. As the son, she turned 'to the animal just as *he* used to do'. (5) The patient then took on the role of her son when *at home* and, *in his role,* stroked her *real* cat, just as *her son* did. Straub (1972, p. 178 ff.) reports that her patient practiced this secretly without the family's knowledge: "Step by step, the patient learned how to interact with the cat via role-play [...]. After seven months, she was ready not only to stroke the cat without fear, [...] but by the end, she even felt a real affection for the cat." Straub believes that taking on the roles of other people in "the technique of role change, was the decisive factor in this treatment. When thinking in the role of her son and emulating his behavior toward the cat, the patient was probably so detracted from her phobic fear that she was relaxed enough to carry out the movements observed in her son [...] with the necessary calmness."

Even in the therapy of "a twenty-year-old [...] with severe exam phobia" and in other cases with phobias, Straub (1972, p. 179) used a similar behavior-oriented approach: "In each case, he designed a treatment plan with the patient and asked them to take on a person's role in carrying out this plan, who they know will be without fear in situations which the patient has reacted fearfully. The patients usually practiced role change in a few sessions. They then carried out their treatment independently according to the plan using the behavioral technique of 'self-regulation'".

In the case of a patient with bacteriophobia and severe compulsive behaviors (see Sect. 7.4, case example 59), Straub (1972, p. 180 ff.) initially centered the treatment on eliminating the bacteriophobia. In the role plays, *the patient* played the role of a young girl, a school friend from the past. As a doppelganger, *the therapist* took on the role of *another* young girl in the patient's role plays. *In these roles, both* made 'half a dozen' *real* trips to the town together. They used public transport, went shopping, 'did not wear gloves (which the patient used to do) and touched anything'. First, the therapist did this in her role as the young girl, and then the patient did it herself. Later the patient did it first, and then the therapist. As a result, the patient's phobic reactions had reduced radically, whereby she continued to play the role of her former school friend for herself 'in the sense of fixed role therapy' at home as well. Only later could she do so *without* playing the role of her school friend.

### *6.8.3 Other Psychodrama Therapists' Approaches to Panic Attacks*

Many psychodramatists (Leutz, 1974, p. 147; Grimmer, 2007, p. 31 f.) let their anxious patients directly re-enact the situations that triggered the panic attacks in a psychodramatic way. In doing so, they use *a trick* to avoid the occurrence of a panic attack: As the patient enters the panic-inducing situation in the play, she symbolizes her 'fear' *externally* as an object or person and thus turns fear into *an object* in the interaction. A group member takes on 'the role of fear' as an auxiliary ego. The externalization of fear enables the patient to enter a fictional psychodramatic dialogue using role reversal with her 'fear'. The patient then negotiates with the 'fear' to find a compromise solution that is tolerable for both sides. Or the auxiliary ego, who plays the role of fear, compresses the protagonist's rib cage 'as the fear does in the patient'. As a result, the protagonist usually begins spontaneously to fight the auxiliary ego physically and forces the 'fear' out of the group room through the door. The therapeutic idea here is: The patient should improve her self-actualization in relation to the symptom of 'fear' and integrate this experience as an action model into her inner conflict resolution processes.

Grimmer (2007) was the first to develop a theoretically justified concept of *disorder-specific psychodrama therapy* for anxiety disorders. He focuses his work on developing the patient's *good inner parenting roles*. In this way, the patients should improve their self-empathy (Grimmer, 2007, pp. 25, 37; Grimmer, 2013, p. 194 f.). While re-enacting childhood scenes, the therapist lets the patient, for example, actively search for memories of earlier *positive* and helpful caregivers and play them out. If such memories are not present, the therapist introduces *positive fictional* figures as new resources and self-stabilizing inner objects. The therapeutic relationship is designed to be sustainable throughout.

Grimmer (2007, p. 23) does *not* work *explicitly metacognitively* (see Sects. 6.4 and 6.5). At the beginning of the therapy, the therapist does a 'fear confrontation with the help of surplus reality'. The patient selects practical situations that trigger her fear and enacts them. The aim is a "systematic, careful encounter with the dreaded feelings of fear. This is intended to reduce the patient's constant self-observation" (Grimmer, 2007, p. 23). Grimmer also lets the patient depict her inner panic with the help of an auxiliary ego on the object level as 'the role of fear' (Grimmer, 2007, pp. 31 f., 35, 40 ff.). The patient then engages in a psychodramatic dialogue with the 'fear'. During role reversal, she also takes on the role of fear herself. The therapist then verbally doubles her in the counter role of 'fear'. However, he suggests to the patient that she *has helpful intentions as 'fear'*: "Actually, I just want to help you!" Grimmer reinterprets the fear as an 'over-committed helper' or a 'clumsy, awkward helper'. In doing so, he uses the therapeutical principle of 'symptom utilization' from hypnotherapy.

Grimmer's approach is similar to that in *cognitive behavioral therapy*. The anxious patient should replace the *unfavorable thought content* "the panic is suffocating me, I am dying of a heart attack" with a more *appropriate cognition.* Such a positive reinterpretation of panic as a 'helper' is therapeutically effective for anxiety patients with neurotic disorder (see Sect. 6.2). The therapeutic process follows the principle of 'anger instead of anxiety'.

***Case example 57***

*A 34-year-old patient with heart phobia begins a therapy session toward the end of the treatment with the statement: "My best friend has come back!" The therapist wonders: "Which best friend?" The patient pats the left side of his chest: "Well, here, my heart!" He continues: "Then I looked: where is the enemy? I noticed what was going on, and I fought back, boom, boom, boom!" The patient imitates a boxing match with his arms as he says this. During therapy, he recognized that his heart problems always occurred when he adjusted too much in his relationship conflicts and did not allow his anger. When his heart palpitations reappeared, he applied this knowledge. He replaced the old thought, "Help! My heart is racing. I'm going to have a heart attack!" with the thought, "My racing heart helps me to notice my anger. This always occurs when I've adjusted too much in a relationship. What relationship is it this time?" He found the right conflict partner and acted out his anger directly at the conflict partner in his fantasy. That stopped his heart from racing.*

But, *in people with structural disorder*, panic attacks express the impending collapse of their internal defense system. Therefore, the *explicit metacognitive approach* mentioned in Sect. 6.5 is more likely to be indicated in the case of these patients. The utilization of the symptom of anxiety improves the patients' self-actualization in conflicts. However, this then activates a masochistic self-censorship acquired in childhood. Thus, erroneous behavior is 'punished' by the destructive superego. The therapist must therefore also work on the defense through self-protection and masochistic self-censorship in the therapy process.

**Exercise 18**

You can understand these considerations and doubts by experiencing Grimmer's approach using role plays. Step into the role of an anxious patient with structural disorder. You will notice that you experience ego confusion using the psychodramatic dialogue with role reversal with the '*role*' *of your fear*.

**Central idea**

Patients with anxiety *and structural disorder, trauma-related disorders, or personality disorders* probably benefit more from the *metacognitive* therapy approach described here.

## References


Grimmer, K. (2007). Psychodrama bei Angststörungen—Überlegungen und Techniken zur Therapie von Angststörungen. In Hintermeier, S. (2016). Psychodramaforschung in Form von Masterthesen–ein Überblick über Themen und Methoden der ersten 8 Jahrgänge der Masterthesen der Universitätslehrgänge Psychodrama Psychotherapie des ÖAGG. In: Stadler, C., Wieser, M., & Kirk, K. (Eds.), Psychodrama. Empirical Research and Science 2. Springer, Wiesbaden. https://doi.org/10.1007/978-3-658-13015-2_21

Grimmer, K. (2013). Die Doppelgängertechnik und die Entwicklung von Sicherheit gebenden ‚inneren elterlichen Rollen', guten Elternintrojekten' - bei Angststörungen. *Zeitschrift für Psychodrama und Soziometrie 12*(2), 189–199.

Heigl-Evers, A., Heigl, F., Ott, J., & Rüger, U. (1997). *Lehrbuch der Psychotherapie* (3rd ed.). Gustav Fischer.

Krüger, R. T. (2020). Ängste und Stress in der Corona-Krise. Praxis und Theorie der störungsspezifischen Behandlung. *Zeitschrift für Psychodrama und Soziometrie 19*, 355–346.

Leutz, G. A. (1974). *Das klassische Psychodrama nach J. L. Moreno*. Springer.

Mentzos, S. (2011). *Lehrbuch der Psychodynamik. Die Funktion der Dysfunktionalität psychischer Störungen* (5th ed.). Vandenhoeck & Ruprecht.

Moreno, J. L. (1945). *Psychodrama and the psychopathology of inter-personal relations*. Beacon House.

Moreno, J. L. (1959). *Gruppenpsychotherapie und Psychodrama. Einleitung in die Theorie und Praxis*. Thieme.

Morschitzky, H. (1998). *Angststörungen. Diagnostik, Erklärungsmodelle, Therapie und Selbsthilfe bei krankhafter Angst*. Springer.

Schacht, M. (2009). *Das Ziel ist im Weg. Störungsverständnis und Therapieprozess im Psychodrama*. Wiesbaden: VS-Verlag. https://doi.org/10.1007/978-3-531-91462-6

Schrenker, L. (2008). *Pesso-Therapie: Das Wissen zur Heilung liegt in uns*. Klett-Cotta.

Straub, H. (1972). Theoretische Anmerkungen zur psychodramatischen Behandlung von Phobien, Zwangsneurosen und anderen psychischen Störungen. In H. Petzold (Ed.), *Angewandtes Psychodrama in Therapie, Pädagogik, Theater und Wirtschaft* (pp.177–194). Junfermann.

Wilkinson, R., & Picket, K. (2010). *Gleichheit ist Glück. Warum gerechte Gesellschaften für alle besser sind* (3rd ed.). Tolkemitt Verlag.

# Chapter 7
# Obsessive–Compulsive Disorders

## 7.1 Obsessive Thoughts, Compulsive Acts, and their Psychodynamic Function

According to the ICD (F42.-), *obsessive thoughts* are "ideas, conceptions or impulses that are recurrent and stereotypically occupy the patient persistently. They are almost always excruciating. The patient often tries unsuccessfully to resist them". *Compulsive behaviors* are repetitive stereotypical acts. "They are neither experienced as pleasant nor are they used to perform useful tasks. The patient often experiences them as a precaution against an objectively improbable event that could harm him or in which he could wreak havoc. [...] Fear is mostly present all the time. If one suppresses compulsive actions, the fear increases significantly." According to Mentzos (2011, p. 104), obsessive–compulsive symptoms function as security measures. In individuals with obsessive–compulsive disorder and a more mature personality structure, the symptoms are "compromises between impulses that must not be allowed and the defense against these impulses. Sometimes it is the impulse [...] and at other times (more often) the defense that predominates the manifest image" (Mentzos, 2011, p. 102).

*Compulsive behaviors* often have the "function of reconciling with the strict superego" (Mentzos, 2011, p.106). In the case of more severe psychological disorders "that border on psychosis", the constant repetition of magical acts serves "to stabilize the self or to ward off greater internal and external dangers" (Mentzos, 2011, p.103). According to Mentzos, the magical acts and rituals, which initially appear mysterious, are a "regressive updating of previous behavior patterns. They arise in times of need. They are very well known to us from the world of children, but also from the world of peoples and other cultures". Thus, the occurrence of a compulsion indicates 'not only a [...]difficult underlying conflict but also the fact that it is about the self that needs to be protected and strengthened'.

Obsessive thoughts and compulsive behaviors are *symptoms* resulting from the acting out of a masochistic defense system in equivalence mode (see Sect. 2.6). They



R. T. Krüger, *Disorder-Specific Psychodrama Therapy in Theory and Practice*,
Psychodrama in Counselling, Coaching and Education 4,
https://doi.org/10.1007/978-981-99-7508-2_7

help them to energetically 'work off' the shame, guilt, and existential fears that arise in everyday conflicts, to maintain an adaptive attitude, and to stabilize themselves when confronted with a threat of disintegration of the self. The creative systemic development of the self (see Sects. 2.4.3 and 8.4.2) is fixed in the masochistic defense system *in everyday conflicts*. The masochistic defense system of patients often leads to disturbances in the therapeutic relationship. The therapist naturally identifies spontaneously with the patient's *defended* process of self-development *against* his sadistic superego in his everyday conflicts. Therefore, she tries to strengthen the patient's self-actualization in his everyday conflicts and intervenes accordingly.

**Question**

Why are early depth psychological interpretations therapeutically unhelpful in the treatment of obsessive–compulsive disorders and can even be harmful?

**Central idea**

Early depth psychological interpretations promote the self-actualization of the patients in their conflicts. In doing so, however, they also actualize the patient's sadistic superego and thus intensify their inner conflict tensions. This can intensify his obsessive-compulsive symptoms. It is possible that the patient *cognitively* knows more about the genesis of his symptoms at the end of the treatment. However, his obsessive-compulsive symptoms are still present because the cause of the symptom was not treated. *The therapist and the patient* are disappointed by the lack of success in therapy, giving rise to corresponding negative transferences and character-related countertransferences (see Sect. 2.10).

The therapist therefore initially treats the patient *metacognitively* in disorder-specific psychodrama therapy. She represents the patient's masochistic defense system involved in the formation of symptoms with chairs. A patient with obsessive–compulsive symptoms unconsciously switches back and forth between *three* different ego states and acts them out.

1. The *dominant defense mode* is the identification with self-destructive internal self-censorship developed in childhood. This is the ego state of 'self-injurious thinking' which gives rise to *obsessive–compulsive thoughts.*
2. The patient *reacts* to the danger evoked by his *obsessive thoughts* with *compulsive behaviors.* In the equivalence mode, the patient *externally* acts as if the threat posed by the *internal* obsessional thoughts is real. The patient acts out his *self-protective behavior through adaptation in his relationship* with his sadistic superego.
3. Unlike people with psychosis, the patient knows that his obsessive–compulsive thoughts and fears are exaggerated or absurd. So he *also* always thinks as a healthy adult.

## 7.2 The Disorder-Specific Treatment of Compulsive Behaviors

As in the disorder-specific therapy of people with personality disorders (see Chap. 4), the therapist works with individuals with obsessive–compulsive patients *explicitly metacognitively* in addressing their rigid defenses in the beginning (see Sect. 2.14). In addition to the two chairs of the symptom scene in everyday life (see Sect. 2.8), she represents the ego states involved in the patient's masochistic defense system with empty chairs and thus makes them the *direct* object of therapeutic communication.

***Case example 16 (continued from* Sect. 2.9*)***
*A 20-year-old patient, Mr. B., has suffered from obsessive thoughts and compulsive behaviors for ten years. These had increased again in the last six months. He complained of 'increased aggression' even though he saw himself as a 'super social person'. In a previous therapy with another therapist, he spoke a lot about his aggression and the problematic relationship with his sister, who was three years older. In the initial interview, he reported that he feared contracting AIDS if he touched a doorknob. But he had informed himself thoroughly. He knew that an AIDS infection usually only comes about through physical contact. However, later he developed the fear that someone in the pedestrian zone of his city might stab him unnoticed with a syringe and infect him with AIDS. So he got some syringes and stabbed himself with them. He wanted 'to know how that would feel' so that he could notice an unwanted puncture more easily. Mr. B. also reported obsessive fear of driving over a pedestrian in his car. Whenever he drove through a pothole, he always looked in the rearview mirror to check the road and allay his fears. He often turned back in his car: "I know that running over a person should feel different. I would have seen the person too." Mr. B. had calculated that 'the probability of such a catastrophic event was only 0.000001%'.*

*To begin with, the therapist concretized the patient's three ego states involved in the patient's ego confusion with three empty chairs: he positioned a 'sadistic tormentor who instigates frightening thoughts' opposite the patient. For this, he placed the hand puppet of an aggressively-looking red devil on the chair in agreement with the patient. The symbolization of his obsessive thoughts as a devil in front of him was deeply moving for Mr. B. He immediately took a picture of the 'tormentor' with his mobile phone. Next, the therapist set up a second empty chair to the patient's left: "This is the chair for your self-protective behavior. First, your tormentor will alert you of the potential dangers. Then you think of some wise preventive measures and implement them. For example, you can turn around in your car. Or you can prick yourself with needles." The therapist then named the chair on which Mr. B. sat: "Regardless of your fears and compulsions, you also think as a healthy adult because you know perfectly well that your fears are unreal. For example, you have found that the probability of such events occurring is quite low. Therefore, the chair you sit in represents your healthy adult thinking." Mr. B. was amazed and relieved that the therapist appreciated his knowledge of the unreality of his fears so positively. After establishing the three ego states, the therapist addressed the 'tormentor' directly. The therapist complained indignantly that he 'made life so difficult for the young man and tormented him so much' (see* Sect. 4.10*).*

*In the following session, Mr. B. shared that he had stopped taking his psychiatrist-prescribed neuroleptic Seroquel on his own initiative. He reported: "I felt much better after the last session! Now I say to myself: 'If something happens, that's how it is. I am just unlucky!' It helped me to see my fears as the devil. It also helped when you called the devil the 'tormentor' and didn't take him so seriously. Now I can already laugh a little at myself! In principle, I don't want to get rid of this fear completely. As a child, I was fearless. I wasn't afraid of anything. But to have no fear doesn't help either." Therapist: "I think it is important that you keep externalizing the sadistic tormentor and view it as a different person. Then you have better control over it. Buy a similar hand puppet for the tormentor and keep it at home! Or use the picture of the tormentor you clicked here."*

*The patient's psychotherapy consisted of only 15 sessions in total. If the patient's obsessive–compulsive symptoms reappeared, the therapist would again work with empty chairs (see* Sect. 4.8*) to address the patient's dysfunctional metacognitive processes. During therapy, the patient repeatedly performed his self-regulation in the three different ego states in the as-if mode of psychodramatic play. He also dealt with the conflicts between his ego states in psychodramatic dialogues with role reversals (see* Sect. 4.10*).*

*The therapist did not interpret the patient's intrapsychic conflicts in depth. Instead, he waited until the patient recognized the relevant connections with the genesis of his conflicts on his own. In the fourth therapy session, Mr. B. spontaneously established a relationship between the 'tormentor' and the sadistic humiliation by his older, behaviorally disturbed sister in his childhood. The therapist validates this connection: "As a child, you were traumatized by your sister. The 'tormentor' reflects the conflict with your sister. If you felt angry as a child, your anger was a healthy reaction to your sister's behavior!" The therapist represented the 'older sister' with an empty chair behind the chair of the 'tormentor' (see* Fig. 4.1 in Sect. 4.2*). He pointed with his hand at the chair for the patient's 'tormentor': "As a child, you learned to discipline yourself in a self-injurious way as a precaution. It protected you from the real external threat posed by your sister. As a result, you were less likely to get in the way of your older sister as a little rival." The therapist placed two empty chairs behind the patient's 'self-protective behavior' on the stage to represent the patient's 'traumatized child' and 'angry child'.*

*The therapist did not deal with the patient's childhood conflicts in this therapy process. Instead, he used the information about the original conflict only to give the patient's defensive behavior a positive meaning. Six months after the end of the therapy, Mr. B's father reported gratefully to the therapist in a telephone conversation: "My son is symptom-free and has passed his final examination." The patient's obsessive–compulsive symptoms had not recurred even three years after treatment. Mr. B. was now working full-time and volunteering in his free time. He'd even confronted his sister about her childhood violent behavior.*

The disorder-specific treatment aims to liberate the patient's creative process of self-development from a masochistic defense system. Therefore, it comprises the following steps (see case example 16 above)

1. The therapist initially centers the therapeutic work on *a typical compulsive act* on the part of the patient in his present day-to-day life. She uses the psychodramatic conversation (see Sect. 2.8) to determine *which self-injurious* thought provokes his compulsive action. The patient is not always aware of it: "You wash your hands repeatedly *because there is an inner voice in you that says: 'You must have been infected by the bacteria on the door handles!'*"
2. The therapist explicitly *names obsessive–compulsive thoughts* as 'self-injurious thinking'. She names it the 'inner sadistic tormentor'—a term *as close to the patient's experience* as possible.
3. The therapist *represents* the 'tormentor' with an empty chair three meters away from the patient as an object image and interaction partner. She places a suitable hand puppet on it, for example, a red devil or a witch: "The tormentor always brings up new, threatening thoughts with a lot of imagination."
4. The therapist gives the compulsive behaviors *a positive meaning* in the context of the patient's dysfunctional self-regulation. She interprets the *compulsive actions* as *appropriate reactions* to the catastrophic fantasies of the 'sadistic tormentor' and as 'self-protective behavior through adaptation to this tormentor': "You avert the tormentor's threats with your compulsive actions."
5. She *externally represents the 'self-protective behavior'* against his sadistic superego with an empty chair and a matching puppet (see Fig. 4.1 in Sect.4. 2 and Sect. 4.8) and places it *next to the patient.*

**Central idea**

The therapist transforms the process of defense through obsessive thoughts and compulsive actions into a *psychodramatic symbolic play*. The patient is supposed to gain ego control over his rigid defense processes. The external representation of the interaction between the *object image* of the inner tormentor and the *self-image* of self-protection through adaptation with chairs is the prerequisite for the patient to be able to free his self-development from being fixed in his defense system.

6. Patients with obsessive–compulsive symptoms already know that their fears are inappropriate and unreal. This knowledge is what distinguishes them from people with psychosis. Therefore, the therapist positively appreciates the patient's insight into the unreality of his fears: "Despite all your problems, you also think as a healthy adult! This is what the chair you sit on stands for." This therapeutic intervention relieves the patient of his fear of going 'crazy' and has an ego-strengthening effect.
7. In conversation, the patient internally switches back and forth between his ego states. With every change, the therapist points with her hand to the corresponding *other* chair and, as a metacognitive doppelganger (see Sects. 2.4.1 and 4.8), verbalizes the special thoughts, feelings, and intentions of the 'sadistic tormentor', 'self-protective behavior', or 'healthy adult thinking' in the as-if *mode of the play.*

8. The patient internally experiences his sadistic superego as a diffuse threat. As in child psychotherapy, the therapist lets the patient develop the form of the 'tormentor' in the symbolic play into a holistic form with typical action sequences, physical sensations, affect, linguistic concepts, and thoughts. The therapist and the patient transform the obsessive thoughts into statements by the "tormentor" and give it a voice: "The inner tormentor is saying it again: 'You must have contracted AIDS!'" They make a list of all the warnings and threats expressed by the 'tormentor' and number them. The patient reads this list aloud to the therapist item by item. In doing this, the patient and the therapist feel the absurdity of the warnings intensely and sometimes have to laugh without wanting to.

**Central idea**

The therapist, as a metacognitive doppelganger, helps the patient to feel the sadistic pleasure of the tormentor in the inner role change. In this way, the patient expands his inner object image of the 'tormentor'. He resolves his projection of the tormentor's good intentions when warning against a threat (see Sects. 2.4.3, 2.9, 8.4.2, and 8.5). This also relaxes the patient's *defenses through introjection* and adaptation. The defense through projection and introjection stabilizes each other.

9. The therapist lets the patient switch to the chair of his 'self-protective behavior through adaptation' and psychosomatically work out the *positive meaning* of his compulsive actions in interaction with the 'sadistic tormentor'. In this way, the patient creates a holistic inner *self-image* in the interaction with the tormentor with action sequences, physical sensations, affect, words, and thoughts. The therapist helps him as a metacognitive doppelganger. Thus, the patient gains psychosomatic access to his own self and resolves his defenses through introjection. He gains ego control of his defenses through adaptation.
10. In the case of *rigid defense through introjection*, the therapist, as a doppelganger, *interacts on behalf of the patient* with his 'tormentor'. She feels the tormentor's threat *externally* on the chair next to her. This spontaneously triggers her resentment against the 'tormentor'. As a doppelganger, she looks directly at the patient's 'sadistic tormentor' (see Sect. 4.8), stands up, rebukes him of her own will, and insults him: "I think you are tormenting Ms. Müller! She has suffered enough already. I don't want it to go on like this!" The therapist asks the patient whether the 'tormentor' reacts. If necessary, she turns the hand puppet representing the tormentor around so that it is facing the wall: "Stop it! You have tormented Ms. Müller enough." The therapist then sits down in her chair again and observes whether *her feeling* of constriction has disappeared. If necessary, she confirms this with the words: "Yes, I feel better now!"

**Central idea**

The therapist must not ask the patient to protest against his 'tormentor' *on his own* because that would trigger his restricting superego and possibly intensify his compulsive actions. The patient should experience *the therapist* as "guilty" from the perspective of the tormentor, and not himself.

11. The patient moves back to the chair of his healthy adult thinking (see Fig. 4.1 in Sect. 4.2). He sees the interaction system between his self-image and his object image of the 'tormentor' from the metaperspective. Thus, he also psychosomatically develops inner distance from his masochistic defense system. This also helps him to represent his defense processes internally and to *think in the as-if mode.*
12. In the next few months, the patient repeatedly acts out *similar or different* obsessive–compulsive symptoms. Together, the therapist and the patient then *repeatedly* represent the masochistic defense system consisting of 'inner tormentor' and 'self-protection through adaption' with chairs and enact them psychodramatically in the as-if mode.
13. The symbolic play enables the patient *to act* against his 'blind sadistic tormentor'. He knows his name and what he looks like. He can buy an appropriate hand puppet and imprison his inner 'tormentor' in a cupboard (see Sect. 8. 5) and lock it. He can get the 'tormentor' out and interact with him of his own free will. He can put the 'tormentor' in his place in the as-if mode of play, and make him answer. He notices himself: "I can obey the 'tormentor''. But perhaps I *don't have to*, or not always, or not so strongly." The patient develops ego control over his adaptation and sadistic superego.

**Central idea**

The symbolic play between the conforming ego and the tormentor liberates the patient's creative process of self-development from his masochistic defense system. The patient *creates, completes, and condenses* his psychosomatic resonance pattern between the memory centers of his action sequences, physical sensations, affect, word concepts, and thoughts (see Sect. 2.7). At some point, this links itself with a psychosomatic analogous resonance pattern of an original conflict (see case example 16 above). This usually is a traumatizing relationship from childhood. The appropriate integration of his masochistic defense system into the childhood conflict liberates his *present conflicts* from undue self-censorship. But his insight should appear like a ripe apple falling from the tree into his hand *on its own*. As long as the patient does not create this connection *autonomously*, his defense through projection and introjection is not sufficiently resolved.

14. The therapist includes elements of trauma therapy in the treatment of relational trauma in childhood (see Sect. 5.6).
15. At the end of the treatment, the patient's inner change must also be integrated into the internal *relationship images* of the present and the past (see Sect. 4.12).

## 7.3 The Treatment of Obsessive Thoughts Without Compulsive Actions

Obsessive thoughts that occur *without compulsive actions* (F42.0) can be attributed to the patient's *own* repressed sexual or aggressive wishes or his 'self-injurious thinking'. The patient dissociates in the service of the ego (see Sect. 7.1), shifts the taboo impulses to a non-integrated, autonomous part of the self, and thereby experiences them as distressing and ego-dystonic. In this way, the patient stabilizes his old adaptive attitude and restrictions from his superego.

The *technique of* projective *personalization* is therapeutically helpful for isolated obsessive thoughts. The therapist takes the following steps with the patient in doing so

1. The therapist symbolizes the patient's *obsessive thoughts* with a larger stone, places it on a second empty chair further away, and explains: "Please imagine a person or a figure sitting there on the chair with the same feelings and impulses that torment you. But these impulses and thoughts are *appropriate and absolutely necessary in the other living environment* of this person to maintain their dignity or their own life. Please look for a figure or person you find suitable for this. You shouldn't know this person. You can choose a person from the Middle Ages, from a fairy tale, or from the world of your fantasy. Who could that be?" As a doppelganger, the therapist must help the patient to find a suitable fictional person. This person is not an amplification of the motto: Other people *have also* experienced conflict. Instead, the *negatively* evaluated obsessions should give *a positive meaning* in the other world of the fictional person according to the motto: The taboo thoughts are totally appropriate *if they occur in this other unique context.*
2. The patient finds a suitable figure or a person. Then, he and the therapist give this fictional figure an appropriate name.
3. The therapist asks the patient to tell a short episode from this other person's life. Like a film script, this episode should have a beginning and an end and describe the plot and interactions in concrete terms. Then, the therapist helps the patient to create the story as a doppelganger.
4. Over the next ten weeks, the patient writes ten short stories from *this other person's* life. In these episodes, the fictional person *must* act out the impulses and thoughts contained in the patient's obsessive thoughts. The patient brings these stories with him to the following therapy sessions.
5. The therapist reads the story each time and asks the patient what he experienced while writing the story. However, she does *not* interpret the story's contents using depth psychology.
6. Sometimes a patient spontaneously makes friends with the inner impulses displaced onto the fictional person at the end (see case example 58). In such a case, the therapist asks him to look for a hand or finger puppet *for the fictional person.* The patient can carry this with him in his everyday life and, if necessary, *consult* with the fictitious person.

***Case example 58***

*A 28-year-old female patient, Ms. A., suffered from obsessive–compulsive disorder. As a result, she had already been in treatment as an inpatient psychiatric patient. By the end of two years of outpatient group therapy, she had generally made good progress. But she was still tormented by her* obsessive *thoughts of 'fuck, bang, suck'. These repeated themselves stereotypically in her head. The therapist challenged the young woman, who appeared to be bourgeois on the outside, to look for a figure or a person who would use these street words. After some thought, Ms. A. named the 'red Zora' from the book with the same title written by Kurt Held. But she modified the story. 'Red Zora' was a 14-year-old girl who lived alone in a hut she herself built in the woods in front of the walls of a medieval town in the seventeenth century. During the day, she would go into town and steal things to eat from the market stalls. If children, especially boys, teased her, she would beat them up. In doing so, she would curse, insult them, and use the above ugly words. She would always win the battles! In the evening, she would go back to her 'home'. The therapist and the patient agreed that she should write ten episodes from 'Red Zora's' life over the subsequent ten sessions. Ms. A. brought the one or two pages long, lively but straightforward stories with her to the therapy sessions. The 'red Zora' was initially alone, but then she gathered a gang around her. While reading the last of the ten stories, the therapist was amazed and delighted: The patient had written in it that she visited the world of the 'red Zora' and 'apprenticed' with the 'red Zora'. Ten years later, Ms. A. reported that the obsessive–compulsive thoughts had disappeared two years after the therapy ended. There were no other obsessive–compulsive symptoms either. She commented on the work at the time with these words: "I didn't even know that I could be so creative! I wasn't sassy enough!".*

The technique of projective personalization specifically resolves the defenses of introjection and adaption to a rigid superego. The patient actively and playfully shifts her own taboo impulses and wishes contained in her obsessive thoughts *to another person, at another time, in another place,* and to the life context of this *other* person. The content and impulses of their obsessive thoughts find a *suitable* framework in that *other* person's difficult life context. The fictional person's thinking and acting are *absolutely appropriate in their difficult situations*. Therefore, he *does not defend* himself through introjection and projection.

**Central idea**

In writing the ten stories, the patient ascribes a *positive meaning* to her own taboo wishes and impulses in another life context. *By definition*, she can identify with her own taboo desires in the *metaphorical stories*. Over time, she thus resolves her own defenses through introjection. However, this does not trigger her strict superego because these taboo wishes and impulses belong to *another* person. As a result, over time, the process of her self-development is liberated from the fixation on the defense of identification with the attacker.

Carmen Kollenbaum (2014, verbal communication) reported on the therapy of a 30-year-old patient whose obsessive thoughts disappeared *after just a few weeks* of working with the technique of projective personalization. The patient had already been treated for severe destructive obsessive–compulsive thoughts three years before that. The current obsessive thoughts arose after having a spontaneous orgasm *during an argument* with her husband: 'All she could think about was that she had to masturbate'. The tormenting thoughts prevented her from relaxing. Meanwhile, the obsessive thoughts also interfered with her sexual intimacy with her husband. The patient was generally very unsettled by this. The previous procedure with the behavioral in vivo confrontation did not bring any lasting relief this time. The therapist, therefore, used this new technique of *projective personalization*. The patient invented three fictional people to whom she attributed her disturbing thoughts and feelings: (1) a 'woman in dreary everyday life who leads a completely fulfilled, never again dreary life through masturbation', (2) a dying woman 'who defeated her tumor for a short time through masturbation', and (3) a prostitute 'who finds it thrilling and exciting to stand on the street and entertain clients'. A few weeks after this work, the patient decided to stop taking the pill and wanted a second child. The obsessive thoughts had disappeared. The patient looked alive again and was full of energy.

**Central idea**

The patient *justifies* her impulse to act on her destructive fantasies *in the life of this other fictional person* and lets this other person carry out the impulse *to the end*. In this way, she indirectly dissolves the existing blockages in her thinking, feeling, and behavior and liberates her creative ego from its constraints.

In the case of masochistic obsessive thoughts, the projective personalization sometimes only succeeds with the other fictional person living in a grotesque world. For example, one patient suffered from obsessive thoughts about wanting to kill her infant. She invented the fictional character of Frankenstein for her murderous fantasies. Frankenstein wanted to kill the monster he created because it wanted to destroy the world. The patient began to cry while telling the story of Frankenstein. She knew, of course, that her child didn't want to destroy the world. She spontaneously linked the interaction pattern "Frankenstein and his monster that must be killed" with the interaction pattern "herself and her infant" internally. In identifying with Frankenstein, she also allowed *the destructive impulses* within herself. This resolved her projection of destructive impulses onto her child. It also relaxed her defense by introjecting the child's *supposed* accusations, "You're a bad mother." She realized that she loved her child and, of course, *didn't* want to kill it. Her child's *demands* bothered her, but not *the child* itself. She discussed with her therapist her difficulties in drawing healthy boundaries.

## 7.4 Self-stabilization and Ego-Strengthening Through Role-Playing

Straub (1972, p. 181), like Mentzos (2011, p. 105), recommends that the therapist focuses on ego-strengthening in patients with obsessive–compulsive disorder. The awareness of repressed conflicts and their causes can lead to an intensification of symptoms or a displacement of symptoms in individuals with obsessive–compulsive disorder.

Straub (1972) used psychodramatic role-plays to strengthen the ego. She integrated her experiences from psychodramatic therapy for children into therapy for adults (Straub, 1972, p. 182). (1) She asked her patients to imagine that they were employed with a television company and had the task of creating *children's programs*: (2) She asked the patients to 'think, if possible, of scenes to be played in the 'television programs''. (3) Next, the patient makes up a fantasy story. This story should have a beginning and an end. (4) The story should *turn out well* in the end. It should include what the child or the inner child of the patient *needs* and *wants.* (5) If the fantasy story does not end well at first, the therapist encourages the patient to think of a *happy* ending. She justifies this with the argument: "Otherwise the children would not like to watch the television programs. They won't sleep well afterward!" (6) The patient enacts the fantasy story psychodramatically and is supposed to play the roles appearing in the 'programs' *himself*. (7) The therapist plays each opposite role. In this way, she helps the patient to differentiate and expand their own roles. She also steers the play in a way that the story ends well as planned. When patients create stories *for children's television*, they often, without realizing it, invent stories that are a metaphor for their *own* inner conflict.

**Central idea**

Straub let her *adult* patients further develop their *healthy inner child* in this way. Like working with the coping fairy tales and the positive counter-images, the role-play *for children's television* strengthens the patient's internal natural self-healing system (see Sects. 5.13 and 5.14).

Straub generally treated her patients with obsessive–compulsive disorder in individual therapy "because then the patient can be activated more intensively in each session than in a group" (Straub, 1972, p. 182).

***Case example 59* (Straub, 1972, p.182 ff.)**

*A patient with a severe obsessive–compulsive disorder "invented [...] the role of the 'little braggart', a roughly seven-year-old boy who confidently dares to take on all sorts of undertakings". First, the therapist suggested scenes 'which she considered important for the patient to create'. 'For example, in one such scene, little braggart persuaded his teacher not to give homework because of the good weather.' In another scene, he 'argued aggressively with his friend's mother for his friend's benefit. The mother was over-anxious and did not want to let him play on the playground. Soon the patient invented 'similar scenes herself and [...] took on some of the associated roles'. She played the child roles in an increasingly carefree manner, was more spontaneous in the adult roles, and restricted her 'children' less because of her concerns. In parallel, the patient felt 'more self-confident and carefree' in her everyday life; she 'hardly interrogated her children when they came home' and 'no longer asked them to constantly [...]change their clothes'.*

*After about a year of individual therapy, one day, the patient wanted to play 'a completely different scene' than usual: "She wanted to enact a scene where a man kidnapped a child. [...] She would play the man's role and 'simply' imagine the child." The therapist should not play along. So it happened. The patient "spoke to a child in the role of the kidnapper, [...] and lured the child to her with the words: "Come, come, I'll show you something beautiful". Then she pulled it away by the hand: 'Just come with me, come with me. [...] Now we are in the forest. [...] I'll show it to you soon. Look, there's a cave; that's where we're going. 'The patient pushed the 'child' in front and continued in a threatening tone: 'So now I have you!' She knelt on the floor, leaned over the 'child', pressed her hands on him, leaned lower, and groaned: 'Ah, now I have you, so, ah, so!'".*

*After the play, the patient was pale and agitated and said hesitantly: "You have to show something like that in children's programs." The therapist replied: "That's probably why you did it". A week later, the patient spontaneously said, "All these ideas were so strange. […] I am very concerned why they came to my mind." The therapist replied to the 'woman plagued by feelings of guilt', that "sometimes all of us have ideas that worry us […] as we cannot see their origin". The therapist had to 'expressly assure the patient that even she would have 'outrageous ideas' occasionally. That 'seemed to put the patient at ease'. The patient changed the subject and invented another television program: This time, she was a nine-year-old boy who went on a flight to see relatives abroad on his own because his parents did not want to come with him. He experiences many exciting things on his trip, and everyone admires him for his independence.*

*In her everyday life, the patient's behavior towards her children was 'becoming more and more normal'. She now […] let them play outside their own house and garden without […] feeling restless. 'In the following conversation, the patient criticized her mother for the first time, who she had described as a loving and understanding mother until then.' Her mother sometimes let her down 'if, for example, a teacher had mistreated her at school'. She always said, "Teachers are always right". The patient did not want to pass on her submissiveness and insecurities to her children. She was, therefore, glad that she no longer restricted her children. Even five years after the end of the treatment, the patient was still 'in a good psychological state, free of anankastic symptoms' (*Straub, 1972, *p.185).*

Straub (1972, p. 184 f.) assumed that the "ego-strengthening role play had reduced the patient's tendency to repress, thereby opening the path to an eruptive discharge of previously repressed emotions (in the role of kidnapper)". Straub interpreted that "the patient invented the child abduction scene also because of the unconscious rejection of her children. Therefore, she felt compelled to play the massively aggressive kidnapper role". She interpreted the role of the child abductor as a *symbolic* image *of the patient's* aggressive impulses. She did not realize that by playing the role of the perpetrator, the patient was *autonomously* resolving her defense by projecting good intentions onto him and thereby indirectly relaxing her defenses through introjection (see Sects. 2.4.3, 7.1, and 8.4.2).

Straub's case example dates from 1972, i.e., when the findings of today's trauma therapy were not yet available. In my opinion (see Sect. 5.5), in this case, the therapist should have asked the patient *directly* whether she experienced sexual assault as a child or whether her mother was traumatized by rape. If necessary, the therapist could then have continued to work within the trauma therapy framework. The following speaks in favor of sexual trauma or secondary traumatization of the patient in case example 59: (1) She had the intense urge to play a scene involving the sexual abuse of a girl. (2) The therapist should not take on any role, unlike the usual format. (3) The role of the abused little girl did *not* come alive in the play. The patient would then have probably seen herself in the 'girl'. That would have ushered her into her old traumatic experience and triggered a flashback. (4) The patient complained to the therapist that her mother sometimes let her down. (5) Like many patients with a trauma-related disorder, the patient acted anxiously and controlling toward her children. (6) At 14, she was 'shocked to learn that men had raped women and girls in many places at the end of the war'. In this context, she would also have heard that some of the raped individuals had become sexually ill." That would have prompted her at the time to 'fear the risk of getting infected herself' (Straub, 1972, p. 181).

In this case, Straub did not work in the narrower sense of trauma therapy. Nevertheless, Straub's approach led to the patient becoming *symptom-free*. It was helpful to concretize the traumatic fears symbolically and give them a coherent framework in a story. The therapist thus became an *implicit* witness of the truth for the patient (see Sect. 5.8). Straub did not leave the patient alone. She empathized with the patient's feelings of horror without trivializing them (see Sect. 5.15). She gave the patient permission to think and feel such complex fantasies. In her approach, Straub specifically dissolved the patient's defense through introjection, but not her defense through projection (see Sect. 7.1).

## References

Mentzos, S. (2011). *Lehrbuch der Psychodynamik. Die Funktion der Dysfunktionalität psychischer Störungen* (5th ed.). Vandenhoeck & Ruprecht.

Straub, H. (1972). Theoretische Anmerkungen zur psychodramatischen Behandlung von Phobien, Zwangsneurosen und anderen psychischen Störungen. In H. Petzold (Ed.), Angewandtes Psychodrama in Therapie, Pädagogik, Theater und Wirtschaft (pp. 177–194). Junfermann.

# Chapter 8
# Depressive Disorders, Masochism and Suicidale Crises

## 8.1 What is Depression?

Epidemiologically depression is the largest group of mental disorders by far (Mentzos, 2011, p. 125). The ICD-10 classifies these into depressive phases in the case of bipolar affective disorder (F31.-), *singular* depressive episode (F32.-), *recurrent* depressive episodes (F33.-), and *persistent* dysthymia in the case of chronic neurotic depression or a depressive personality disorder (F34.1). Depressive episodes can be *mild, moderate, or severe.* There are *severe episodes without* psychotic symptoms or *with* psychotic symptoms, such as hallucinations, delusional ideas, psychomotor inhibition, or stupor. Persistent dysthymia is characterized by a depressive mood lasting for at least a few years.

A variety of clinical psychopathological symptoms are included in these diagnoses. Therefore, according to Mentzos (2011, p. 125), "it would make more sense… not to speak of depression but of the group of depressions. […] In fact, the depressive mood is the common denominator of all variations in depression". Other symptoms can include psychomotor inhibition, listlessness, pronounced tiredness after the slightest exertion, sleep disturbances, decreased appetite, difficulty in concentrating, waking early, feeling low in the morning, helpless clinging tendencies, self-destructive behavior, suicidality, loss of interest in the outside world, and anhedonia, the inability to experience pleasure. There can also be a decrease in one's self-esteem and self-confidence. Feelings of guilt can arise and intensify into delusions of sin or impoverishment (Mentzos, 2011, p. 125 and ICD-10).

**Central idea**

The psychodramatic *idea of the spontaneously creative person* suggests that depressive states, according to Mentzos (2011, p. 126), should be understood as an indicator of "active but pathological processing of conflicts, trauma, and other stresses". The depressive affect signals the hopeless entanglement in seemingly unsolvable conflicts and an impending standstill in the ongoing half-conscious, half-unconscious conflict processing (Mentzos, 2011, p. 126).



R. T. Krüger, *Disorder-Specific Psychodrama Therapy in Theory and Practice*, Psychodrama in Counselling, Coaching and Education 4,
https://doi.org/10.1007/978-981-99-7508-2_8

In the *constant conflict* between self-actualization and adaptation, those affected lack the ability for *adequate self-actualization.*

**Important definition**

Rogers (2009, p. 26 f.) describes *self-actualization* as "the organism's inherent tendency to develop all its possibilities; and in such a way that they serve to maintain or promote the organism. This tendency includes not only [...] the basic needs [...]but also [...] the ability to differentiate itself and its functions. It includes expansion in the sense of growth". The *self is a dual system.* It consists of the inner self-representation and individual object representation in the present, past, or future situation.

**Central idea**

The human *self is a dialogic process.* This process realizes constructing and representing the inner self-image and object image, appropriately to the *external* current situation, and interacting and rehearsing dialogically between the self-image and object image (see Sect. 2. 9). Psychotherapy should therefore be bifocal and progressively develop both, the *inner* self-image as well as the *inner* object image, in the current *external* situation.

Appropriate self-actualization in a given external situation provides a *feeling of self-efficacy.* It is *not* to be equated with *external self-realization.* People become depressed when their self-actualization is severely restricted or blocked by external or internal pressure to adapt. With *conscious adaptation*, the affected person still has internal access to his internal self-actualization. Therefore, in an emergency, he can make an active choice to adapt. In the case of *unconscious adaptation*, however, the affected person does not even notice that he is adapting. Three different adaptation constraints can restrict self-actualization:

1. In a current conflict (see Sect. 8.3), self-actualization is restricted by *real external pressure to adapt*, for example, by the loss of a job or by the restrictions on physical contact during the Covid-19 pandemic.
2. Self-actualization is restricted by one's *neurotic inner compulsion to adapt.* In the current conflict, the affected person fights off appropriate self-actualization by identifying with the aggressor (see Sect. 8.4.2).
3. Self-actualization is also restricted by one's *internal structural pressure to adapt* (see Sect. 4.7). In such a case, the affected person defends himself by identifying with the system (Krüger, 1997, p. 211 ff.). According to Parin (1977), he identifies himself blindly in the present, as it were,

   (i) *With the role* assigned to him by his system of relationships, his institution, or society. He receives narcissistic gratification from the concerned system for taking on this role.
   (ii) *With the planning* of the relationship system.
   (iii) *With the explanation patterns* of the relationship system.
   (iv) With the goals, values, and norms of the relationship system.
   (v) The affected person and the members of his relationship system affirm each other narcissistically in their role behavior. The affected person unconsciously denies the *naturally existing* conflict between his self-determined role and the role determined by his partner's expectations. He feels identical

to the role assigned to him. But he becomes depressed when the narcissistic gratification for the role assigned to him is missing in his relationship system or when he loses that role, for example, when he is no longer the admired son of his family.

## 8.2 The Different Forms of Depression

The disorder-specific psychodramatic approach to treating people with depression comprises *three different methods*. These are determined by *how* the patient's *self-actualization is confined* in his current conflicts:

1. In the case of *current conflicts*, there is real external pressure to adapt, which forces an external and internal change, for example, the death of a relative, cancer, or a workplace conflict (see Sect. 8.3). In such a case, the therapist works with the psychodramatic dialogue with role reversal or the two-chair technique in a potentially traumatic situation (see Sect. 5.8).
2. In the case of a *neurotically induced conflict*, the therapist works on relationship conflicts using the seven steps of the psychodramatic dialogue (see Sects. 8.4.2–8.4.7). They systematically resolve the defense through identification with the aggressor, which restricts self-actualization.
3. In the case of *an internal structural pressure to adapt* (see Sects 4.4 and 8.5), the therapist also works on the patient's rigid defenses of splitting and denial in an explicit metacognitive manner (see Sect. 4.7). For example, when the patient *behaves masochistically*, she focuses on talking about the *general principle*, bringing forth the contents of the patient's self-injurious thoughts.
4. *Severe depression bordering on psychosis* (see Sect. 8.6) occurs in patients with severe deficit experiences in childhood or those with trauma-related disorders. The patient's capacity to mentalize has collapsed. As a result, the patient's ego can only be found in the patient's self-regulation *of his depressive mood* (see case example 71 in Sect. 8.6). The patient is unable to internally connect his depressive mood with the triggering interpersonal conflict that has caused it.

In the *initial interview*, the therapist uses the method of diagnostic psychodramatic conversation (see Sect. 2.8). In doing so, she concretizes the conflict stated by the patient with two empty chairs *externally* in the therapy room. But the patient does not shift to the chairs of this symptom scene. During the diagnosis, the therapist looks, shoulder to shoulder with the patient, at the two chairs of the symptom scene. She attunes her intuition with the holistic process of the patient's intuition (see Sect. 2.5) and lets him retrace the chronological course of *interaction sequences* in his inner conflict image from memory from the observer position. Thus, the patient resolves his defense through denial (see Fig. 2.5 in Sect. 2.3). As a cognitive doppelganger, she uses interviews and verbal doubling to help him create a psychosomatic resonance between his actions, physical sensations, affect, linguistic concepts, and thoughts and to fill gaps in the psychosomatic resonance (see Sect. 2.7). She then asks him about

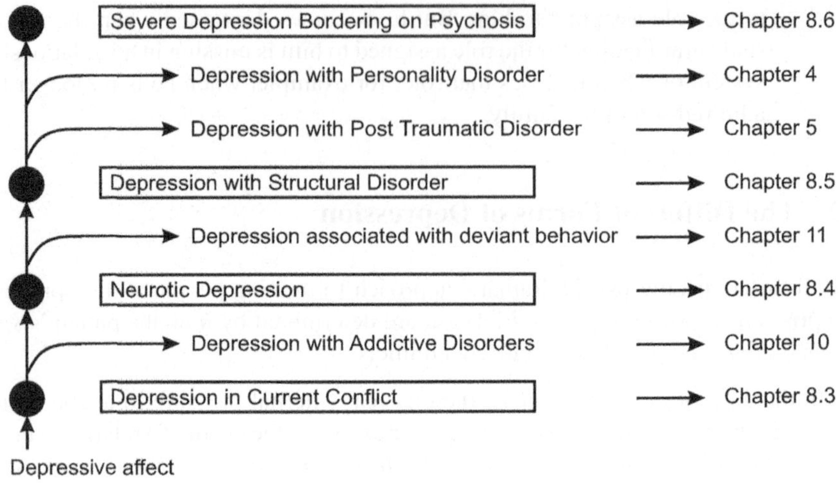


**Fig. 8.1** Exclusion procedure in the diagnosis of depression

the onset of his depression: "For how long have you been feeling so exhausted and tired? When did this start?" She helps the patient describe the interactional framework in which his self-actualization was narrowed.

The therapist intuitively uses *the elimination procedure* for the diagnosis (see Fig. 8.1 below). She first looks for high-energy conflicts in the present (see Sect. 8.3). However, often one *cannot* explain depression in terms of a response to a current conflict *alone.* The current conflict would result in no depression or significantly mild depression *in other people.* This indicates that depression is also partly caused by neurotic conflict patterns (see Sect. 8.4). Even then, the therapist cannot understand the cause of the depression in some patients. Despite all efforts, she remains disoriented. This is a diagnostic indication that the patient's depression is partly due to a *structural* disturbance (see Sects. 4.4 and 8.5).

Indications of depression due to structural disturbances: (1) The patient keeps changing the subject and the reason for his problem (see Sect. 2.8). He *cannot* describe his conflict in a comprehensible manner. (2) The therapist herself repeatedly feels confused. (3) When working with the table stage (see below), the patient lays stones symbolizing elements of his inner conflict area in a row next to one another. This rationally *controlled* order depicts the patient's *inability* to think *in pictures.* (4) The therapist quickly senses a latent disturbance in the therapeutic relationship. She cannot resolve this disturbance in psychodramatic self-supervision (see Sect. 2.9). She must include the constellation work with the ego states in the self-supervision. These are steps 13–17.

In the case of *depression bordering on psychosis* (see Sect. 8.6), the patient's mentalizing has collapsed. Therefore, as a doppelganger, the therapist first helps the patient improve his sense of self and authority in the process of self-regulation in

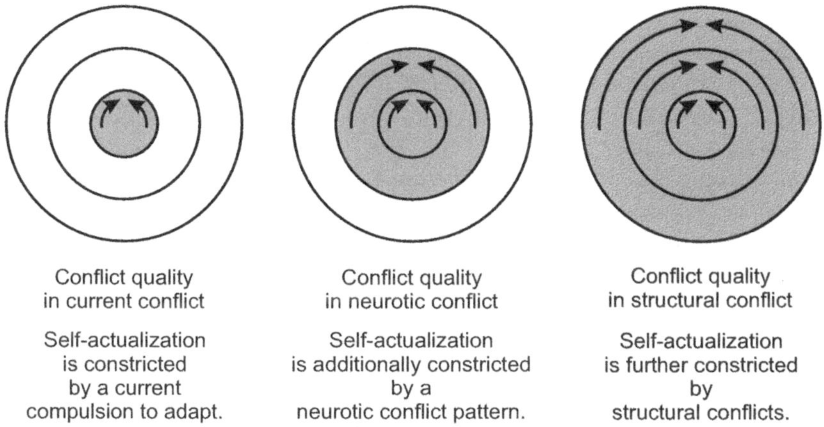


**Fig. 8.2** The three different conflict areas in depressive disorders

his *everyday life*. It is a prerequisite for him to relate his depression to triggering interpersonal conflicts (See Fig. 8.2).

The therapist can *also use the table stage* for diagnostic work (Sect. 5.10.10). In doing so, she uses the language *of symbols* in addition to *verbal* language. When working with the table stage, the patient and the therapist get an overview of the *connection between the patient's various conflicts*. For this purpose, they build the symbolic image of their 'soul landscape' together during the conversation (Krüger, 2005, p. 266 ff.) and represent it with stones and wooden blocks on the table: (1) The patient's ego, (2) His feelings, (3) Other people involved in his conflicts, (4) The institutions involved, (5) Important objects such as the bed in which the patient lies at home until noon, (6) His ideals and values. (7) The development of his depression is symbolized as a *timeline* with three stones, one for the beginning of the conflict, another for the current situation, and a third for future development. The therapist moves the stone that represents the patient forward or backward along this timeline on the table during the therapeutic conversation. She empathically names the patient's affect, differentiates them verbally doubling together with him, and represents them on the table with matching stones. The therapist and the patient, together, look at the symbolic soul landscape of the patient represented on the table, from a *meta-perspective*. In the last third of the therapy session, the therapist can point with her hand at the symbolic picture on the table and ask the patient: "Do you always do it this way?—And if you do, why is it the best solution for you? Are you afraid of something?" The collaborative work with the table stage activates the patient's *inner* perception and processing of conflicts.

In the case of *structural conflicts* in the patient, the therapist also names and symbolizes the patient's rigid defense, for example, his self-injurious thinking, with the help of chair work (see Sects. 4.7 and 4.8), thus making it the subject of therapeutic communication.

***Case example 60***
*In the first interview, the 42-year-old Ms. A. reports: "I've had problems for a long time now, more than ten years. My problem is that I always have to apologize for my existence!" Therapist: "So you deny your right to life. I am putting a chair across from you for your inner judge." Ms. A: "Yes, I have to do everything one hundred percent. Nothing is good enough!" Therapist: "How old is your inner judge?" Ms. A: "It's always been there since school." After extended maternity leave, the patient is now working part-time in a nursing home. Therapist: "But you are not able to show yourself at work? You pretend as if there is no problem?—I'll put another chair next to you for your self-protection behavior that pretends as-if." Ms. A: "That's right. Once, when I had to ask my supervisor something, she said: 'You don't need to sneak up like that! Just be open and say what you want!' That was when I realized that I had had depression for ten years. But I only realized that afterward."*

*The therapist evaluates this realization of the patient as inner progress: "That's when you saw yourself through a different set of eyes and took yourself seriously." Ms. A: "Ten years ago, we moved into our own house on the outskirts. But that was just a shell structure. Even at Christmas, we sat amidst unpacked boxes. Before that, we lived in a nice little apartment in the city. I couldn't sleep after moving. I would wake up at four in the morning, electrified. Then I had destructive thoughts in my head. I was depressed for a year. Most of the time, I sat at home and just cried!" The therapist points to the chair for her self-protection through adjustment: "Secretly!" Ms. A: "Yes, secretly, I can do that very well!" Therapist: "What were these destructive thoughts?" Ms. A.: "Oh, I thought: 'If only you hadn't moved in here! If only I could get sick.' Or: 'If my husband gets sick and dies, then I will move out from here!'" Therapist: "Oh, you were angry with your husband too. You got in touch with your inner angry child! I will put an extra chair over here for this angry child. But of course, such thoughts do not go well with your strict conscience! Were people very strict with you in childhood? As strict as you are with yourself now?" Ms. A: "Yes, my parents, they were teachers. My father was often in a bad mood and choleric. He always insisted that one be the best at everything in school. I didn't do everything well enough for him. For example, I wasn't allowed to mow the lawn because I didn't cut the edges well enough. My mother was also impatient, and she always took everything from me. If you wanted to help, you couldn't. We always had 16-year-old interns to look after us children. They changed every year."*

## 8.3 Therapy for Depression in Current Conflicts

In the case of current conflicts, self-actualization is restricted by *an actual* stressor or a need to adapt to everyday life (ICD-10 F32.-, F43.0, and F43.2). This stress often leads to burnout or severe exhaustion. Triggers can include serious physical illness, a pain syndrome, serious relationship conflict, separation conflict, grief reaction after the death or loss of a close one, or the loss of a job. In such a case, the therapist and the patient collaboratively grasp the *real conditions* in his current conflict and the *real magnitude* of the current pressure to adapt. They look for the patient's self-developed coping strategies and appreciate them. This activates the patient's conflict processing and recognizes his ability to resolve conflicts.

***Case example 61***
*A 54-year-old man, Mr. B., is in a sanatorium because of chronic lung disease. He is suffering from chronic reactive depression (ICD F32.2). During the diagnosis, with the help of the table stage, the therapist learns that his wife died nine years ago. Six years ago, he lost his job as a truck driver due to lung disease. His children live in a different city. Mr. B. ekes out his existence in poor circumstances as an early retiree. Despite his good ego strength, the need to adapt to his severe lung disease blocks the transition to better self-actualization. Mr. B. suffers from threatening attacks of shortness of breath. He puts a four-centimeter large stone for his 'lung disease' next to the two-centimeter small stone representing his ego on the table stage. The therapist allows herself to be empathically drawn into the patient's hopelessness. But then she notices that she is defending herself internally against the patient's paralysis. As a doppelganger, she reaches for a wastebasket in desperation, takes the stone for the 'lung disease' from the table, and puts the wastebasket in its place: "This is your lung disease. You have no choice; you must submit to your lung disease—Crap! Crap! Crap!—Is the wastepaper basket big enough for you? How did you manage to cope with this serious illness at home? What possible solutions did you find?" The patient shares many small creative solutions that he has newly developed to cope with his life. The therapist appreciates the patient's ingenuity. Symbolizing the lung disease with the wastebasket made the existential quality of his disease clear. At the end of the therapy session, everything essential in the patient's current life situation is symbolized by stones outside on the table. His various areas of conflict and his resources are visible side by side. The depressed patient perceives the abundance and diversity of his externally restricted life. That helps him reconcile a little with himself.*

Patients whose depression is caused *solely by current conflicts* have, *by definition*, an excellent ability to mentalize. They can *play and change roles*. They can internally grasp and report on the conflict causing their depression. The therapist first identifies *the temporal development of the current conflict* with these patients. To do this, she uses protagonist-centered plays in group therapy, and the psychodramatic conversation (see Sect. 2.8) and the table stage in individual therapy.

If necessary, the therapist verbally *doubles* or interviews the patient during a psychodramatic dialogue with her conflict opponent in *the two* complementary roles (see Sect. 8.4.2). Soliloquy in his role, verbal doubling, the interview, and the role feedback improve his *inner* mentalization and fill gaps in his inner psychosomatic resonance between sensorimotor interaction patterns, physical sensations, affect, linguistic concepts, and thoughts. The *sharing by others* or *amplifying interpretations* during the debrief stabilizes the patient's self-actualization in his conflict. *Amplifications* are fairy tales or stories from social contexts that reflect a similar life experience. The patient recognizes himself as the hero or the heroine of the story. With his *individual* conflict, he is no longer different from everyone else. He no longer feels excluded from the human community. This helps him to give legitimacy to his feelings and desires.

In the psychodramatic processing of an actual conflict, the therapist can orient herself on the 12 steps of psychodramatic self-supervision (see Sect. 2.9). The therapeutic effect primarily arises from role reversal. Once a patient perceived herself as a 'lump of grief' through the eyes of her conflict partner while reversing roles. The therapist confirmed that she had actually behaved in this way. This perception led to a change in her behavior *in all of her intimate relationships*. Ziehm-Kossatz (2013, p. 264 f.) once helped a patient, as a general practitioner, psychodramatically in only two sessions of 20 min each to cope with a serious current conflict.

***Case example 62***

*"A 36-year-old, slightly overweight orthopedic shoemaker comes to my general medical consultation for the first time. He immediately gushes off: 'I've had a new job in my company for three months. A predecessor was fired because he got bogged down and left some important jobs behind. I am now doing one and a half person's job. [...] I feel overwhelmed. I have trouble sleeping. I can't go on.' I ask him how he thinks I can help him. He says: 'I would like to take sick leave.' From what I've heard, that doesn't seem like a good solution. I ask him what it will be like when he returns to work after his sick leave is over. The patient: 'Then my workload would have doubled because no one else can do my work. So this would not be a good solution!' I affirm what he says and place a chair next to him [...]: 'This chair represents a part of your personality that is a kind of advocate for your interests and protects you from being overburdened and ultimately falling ill'". (The therapist used the technique of a fictional doppelganger that supports the patient's healthy adult thinking. Supplement by the author). "This part also made sure you got an appointment with me. But, you are now sitting in the chair of the well-functioning employee [...]. Unfortunately, I cannot help this part because I always get sick when I overload myself." (The therapist herself offers a sharing. Supplement by the author.) "But I could support your advocate! Would you please sit in the advocate's chair and tell me what your client really needs?' The patient sits on the advocate's chair and reports: 'This year (it is now the beginning of November), I have only had five days of vacation. I really need a vacation!'.*

*Therapist [...]: 'Could you help your client enforce the legally guaranteed right to vacation?' Patient as an advocate: 'I can try.' As a therapist, I set up an additional chair for the boss. The patient describes this boss as a young, self-confident, and dynamic person. The patient presents his concerns from the role of an advocate: 'I would like to apply for two weeks' leave.' At my instruction, the patient changes into his boss's role and [...] replies [...]: 'But you still have to train the new colleague.' There is another role reversal. Patient: 'Others will have to take care of that, I feel drained, and I'm afraid of falling ill. I urgently need some rest so that I can do my job well.' In the rest of the play, 'the boss' approves of the vacation.*

*Two weeks later, the patient returns with a [...] flight booking to Gran Canaria. He reports that it gave him a lot of strength to have 'an advocate by his side'. He made it clear to the boss that he urgently needed a vacation. We work psychodramatically again for twenty minutes and use the table stage to determine which tasks he urgently needs to be relieved of and how to deal with the overtime hours. I saw the patient again just before Christmas. During his vacation, the work areas were redistributed. He is now working on field and is completely satisfied with it. [...] He can do his job well." In this therapy, the therapist understood the patient's symptoms of exhaustion as an expression of a current workplace conflict. She defined the conflict as a relationship conflict between the patient and his employer. She let the patient fictitiously carry out this conflict as a psychodramatic dialogue and placed an inner, fictional doppelganger at his side in the form of a 'personal advocate'. The 'advocate' helped him improve his self-actualization in the conflict with the boss.*

## 8.4 Therapy for Depression Caused by Neurotic Conflict Processing

The constriction of self-actualization in patients with depression can result from neurotic development (ICD F34.-, F32.-, or F33.-). In these cases, they had to learn to *adapt* and *not* notice their wishes and needs *in their childhood*. They defend through introjection, denial, projection, and identification with the aggressor in conflicts. These forms of defense were the best solution for them *in their childhood*. But the patients continue to practice these *old* solutions *in their current relationships* without any awareness.

**Important definition**

Anna Freud (1984, p. 88) understood the defense through 'identification with the aggressor' as *a combination of the defense through introjection and the defense through projection.*

When interacting with others, each person develops an *inner image* of the conflict partner as well as an *inner image* of himself. He then acts in the *external* relationship as determined by his *inner image* of the relationship.

1. In the case of *defense through introjection* (Ferenczi, 1970, p. 100) (see Sect. 2.4.1), the patient *automatically* takes over parts of the reality construction *of his opponent* and makes them his own during a conflict. He, therefore, also perceives the opponent's misperceptions as his own *without realizing it*. For example, he also integrates the attributions and expectations of *his opponent* into his inner self-image. The patient in case example 63 (see below) constantly felt a latent tension in her relationship with her husband. Whenever she brought up the conflict, her husband always grumbled: "You're crazy. This emotional talk is never-ending!" The patient then defended by introjection and thought: "I'm crazy. I'm too emotional." "I do not feel well. So *I* am a problematic person." The patient was trapped: The further development of her inner self-image was fixated

in a 'false' self-image through introjection. This hindered her from validating *her own emotions* and resolving the conflict.

2. In the case of *defense by projection* (see Sect. 2.4.2), the person concerned is fixated on a particular object image of his conflict partner *without reviewing it any further*. Over time, by holding on to this 'false' object image, he pushes his opponent into a role complementary to his own behavior. As a result, he fights in his conflict partner what he defends in himself. The patient in case example 63 (see below) projected her *own* sense of suffering onto her husband and excused the husband's unreasonable behavior: "My husband suffers from my emotions and my *abnormal* need to talk. *That's why* he reacts so contemptuously." The further development of her object image of her husband was fixed on the image of suffering. Therefore, it did not occur to the patient to name his indifference toward her and check whether, for example, he was unable to love or perhaps had a lover.
3. In *defense through identification with the aggressor* (see Sect. 2.4.3), the person affected is firmly fixated on a specific self-image and object image through *the combination* of defense through introjection and projection. Anna Freud (1984, p. 92) defined defense through identification with the aggressor as *an unconscious "exchange between the aggressor and the attacked person"*. The hare shoots the hunter, as it were. The patient in case example 63 believed that *she was aggressive* when talking to her husband, and *her husband suffered because of her*. But in fact, she *suffered* because of her husband and *her husband was the aggressive one*.

   A patient who adapts neurotically and defends himself by identifying with the aggressor decompensates into depression,

   1. If the pressure to adapt increases even further in a situation of failure.
   2. If the external gratification for an exhausting adjustment is missing, for example, gratification for being a habitual helper.
   3. Or when the patient becomes aware of the joylessness of his life in a situation of temptation but thinks that he cannot or should not change anything.

***Case example 63* (Krüger, 2003, *p. 95 ff., abridged)***

*As a child, 49-year-old Ms. C. had "never done anything forbidden". She met her husband when she was sixteen. She was emotionally drawn to him because he was reliable. So he stabilized her adaptive attitude in the first instance. However, the couple had grown increasingly distant in the almost thirty-year marriage. The husband bought a motorcycle, drove it through the United States, and wanted to camp with her. But the patient did not want to go along, ultimately because of her chronic back pain. Ms. C. increasingly became aware that something was amiss in their relationship. But the husband "didn't want to talk". One day her husband suddenly separated from her and said: "I don't want to lead a life like this!" The patient was utterly shocked. She collapsed mentally and physically and reacted with massive, prolonged depression and suicidal fantasies (ICD F32.2). She was treated medically by a psychiatrist. Before the separation, Ms. C. had "always given her husband his freedom" in order to avoid arguments: "He was allowed to do everything, and I was not allowed to do anything!" She had increasingly submitted to him and took his devaluations of her in her self-image. However, that didn't prevent the breakup of their relationship. An inpatient convalescence treatment stabilized the patient a little. In the subsequent outpatient psychotherapy, the somewhat large, clever woman would cry immediately every time she spoke about her "husband" (continuation in* Sects. 8.4.2 and 8.4.3).

**Exercise 19**

Try to experience being depressed *by conscious introjecting*: Think of a relationship conflict that you have already resolved. Re-enact the conflict with your 'conflict partner' in a psychodramatic dialogue with role reversal (see Sect. 2.4.3). Please adapt yourself entirely to the expectations of your ´conflict partner´: Imagine that your opponent "naturally" *cannot* feel, think, and act *differently* and that he would suffer from your protest. Adopt the explanations he uses to justify his actions toward you as your own. Fade out from your perception all behaviors of your "conflict partner" that trigger aggression in you. Think about eliminating the disturbance in the relationship "*without* hurting your conflict partner". You will notice that you are starting to feel depressed.

## *8.4.1 The Basic Principle of Psychodramatic Therapy for Depressed People with Neurotic Conflict Processing*

**Central idea**

In persons with neurotic depression, self-actualization is blocked in conflicts. The inner representing of the self-image is fixed in a 'false' self-image as a result of defense through introjection. A 'false' self-image always provokes a fixation in the inner object image, too. This further results in defense through projection (see Sect. 2.4.2). Therefore, the therapist works with two focal points: She tries to free the patient's inner self-image as well as the inner object image from their fixations using the psychodramatic dialogue with role reversal.

The psychodramatic dialogue with role reversal realizes the four metacognitive tools of natural mentalization in producing inner relationship images in the as-if mode of play, thereby freeing mentalization from its fixations (see Sect. 2.2 and Fig. 2.5 in Sect. 2.3). The internal *representing* of the relationship is fulfilled through the external scene construction, the internal *interacting* through external role play in the relationship picture, the internal *rehearsal* through the external role reversal and the internal *integrating* of a neurotic affect or behavior into other conflict images through the external change of scene.

In patients with neurotic depression, the inner processing of conflicts is blocked by defense through introjection, projection, and identification with the aggressor. The psychodramatic dialogue frees their conflict processing from their blockades. As a result, his conflict-solving abilities are again freely available to him in the next real encounter with his conflict partner. He can reorient himself and *look for a new appropriate response to the situation.*

From 1936, Moreno initially worked 'only' with role-plays (see Sect. 6.8.1) in his development of psychodrama therapy in his sanatorium. He was not yet familiar with the direct exchange of roles between the patient and an auxiliary ego which takes on the role of the conflict partner in the play (Moreno, 1945, p. 11 ff.; 1985, p. 185 ff.; 1959, p. 221 ff.). It was in 1959 that he first described the *role reversal* in protagonist-centered plays in the writings accessible to me (Moreno, 1959, p. 248 ff.). At that time, he reported on a treatment described by Robert Drews (Group Psychotherapy VI, 1952, quoted in Moreno, 1959, p. 248), which had taken place in 1946.

***Case example 64***

*The therapist healed a patient, Mr. Rath, in only three therapy sessions. He had suffered from writer's cramp for fifteen months and thus could not work. Three of his fingers on the writing hand, "the middle, ring, and little fingers were bent in various positions". As a result, the patient was incapacitated in his job as a court reporter, and his income became meager.*

*During the first therapy session, Mr. Rath told the therapist about a relationship conflict with his superior, a judge. He had initially supported the judge when he was conspicuous in court due to his alcohol addiction. However, the judge increasingly despised the patient and ended the friendship. Until the initial therapeutic conversation, the patient had "not expressed his feelings to the judge or anyone else for that matter".*

*The therapist let the patient take on the role of the judge in the first therapy session. The therapist himself played the role of Mr. Rath, imitated him by doing his paperwork, and was submissive and humble. He thereby mirrored the patient in an unexpressed manner. In the role of the judge, Mr. Rath was at first humorous and witty but then increasingly tense, angry, and hostile. Finally, he turned red with anger, raged, and insulted Mr. Rath, played by the therapist. He knows too much. That would be enough to bring him, the judge, to the gallows.*

*The therapist and the patient changed roles. The therapist himself took on the role of the judge. In his role, Mr. Rath began "to attack the judge […] in coherent, profane, and hurtful language. He walked around the room with quick steps, sweating, cursing. […] He spontaneously clenched his right fist with his cramped fingers and hit the table with such force that the glass plate cracked. About five minutes after the discharge […], he started crying and yelling that he had been a damn coward for enduring this miserable comedy for so long […]. Then he sat down […] and wept silently to himself. […] Then, the patient got up again and noticed that his 'paralyzed' fingers were free, flexible, and relaxed. Delighted, he exclaimed: 'My God, I am healed!'" He called his wife and told her.*

*A catamnestic survey in 1952, seven years after treatment, discovered that 'his hand was in perfect shape'. His relationship with the judge had changed. The patient had been accepted into a legal firm on the judge's recommendation and was 'now the successful head of a staff of court reporters'. What is remarkable about this case example is that for the treatment to be successful, it was not necessary to link the patient's compliance with an authority figure with similar experiences in his childhood: There was 'no psychogenetic penetration of his life experience outside of the patient-judge relationship'.*

The patient was fixated on defense through identification with the aggressor, i.e., in the combination of defense through introjection and projection (Freud, 1984, p. 88). He had *defended through introjection* and, in doing so, adopted the judge's accusation and felt guilty without realizing it. He also *projected* his perfectionism and sense of justice onto the judge and submitted to it.

The therapy was successful because the patient reenacted, reviewed, and changed his inner self-image, object image, and causal construction in the relationship conflict with the judge. He did so with the help of the psychodramatic dialogue with role reversal in the as-if mode of play (see Sect. 2.4.3).

(1) The therapist first invited the patient to change to the opposite role and explore the inner reality of the judge in the relationship through *psychosomatic acting*. It helped him dissolve his projection of perfectionism and sense of justice and his denial of the judge's inhuman behavior. (2) First, the therapist himself enacted the behavior of the docile patient as an auxiliary ego. The patient perceived his own behavior through the eyes of the judge as cowardly. That didn't fit with his self-image. He felt angry with himself for conforming, and angry at the judge for his unjust behavior. (3) In his role, he allowed his previously suppressed anger toward the judge beyond the previous reality. In this way, he self-actualized in relation to the judge and dissolved his defense by introjecting the blame. The cathartic psychosomatic integration of his anger into the relationship image made his writer's cramps disappear. The patient became spontaneous through the dissolution of his defense through identification with the aggressor in the relationship with the judge (Moreno, 1974, p. 13). He *internally* perceived the judge anew in the following encounters in real everyday life. He, therefore, also *externally* behaved in a new way toward him and appeared more courageous. This made the judge respect him again, or at least fear him more. As a result, the judge even advanced the patient's career.

**Central idea**

In patients with *neurotic depression*, *internal role reversal* is blocked in a conflict. In relationship conflicts, they have relatively rigid images of themselves and of their conflict partner through a combination of their defense through introjection and projection. However, with the help of psychodramatic dialogue and *free external role reversal*, they can liberate their object image and self-image from their neurotic fixations. This, in turn, liberates the patient to *reorient* himself *in real life* in the encounter with his conflict partner and to look for a more appropriate solution. *Without planning it,* he spontaneously acts more appropriately in his relationship conflict and becomes more self-confident and expansive.

### 8.4.2 The Seven Steps of Psychodramatic Dialogue in Neurotic Depression

**Recommendation**

In the therapy of people with a neurotic arrangement of relations, the psychodrama therapist uses the technique of *diagnostic psychodramatic conversation to lay the foundation of the therapeutic work* (see Sect. 2.8 and Fig. 2.9). She represents the patient's symptom scene with two additional chairs in the therapy room for self-image and object image in his everyday conflict. As a result, the patient and the therapist view the patient's relational conflict from the meta-position. The patient perceives himself from the outside as interacting *separately from* his conflict partner and becomes a doppelganger for himself.

In the psychodramatic dialogue with role reversal, the patient further develops his self-image and also his inner object image through psychosomatic acting in the as-if mode of play. In doing this, he complements his psychosomatic resonance patterns between his memory centers of sensorimotor interaction patterns, physical sensations, affects, linguistic concepts, and thoughts (see Sect. 2.7). *Psychosomatic participation* is the difference between psychodramatic dialogue and psychodramatic conversation. Therefore, Moreno (1959, p. 98) says: "Speech is important. However, action precedes and includes speech." The *psychodramatic dialogue with role reversal* is always a joint effort between the patient and the therapist. The therapist uses her intuition to follow the patient's psychodramatic conflict processing and, if necessary, intervenes with psychodramatic methods. When working with the psychodramatic dialogue and role reversal, the therapist uses *seven different steps* to improve the patient's self-actualization in the conflict, if necessary. These liberate the inner self-image *as well as the inner object image* from their fixations in conflict:

1. *The therapist* herself takes on the role of the patient in the psychodramatic dialogue and *acts on his behalf* as his doppelganger. The patient changes into the opposite role of his conflict partner.
2. In his role and in changing the role, the patient *reenacts* a confrontation from memory with the associated interaction sequences in chronological order.
3. In a hypothetical psychodramatic dialogue with role reversal, *the patient* behaves *more expansively of his own volition* in the relational conflict and tries something new by going beyond reality.
4. The therapist and the patient discuss the previous psychodramatic play. In the *focal role feedback*, they look for what has been new or has become more apparent in the last play. In doing so, they validate the expansion of the patient's self-image and object image in his conflict, if available.
5. Mirroring from the meta-perspective: The therapist and the patient jointly name the behavior of the patient's conflict partner from the meta-perspective and look for amplifications for the conflict.
6. The therapist takes on the role of the patient in the psychodramatic dialogue, if necessary, and *mentalizes as a doppelganger on his behalf*. In his role, she expresses, going beyond reality, what she thinks, feels, and perceives in the

interaction with his conflict partner. The protagonist takes on the role of his conflict partner in the play.

7. As a doppelganger, the therapist *conducts contract negotiations* with the patient's "conflict partner". *As a doppelganger*, she tries to negotiate a more appropriate balance between giving and taking in the patient's relationship conflict and thus to make the relationship *systemically fair*.

In each therapy situation, the therapist only applies the steps of the psychodramatic dialogue indicated currently. The more patients with depression are fixed in the defense through introjection and projection, the more they need the therapist's or group members' help (see Sect. 8.4.5).

1. *The therapist, as a doppelganger, takes on the patient's role in the psychodramatic play.* Depressed patients often protest about what happened to them. They express their *suffering* from the event but do not name their *own feelings* in the conflict situation because they defend themselves self-injuriously through introjection. In doing this, they often project their strict or sadistic superego onto their conflict partner. Patients who think masochistically often refuse to work through their conflict psychodramatically because the inner representation of their self-image in the conflict is blocked by an authoritarian conflict partner (see case example 15 in Sect. 2.14 and case exmample 70 in Sect. 8.5).

**Central idea**

Projection and introjection stabilize each other and add up to defense through identification with the aggressor. The patient projects his own positive characteristics onto the conflict partner, otherwise, he would not be able to maintain his defense through introjection.

When there is a blockage in the inner representation of the self, the therapist first tries to free the patient's *inner object image* from its fixation through projection. Thus, the defense by introjection is no longer stabilized by defense through projection. The therapist herself plays the role of the patient and, as a doppelganger, verbalizes what she thinks and feels *on behalf* of the patient. The patient himself assumes the role of his conflict partner and reacts as he thinks he would act. It usually turns out that the conflict partner is *different* from the patient's own sadistic superego. Or the therapist and the patient realize that the conflict partner is truly as bad as the patient described him. For instance, the patient in case example 63 immediately panicked due to the projection of her severe superego onto her husband when asked to assume her own role in the psychodramatic dialogue with her 'husband'.

***Case example 63 (1st continuation, see* Sect. 8.4*)***

*During therapy, Mrs. C. decides to deal with her marital conflict psychodramatically. The therapist represents her inner relationship picture with two empty chairs. At the beginning of the play, Mrs. C. wants to take on her own role in relation to her 'husband' on the empty chair. But she immediately begins to cry helplessly. Therefore, the therapist himself takes on the role of the patient as her doppelganger. He asks her to switch to the role of her husband. The therapist assumes her posture. He verbalizes her thoughts and feelings toward her husband on her behalf. In terms of content, he adheres to the information that Mrs. C. had previously given in the therapeutic conversation: "I cannot live like this. I know nothing of you. I trust your promise. But when I am in need, you are not reachable. I'm desperate and disappointed!" In doing this, the therapist expresses the patient's inner despair through his gestures, facial expressions, and inner attitude. Mrs. C. has changed to the role of her husband. But she remains herself: "Now my husband would be leaving the room. He always says I shouldn't be so emotional!" The therapist doesn't want to force anything. So he interrupts the play and moves on to the debriefing: "When in your role, I noticed some anger rise in my stomach from deep down below. I was petrified of this anger but was also fascinated by it." Mrs. C.: "I'm feeling sick!" The therapist interprets her body sensation as a psychosomatic reaction to the relationship conflict: "It's as if you get a poisoned apple from your husband and swallow a bite of it, just like Snow White did from her stepmother".*

*After the play, the therapist and the patient used psychodramatic conversation (see* Sect. 2.8*) to discuss how the marital conflict had come about: What had the patient experienced in the conflict with her husband so far? In retrospect, what did she see as the cause of the conflict? During the debriefing, the therapist repeatedly pointed to the patient's chair on stage or, if necessary, to her husband's chair. He supported her in verbalizing her feelings. (2nd continuation below).*

In the play, the therapist *acted as* the patient's *doppelganger. He* freely expressed *his* experience in *her* role. In the role of her husband, the patient perceived herself, played by the therapist, as a tormented person from the outside. In doing so, she developed empathy for her own feelings. Patients with neurotic depression are often deeply touched when the therapist, as a doppelganger, authentically plays out their feelings of suffering in their relationship conflict. They are amazed that another person understands them so well and can put their feelings into words (see case example 15 in Sect. 2.14 and 19 in Sect. 4.4).

**Question**
Why does the patient integrate the therapist's statements as a doppelganger into his self-organization?

**Answer**
Because the statements made by the therapist as a doppelganger perfectly complement the patient's psychosomatic resonance pattern in his conflict. In doing this, the therapist must fully identify with the patient and bring the patient's thinking and feeling, on his behalf, into the as-if mode of thinking. She should not want the patient to be different than who he is.

2. *Re-enacting a memory*. The patient and the therapist work together to reproduce the patient's inner construction of reality in her past conflict in the as-if mode of play. A group member or, in an individual setting, the therapist himself takes on the counter-role as an auxiliary ego (see Sect. 8.4.4). In a psychodramatic dialogue with role reversal, the patient shows the *temporal* sequences of interactions in a *recalled* confrontation with her conflict partner in both roles. That dissolves the

defense through denial (see Sect. 2.4.2). Taking on the counter-role also dissolves the defense through projection (see case example 63, 4th continuation below). In the counter-role, the patient reproduces the inner sensorimotor interaction patterns, physical sensations, affect, linguistic concepts, and thoughts of her conflict partner *psychosomatically*. She thereby expands her image of the object and liberates it from its fixation. Thus, she recognizes anew how her conflict partner ticks. She thus perceives the reality of her conflict partner in a new way in everyday life.

3. *The patient tries something new out of her own will in a psychodramatic dialogue with role reversal with her conflict partner.* The therapist asks the patient to rehearse her conflict in the as-if mode of play: "Do you want to express your thoughts and feelings to your husband here in the role play?—It's not about whether you *do* the same to him *in real* everyday *life*! We are only working on your inner picture of the relationship. We will pretend that your husband is sitting across from you. In reality, of course, your husband is sitting at his computer at his place of work." *In the as-if mode of play*, the patient verbalizes *what he feels and thinks, beyond the previous reality,* and demands what he needs. In this third step of the psychodramatic dialogue *in the as-if mode of play*, the patient *tries a new action* of his own volition in the conflict. In doing so, he expands his self-actualization in his inner conflict image and dissolves his *defense through introjection*. The patient should "only" communicate *his truth* to his 'conflict partner'. There is the *subjective truth of the conflict partner* and the subjective truth of *the patient*. It is not about blaming the conflict partner.

The therapist *often* has the patient *reverse roles* during the *rehearsal*. In the opposite role, the patient shall develop the appropriate response to *each* of her own statements. In the role of her conflict partner *in role reversal*, she assumes *his* posture to get well settled into his holistic self-organization.

**Recommendation**

If necessary, the therapist *verbally* asks the patient how she feels in the conflict partner's role. In the play, however, as an auxiliary ego, he only repeats what the patient truly said in the conflict partner's role. Thus, in the role of her conflict partner, the patient may discover a possible *discrepancy between* the thinking and acting of her conflict partner.

The mental rehearsal expands the patient's knowledge of cause and effect in her relationship conflict. In the subsequent encounter with her conflict partner *in real everyday life*, she will then know how her conflict partner would react to her *old* behavior. But she *can* also leave out her old behavior and look for new, more appropriate behavior in the relationship. The dissolution of the defense through identification with the aggressor results in the patient spontaneously changing her behavior toward her conflict partner.

**Central idea**

Role-theory-oriented psychodrama therapists focus mainly on the patient's role development *in his own role, i.e., on the development of the role of self-representation* (see Sect. 2.14). In this way, they fail to resolve the projection that stabilizes the patient's fixation in a self-injurious self-image. But, the patient must liberate her *object image* from fixation, too. In this way, she recognizes appropriately whether and how *she* can influence the behavior of her conflict partner.

Empathy cannot replace the external role reversal with the conflict partner. In a role reversal, the protagonist *psychosomatically* experiences how her conflict partner ticks *internally*. She assumes her conflict partner's role and retraces the neuronal connections between his memory centers of sensorimotor interaction patterns, physical sensations, affect, linguistic concepts, and thoughts. The *psychosomatic* experience in his role gives her experience a greater degree of certainty than a mere *internal* role reversal.

***Case example 63 (2nd continuation, see above and Sect. 8.4)***
*For the first time, Mrs. C. takes on her own role in a psychodramatic dialogue with her husband. The therapist takes on her husband's role as an auxiliary ego and insults Mrs. C. according to her instructions: "You're crazy! This emotional talk is never-ending!" Ms. C. answers and directs the conversation to their son Walter: "When you talk to him on the phone, you don't even ask him how he's doing!" Mrs. C. and the therapist switch roles. Mrs. C. responds from her husband's role: "Walter doesn't even want to talk to me anymore. You are raising him. That is your bad influence!" Back in her own role, Mrs. C. defends herself desperately from her husband: "I tried to persuade Walter to call you. But he didn't want to. Now I stay out of it!" The therapist changes into the role of Mrs. C. and repeats her statements. The protagonist remains rigid in her husband's role: "That is your influence, that is the result of your upbringing!" The therapist and the patient recognize that Mrs. C.'s husband does not seem to be or is no longer willing to question his behavior for her sake. Her husband's negative attitude is evidently a reality and not a projection. (3rd continuation below).*

The therapist can use a *short form* for the 3rd step of the psychodramatic dialogue. She instructs the patient to adequately practice the 12 steps of psychodramatic self-supervision (see Sect. 2.9) in the therapy room. This method includes the 3rd and 4th steps of the psychodramatic dialogue. It only takes 15–20 min.

4. *Intermediate discussion with focal role feedback and psychodramatic conversation*: In *focal role feedback*, the therapist specifically asks the patient: "Did you experience something *new in the play* in your conflict partner's role or your role? Or has something just *become clearer* to you in the play?" With these questions, the therapist prompts the patient to compare her experience in the play with her experience in everyday life *and* to recognize differences autonomously. Thus, the patient learns to perceive differences in her psychosomatic experience in everyday life. The therapist actively gives her responsibility *for her own* mentalizing in conflict. The patient writes down her answers to the two questions on a piece of paper (see Sect. 2.9). She then verbally communicates them to the therapist. Sometimes the patient does *not* recognize a new experience *herself*. In such a case, the therapist draws the patient's attention to what she herself said in the play: "Did you know, *before the play,* that your conflict partner is afraid of your spontaneity?".

**Central idea**

It is important to quickly write down the seemingly small *new* experiences in the two roles in the play because protagonists forget their new *psychosomatic* experiences in the roles within a few hours. They often "only" remember the *interpretations* they have derived from them. But, a new *psychosomatic experience* in one of the roles changes the inner relationship image and has a more lasting effect than an interpretation.

The therapist validates the patient's *new* experiences and thereby gives them importance. Then, if necessary, he explains to her *how* her new experience could possibly change the relationship with her conflict partner *in real everyday life*: "In the play when in the role of your boss, you noticed that his distant behavior is only for *self-protection* and that he *does not reject* you. Believe it! You will notice: this perception changes your relationship with your boss when you meet him again."

The therapist repeatedly uses the method of *psychodramatic conversation* in the interim discussions (see Sect. 2.8). To do this, he places chairs for the patient's self-representation and object representation in their conflict outside in the therapy room (see Fig. 2.9 in Sect. 2.8). By looking at the symptom scene, the protagonist experiences her own truth in the relationship as well as that of her conflict partner as *existing side by side*. She perceives the conflict between herself and her conflict partner *systemically* as a *relationship conflict* and no longer just her individual problem.

5. *Mirroring from the meta-perspective and searching for amplifications*. If necessary, the therapist and the patient look at the two chairs representing the relationship conflict from the outside. They describe what happens between the two conflict partners and how they perceive the conflict partner's external behavior from the meta-perspective. "How would you describe your conflict partner's behavior?" This is the technique of mirroring. Sensitive patients often use a term in their response that describes the *absence of a positive quality*. For example, they say 'he is unempathetic' or 'he is disrespectful' instead of 'he is selfish' or 'he is arrogant'. They avoid calling the negative or evil by its name. This helps them deny their own negative affect toward the egoistic conflict partner. In such a case, the therapist asks the patient: "No, please do not use the term 'unempathetic' and 'disrespectful'. Say *what is* and *not what is not*!" By using an adequate term, the patient gives herself permission to perceive her conflict partner's negative behaviors and characteristics and react emotionally appropriately (see case example 63, 4th continuation).

If necessary, the therapist and the patient also look for *amplifications* for the patient's conflict in the psychodramatic conversation. For example, it can be a relationship image from a fairy tale. Or the therapist talks about other patients who have had similar experiences and how they dealt with such a conflict. Or she describes symbolic images from social references. The sharing of participants in a *group* setting (see Sect. 8.4.5) also have a similar function as the amplifications of the therapist in the individual setting. The *amplifications* positively confirm the patient's self-actualization in her conflict. The patient learns to validate her feelings and perceptions.

***Case example 63 (3rd continuation, see above and Sect. 8.4)***
*At the beginning of the session, Mrs. C. says: "I don't know what to say. Actually, I'm fine now, much better than a year ago. But when the conversation turns to my husband, I keep crying." Spontaneously she adds: "I have always avoided any points of friction that could have led to arguments in my relationship with my husband. I've always felt like I'm not normal. Whenever we fought, I was always told: 'You're crazy! This emotional talk is never-ending!' But if my husband was in a bad mood, for example, because of something at work, he could let it all out. I couldn't!" The therapist: "It seems to me that your husband is behaving like a tyrant. But Gandhi already said: "Tyranny is not the fault of the tyrants but of the oppressed! For if you would not allow yourself to be oppressed, there would be no tyrants'" (4th continuation below).*

6. *Vicarious mentalization as a doppelganger*. In the case of *a strong neurotic fixation*, the patient often remains stuck in the defense through introjection and projection. The patient *also* does not dare to openly share her truth with the conflict partner, *even in the play*.

**Central idea**

In such a case, the therapist identifies *spontaneously* with the oppressed self of the patient in her conflict and *feels constricted on her behalf*. He then often reacts with countertransference and would like the patient to be different from what she is. For example, he *verbally* asks the patient to be more expansive in her role. However, the patient then often feels criticized and develops a negative transference to the therapist.

**Recommendation**

It is therapeutically more productive if the therapist experimentally takes on the patient's role and makes *his protest* useful for the therapy. For example, as a doppelganger, he integrates his affect into the patient's conflict image *on behalf of the patient* on trial in the as-if mode of play. In doing this, the patient plays the role of her conflict partner. The patient and the therapist thus *jointly* answer the question of cause and effect in the relational conflict: Does the patient's conflict partner behave in such an authoritarian manner only because she demonstrates no resistance? Or does she adapt to him because her conflict partner is so authoritarian? (see case example 15 in Sect. 2.14)

In *vicarious mentalization as a doppelganger*, the therapist mindfully verbalizes *his* true physical sensations, affect, motivation, and thoughts toward the "conflict partner". He actively justifies, on behalf of the patient, why it *is the best solution* for the patient to think, act, and feel so inhibited. As a doppelganger, he states his motivation, and, in the process, integrates ethical values and personal necessities into his argument. The patient is mostly fascinated by being understood so well (see case example 19). In this way, the therapist and the patient together assess whether the "conflict partner" *would* react empathetically with the patient verbalizing their feelings and thoughts. That would be the case in a loving or respectful and not merely functional relationship (see case example 5).

***Case example 63 (4th continuation, see above and Sect. 8.4)***

*The therapist requests the patient: "I would like to try something different with your husband in your role in the play. Please play your husband's role and try to react the way your husband would!" The therapist takes on the patient's role and turns to her 'husband': "You have changed: In the past, one could rely on you. We got married, built a house, and started a family. You thought it was good back then, just like me! Now I don't even know you anymore! You want to be the father of our son, but you ignore him. What do you feel about it?" Mrs. C. as her husband: "I think Walter could care a little more for me!" Therapist as doppelganger: "No, I do not want to know what you think. I want to know what you are feeling!" Mrs. C. slips out of the role of her husband: "My husband would have left the room long ago!" The therapist: "You are your husband. If he would have walked out, then you go too!" Mrs. C. gets up from her chair. In the role of Mrs. C, the therapist feels disappointed and angry. He yells: "You are a coward! You are a coward! A motorcyclist but such a coward! When things get tough, you always just run away!".*

*In the debriefing, Mrs. C says: "I didn't feel anything in my husband's role!" The therapist confirms: "When I played your husband's role, I felt the same way. What you said did not affect me very much. I held a shield in front of me and was careful not to let my wife's allegations hit me. In truth, my thoughts were elsewhere. I hoped the conversation would soon be over because my girlfriend was waiting." Mrs. C.: "Actually, after my treatment in the psychosomatic clinic, I decided: 'I don't want to understand my husband anymore.' Do I need to understand him?" The therapist: "No, you shouldn't learn to understand him by playing his role here. The point is that you should recognize its inner reality! That you know how he functions on the inside! Because if you know how he thinks and feels, it is easier for you to assert yourself against him!" Mrs. C.: "I once went after him and asked him why he wanted to separate." The therapist: "I think you know why he's leaving, and you don't need to ask him anymore, do you? He's afraid of losing his freedom! He thinks that he is a great guy. He is uncomfortable with being questioned by you. He is a coward! You should dare to call a spade a spade, at least in front of yourself." Mrs. C.: "Maybe I should tell him he is a coward!" (5th continuation in Sect.* 8.4.3*).*

7. *Vicarious contract negotiations.* If the "conflict partner", *enacted by the patient*, continues to react uncompromisingly and authoritatively *in* the first six steps of the psychodramatic dialogue, the therapist moves on to the 7th step, the vicarious contract negotiations. Doing this, the therapist, as a doppelganger, demands *a different external behavior* from the "conflict partner" in the relationship. The therapist does not need to or have to know *before* the play what he wants to ask of the "conflict partner". He may initially engage in the *soliloquy* in the role of the patient. In doing so, he integrates all the information he has from her in his actions, physical sensations, affect, and thinking *in her role*. In this way, he feels the patient's *actual needs and desires* (Krisztina Czáky-Pallavicini 2014,

only orally communication). While in the patient's role, he intuitively searches for what she would need from the conflict partner to improve the *quality of the relationship*. The *demand* can seem small: "If you want to end our friendship, I wish that we agree, nevertheless. Please allow me to email you at least every two months and ask how you are. And I would like you to reply to me with one sentence. Is that possible for you?" Or: "I'm allergic to your contemptuous tone. I got enough of that from my mother when I was a kid. I didn't need that again. I want you to be caring with me." In the role of her conflict partner, the patient responds the way she believes the conflict partner *would*.

The therapist *ethically* justifies his demands toward the patient's "conflict partner" with general human values and norms. He demands, for example, "respect for the other" or "fairness in giving and taking". In this way, he investigates whether the patient's "conflict partner" would take the patient's wish *seriously* because of rational factors and whether he would be willing to come to a concrete compromise. The goal is a *systemically fairer relationship*: "I want and need from you … and I am also ready to give you this and that."

**Important definition**

There are two types of justice, legal and intersubjective. Legal justice is determined by external rules or laws. But *intersubjective justice* has to be renegotiated in every new situation. Ultimately, relationships only succeed if both partners *try to do justice to one another and themselves*. Only then will the resources of *both* relationship partners be fully used in the situation. A hiking group can, for example, set up the rule that each group member should carry the *same amount of weight* in their backpack. However, if *one* hiker has a fever, it is intersubjectively fair for *another* hiker to take some of the sick person's luggage, unlike the day before. In this way, everyone moves forward better together.

*Intersubjective, systemic justice* is already described in the Christian Bible as a central development principle for relationships. The focus of systemic justice is inherently emancipatory. It helps to hear the voices of the oppressed and the excluded and to make their experiences fruitful as a resource for social contexts. The doppelganger technique and role reversal can help to process this systemic development principle in a relationship conflict (Krüger, 1997, p. 174). *Sustainable* conflict resolution is about *cooperation* and not victory or defeat. The seven steps of psychodramatic dialogue in the as-if mode of play systematically help widen the possibilities for *cooperation in the conflict* (see Sects. 2.1 and 2.9).

**Central idea**

Self-actualization *succeeds* when the individual lives their *abilities* and limits in the relationship (Ciompi, 2019, p. 186) and integrates themselves into the *community's well-being* (see Sect. 2.1). It is a *dialogical process of self-organization*. This process includes the development of the inner self-image and object image in the given situation. The inner self-image and object image constantly change as the external situation is continually evolving. A *sustainable solution* to the conflict comes about when *both* conflict partners free their inner self-image and object image in the conflict from their fixation through the defense and develop them further to suit the external reality. Thus, they can *cooperate* in shaping external reality.

The vicarious contract negotiations are therapeutically fruitful even if *the therapist* fails with his request to the "conflict partner". If the patient, in the role of her "conflict partner", rejects *every* suggestion from her doppelganger, it indicates that she is indifferent to her conflict partner. The "conflict partner" doesn't see any advantage if he were to respond to her wishes. The patient then *realistically* assessed her conflict partner before the play and *does not* defend through projection. The therapist and the group members recognize *the true extent* and the drama of the patient's relationship conflict for the first time. They positively affirm that the patient thinks, feels, and acts appropriately toward his conflict partner.

But if the "conflict partner" is ready for a systemically more equitable solution to the conflict, the patient realizes psychosomatically, in the counter-role, that there is *more room* in the relationship *for her self-actualization* than she previously thought. She expands her inner image of her conflict partner and dissolves her defense through projection. In the subsequent encounter in real everyday life, she will see him with a different set of eyes and behave more demandingly on her own. Because she knows that he would respond to her wishes, even if perhaps reluctantly (see case example 15 in Sect. 2.14).

After steps 6 and 7 of the psychodramatic dialogue, the patient does *not change back to her role*. She should *not practice* the behavior demonstrated by the therapist. That would be premature pushing. It could trigger the patient's superego prohibitions and, thus, worsen her depression. *The therapist* should take responsibility for *his* expansive behavior *in the patient's role* because *he* wanted to rehearse and investigate the cause and effect in the conflict and whether the patient 'only' defends through projection. The patient experiences that, *in the role of her conflict partner,* she does not break down, become violent, or end the relationship if her doppelganger, the therapist, behaves more expansively. Her physical and emotional experience in the role of her conflict partner differentiates and expands her inner image of him and liberates her object image from its fixation. She becomes internally free to perceive her conflict partner without projections in everyday life. As a result, she then *autonomously* finds a new and appropriate behavior for the current situation. She must *not rehearse* a new behavior. A new behavior, recommended by the therapist or group, would hinder her from behaving appropriately in the current situation in everyday life.

**Central idea**

Some therapists who observe the psychodramatic vicarious mentalization and contract negotiations in a seminar, rate these procedures as a *directive style*. In doing this, they get caught in internal-external error (see Sect. 2.14). The therapist and the patient work together on the patient's *inner images* and do not modify his *behavior in real everyday life*. I have never had an experience where a patient simply adopts the therapist's arguments and negotiation goal from the representative contract negotiations. In steps 4–7 of the psychodramatic dialogue, the therapist adheres to the *rule of abstinence* more clearly than if he would *verbally* suggest a different role behavior toward the patient's conflict partner.

## Exercise 20

You cannot understand these processes just by reading them. The therapist develops his therapeutic impulses from his *psychosomatic perceiving* in the encounter with the patient. Therefore, try to apply steps 6 and 7 of the psychodramatic dialogue in counseling or therapy. You will notice: There is a difference between *watching* steps 6 and 7 from outside as an observer or *psychosomatically acting them* as a doppelganger. Your acting as a doppelganger liberates the patient from defense through projection. By changing her inner object image, the patient *autonomously* finds a new appropriate solution for the current relationship conflict in her everyday life *without* any therapeutic help.

**Central idea**

*Defense* is a dysfunctional *metacognitive* process, which produces the same old dysfunctional thinking, feeling, and acting in new conflict situations. If the patient dissolves the defenses in his conflict with the help of *metacognitive psychodrama techniques*, he will automatically arrive at new thoughts in the process of dealing with the conflict. We call this new thought process the 'surplus reality'. The patient then *perceives* the reality of his conflict in everyday life with a fresh set of eyes and, *therefore, also acts differently and more spontaneously* in his conflict in everyday life. That is the secret of the therapeutic effect of the psychodramatic dialogue with role reversal.

### *8.4.3 The Integration of Improved Self-actualization in Relationship Images from Childhood*

**Recommendation**

In treating people with depressive disorders, the therapist initially addresses the patient's *current* conflicts in a *solution-oriented* manner by applying the psychodramatic dialogue with role reversal. In steps 6 and 7 of the psychodramatic dialogue, the patient resolves his defense through introjection and projection and experiences that he *can influence* the external behavior of his conflict partner and change it. However, many patients wonder why it is so difficult for them. This experience then lets them *spontaneously* search for *why* they have always adapted so strongly to the expectations of others *until now*.

***Case example 63 (5th continuation, see Sect.* 8.4 *and* 8.4.2)**

*In the following one-on-one session, Mrs. C. starts by saying: "I asked my father whether he actually wanted a boy. He was furious! He said: 'That was your grandmother! When you were born, she said: 'Another girl!'" The therapist: "So you have a permanent place in your father's heart!" Mrs. C. spontaneously: "Yes!" She radiates heartfelt joy at this thought: "Yes, my father never really liked my husband. He found him brash and naughty." She continues: "My mother told me: Until I was five years old, I was always a delightful child, and I laughed a lot. My cousin's husband also said: 'You were always so friendly!' Somehow others seem to see me differently than I see myself!" Mrs. C. is on the way to rediscovering herself. The therapist: "Are you amazed?" Mrs. C: "Yes. If I relate that to what my husband said, that I keep bickering and nagging, I feel a bit stuck, and it still impacts me. Sometimes I still feel worthless. But sometimes, I can snap out of it again!".*

*In the following therapy sessions, the therapist and the patient use psychodramatic dialogue to explore further the causes of the failure of the marital relationship. Mrs.*

*C.: "In my relationship with my husband, I was always made to be the ass! Now my mother has also said: 'He was very dominant.' Over time, it seems like that to me as well. Years ago, a friend said that my husband was a maverick with a wife and a child!" In the following therapy session, Mrs. C reports: "I visited my parents on the weekend. Even there, we talked about my husband. I said, 'He was a prick!' My mother laughed. But my father made telescope eyes like that!" She playfully holds her hands to her own eyes and shows how she imagines telescope eyes. As a child, the patient had never done anything forbidden. But now, she feels fun shocking her bourgeois father with her choice of words.*

*After a four-week vacation, Mrs. C. ponders during the therapy session: "I'm thinking about whether my son and I should move out of our house. I don't particularly appreciate that my husband can walk into our house and behave in any way he wants. I'm fine. I am blissful. I simply have to be careful not to lose the ground under my feet. Only in the last few weeks have I realized that the people I am with support me. So many say: 'Do it! Move out of your house! We'll come and help.' I think they've been supporting me all along. But I am only noticing it now! When I recently called my husband about a tax payment, I told him I was looking for a new apartment. And that we have to think about whether we should get a divorce. He went very quiet and only said yes or no. When I hung up, I didn't feel as cramped and uncomfortable as I usually did after using the phone." The therapist: "Now the buck lies with your husband. Now he has to decide and respond!".*

Many psychodramatists let their depressed patients switch to childhood scenes relatively quickly when dealing with *current* relationship conflicts psychodramatically. Together, they explore *the childhood scenes* for reasons that may explain their patients' strong willingness to adapt in the present. This process tempts the patient and therapist to believe that the current conflicts would *not exist if the patient had had a "better childhood."* In extreme cases, the patient finally knows a lot about the genetic causes of his current conflict but he has changed little (see Sect. 7.1). Or he tries, with a positive confirmation from his therapist, to assert his needs without any consideration for the needs of their conflict partner.

**Central idea**

When reenacting scenes from childhood, the patient psychosomatically experiences that his mother, for example, didn't take an interest in his thinking and feeling as a child. He then knows *why* he is so allergic to his wife's distancing. However, he doesn't know if his wife would accept him asserting himself. Reenacting scenes from childhood doesn't resolve the defense through projection in *current* conflicts. The patient remains fixated in the old object image of his conflict partner. With the help of the psychodramatic dialogue with role reversal, the patient must *check if* his conflict partner behaves dominantly because *he* always adapted, or if *he* adapted because his authoritarian conflict partner allows no compromises.

The black-and-white pattern of *either* self-fulfillment *or* adaption doesn't apply in relationships. They always exist side by side. A relationship conflict must be resolved *systemically* if the solution is to succeed in the long term. *Both* partners in a *couple relationship*, for example, benefit from the relationship in the beginning through mutual love and appreciation. After a while, however, they enter the second phase of the relationship, the *battle for resources*. Who is allowed to realize their *own interests* to what extent in the relationship? The battle for resources triggers old neurotic solution patterns in both partners. As spouses feel connected, they learn to resolve most of these conflicts with one another over time. However, despite all love, a *mutual neurotic allergy* sets in (Krüger, 2010). Two things come together: (1) What is progress for the *inner child of the husband* triggers an old neurotic wound *in his wife* and gives rise to negative transference in her. (2) *In addition, however,* what is progress for the *inner child of the wife also* triggers an old neurotic wound *in the husband* and *also* leads to a negative transference *in him*. In this situation, there is only one solution: If the relationship is to survive, the partners must inform each other about their neurotic or traumatic wounds and try to be mindful of the other's wounds. In this way, the partners free the blocks in their inner role reversal. They can come to an agreement: If the *husband* doesn't keep an appointment, *he* should tell how important his other duty is *for him* on a scale from 1 to 10. If he says 10, the wife must let him go. However, the wife should also say how important it is *for her* on a scale of 1–10 that he stays, because otherwise, her childhood trauma film of being an unwanted child will come alive. If *she* says 10, the husband *must* stay with her no matter how urgent his other duty is. This agreement empowers both partners to act mindfully *in a potentially retraumatizing situation*. They don't have to separate from one another to protect themselves.

***Case example 65***

*A patient had realized during therapy that she would decompensate into a trauma film whenever her husband distanced himself from her in an argument and frowned. She worked through the marital conflict with the help of psychodramatic dialogue. However, the first six steps did not lead to a solution. The therapist, therefore, continued to the 7th step of the psychodramatic dialogue (see* Sect. 8.4.2*). As a doppelganger, he informed the "husband", played by the patient: "When you frown, I always slip into a trauma film. I need three days to feel stable again. You know how it was for me in my childhood with my hot-tempered father. So if you frown, may I ask you what you are feeling and thinking in the moment? Would you be ok with that? You also benefit if I don't feel depressed and withdraw for three days." In her husband's role, the patient noticed that he was happy to agree to this new compromise. She was amazed in the debriefing: "It would never have occurred to me to ask my husband that. It's in fact very easy!".*

**Central idea**

The happiness in a marital relationship is love. The *drama*, however, is that you are not one but two.

In the treatment of depressed people with neurotic conflict processing, there is a risk that the neurotic solution patterns in the relationship images from childhood will spread to the current relationship images over and over again. The patient should, therefore, also integrate her improved self-actualization, *free from defenses* in the present, into her inner relationship images from childhood.

As with the patient in case example 63 (see Sects. 8.4, 8.4.2 and 8.4.3, this often happens spontaneously. Otherwise, the therapist will occasionally ask *specifically* about the age of the adaptive attitude (see case example 53 in Sect. 6.3): "Since when have you been blindly meeting the expectations of others?" This question prompts the patient to link her new experiences in the current relationship conflict with her childhood experiences: "As a child, I always had to function no matter what. My brother was sick. I didn't want to burden my parents anymore!".

If necessary, the therapist supports the patient in further developing her inner images from childhood: For example, he asks her to write a *fictional letter* to a person from childhood (see Sect. 4.12). The patient informs this caregiver that she is depressed as an adult because of the adaptation she learned in childhood. She also shares what she would have needed as a child instead. Or the therapist lets the patient, as the adult she is now, engage in a hypothetical psychodramatic dialogue with role reversal with the caregiver from childhood (see Sect. 4.12). In this way, the patient can integrate her *new* insights into her *old* inner relationship image from childhood.

*At the end of her therapy*, the patient should develop a coherent answer to the question: "What do I have to do to feel depressed again?" In answering this question, the patient grasps the *old path of her neurotic self-regulation* that led her to depression. She should write this insight in her dream and self-experience book. Later, when she feels depressed *again*, she can read the book and discover what *she did or did not* do before her decompensation.

**Recommendation**

*In short-term therapy* or counseling, the therapist works with the patient or the client on the systemically equitable structuring of relationships in their *current* relationship conflicts due to the shortness of time (see Sect. 3.3). Thus she works in a *solution-oriented* manner.

**Central idea**

*In long-term therapies*, the following rule applies: *the more tumultuous* the conflict between adaptation and self-actualization in a current relational conflict, the more the therapist should limit his work to the present conflict *alone*. However, *the less* patients with depression suffer from the imbalance between adaptation and self-realization in their current conflicts, the more the therapist has to go with them psychodramatically into their inner relationship images from childhood, address their old defense patterns (see Sect. 4.8) and change them.

### *8.4.4 The Therapist's Participation as a Doppelganger and an Auxiliary Ego in the Psychodramatic Dialogue*

In psychotherapy, the therapist combines *her intuitive process* with the *patient's* intuition (see Sect. 2.5). She identifies concordantly with *the patient's* self-actualization at one point and complementarily with the self-actualization of *his "conflict partner"* at another time. The group members (see Sect. 8.4.5) perform this changing identification as auxiliaries in the as-if mode of play also by reversing roles. In individual therapy, the therapist potentially takes on *three different roles* in the individual setting: (1) The role of the leader in the therapeutic *meta-position outside the scene* (see Fig. 2.9 in Sect. 2.8), which is the *standard position* of the therapist during the psychodramatic dialogue, (2) The role of the protagonist's doppelganger when he changes into the opposite role, and (3) As an auxiliary ego also the role of the protagonist's conflict partner.

Inexperienced psychodramatists easily get stuck in identification with one of the two complementary roles of the patient when they play along in the psychodramatic dialogue, and lose the overview. It is then helpful to return to the therapist's standard position, the *therapeutic meta-position outside the scene.*

**Exercise 21**

If you are a beginner in psychodrama, please accompany your patient in their play *"only"* from the meta-position initially. If the patient is currently in his *own* role, position yourself slightly *on the patient's side* and look at his "conflict partner". However, if the patient takes on the role of *his conflict* partner in a role reversal, position yourself slightly *on his "conflict partner's" side* and look at the "patient". In this way, you *energetically activate* your patient's thinking, feeling, and acting *in his two complementary roles.* The meta-position helps you to *internally* keep an overview of the dialogue between the two conflicting partners, thanks to the *external* distance to the scene. You remain in the professional role of yes-but and focus on the *process between the conflicting partners.* Thus, you do not forget to ask the patient to reverse roles.

Beginners in psychodrama can *gradually practice* their leadership skills:

1. The therapist initially directs the patient's psychodramatic dialogue *only* from the meta-position outside the play scene. She *herself* does not take on *any roles* in the protagonist's play. She "only" helps him realize the 12 steps of psychodramatic self-supervision in his play (see Sect. 2.9).
2. In the next step, the therapist also takes on *the protagonist's role* when the protagonist is playing the role of his conflict partner in role reversal. The therapist's action in his role helps the patient to arrive at the counter-role and to *psychosomatically* experience how her conflict partner feels (see Sect. 8.4.2).
3. If the therapist feels reasonably safe in this work, she gradually takes on also *the role* of the patient's *conflict partner*, if necessary, and enacts it. In doing so, she can vary her *enactment in the counter-role*: (1) She stands *outside the scene* and only *verbally repeats* what the patient said in the role of his conflict partner. (2) She stands *behind the chair of his conflict partner* and repeats what the protagonist said in this role. (3) She sits *on a second chair next* to the chair of his conflict partner (see Sect. 8.4.7) and plays her role according to the patient's instructions. (4) Or she sits on the chair of his conflict partner and plays his counter-role. As an auxiliary ego, like the protagonist himself in role reversal, she always adopts the posture of the patient's conflict partner and imitates their gestures and facial expressions.

**Recommendation**

The therapist follows her own *intuition* when deciding *whether and how* she wants to take on the counter-role, as an auxiliary ego, in the patient's play in the individual setting.

The more heated the argument in the conflict and the more actively the patient deals with his "conflict partner", the more likely she is to take on *the respective counter-role.* Because even people who can imagine well have a hard time arguing with an empty chair. The therapist's enactment in the opposite role activates the protagonist's physical sensation, affect, and thinking in his own role. This increases the authenticity and depth of his self-experience in the play.

**Central idea**

In both roles, as auxiliary ego and doppelganger, the therapist internally complements the relationships between actions, physical sensations, affect, thinking, and language intuitively to a holistic psychosomatic resonance pattern (see Sect. 2.7). As a result, she understands more quickly and comprehensively how each of the protagonist's conflict partners ticks. This further helps her to emphasize important statements in the roles by modulating her language and leaving out unimportant sentences.

The therapist should not play a counter-role in protagonist-centered plays of *patients with severe structural disturbances* because these patients think in the equivalence mode (see Sect. 2.6). The patient may then make no distinction between the *role played* by the therapist and the *real therapist* (see case example 19 in Sect. 4.6). In such a case, when the therapist *in the role of the conflict partner* says, "I am angry with you", the patient believes *the therapist herself* is angry with him.

### *8.4.5 Psychodramatic Group Therapy for Patients with Depression*

***Case example 66* (Krüger, 1997, *pp. 86 f., 143, 226 f., Modified*)**
*Mr. D., a 27-year-old social worker, was referred to a psychotherapist by a neurologist with the diagnosis of "endogenous depression". He suffered from severe depression and endogenous eczema on his hands and forearms. His breathing was slightly asthmatic. The therapist was shocked by the intensity of his conflict with his father when taking the patient's history and felt: "If Mr. D. realizes his authority issues with his father, he'll kill his father." After two years of psychodramatic group therapy, the patient's depression and physical complaints had disappeared. He had rebelled at work and made himself heard by his top boss. Moreover, he implemented a new way of distributing tasks to various professional groups. He also recognized the neurotic background of his depression and linked his depression with his pathogenic family dynamics.*

**Exercise 22**
What do you think led to the success of Mr. D's treatment? *How often* has the patient dealt with present-day conflicts or with childhood problems in protagonist-centered psychodramatic plays? How often has he enacted in a fairytale or impromptu play in the 80 sessions of his group therapy? Before reading any further, please write down your responses on a piece of paper.

***Case example 66 (continued)***

*The therapist asked these three questions to the psychodramatists present at a staff meeting of the Moreno Institute Überlingen. The co-workers of the institute organized themselves sociometrically according to their various answers. Thirty-three colleagues stood in place of 'protagonist-centered plays for childhood conflicts', three stood in place of 'fairytale and impromptu plays', and four stood for other therapeutic approaches. To everyone's astonishment, Mr. D. had worked with protagonist-centered plays only twice in his two-year treatment. He never switched to a childhood scene. In his first protagonist-centered play, he showed how he took the train home from Munich to Hannover three days before the group meeting. But he stopped the play and panicked. In his second protagonist-centered play, at the end of his treatment, he successfully dealt with a 'psychologist' from his current field of work.*

*But how could the patient's treatment success be explained if he had seldom dealt with his conflicts in a protagonist-centered manner? The therapist had written detailed group notes. They included insights such as (1) Mr. D. participated in impromptu plays several times. (2) He was elected to play the role of 'angry' or dominant male opponent 12 times by other group members in their own plays. At first, he maintained during the debrief: "I can't argue!" But, as an auxiliary ego, he played the male roles offered increasingly in more authentic and differentiated ways. In a role reversal, he also took on the roles of the inhibited and adapted protagonists. In doing so, he worked on his serious conflict of authority vicariously through the plays of other group members. (3) After the protagonist-centered plays of other group members, Mr. D. repeatedly complained about the egoism of their conflict partners and said to the protagonist: "It can't stay that way! You have to defend yourself more!" As a result, he became the action leader for the topic of 'self-actualization in the relationship with a dominant conflict partner'. (4) In such a situation, the therapist often asked Mr. D.: "Show Eva how you would behave in her place! Eva, you can take on the role of your husband!" In these plays, Mr. D. openly dealt with their authoritarian "conflict partners" as the protagonists' doppelganger.*

*The patient has differentiated his inner object images of 'angry' dominant men by frequently playing roles of 'angry' dominant males and, thus, loosened his defense through projection and denial. Additionally, as a doppelganger, he differentiated his self-image psychosomatically in authority conflicts. In doing so, he dissolved his own defense through introjection. Hence, he weakened his defense through identification with the aggressor by frequently playing roles in others' protagonist-centered plays. At the end of therapy, he spontaneously recognized the connection between his depression and childhood conflicts. He distanced himself from his father's patriarchal intent that he should have become a doctor. As a result, he gained significant recognition in his chosen profession. This development occurred even though Mr. D. had never once dealt with his father/authority conflict psychodramatically.*

In psychodramatic group therapy, depressed patients defend through introjection and often remain stuck in their inferior position vis-à-vis their conflict partners in their protagonist-centered plays. The therapist then often unconsciously identifies with the protagonist's self and tries to empower the patient in his obstacles in the play. She then doubles the protagonist, for example, *suggestively*: "I'm angry!" "I am sad and disappointed!" Or she works *cognitively psychodramatically* (see Sect. 2.14) and encourages him to adopt a more expansive role behavior.

**Recommendation**

In such a case, it is more appropriate to end the protagonist-centered play early and proceed to the debriefing. The more inappropriately the protagonist behaves in the play, the more likely the group members will protest against his way of resolving conflict in the debrief: "But that's not how it works! Defend yourself!" "I would speak my mind!" The therapist then asks the protesting group members to become the patient's doppelganger and deal with his "conflict partner" *on his behalf:* "Step into Klaus's role and show us how you would behave in his place!" (see Sect. 2.11)

**Central idea**

Each group is *a self-organizing system*. Inappropriately submissive behavior on the part of the protagonist in his play *always* provokes protest from the other group members (see Sect. 2.11). The therapist uses this protest therapeutically for the 6th and 7th steps of the psychodramatic dialogue (see Sect. 8.4.2). The protagonist *himself* always takes on the role *of his conflict partner* in such a play.

The group members and the patient collaboratively test whether and to what extent the patient's "conflict partner" would be willing to form a systemically just relationship. This process is therapeutically *successful in any case*, regardless of the result: (1) If the protest of the group participant were *inappropriate*, the group participant playing the role of the protagonist would fail in his interaction with the protagonist's "conflict partner", just like the protagonist himself. The group then recognizes, perhaps for the first time, the real drama of the protagonist's conflict and acknowledges his plight. (2) However, if the group participant's protest was *appropriate*, playing the alternative solution dissolves the protagonist's fixation in his defense through introjection, projection, and identification with the aggressor. The protagonist thus becomes internally free to look for a *new solution* to his conflict in everyday life. But, the group participants also learn in the process (see case example 66 above). This approach in the *treatment of patients with depression* surprisingly gives everyone involved considerable pleasure. There is a lot of laughter in the group.

In Moreno's tradition (1959, p. 238), some psychodramatists interpret the group participants' authentic and enjoyable experience in playing destructive counter-roles as the group member's *own* desire to be cruel and his *own* tendency for sadistic behavior. However, this interpretation assumes that the group participant cannot distinguish between play and reality.

**Central idea**

Anyone who can play *a destructive counter-role* well has *more* control over their destructive impulses than someone who strictly rejects this for ideological reasons or because of their own inhibition. Because they can *think* of evil in the *as-if mode* and do not act it out at the first opportunity in the *equivalence mode* (see Sect. 2.6). According to Gandhi: "Only those can offer non-violent resistance, who *can* use violence and then renounce it."

Some psychodramatists falsely assume that when playing the counter-role of a sadistic conflict partner in a role reversal, the protagonist "feels the inner energy of the perpetrator and then integrates it into his own role". But, the reason for the protagonist's increased courage is different. The role reversal helps the protagonist liberate his object image from its fixation. In the counter-role of his conflict partner, the patient establishes a connection between his conflict partner's actions, physical sensations, affect, thinking, and speaking. For example, he psychosomatically perceives his indifference or lust for power. In this way, he breaks his defense through projection (see Sect. 2.4.2). He is outraged by *the opponent's* desire for power. That makes him more courageous in his interaction with the conflict partner.

### *8.4.6 Therapy for Depression in Separation Conflicts*

Separation conflicts arise when a person leaves an old relationship system or when it breaks. For example, *adolescents* experience physical and emotional development spurts during puberty. They come together in peer groups and face challenges *outside* of the family. However, they can become depressed if they fail to separate from their original family. They are fixated on an old self-image, characterized *by defense through introjection.* For example, a 20-year-old woman discontinued her studies in a faraway city after six months and returned to her parents' house. One of the reasons she failed was that she couldn't go shopping at the supermarket in her place of study. This was because she had blindly adapted to her mother's addiction to control. If the young woman wanted to buy yogurt, she couldn't decide which was the healthiest option, and half an hour later, she would leave the shop without any yogurt. *Adults* are more likely to become depressed as a result of separation conflict *because of the defense through projection.* When a child leaves home, adults are fixated in an old beloved object image of their child. A separation conflict can be triggered by a divorce, loss of work, or when a close friendship ends. For example, from 1913 to 1918, Jung (1985) encountered a severe depressive crisis after separating from his teacher and friend, Sigmund Freud.

**Central idea**

A separation conflict in adolescents is the result of a change in inner self-image; in parents, it is the result of a change in the inner object image. In long-term separation conflicts, this change doesn't succeed spontaneously. The patient defends through introjection and projection. The defense through introjection stabilizes the defense through projection. Or the defense through projection stabilizes the defense through introjection. The fixation in an old *inner* self-image and an old *inner* object image must be resolved. Therefore, the psychodramatic dialogue with role reversal is indicated in disorder-specific approaches.

***Case example 67***

*The 35-year-old Mr. E. sought group therapy because of reactive depression and a neurotic self-esteem problem. One day he reports: "I have problems with my mother. She called me six weeks ago. She also asked me if I was in a new relationship. I answered 'no'. But the truth is, I have had a new boyfriend for three months, and I feel very comfortable with him. I don't even know why I lied." Mr. E. clarifies the relationship with his mother in a psychodramatic dialogue (step 3 of the psychodramatic dialogue, see* Sect. 8.4.2*). He sits on his chair during the play and looks at* *the mother. She looks dismissively at the window. Mr. E.: "We're so far apart, I don't understand!" Mr. E. reverses roles and steps into the role of his mother: "You don't come home like you used to. Everything has changed! The neighbors' children always come for a visit. They have grandchildren. It's different for us. I can't even imagine how it will be with us."*

*Mr. E. is gay. The therapist interviews Mr. E. in the role of his mother: "Mrs. E., have you ever dealt with the subject of homosexuality? Do you know what that is?" Mr. E. as the mother: "Yes, of course. But I want us to maintain the image of a 'normal' family, at least outwardly. I want Jörg to visit me and call me regularly." Again in his own role, Mr. E protests: "Actually, you don't want me to visit you with my boyfriend. I always have to be who you want me to be. That's why I always come to visit you alone. You distance yourself from me!" Mr. E. takes on the role of his mother again: "I have already read something on the subject of homosexuality. And I've seen films about it on TV. But it's hard for me to imagine that you are with a man like I am with dad. I cannot imagine that! And besides, children simply visit their parents!".*

*Mr. E. changes back to his own role. As an auxiliary ego, a group participant repeats the 'mother's' sentences. The therapist asks Mr. E: "What are you feeling physically and emotionally in your role?" Mr. E: "I feel distressed." The therapist: "Where in your body do you feel this? In the head, in the chest, or the stomach?" Mr. E.: "More in the throat, it's tight, I feel a lump." The therapist: "Can you tell your mother that the argument with her causes a lump in your throat?" Mr. E. to his 'mother': "I don't understand why you don't accept it. You've known that I'm gay for five years now. You always say you accept it. But I don't see it." In the debriefing session, one of the group participants tells Mr. E.: "Talk to your mother in plain language!" The therapist asks this group participant to take on the role of Mr. E. and to try it on his behalf (steps 6 and 7 of the psychodramatic dialogue). Mr. E. changes into the role of his mother and shows how she would react to it. The group participant in Mr. E's role: "When you talk about how I should be like others, I feel my throat tighten. I think the distance between us is quite right. I don't see any other possibility at the moment!" In the role of his mother, Mr. E. reacts surprisingly excessively: "But then why don't you tell me that you have a boyfriend! You know that I notice everything and know everything about you anyway! You are my son! And I am your mother! You can't hide anything from me anyway!".*

*In the debriefing, Mr. E. spontaneously says: "I have noticed that my mother wants me to be like I was as a child. She doesn't accept who I am today. She doesn't understand anything! I think the distance might be good for us." The group participant who took on the mother's role as an auxiliary ego: "As a mother, that was obvious to me. I was disappointed not to have any grandchildren!" The therapist: "I suspect your being gay has created an existential gap between the two of you that cannot be bridged! This concerns not only your identity but also your mother's! But one can only overcome an existential gap by recognizing it. Besides, I think it is important for you not to lie to your mother. Because lying often leads to feelings of inferiority and makes you depressed!" After two group sessions, Mr. E. spontaneously says: "I have thought about it, and I think I want to re-establish the relationship with my sister. I want to have a conversation with her about our family. My sister lives five hundred kilometers away. She had a fallout with my mother a long time ago. I want to know how my sister is doing in relation to my mother now."*

In a separation conflict, the patient expresses everything he feels and thinks toward his attachment figure in rehearsing a psychodramatic dialogue. In this way, he frees his inner self-image from fixation in the conflict, develops it further, and dissolves his *defense through introjection* (see Sect. 8.4.1). In the role of his mother, he psychosomatically experiences why the separation is so difficult for her. He psychosomatically learns something about her values and norms, her open or hidden contracts, her inner conflicts, and her defenses. He looks for answers to the questions: "Who *was* my mother really? Who would she have *wanted* to be? Who *could* she have *become* in other circumstances? *What* prevented that?" In doing this, the protagonist resolves his *defense through projection*. This helps him to refrain from automatically doing what his mother introject asks him to do. Instead, he asks himself: "Do I want what I want, or does my inner mother want that?" Then, he *can choose again* and is free to develop his *own* norms and ideal values (see case example 68 in Sect. 8.4.7).

**Central idea**

"True emancipation always requires a further development of the *inner* image of the conflict partner" (Krüger, 1997, p. 232).

The detachment from restrictive family relationships is easier if the person concerned knows any *family secrets* that may exist. He then no longer identifies himself, *unknowingly through introjection*, with the taboos, guilt complexes, and defensive patterns associated with the family secret. Awareness of a family secret often triggers a developmental boost in those concerned. For example, Bode (2009, p. 55 f.) reported on a man who had learned new information about his parents' life story: He "understood that the persistent feelings of guilt he felt came from his grandfather." The man had told the author, Mrs. Bode: "There is a saying in our family: 'If it is too good for you, life punishes you!'" The grandfather was a farmer in East Germany. In 1945 he hesitated to flee the Russian army because he had hoped the American military would advance. That "was the decisive mistake of his life. He lost everything he owned, and the Soviet soldiers also forced him to watch them raping his wife and mother. [...] I know most people think: I don't want to burden myself with my parents' war experiences. But I was relieved when I finally knew the truth. It was a weight off my shoulders! [...] It was only after I knew the secrets that I understood a lot: Why we were always so afraid, why my father behaved so well-adjusted, his extreme preoccupation with safety, his insistence on saving, saving, saving." Bode writes: "Since he can see his parents as people who were broken by the war, he is better able to endure his mother's strange behaviors, which used to upset him earlier." The man concerned reported: "Among other things, I have more respect for my parents' life achievements, and I no longer judge them for their fearfulness and adaptability. [...] I can simply detach myself." According to Bode (2009, p. 56), this man's mother *learned much about herself* through her son's separation, and the confrontation with him. Now, unlike in the past, she can allow herself to enjoy some things in life.

### 8.4.7 Therapy for Prolonged Grief Reactions

The self-actualization and adaptation of an individual are entangled in a *long-lasting relationship* with the self-actualization and adaptation of his *reference person*. This happens through the diverse empathy, interaction, and agreement processes and the associated delegations, introjections, and projections.

**Central idea**

The death of a loved one changes the balance between one's self-actualization and adaptation in the *inner relationship image*. However, people usually hold on to the old relationship image to avoid losing the loved one internally. The loss must be integrated into the inner object image and the inner self-image (Krüger, 2003, p. 102 ff.).

In bereaved persons, depressive mood swings are still *appropriate* reactions *in the first year* after the death of a loved one and are not considered pathological. Signs of a pathological grief reaction are: (1) A bereaved person is unable to work for more than six weeks after the death of the loved one. (2) He withdraws from all his relationships, and/or (3) The grief reaction lasts longer than a year.

Prolonged or severe grief reactions occur when the bereaved cannot change their old inner relationship image with the deceased *on their own*. The patient reacts with guilt if he is doing well. He projects his own criticisms, resulting from the loss, onto the dead. But, he introjects his accusations. So he defends by identifying with the aggressor (see Sect. 2.4.3 and 8.4). This helps the patient to internally hold on to the relationship with the deceased. Therefore, the counselor or the therapist supports the change of the inner self-image and object image using the fictional psychodramatic dialogue. Blatner (2001, p. 41 ff.) suggested a structured method for counseling the bereaved, which he called the *"last encounter"*. This method consists of five steps:

1. In the psychodramatic dialogue, the therapist lets the patient remember the "dead person", and, *in his own role*, share his memories with them.
2. *By reversing roles with the deceased*, the mourner recollects *their* memories of the patient and shares these out loud to himself.
3. *In his role*, the patient formulates answers to the question: "What did the deceased mean *to me*?"
4. By reversing roles, he formulates *in the role of the deceased* an answer to the question: "What did I mean to the deceased in their lifetime?"
5. The patient deals with an unfinished business in the "last encounter". He asks or says, for example, what he has always wanted to ask or say to the deceased but didn't yet, and generates a coherent response from the loved one through role reversal.

The patient can no longer directly resolve conflicts with a deceased person *after their death*. The patient may feel guilty. Or he may have never told his mother that he loved her. Unfinished business can, in retrospect, weigh heavily on the memories of the deceased and color them negatively. In such a case, the bereaved should clarify the relationship with the deceased person in the as-if mode of psychodramatic play. The grief work in the as-if mode of play along with the last messages and questions helps the patient to appropriately develop a new inner self-image in the relationship and to resolve his defense through introjection. In a role reversal, in the role of the deceased, the patient also resolves his inner object image from the fixation and, thus, resolves his defense through projection (see Sect. 8.4.2). In doing so, the therapist accompanies the patient in small steps. The inner transformation often takes more than one session. A 70-year-old man, for example, was deeply shaken when he imagined his 'wife', who had just died, in the empty chair in front of him. In the first session, he only looked at the empty chair and *shared his* memories of his wife *with the therapist*.

The five steps of the grief work do not have to be carried out *in precisely the same order* as described above. But, this process model can *help the therapist* check whether one or more steps of grief work are still missing.

***Case example 68***

*The 50-year-old Mr. F. asks his father, who died four years ago (5th step of the grief work), in a fictional psychodramatic dialogue: "You have always been so distant from me. Why haven't you ever talked to me about personal matters?" Mr. F. in the role of the father: "I couldn't!" Mr. F. as the son (1st step of the grief work): "But I always tried so hard. For example, I always tried to do particularly well at school just to make you happy." Mr. F. as the father: "Yes, I noticed that. I was proud of you!" Mr. F. as the son, getting louder: "But why did you never tell me that!" Mr. F. answers in the role of his 'father' without any emotion but clearly suffering (2nd step of the grief work): "I couldn't; I'm different!" In his childhood, Mr. F. had always put his wishes for his father's recognition and affection on the back burner. He tells the therapist: "At first, I idealized my father for many years. Later I devalued him!".*

*The protagonist continues the psychodramatic dialogue and expresses anger toward his father through soliloquy. But he acts very cautiously in the game. Therefore, the therapist takes on Mr. F's role and moves on to step 6 of the psychodramatic dialogue. Mr. F. plays the role of his father. The therapist verbalizes his anger as a doppelganger (see* Sect. 8.4.2*). Despite his 'son's' anger, Mr. F remains distant as the 'father'. In an interim debriefing, the therapist shares his experience as a doppelganger with the protagonist: "When you, as a father, said 'I can't do this!', my face went numb. Then I felt myself getting angry. Perhaps I felt something in myself that you do not allow yourself to feel?".*

*In the continuation of the psychodramatic dialogue with the father, the therapist moves on to step 3 of the grief work and asks in the role of the protagonist: "What did I mean to you?" In his father's role, Mr. F. looks for an answer for a long time (4th step of the grief work). But then he says with a warm, intense look and a firm voice: "You are my son!" Mr. F. and the therapist reverse roles again. In the father's role, the therapist internally allows himself the high emotional intensity in the father's statement. He tries to express this when he responds to the son: "You are my son!" Mr. F. is very touched. He responds from the heart (3rd step of the grief work): "And you are my father!" He turns to the therapist and says: "I would love to hug you now!".*

*During the debriefing, the therapist asks the patient: "Do you know why your father was so distant?" Mr. F. talks about his father's life. He was a hard-working, well-respected man who kept a distance from everyone. The further report by Mr. F. suggests that his father was traumatized as a soldier in World War II. The therapist: "This is a common symptom in traumatized people: those affected can no longer allow themselves to feel their emotions. In the traumatizing situation, they learned to suppress their emotions in order to function and remain capable of acting. Even if they want to feel their emotions at a later stage, including positive feelings such as love, they suffer because, tragically, all unprocessed feelings from the trauma situation come to the surface along with the positive ones. If the traumatized person were to allow that, they would lose control of themselves. That might make them incapable of coping with the demands of everyday life. That is why many traumatized people unconsciously split off their feelings in the long run. They then suffer from numbness and cannot change that. This then leads to severe disturbances in their personal relationships."*

The patient in the case example above introjected, in his childhood, his traumatized father's fear of closeness and his compensation through performance. In rehearsing the psychodramatic dialogue, however, he openly shared his unfulfilled need for closeness with his father. In this way, he further developed his inner self-image in the relationship with his father and resolved his defense through introjection. In the role of father, this rehearsal allowed him to *psychosomatically* feel his fear of closeness and loss of control. This expanded his inner object image and resolved his projection of rejection. The psychodramatic grief work helped him understand his father's distant behavior as *self-protection* against flashbacks of the war. Clarification of the relationship and 'joint' mourning over the joint fate made it possible for him to distance himself from his father's defense system four years after his father's death. He took the courage to live his own life in a more self-determined and relational manner.

In the "last encounter" of a patient with a 'deceased' in psychodramatic dialogue, the therapist or the auxiliary ego *also* takes on the patient's *counter-role* sensitively and carefully in gradations. She usually sits on an additional chair *next* to the deceased's empty chair. In doing so, she pays tribute to the existential level of the "last encounter". Sometimes the therapist 'only' steps behind the deceased's chair and repeats the protagonist's last sentences in the opposite role. However, the more intense the discussion between the protagonist and the 'deceased' becomes, the more critical it is that the therapist, as an auxiliary ego, actually plays the opposite role. The protagonist thus activates and integrates his actions, physical sensations, affect, and thinking *more holistically in his own role* (see Sect. 8.4.4).

The first two steps of the grief work with questions such as: "What did I experience and share with you?" and "What did you experience with me?" specifically open the reservoir of memories for the *old* relationship experiences with the deceased. In doing so, the patient processes his memories into a *relationship story*. He works out the mutual balance between self-actualization and adaptation, and the values and norms of *each* relationship partner. If necessary, he can specifically return expectations that the deceased has delegated to him in the play.

The 3rd and 4th steps of the grief work with questions such as "What did you mean to me?" and "What did I mean to you?" stimulate the protagonist to re-examine the *holistic meaning of the loved one* in his own life and development and also to grasp *one's own importance* in the life of the deceased. In both roles, the patient condenses all his relationship experiences into a symbolic image or sentence. As a doppelganger, the therapist helps him sensitively and creatively. The *existential* dimension of the subject of 'death' and the loss of a loved one usually leads to emotionally touching psychodramatic plays. The group members intuitively interact mindfully in a coherent and honest manner with themselves and others. They often respond with profound sharings, which offer support and security to the bereaved in the group.

If necessary, the therapist also uses therapeutic elements in the therapy for a *pathological grief reaction*, similar to those used in therapy for post-traumatic stress disorder (see Sect. 5.8). For example, she uses the *two-chair technique*: She places an empty chair next to the patient for his 'competent everyday ego', which is currently paralyzed by the death of a loved one. She names the chair on which the patient sits, 'the chair for the grieving Karl'. In the further conversation, she lets the patient switch back and forth between his 'competent everyday ego' and his 'grieving ego', depending on his current condition. This turns the 'either-or' between grief and coping with life into an 'as well as'. If necessary, the therapist also uses *self-stabilization techniques*. For example, the patient symbolizes his resources with stones and wooden blocks on the table stage. Or he develops a safe place with the therapist's help (see Sect. 5.10.5) where he can stabilize himself using transpersonal images. Unfortunately, we in the Western industrialized nations rarely take the necessary time to mourn and make appropriate internal changes after the death of our loved ones. This eventually hinders our own internal maturation process.

***Case example 69***

*An 84-year-old patient reported that 'the subject of death is taboo' for old people in a retirement home she stays at. She had bought a place for her own casket in an old cemetery next to a beautiful old tree. When she told other residents about this, they fearfully changed the topic.*

The grief work after the death of a loved one includes facing the fear of one's own death. The older the bereaved, the more one fears *one's own death*. The therapist will address this issue if necessary. Frede (2009, p. 35) suggests that, in such a case, the patient should engage in a psychodramatic 'dialogue with death'. The therapist turns to the patient and says: "I'm just imagining that death is sitting here with us—maybe on this chair. [...] What would you want to say to death?" The therapist doubles the patient in this dialogue and invites him to reverse roles: "If death could answer, what would it say?".

According to Frede (2009, p. 36), everyone has "certain ideas about death. A dialogue with death helps define these ideas and contextualize them to one's own life situation". Frede (2009, p. 36) differentiated this work into the 'association sociogram' technique on the subject of death. The therapist asks the patient to draw a circle on a piece of paper: "Please write the word death in the center! When you think about death, what comes to mind? [...] Make a circle around each association and connect it to the center. [...] Just imagine that death could join our conversation. [...] Out of all these associations, what would death talk to you about?" Because "the protagonist familiarizes himself with the various aspects of his idea of death", "these lose some of their paralyzing power over him". By talking about his ideas of death, the patient gains "a certain distance, which makes it easier for him to observe his thoughts and feelings associated with one's own idea of death [...] without judging them, holding onto them or evading them. [...] The I is no longer identified with fear, sadness, or worry about the future: I *have* certain feelings, but *I am not* these feelings. [...] Because there is a part of me that observes these feelings (Wilber, 2006, p. 113)." This work helps people develop "not only their own idea of death but also their personal reactions to it. One can at least partially counter some fears. [...] The *open* discussion about death in therapy helps the bereaved at least lose the fear of these fears and learn to accept them as part of human existence: 'Everything that lives will one day cease to be—including me'. In dialogue, many patients no longer see death as an enemy, but as an ally for life [...] who shows them what is really important" (Frede, 2009, p. 36).

## 8.5 Therapy for Masochism and a Pathological Superego

Masochistic thinking and behavior occur in various mental disorders, for example, severe depressive disorder, trauma disorder, obsessive–compulsive disorder, addiction disorder, or borderline personality disorder. Usually, persons with masochistic behavior were traumatized in childhood or secondarily traumatized in relationships with traumatized parents (see Sect. 5.2). The patients must have had to learn to block their self-actualization *through self-censorship* in their relationships as a child. Otherwise, they would have been beaten, rejected, devalued, or abandoned or they would have destroyed the equilibrium in their family leading to a family crisis. Self-censorship was a creative solution that helped the child to survive psychologically. It was therefore not possible for the child to develop healthy narcissism and the ability to self-actualize appropriately in relationships.

Patients with masochistic behavior block their self-actualization *even as adults*, although there is *no* external force to think self-injuriously. Rohde-Dachser (1976, only orally communicated) describes *masochism* as a "cry for empathy". People with masochistic, depressive, or dependent personality disorder (F.34.1, F60.7) are trapped in a defense system. This consists of self-protection through adaptation or grandiosity *and* masochistic self-censorship (see Sects. 4.7–4.10). The defense system creates a split in the process of self-development. Allowing the self to emerge would retraumatize the patient. Even the idea of a wish is taboo. Patients come into therapy when their defense system can no longer block their self-actualization adequately. The external pressure to conform becomes overwhelming. Or a favorable external situation allows one to live on their own terms.

**Central idea**

The masochistic self-censorship and the defense through grandiosity and perfectionism mutually stabilize each other. The patient's 'inner soul killer' is quiet only when the patient is grandiose and perfect. He is not allowed to be a normal human with emotions, strengths, and weaknesses.

Masochistic thinking and a pathological superego can be recognized by the following indicators: (1) The patient devalues himself and reacts prematurely with feelings of guilt. He experiences his inappropriate self-deprecation and self-accusations as *appropriate*, as they are part of his identity. (2) He cannot defend himself adequately and set boundaries in important relationships. (3) He strives to be a perfect or grandiose person in order to defend his inner masochistic self-censorship. If he didn't do that, he would get depressed. (4) Some patients become angry with themselves and bottle up their anger. But, at some point, the anger erupts. This eruption then confirms their inappropriate self-accusations and self-doubt in the process. (5) The patient may not be able to break free from the relationship with a damaging attachment figure. (6) He expects unreasonably serious personal and social problems in his future.

***Case example 70***

*The 53-year-old Mrs. Z. has been retired for six years now due to depression and exhaustion as a consequence of a structural disorder. She suffers from migraines for about thirteen days a month (F34.-, G43.0). Mrs. Z. spends most of her life at home. Her social contacts are limited to a few activities with her husband. He suffers from stress syndrome, and high blood pressure, and is overweight due to his high-stress job and many hobbies. When he gets home from work at 10 p.m. or later, he first reads his e-mails before the couple 'sits together for an hour or two' and then goes to bed at 1.30 a.m. Mrs. Z. expresses indifferently: "That's just how it is." When the therapist draws the intelligent patient's attention to the absurdity of these systemically opposing lifestyles, Mrs. Z says: "I don't want to restrict my husband's activities. He is very popular everywhere." In another context, however, she says: "I feel out of breath when he comes home for lunch sometime for twenty minutes."*

*As a child, Mrs. Z. had to stabilize her traumatized parents. She was brought up with strict rules. Her own feelings and needs were not seen. As a result, when she was six months old, she was hospitalized for an eating disorder for three weeks. Even now, at over fifty years of age, Mrs. Z. immediately associates her own emotions and wishes with a feeling of senselessness and helplessness. She often cries desperately in therapy sessions when she realizes that she here actually has time and space for herself but cannot express herself verbally.*

*The therapist wanted to help Mrs. Z improve her self-development (see* Chap. 1*). He asked Mrs. Z to write a coping fairy tale about her childhood trauma (see* Sect. 5.14*). In the following therapy session, Mrs. Z complained: "It was incredibly difficult to even remember events from my childhood. I experienced a mental block. As if a doorman was standing in front of the door and said: 'You can't come in!'" The therapist represents the 'doorman' with the hand puppet of a sadistic laughing devil on a chair three meters away from the patient.*

Patients with a depressive personality disorder are, as it were, under the spell of the evil mountain spirit from the fairy tale "The Traveling Companion" by Hans Christian Andersen. Many princes have wooed the beautiful princess in an attempt to marry her. She promises marriage to the suitors if they solve her three riddles. If a suitor fails to do this, he will be beheaded. When the hero of the fairy tale comes to the princess's castle, he sees ninety-nine male heads impaled on the bars of the fence surrounding the castle. Verena Kast (1980, p. 52 ff.) interpreted this fairy tale as a tale of masochism. Like the hero of the fairy tale does with the princess, the therapist strives for a good relationship with her masochistic patient. But she is repeatedly left feeling puzzled. She fails in *all her attempts* to help him. The many heads of the suitors in the fairy tale symbolize the therapist's failed attempts to resolve the patient's masochistic self-censorship. The patient keeps beheading his therapist through his masochism, so to speak.

The diagnosis of a depressive or masochistic personality disorder often only results from the shared experience of the therapist and patient in the therapeutic relationship:

1. The more a patient accepts an imbalance between self-adaptation and self-actualization *and* the less aware he is of this imbalance, the more likely he is to suffer from masochism and a pathological superego (see case example 70 above).
2. The patient's childhood trauma is recognized and named. However, without realizing it, the *therapist* does not give sufficient meaning to his trauma.
3. The therapist attempts to encourage the patient's self-actualization in relational conflicts, for example using the seven steps of the psychodramatic dialogue (see Sect. 8.4.2). But, she fails because of the patient's inability to reverse roles. Or the patient had improved his self-actualization only *for a short time*. There is no progress in therapy over time.
4. The patient defends himself through *projective identification* (see Sect. 2.4.4). This defense leads to a *disturbance in the therapeutic relationship*: (i) The patient thinks and acts in a self-injurious manner. (ii). The therapist identifies with his repressed self and contradicts him. (iii) A latent power struggle develops between the hopeless patient and the therapist, who protests against his hopelessness. iv. The therapist feels strained, annoyed, and thwarted in her efforts. She thus *feels* what the patient represses, on the patient's behalf.
5. The therapist often takes over the systemic role assigned to her by the patient and represses her feelings of disappointment, sadness, helplessness, and anger. She acts out her *countertransference* (see Sect. 2.10) and continues to be *only* the good, supportive mother.
6. The therapist repeatedly represents the patient's self-injurious thinking and inner child as chairs and puppets (see Sect. 4.8). However, the work on the self-injurious thinking (see Fig. 4.1 in Sect. 4.2) encourages the patient *only briefly* because of his rigid defenses. The therapist is drawn into the conflict between the patient's self-actualization and pathological superego. She *unilaterally* identifies with the patient's repressed self and tries to strengthen it. However, she "forgets" to deal with the patient's defense system and feels frustrated.

7. The therapist finds it increasingly difficult to endure the patient's self-blockage. She feels tormented by the patient because he keeps repeating his old defense pattern and reporting new failures. In the end, the patient even wants to work through some relationship conflicts *that have already been dealt with.* The therapist is disappointed with the lack of success in therapy.

**Central idea**

Patients with masochistic disorder tempt the therapist into being therapeutically *inconsistent*. The lack of progress in therapy then alerts the therapist that the patient continues to be fixated on his defense of self-protection through adaption or grandiosity and masochistic self-censorship.

Patients with a depressive personality disorder or masochism suffer from *metacognitive confusion* between their healthy adult thinking, their self-protection through adaption or grandiosity, and their self-injurious, masochistic self-censorship. They must therefore also be treated *metacognitively* (see Sect. 4.8).

**Central idea**

It is *part of being a therapist* to allow yourself to be tormented once in a while. However, the constant willingness to do so leads to the therapist and the patient *jointly* denying the reality and truth of their relationship. Then they both act masochistically. The patient torments *the therapist* as he torments himself in everyday life. The therapist then reacts by openly or latently devaluing the patient. Transference and countertransference block progress in therapy. The therapist must again self-actualize in the therapeutic relationship in order to resolve her countertransference. In the therapy of people with masochism, the *new beginning begins with the therapist*.

Therefore, the therapist takes the *following* therapeutic *steps*:

1. The therapist engages in *psychodramatic self-supervision* with steps 1–17 (see Sects. 2.9 and 4.8). In the *fictional* psychodramatic dialogue, she names *her feelings* of resignation, tiredness, annoyance, anger, listlessness, and helplessness. She attributes the "patient's" external actions, which trigger these feelings in her, to the patient's "self-injurious thinking" (see Sect. 4.8). She symbolizes it externally with a chair for the 'blind soul killer' or 'tormentor' and places this chair opposite the patient. As a result, she perceives the "patient" as *a victim of his "inner soul killer"* in self-supervision and can empathize with him internally again. Her resignation and anger disappear.
2. The therapist names the patient's unfavorable approach to himself as "self-injurious" in the real encounter and sets up a chair in the room opposite him on the object level for his inner "blind tormentor" or "blind soul killer" (see Fig. 4.1 in Sect. 4.2).
3. The therapist explains to the patient the meaning of the terms "self-injurious" or "masochistic". She describes the *positive function* his self-censorship had in his childhood: "Your self-injurious thinking was a wise *solution in childhood*. Both your parents were traumatized and addicted. You were creative as a child and *censored your own desires* to cope with the unbearable situation."

**Central idea**

The therapist additionally represents the two other metacognitive processes involved in the defense system, namely self-protection through adaption or perfectionism and the rejected negative emotions (the inner child). The masochistic self-censorship is stabilized by self-protection through perfectionism, which helps to avoid a flashback.

4. The therapist places the chair representing the adaption near the patient (see Sect. 4.8 and Fig. 4.1 in Sect. 4.2): "This chair symbolizes your self-protection through adaptation. You try to meet the expressed and unspoken expectations of your significant others most perfectly. You always have to be a good person, know everything, and present everything calmly. I will place this hand puppet of a white knight onto the chair, representing your high expectations of yourself." Or: "You control the current situation because you can't stand it if something bad happens to someone near you."
5. The therapist points at the chair of 'self-injurious thinking': "Self-censorship has helped you to adapt and to *not* amplify the chaos in the family with your feelings and problems. However, the problem is that you censor yourself *even now*." The therapist places another chair behind the chair of self-protection through adaption: "You have to devalue yourself and perfectly meet the expectations of others, otherwise you are not able to deal with the negative emotions evoked in you. Feeling insecure, exhausted, annoyed, or resigned is taboo. In such a case you would experience a flashback." The therapist positions the chair representing the negative feelings far away in the corner of the therapy room."

**Central idea**

The therapist must explain to the patient the *positive function of his defense system* in his holistic process of self-regulation.

6. The therapist *steps next to the chair* for the soul killer and lends him a voice as an auxiliary ego. She converts the patient's many *self*-reproaches, *self*-accusations, or *self*-denigration into you-statements for the soul killer. As a result, "I'm worth nothing" becomes: "You're worth nothing, look at you!"
7. The therapist also symbolizes the self-injurious thinking with an *additional* matching hand puppet on the chair. Thus, the patient looks at his own self-injurious thinking *as an interaction* partner from the outside. He experiences himself anew *as* a *victim* of his inner soul killer.
8. She works with the patient to find an *appropriate name* for the character that will represent his self-injurious thinking. This name is intended to consolidate the patient's personal self-injurious statements into one symbolic concept: the blind sadistic critic; the blind prosecutor who mocks the patient's feelings; the blind judge; the blind soul killer who denies the patient's right to exist if he doesn't conform to external expectations; the blind cold-hearted governess; the blind accuser; the child wrecker.
9. Patients with severe structural disturbances are often internally paralyzed by the external appearance of the 'sadistic critic' as an interaction partner. The empathic therapist is paralyzed too. In such a case, the therapist defends herself, *as an interacting doppelganger* (see Sects. 2.4.1, 7.2 and 9.8.8) for the patient, against the patient's 'blind inner prosecutor'. For example, she screams directly at the chair and the puppet (Arntz and van Genderen, 2010, p. 53 ff.) and

puts him in his place: "Don't you see how Christa is suffering? Why are you tormenting her then? Stop that! She has suffered enough as a child. She doesn't need it anymore! Just go!" If necessary, the therapist even turns the sadistic prosecutor's chair such that the puppet faces the wall. Or she carries him out of the room with his chair. Often, the patient wonders about such *direct* help from the therapist against his 'self-injurious thinking'. He is irritated and laughs a little. During debrief, however, he reports that he suddenly could 'breathe more freely'. The patient *shouldn't put away* his inner 'soul killer' *on his own* because that would activate his sadistic superego.

10. The therapist and patient make *a list* of the patient's self-injurious statements and number them. To do this, they convert the patient's various self-deprecating thoughts into *statements made by the blind accuser* or the soul killer. The "I" should always become a "you". "I can't do it" becomes "You can't do it!" Some patients self-injuriously write down the statements of their 'soul killer' as I-statements. They then tell the therapist: "I didn't feel well with the list at home." In such a case, the patient should definitely convert the statements of the 'soul killer' into "You" statements. One patient reported: "It was very exhausting for me. But it helps. Once I felt like I was in a stupor. Then I took the list out and I thought, 'What is the soul killer's voice saying right now? What do you hear him saying?' My head suddenly cleared up."
11. For six months, the patient collects statements from his soul killer and makes a list. He reads them out to the therapist. One patient collected 42 self-injurious accusations from his sadistic superego. Some of these contradicted each other. He read them out in group therapy. Another group member, a writer, exclaimed enthusiastically: "That's literature, what you wrote there!" Three weeks later, the patient drove with that list to his childhood hometown. As a 50-year-old well-dressed gentleman, he crawled between trees alongside a small river in the forest. He had always played there as a child. He took out the list of his self-devaluations from his pocket, lit them with a match stick, and burned them in a ritualistic manner.

**Central idea**

In patients with narcissistic personality disorder, grandiosity is the dominant defense pattern (see Sect. 4.2). This is stabilized through masochistic self-censorship. In patients with masochism, the dominant defense pattern is the masochistic self-censorship. This is stabilized through self-protection through adaption and perfectionism. In each case, the therapist first works to resolve the dominant defense pattern. In doing this the therapist gets therapeutic access to the other defense patterns as well (see Sect. 4.10)

Masochistic thinking patients act out their self-injurious thinking in equivalence mode (see Sect. 2.6). The patient doesn't consider *whether* he is inferior. He *knows he is*. He knows that his friend will break up with him if he said: "I can't listen to your complaints any longer." In metacognitive therapy, the patient learns to integrate the as-if mode in equivalence mode (see Sect. 2.6): (1) He *names* his defense pattern 'inner soul killer'. Thus, he neuronally connects his self-injurious thoughts with the generic term 'masochism'. (2) He *represents* his defense pattern *externally* as a puppet on another chair. (3) He curiously *collects the statements* of the 'soul killer'. In this way, he tracks down the soul killer's presence like a detective looking for a murderer. (4) He reveals his masochism by reading aloud the statements of his soul killer to other people. In doing so, he notices the grotesque, contradicting, *sadistic pleasure* of the soul killer in the statements. Thus, he resolves the feelings of helpfulness he projected on his soul killer. This loosens his defense through introjection and frees his self-development from fixation in masochistic self-devaluing. (5) As an *interactional doppelganger*, the therapist helps the patient to free his self-development. Thus, over time the patient develops *ego control* over his self-injurious thinking. He doesn't think self-injuriously as often and for as long and can sometimes even laugh about it (see case example 8 in Sect. 2.6).

**Central idea**

The patient recognizes the *general metacognitive principle* that gives rise to *many of his different* self-reproaches and self-deprecations. He, along with the therapist's help, gives this general principle a name: "This is my self-injurious thinking." Naming the general metacognitive principle helps him to stop his self-injurious thoughts. He *no longer* has to speculate *over every single* self-injurious thought.

12. The therapist asks the patient about *the age of his self-injurious thinking*: "Since when have you been thinking that you are worthless and that you have no right to live? When was the first time?" She then sets up a chair for the internal 'traumatized child' and places the puppet of a four to eight-year-old boy on it (see Fig. 4.1 in Sect. 4.2). The sight of the puppet can retraumatize the patient. The therapist therefore immediately asks the patient what the sight of the 'little boy' triggers in him. If necessary, the therapist takes the chair for the traumatized child out of the room and puts it in the hallway (see Sect. 4.8).
13. The therapist uses elements from trauma therapy (see Sect. 5.6), if necessary.
14. Associating the patient's masochistic thinking with his childhood helps him to understand himself better. In the next 15–30 sessions, however, the therapist works on the patient's core problem in the present, his *current* masochistic self-censorship.
15. The therapist tells the patient: "Your self-censorship is allowed to die. You are a moral person even without the self-injurious self-censorship and you have a conscience even without it." This message frightens some patients. They experience the disappearance of the 'soul killer' as a loss. The therapist understands this fear as fear of *a loss of identity*. Although this identity is *negative*, it gives the patient a sense of identity. The patient has lived with this self-censorship since childhood. He doesn't know how to be without it. He has to learn that first.
16. The therapist places an *extra chair behind* the 'soul killer' chair for the *harmful attachment figure from childhood* (see Fig. 4.1 in Sect. 4.2): "I want you to separate the inner soul killer's self-censorship from your parents' images. The internal images of your inadequate parents will continue to live on in you." The therapist soon removes the chair for the "alcoholic father" to avoid retraumatizing the patient. In metacognitive therapy, the therapist does not work

on the relationship with the *pathological introject*, but rather on the patient's *old self-censorship,* developed in childhood, in the encounter with his harmful attachment figure.

17. The patient should buy a puppet for his 'blind soul killer' or his 'blind governess' who controls him. He puts this puppet *in a closet* at home and locks it. The soul killer belongs "in jail" so to speak. He should 'not be able to get out again *at any point in time'*. The patient should not put his inner soul killer on his desk and then always see it in front of him. The therapist interprets this as masochistic: "You have to constantly expend energy to block out the sight of the soul killer while you work!"
18. The patient should take his "soul killer" out of the cupboard *once a day*, look at it for five minutes, and feel when the soul killer devalued him again that day. He adds *new* statements from the soul killer to his list. He then puts the soul killer back in the closet and locks it. This ritual in the as-if mode of play helps the patient to *neurally connect the external distancing* from their self-injurious thinking in their memory. One patient had symbolized her 'inner soul killer' with the hand puppet of a robber. If she struggled to sleep in the evening, she would place the puppet in front of her and let the sight sink in. Then she would grab her 'inner soul killer' and carry it out of the room. She locked it in a closet in the farthest corner of her apartment. She would then go back to her bedroom and lay down in her bed. This ritual helped her to alleviate her nocturnal psychosomatic crises.
19. In the course of the therapy, at the beginning of a therapy session, the therapist always sets up the two chairs for the *symptom scene* in her room (see Fig. 2. 9 in Sect. 2.8). It is only when the patient in the therapy session thinks and acts in a self-injurious manner, that she places a second chair opposite him for his blind sadistic critic, persecutor or soul killer. She then points to this chair with her hand and rephrases the patient's statement. The patient's statement "*I* can't do anything!" becomes the soul killer's statement "*You* can't do anything anyway!"
20. If necessary, the *therapist* verbalizes *her negative affect*, triggered by the patient's self-injurious thoughts and actions. She gestures at the "blind soul killer": "I feel sad and annoyed because you are blocking all my efforts with your self-injurious thinking. You keep biting my head off, so to speak. I think I feel within myself the feelings that you are repressing in yourself." The patient does *not* feel devalued by this feedback because the therapist is standing *shoulder to shoulder* with him and looking *at his "inner blind soul killer"*. He feels seen and validated. The therapist must *repeatedly* justify her own negative feelings in the therapeutic relationship and make them beneficial for the therapy.
21. Sometimes, when the therapist verbalizes her negative affect, the patient responds with a *negative transference*. In such a case, the therapist places a chair next to her for the transference figure from childhood and actively works out the difference between herself and the transference figure (see Sect. 2.10): "I'm annoyed with you, as your mother often was. It's true. But then your mother always cut off from you and didn't speak to you for days. I *don't want*

to end therapy with you. My motivation for sharing my feelings with you is that I want to be honest and take you seriously as a person. Would you rather have a therapist who pretends nothing is wrong? We have a therapy contract for another 28 sessions. We're in the same boat and must get along somehow. I make sure I'm okay. Otherwise, you can't learn anything from me. Now that I've expressed my feeling, I feel better immediately."

22. Patients who repeatedly act masochistically often project their own sadistic superego or soul killer onto those they relate to (see Sect. 8.4.2). The therapist, therefore, teaches the patient *psychodramatic self-supervision* (see Sect. 2.9). The patient should use this method alone at home in order to distinguish the *real person* of his conflict partner from the figure of his inner soul killer in current relationship conflicts. In the role of his respective conflict partner, the patient repeatedly explores his true thoughts and feelings and thus dissolves any existing projection of devaluation. Thus, some patients learn, for the first time, how different people are and how differently they tick.

**Central idea**

There is a close connection between the patient's self-actualization and the actualization of his masochistic thinking. If the patient dares to take a small step forward in self-actualization, the patient's inner soul killer or prosecutor also becomes active again and pushes him back into adaption. The devil doesn't care about the souls roasting in the fire. But when a soul tries to escape from the underworld to go to heaven, he chases after it.

23. The therapist tries to relate the patient's *emerging* depressive moods in therapy to small advances in self-actualization: "Your soul killer is active again *because you dared to be* yourself, and not only to function well as a father / because you moved in with your partner / because you are successful / because you took it easy." One day a patient wanted to break up with his partner, a pretty young woman, "just like that". The therapist was taken aback. But he recognized, "You're not used to just enjoying when you're feeling good. If you have these thoughts again, please try to simply let yourself enjoy for three more hours!" In the next session, the patient reported with shining eyes: "It worked. It was beautiful!"
24. Some patients use a form of self-stabilization technique *at the end of their therapy* when the soul killer or inner prosecutor emerges. They list out loud to themselves everything positive they have done recently—first, second, third... Even small things count. One patient always patted himself on the back. Visualizing the real positive small victories can help push the self-injurious thoughts aside.

**Central idea**

The therapist cannot gift the patient his self-actualization. The patient has to acquire it himself, laboriously and in small steps. An inner transformation of masochistic thinking and acting therefore usually requires a long-term therapy of 50 sessions or more.

25. When the patient defends through grandiosity, the therapist points to his self-image in the symptom scene (see Sect. 2.8 and Fig. 2.9) and draws his attention

to the contrast between self-protection through grandiosity and *being normal in everyday life*: "To be normal means to allow oneself to be how you are. Normal people are allowed to feel *insecure* in an *unsettling* situation. Normal people get angry when there is a reason to be angry and feel sad when there is a reason to be sad. It says so already in the Psalms in the Bible. But your blind inner soul killer forbids you from being a person with *normal* feelings, a person who has strengths but also makes mistakes. Maybe you don't even know what it's like to be normal. How would a normal father react to the situation at the parents' conference? Do you know what I mean by 'normal person'?" Many masochistically fixated patients are puzzled by this question: "No, actually I don't. I always think I am wrong, instead!"

26. The patient consciously practices being a "normal person" in his everyday life and also gives permission to his blocked feelings. This can be a long journey of practice because "being normal" means allowing oneself to be. However, doing this often actualizes the patient's self-injurious thinking.
27. The therapist explains to the patient that his therapy is so lengthy because of the deficits and trauma in his family of origin: "You feel guilty in the present because you violate a *rigid defense from your family of origin* with your completely normal wishes. There was a taboo on talking about feelings in your family. No one was allowed to address problems and expect others to deal with them. So now you are the first in your family to break the taboo. It's a big, tough job."
28. *Masochism also gives something*. Masochism is a prison, but the rules in this prison are simple. The patient *always* only thinks: "I am nothing, I can do nothing, I am good for nothing." If necessary, the therapist informs the patient: "It is also comfortable to think masochistically. Because you know your way around. If you omit perfectionism and self-injurious thinking, you have to reassess what the *respective* conflict partner *really* means in his statement, how he *really* ticks, and what he *really* wants in *every* conflict situation. That's exhausting. If that is too exhausting for you, you can of course remain in your masochistic thinking and acting."
29. As patients make progress in therapy, they sometimes feel that they are missing something *without* the masochistic self-censorship: "Life has become dull and boring! I don't have to maintain balance all the time anymore." The patient misses his constant state of hyperarousal, the rigid fixation on grandiose or perfect goals, and his failure to meet these demands. The therapist re-interprets this message positively: "Previously, you were trapped in your self-injurious thinking and your adaption to the assigned systemic role. If you let go of your masochistic self-censorship you are spontaneous and free to seek an appropriate solution in the respective situation. In the beginning, it is exhausting to be free. But you will learn it through practice."
30. The patient often only realizes during therapy that, contrary to his original assessment, he did not have a "beautiful childhood". He also recognizes that his problem with his inner killer or prosecutor shows up in *all* his relationships, even with his beloved children. The therapist appreciates the patient's strenuous work: "You're dealing with a *character change*. It takes at least two years for

the new solutions to be neurally wired in your brain. If you think this work shouldn't be exhausting, write that expectation on the list of what your inner killer says, 'This is far too exhausting for you. You can't do it anyway!'"

31. Some patients develop grandiose abilities as fathers, husbands, or co-workers *by adapting* to the accusations of their 'blind soul killer'. They are narcissistically abused, humiliated, and devalued by caregivers and *still try to function perfectly* in the assigned systemic roles in the present. In this case, the therapist has the patient engage in a psychodramatic dialogue with their damaging caregiver in the present. As a doppelganger in the 6th and 7th steps (see Sect. 8.4.2), she tells the caregiver, who is played by the patient: "I don't need this anymore. I have experienced enough humiliation, loneliness, and abandonment in my childhood. I'm traumatized by it. I don't need this again. Stop! Stop doing that. I am allergic to it. I want you to be mindful of my vulnerabilities. Let's agree on how you can tell me something in peace. But I can't take it anymore if you react emotionally to me! Stop!" In the role of his attachment figure, the patient often feels that this is the first time that he has respect for him. This experience *completes* his inner picture of his conflict partner. In the *next real encounter* with him, he will therefore behave differently on his own (see case example 15 in Sect. 2.14).
32. It is not uncommon for patients or clients who act masochistically to try to have their unfulfilled childish needs fulfilled by their *elderly* parents in the *present*. But they keep getting a bloody nose, break off contact from time to time and then try again and again: "I want to improve the relationship with my mother!" In such a case, the patient is not really separated from the parent concerned. The therapist, therefore, allows him to integrate his progress and findings from the therapy *in psychodramatic dialogues* with role reversals *into his inner relationship with the childhood attachment figure.* True detachment only succeeds if the patient develops his inner self-image and *also the inner object image* of his attachment figure through rehearsal with role reversal (see Sect. 8.4.6): Who was the mother really? How does she tick in the relationship? What were her values and norms that determined her actions in my childhood? What defense am I running into against her at the moment? When did her defenses arise? Who could she have become if she had grown up differently? If necessary, the patient can also write a coping fairy tale *for his mother* (see Sect. 5.14). In this process, he recognizes the familial defense structures of his family of origin and can then break away from them more easily.
33. Some therapists identify with the patient's inner abandoned or traumatized child in therapy without realizing it. They become impatient or can no longer stand the extent of the patient's masochistic self-censorship. They then introduce a fictional helpful doppelganger to aid in the patient's self-actualization against his inner 'soul killer'. It is usually more appropriate to apply the described procedure *more consistently,* to adequately appreciate the severity of the patient's childhood trauma experiences, and to integrate elements of trauma therapy into the work (see Sect. 5.8).

## 8.6 Therapy for Severe Depression Bordering on Psychosis

A severe depression bordering on psychosis (ICD F31.4, F32.2, F33.2) occurs when an old defense system has collapsed. The patient's inner fantasy space collapses, and their mentalization is profoundly paralyzed or deficient. They cannot connect their depressive affect with past or present conflicts because they can no longer represent their conflicts internally (Krüger, 2012, p. 301). Therefore, they do not understand themselves or *any depth psychological interpretations*. It is difficult to connect with these patients psychotherapeutically because of the severity of their depression.

***Case example 71* (Krüger, 2004a, *p. 257 ff., Revised)***
*A 48-year-old social worker, Ms. H., seeks outpatient therapy fourteen days after a seven-month long (!) treatment in a psychiatric clinic with a discharge diagnosis of 'Severe depression with psychotic symptoms' (F32.3). She is, she says, "doing just as bad as she was before the inpatient treatment". She takes antidepressants, sedatives, and neuroleptics as medication. The year before, Ms. H. had had a mental breakdown triggered due to harassment at her workplace (current conflict). She slowly enters the therapy room with small steps and sagging shoulders. She is startled by the smallest of external irritations. Ms. H. fell ill after obeying her boss's unreasonable instructions for a long time. Her boss seemed to have a noticeable disturbance in her own personality. However, despite her intelligence, Ms. H. is unable to relate her depression to the harassment at her workplace internally. Despite her severe depression, she wants to go back to work immediately.*

*In reality, Ms. H. was creatively gifted. As a child, she had a good intuitive sense of discrepancies in her family of origin and was, as she later said, "always curious, open, and honest". Tragically, this led to her being considered "the difficult one" in her family. She was repeatedly devalued and shamed in her family. As a child, Ms. H. unintentionally identified with this role of being the difficult one in a family where the perception of emotions and conflicts was taboo. Her father was traumatized by the war. Her mother had ulcerative colitis. Empirically, these two diseases are known to be accompanied by a splitting-off of emotions. The family suppressed emotions by assigning roles and ideological rationalizing with the help of a Christian justification of love. Her father worked in a Christian community. He once wrote to her in a letter: "There is always a black sheep in every four or five siblings. But one can also love a black sheep." Ms. H. was therefore not excluded in her family as long as she was at home. In fact, she received narcissistic gratification from taking on the role of the 'difficult one".*

*At the age of nineteen, the patient decided, as part of her separation from her parents' home, "to no longer be difficult" because she hated being 'funny' and 'dramatic'. As a result, later in life, she was always left feeling that she was 'not right'. She said: "I doubt myself so often. But others seem to feel so safe with themselves. This is my deepest question." Ms. H. learned a profession in which she helped children with mental and physical disabilities. She also married a widower with a difficult family. These two areas of conflict triggered the patient's intrapsychic conflicts due to the external pressure to adapt. She had psychosomatic complaints for many years before she broke down mentally at the age of 47.*

*The therapist and the patient could not agree on the cause of her depression in the first two therapy sessions. The patient fought against the role of the 'difficult one'. She completely ignored the cause of her breakdown and workplace harassment and went back to work immediately, severely depressed, against the therapist's advice. However, her boss immediately sent her home because of her severe depression. (For continuations, see* Sects. 8.6.1–8.6.6*).*

**Central idea**

The ability to mentalize collapses in patients with severe depression (see case examples 71 above and 89 in Sect. 9.8.1). Life happens to these patients. There is no inner self that could oppose the conflict partner in a conflict. Unfortunately, the ego is busy regulating the symptoms of depression. Therefore the therapist does *not* initially focus his work on the patient's interpersonal conflicts. Instead, he should validate the patient's *suffering from her depression* and, as a doppelganger, actively accompany her in her attempt to regulate the symptoms of depression. This activates her sense of self and authority *in regulating her symptoms*.

In case example 71, the therapist used six intervention techniques: (1) He exchanged roles with the patient and *mentalized* her thinking and feeling in the therapeutic relationship *on her behalf*. (2) Together with the patient, he implemented the process of self-regulation in her suicidal fantasies and asked her to think through her suicidal fantasies *right up to the end*, with all the consequences included. (3) Together with her, he implemented the process of *self-regulation* in her everyday life and thus activated her sense of self and authority in her actions. (4) He used the power of symbolizing in *nocturnal dreams* as an amplification to understand the patient's self-regulation during the day. (5) He symbolized *the sadistic superego* of the patient with an object and fought against it as her doppelganger. (6) He helped her to integrate her self-actualization, which improved in therapy, *into her inner relationship images*.

## *8.6.1 Vicarious Mentalization in the Therapeutic Relationship*

***Case example 71 (1st continuation, see* Sect. 8.6*)***

*At first, the therapist could not get in touch with Mrs. H. because of her severe depression. In order to better understand her internally, he asked her: "May I change into your role? I want to know what it is like to be, feel, and think like you." The patient and the therapist changed places. The therapist assumed her slumped posture and re-enacted her role. He verbally repeated what she had said. As her doppelganger, he allowed himself to experience her role physically, mentally, and cognitively vicariously and expressed it verbally. In doing so, he recognized that the grave 'feelings of panic' Mrs. H expressed were actually 'feelings of guilt' for not functioning adequately' in his own subjective experience: "I feel the guilt and panic go through my arms and chest down to my navel." Mrs. H corrected: "I feel it as a cramp that goes down to the lower abdomen."*

*During vicarious mentalization, the patient realized that her physical and mental experiences could be put into words and understood by someone else. This process indicated to the patient: She is allowed to be difficult in the therapeutic relationship. This dissolved the blockage in the therapeutic relationship. In the next therapy session, Mrs. H. was able to report her suicidal thoughts openly for the first time. These had already existed for several weeks (continued in* Sects. 8.6.2–8.6.6*).*

## *8.6.2 The Activation of a Sense of Self-regulation in the Symptom of Suicidal Fantasies*

Mrs. H. was experiencing a pre-suicidal syndrome (see Sect. 8.8.3) due to her suicide fantasies. She thought in the equivalence mode (see Sect. 2.6) and was experiencing her *external circumstances* as depressing as *she felt within.*

**Central idea**

The patient's mentalizing and her inner fantasy space had collapsed. The patient experienced herself as someone to whom life happens. She felt she was at the mercy of her depression and could only react. The therapist, therefore, retraced her process of self-regulation, with her, in the symptom of suicidality. The aim was for her to develop a sense of self-regulation (thinking, feeling, and perception) in her actions and restore her inner fantasy space.

In doing this, the therapist asked her to think of her plan for suicide step by step, including the time, place, *and all the consequences.* In this way, the patient integrated the as-if mode of play into her thinking in the equivalence mode (see Sect. 2.6). That resolved her pre-suicidal syndrome. She could internally connect with her self-actualization in the symptom of suicidality.

***Case example 71 (2nd continuation, see Sects. 8.6 and 8.6.1)***

*After Mrs. H. had reported her suicidal ideation, the therapist asked her to imagine the course of her potential act of suicide with all the consequences. Mrs. H's fantasy was to jump out of her friend's apartment window, which she regularly cleaned without pay, to structure her everyday life'. The apartment was on the 23rd floor of a high-rise building. Together, the therapist and the patient imagined how she would think and feel and what she would experience in her body during the act of suicide moment by moment. The patient and therapist recognized that it was about flying for her. Flying would allow her to leave the suffering behind and 'feel freedom'. The therapist asked the patient to go even further in her imagination of the suicide: "And when you come down on earth, what will happen? What do you think?" It was only then that Mrs. H. realized how this act of suicide would completely destroy her physically. She would also emotionally hurt her friend and her loved ones. This horrifying imagination terrified her to the depths of her soul (continued in* Sects. 8.6.3–8.6.6*).*

The imaginative realization of the suicide fantasy helped the therapist to *diagnose* the patient's suicidal risk. If the patient hadn't felt terrified in the end, the therapist would have had to admit her to a psychiatric clinic in an emergency. Thinking through to the end of the suicide fantasy *in the as-if mode* helped Mrs. H. to recognize the difference between her wishful fantasy and the horrible reality of the act of suicide *with its real consequences.* She developed internal distance from her suicidal ideation and her pre-suicidal syndrome was resolved.

### 8.6.3 Rebuilding the Inner Fantasy Space in Everyday Life

***Case example 71 (3rd continuation)***
*From the sixth therapy session onwards, the therapist would ask the severely depressed patient to report specifically about her present everyday life. In doing so, he walked through, together with her, her actions, physical sensations, affect, and thoughts in the process of her self-regulation in depression, step by step: "What did you do after you woke up in the morning? What did you think? What did you feel? Then what did you do?..." The therapist and the patient represented everything that she reported with stones and blocks of wood on the table: her own self, her feelings of guilt, her sense of duty, her bed, her husband, and other relatives. Like a naive, curious child, he let Mrs. H show him the way of her self-regulation today. He doubled her verbally and helped her put her feelings and thoughts into words. In doing so, he always pointed out to her when she had made a choice. For example, he stated: "Ah yes, you drank tea for breakfast but didn't eat anything." Once, Mrs. H. lay in bed for two days until her husband persuaded her to get up. The patient felt that she was an imposition on others. She was living in the role of the 'difficult one' in her present family, even though this role was initially created for her survival in her family of origin. The bed had become a cave for her, in which she felt safe with her cuddle pillow. The therapist commented: "If it felt more comfortable for you to turn on your left side in bed, then that was the best solution for you!".*

*Retracing the chronological sequence of interactions in depression, resolved the defense through denial (see* Sect. 2.4.2*). It revealed that Mrs. H. had been suicidal in the car on her way to the therapy session. She had had the idea of crashing into a truck. The therapist was startled. But he saw Mrs. H. sitting in front of him alive. He, therefore, asked her to tell him exactly how she had regulated her suicidal tendencies: "What did you think and feel after the thought of crashing into a truck? Something must have caused you to distance yourself from this idea!" Mrs. H.: "I thought that you were waiting for me." At that moment, the therapist experienced Mrs. H. as naively trusting as a child. He felt connected to her. That calmed him down a little. However, he increased the number of therapy sessions to twice weekly and thus made the therapeutic setting more stable than before. He did not admit the patient to a psychiatric clinic because she had recently been hospitalized for seven months without any improvement in her condition (continued in* Sects. 8.6.4–8.6.6*).*

**Central idea**

The patient's inner fantasy space had collapsed. Life happened to her. The patient first had to develop a sense of self-regulation in her actions. So this work was not about the content of her thinking, but about reviving her mentalizing ability.

During this work, the therapist met the patient with an inner attitude: *When it's about living*, there is no right or wrong. *Every* action the patient takes is a solution. The patient's current solution may not be a *good* solution, but it is the best possible solution for her *right now* because *the patient's soul doesn't do anything for free.* The therapist accompanies the patient in understanding her actions in everyday life as an implicit doppelganger shoulder to shoulder. He interviews her: "What do you feel and think when you do that?" And he verbalizes *his own* actions, feelings, affect, and thinking *as her doppelganger*. In this way, he fills gaps in *her* inner psychosomatic resonance (see Sect. 2.7) and marks meaningful thought contents. The collaborative mentalization of the patients' experiences in their everyday life has an ego-strengthening effect.

Working with the table stage helps the therapist to get an overview of the patient's psychological crisis together with the patient.

**Recommendation**

The more distressed a patient is, the more likely it is that the therapist *himself,* as a doppelganger, has to represent and re-enact the patient's experience externally with stones on the table when working with the table stage.

The patient's ego stone in her soul landscape represents the center of her self-regulation: "It is your ego that feels guilty". The *external* play in the as-if mode with the stones on the table stage improves the patient's *inner* capacity to think in the as-if mode via the feedback loop between the external psychodramatic play production and inner mentalization (see Sect. 2.3). The patient looks at *the symbolic image of her self-regulation* in her crisis from the meta-perspective. This sets up her inner fantasy space again and strengthens her cognition. At the end of therapy, Mrs. H. paid tribute to the *small-step* therapeutic work on the process of her self-regulation with the comment: "Whenever I said that I wasn't doing so well, you would always ask me pointedly. That's when I noticed what I really *felt.*"

### 8.6.4 Symbolizing in Nocturnal Dreams as an Amplification for Understanding the Patient's Self-regulation in Everyday Life

Some patients with severe depression continue to process their conflicts in nocturnal dreams *despite their mental breakdown.* However, the dream work must not be severely impaired by a high dosage of psychotropic medication. The therapist uses the power of symbolic images in the nocturnal dreams *therapeutically* as a resource for self-regulation in mentalizing. He appreciates the *inner creativity* of the patient that may be recognizable in the dreams. This activates the patient's inner ability to mentalize in everyday life.

***Case example 71 (4th continuation, see Sects.* 8.6–8.6.3)**
*The first sign of progress in Mrs. H's therapy was visible in the 10th session. She narrated a dream in which a house had collapsed above her. The debris had fallen on her. A week later, she even dreamt of a large church that had collapsed above her. She resignedly interpreted these dream images as symbols for the collapse of her hope for healing. The therapist knew, however, that if a patient symbolically converts their clinical symptom into a scenic dream image, it is to be seen as progress in psychotherapy (*Plassmann, 1999*). Therefore, the nightmares described by Mrs. H. gave him confidence that Mrs. H. could benefit from psychotherapeutic treatment. He communicated this assessment to the patient through a 'space interpretation' (*Plassmann, 1999*): "I think your creative powers are gaining some strength, at least in your unconscious. Because your unconscious is able to symbolically represent your mental breakdown through images and deal with it."*

*The appreciation of the creative powers of her unconscious brought about further progress in the patient. However, this was demonstrated in the following therapy session in a somewhat grotesque manner. Mrs. H. reported a new dream: "My brother-in-law put a pistol in my hand. In the dream, I held it to my head and pulled the trigger. But nothing happened. I felt very disappointed in the dream and said: 'That doesn't work!'".*

*In contrast to the dream images of the collapse of the house and the church, death in this dream no longer 'simply' fell upon the patient as a matter of fate. She was now trying to kill herself in the dream. This indicates that, at an unconscious level, she was now feeling in control of her suicidal fantasies. At the same time, however, similar to real life, she did not succeed in putting this into practice. The therapist interpreted the dream: "In the dream, your unconscious gave you a pistol without any bullets, and the suicide attempt failed. Perhaps this indicates that there is a part in you that wants to live?" Mrs. H. found this dream interpretation to be true but also restrictive. She groaned, "If committing suicide is not possible anymore, what then? Then it will be really difficult!" The possibility of suicide had given the patient a feeling of freedom and the ability to act, which has now disappeared. (Continued in* Sects. 8.6.5 *and* 8.6.6*).*

## *8.6.5 The Doppelganger Technique in Self-injurious Thinking*

***Case example 71 (5th continuation)***
*At the beginning of the 14th therapy session, Mrs. H said: "It was challenging for me to come here today. Just thinking about it as I lay in bed was a nightmare. But my husband made sure that I got up and came here." The patient radiated deep suffering. As with focusing (*Gendlin, 1998*), the therapist asked the patient to exactly describe*

*her experience of the 'nightmare': "Where do you feel the nightmare? What color does it have? Which shape? What consistency?" Mrs. H. experienced her nightmare as a square, a brown-black stone weighing about ten kilograms lying on her chest. The therapist remembered a similar stone lying in a closet behind him. He turned around, picked up the stone, and placed it on the table: "Is the stone like that?" Mrs. H. turned completely white in the face and stared at the stone: "You have such a stone!—I can't even look at it!" The therapist: "Would you like to do something?" The patient: "I would rather take it and throw it away." Therapist: "Do that!" Mrs. H hesitates: "No, it does not work like that. I'd have to throw it through the window."*

*The therapist seriously considered doing this on behalf of the patient. But then he dreaded the effort of having to repair the window. He saw the stone on the table in front of the patient and hesitated. Then he felt: He couldn't stand the sight of this threatening stone in front of him on the table. As a doppelganger, he took the stone on behalf of the patient and held it in his hands: "We can also take the stone away. How far away does it have to be?" He got up, took the stone to the far corner of the room, and laid it on the floor: "Is that okay? Mrs. H: "Yes, that's fine. I can't see it now!" The therapist went back to his chair. He sat down. He felt that the situation had eased for him.*

*But, a short while later, he felt blocked again: The nightmare stone was still threatening him from the corner of the room and paralyzing his inner contact with the patient. So he followed his impulse to act as a doppelganger and stood up: "I can't stand it!" He fetched the stone from the corner of the room and carried it out of the room through the corridor into the examination room of his practice. There, he placed it on the floor in the furthest corner. Then he went back to the therapy room. He explained his actions to the patient: "It's not just about working, but also about feeling good." The therapist sat down on his chair and felt differently in the changed situation: "Yes, that's better for me." A deep, long-lasting silence emerged in the therapeutic relationship.*

*The therapist felt more comfortable. Suddenly he saw that Mrs. H. was beginning to cry cathartically from deep inside her body. Her breathing was restricted like in an asthma attack, and she groaned: "I feel so empty from within, so empty, so empty!" The therapist told her what he had experienced: "I have great respect for the depth of your feelings. You do a lot of work when you allow your feelings here." Mrs. H: "I always feel so guilty that I don't do anything here during the session!" The therapist gave the patient plenty of time. She slowly relaxed. Then she spontaneously said: "I have always lived against my feelings in my relationship with my stepdaughter. I've always tried to fix everything and do everything. But my stepdaughter didn't like me. She always only wanted her dead mother. I have never been able to talk to my husband about these feelings." For the first time, the patient internally linked her suffering with her own relationship conflict through these statements. The therapist affirmed this as a therapeutically significant step: "Linking your feeling of emptiness with the knowledge that you have always acted against your own feelings makes a lot of sense." (6th continuation below).*

**Recommendation**

The therapist should constantly *positively affirm new solutions* that *appear spontaneously* in the patient's crisis. This helps those affected to integrate the new solution into their self-organization and to stabilize it over time. If a new solution is not positively affirmed from inside or outside, it is mostly lost again in the chaos of the crisis (Schacht, 1992, p. 125). This is a finding from the chaos theory (see Fig. 2.1 in Sect. 2.1).

**Central idea**

Improving one's sense of self in acting can *worsen* severe depression. In such a case, the improved sense of self intrapsychically triggers an internal pathological introject or a sadistic superego. In such a case, *the therapist* must not be confused in assessing the patient's progress.

***Case example 71 (6th continuation, see Sects.* 8.6–8.6.4)**

*At the beginning of the next therapy session, Mrs. H. was in a completely unexpected state, depressed and by no means relieved. She groaned: "I feel so bad and guilty because I portrayed my husband so negatively here in therapy." She defended through projective identification (see* Sect. 2.4.4*). She identified with the role of the good mother ascribed to her in her current family. The therapist should help her be a good mother and not cause trouble for her family. By acting out this defense, she delegated her own sense of self to the therapist. The therapist felt internally blocked, resigned, and lost on the patient's behalf. In this situation, however, he made his own emotional reaction fruitful for therapy. He symbolized the patient's self-accusation and his inner protest against it with two stones in a symbolic image. He placed the five-kilogram nightmare stone from the 14th therapy session on the table in front of him and clamped a cherry-sized, green semi-precious stone underneath it: "The big stone here is your feeling of guilt, which is depressing you. The small stone is you!" (7th continuation see Sect.* 8.6.6*).*

The *interpersonal* conflict between the patient and the therapist was transformed into an *intrapsychic* conflict of the patient through the external representation of her interacting self-parts. From the meta-perspective, they both perceived the patient's conflict *as an intrapsychic conflict* outside on the table stage. The patient's 'self' was the victim of the big stone of guilt. In this way, she was able to admit her will to exist, suppressed by her large, sadistic superego.

**Recommendation**

When symbolizing a sadistic superego on the table stage, the therapist should keep replacing the object symbolizing the superego with a *larger* object until the patient protests: "No, the previous stone is big enough!" The following rule applies: the larger and more powerful the superego stone looks in relation to the small ego stone, the more likely it is that *the patient* will develop compassion for her suppressed and frightened self and empathize with herself.

The treatment of Mrs. H. took place more than 30 years ago. At that time, I had not yet developed the models of disorder-specific therapy for people with trauma-related disorders and structural disorders presented in Chaps. 4 and 5 of this book. Today I would treat the patient's dysfunctional metacognitive processes with the *chair work* on the room stage instead of stones on the table stage (see Sects. 4.7 and 4.8) *from the point at which* Mrs. H. was able to relate her depressive affect on her own with her current relationship conflicts.

### *8.6.6 The Integration of Improved Self-actualization into the Inner Relationship Images*

***Case example 71 (7th continuation, see Sects.* 8.6–8.6.5*)***
*The therapist symbolized Mrs. H.'s intrapsychic guilt conflict in the following twelve therapy sessions patiently and consistently with the same two stones on the table. This helped to center the therapeutic conversations thematically on the intrapsychic conflict. When the patient talked about her current negative feelings and body sensations, she saw her 'sadistic superego' lying heavily on her 'little self' on the table and spontaneously associated various relationship problems from her life story in which she had felt guilty. Unlike at the beginning of the therapy, the patient now linked her depressive affect with inner relationship images. She redefined herself in her thinking as "someone who dares to be difficult for the other, at least in her thinking, and then feels guilty toward the other".*

*In this therapy, the therapist learned that an internal structural change takes a lot of time. The new paths must permanently interconnect and nestle in the memory structures of the human being in order to become part of a new dynamic balance of the soul (see* Fig. 2.1 in Sect. 2.1). *Mrs. H. needed another twelve therapy sessions with consequent 'linking work' (Fuhr, 1994, verbal communication). It was only after six weeks, in the 25th therapy session, that she explicitly confirmed to the therapist that her condition had improved: "In the last session when I went out, I felt something light inside me for the first time."*

*The sight of the small suppressed ego stone under the large 'guilt-stone' helped the patient justify her feelings in relation to her conflict partners. She spontaneously linked her feelings of powerlessness and helplessness with the traumatizing workplace conflict that had triggered it. She no longer wanted to be 'the difficult one'. She had, therefore, not spoken to anyone about the harassment at her workplace. But now she told the therapist: "Back then, as a social pedagogue, I failed in my creative style of work with differently-abled people. I had to re-dress them whenever they would wet themselves. Some youngsters have beaten me on several occasions. My colleague, who was part of the group, would run to the toilet for an hour whenever it got difficult." Mrs. H had asked her boss for help in this emergency. But the boss had obviously been overwhelmed with this situation herself. So in response to Mrs. H, she had given absurd suggestions to practice specific exercises in arithmetic, biology, and other subjects with the youth. Each exercise should last a quarter of an hour. Mrs. H. had been asked to record her work and its successes in detail and submit these records to the boss for supervision every day. Mrs. H. resignedly said: "The others in the facility didn't bother the boss. They just went along with it somehow! But I was constantly afraid!" 19-year-old Mrs. H.'s plan to 'no longer be difficult' was a disaster in this situation. She should have been difficult with her boss in order to protect herself mentally. It is fitting, that a few years later, Mrs. H's boss took early retirement due to a mental disorder.*

*After three months of explicit metacognitive work on the intrapsychic conflict between herself and sadistic superego, Mrs. H. named the small green stone that was so unbearably burdened by the big guilt-stone on the table stage, 'my feeling ego': "It is my own will, which was buried in me." She added a third stone to the outer symbolic image of the two stones for her 'adapted ego' and said: "I hadn't even noticed it before. I just did everything all the time." Mrs. H. tried to find out in which of the three ego states she was in her relationship conflicts respectively, whether in her punishing superego, in her 'adapted ego', or in her own feeling as a healthy adult woman (see* Sect. 4.7*). The external image of her ego states on the table helped her work through her relationship conflicts. As a result, she learned to assert herself better in everyday conflicts.*

*For example, in the 81st therapy session, Mrs. H. reported that her husband had advised her "to go back to work because of her self-esteem problems". But she immediately protested: "I'm not bored at all. I am fulfilled. I am rediscovering a lot of things for myself right now. I paint. I am learning English. And for the first time, I am also enjoying the household chores. I have developed interests! I don't want anyone telling me what to do!" The therapist appreciated her new self-determination in the conflict with her husband as 'personal progress'. Mrs. H. appeared quite distressed upon hearing this positive appreciation and said: "The work in the institution for differently abled had left me with a lot of self-doubts!" She started weeping cathartically and groaned: "I am never enough! I do not want to feel like that anymore! I don't want to be determined by idiots anymore!" This sentence became the focus of her further development in psychotherapy: "I don't want it anymore! I don't want to be determined by idiots anymore!" (8th continuation below).*

Over time, the patient developed awareness of her defense through identification with the system (see Sect. 2.4.4), and through the explicit metacognitive work on her intrapsychic conflict (see Sect. 4.8). She realized that even as an adult, she was still identifying with the role of the 'difficult one' from her childhood. Over time, by working on her identity conflict, she learned to justify *her feelings* even more and relativized the power of her sadistic superego. In doing so, she dared to feel what she is feeling. She no longer had to ignore the 'evil' in her loved ones. At the end of therapy, Mrs. H. stated: "My husband always said that he would like to have a *normal* family. I had tried everything to achieve this goal. But the family *was not* normal. It was difficult. The daughter always wanted her dead mother back. I should have said to my husband: 'But this is not a normal family, this is a *difficult family*!'".

***Case example 71 (8th continuation)***

*At the end of her therapy, the patient dreamt of a newly built house she had moved into. This indicates that she had established a new inner self after her old adjusted self had collapsed. Mrs. H. had retired for three years due to her severe depression. However, two years before the end of her five-year therapy, she decided to return to work in her old institution. She fought against all opposition and ensured that she only worked with individuals and no longer in groups. At the end of therapy,*

*Mrs. H. shared a dream: She is standing with her 'therapist' on a mountain meadow and talking. Then she says goodbye of her own accord and "drives away in her Triumph sports car". In the 1950s, there was a sports car called "Triumph". Mrs. H. herself was driving the car in the dream. So she could now steer herself and leave the therapist figuratively 'in triumph'. In the continuation of the dream, she then switched to a bicycle and thought: "But now you need a lot of time!" Mrs. H. then decided: "Now I want to take my time in my everyday life, too". Ten years after the end of her psychotherapeutic treatment, the patient informed the therapist that she had not been mentally ill ever again in the last ten years.*

The *psychotherapeutic treatment* of a patient with severe depression with structural conflicts should proceed in small steps and offer stability, in the beginning, considering the patient's internal blockages and inner chaos. We, therefore, recommend two 50-min sessions per week for the first 3–6 months. The frequency of the sessions can be reduced to one session per week once the patient's condition has improved. The treatment for *severe depression with structural conflicts* can last for five years. However, it can be phased out at a lower frequency in the last two years. In the case of *chronic disorders*, the therapist must continue to accompany the patient for many years after the end of the intensive phase of psychotherapy. A 50-min session once every four weeks is sufficient for this. The stability in the therapeutic relationship often stabilizes the patient in their professional life, personal relationships, and in dealing with themselves. Many therapists underestimate the therapeutic effect of a long-term, stable therapeutic relationship with their patients. During these subsequent years, the patients sometimes take important developmental steps despite the limited therapy hours.

## 8.6.7 Limitations in the Therapy of People with Depression

In the psychotherapy of patients with severe depression, everything that helps alleviate their *suffering* is ultimately good. Sometimes it helps if the therapist firmly asks the patient to take an absurdly small step in the right direction.

***Case example 72***

*A 48-year-old housewife, for example, had been suffering from severe depression and schizoaffective psychosis (F25.1) for a long time and had developed a helplessness syndrome. Her husband was very caring and did all of the household chores for her. The therapist witnessed this absolute protection of the patient during a home visit and experienced it as exaggerated and absurd. Therefore, he asked the patient to carry at least one spoon from the dining room into the kitchen after lunch every day from that day onwards. The patient gradually emerged from her depression from the moment she did as told by the therapist.*

The clinical symptoms in patients with severe depression are sometimes difficult to influence psychotherapeutically. Nevertheless, the therapist should *continue* to provide psychiatric and psychotherapeutic support to the patient. Sometimes the symptoms improve surprisingly. It can help, for example, if the therapist answers psychodramatically (see Sect. 4.13) and expresses his feelings openly *after having endured the patient's suffering for a long time*: "I feel helpless in my relationship with you as a person. That doesn't mean that, as a therapist, I want to stop therapy. You are in therapy with me, and we are in the same boat. I just want to tell you honestly how I am doing with you."

***Case example 73***

*Mrs. I., a middle-aged nurse, was severely depressed. She sought outpatient psychotherapy after several admissions to psychiatric and psychosomatic clinics. After two operations, she was sick for three years and was thus unable to work. During these three years, all her therapists in inpatient and outpatient care were in despair due to her repetitive sentence: "I can't think, I have become stupid!" The therapist willingly tried out various therapeutic approaches for six months. In his desperation, he even gave her a foot massage for 30 min. But, the patient did not start again until the therapist gave up his helper attitude and took her 'saying' seriously. He told the patient openly: "I don't know what to do next. I think it's true: Maybe you do have brain damage!" The therapist's surrender led to an inner turning point in the patient and a new beginning in her ability to think. The therapist only realized much later that her statement was true in a figurative sense! The patient had almost died in two emergency operations due to medical errors and was only saved by the mindfulness of her life partner. In addition, she was also psychologically traumatized due to a subsequent chronic physical illness. The patient's statement, "I can't think, I have become stupid!" was an accurate description of the frozen state of her traumatized mentalization.*

This book does not describe psychotherapy for depression in the context of bipolar affective disorder (ICD-10 F31.-). In bipolar disorder, the patient experiences episodes of mania and depression alternatingly. According to Mentzos (2011, p. 213), mania is to be understood "as an antidepressive defense. [...] The sequence of depression and mania corresponds, on the one hand, to repetitive sequences of a self-degrading submission to the superego and fate and, on the other hand, to the illusory, manic denial and excessive self-overestimation, which can only last for a short time." Depressive and manic psychoses "often don't break out of the blue, they are at least partially triggered by difficult breakups, illnesses, or losses" (Mentzos, 2011, p. 312). Even before this disorder is diagnosed, patients experience fragile disturbances in their self-esteem regulation. "Traumas, disappointments, and frustrations experienced by these patients in childhood have made them hypersensitive to the triggers mentioned above." This hypersensitivity leads to the onset of depressive or manic phases in the presence of new triggers. According to Mentzos (2011, pp. 212 and 214), a certain organically induced over-excitation or biological instability can be assumed in bipolar patients.

In my experience, psychiatrists diagnose 'bipolar disorder' too often. One reason for this may be that the therapist's time and professional resources are limited. If the doctor assumes a biological psychotic condition, it is easier for him to justify to himself that he is largely confining himself to the administration of medication.

Severe depression in the context of 'bipolar disorder' (F31.-) is often depression in the context of a borderline personality disorder, a dissociative disorder, or a trauma-related disorder (see case example 71 in Sects. 8.6–8.6.6). For example, the manic decompensation of Mrs. H's husband (see case example 71) occurred 15 years after her treatment, after he heard gunshots in a war zone in Syria outside his hotel. His manic decompensation served the function of countering a flashback from childhood trauma.

## 8.7 Treatment with Psychopharmacology

When patients with *severe* depression are discharged from a psychiatric clinic and come to outpatient psychotherapy, they are often found to be consuming very high dosages of psychotropic drugs. Psychiatrists often *combine* antidepressants, sedatives, and neuroleptics. They may then supplement these medications with anti-epileptic drugs "to prevent bipolar mood swings". For example, the patients in case examples 71 (see Sects. 8.6–8.6.6) and 73 (see Sect. 8.6.6) were more or less rigid in their facial expressions and gestures, had swollen faces, and walked in small steps without moving their arms when they came to their first psychotherapeutic interview. Psychotherapists, even if they are psychologists, are *jointly responsible* for their patient's medication. When in doubt, a psychotherapist should follow their intuition and communicate their doubts to the prescribing doctor. A high dosage of psychotropic medication should be *reduced to an appropriate level* as early as possible in cooperation with a psychiatrist. The reasons for this are: (1) A psychotherapeutic relationship giving a sense of security replaces a part of the medication. (2) Patients may not be able to make adequate use of psychotherapy due to the effects and side effects of the medication. For example, psychotropic drugs often limit one's cognitive abilities. However, the patient needs his cognitive abilities in order to process his experience *in psychotherapy*. (3) The pathological mental states of the patient must be acted out in the relationship with the therapist so that they are accessible for psychotherapeutic interventions.

**Recommendation**

When prescribing psychotropic drugs, the general rule applies: the closer the therapeutic relationship, the lesser the amount and dosage of drugs required. For example, if a patient is in twice-weekly therapy, his medication can be decreased even more than if he were in *once*-weekly therapy.

Psychotherapy sessions save a lot of money when compared to the often very expensive psychotropic drugs. Medicines mainly 'only' improve the symptoms. But psychotherapy heals at a deeper level. It often prevents illnesses from becoming chronic, resulting in extended sick leave and early retirement. Even if *all* complementary economic costs are included, psychotherapy is probably no more expensive than a purely biomedical treatment over many years. In Germany, health insurance companies cover the costs of psychotherapeutic treatments at the therapist's request because it helps them save money. This was an outcome of a scientific study by

Dührsen (1962). This study indicated that patients who had engaged in psychoanalytic psychotherapy were sick and *incapable of working for fewer days every year* than the average population. The number of sick days also included all physical illnesses. The financial expenditures of the health insurance companies for medical care had therefore decreased.

## 8.8 Suicidal Crises

### *8.8.1 Fundamentals of Suicidal Crises*

Suicidal tendencies are scary because healthy people find it absurd to seek the great, real death instead of dreading it. A successful suicide always indirectly hurts other people in the social environment. This is because suicide is a breach of taboo and a violation of the deeper meaning of the human community. One of the tasks of a community is to ensure the survival of the *individual* members of the community. A community can be the family, the employees at work, a circle of friends, or the neighbors. A suicide attempt is often an *unspoken* message from the individual to the community that it has failed or is about to fail in an important task. A successful suicide always calls the community's identity into question. Many families break apart after a family member kills themselves.

In exceptional cases, suicide can be an *appropriate* solution to a conflict, for example, in a serious, incurable disease. Suicide is perhaps the only way for those affected to maintain their *dignity* (see Sect. 8.8.4). Paragraph 1 of the German constitution also applies here: "Human dignity is unimpeachable." In most cases, however, the prerequisite for suicide with dignity does not exist.

Everyone has the right to kill themselves. But only a few people attempt suicide even when in full possession of their mental and emotional powers. A good example of suicide with dignity is Moreno himself, the father of psychodrama: "In late April of 1974, a series of minor strokes had weakened him. At the age of 85, he was bedridden, he could [...] only speak slowly [...]. Because he was in pain from eating solid foods and knew he would die soon anyway, he decided to hasten the end and die with dignity. He decided not to eat anymore and to live only on water" (Yablonsky, 1986, p. 247 f.). His family and many of his students from around the world said goodbye to him one by one in his home. He died after about six weeks of fasting.

### *8.8.2 Constricted Thinking in the Pre-suicidal Syndrome*

In a *pre-suicidal syndrome,* people at risk of suicide are usually in a psychological state of emergency through the encounter with the great real death.

**Important definition**

A pre-suicidal syndrome involves the following (Ringel 1953, quoted from Reimer, 2007, p. 599): (1) The individual's thinking is fixated on death fantasies up to and including the longing for death, *without* thinking through the consequences of the imagined suicidal act. (2) The inner mentalization, the self-actualization tendency, and the ability to imagine or fantasize are constricted. The closer in time suicidal patients come to their suicidal act, the more they think in equivalence mode (see Sect. 2.6). They then see their outer world as negatively as their inner construction of reality suggests. They, therefore, see no other way out except for suicide, even if there was a way out. They can no longer feel the relationship with those close to them.

Sometimes an unplanned event pulls a suicidal person out of their pre-suicidal syndrome.

***Case example 74***
One patient told his psychiatrist, "I went into the woods with a rope to hang myself. There I met a man with a big black dog. The dog suddenly barked terribly at me. The man couldn't calm him down and kept apologizing to me: 'My dog is not usually like that. I didn't even know that he could be so aggressive! I'm sorry!' This other man, unsuspectingly, engaged me in a conversation. We talked for twenty minutes. I didn't tell him about my plan. But after that, I could no longer carry out my plan. I went home and talked to my wife. She then made this appointment for me with you."

Some suicidal people delay their suicidal act *on their own* initiative until the pre-suicidal syndrome and the suicide fantasy dissolve.

***Case example 75***
*A 50-year-old patient had been traumatized in the first year of his life by being hospitalized for six months in the post-war period. As a funeral director, he always became suicidal when he was exhausted and happened to have a "suicide" coffin as well. In four years of therapy, he had secretly gone into the cellar at night a total of twenty times with a rope to kill himself. But he would always take his time there. He would sit on the cellar stairs and wait. He always waited until he thought of his daughter. Sometimes this would take up to three hours. Then he would curse himself: "You are a pig! You just want to slip away!" Then he would put the rope aside, go upstairs to his apartment, and resume his daily chores. The therapist only realized much later that the patient began the act of suicide whenever he found himself feeling empty and senseless. The encounter with the great death helped him wake up from a flashback and the pre-suicidal syndrome. Then he would feel his body again and could enjoy the little things in life until the next crisis.*

### 8.8.3 Criteria for Assessing the Risk of Suicide and the Need for Therapy

There are many reasons why someone attempts suicide. The therapist can evaluate the risk of suicide and why one needs therapy by examining two questions *after a patient has attempted suicide*:

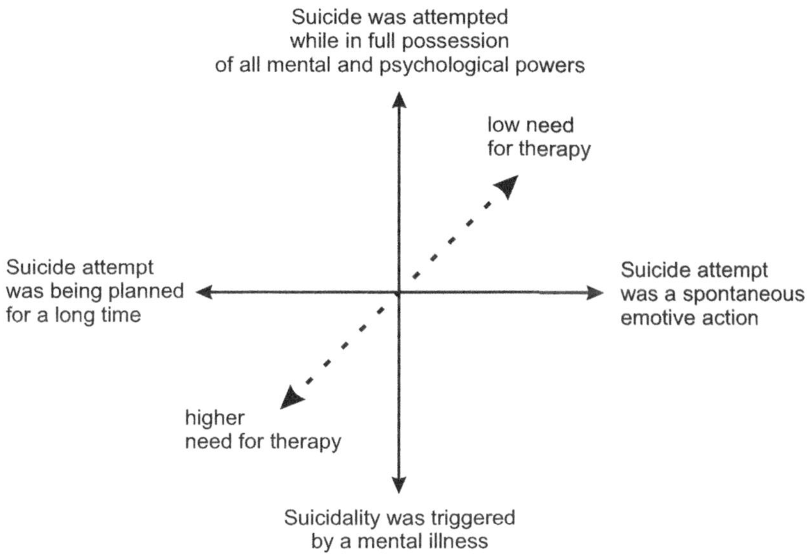


**Fig. 8.3** Criteria for the risk of suicide and the assessment of the need for therapy after a suicide attempt

1. Is the attempt at suicide more of an 'emotional act' or a 'long-planned attempt to end one's own life'?
2. Is it a suicide attempt with the individual being "in full possession of all mental and emotional powers" or a "suicidal act caused by mental illness"? (See Fig. 8.3).

The risk of death of a suicidal patient and their need for therapy is generally more significant when they have been planning the act of suicide for a long time, and the individual is severely distressed. People with suicidal thoughts must be taken seriously because of the mortal danger associated with their suffering and considered at risk, *even if* a suicidal act appears to be 'simply' demonstrative. Because even a 'simply' demonstrative attempt at suicide can lead to death. The therapist, together with the patient, looks for answers to the following questions during diagnosis and crisis intervention (see Sect. 8.8.5):

1. When did the patient *first think about* ending their life before attempting suicide? The longer it has been, the more dangerous the suicide fantasies. The greater the time interval, the more time the patient has had to reconsider his suicidal intention and examine it based on what has been happening in his everyday life. But the shorter the time interval, the more likely it is a question of a poorly thought-through emotional act.
2. *In which context did the suicidal thoughts arise for the first time?* How did the crisis develop *over time*? The greater the patient's external distress in his *real* everyday life, the less likely his suicidality is due to an already existing

mental disorder. The risk of suicide is exceptionally high for those whose therapists *cannot* establish an understandable reason for their suicidal act or suicidal intention *during therapy*. Young adult males, for example, are more likely to kill themselves without a suicide note and seemingly for no reason. These young men have the following factors in common: (1) They are going through a transition internally and externally. For example, they have just finished school. (2) They hide their loneliness behind a facade that appears to be perfect on the outside. (3) Their families never talked about feelings and problems. As a result, they lack the imagination and spontaneity required to find *another* solution to their conflict. Seemingly random suicide attempts are very dangerous. If the therapist can empathize with the patient's conflict, she can act and find ways out of this particular conflict with the patient. However, this possibility does not exist if the patient does not know the reason for his suicide attempt. The triggering conflict situation then remains latent and can reoccur or even intensify *at any point in time*.

3. *When did the patient start planning their suicidal act?* What ideas had he developed about this? A cruel suicide plan indicates a severe mental disorder in the patient. The more the patient thinks about the threat to *others*, the less likely it is a mere emotional act.
4. *What did the patient think and feel when he began his suicidal act?* And then when he did it? And before he passed out? The answers to these questions provide insight into the patient's self-regulation process in the symptom (see case example 71 in Sects. 8.6-8.6.6) and his internal conflict processing.
5. What did the patient *feel shortly after stopping their suicidal act*? What did he think next? Then what did he do? The answer "It didn't work, there was a barrier" has a *high therapeutic value*. Because the patient suddenly recognizes that he is about to confront *real* death. The constriction in his thinking *spontaneously* dissolves when faced with the choice of whether to live or die. He is potentially ready to 'capitulate' and challenge his old intrapsychic equilibrium for the sake of his own life.
6. What did the patient *think and feel when he regained consciousness after attempting suicide*? What if he could think clearly again after taking the tablets? The response "Luckily, it didn't work!" indicates that the patient has found a way out of his constricted thinking *after* his suicide attempt and is ready to rethink.
7. Sometimes, during crisis intervention *immediately after a drug overdose*, the therapist feels that she is having a 'normal' therapeutic conversation with the patient. However, often, the patient can *hardly remember anything* when they meet again because his ability to think and short-term memory had been severely impaired chemically due to the drug overdose. The therapist didn't notice it in the first conversation.
8. *Does the patient have a supportive network of personal and social relationships?* How did people in his network react to the information about suicidality or his suicide attempt? The more close-knit the network of friends and family, the easier it is for people to cope with crises.

9. *Has the patient already spoken to at least one person about their attempted suicide?* The less a patient talks about his crisis to others, the less likely he will deal with it internally. And the more likely he continues to be at risk.

***Case example 76***

*The 45-year-old Mr. N. sought initial psychotherapeutic consultation after his admission to a psychiatric clinic. He had suddenly been fired from his job after a prosperous professional career. For two years after that, Mr. N. had lied to his family that he had a new job. He pretended to drive to work every day but spent his time somewhere no one saw him, for example, in a parking lot on the highway. The patient had resolved to kill himself if his family discovered his lie: "I knew that my web of white lies would break at some point! I longed for some peace and quiet." After two years, his wife discovered that his previously well-stocked bank account was now empty, and she confronted him. Mr. N. decided that the time had come to act: "I took the rope, went into the forest, and threw it over a tree there. The rope was hanging there. I took my time. At some point, I realized: 'I can't do it!' I was surprised. Afterward, I accused myself of being a coward! I didn't know that in my life. I had always been a courageous man at work, especially during a crisis. I would be extremely cool there. I was a doer. I would always step in and connect with people!—I stayed in the forest for three days. My family believed I was dead." When Mr. N. returned home from the forest, his daughter greeted him with relief with the words: "You are my father! I'm glad you're not dead!" Mr. N: "I'm proud of my daughter!" The therapist interpreted the patient's feeling, "I can't do it!" radically positively: "That wasn't cowardice! You discovered your will to live there in the wood! All living beings have this natural will to live! The desire to live is an existential right. The right to life is a law in the United Nations Charter of Human Rights. It is free from all external norms."*

### *8.8.4 The Encounter with Death as a Wake-Up Call and an Impetus for a New Beginning*

**Recommendation**

In crisis intervention with suicidal people, the therapist should use the patient's encounter with the real great death as a wake-up call and an impetus for the patient's inner change. The thought, "He just wants attention!" is therapeutically unproductive. The therapist must not adapt to the patient and join him in trivializing his suffering: "No, it's not that serious!" That would potentially increase the patient's risk.

A person with thoughts of suicide is in *real* danger of death. But a suicidal crisis is also an opportunity. The *existential* character of the situation can present him with the freedom to let go of old ways and try new ones. He has the chance to develop a new kind of conscience.

**Central idea**

According to Dürckheim (1976, p. 110), there are three types of conscience: (1) The child's conscience, (2) The community conscience, and (3) The absolute conscience. If an individual obeys the child's conscience, he is afraid of punishment. If he obeys the community's conscience, he is afraid of being different from the others, breaking the community's laws, and being cast out for inappropriate behavior. But there is also a transpersonal conscience: "Here I stand, I can't help it!" The person concerned then sometimes *consciously* violates familial or institutional norms for the sake of *transpersonal truth* and accepts the consequences of his actions.

***Case example 77***
*In the United States, a Catholic priest climbed the fence of a nuclear missile depot in the presence of press reporters and hit the silo of a missile with a hammer. Naturally, he was arrested by the police, sentenced by a judge, and sent to prison. But the priest wanted to set an example. He had stood up for a transpersonal truth greater than his parents' truth and more comprehensive than the state law.*

Similarly, people with suicidal fantasies have the right to review the rules of their community and break them to sustain their own life, if necessary, in an attempt to defend or restore their human dignity.

***Case example 78***
*The 17-year-old Lisa, an outwardly attractive student, comes to the counseling center because she has refused to attend school. The accompanying mother complains: "At home, she is just lying in her bed." The therapist uses the table stage for her therapeutic work with the girl. On the table stage, she uses stones to symbolize a timeline for the development of the girl's psychological crisis. For the last three years, Lisa has thought about killing herself over and over again. Her suicide fantasies intensified after an abortion six months ago: "I hate my boyfriend for doing this to me!" The student adds: "My mother advised me to have the abortion. My mother had her first child when she was fifteen and wanted to protect me from going through the same experience." At present, Lisa is severely depressed and remains indoors all the time. In her bed, she dreams of her relationship with her former boyfriend. Everything seems pointless and empty to her: "I just want to die."*

*While looking at the table stage, she also mentions a new friend: "If I go out with him, then I don't think about dying. I'd like to have a child from him someday! But my mother forbids me to contact him!" The therapist places a stone for the new friend and another one for the child she wants. She positions the stone for the child further away from the stone for the present on the timeline. The small black stone for "suicide" is very close to the stone that marks the present. The therapist is concerned for the girl's life. She feels helpless. But then, as an implicit doppelganger, she consistently thinks ahead of the girl's suicide fantasy along the timeline. She points with her hand at the stones for the friend and the child: "If you kill yourself, you have to say goodbye to your future, to your new friend and the child you want! That's how you want it to be, isn't it?—However, there might be another option: You run away from home and try to live with your boyfriend. If that doesn't work then, you can still kill yourself. Ultimately, nobody can stop you from dying. But once you are dead, you can no longer try what it would be like to live with the new boyfriend and your own child! You know, it's really about your life! I think: your life is more important than you obeying your mother!" The therapist then narrates the fairy tale of Rapunzel as an amplification interpretation. Rapunzel had also been locked in a tower by her 'mother'. The mother wanted to save her from the evil world. But then a prince climbed up to join her in the tower. Rapunzel became pregnant by the prince. Her 'mother' found the prince, and pushed him down from the high tower. He injured himself gravely. She shunned the pregnant girl. Rapunzel and her two children searched for the prince for two years, and then she found him again. Her tears fell on his blind eyes and he regained his sight."*

In the case example, the therapist strongly represented the belief that the girl could and should find new solutions in her encounter *with real death.* If it helps her live, she should leave her family and 'sin' against her mother's rules. A community's laws, values, and rules exist to protect the community members from hardships. But they have to fulfill their function. They lose their meaning when they lead to the loss of human dignity and death. Therefore, the therapist aggressively represented the transpersonal quality of conscience for the 17-year-old girl to dissolve *the block in her fantasy through adaptation.*

Patients with thoughts of suicide often get stuck in an old, rigid defense system. Suicide becomes the way to avoid having to change one's old intrapsychic equilibrium.

***Case example 79***
*An artist committed suicide six months after the end of his psychotherapeutic treatment. He was unable to accept the failure of his grandiose ideas about himself in therapy. Despite all his friends' efforts, he couldn't capitulate. He 'preferred' the real great death to the small death of inner change. After his real death, however, it was too late for him to break out of his old intrapsychic equilibrium and find a more humble path for his life.*

***Case example 80***
*A 50-year-old patient, Ms. K, was traumatized in childhood. She only found a new beginning after five years of psychotherapy through a suicidal crisis in her life (*Balint, 1970*). She had long resisted an inner change with the help of her grandiose self-image. In the end, she had a mental and physical breakdown due to psychosomatic fever attacks. Nothing seemed to work anymore. She was filled with despair and, thus, considered suicide. However, during the crisis, Ms. K. spontaneously found a new solution to end her suffering. She just did what was good for her, following the motto of the Bremen Town Musicians: "You will definitely find something better than death!" After a long time, she called her former partner again. Unlike before, she spoke to him openly about her feelings. To her astonishment, she spontaneously felt understood by him. Her inner 'blind sadistic governess', with traits similar to her birth mother, lost her power over Ms. K in her encounter with the real death. The 'blind governess' disappeared in the following years, apart from a few 'relapses.'*

Many suicidal people only begin to look for a new way of living *after a crisis.* "Avoiding or combating suffering is natural. But when we are suffering, the point is to accept it and use it to create something beyond suffering. [...] We have to accept defeat and not pretend as if nothing has happened. We must overcome our resistance"

(Dürckheim, 1982, p. 88 f.). The fear of the real great death can help to let go of an overwhelming life principle, and we can humbly try to *live* a simple life. This is, for example, the core experience of Alcoholics Anonymous at their mental and physical 'rock bottom' (see Sect. 10.7). People with alcohol addiction cannot imagine a life without alcohol. But if they are at risk of confronting the real great death because of alcohol, it often helps them become abstinent and 'simply' stop drinking. One day and another and another. And so on.

***Case example 81***
*A 45-year-old patient, Mrs. L., sought therapy for a year after her 18-year-old son's suicide. She was always dressed in black and wanted nothing more than 'to go to her son's grave'. Her son had been differently-abled right from childhood. At the age of 18, he poured gasoline over himself, lit fire to it, and died a brutal death. Mrs. L made no noticeable progress during the one-year treatment and discontinued therapy. A year later, she was diagnosed with breast cancer. In this situation, she suddenly had to decide whether she really wanted to die. She chose the operation. She then made sure that her mother-in-law moved out of her home. She also motivated her alcoholic husband to face his illness and become abstinent. She even co-founded a self-help group for people with addiction disorders, along with her husband.*

## 8.8.5 Therapeutic Interventions in the Event of Risk of Suicide

A therapist who treats or counsels people at risk of suicide *cannot* save them *all* from dying. Their experience is similar to cardiologists who treat patients after a heart attack. *Not every* patient survives a heart attack. Nevertheless, the death of a patient by suicide is always a shock for the therapist. The therapist intuitively rethinks her therapeutic actions in retrospect. I drew the following conclusion from the suicide of some of my patients: "In the future, I would like to act more courageously and unconventionally with those at risk of suicide because of their *existential* threat. If necessary, I would like to offer them help *even outside of the customary pathways*." Treating patients at risk of suicide includes admitting them to a psychiatric facility against their will if their life is otherwise at risk. For example, a young patient, Ms. J., acutely decompensated in a psychotherapy group and was psychotic. She appeared suicidal, and no one could reach her. Finally, the therapist forcibly sent her to a psychiatric clinic directly from the group. The police carried the struggling, screaming young woman from the therapy room down the doorway to the street and used reasonable physical force to get her into the ambulance. Twenty years later, Mrs. J. is still alive today. She is working and regularly comes for therapy along with her husband. She is always happy to see the therapist. Her husband also smiles at the therapist.

It is a matter of life and death for people in suicidal crises. The therapy process demands empathy from the therapist and, at the same time, also requires them to call things by their names and speak clearly. *Crisis intervention* for people at risk of suicide involves diagnosis and therapy simultaneously. Together with the patient, the therapist retraced his *self-regulation process in the development* of his suicidal thoughts (see Sects. 8.6.2 and 8.6.3). As a *doppelganger*, she helps him to understand his self-regulation in his crisis. She verbalizes his actions, physical sensations, affect, and thoughts (see case example 71 in Sect. 8.6.3). She does not *oppose* the patient's suicidal impulses with her interventions. Instead, she retraces *shoulder to shoulder* with him, step by step the chronological sequence of interactions, to find out how his suicidal thoughts came about and how he dealt with them. In doing so, she resolves the suppression of interaction sequences (see Sect. 2.4.2). She works according to the principle: "The patient's soul doesn't do anything for free." She draws the patient's attention to the point in time when he decided on his way through the crisis. She searches without prejudice for why his solution has always been the best solution for him. This process expands his equivalence mode by thinking in the as-if mode (see Sect. 2.6). The patient no longer blindly concludes from his *inner* despair that *the outer world is also* full of despair. He can once again distinguish between his *inner* despair and the *outer* world, which simply goes on. He experiences anew that his suicide would be an act of his *own free will*.

**Central idea**

During the crisis intervention, the therapist understands the patient as a person who in his inner conflict processing, consciously or unconsciously, concluded: "I cannot live like this!" But she completes the sentence internally in the as-if mode: "I cannot live like this, but maybe *I can live differently*!"

This therapeutic attitude helps the therapist protect their spontaneity and fantasy from the patient's constricted thinking. The following rules and techniques have proven effective in crisis intervention for patients at risk of suicide:

1. Whenever the therapist has the idea or an indication that a patient *may be* secretly thinking about suicide, she should *immediately ask about suicidal thoughts*. This applies even if, when treating a patient, she 'only' has the intuitive idea: "He *can't* live like that in the long run." It is better to ask one too many questions than too few. This is therapeutically important for the following reasons: (1) It helps evaluate the extent of the risk of suicide. Or it relieves the therapist of possibly unfounded fears. (2) The therapist marks the danger of the situation and makes it accessible for therapeutic communication. (3) Inquiring about suicide fantasy dissolves the patient's constricted mentalization in the pre-suicidal syndrome. As a result, his death fantasies lose their possibly illusory character (see case example 71 in Sect. 8.6.2). (4) The open therapeutic conversation about suicidal fantasies often integrates the patient's suicidal impulse with the associated conflict. (5) The patient is no longer alone in the space of his suicidal fantasy. (6) The patient's existential suffering is appreciated.
2. The therapist sets up a timeline with three chairs in the therapy room in conversation with the patient. She places the first chair in one corner of the room to represent the patient's birth time, the second chair in the opposite corner of the room for his likely natural death at around 80 years of age, and the third chair

between these two chairs for his present life (see Sect. 8.8.4). She points to the respective chair with her hand: "You are now 50 years old and are still physically healthy. Statistically speaking, you still have 30 years to live. That's about 10,000 days. Every day your lifespan reduces by one day." The patient and the therapist look at the timeline from the meta-perspective. The patient becomes aware of the natural finiteness of his life and realizes that if he were to kill himself, he would be giving away 30 years of his life. The therapist can also symbolize this timeline with three stones on the table stage. In his film 'Guide to Happiness', Yalom said that he often illustrated the *existential dimension of his patients' lives* for them in a similar manner. First, he would draw a line on a piece of paper and mark the patient's time of birth and the possible time for his natural death. Then he would ask the patient to mark the point in time where he could see himself right now. In doing so, the patient would recognize the finiteness of his life and feel encouraged to *evaluate whether he really wanted to live the way he lives in the present.*

3. When working with the table stage, the therapist can add to the lifeline between birth and natural death stones for (1) The time of the initial *arrangements* for the suicide attempt, for example, the date on which the patient bought the tablets, (2) The *beginning* of the suicidal act, (3) *Waking up* from unconsciousness or *stopping* the suicidal act, and (4) The time at which the patient met his loved ones again. The therapist asks the patient to describe their thinking, affect, physical sensation, behavior, and wishes *for each of these points in time* in detail. Together they trace his thoughts, feelings, actions, and sensations along the timeline. They look at each bead on a string of beads, as if they wanted to write a film script together. Then, the therapist re-enacts the crisis concretely with the stones on the table stage. For example, she takes the stone for the patient's ego and lets him 'go to the train tracks': "What did you think and feel on the way?" In this work, the therapist works shoulder to shoulder with the patient in implementing his self-regulation process in his development of suicidality (see Sect. 8.6.3). She makes the patient aware of his decisions and calls things by their names. If necessary, she represents the patient's rigid defense patterns with empty chairs (see Sect. 4.8).

**Central idea**

In doing this, the therapist implicitly assumes that the patient's suicidal thoughts result from *subjectively coherent* conflict processing. Therefore, together with him, she searches for the meaning that his suicidal thoughts have *for him* in his life.w

4. Some patients stop their suicidal actions. They may then interpret their actions with the words: "I was too cowardly" (see case example 76 in Sect. 8.8.3). The therapist re-interprets such an interpretation in a radically positive way: "Maybe *your body* didn't want to die and signaled to you: 'But I want to live!'"
5. While the patient is processing his self-regulation in the crisis, the therapist points to *alternative options for action*: "You have always been a strong, independent woman. If your partner worries about you after you attempted suicide, it may indicate that he loves you. Admit it! Enjoy his attention! You've always

longed for love!" *In rare cases*, an act of suicide is part of a macabre game with own life and, as it were, Russian roulette. In such a case, the life-threatening acts are *masochistic* or addictive. Those affected obtain the existential *feeling of being alive* through the emotionally intense kick of the *danger to life*. In doing so, however, they often self-injuriously and ignorantly repeat old destructive relationship patterns from childhood.

6. In the case of suicide fantasies, the therapist works with the patient consistently to identify *the possible consequences of his planned suicide act* (see case example 71 in Sect. 8.6.2). Nowadays, driving your car into a tree is no longer lethal. However, it can lead to a lifelong disability or harm other drivers. If the patient throws himself in front of a train, it often traumatizes the train driver. Thinking *about the consequences* of one's actions activates the patient's sense of self in its restricted conflict processing. It dissolves the constriction of thinking in the pre-suicidal syndrome. The patient can now consider whether or not he wants to accept the identified negative consequences of his actions (see case examples 71 in Sects. 8.6–8.6.6, 75 in Sect. 8.8.2, and 78 in Sect. 8.8.4).
7. Many patients come to therapy only *after attempting suicide*. The therapist then works with the patient to identify the potential risk of death in his type of suicide attempt. Ten headache pills are not going to kill a person. Most people know this. On the other hand, it is life-threatening to drive off in a car when intoxicated and suicidal. Intoxication with alcohol and tablets *together* is more dangerous than a suicide attempt with alcohol or pills *alone*. The therapist informs the patient of the *real* risk of dying they were taking. The higher the risk, the more likely it is that the act of suicide will be a wake-up call to life. The lower the risk, the more the therapist can positively re-interpret the failure of the patient's suicide attempt: "You are intelligent. I think a part of you didn't want to die! It would have been quite easy for you to plan the suicide attempt more precisely if you had wanted to."
8. The therapist uses the basic human fear of death and her own insight into the value of life as *an impetus* for a possible inner change in the patient (see case example 78 in Sect. 8.8.4): "Life is too short. What comes after that takes a long time. It would be a shame if you *just happened* to be dead without really thinking about what death is!" The patient should take himself seriously when he feels, "I can't live like this". He should take his time to think about *whether he could live differently*.
9. The therapist does not allow the patient to go home *after* a suicide attempt *until* they have worked together to develop an appropriate plan for continuing therapy. For example, she proactively books another appointment for him. Or she arranges a consultation with a professional in a counseling center or with another psychotherapist. If the patient refuses to come for future appointments without a plausible reason, it may be a *diagnostic* indication that he is still at risk of suicide. The *patient's decision* to continue with therapy gives him *inner* support in the event of future risk. The offer of help may encourage the patient to look for a way out of his crisis.

10. The therapist develops ideas for a therapy plan together with the patient. She defines the causes for his suicidal thought and shows him how he can continue to work on his problems if necessary. For example, she justifies the suicidal thoughts of an alcohol-dependent person with his alcohol problem and tells him what to do about his alcohol addiction. If necessary, she informs him about inpatient treatments, health resorts, short-term outpatient treatments, outpatient psychiatric or psychotherapeutic treatments, or the possibilities of drug therapy.

    About 80% of patients who have attempted suicide need further psychotherapy or psychiatric treatment. But some people *do not need any after-care*. These are people to whom *each of the following three points applies*: (1) The suicide attempt was 'only' related to an actual conflict. (2) The person has a reliable family and social environment. (3) The patient *spontaneously* became afraid for his own life upon encountering real death. *In another case*, the therapist advises the patient of therapy options.
11. Many therapists have the patient sign a contract to ensure that the patient *will not* attempt suicide until a point in time specified therein. The consultation about the planned contract helps *the therapist* protect himself *legally*, assess the suicidal risk diagnostically, and talk about the subject of life and death with the patient. However, such a contract does not relieve the therapist of their responsibility for the patient's life. Therefore, the therapist should also decide *for herself* whether she considers the patient to be at risk. If she is unsure, she must find reliable help.
12. Sometimes the therapist has to admit a patient to a psychiatric clinic *against* his will. If necessary, she can motivate the patient with the following sentence: "Give yourself a chance by staying in the clinic! If you still want to die *after your stay in the clinic*, nobody can stop you!" The patient then has time to reflect on his conflicts during his inpatient treatment. He can consider whether suicide is the appropriate solution to his conflicts. He can look for alternative solutions and life options in discussions with fellow patients, therapists, and family members or friends.

## References


Arntz, A., & van Genderen, H. (2010). *Schematherapie bei Borderline-Persönlichkeitsstörung*. Beltz.

Balint, M. (1970). *Therapeutische Aspekte der Regression*. Klett-Cotta.

Blatner, A. (2001). Psychodramatic methods for facilitating bereavement. In P. F. Kellermann, & M.K. Hudgins (Eds.), *Psychodrama with Trauma survivors. Acting out your pain* (pp. 41–50). Jessica Kingsley Publishers.

Bode, S. (2009). *Kriegsenkel. Die Erben der vergessenen Generation*. Klett-Cotta.

Ciompi, L. (2019). *Ciompi reflektiert. Wissenschaftliches, Persönliches und Weltanschauliches aus der Altersperspektive*. Vandenhoeck & Ruprecht.

Dührssen, A. (1962). Katamnestische Ergebnisse bei 1004 Patienten nach analytischer Psychotherapie. *Zeitschrift Für Psycho-Somatische Medizin, 8*, 94–113.

Dürckheim, K. G. (1976). *Vom doppelten Ursprung des Menschen* (3rd ed.). Herder.

Dürckheim, K. G. (1982). *Der Weg, die Wahrheit, das Leben. Erfahrungen auf dem Weg der Selbstfindung. Gespräche über das Sein mit Alphonse Goettman*. Scherz.

Ferenczi, S. (1970). *Schriften zur Psychoanalyse I*. Fischer.

Frede, U. (2009). Die Bedeutung des Psychodramas in der Begegnung mit alten Menschen. *Zeitschrift für Psychodrama und Soziometrie, 8*(1), 25–39.

Freud, A. (1984). *Das Ich und die Abwehrmechanismen*. Fischer Taschenbuch Verlag.

Gendlin, E. T. (1998). *Focusing*. Taschenbuchausgabe. Rowohlt.

Jung, C. G. (1985). *Erinnerungen, Träume, Gedanken von C. G. Jung. Aufgezeichnet und herausgegeben v. A. Jaffé*. Walter Verlag.

Kast, V. (1980). Die verwünschte Prinzessin. Zum Problem des Sado-Masochismus. In M. Jacobi,V. Kast, & I. Riedel (Eds.), (1990) *Das Böse im Märchen* (2nd ed., pp. 67–89). Bonz.

Krüger, R. T. (1997). *Kreative Interaktion. Tiefenpsychologische Theorie und Methoden des klassischen Psychodramas*. Vandenhoeck & Ruprecht.

Krüger, R. T. (2003). Indikationen und Kontraindikationen für den Rollentausch in der psychodramatischen Psychotherapie. *Zeitschrift für Psychodrama und Soziometrie, 2*(1), 91–116. https://doi.org/10.1007/s11620-003-0011-y

Krüger, R. T. (2004). Schöpferisch sein – wieder schöpferisch werden. Kreativität als Ressource des Menschen und als Mittel der Heilung in der Psychotherapie. In S. Gunkel, & G. Kruse (Eds.), *Salutogenese und Resilienz – Gesundheitsförderung, nicht nur, aber auch durch Psychotherapie?* (pp. 257–249). Hannoversche Ärzte-Verlags-Union.

Krüger, R. T. (2005). Szenenaufbau und Aufstellungsarbeit, Praxis und Theorie, Variationen und Indikationen im Gruppensetting und in der Einzelarbeit. *Zeitschrift für Psychodrama und Soziometrie, 4*(2), 249–274. https://doi.org/10.1007/s11620-005-0091-y

Krüger, R. T. (2010). Der Durchgang durch die gegenseitige neurotische Allergie in längeren Paarbeziehungen. *Zeitschrift für Psychodrama und Soziometrie, 9*(1), 83–92.

Krüger, R. T. (2012). Kreativität als Mittel der Heilung in der störungsspezifischen Einzeltherapie einer schwer depressiven Patientin. *Zeitschrift für Psychodrama und Soziometrie, 11*(2), 297–310.

Mentzos, S. (2011). *Lehrbuch der Psychodynamik. Die Funktion der Dysfunktionalität psychischer Störungen* (5th ed.). Vandenhoeck & Ruprecht.

Moreno, J. L. (1945). *Psychodrama and the psychopathology of inter-personal relations*. Beacon House.

Moreno, J. L. (1946/1985). *Psychodrama, Volume I*. Beacon, N. Y.: Beacon House. Seventh edition.

Moreno, J. L. (1959). *Gruppenpsychotherapie und Psychodrama. Einleitung in die Theorie und Praxis*. Thieme.

Moreno, J. L. (1974). *Die Grundlagen der Soziometrie. Wege zur Neuordnung der Gesellschaft* (3rd ed.). Westdeutscher Verlag.

Parin, P. (1977). Das Ich und die Anpassungsmechanismen. *Psyche – Zeitschrift für Psychoanalyse und ihre Anwendung, 35*, 481–515.

Plassmann, R. (1999). Körperpsychologie und Deutungstechnik – Die Praxis der Prozessdeutung. In W. Kämmerer (Ed.), *Körpersymptom und Psychotherapie. Der Umgang mit dem Symptom: Zur Spannung zwischen krankem Körper und Person*. VAS.

Reimer, C. (2007). Psychotherapeutischer Umgang mit suizidalen Patienten. In C. Reimer, J. Eckert, M. Hautzinger, & E. Wilke (Eds.). *Psychotherapie. Ein Lehrbuch für Ärzte und Psychologen* (3rd ed., pp. 595–609). Springer.

Rogers, C. R. (2009). *Eine Theorie der Psychotherapie*. Ernst Reinhardt.

Schacht, M. (1992). Zwischen Ordnung und Chaos. Neue Aspekte zur theoretischen und praktischen Fundierung der Konzeption von Spontaneität und Kreativität. *Psychodrama, 5*(1), 95–130.

Wilber, K. (2006). *Einfach »Das«. Tagebuch eines ereignisreichen Jahres* (3rd ed.). Fischer Taschenbuch Verlag.

Yablonsky, L. (1986). *Psychodrama. Die Lösung emotionaler Probleme durch das Rollenspiel*. Klett-Cotta.

Ziehm-Kossatz, H. (2013). 20-Minuten-Psychodrama in der allgemeinmedizinischen Sprechstunde. Das Doppeln in der psychotherapeutischen Beratung. *Zeitschrift für Psychodrama und Soziometrie, 12*(2), 263–267.

# Chapter 9
# Psychotic Disorders

The mentalization-oriented, disorder-specific psychodrama therapy helps *people experiencing psychosis*. However, it also expands *the psychotherapist's* experience and knowledge of fundamental questions, such as: How do people process conflicts? What is mentalizing? How does healing happen? What is therapeutic abstinence? What is creativity? What is resistance? What is the doppelganger technique? What is spontaneity? What does "meeting at eye level" between therapist and patient mean? The therapist enhances her flexibility and intuition when working with people with psychosis. She learns to ascribe positive meaning to what seems absurd and acts with the belief that *the patient's soul does nothing for free*. This skill is also helpful in the psychotherapy *of other* severe mental disorders: rigid defense patterns in personality disorders (see Sect. 4.8), suicidal fantasy (see Sect. 8.8), severe depression (see Sect. 8.6), anxiety and obsessive–compulsive disorders (see Sects. 9.6 and 9.7), non-substance-related addictions (see Chap. 10), or pathological deviant behavior (see Chap. 11).

## 9.1 The Historical Development of the Treatment of People with Psychosis

Psychiatrists use the term "psychosis" to refer to a *whole group* of severe mental disorders. The loss of touch with the reality of thought content is common in these disorders. The patient's thoughts and behaviors do not make sense in the context of their life history. The disorders contained in the term "psychosis" differ in their symptoms, cause, course, and need for therapy. The ICD-10 classifies them under the terms schizophrenia (F20), schizotypal disorder (F21), persistent delusional disorder (F22), acute transient psychotic disorders (F23), induced delusional disorder (F24), and schizoaffective disorders (F25). The disintegration of the systemic process of



R. T. Krüger, *Disorder-Specific Psychodrama Therapy in Theory and Practice*, Psychodrama in Counselling, Coaching and Education 4,
https://doi.org/10.1007/978-981-99-7508-2_9

self-development, illusionary misjudgments, and the resulting disturbances in relationships are common to this group of disorders. The psychiatric treatment of people with schizophrenia is more successful than is often assumed. Ciompi et al. (2010) proved that the dictum "once a schizophrenic, always a schizophrenic" is wrong. In a follow-up examination of almost 300 patients, a good quarter of them had gradually healed, and another quarter had improved significantly after an average of *36.7 years post their first hospital admission.* More than 20 other follow-up studies worldwide have substantiated this finding (Ciompi, 2019, p. 100).

Unlike any other disorder, inadequate knowledge and violence characterized the treatment history of people with psychosis in Europe until the nineteenth and twentieth centuries. Working with people with psychosis in Germany again reached a terrible climax in the murder of many patients during the National Socialist era. Psychiatry only developed into a *scientifically based* discipline in the nineteenth and twentieth centuries. The development of many effective medications and modern social psychiatry has made the treatment of patients with psychosis more humane and successful over the past 60 years.

**Central idea**

Humane psychiatric treatment methods are a social achievement that must be secured and defended against the basic human fear of the "crazy" *at all times*. People who fall outside the societal norms and *cannot* protect themselves adequately are easily marginalized and disadvantaged.

Despite the equally severe consequential damage, society spends less money on people with mental health concerns than on those with physical illness. In 1971, the nursing rates in the psychiatric hospitals of Niedersachsen in Germany were half those in a general hospital with the most basic facilities. Nevertheless, the country made a profit of 4.7 million German marks with its psychiatric clinics that year. On the other hand, *other* medical hospitals received substantial grants (Krüger, 1974, p. 19). Furthermore, only 12 of the 25 medical posts at the psychiatric state hospital in Wunstorf were occupied. Today, 50 medical posts exist for only half as many patients.

The 1970s marked the beginning of modern social psychiatry in Germany. The state downsized large psychiatric hospitals and built new *community-based* clinics. In addition to pure psychiatric treatment, the patients in the clinics received group therapy and occupational therapy. The nurses, social workers, and pedagogues received further training in social therapy. Some clinics applied the therapeutic community principles in some of their wards. In addition, there was also a rise in day clinics, dormitories, and assisted living for people with mental disorders.

Beginning in 1936, Jacob Levy Moreno developed psychodrama as a method of psychotherapy at a private hospital with 12 beds in Beacon, New York. Even then, the clinic functioned according to the therapeutic community principles. About 8 of the 12 patients were experiencing psychosis. Beginning in 1948, Manfred Bleuler, Gustav Bally, Medard Boss, and Marguerite Séchehaye, together with Gaetano Benedetti from Italy, Christian Müller, Martti Siirala from Finland, and Norman Elrod from the USA, developed "psychoanalytic psychotherapy for schizophrenia" in the Psychiatric University Clinic in Zurich (Red, 2018, p. 329 ff.). Benedetti's therapeutic approach is similar to that of Moreno. He lived with the patients wholeheartedly in their madness and, at the same time, maintained transmodal control over the therapeutic situation (Red, 2018, p. 336). Séchehaye rewrote her patient's delusional reality into a story of coping with the help of symbolic realization and wish fulfillment. This led "to changes in both the patient's and the analyst's life" (Red, 2018, p. 341). In Germany, there has been a working group for psychodynamically oriented psychotherapy for psychoses since 1975 (Nowack et al., 2018, p. 377). This group later became part of the German section of the "International Society for Psychological and Social Approaches to Psychosis" (ISPS).

Today, the most commonly used psychotherapy methods for psychoses are cognitive behavioral therapy (Lincoln & Heibach, 2017) and family therapy (Neraal, 2018a, 2018b, p. 29 ff. and 229 ff.). Since 2002, experts have increasingly recommended them in national guidelines in various countries. From 2014, health insurance companies will cover psychotherapy costs for patients with psychosis in Germany upon application. However, Lincoln and Heibach (2017, p. 2) state that the realization that one can treat symptoms such as delusions and hallucinations with psychotherapy has made little headway in psychotherapeutic practice. Many older psychotherapists do not have sufficient training for this. There are also false assumptions about the prerequisites for successful psychotherapy, for example, the idea that patients with schizophrenia have to have sufficient insight into the illness before starting treatment. The *psychotherapy* of people with psychoses still depends on the commitment of a few therapists on site. As a result, advances in the treatment of psychoses are repeatedly lost. The usual external organization of psychotherapies in Germany is often too rigid for the distinctive characteristics of patients with psychosis.

Psychotic disorders are expressions of *metacognitive disorders*. Therefore, the disorder-specific psychodrama therapy described in this book treats psychotic disorders *metacognitively*. The *two* qualitatively different processes of the patient's conflict processing—conflict processing in everyday life and conflict processing in delusion—are designed, differentiated, and executed *separately* in the as-if mode. The therapeutic conflict processing in a state of delusion is not centered on the *delusional content and insight into illness* but on the *change and expansion of the metacognitive process* with which the patient produces his delusional content. Moreno's psychodramatic methods and psychotherapy findings for psychosis (see Sects. 9.5 and 9.6) date back to 70 years ago. In the following text, I will demonstrate how they can also be used in today's therapy and develop them further.

## 9.2 Blockages in the Therapeutic Relationship in Psychiatric Treatment of Psychosis

In *conventional psychiatric treatment*, the therapist tries to make the patient's psychotic *symptoms* disappear, mainly with *psychotropic drugs*. However, a therapy process centered on drug treatment is "equivalent to an amputation" (Benedetti, 1983, p. 190). As soon as the ego of psychotic symptom production "is amputated, nothing remains but a defect, a shriveled ego that understands itself only insofar as it pays the high price of giving up any future-oriented possibility of growth."

Even in modern social psychiatry, the goal of therapy remains that the patients should accept their delusion *as an illness* and reduce their psychotic symptoms by taking the prescribed medication. They are supposed to learn *how to live*, structure their day, work, manage relationships, and spend their free time 'under the protection of the medication'. Ideally, their family and social environment will support them in doing so. Therapeutic communities in clinics, day clinics, leisure clubs, outpatient individual or group therapy, or assisted living are also helpful.

The fundamental problem in the treatment of patients with psychosis is that they *naturally* evoke disintegration-related countertransference (see Sect. 2.10) in their therapists. According to Hartwich (2018, p. 202), this is 'resistance by countertransference'. This countertransference leads to a block in the relationship between the patients and their therapists:

1. The patient tells the therapist about his problems. While listening, the therapist *internally* absorbs the patient's physical, psychic, and verbal information and tries to empathize with his internal conflict processing as an implicit doppelganger.
2. But at some point, the patient narrates bad influences, strange events, or harassment.
3. The therapist is confused and alienated by the patient's communication and feels afraid. Her emotion fixes her inner object image of the patient in the perception that 'he is crazy'. She unconsciously suppresses other actions of the patient and his suffering as a human being. Thus, she sticks to her biased perception. She asks skeptical questions and draws the patient's attention to contradictions in his descriptions.
4. The patient does not feel understood by the therapist and is irritated. As a result, he shuts himself off internally and distances himself. In this way, he acts out his existential dilemma in the therapeutic relationship between his desire for closeness and his refusal of intimacy (Mentzos, 2011, p. 223 ff.) due to his fear of disintegration. A vicious circle develops between the therapist's biased perception and the patient's distancing.
5. The *conventional psychiatric therapist* doesn't *use* her feelings of confusion and fear *psychotherapeutically*. She sticks to her biased inner object image 'he is crazy' and ascribes the label of "psychosis" to the patient. She inquires about the history *of his illness*: "Have you ever received psychiatric treatment? Do you take medication?" Then, she diagnostically records the patient's *psychotic symptoms*, classifies them using Bleuler's list of symptoms (1983), and documents them as

*psychopathological findings*: "The patient suffers from auditory hallucinations, derealization, depersonalization, and audible thoughts."
6. The patient feels that the therapist is not interested in his *actual suffering* and his fear of going insane *as a human being*. Or that the mafia is threatening him. Or that he will be poisoned. Or that his neighbors film him with a video camera. He is alone in his subjective suffering.
7. In this situation, he only has the choice between two evils: Either he sticks to his delusional experiences. However, this puts him in conflict with his social environment. Therefore, he withdraws from the therapeutic relationship and his other relationships. As a result, many people with psychosis become homeless. 15–30% of the homeless have psychosis. *Or* the patient blindly accepts the therapist's interpretations, adapts, and learns *the role of the patient*. As a "sick person", he takes the prescribed medication. He learns not to talk about his delusional experiences and trivializes them, even when interacting with the therapist.

**Central idea**

In a conventional psychiatric relationship, the patient is the ignorant one, and the therapist is the knowing one. The patient becomes the *object of treatment*. The therapist's authority blocks the therapeutic relationship. The therapist acts out a disintegration-related countertransference, a "countertransference resistance" (Hartwich, 2018, p. 202).

Modern social-psychiatric treatment of patients with psychosis is a significant advancement compared to the treatment eighty or a hundred years ago. At that time, therapists compensated their feelings of powerlessness and inadequacy toward their patients with psychosis with devaluation or grandiose feelings of helping or rescuing. They often used violent psychiatric treatment methods: insulin shocks, cold baths, or electroconvulsive therapies. Such therapeutic measures harmed not only the patients *but also the therapists themselves*. In 1941, for example, Boss (1979, quoted from Red, 2018, p. 339) examined 21 nocturnal dreams of 10 different shock therapists. In their dreams, they developed strong fear and intense feelings of guilt. The shock therapists suffered from "a threat to *their own* mental structure and the psychological imbalance caused by electroconvulsive applications".

Due to the therapist's *natural* disintegration-related countertransference, psychiatric clinics often tend to return to the mechanisms of the old institutional psychiatry even today. "The dynamics of acute psychotic disorder and the institutional behavior are mutually dependent and become a form of institutional defense" (Putzke, 2018, p. 300). The therapists unconsciously take over healthy adult thinking on behalf of the patients. In their desperation, they focus purely on pharmacological treatment, and otherwise only manage the patient's symptoms.

## 9.3 Mentalization Disorders as the Cause of Delusional Production

As a psychodramatist, I define mentalizing as the *creative inner process work* with which humans remember, with which they create an image of themselves and others in the current situation, control external actions, plan behaviors, and process conflicts. Humans use four tools for this purpose (see Fig. 2.3 in Sect. 2.2): representing, interacting, rehearsing, and integrating (see Sect. 2.2).

**Exercise 23**

Explore mentalizing for yourself. Please think about a relationship conflict of your own for 1–2 min. *What* did you think about? *How* did you think about it? Which metacognitive tools of mentalizing did you use? You will notice:

1. You *represented* the conflict in your imagination as an image,
2. You reconstructed memories internally and *interacted* with the conflict partner,
3. You may also have looked for a new way of behaving to resolve the conflict. This process is called *mental rehearsing.*
4. You may have even connected your conflict with other conflicts "I experience the same in relationships, as in my childhood." This process is referred to as *inner integrating.*

*Defense* is a protection against the disintegration of the self and needs a certain ego strength. If a person has insufficient ego strength when experiencing a high-energy affect, they experience a breakdown in the inner process of self-development. *The self* is a constant creative process of development. This process includes the development of the *inner* self-image and the *inner* object image in the current situation. The process of self-development is mediated through mentalizing.

**Central idea**

In psychotic decompensation, the patient loses ego control over his process of self-development. This disintegration is triggered by a high-energy affect that overwhelms the patient's processing system. The patient experiences dissociation in his psychosomatic resonance patterns (see Sect. 2.7). There is a split between the patient's cognitive ego (thoughts and linguistic concepts) and the psychosomatic ego (sensorimotor interaction patterns, physical sensations, affect) (see Fig. 2.4 in Sect. 2.2). The patient experiences a nameless horror and cannot find the appropriate words and thoughts. The disintegration of the systemic process of the self draws the tools of mentalization into the vortex of dissolution. As a result, the tools of mentalizing only work as *mechanisms of dream work* in emergency mode (Krüger, 1978, see Fig. 2.5 in Sect. 2.3) and produce delusional content.

There is a *metacognitive confusion* between the patient's delusional thinking shaped by the dream mode and their everyday thinking.

1. The tool of inner *representing* becomes the dream mechanism of '*perceiving inner thoughts as external reality*' (Freud, 1975, p. 177). Thus, patients with psychosis mix the *inner and outer* worlds in their delusional reality. Panic turns into paranoia (see case example 95 in Sect. 9.8.8). The feeling of losing control

over one's own life turns into the imagination: A thief has burgled my home. Desires become delusions of grandeur (see case example 86 in Sect. 9.7).
2. The tool of *interacting* becomes the dream mechanism of '*shifting*': The logic of the chronological interaction sequences in conflict processing is disintegrated. It keeps changing to match the high-energy affect. When interacting internally, the patient forgets interaction sequences and experiences that relieve feelings of guilt. In the case of delusions of grandeur, he ignores limiting factors. According to Freud (1966, p. 177), an element is "replaced by something remote, that is to say, the emotional emphasis is moved from an important element to an unimportant element, and the strange dream appears". Thus, the high-energy affect is moved to other inner images.
3. The inner *mental rehearsal* becomes the dream mechanism of '*reversal into the opposite*': "In the nocturnal dream, the rabbit often enough shoots the hunter" (Freud, 1966, p. 183). The relationship between inner self-images and inner object images disintegrates. The self-images and object images move freely in space and rearrange themselves into delusional relationship patterns. The self-deprecation (self-image) turns into the voices of neighbors (object image) talking about the patient (see case example 96 in Sect. 9.8.8). The desire for help and salvation from another person or God (object image) turns into the delusion (self-image) of "I am Jesus."
4. The tool of inner *integrating* becomes the dream mechanism of '*consolidation*'. This merges two inner images, that have something in common, into one (Freud, 1966, S. 174). For example, the patient wants to disrupt the petty-bourgeois thinking in his family. This wishful thinking merges with his image of TV stars who can do it. The patient then torments the family and therapist with his delusion that "soon he is "going to be the greatest entertainer in the world" (see case example 86 in Sect. 9.7).

*Even healthy people* can think, feel, and act in dream mode. However, they control their symbolizing in dream mode through mentalizing in the *as-if mode* (see Sect. 2. 6). They *know* that their absurd fantasies are *only inner fantasies* and do not reflect the outside world's reality. Modern artists like Joseph Beuys, the composers of contemporary music, storytellers, some writers, and many theater directors could and can allow the dream mode of mentalizing *in the service of their ego* (Balint, 1970, p. 187 f.), thereby making them *particularly creative.*

Recent research suggests that *everyone* who *dreams at night* thinks, feels, and acts in the dream mode to process conflict. In dreaming, people integrate memories from everyday life with their previous experiences and memories stored in their brain. Dreamwork also expands the memory content *alogically,* leading to the freedom of thought necessary to create new solutions. Experiments show (Robert Stickgold and Erin Wamsley, quoted in "Die Zeit" No. 32, p. 27, August 4, 2011) "that dreams not only strengthen memories but can also offer varied new insights. As the brain replays the day's experiences, it looks for new solutions. At night we reenact what we experienced during the day. However, few dreams are true replicas of waking experiences. Instead, most pick up memory fragments and combine them into new, often bizarre images to create nocturnal mental cinema. But why? [...] The researchers' experiments are now pointing in a clear direction—the nocturnal mental cinema makes us fit for reality."

**Central idea**

In the case of patients experiencing psychosis, the deficits in their mentalizing ability and the disintegration of the systemic process of self-development are *indirectly* reflected in their reduced ability to act in the *as-if mode of play* (see Sect. 2.6).

When *people with psychosis* enact a fairy tale in group therapy, they usually stop after 5–10 min. They enact the contents of the fairy tale concretely and try to do everything right. *People with neurosis* or psychologically healthy people, on the other hand, spontaneously activate *their own inner conflicting relationship images* through their actions in the fairy tale play. These patterns become a part of their fairy tale, analogous or compensatory, and differentiate and expand their actions in the play. As a result, their enactment of a fairy tale usually lasts 45–90 min. It is fitting, that patients with psychosis often do not understand jokes or depth-psychological interpretations because of the deficits in their mentalization. They perceive symbolic images and metaphors in the equivalence mode as a *concrete* description of external reality. For example, healthy people often use the metaphor "I'm not here anymore" when they feel exhausted. People with psychosis, on the other hand, believe that they no longer exist *in reality* when feeling exhausted (see case example 82 below and continuation in Sect. 9.9).

Delusional patients secure their internal delusional construction by *thinking in the equivalence mode* (see Sect. 2.6). They do not differentiate between their *internal symbolic image of the conflict* and *the external reality. Patients* thinking in the equivalence mode assume that their *inner* construction of reality adequately reflects the *outer reality*. Thus, as Fonagy, Gergely, Jurist, and Target (2004, pp. 96ff.) say, "they confuse internal states (such as thoughts, fantasies, and feelings) with external reality and experience it *as reality* rather than as mere *internal representations of reality*."

***Case example 82***

*As an officer on his ship, Mr. B. discovered that he was missing 100 marks in his cupboard. He suspected someone from the ship's crew had stolen his money. But at the same time, he was afraid of wrongly accusing someone. This dilemma caused him to panic. His mentalizing disintegrated. He feared being debarred from his crew if he made a false accusation. He was thinking in the equivalence mode, believing that the ship's crew members wanted to get rid of him. He jumped off the ship into the sea in the middle of the English Channel between France and England as a reaction to the suspected exclusion from the community. Luckily he was seen by a sailor. The crew rescued him and took him to a psychiatric hospital in the nearest port (continued in* Sect. 9.9*).*

Similar to the nocturnal dream images, the contents of a patient's delusion are often a *symbolic* image of the patient's existential need in the conflict that triggered it: (1) The patient feels, for example, that his mother restraints and abuses him. But *he thinks in equivalence mode.* Therefore, he experiences this internal feeling as an external reality and believes that his mother is *actually* poisoning him. (2) Another patient believes he is the real Jesus in the equivalence mode. He does not understand his thoughts *as a symbolic image* for his feeling in his current living environment: "*Like Jesus*, I make others' suffering my own and perish because of it." (3) People with psychosis *lose* control of their internal conflict processing and believe that their *social environment* controls their lives, watches them, and eavesdrops on them. (4) A 35-year-old patient (see case example 96 in Sect. 9.8.8) felt inferior because she hadn't gone to college and "didn't manage her life the way others do." In her delusion, she experienced her feelings of inferiority in the form of external voices of *"neighbors" who spoke negatively about her.*

## 9.4 The Psychodynamics of Psychotic Decompensation

There are *genetic and environmental* factors involved in the occurrence of psychosis. Twin research shows that if one parent experiences psychosis, there is a twenty percent chance that *one of their children* will also experience psychosis (Mentzos, 1999, only oral communication). However, the occurrence of a psychotic disorder *also depends on environmental factors*. Under advantageous circumstances, children of parents with psychosis can develop unique talents instead of becoming ill. This finding was possible with the help of Finland's highly differentiated population statistics. There are a hundred children of parents with psychosis who are *identical twins* and were each *adopted by different families*. If the relationships in the new families were *stable and flexible*, the children developed sufficient inner ego strength and unique talents.

About one percent of people *in all countries and societies on Earth* experience psychotic disorders. Therefore, unfavorable social and family conditions cannot solely explain the risk of developing psychosis. In the course of evolution, man has had to cultivate special cognitive abilities to survive and spread out all over the world. This ability is so complex that the mentalization of sensitive people with deficits or childhood trauma *worldwide* can implode in conflicts in adulthood. However, the risk of psychotic decompensation has not blocked the evolution of mentalization in humans. The advantage of saving energy by processing conflicts in the as-if mode was too great.

The decompensation into psychosis can be explained as follows: People with psychosis react more *sensitively* to stress and conflicts than other people (Zubin & Spring, 1977): "People at risk of psychosis often have a history of emotionally difficult experiences such as sexual trauma, neglect, or serious discontinuities" (Ciompi, 2019, p. 105). They have developed rigid defensive patterns due to childhood deficits or traumatic experiences. It is, therefore, difficult for them to withstand conflicts and psychological stress. For example, they adapt to the family system (see case example 87 in Sect. 9.8.1) and take on the role assigned to them by others. Such self-protective behavior spares them the intrapsychic conflict between their *systemic role* in the family and their *inner self* in conflict situations (see Sect. 2.4.4). In doing so, however, they do *not* learn to process internal and external conflicts *adequately*. Psychotic decompensations are then triggered by traumatic crises, physical illnesses, or challenging situations in life, for example, the first romantic relationship. The old, functional role that provides support is lost. The old defense system collapses. The loss of a *negative* identity can also trigger decompensation, for example, the loss of the eccentric role or the role of the 'difficult child' (Mentzos, 2011, p. 206). People with psychosis decompensate when their emotional stress exceeds a critical level in an identity conflict (Ciompi, 2019, p. 104). Drug abuse or retraumatizing situations are often involved in the breakdown.

Neraal (2018a, 2018b, pp. 29 and 38) suggests a *significant relationship dynamic* in the context of psychotic symptoms: "The person with psychosis represents the *family's* 'overflowing vessel of emotions, so to speak." The psychotic thought content is often symbolic images of *conflicts* hidden *in the family or by society*. The example of Greta Thunberg's family helps us understand the significance of a relationship dynamic in severe psychological symptoms. Greta Thunberg didn't experience psychosis. But she was autistic and severely anorexic for two years, from the age of 12–14. Thus, she acted out the meaninglessness of her own life in the face of the climate crisis and unconsciously protested from the omega position against the high energy consumption in her family's lifestyle: Her mother is a world-famous opera singer. As a result, the family lived alternately in Japan for a few months, then again in New York or Paris in the past. At one point, they *sought family therapy*. As a result, the family members learned to take Greta's feelings and fears seriously and listened to her. Greta Thunberg is a sensitive person with Asperger Syndrome. She heard about climate change and let it impact her emotionally and existentially. However, due to her mental strength, she developed a *transpersonal conscience* during therapy *instead of* experiencing psychosis.

Anyone with a *childlike conscience* is afraid of punishment from their parents. Those with a *community conscience* are afraid of being excluded from the community. But a person with a *transpersonal conscience* follows the greater truth (Dürckheim, 1976, p. 110) and protests against the community's norms when necessary, even if it means breaking the law and being penalized. Greta Thunberg drew new strength from her transpersonal conscience. For the first time at 16, she demonstrated, *against her parents' will*, in front of the Swedish parliament in Stockholm against the inaction of politicians concerning the climate crisis. The family members continued to listen to Greta. They integrated Greta's fears into their *own* lives *as a complementary truth*. Her father now lives a vegan life. As an opera singer, her mother only accepts invitations to places she can reach by train. With her inner mental change, Greta Thunberg gave *a positive meaning* to her *denial* of the world, expressed through her symptoms. She became a role model for hundreds of thousands of people.

In social relationships of people with psychosis, Mentzos (1992, p. 10 f.) observed "pronounced dramatic escalations of the clash of opposing intrapsychic tendencies [...] in people with schizophrenia, for example, the bipolarity between the *self-related* and the *object-related* [...] tendencies. The resulting [...] conflict only allows for two [...] 'solutions': extreme narcissistic withdrawal or the dissolution of ego boundaries and the fusion with the object. Affective psychoses [...] are characterized by the bipolarity of (normally by no means mutually exclusive) self-worth and object worth. Even here, there are only two possible [...] 'solutions' to the resulting frozen conflict: absolute domination of the archaic, [...] overpowering superego (depression) or the superego being 'thrown overboard', i.e., the dominance of grandiose self (mania)." The dilemmas described by Mentzos reflect the *existential quality* of the inner conflicts of a patient experiencing psychosis. It is a matter of existence/non-existence, being/not being oneself, or dignity/indignation.

In people who decompensate into *psychosis,* the process of self-development disintegrates due to excessive emotional tensions (see Sect. 9.3). Thus, the tools of mentalizing work as mechanisms of dream work in emergency mode. The process qualities (Plassmann, 1999) of space, time, logic, and sense (see Fig. 2.5 in Sect. 2.3) dissolve in the internal construction of reality. In Moreno's words (1939, p. 4f.), "a break-up and distortion of the tele-relations (internal images, added by the author) take place, a breaking up of the auto-tele (relation to oneself, added by the author). The sense of time and space may also become blurred." In response, the self constructs the *auxiliary reality* of delusion to stabilize the systemic process of self-development.

"What we consider as disease production is, in reality, the attempt at healing, the reconstruction" (Freud, 1910, quoted in Hartwich, 2018, p. 180) and Grube (2018, p. 167 f.) speak of hallucinations as "paralogical constructions". They are "to be interpreted as counter-regulation patterns to disintegration, ego threat, and risk of decompensation". As early as 1847, Ideler (quoted from Hartwich, 2018, p. 180) understood delusion as "hard work on the reorganization of consciousness". Scharfetter (1986, only *as being quoted* in Hartwich, 2018, p. 180) understood delusion as an "autotherapeutic endeavor". In 1992, Benedetti also recognized delusions as "attempts at recompensation and reconstruction".

But the inner auxiliary reality of delusion is *not positively confirmed* in everyday life. The patient notices it and develops an *existential fear of becoming* insane. The relationship partners distance themselves from the patient's perception of reality. The patient is existentially afraid of being excluded from the community. The secondary existential fears *traumatize* his soul. He *cannot flee* from his voices or the "persecutors" or *fight* them. A traumatizing situation (see Sect. 5.2) causes tremendous stress to the human brain. Old neural connections dissolve. The processes of conflict management disintegrate even more. As a result, the inner conflict processing repeatedly produces new bizarre inner auxiliary realities—the delusional content. A vicious circle develops between (1) the production of delusions, (2) the lack of positive confirmation of the delusional reality from outside, (3) the existential fear of becoming insane and/or being excluded from the community, and (4) the disintegration of mentalizing.

Imaging procedures can demonstrate the neurophysiological consequences of decompensation into psychosis as *dysfunction of the brain structures relevant to the working memory* (Frith, 1992; Goldman-Rakic, 1994). For example, in examining patients after the first appearance of schizophrenia, Schneider, Habel, Reske, Kellerman et al. (2007) found: *The less* the working memory structures were activated in patients with psychosis, *the more* their illness deteriorated in the following year.

Despite their delusion, many people experiencing psychosis want to continue functioning in their everyday lives and try to cope with their tasks. They act as if nothing is wrong and separate their delusional life from their daily experience. They develop a *secondary defense by splitting the* self into an "everyday ego" and a "dream ego" (see Sect. 9.8.1). The patients can still meet many of their everyday needs as healthy adults. However, their ego is trapped in the production of delusional content.

In the event of an *unfavorable development*, the disintegration of the process of self-development and the psychosomatic resonance patterns in the brain's memory centers continues to spread. Patients cannot adequately process their high-energy affect. In this way, patients develop chronic schizophrenia from *acute* psychosis. However, people with acute psychosis are *seemingly less likely to develop* chronic schizophrenia with intensive and adequate psychotherapy (Aaltonen et al., 2011, p. 179). In psychotherapy, the patient's problems in conflict processing are taken seriously. This experience equalizes their narcissistic deficits and stabilizes their soul. They possibly develop a new identity.

In the early 1940s and 1950s, Moreno (1939, p. 3 ff.) described the psychodynamic processes involved in psychotic decompensation as follows: "In the case of a hallucinatory psychosis … a break-up and distortion of the tele-relation take place, a breaking up of the auto-tele…The sense of time and space may also become blurred…As the psychological organization of time and space are disorganized, the spontaneity states, instead of following one another in rapid frequency, producing the sense of time with the dimensions of a past and future, flow freely into space since there is no barrier to prohibit this." Sigmund Freud (Freud, 1917, p. 423, only quoted from Böker, 1992, p. 146) understood the processes involved in psychotic decompensation similarly: "The ego reacts to an unbearable loss by denying it with the psychotic symptoms: the ego breaks off the relationship with reality, it withdraws the cathexis from the system […] and disintegrates."

## 9.5 Moreno's Secret in the Psychotherapy of Psychoses

In 1936, Moreno founded a 12-bed sanatorium in Beacon, New York. Eight of these beds were usually occupied by people with psychosis. There were no neuroleptics for treating psychoses in the 1930s and 1940s. So Moreno had to develop *psychotherapeutic* approaches if the symptoms of his patients with psychosis were to improve. In the therapy of his patients, Moreno used his experiences from the treatment of an actress in his improvisational theater from 1921 (see case example 15 in Sect. 2.6). He summarized this experience in the sentence: "Every true second time is a liberation from the first" (Moreno, 1970, p. 77). Moreno concluded from these experiences: The patients had to gain ego control over their deviant thinking and feeling through *acting* in the as-if mode of play (see Sect. 2.6). Thus, they learn to distance themselves from their dysfunctional thinking and feeling and modify or stop it.

Moreno's clinic functioned based on the therapeutic community principles (Straub, 2002, only oral communicated). For example, the therapists ate their meals *together* with the patients. They also accompanied them to the hairdresser. Moreno arranged for his patients to enact their delusions in *role-plays*. He had auxiliary therapists take on complementary roles in the patient's delusional system. The auxiliary therapists acted out the delusion with the patients. As a result, the patient's symptoms improved. This experience fascinated Moreno so much that he asked to have his tombstone written before his death: "Here lies the one who brought laughter to psychiatry." Moreno (1939, p. 5 f.; 1945a, p. 3 ff.) called the form of *psychodramatic individual therapy* he developed for people with psychosis "the auxiliary world method". In the following case example, Moreno & Moreno (1975a, p. 193 ff.) treated a man with psychosis who believed he was Adolf Hitler *at the beginning of the Second World War in 1939*. The patient had emigrated from Germany to the USA.

***Case example 83***
*The patient came to Moreno for a consultation. He had a trimmed mustache on his upper lip. Moreno asked him his name. Then the man got angry: "Don't you know who I am?" Moreno was startled. But then he remembered: the patient's wife had called him on the phone and said that her husband believed he was Adolf Hitler. Moreno promptly touched upon the patient's delusion: "Of course, now I recognize you, Mr Hitler!" In response to Moreno's accepting attitude, the patient complained that the man in Germany who called himself Hitler was taking everything from him. "He took my name... he took everything I have, my inspiration, my brainpower, my energy. This other man also claims to have written the book 'Mein Kampf'. I wrote 'Mein Kampf'." Moreno picked up the phone and called two nurses. When they arrived, he introduced them to the patient as "Mr. Goering" and "Mr. Goebbels." The patient had actually come at an inappropriate time. Moreno was about to speak to his students in a lecture hall. He, therefore, seized the opportunity and informed those present: "Mr. Hitler wishes to make an announcement to his people." The patient promptly followed the request.*

*In this case report, Moreno describes how he treated the patient in individual therapy for three months. The two nurses who played Goering and Goebbels maintained their doppelganger roles in their everyday interactions with the patient. They also interacted with him in the as-if mode of play. They didn't reverse roles with him. There was also no debriefing of the psychodramatic play. Initially, the patient "Hitler" behaved aloof towards his "comrades," but then he began to become more familiar: "During an intermission of one session, he said to Goering: 'Hello Goering, what do you think of the joke I made on stage today?', and they laughed together. But suddenly, Hitler swatted Goering. Goering responded similarly, and a regular fistfight took place on the spot, during which Hitler took a bad beating. Later they enjoyed a glass of beer together. From then on, the ice between them gradually began to melt." The patient slowly changed as a result of the treatment. Finally, he shaved off his mustache and, at the same time, began to cry bitterly. Later, he also requested that people call him Karl and no longer Adolf. The patient, a master butcher, could reintegrate well socially after the treatment. He returned to Germany a few years later.*

During my training as a psychodrama therapist, I read various case examples of Moreno's therapy of people with psychosis (Moreno, 1939, 1945a, 1959, pp. 253–317; Moreno, 1975a, pp. 191–206). I found the descriptions fascinating. But I didn't want to pretend to my patients at first that I shared their delusional reality and then distance myself from their psychotic experience. I didn't want to lie to them. I would have been helpless if they had asked me if I believed their delusional reality.

**Central idea**

Today I know: It counts as therapeutic *malpractice* to tell patients, directly or indirectly, *after a joint psychodramatic enactment* of their delusion, that their delusions do *not* correspond to reality. This disrupts *the stabilization* of the patient's inner process of self-development in the as-if mode of play (see Sect. 9.6). The patient feels even more alone than before the enactment. The high-energy affect that led to their decompensation into psychosis is actualized, thereby aggravating the patient's symptoms, because their stabilizing auxiliary reality has been called into question (see Sect. 9.4).

***Case example 84* (Bender & Stadler, 2012, *p. 89*)**
*A patient recently admitted to the clinic talked about his paranoia in group therapy and partially enacted it psychodramatically. In the debriefing, the group "expressed, with shock and tact, that the story actually sounds fantastic and improbable." None of the therapists in this situation supported the protagonist's experience of reality as a doppelganger. They didn't follow the basic principle "Be with your protagonist" (Dean Eleftery, 1973, verbal communication). The group members wanted to help the patient improve his insight into the illness through their feedback. However, their distancing from the patient's reality experience intensified his psychotic symptoms. The patient "fled from the clinic that same evening [...]. Two days later, he was found drenched in the rain and brought back by the police in an agitated and confused state."*

## 9.6 Moreno's Metacognitive Approach in the Psychotherapy of Psychoses

**Central idea**

Many therapists focus their work on changing the *inappropriate thought content* in the delusion of patients experiencing psychosis. They address the *cognitions*. *Metacognitively oriented* therapists try to free the patient's creative inner process, which *produces* their *inappropriate thought content*, from its blockage and halt the whirlpool of disintegration of the systemic process of self-development.

Like most psychodrama therapists, I did not dare to use Moreno's auxiliary world method in the treatment of my patients for many years. An experienced psychiatrist and trainer in psychodrama (Wolfgang Gerstenberg, 1974, verbal communication) once told me: "I tried it, but it did not help my patients. Moreno could do that because he was a special person. That is not me. That's why I don't need to be able to do that either." But in his psychodramatic approach, Gerstenberg empathically followed the fleeting psychotic *thoughts* of his patients with frequent psychodramatic scene changes. He did *not* work *metacognitively*. He did not treat the everyday conflict processing *and* the conflict processing in delusional conflicts *separate from each other*. He did not try to construct *individual delusional scenes* together with the patient and transform them into a story of coping (see case examples 85 in Sect. 9.6, 88 in Sect. 9.8.1, and 96 in Sect. 9.8.8).

**Central idea**

The ability to provide psychodrama therapy to people experiencing psychosis does *not* depend *only* on the therapist's personality. In my opinion, Moreno did *not fully describe* his *practical approach* in his case examples 70 years ago. Therefore, one *cannot successfully imitate* his approach as a therapist. The description of the doppelganger's dialogue is missing (see case examples 85 in Sect. 9.6 and 86 in Sect. 9.7).

Moreno's disorder-specific approach in the psychotherapy of psychoses contradicts contemporary *psychiatric* thought. *Not every* psychodrama therapist is so spontaneous and self-assured that he can and wants to flexibly accompany his patients *in their delusional world*. *Psychodynamic psychotherapists* have the same problem in working with people with psychoses. Psychoanalysts also make little use of the practical disorder-specific approach of Benedetti and Séchehaye today.

As a psychodrama therapist, I initially limited my work to treating my patients "only" from a *social-psychiatric* perspective. I used *practice role-play* in group therapy (see Sect. 9.12), and the patients made progress. Many of them stabilized mentally, socially, and in their family lives. What irritated me, however, was the poor sustainability of the therapy. The accompanying pharmacological treatment made the psychotic symptoms of the patients disappear. However, after stopping the neuroleptics, the symptoms usually returned after 4–8 weeks, sometimes even after three days.

It wasn't until 1998 that I understood Moreno's 'auxiliary world' method in the therapy of people with psychosis. It was a creative leap in my therapeutic approach to the experience of people with psychosis and Moreno's theory of 'spontaneity'. At that time, I met with some psychodramatists from the German Professional Association for Psychodrama (DFP) in a working group on "Psychodrama in Therapy for Psychosis". We exchanged our experiences and experimented. For the first time, we recognized how Moreno proceeded *practically* in the psychotherapy of patients with psychosis and why his disorder-specific approach has a *healing* effect. The new insight came when we role-played a report by Schindler (1996, p. 9).

**Exercise 24**

Try to reenact the following case example in small steps together with a colleague in a role play. Then you will understand the secret to healing psychosis *psychosomatically*.

***Case example 85***

*In the early 1950s, Moreno came to the University Psychiatric Clinic in Vienna to demonstrate his therapy method in practice. He had been asked if he wanted to speak to the patient beforehand. Moreno renounced it. The clinicians then selected a patient with a depressive stupor for the demonstration. As a result of her severe mental illness, this woman "did not respond to the doctors' questions. She was mentally absent and lost." Schindler reports: When the patient was led into the lecture hall, she "stopped after a few steps. But then Moreno approached her, greeted her loudly, and took her hand. Then he stood next to her and explained that the doctors in the auditorium were like students. And that they should learn about her situation from her perspective [...]" (continued below).*

**Central idea**

In the therapeutic conversation with the patient, Moreno shifted from the usual face-to-face position to the shoulder-to-shoulder position. I imagine he grabbed her left hand with his right hand, stood at her side, and turned his gaze, *together with her*, toward the auditorium. Together, they looked at the doctors sitting in rows in the lecture hall. The audience probably looked at the two expectantly. Moreno then explained the situation *to the patient* shoulder to shoulder. *As her metacognitive doppelganger,* he verbalized what he perceived in the identification with her. He thus activated and structured the mute patient's inner thinking. Schindler further reports:

***Case example 85 (continued)***

*Moreno asked her name almost casually. To our amazement, she told him her name without any inhibitions. Moreno repeated the name slowly and found it was nice. He made an association that I've now forgotten, which didn't fit either. The patient corrected him, and he immediately accepted her perspective and offered an extension. This is how a thoroughly trivial conversation developed between the two, emphasizing the importance, supported by an expression of personal interest and without any objective justification. The patient's stupor seemed to have fallen off, and a conversation about their life situation developed. Moreno rarely asked any questions. He offered her his ideas and let her guide him through corrections. So the patient was actually helping him. She imagined some family members who wanted to withdraw. Moreno wouldn't tolerate that.*

We then practiced applying Moreno's practical approach to *our own patients'* treatment through role-plays in our working group. One of us played the role of our own patient, and another tried being a therapist. Like Moreno, we stood *shoulder to shoulder next to the "patient"*. As doppelgangers, we tried together with the "patient" to playfully participate in her *internal production* of delusion and actively develop it beyond reality. In the therapeutic relationship, we had to think, feel and act *transmodally in the equivalence mode*, as if the patient's delusions were reality (see Sect. 9.7). I call this method "Doppelganger Dialogue" (Krüger, 2001a, p. 257 ff., see Sects. 9.8.2–9.8.5). Moreno (1959, p. 85) once described the *doppelganger method* in his poetic language with the words: Due to psychosis, the patient is "in such a mental state that communication is challenging, and neither the doctor nor the nurse can establish contact with her. [...] But if she could talk to herself, to the person closest to her and who knows her best, she would have someone to form a connection with. In order to enable her to do this, we reproduce her 'doppelganger' for her on stage, with whom she can identify most easily and with whom she can talk and act together. That is the purpose of the doppelganger method in psychodrama." Moreno's definition seems like he was thinking of this patient with a stupor in the Vienna University Clinic.

## 9.7 The Transmodal Relationship with Patients Experiencing Psychosis

Schindler's report (see case example 85 in Sect. 9.6) *fills a gap in Moreno's description* of his practical approach to the therapy of people with psychosis. Moreno understood the psychotic symptoms of his patients as an invitation to *encounter*. Plassmann (2019, S. 55ff.) calls such an offer the "present moment". The patient acts out a dysfunctional thought and behavior and, thus, *unconsciously asks* the therapist for help to resolve this dysfunctionality. The encounter with patients suffering from psychoses fails by definition. If the encounter is to be successful, the therapist has to enter the patient's delusional world as a metacognitive doppelganger (Moreno & Moreno, 1975a, p. 193 ff.). In case example 83 (see Sect. 9.5), Moreno called two nurses and introduced them to the patient "Hitler" as "Mr. Goering" and "Mr. Göbbels". I suspect that, *as a doppelganger*, Moreno immediately turned to the two nurses and addressed them: "Mr. Goering, we're waiting for you! Why are you so late?—Ah, yes, Mr. Göbbels, nice to have you here! I hope you bring good news to Mr. Hitler!" The two nurses immediately accepted this role assignment as trained auxiliary egos *without asking* any questions and went transmodally into the delusional reality of the patient "Hitler". Therefore, the patient had no choice. He had to get wholly involved *in his own delusional reality*, taken over by Moreno, and act as "Hitler". Otherwise, he would have betrayed his *own* delusional reality.

**Central idea**

The *doppelganger dialogue* (see Sects. 9.8.2–9.8.5) is the basis of the disorder-specific psychodrama therapy of people with psychosis. Through doppelganger dialogue, the therapist helps the patient to gain ego control over the work of his mentalizing tools. As a metacognitive doppelganger, the therapist actively affirms the *positive stabilizing function* of the patient's delusional production in the holistic process of his inner systemic self-regulation (see Sect. 9.8.5).

The therapist steps *shoulder to shoulder* with the patient *transmodally* into the patient's delusional scene and actively shapes it.

***Case example 86* (Krüger, 2001b, *p. 49 f., changed*)**

*A 40-year-old patient, Mr. A., had been in outpatient psychiatric-psychotherapeutic treatment since the onset of his illness eleven years ago. During this time, he decompensated into acute psychosis and was hospitalized seven times. In eleven years, he spent a total of 350 days in hospitals. He was forcibly admitted six times. He had graduated from high school, was a skilled craftsman, and was on early retirement for five years. He had had a legal guardian for six years to manage his financial affairs. Mr. A. was overweight and diabetic and consumed a lot of alcohol when ill.*

*In January 2000, the patient's father came to see the therapist and reported: "My son has changed again. He has spent 1,000 marks in the last three days." The therapist telephoned the patient and asked if he could come and talk to him. Mr. A. answers the phone and replies cheerfully: "I can swing by sometime." The therapist is treating another patient when a staff member calls him out into the hallway to see Mr. A. Meanwhile, Mr. A. is standing there, comfortably resting his arm on the counter, and greets the doctor in a friendly and cheerful manner: "Hello, Mr. Krüger!" Therapist: "Hello, Mr. A. Nice that you have come!" Mr. A.: "Yes, it's good to meet you again!" Therapist: "Yes, your father is worried!" Mr. A.: "Oh! the old man, he's being stingy with the money again!" The therapist does not admonish the patient that he must also understand his father. Instead, as a doppelganger, he enters the patient's delusional world and shapes his delusional reality with the doppelganger dialogue: "You seem to be fine!" Mr. A.: "Yes, no reason to complain!" Therapist: "So it's starting now, yes?" Mr. A.: "Yes, because I am chosen!" Therapist: "Oh, you are going to be great!" Mr. A. teasingly: "Yes, I am about to become the greatest entertainer in the world!" Therapist: "You will come on TV." Mr. A.: "Yes, it is only a matter of time. They chose me." Therapist: "It's like winning the lottery! You received a letter confirming that." Mr. A.: "Yes, it's going to start soon!" Therapist: "And when you watch the news on TV, the newsreader has already announced: 'Arthur A. is the new entertainer for TV! It's still unclear who Arthur A. is, but it'll start soon!'" Mr. A.: "They're eavesdropping at the moment!" The therapist: "The TV people!" Mr. A. laughs cheerfully and underlines his statement with a hand gesture: "No, all people in the world." Therapist: "And then you will be free of all your worries! You have money! You are the greatest entertainer in the world! You make music and jokes, and you make people laugh!" Mr. A. somewhat arrogantly: "No more problems, Mr. Krüger." He adds hesitantly: "I just have to be careful not to slip and become sick!".*

*At this point, the patient unexpectedly shifts from the equivalence mode to the as-if mode in thinking about his identity as the world's greatest entertainer and recalls his earlier decompensation into psychosis. The therapist follows this change immediately without commenting on it. He thinks, feels, and acts "normally" as a psychiatrist: "Shall I give you an injection?—I can do that." Mr. A.: "Well, maybe that's better!" Therapist: "Okay, come with me!" Mr. A. accompanies the therapist into the examination room and gets injected with a depot neuroleptic. He doesn't pay attention to the dosage. The therapist and the patient schedule another appointment to see how the depot injection works and whether he experiences any side effects.*

In the doppelganger dialogue, the therapist and the patient internally *represented* the delusion scene between the patient and his future employer as if writing a film script. They *interacted* with his interaction partners and developed his delusion into a holistic story of coping through *mental rehearsal*. However, a story of coping with a delusion is always absurd by definition. Thus, the patient psychosomatically felt the absurdity of his coping story. He noticed that his identity as the world's greatest entertainer is only *an inner representation* and probably cannot be realized in the external reality (see Sect. 2.6). In doing so, he thought of his desire in the as-if mode and no longer in the equivalence mode. Thus, he developed an insight into his illness (see Sect. 9.8.5).

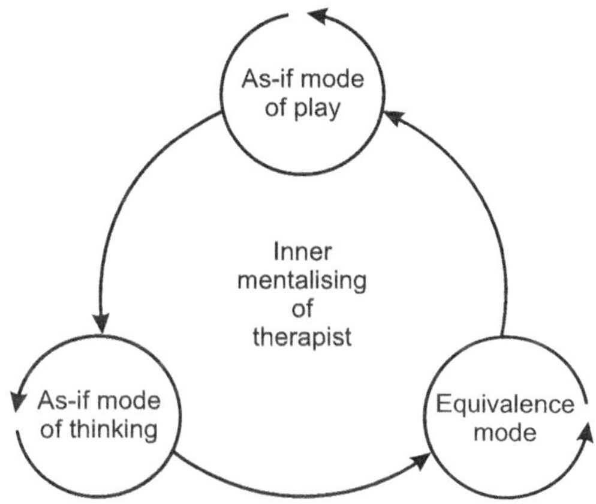


**Fig. 9.1** The therapist's transmodal thinking and acting as a doppelganger

**Important definition**

The therapist *freely switches* between three modes of mentalizing—the *equivalence mode*, the *as-if mode of thinking*, and, if necessary, the *as-if mode of play—without* integrating them (see Fig. 9.1 below) in the *transmodal relationship* with patients experiencing psychosis (see Sect. 2.6). As the patient's metacognitive doppelganger, she does *not* draw the patient's attention to the contradictions between his various thought contents.

**Central idea**

The patient's high-energy affect in the current conflict disrupts the systemic process of his self-development. His ego control over the work of his tools of mentalizing breaks down. Therefore, the therapist *enters his delusional world* as a doppelganger. As a metacognitive doppelganger, he works together with the patient to restore his ego control over his mentalization. In the doppelganger dialogue, the therapist carries out the patient's representing, interacting, and rehearsing in the patient's delusional world shoulder to shoulder with him, or implements it anew, using *her own* mentalizing (see Sect. 2.2). In doing so, she helps *the patient* organize his mentalization process spatially, chronologically, and logically in his delusional production and, thus, stops the disintegration of his inner systemic self-development (see Sect. 9.8.5).

Relating to the patient transmodally does *not* mean the therapist *only avoids* contradicting the patient. The therapist does *not* announce in advance that she "now wants to address his delusion". She does *not* ask the patient's *permission* to talk to him differently. She does *not debrief* the joint shaping of the delusion with the patient. These actions would *indirectly* define the patient's delusional reality as mere *fantasy*, and the collaborative transmodal relationship and encounter would fail.

*Moreno's* approach to the *psychotherapy of psychoses*, which he developed since 1936, seems strange to us "rational" people today. However, his unique way of dealing with people with psychosis is well-known in other contexts. As early as 1788, *Goethe* described the "healing of insanity through a psychic cure" in his "Lila" using a very similar procedure (Diener, 1971). In the story, a healer lets the family and the domestic staff of a woman experiencing psychosis act out the characters that appear in her delusional world for three days. Thus, the woman is no longer alone in her delusional experience and is no longer afraid of going crazy. This stabilizes her systemic process of self-development and halts its disintegration. For the first time, she can *externally* perceive her delusional figures in the as-if mode of play, actively *interact* with them, and *rehearse* relating to them and influencing their actions. Thus, she re-establishes ego control over her representing, interacting, and rehearsing in her delusional world. In Goethe's story, she gains insight into her illness and is healed.

Transmodal communication in doppelganger dialogue and the auxiliary world method have long been practiced as therapy methods even *in other cultures*. For example, a medical student from Africa once told me (Krüger, 1997, p. 112) that he had witnessed how a medicine man in his homeland treated and healed a tribesman with psychosis: the tribesman believed that other members of his tribe had stolen from him. Together with the "victim" and the other villagers, the medicine man staged a major search for the "stolen" objects. The whole village and the patient went shouting from hut to hut with great effort. They looked for the stolen objects in all corners. In doing so, the healer did not distance himself from the apparent absurdity of the patient's delusional fantasies. Instead, he *thought transmodally with him in the equivalence mode* and acted with him and others as doppelgangers in the as-if mode of play, as if the patient's delusions were real.

The transmodal relationship with patients suffering from psychosis can be found under different names and with modifications in *other psychotherapy methods* for psychosis, for example, Sechehaye (1956) or Benedetti. According to Séchehaye (Elrod, 1991, quoted by Red, 2018, p. 341), the psychotherapy of psychoses is *not* only about "helping the patient with schizophrenia face social reality but also about creating a new reality together with him…through symbolic realization, leading to changes in existence in both the patient and the analyst."

## 9.8 Why Metacognitive Psychodrama Therapy Can Causally Stop the Delusional Production

**Question**
Why are early psychodynamic interpretations of delusions as symbolic images therapeutically ineffective or even harmful?

Before I understood Moreno's approach (see Sect. 9.5), I treated a 40-year-old patient with chronic paranoid psychosis (ICD10: F20.0) in 160 sessions over three years *without participating in her delusional world* (see case example 87 in Sect. 9.8.1). I tried to interpret the delusional content with a depth psychology lens. This approach stabilized the patient in her family and social life. She *did not need hospital treatment*. However, despite continuous treatment with neuroleptics, the patient's core disturbance, her delusions, did not disappear. Other therapists have had similar experiences. Schwarz (2018, p. 107 ff.) stabilized a patient with psychosis in 20-year psychoanalytic *psychotherapy* and "saved his life". However, after the end of therapy, the patient made two serious suicide attempts and was hospitalized several times. He stabilized later and lived with his partner as an early retiree.

Depth-psychological interpretations aren't wrong. But, they don't help the patients Often, delusions are a *symbolic expression* of an existential conflict in the patient's family or social environment. If the patient believes he is poisoned by his mother, it may be that his mother restricts him with excessive care. Early depth-psychological interpretations follow the theoretic idea: As far as possible, the patient should recognize that his delusion is "only" a symbolic image of his everyday conflict. Thus, he should distance himself from his delusion. The problem is that *a patient experiencing psychosis* finds *no* resemblance between the mother who threatens him in his delusion and the mother who worries about him in everyday life. *He cannot understand symbolic images* and metaphors as figurative. He thinks of his delusion in the equivalence mode and considers it real. If the patient *were to understand* the symbolic meaning of his delusional content, it *would* actually harm him. This is because it would trigger his negative affect toward his mother which has disrupted his ego control over his mentalizing and caused him to decompensate into psychosis in the first place (see case example 31, Sect. 4.14).

For the same reason, *a psychodramatic relationship clarification* with role reversal with important attachment figures is contraindicated in the treatment of patients with psychosis. Better self-actualization in the as-if mode of play actualizes the patient's desire for distance and aggression that had led to the breakdown of his ego.

**Central idea**

According to Winnicott (1985, p. 63), "People who cannot play must first learn to play. They don't understand interpretations. [...] Premature interpretations, therefore [...] sound like instructions and lead to adaptation." According to Auchter (1995), it is important for a psychotherapist to "develop the ability *not knowing*, not knowing immediately, and not knowing everything."

People decompensate into psychosis when a high-energy affect in the triggering conflict situation traumatizes their souls (see Sect. 9.4). They are afraid of going insane. This existential fear disintegrates the systemic process of self-development. As a result, the tools of mentalizing work in emergency mode as mechanisms of dreamwork (see Sect. 9.3) and produce delusions. Thus the tools of mentalizing become mechanisms of dreamwork (see Sect. 9.3) and produce delusional production. The cause of the disorder is not the delusional *content* but the dysfunctional *metacognitive processes that produce* the delusional content. In metacognitive psychodrama therapy, the therapist and the patient convert the mechanisms of dreamwork back into tools of mentalization by mentalizing together in the doppelganger dialogue and using them appropriately in the delusional scene. This stops the current delusional production or reduces it (see case examples 94 in Sects. 9.8.6 and 9.8.8 and 95 and 96 in Sect. 9.8.8).

In doing so, the therapist uses the following steps:

1. The therapist and the patient construct *a delusional scene* from the patient's most important delusional content and *represent* it externally with the help of chairs and hand puppets. This *differentiates* the subject and object in the delusion (see Sect. 9.8.4). The *object* can be, for example, a voice heard by the patient. he feeling of threat gets a suitable conflict partner as the object, the 'persecutor'

(see case example 95 in Sect. 9.8.8). Or *the object image* of the voice gets the appropriate *self-image*.

2. The therapist and the patient psychodramatically play an *individual delusion scene*. They both *interact* in the conflict as the doppelganger and protagonist. Thus, through their actions, they expand their respective inner psychosomatic resonance patterns between the memory centers of sensorimotor interaction patterns, physical sensations, affect, linguistic concepts, and thoughts. Moreno says (1959, p. 98): "Talking is important. But acting precedes and includes talking."
3. If necessary, the therapist *rehearses* as a metacognitive doppelganger on the patient's behalf without being daunted by the contradiction between delusion and reality. For example, she loudly berates the 'mother', symbolized with an empty chair, as a 'bad mother who wants to kill her son', and forbids it explicitly (see case example 95 in Sect. 9.8.8). In doing this, the patient feels *psychosomatically* relieved through the acting of the doppelganger. But, he also remembers that his mother loves him and cares for him. He experiences his inner object image of his mother in everyday life *differently* than the therapist's cruel image of his mother. Therefore, he begins to doubt his delusion of being *poisoned* by his mother.

**Central idea**

The repeated interruption of the current delusional production precedes the development of insight into the illness. It is not to be equated with insight into illness (see Sect. 9.8.5).

**Question**

Why does the joint therapeutic development of delusion also improve the patient's ability to deal with conflicts *in his everyday life*?

Metacognitive therapy reduces or stops the current production of delusion (see case examples 94 in Sects. 9.8.6 and 9.8.8, and 95 and 96 in Sect. 9.8.8) thereby improving the patient's ego strength. A 40-year-old patient had been planning to leave home for three years. Together, the therapist and the patient developed her delusion metacognitively in a therapy session. The patient then left home *without* discussing her desire to move with the therapist again. The therapeutic stabilization of the systemic process of self-development in delusion production *automatically* improves the patient's ability to deal with *everyday conflicts*. The therapeutic principle of strengthening the ego through self-development is also practiced in the psychotherapy of children. In their *free symbolic play*, the children shift their high-energy affect onto roles in a story and help the heroine to overcome danger: the cat, who is being treated cruelly, must be saved. The conflict is further developed into a story of coping in the symbolic play. Free play promotes the children's ego strength and self-healing (see Sect. 5.13). At the beginning of group therapy, they often only play for a few minutes and are otherwise standing outside the scene of the play. By the end of therapy, if they can play along for the whole session, their symptoms of illness will have disappeared in everyday life.

### 9.8.1 The Separation of the 'Dream Ego' from the 'Everyday Ego' Using the Two-Chair Technique

Mentalization-oriented metacognitive psychodrama therapy is more successful in new patients with a *first* psychotic episode than chronically ill patients. Therefore, new patients may even heal. Their delusional world is still fresh and not yet branded into their memories. They have *not yet* identified with the role of the sick person or the diagnosis assigned to them in the psychiatric system. The *secondary* damages caused by treatment traumata and medication are still minimal. But the *chronically ill also* benefit from metacognitive therapy.

Patients with *acute psychosis* often confuse the therapist with rapid changes in the topic of discussion and the chaos in their delusional life. In such a case, the therapist should justify her own feelings of disorientation and actively orient herself by using empty chairs in the therapy room. In doing this, she *also helps her patient*. When working with the table stage, she represents the dream ego and the everyday ego side by side with two stones. Together with the patient, she represents everything that currently makes up his life with stones and wood blocks, namely *his feelings*, his friends, family members, and other significant things. In the *case of acute psychosis*, the work with the table stage slows down and relaxes the interaction in the therapeutic relationship.

***Case example 87* (Krüger, 1997, *p. 44 f., abridged*)**
*40-year-old Mrs. E. came to the initial consultation in a severe state of psychosis. She spoke about magicians stealing her aura at night, raping her, and sending her back. These magicians would influence her over the radio. She suffered from physical discomfort and much more. The therapist was truly confused with all the information. He agreed with her to start a drug treatment with neuroleptics. In the second therapy session, he asked the patient: "Could you please represent the important elements of your life by using different stones and placing them on the table? Take a stone for yourself as well!' Mrs. E. placed a small I-stone on the table. Next, she put two larger stones at some distance for two 'evil magicians', one for a man and one for her former professor. She had fallen in love with her before her mental illness. Then she placed a stone for their partner behind these two stones. The therapist asked: "Is that all?" Mrs. E.: "Yes, that's all!" But, the therapist also had her represent her everyday ego on the table stage: "Mrs. E., but you still exist in everyday life. You function as if nothing happened! You have children and a business too. Please add a stone for your everyday ego!" The patient placed a second stone next to her first "I-stone", symbolizing her "everyday ego". She then completed the symbolic image by adding stones to represent her husband and two children.*

*Together, the therapist and the patient looked at the symbolic life image of the patient on the table. Mrs. E. referred to the dream ego as her "feeling ego" and the everyday ego as her "functioning ego". As she saw the two stones, she suddenly fell silent and burst into tears: "Actually, I've only functioned my whole life!" Despite chaotic family circumstances, Mrs. E. had energetically mastered her life during her childhood. But she had married a man who was not very good with people. He now had an alcohol problem. Mrs. E. had split off her feelings in her marital relationship in a similar way as in her childhood. However, after a gynecological illness, she fell in love with her professor. When the professor did not reciprocate her love, she decompensated into psychosis. Mrs. E reported in the following therapy session: "I just cried for three days after the last session."*

***Case example 88***
*A 32-year-old craftsman, Mr. F., had been delusional for six months. He believed he was being bugged and filmed in his apartment. In the first session, the therapist succeeded in convincing the patient that he should take one neuroleptic tablet every evening for four days for "his excessive sensitivity". The therapist used the doppelganger dialogue to communicate with the patient and, in doing this, recommended that he file a complaint with the police. In the second therapy session, Mr. F. reported: "It has become much calmer now. By the way, I also went to the police. But they said they needed evidence or a witness." The therapist: "Oh, yes, of course. That makes sense!" Mr. F: "But I don't have that!" The therapist: "Oh, what a pity!" Four weeks later Mr. F began to have doubts: "Perhaps I just imagined it all." The therapist deliberately ignored the patient's growing insight into the illness. But he represented the contrary psychotic logic of the patient next to him with an empty chair: "You say you may have only imagined it. But I think what you experienced with your neighbors remains valid and significant. So I am placing this empty chair here next to you for the part of you that experienced the filming and bugging. You can call it your dream ego if you want. Our nocturnal dreams appear unreal during the day but true during the night." The patient then spontaneously decided to write down a list of his everyday experiences for the next four weeks. He divided these experiences into two groups and titled one group "real" and the other group "just imagined."*

In the two-chair technique, the chair on which the patient sits represents his 'everyday ego,' and the chair next to him represents his 'dream ego'. The therapist gives the patient's dream ego a personally appropriate name: "This is the part of you that is being bugged," or "This is the part of you that the neighbors harass," or "This is your entertainer self" (see case example 86 in Sect. 9.7). Then in the therapeutic conversation, the therapist actively assigns topics to his everyday ego *or* his dream ego *by pointing to the respective chair.*

The *two-chair technique* with the "everyday ego" and the "dream ego" is helpful in the psychotherapy of people with psychosis for the following reasons:

1. The external spatial separation of the psychotic experience from healthy adult thinking restores the patient's dignity as a human being. She is not only "a psychotic" but a woman, who *among other things, also* thinks psychotically. As with the chair work of patients with personality disorders (see Sect. 4.8), the psychotic experience is "only" *an individual character trait* of the patient. The therapist gives the patient's delusional life in the as-if mode of play a right to exist through the *external* representation of the "dream ego". A delusional life is allowed. The patient develops self-empathy for her pain.

2. The *external juxtaposition* of the "dream ego" and the "everyday ego" dissolves the patient's *secondary* defense through the splitting of the self and denial of the delusional content (see Sect. 9.4). Together, the therapist and the patient look at her disturbing psychotic experience from the meta-perspective. The place and time of the current therapeutic relationship and that of the occurrence of the psychotic experience is externally separated in a psychosomatically perceptible way. Thus the therapist and the patient deliberate on psychotic thinking and, in doing so, think concretely metacognitively.
3. In communicating with each other, the therapist and the patient sort out what belongs to the patient's everyday reality and her delusional reality. In doing so, they *internally* delegate all of the patient's *psychotic* experiences with their high-energy affect to *the chair of the "dream ego" outside*. They thus reduce the pressure of conflict in the therapeutic relationship. In doing so, the patient's everyday ego is indirectly defined as 'healthy'.

**Central idea**

In patients with psychosis, the tools of mentalizing work in emergency mode as mechanisms of dream work. Therefore, they aren't able to *appropriately* represent their delusional experience *internally* as a scene and to process the delusional conflict (see Sect. 9.3): Who with whom, how, and why. This results in *metacognitive confusion* between their delusion and external reality. But, the separation between the imaginary world and the external reality is the basis for inner conflict processing. The two-chair technique implements the necessary separation of the imaginary world and the everyday world *externally* in the as-if mode of play. This strengthens the patient's cognition and ego control over her psychotic thinking because she can choose freely. She can change chairs internally and think psychotically, but she can also remain seated on her chair internally. Thus, the two-chair technique untangles the patient's metacognitive confusion between his everyday thinking and his delusion production *also internally*.

4. The *therapist* develops *two opposing parallel* empathy processes without resolving their opposition and alternates between them. As a metacognitive doppelganger, he empathizes with the patient's suffering as a victim of her persecutor or her voice in the delusion. He actively carries out her delusional production consistently until she says: "Yes… but…" and spontaneously shifts back to her everyday thinking (see case example 86 in Sect. 9.7). But as a *doppelganger* of her healthy adult thinking, he also develops compassion for her suffering from her symptoms of illness in her everyday life thinking. Alternating between the two empathy processes resolves the block in the psychiatric relationship and the metacognitive countertransference (see Sect. 9.2). The therapist feels *free* to switch between thinking with the patient in her delusion as well as in her everyday conflicts and remains creative, if necessary.
5. Collaborative therapy planning becomes more manageable. The 'everyday ego' represents the *working space of social-psychiatric therapy*. The second chair for the 'dream ego' represents the *psychotherapeutic work on the delusion scene*. The actual *external* co-existence of the dream ego and the everyday ego makes it easier for the therapist and the patient to realize *both therapeutic approaches on an equal footing* side by side (see below).

6. As a metacognitive doppelganger, the therapist tries together with the patient to liberate the patient's internal process of self-development from the whirlpool of disintegration. He lets the patient switch to the chair of her "dream ego" and tries to integrate individual elements of her delusional world into a *delusion scene* with the help of the auxiliary world and develops it into a holistic history. The chair for her realistic "everyday ego" remains noticeable in the therapy room. The *external* psychosomatic presence of the 'everyday ego' as a chair gives the therapist and the patient a feeling of security when using the auxiliary world technique. The external 'everyday ego' is an anchor in reality for both of them. Because *after* the collaborative work in the auxiliary reality of the delusion, the patient can switch back to the other chair of her 'everyday ego' at any time.

**Recommendation**

*In disorder-specific psychodrama therapy* for people with psychosis, the therapist acts bifocal. She treats the patient's conflict processing in everyday life *separately* from the conflict processing in his delusional experience.

Psychotherapy of patients with psychosis comprises the following successive steps: (1) the doppelganger dialogue (see Sect. 9.8.2) and mentalizing in dream ego, (2) separation of the patient's 'dream ego' from his 'everyday ego' with the help of the two-chair technique, (3) support for the 'everyday ego' through psychopharmacological treatment and social-psychiatric measures, (4) collaborative therapy planning, (5) constructing the patient's delusional content into a delusion scene and developing it into a story of coping with the help of the auxiliary world technique (see Sect. 9.8.8). (6) *Thereafter,* if necessary, the therapist interprets the symbolic meaning of the delusional contents in the context of the patient's life history and (7) helps the patient improve his ability to deal with conflicts in everyday relationships in the present directly. (8) *Chronically* ill psychotic patients often need to be stabilized through monthly therapy sessions for many years.

The *social-psychiatric interventions* help the patient find his way in his social relationships and cope with *everyday life* appropriately. For example, the therapist prescribes medication (see Sect. 9.8.6). She includes family members in the therapy process. She refers the patient to a clinic if they are at risk of hurting themselves or others. However, in social-psychiatric therapy, the patient's ego remains trapped in its delusional production. *Only metacognitive* psychotherapeutic interventions can liberate the patient's ego from its delusional production (see Sect. 9.8.1–9.8.9).

### *9.8.2 The Doppelganger Dialogue in the Initial Psychotherapeutic Consultation*

In the first meeting, the therapist engages in a routine diagnostic and counseling conversation with the patient. In doing so, she usually represents the patient's symptoms and conflicts in his everyday life from a few days or weeks ago externally with two additional empty chairs in the therapy room (see Sect. 2.8 and Fig. 2.9).

She waits until the conversation with the patient reveals a window to his delusional world. She notices that the patient's thought content appears strange or she feels confused (see case example 86 in Sect. 9.7). For example, the patient may say: "I hear voices!" or "The neighbors are watching me!" If the patient does *not* share *any* psychotic thoughts of his own accord, the therapist *herself* directs the conversation toward such a window. For example, she asks the patient, "Can you sleep at night?" If the patient has not been able to sleep *two nights in a row*, this is often an indication of nocturnal delusions. The therapist then switches to the doppelganger dialogue *without* giving any reason. She points to the empty chair of the patient's *self-image* in the symptom scene (see Fig. 2.9 in Sect. 2.8): "Then you lie in bed and want to sleep!" She then points to the opposite chair of his *interaction partner*: "But then you hear your neighbors gossiping about you." Depending on the content of the conversation, the therapist uses the second chair for the patient's problems in his everyday life or his psychotic experiences.

***Case example 89***

*54-year-old Mrs. K. comes for the initial consultation. She reports that she cannot sleep at night. Therapist: "It's too loud; the neighbors are talking about you." Mrs. K.: "No, I'm afraid." Therapist: "You're being threatened by strangers." Mrs. K.: "Yes, when I went home yesterday, many things in my apartment were in a completely different space than usual." Therapist: "There was someone in your apartment." Mrs. K.: "Yes." Therapist: "A man who wanted to steal things from you." The therapist points to the chair for her inner object image in the delusional world. Mrs. K.: No, I think it was a woman. Therapist: "The woman came into your apartment but didn't steal anything. She just took everything in her hands and looked at it." Mrs. K.: "Maybe she wanted to see if there was anything valuable." Therapist: "And then she went away again and planned a burglary." Mrs. K.: "But I don't have anything valuable in my apartment." Therapist: "You don't have any jewelry or money." Mrs. K.: "Yes, I've been unemployed for a long time." Therapist: "So you only have a television. Of course, one can also sell that. Perhaps it fetches around 100 euros at the flea market." The therapist takes the chair representing the object image of "the other woman" and places it four meters away: "The chair is too close for me. That feels spooky. Slightly further away is better for me. So the woman left and will come back soon." Mrs. K.: "No, I think she told a man." Therapist: "And then the man comes at some point and breaks into your apartment." Mrs. K.: "Yes." Therapist: "Then he will steal your TV and maybe other things from your kitchen." Mrs. K.: "I don't know. Maybe he'll attack me too."*

*Therapist: "You are scared of being attacked. I suggest you ask your neighbor if you can give her a call at night if you hear something at your front door." Mrs. K.: "No, I can't. She is already annoyed with my stories." Therapist: "But you have other friends or relatives you can call in an emergency." Mrs. K.: "Yes, my son. But he's sick. He has enough on his plate already." Therapist: "But if you are in trouble. What illness does he have?" Mrs. K., in a somber tone: "He has prostate cancer." Therapist: "But your son is still young. He'll survive." Mrs. K.: "No, he already has metastases in his shoulder." Therapist: "Oh, I'm sorry to hear that. That's terrible for him. And for you. Do you have any other children?" Mrs. K.: "No."*

*The therapist feels shocked and paralyzed on behalf of the patient. In her questions about the patient's everyday reality, she switches from the equivalence mode back to the normal psychiatric relationship. She understands the patient's symptoms indicate acute transient psychotic disorder (F23.8) and traumatic crisis (F 43.1). In her delusion, she experiences that the order of things in her apartment has changed. This experience symbolically expresses the inner fragmentation of her soul due to the impending death of her son.*

In the as-if mode of play, the therapist and the patient (1) *represented* the delusion scene, (2) transformed its *interaction sequences* into a logical story, (3) redesigned it into a copying story through *rehearsal* and (4) *integrated* it with the patients's serious everyday conflict. Thus, they stopped the patient's delusion production.

**Central idea**

Even short doppelganger dialogues improve the therapeutic relationship. The patient is no longer lonely in his delusional reality. In the distress of his delusional reality, he feels seen, taken seriously, and understood by the therapist *as his doppelganger* even though he doesn't understand himself. The patient's delusion *usually* ruins the encounter between the patient and his therapist. However, the encounter succeeds in the doppelganger dialogue. The doppelganger dialogue is the basis for Encounter Focused Therapy in the treatment of people experiencing psychosis.

In doppelganger dialogue, the patient carefully develops trust in the therapist. Trust also facilitates the patient's *social-psychiatric* treatment.

***Case example 90***

*Mr. D is a patient with chronic psychosis and emotional rigidity. Mr. D. had sent in an early application for a promotion at his office. However, when he didn't receive the expected promotion, he developed delusions of grandeur (ICD F22). He thought he had been appointed head of the office. A few weeks later, he assumed he had been appointed head of a state office and even the CSU chairman, a great political party in Germany. Mr. D. went to work in a black suit every day. He worked at his job there, constantly waiting to receive the appropriate certificate of appointment. The therapist placed one stone on the table in front of him for his 'everyday ego' and another for his' dream ego': "On the one hand, you have received the information that you will be appointed today. So you go to your office in a black suit! I am placing this round stone here to represent this experience. We can call it 'the promotion stone'. On the other hand, when in office, you have to act as if nothing has happened and as if you know nothing. I represent this experience with this squared stone here. You then try to go about everyday work in your office in a black suit. That must be very tiring!" The otherwise unemotional man suddenly began to cry and groaned: "You can believe me!" He felt deeply understood by the therapist. His cooperation with the therapist greatly improved in his social-psychiatric treatment.*

### 9.8.3 The Doppelganger Dialogue for Crisis Intervention in Patients with Acute Psychosis

**Question**
In the doppelganger dialogue, the therapist *himself enters* the patient's delusional world and, together with the patient, develops it further. Why doesn't that *reinforce the patient's delusion production*?

In *crisis intervention* for patients with acute psychosis, the doppelganger dialogue transforms the mechanisms of dream work back into tools of mentalizing (see Sect. 9.8). This halts the current delusion production thereby improving *the emotional contact* with the patient. The transmodal relationship helps, for example, to execute involuntary admissions to a psychiatric clinic *without* traumatizing violent measures by the police.

**Recommendation**

The therapist does *not* use the two-chair technique in the crisis intervention (see Sect. 9.8.1). Instead, *as a metacognitive doppelganger*, as in the auxiliary world, she directly enters the patient's delusional world through *psychosomatic action* (see Sect. 9.8.8). Doing this, she actively tries to support him in fulfilling his supposed task in his *delusional scene* or to protect him from a supposed threat.

***Case example 91 (Gudrun Runge, 2014, only orally communicated)***
*A general practitioner had learned the technique of doppelganger dialogue in a seminar. During supervision, she shared how she used this technique for crisis intervention with a patient: She was called to a patient's home for an emergency at night. There was an ambulance and a police car in front of the patient's house. In Germany, only police officers are allowed to touch a sick person physically and, if necessary, force them into the ambulance against their will. Nurses are not allowed to do that.*

*The nurses and police officers provide the doctor with all the necessary information while standing in front of the patient's house. Then the doctor goes through the house to the patio behind it. She sees a 50-year-old man standing there. He is looking up at the sky and intently watching something. The doctor stands to his left shoulder to shoulder with him. She also looks up into the sky: "There are a lot of stars today!" The man: "Yes." The doctor: "You have to pay attention!" The man: "Yes." He makes a big arm movement from the top left to the bottom right toward the ground. The doctor imitates the movement as a doppelganger. She thinks and feels transmodally in the equivalence mode and boldly gives meaning to the arm movement: "Ah, you have to pay attention to ensure that the celestial bodies there" she points to the stars visible in the sky, "do not hit us directly here on Earth!" The man: "No, that's where UFOs land." The doctor: "Oh yes, you show the UFOs where they should land." The man: "Yes, I'll instruct them." The doctor is startled. She thinks for a moment. Then she says empathetically: "You have a huge responsibility. That must be exhausting!" The man groans: "That's right!" The doctor seriously engages with the patient's delusional reality internally and externally. She continues to watch the sky with him. Then she has a creative idea: She points to the left with her hand: "There, there's another UFO. You forgot that one!" The man: "Oh!" With his right arm, he again shows the "UFO" the way to the "landing pad" with a big movement.*

*The doctor keeps looking at the sky. After a while, she says rehearsing mentally: "I don't see any UFOs anymore. Do you see another one?" The man: "No!" At that moment, the doctor flexibly switches from thinking in delusional logic to thinking in everyday logic without being bothered by the contradiction between the two logics: "Can we go then?" The man: "Yes." As if naturally, he goes through his house to the ambulance together with the doctor and sits in it without protesting. The police officers do not have to intervene violently. The patient's nosy neighbors do not see the patient screaming and punching when the police put him in the ambulance. The patient is not additionally traumatized by the involuntary admission. The joint interaction with the UFOs and the joint rehearsing in the delusion scene stopped the current production of delusion (see case example 88 in Sect.* 9.8.1*).*

***Case example 92 (Luzia Amrein, 2020, oral communication)***
*A 45-year-old patient with severe exhaustion and paranoia refused his family doctor's advice to get admitted to a psychiatric clinic. The family doctor asked a psychotherapist for help. The patient came to her office. He immediately began drawing the curtains in the therapy room. The therapist immediately switched to the doppelganger dialogue and helped him do it: "Yes, they have to be closed!" Patient: "Otherwise, they can look in here!" Therapist: "Yes, otherwise, they can see us here. That would be dangerous." The therapist also helped the patient to carefully close the shutters. They both could no longer see outside. Therapist: "It must be exhausting for you, constantly hiding from the Islamic State people." Patient: "No, they are people from my place of work." Therapist: "Oh, I understand. The people from your workplace are after you and want to spy on you. And it's been like this for one week now." Patient: "No, for three weeks." Therapist: "They've been after you for three weeks. Then you are probably having trouble sleeping at night." Patient: "That's right, I'm completely exhausted." The therapist: "Then it would be good for you to go to a clinic! You will be protected from your colleagues' influence. You could take a week or two to rest well and recuperate." The patient: "Yes, I think that would be best. I can't stand it any longer at home." The therapist switches to everyday logic: "Then I'll call the clinic immediately and ask if there's a bed available for you." Patient: "Yes, that would be great."*

*The father-in-law had come along with the patient and sat in the waiting room. The patient, the therapist, and the father-in-law left the practice together. The therapist locked the practice door behind her. She checked again with her hand whether the door was closed. The patient laughed, "Yes, that's good if you protect yourself from them. Not that they are going to steal your documents." The patient allowed his father-in-law to drive him to the clinic without resistance. After an extended stay in the hospital, he contacted the psychotherapist and thanked her for her understanding. He then engaged in intensive psychotherapeutic work with her and successfully reintegrated into his workplace.*

The therapist and the patient represented the delusion scene between the patient and his persecutors in the therapy room and interacted together with his persecutors in the as-if mode. This reduced the patient's panic and strengthened his cognition. He gained psychosomatic awareness of his distress.

The doppelganger dialogue also makes it easier to diagnose obscure clinical pictures. The therapist and the patient's attempts in constructing a delusional scene together help to discover or rule out psychosis.

***Case example 93***

*During supervision, an experienced psychiatrist described the case of a 25-year-old patient "with severe depression, anxiety, and borderline syndrome." Her patient had already made many severe suicide attempts. She has been in psychiatric inpatient treatment for 24 months in the last five years. Despite the intensive treatment, her symptoms had not improved. The supervisor, therefore, recommended that the therapist review the diagnosis: "But please use the doppelganger dialogue method for this!" The therapist and the supervisor practiced the doppelganger dialogue together in a role play. The psychiatrist herself took on the role of her patient, and the supervisor played the role of the therapist.*

*The psychiatrist felt amazed, happy, and relieved in the next supervision session. She reported: "I used the doppelganger dialogue with my patient. It turned out that the patient was hallucinating and had an extremely destructive delusional system." The doppelganger dialogue revealed that the patient suffered from chronic paranoid-hallucinatory psychosis (ICD: F20.0). Thanks to the new diagnosis, the psychiatrist could treat her patient appropriately with medication for the first time after five years of therapy.*

*After that, the therapist sometimes visited the patient at home for crisis intervention during outpatient treatment. Each time she would find the patient sitting on the floor in the corner of the room in a state of severe psychosis. The therapist would then place a chair in the other corner of the room, representing the voice of Satan molesting the patient. As an interacting doppelganger, the therapist yelled at him: "Leave Mrs. Krämer alone! She can't take it anymore!" Representing the persecutor and interacting with him relaxed the patient and helped re-establish contact in the therapeutic relationship.*

### 9.8.4 Practical Implementation of the Doppelganger Dialogue

The doppelganger dialogue technique is the basis of the metacognitive psychotherapy of psychoses, because patients with psychosis cannot process the conflicts in their *delusion* due to the breakdown of their ego control over their tools of mentalizing (see Sect. 9.3). Together with the patient, the therapist can lead the doppelganger dialogue purely verbally in the as-if mode of thinking (see case example 86 in Sect. 9.7). Or

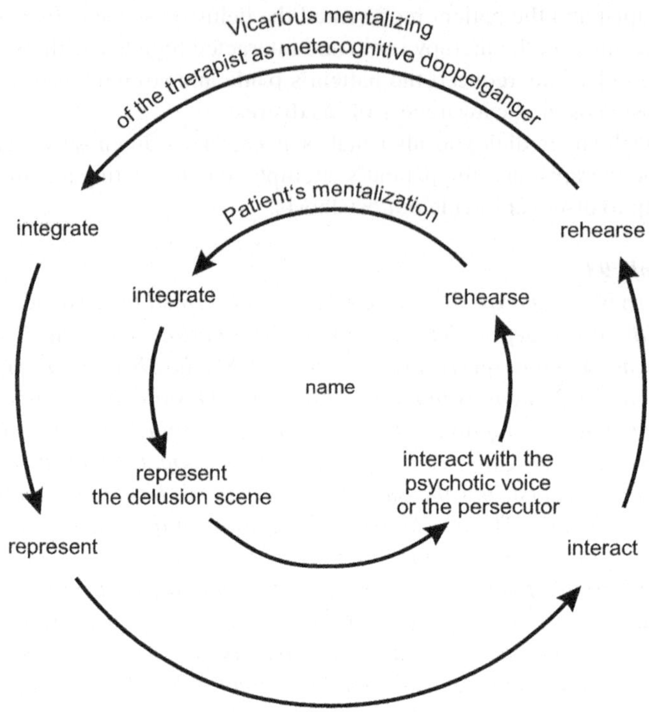


**Fig. 9.2** Vicarious mentalizing of the therapist as a metacognitive doppelganger

she combines it with the auxiliary world method and uses it in the as-if mode of play (see case examples 91–96 in Sects. 9.8.3 to 9.8.8).

**Central idea**

During the conversation, the therapist feels confused on behalf of the patient experiencing psychosis. Therefore, together with him, she orients herself to his chaotic delusional thoughts in a doppelganger dialogue. *Acting* as a metacognitive doppelganger, she realizes *her* tools of mentalizing in his delusional production. Together with him, she *represents* individual delusion scenes, creates the chronological sequence of *interactions* in them, and tries to *develop* logic and meaning in them.

The doppelganger dialogue method *looks quite simple from the outside*. In truth, however, the therapist thinks and acts in a very complex way (see Fig. 9.2):

1. The therapist waits until the conversation with the patient reveals a window into his delusional world. She then goes *inward* with the patient into his *delusional life* and stops at an emotionally charged delusion content.

**Important definition**

Together with the patient, the therapist *verbally* reconstructs important content from his delusional reality into a *delusion scene* (see Fig. 9.3). They develop a conflict space where the patient's self-image and object image interact with one another. As a victim, the patient

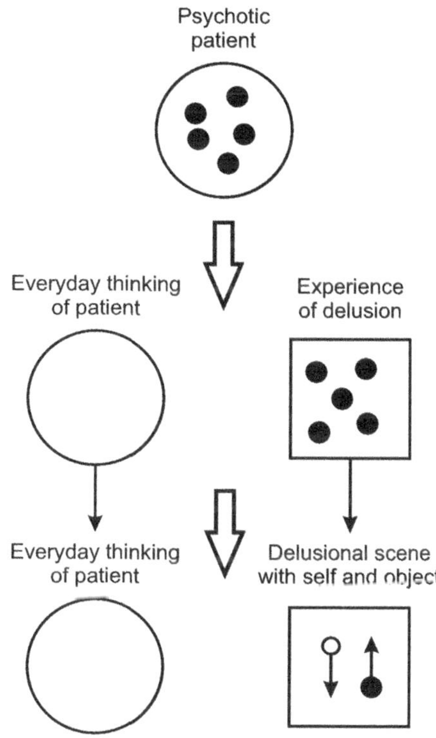


**Fig. 9.3** Construction of a delusion scene using the two-chair technique

feels he is being followed, watched, spied on, or hears voices talking about him. The delusion scene then includes the patient's self-image as a victim and, the object image of an interaction partner who persecutes or observes him, or spies on him. The co-construction of a delusion scene is the first step in the patient regaining ego control over the work of the mentalizing tools in the delusional production.

2. Together, the therapist, as a doppelganger, and the patient describe the people interacting in the delusion scene and retrace the *chronological sequence* of actions and reactions *step-by-step*. Action and reaction should interlock like the hooks of a zipper.

**Central idea**

The therapist and the patient write a script for a film, so to speak. Together, shoulder to shoulder, they always implement only the next logical step in the chronological interaction *sequences* in the delusion scene. In this way, the patient *himself* notices that he *cannot remember* many concrete actions in his delusion scene. As a result, he wonders whether he has merely imagined the psychotic events and gets *insight into his illness*. The *step-by-step* approach helps the therapist, *as a metacognitive doppelganger*, to individually determine the patient's dysfunctional logic and avoid 'false' assumptions.

3. The therapist *only* makes *statements* in the doppelganger dialogue. Unlike other times, she *doesn't ask* any *questions*. It is very unusual for a therapist only to

make statements and not ask questions. Even experienced psychodramatists have to practice the doppelganger dialogue in the beginning.

**Central idea**

People must process a question in the as-if mode of thinking to answer it *appropriately*. However, patients with psychosis think, act, and feel *in the equivalence mode*. They experience their internal thinking as external reality (see Sect. 2.6). *If asked a question*, a patient with psychosis would feel insecure and shut down. Internally, he would shift from the shoulder-to-shoulder position to the face-to-face position. The joint transmodal construction of delusion wouldn't succeed. In contrast, however, when thinking in equivalence mode, the patient understands the therapist's *statements* as descriptions of 'external delusional reality'. This allows him to agree or disagree with the therapist's statements. He becomes the person who knows, and the therapist becomes the one who doesn't know.

4. The patient's mentalizing disintegrates in his delusional production and works in emergency mode as dreamwork (see Sect. 9.3). As a result, he mostly knows little about his delusion scene. Therefore, the therapist often goes one step ahead of the patient *in the joint orientation* in the delusion scene. For example, when the therapist wishes to ask if the voice is male or female, she turns the question into a statement, "The voice is male." The patient hesitates, then states, "I don't know. No, I think it is female." In another case, the therapist suspects, "The one blessing you is an enlightened one." The patient: "No, a ghost!" Therapist: "Then he is like a Jinn, a blue Jinn." The patient: "No, it's red." The therapist: "Ah, yes. His color is not blue but dark red."

**Central idea**

In the doppelganger dialogue, the more specific and action-oriented the interactions and logic in the patient's delusion scene, the more likely the patient notices that his delusional reality *doesn't match* his everyday reality and is therefore 'only' a fantasy.

5. As a metacognitive doppelganger, the therapist consciously thinks a little *more absurdly than the patient* in the joint development of the delusion scene. This 'false' presentation motivates the patient to correct the therapist and narrate his own delusional reality. Naturally, he is better acquainted with the action sequences, bodily sensations, emotions, linguistic concepts, and thoughts related to his delusion than the therapist. Thus, the patient completes the psychosomatic resonance pattern associated with his delusion (see Sect. 2.7) between his different memory centers. By distancing himself from the therapist's statement, the patient feels he is separate from the therapist as a doppelganger. The *patient* becomes the one who knows, and *the therapist* is the one who doesn't know. The result is *an encounter on an equal footing*. The therapist always immediately integrates the patient's corrections into the joint construction of his delusion scene.

**Central idea**

The doppelganger dialogue realizes the patient's longing for a supportive relationship. However, it *also* protects the patient from the dilemma of seeking intimacy and avoiding it simultaneously, as described by Mentzos (see Sect. 9.4). By slightly exaggerating his delusional reality willfully, the therapist repeatedly allows the patient to contradict her and thus *distance himself from her.*

6. In the doppelganger dialogue, the therapist does *not empathetically* verbalize the *patient's affect alone*, as in Rogerian psychotherapy: "You felt threatened and powerless." *Empathic doubling* or mirroring of the affect amplifies the patient's fear of symbiotic closeness with the therapist. The therapist, therefore, *always immediately* and willingly describes the interactional frame that *she suspects* belongs to the emotion in his delusion scene: "You felt threatened *by the rays* that came out of the socket and hit you." This description gives the patient the opportunity to distance himself from the therapist's statements, correct them, and further develop the interactions in the delusion scene beyond reality.
7. The therapist *does not ask* the patient *diagnostic questions*: "Do you think other people can hear your thoughts?" Instead, she transforms these questions into an appropriate interactional scene from the patient's life, in which the patient *might* experience the psychotic symptom she suspects: "And when you were waiting at the tram stop, you felt that other people around you could hear your thoughts!".
8. Some of the therapist's ideas in the doppelganger dialogue are new to the patient. He *needs time* to internally fit them into his thinking and feeling in his delusional reality and correct them if necessary. The therapist, therefore, repeatedly pauses in the doppelganger dialogue.
9. The therapist herself is often unsure and doesn't know what to do next in the doppelganger dialogue. In such a case, she conducts a soliloquy in the patient's presence: "I'm confused right now, and I need to think a little. It's hard feeling threatened like that. I'm just thinking about what I can do against the danger. Give me some time. I am thinking!' Such communication humanizes the therapist in the patient's eyes because she feels at a loss, too. In such a soliloquy, the therapist often vicariously verbalizes the patient's feelings.
10. Patients with psychosis often ask the therapist at some point if they share their delusional perception of reality: "Do you believe what I told you?" In such a case, the therapist does *not* answer with a yes or no. Instead, she remains in the role of the metacognitive doppelganger in his delusional reality: "But you yourself told me." Then she reframes his feeling of insecurity *in the context of his delusion scene* and immediately elaborates on the scene: "You are insecure. Everyone is pretending! You feel unsettled and scared. You don't know who is behind it and pulling the strings. Maybe it's the secret service!".
11. The therapist avoids *symbolic images and metaphors* in her statements. For example, she does *not* say, "Your husband's negligence was a slap in the face!" Patients with psychosis comprehend metaphors concretely in equivalence mode. So they interpret the above metaphor as "Your husband slapped you in the face!" Metaphors and symbolic imagery unsettle patients unnecessarily. Therefore, the therapist formulates her empathetic comments *as a scenic interaction*: "Your husband did not keep his promise. You were very disappointed."

12. Patients with psychosis experience their delusional world as reality. Time and again, they try to accommodate the demands of their delusional reality, such as obeying the voices or fulfilling their delusions of grandeur. But they don't succeed; otherwise, it wouldn't be a delusion. Nevertheless, the patient feels threatened. Or he is completely overwhelmed when, for example, he believes he is Jesus. In such a case, the therapist expresses her sympathy for the patient's suffering *in his delusion* scene: "Yes, really, you have a huge responsibility!" "But it is very exhausting to have to pretend as if nothing is wrong!" (see case example 90 in Sect. 9.8.2) Expressing compassion for the suffering in the delusional world improves the patient's trust in the therapist.
13. In the last third of the doppelganger dialogue, together with the patient, the therapist derives a logical consequence from his delusional reality *for his mental rehearsal in his everyday reality*: "You surely have already inspected everything in your living room for bugs!—No? Then do that!" "Maybe you should go to the police and report your neighbors because they are making videos of you! That violates your privacy rights." One patient actually went to the police and later told the therapist, feeling very disappointed: "The police officers asked if I had any evidence of my suspicion that the neighbors were spying on me and filming me in my apartment. But I don't have any evidence!" The therapist replied empathically: "Yes, that's right. This must be hard for you." The integration of delusional reality into everyday reality *cannot succeed*. Because if it were to succeed, the delusional reality would indeed not be *a delusion*. The patient recognizes the *difference* between his delusional world and everyday reality through external rehearsal in his delusional world.
14. In the doppelganger dialogue, the therapist does not make false promises to the patient about his everyday reality and does not lie to him. She is his metacognitive doppelganger in mentalizing the delusion scene, but *not his active helper in everyday life*. For example, she doesn't promise him that she will go to the police *with him* and file a complaint against the mafia.
15. At the end of the conversation, the therapist returns from the doppelganger dialogue to everyday reality (see Fig. 9.1 in Sect. 9.7) and assumes responsibility for her role as therapist, psychologist, or psychiatrist. She plans, for example, appropriate drug treatment and socio-psychiatric aid. Or she motivates him to go to a hospital or a day clinic. The patient feels taken seriously and understood by the therapist because of the previous encounter in the doppelganger dialogue. The therapist did not leave him alone in his suffering. He is, therefore, often more willing to accept the therapist's recommendations. The transmodal relating to the patient is not folie à deux (a delusional disorder shared by two).

**Exercise 25**

Experience the doppelganger dialogue technique through *psychosomatic acting*. You cannot understand it just by reading about it because your impulses to act therapeutically arise *from your psychosomatic experience* in the direct encounter with your patient. Try to do a role-play with a colleague and, as a "therapist", go into the delusional production of a "patient" with psychosis and verbally develop a delusion scene, together with the "patient", in the doppelganger dialogue. The colleague is supposed to play the role of one of his patients with psychosis.

You will notice (1) As a therapist, you initially fail at making statements instead of *questions*. You have to practice this first. (2) The doppelganger dialogue requires courage, spontaneity, good intuition, and, last but not least, also humility. As a therapist, you are *spontaneous* when you live in the moment and try to act appropriately in the current situation without prejudice, interpretation, prior determination, and expectations. (3) Firstly, you will fail at this goal. Many therapists feel insecure when they accompany their "patient" as a doppelganger and "falsely" describe the delusion. But you don't have *to succeed* in the doppelganger dialogue. All that matters is that *you make an effort* to succeed. (4) Even if you make "mistakes" in the doppelganger dialogue, your "patient" will react positively *to your efforts alone.* As a result, the therapeutic relationship begins to flow again. Patients with psychosis feel incredibly lonely in their delusions. But the doppelganger dialogue eliminates this loneliness. An existential encounter takes place. Sometimes this encounter is a sacred moment for the patient and the therapist (Luzia Amrein, verbal communication 2020). (5) The doppelganger dialogue reduces the "patient's" mistrust of the therapist. For the first time, the patient experiences that someone is genuinely interested in the content of his delusion.

**Central idea**

The therapist should *allow and accept* her own feelings of insecurity. This is the only way for her to remain capable of acting in the therapeutic relationship. She should not personalize it and conclude: "I am incapable of psychotherapeutically treating people with psychosis," because the insecurity is a justified, *appropriate* reaction to the patient's behavior.

When the therapist *herself* is part of the patient's delusional system, it is much more challenging to communicate with the patient in doppelganger dialogue. For example, the patient may be delusional and believe the therapist loves him. In such a case, the patient wants to engage in a *real* partnership with the therapist. He would like a concrete answer about how should their romantic relationship continue *in everyday reality*. The shoulder-to-shoulder position of the doppelganger dialogue automatically turns into a *face-to-face position.* In such a case, the therapist can try to tell the patient that she does not want a relationship with him *in everyday life.* But then, she should *immediately* shift to *another delusion* in the doppelganger dialogue and actively work on it with him. In this way, she once more encounters the patient as his doppelganger *shoulder to shoulder*. Or she can refer the patient to another therapist.

The therapist can use the metacognitive therapy with the help of the doppelganger dialogue in many formats, such as the initial consultation (see case examples 88, 89, 90 in Sects. 9.8.1 and 9.8.2), crisis intervention, for diagnosis (see case example 93 in Sect. 9.8.3), during hospital admission (see case examples 91 and 92 in Sect. 9.8.3), home visits, doctor's visits in the hospital, and long-term psychotherapy. The doppelganger dialogue is indicated for people with *acute* psychosis, *chronic* psychosis, and in the state of remission *after* psychotic decompensation.

Encountering patients with psychosis in doppelganger dialogue improves the patient's ego strength and the *therapeutic relationship* and, thus, makes *socio-psychiatric therapy* more successful. Patients are less likely to be admitted as inpatients, or even when they are, the duration is shorter. Disorder-specific psychotherapy of delusional disorder reduces the *treatment costs* through fewer and shorter hospital stays and reduced intake of medications.

### 9.8.5 The Theory of the Therapeutic Effect of Doppelganger Dialogue

A psychiatrist reported in a working group for psychosis therapy: "I tried the method with a patient with psychosis in my outpatient clinic. I represented her voice with a chair across from her and then, as her doppelganger, loudly berated the 'voice': "Stop it! Don't you see that Mrs. E. is already exhausted? I forbid you from talking to her. 'Stop tormenting her!' Then I carried the chair out of the therapy room, came back in, and closed the door. The patient's delusional voices disappeared over the next weeks."

**Question**
Could the therapist do magic? Explain theoretically: Why did the patient stop hearing voices without additional medication? (see case example 95 in Sect. 9.8.8).

Psychotic experiences traumatize the human soul. In a delusion, the patient cannot fight against his persecutors or against those whose voices he hears. But he can't flee from them either. His *action* is blocked. Even a patient experiencing delusions of grandeur fails in his grandiose task repeatedly. At the same time, patients experience existential fears. Patients with psychosis are at the mercy of basic human fears: the fear of being left out, the fear of absolute loneliness, the fear of going crazy, and the fear of losing their dignity as human beings. The resulting panic blocks the work of their tools of mentalizing, allowing them to work in emergency mode as mechanisms of dreamwork.

The doppelganger dialogue reduces these fears to a tolerable level. The patient no longer feels incredibly lonely. He has someone to talk to, someone who doesn't question his perception of reality and, if necessary, fights his adversary on his behalf. The therapist acts on the patient's behalf (see case example 95 in Sect. 9.8.8) and defends his dignity, his right to live, and his right to mental and physical health care. Thus, the patient internally regains his capacity to act in his traumatizing situation. The traumatizing quality of the situation is thus resolved thereby stabilizing the patient's self-development. The patient's hyperarousal subsides, and he becomes calmer. His panic reduces. As a metacognitive doppelganger, the therapist *freely and actively* uses the tools of *her* mentalizing in *his* delusion production. Thus, she helps the patient to convert his mechanisms of dream work to tools of mentalizing and in doing so, reduce or stop his current production of delusion (see Sects. 9.8.2–9.8.4). Therefore, even *an inept* attempt improves the patient's ego strength and the therapeutic relationship.

**Question**
Why does the patient develop *insight into his illness* through the doppelganger dialogue? Why doesn't it reinforce the patient's delusion when the therapist enters their delusion world?

The *free interaction* with the persecutor or the voices activates a psychosomatic resonance between the memory centers of his sensorimotor interaction patterns, physical sensations, affect, linguistic concepts, and thoughts (see Sect. 2.7). As a result, the patient's associations in the delusion scene become more complex. This process makes it easier for him to find a new solution in a targeted or consistent manner *or* to give up this search (Moreno, 1939, p. 25). The doppelganger dialogue implements the as-if mode into the patient's thinking in the equivalence mode. In this way, over time, he regains ego control over his delusional production (Moreno, 1945a, p. 3f). Interacting and rehearsing in a delusion scene reduces or stops the current production of delusion. The mechanisms of dreamwork function freely as mentalizing tools again (see Sect. 9.8). The patient *independently* notices that, *despite intensive collaborative efforts*, there is *no* logic in the delusional events or that the jointly developed reason also *seems absurd to himself*. Initial insight into the condition emerges. For example, Mr. A. (case example 86 in Sect. 9.7) noticed the absurdity of his delusion of grandeur through the doppelganger dialogue and suddenly said: "But I have to be careful not to veer off."

**Recommendation**

The therapist remains in the transmodal relationship mode *until the end of therapy*. As a metacognitive doppelganger, she actively confirms, if necessary, the *need for* the existence of the patient's two opposing realities *side by side* (see Sect. 9.8.1).

**Important definition**

In the metacognitive doppelganger technique, the therapist activates within herself the sensorimotor interaction pattern, physical sensation, affect, linguistic concepts, and thoughts that belong to the development of the patient's inner self-image in his delusional scene. She completes this psychosomatic resonance pattern *internally* on behalf of the patient to form *a holistic psychosomatic resonance pattern*. This makes the therapist flexible in the doppelganger dialogue and gives the patient stability in his delusional scene.

**Central idea**

The transmodal relationship mode is necessary until the patient has developed the psychosomatic resonance pattern associated with his delusional scene into *a holistic resonance pattern* with sensorimotor interaction pattern, physical sensation, affect, linguistic concept, and thoughts (see Sect. 2.7). If the delusion is interpreted as a fantasy too quickly, the neuronal connections in the psychosomatic resonance pattern of the delusional scene break down once again. The completion of the neurophysiological interconnection between the corresponding five memory centers makes it more likely that the patient will, at some point, *autonomously* link the delusion with similar psychosomatic resonance patterns from his life history (see Sect. 2.7). Through this integration, the patient then experiences his delusion as an *inner representation* of reality and not directly as the outer reality itself.

The therapist continues to talk to the patient about the delusional content in equivalence mode, *even when* the *patient himself* begins to doubt the reality of his delusion (see case examples 86 in Sect. 9.7, 88 in 9.8.1, and 95 in Sect. 8.8.8). She reinforces the work of his mentalizing tools in his *current* delusional production in order to stop it. The patient's insight into his illness is *a result* of the end of delusion production and *not* a prerequisite. As a metacognitive doppelganger, the therapist strengthens the patient's ego until the patient gains ego control over his delusional production and insight into his illness all by himself.

**Important definition**

Ego control means that the patient can think of his delusion in the as-if mode and experience it as his inner representation of reality, but not external reality itself. So it doesn't have to be 'normal'. He is free to think and behave in strange ways if he has accepted his traits only as his *personal idiosyncrasies*.

The therapist's acting in the doppelganger dialogue may seem directive from the outside. In truth, however, the therapist develops a profoundly abstinent attitude. Her abstinence is more genuine than, for example, early psychodynamic interpretations (see Sect. 9.8) or cognitive behavior therapy (see below).

Patients with psychosis need at least one year of disorder-specific metacognitive psychotherapy to develop *long-term* insight into their illness (see case examples 94 and 96 in Sects. 9.8.6 and 9.8.8). There are many minor setbacks along the way. That's because of new crises the patient's delusional life can actualize again, *despite* a brief insight into the illness. In case of another decompensation, the patient would remember that the therapist had questioned the reality of his delusion. That would be proof that the therapist doesn't believe him after all. Loneliness and existential fears of going insane would nullify the stabilization of his process of self-development. His process of self-development would disintegrate further. *In retrospect*, he would feel betrayed and humiliated. His relationship of trust with the therapist would suffer *permanent* damage.

**Central idea**

The patient *himself* has to gain insight into the illness again and again if it is lost. The *lack* of insight into one's condition is an indication that the patient's mentalizing still works in emergency mode as dream work. The patient needs the auxiliary reality of the delusion for stabilizing the systemic process of his self-development. The patient must learn to think about his delusional world in the as-if mode and understand it as an *inner representation* (see Sect. 2.6). Then, he can differentiate his delusional reality from his everyday reality *all by himself*.

In psychotherapy of people with psychosis, the doppelganger dialogue *helps therapists* transform *their feelings* of powerlessness and helplessness into *action* in a therapeutically effective way. The *theory of metacognitive interventions* described here gives the therapist security and is a map for orientation in her practical work.

The practical implementation of the doppelganger dialogue is full of surprises. When using the doppelganger dialogue, the therapist acts in the here and now *without prejudice, interpretation, prior determination, and expectations.* Her acting is similar to the famous Zen Buddhist parable: the therapist sees the patient with delusion like someone catching fish *with a wicker basket* in the river. But she *doesn't* say: "That won't work!" Instead, she grabs a second wicker basket, steps into the river, and "catches trout" too. She comments on her actions: "There, a shadow! Heck, the trout is gone; it just took off!—It probably saw me.—The water is pretty cold.—The trout probably just swam to the other trout and warned them about us!—I wonder if trout communicate with each other like whales?" In metacognitive psychodrama therapy of people experiencing psychosis, the therapist learns the art of failure. As a doppelganger, she actively tries to successfully develop the reality and logic in the delusional story together with the patient. But, she fails. Otherwise, the story wouldn't have been a delusion.

As a psychodynamic psychotherapist, Benedetti (1983, p. 199 f.) *also* designed the therapeutic relationship with patients with psychosis transmodally. His statements seem to explain the *psychodramatic doppelganger dialogue*. He recommended that the therapist must consciously absorb his patient's delusional symptom and, *by acting together in the symptom*, "enrich it with feelings and ideas of his own, which continue and modify the patient's suffering simultaneously. [...] The therapist's fantasy transforms the patient's self-image [...] into a new one that does not negate the first, but rather connects with what is creative in the therapist's experience." Benedetti (1983, p. 297 f.) thought that "the *therapeutic identity confusion* can be a way to overcome the identity confusion in which the psychosis is grounded. The first is the reversal of the second." The doppelganger function of the therapist in the patient's delusional production results in a *"dualization of the patient's autistic psychopathology"*: "The resulting relationship, in turn, develops a dynamic based on the ability to transpose the patient's psychopathological experiences into a dialogue without at the same time negating them or dismissing them as 'abnormal'. But then the patient may open up to the therapist and let him peek into his inner world. This breakthrough is made possible precisely through the therapeutic experience of and participation in the preceding autistic isolation." The therapist should be able "to incorporate the patient's identity and shelter it without losing herself in the process" (Benedetti, 1983, p. 194). The psychodramatic doppelganger dialogue and its theory could help psychodynamic psychotherapists apply Benedetti's recommendations more frequently.

*Cognitive-behavioral* therapists stop halfway in their treatment of people with psychosis. They also have their patients describe the interactions in their delusional world scenically and playfully identify with the patient's ego in his delusional production. They also verbalize the patient's feelings and construct an interactional delusion scene with self-image and object image: "You feel persecuted. The person up there is certainly one of the persecutors." However, the therapists *do not* enter the patient's delusion production in the doppelganger dialogue to develop it and, thus, stop it (see Sect. 9.8). Instead, together with the patient, they patiently and paradoxically search for evidence of reality in the delusion. However, by definition, this is not possible. They, therefore, offer *alternative* explanations to replace delusional thoughts (Lincoln & Heibach, 2017, p. 53). In cognitive behavioral therapy, the patients should "question their dysfunctional assumptions about reality" (Lincoln & Heibach, 2017, p. 47). The therapist hope that the *insight into illness* would reduce or stop the production of delusion over time. The therapist tries to improve the patient's *ability to distinguish between* reality and delusion from a position of maternal acceptance.

**Central idea**

In psychotic decompensation, the tools of mentalizing work in emergency mode as mechanisms of dreamwork (see Sects. 9.3 and 9.6) and, therefore produce delusions. Cognitive-behavioral therapy does not treat this *cause* of delusion production. On the contrary, *metacognitive psychodrama therapy* for psychosis tries to change the patient's *metacognitive process* which produces his dysfunctional delusional thought content. The psychodramatic conversion of mechanisms of dreamwork into tools of mentalizing stops or reduces *the current production* of delusional content. Patients regain ego control over the function of their mentalizing tools. In doing so, the patient *autonomously* develops *an insight* into his illness and *searches* for new solutions in dealing with his conflicts.

### *9.8.6 Psychopharmacological Treatment and Personal Emergency Plan*

Drug treatment with neuroleptics helps people with psychosis reduce their *sensitivity* to conflicts and, thus, *indirectly* strengthens their ego in everyday life. The problem, however, is that after stopping the neuroleptics, they often decompensate into psychosis again within a few days or weeks. Neuroleptic drugs do *not* 'glue' self fragments of patients with psychosis, as Hartwich assumes (2018, p. 179). They only paralyze the *dysfunctional* metacognitive processes producing the delusion. But, *mentalization-oriented, metacognitive action methods* develop Hartwich's desired "bonding qualities between the self-fragments" (Hartwich, 2018, p. 179) in the psychotherapy of psychoses. Constructing the delusion scene and joint interacting and rehearsing in the delusion scene bind the self-fragments to each other. For this purpose, in psychodrama, we use the doppelganger dialogue, the symbolizing of the dream ego alongside the everyday ego (see Sect. 9.8.1), the auxiliary world method (see Sect. 9.8.8), and hand puppetry (see Sect. 9.10).

In mentalization-oriented therapy, the therapist offers drug treatment from a transmodal attitude as it implicitly questions the patient's delusional reality. Otherwise, there will be a struggle for reality between her and the patient. Medication should make sense for the patient *within his subjective experience of reality.* Therefore, the therapist looks for a symptom of distress in the patient's *everyday life* that is treatable with neuroleptics. For example, insomnia or the inner agitation and stress caused by the voices: "It must be difficult for you to hear your neighbors talk about you incessantly and still go on with your life as if nothing is wrong. Especially when you are sensitive to conflicts. However, there is the option of taking medication, for example, one tablet of Amisulprid 100 mg daily. This drug makes you less sensitive to conflict. Then you wouldn't feel so agitated when your neighbors talk about you. Anyhow you would still be able to drive a car."

***Case example 94***
*A 20-year-old student, Mr. C., comes for an initial consultation because of drug-induced psychosis (ICD F12.5). He keeps hearing voices, although he says it's been six months since he last used illegal drugs. When asked, he confirmed that he had consumed excessive hashish for five years. He considers himself an addict. But he is now abstinent and never wants to use illegal drugs again. The patient has superficial insight into his illness concerning his psychotic experience. However, after being discharged from the clinic, he had not taken the prescribed psychotropic drugs for three months. As a result, he has decompensated again. In the second therapy session, the therapist explains to the strong rational young man: "Your psychosis probably came about because your ego strength has weakened through years of heavy hashish consumption. The drugs have diminished your ability to process conflict internally. That's how hashish work. My approach in psychotherapy aims to improve your ego strength again. In psychotherapy, we rebuild your ego strength together. But when you hear voices, you are torn between your delusional world and your everyday world. Your laboriously improved ego strength keeps collapsing and is unable to grow. I, therefore, make it a condition of psychotherapy that you take a small dose of neuroleptics, at least in the first phase of treatment. The dosage should be high enough that your voices disappear. The medication should have little or no side effects. First, you can try the tablets for three days. Tablets are not the same as depot injections. So you can simply stop taking the tablets if you experience any side effects. Come back after three days and then tell me whether you noticed any positive effects of the medication and, if so, what those were!" (continued in* Sect. 9.8.8*).*

**Recommendation**

The therapist should *only* begin long-term outpatient psychotherapy with a *patient with psychosis if* the patient has at least attempted low-dose drug treatment with neuroleptics in tablet form within the first five sessions of psychotherapy.

If the patient takes neuroleptics *in tablet form* during the initial phase of treatment, he is *involved* in the decision-making process about the type and amount of medication (see case example 94 see above). In patients with an initial psychotic decompensation, the fourteen-day depot injection is used *only in acute crises* because many patients do not know the consequences of their consent to depot injections. It can temporarily lead to severe side effects. *Side effects* of neuroleptics include muscle cramps, movement disorders, visual disturbances, fatigue, sexual disturbances, hand cramps when writing, and cognitive impairment, among others. Therapists, including psychologists, should *actively look* for such side effects and ask about them during treatment with psychotropic drugs. Psychiatrists should reduce the medication as much as possible in the event of side effects. In the psychotherapy of psychoses, Benedetti and other therapists from the Zurich School have "always advocated that, depending on the situation, drug treatment can very well support and promote psychotherapeutic care" (Red, 2018, p. 347).

*Treatment* with neuroleptics *reduces the patients' sensitivity to conflicts.* That is the goal of taking the medication. But *excessive medication* paralyzes the patient's inner conflict processing *in psychotherapy.* As a result, psychotherapy is then less effective. However, *too little medication* also impedes progress in psychotherapy. The patient's working memory is overwhelmed with strong emotions and unresolved conflicts. The patient's mentalization ability, which had improved in psychotherapy, breaks down time and again.

**Recommendation**

Neuroleptics should be prescribed in adequate amounts to stop auditory hallucinations *largely* because continuous hearing of voices traumatizes the patient's soul. Hearing voices indicates that the patient's psychological process structures *are still disintegrating in the present.* On the other hand, it is advantageous if the patient hears one or more voices once every two to four weeks. The therapist and the patient can then *enter into the acute delusional production together* and work through the conflict in the delusion scene. In this way, the patient learns to deal actively with his current voices. He can also practice this directly in his everyday life (see case examples 94 and 96 in Sects. 9.8.6 and 9.8.8). At the end of psychotherapy, patients with psychosis should have lived *without psychotropic drugs* for six months if possible. Or the patient takes the smallest possible amount for him in the long run.

In exceptional cases, patients must be admitted to a psychiatric clinic. In the case of self-harm or danger to others, even *involuntary admission is crucial. After the hospital stay,* the therapist should discuss with the patient the shared experience of the process of involuntary admission in *psychotherapy*: She asks him what he experienced during the admission and how he judges the admission retrospectively. She justifies her actions once again. She openly names the fear she had for him as a person and acknowledges her limits: "I would like to be a grandiose therapist. But I've realized that I've failed whenever I tried to be grandiose."

People with psychosis often have difficulty remembering their *therapy experiences* because of their mentalizing disorder. The therapist thus becomes the patient's memory *vicariously.* She actively reminds him of such shared experiences when needed. Additionally, she invites the patient to draw up a *written crisis plan* collaboratively as her *own* memory aid. This crisis plan should include the following information: (1) What specific signs can help the patient recognize that he is beginning to decompensate? If he doesn't sleep *one* night, it may be a coincidence. However, the danger is imminent if the patient cannot sleep *two nights in a row.* The patient is also at risk when other people "can hear the patient's thoughts again" or when "the neighbors are talking about him again". (2) Which medications will help him in *crisis*, and what dosage? (3) What will he do if he feels unwell again? For example, the patient can decide that if a particular event occurs, he will immediately consult a doctor and tell him that he is afraid of experiencing psychosis again. (4) Patients who have advanced in therapy can plan to feel angry toward their voices, interact with them internally, and influence them suggestively (see case examples 94 in Sects. 9.8.6 and 9.8.8, and 96 in Sect. 9.8.8). The therapist recommends that the patient *always carry* his crisis plan in his wallet.

### 9.8.7 Collaborative Therapy Planning

After the initial five sessions of therapy, the therapist decides if she wants to work psychotherapeutically with the patient on a long-term basis. In the first session, she uses the doppelganger dialogue for diagnosis and crisis intervention, or 'only' for the improvement of the psychiatric relationship. A crisis intervention needs 1–2 sessions, short-term psychotherapy or trial therapy includes 25 sessions, and long-term psychotherapy needs 100 sessions or more.

**Central idea**

In making this decision, the therapist *also* relies on her feelings for guidance: "Do I connect with the patient? Does the patient's suffering touch me? Do I have the courage to engage with the patient despite all the insecurities?" These are indications that the therapy could go well. Sometimes, the therapist's intuition is wiser than her mind.

The severity of illness experienced by patients with psychosis varies greatly. While a single hospital stay or brief disorder-specific therapy is sufficient for some patients, others need 100 to 200 therapy sessions or longer. The therapist *can't make* the patient heal. It happens autonomously. But the therapist can create good external conditions which promote healing. How healing occurs is ultimately a mystery. An excess of something good doesn't always heal more. The disorder-specific therapeutic techniques must be subordinate to the therapist's intuition. The therapist must be patient and intervene in the right place at the right time. In doing this, the theory *extends* the therapist's stability. The *spontaneity and creativity in the therapeutic relationship* between the patient and the therapist and the stability and flexibility in the therapeutic relationship are central to the healing process. Appropriate therapeutic techniques must be used *for the specific person in the current moment.* Only then they are therapeutically effective.

The goal of psychotherapy for psychoses is not always *total* healing. However, it means a lot for people with psychosis, their families, and society, (1) if hospital admissions can be avoided or shortened, (2) if the amount of psychotropic drugs is low, which in turn results in fewer long-term side effects, (3) if a person can avoid a decade-long career as a psychiatric patient, (4) if the patient remains part of his family, (5) if he does not have to retire, and (6) if he does not kill himself.

**Central idea**

Psychotherapy for psychoses is emotionally exhausting for therapists because of the patient's metacognitive confusion. But the therapist gains a lot. In her existential encounter with the patient, the therapist develops her intuition, her inner flexibility, her creativity, and her sensitivity to the truth of the soul. She learns anew to attribute a radical positive meaning to the absurd. These skills are also helpful in the therapy of less severely disturbed patients. For example, they are fundamental in dealing with defense and resistance therapeutically and in the therapy of patients with personality disorders (see Sect. 9.4) or addiction disorders (see Sect. 9.10).

The therapist should initially treat only one or two patients with psychosis in long-term psychotherapy, preferably with accompanying supervision. In inpatient treatment, the therapist should discuss the psychotherapeutic approach with her superiors and the team. The team must want to support the psychotherapy process. Otherwise, the therapist and her patient will attract projections that are likely to burden the treatment.

### *9.8.8 Moreno's Auxiliary World Method in Contemporary Form*

**Question**
Why does a patient with psychosis also have to *act psychodramatically* in his auxiliary world and not just verbally in the double dialogue?

Moreno's auxiliary world method was a form of individual therapy. Assistant therapists, as auxiliary egos, would enter the patient's *delusional reality* for several weeks and realize it in the as-if mode of play together with the patient *in the everyday reality of the clinic* (see case example 83 in Sect. 9.5) as if the delusion were real. Today, the auxiliary world method would strain most clinics' human and time resources because of the tremendous effort involved. However, one can implement it with less effort, even in outpatient therapy. Today we use *chairs and hand puppets* instead of the assistant therapists to represent and enact the interaction system of the delusion outside in the therapy room.

**Central idea**

The core disturbance in people experiencing psychosis is the disintegration of the inner systemic process of self-development and the dissociation of internal psychosomatic resonance patterns (see Sect. 9.3). Thus, the tools of mentalizing work in emergency mode as mechanisms of dream work and produce delusion content (see Sect. 9.4). Patients with psychosis even fail in the first step of mentalizing—the *internal representing* of self-image and object image in the delusion scene.

For example, patients who feel persecuted *cannot* perceive the persecutor as a *real* person in the external world. Therefore, as reasonable persons, they do not *interact* with him. Their conflict processing is blocked. The therapist, therefore, *represents* the patient's 'ego which is persecuted' with a chair next to him *and* the 'persecutor' as an interaction partner facing him, with a chair and a hand puppet. Thus, the patient sees his 'persecutor' externally and can *interact* with him *psychosomatically* in the as-if mode of play. The therapist accompanies him as a metacognitive doppelganger. This interaction can also happen in the initial interview (see case example 95).

**Case example 95 (Alfons Rothfeld, 2018, only communicated as E-Mail)**

*After the psychosis seminar, I soon had the unexpected opportunity to use the auxiliary world method on a patient. This patient felt watched and controlled by signals. I placed two chairs in the therapy room, one for herself and one across from her, for the unknown person watching and controlling her. I actively turned to this unknown person and spoke clearly and distinctly as a doppelganger: 'I, Dr. Rothfeld, disapprove of your behavior towards Mrs. G. You are violating Mrs. G.'s human dignity! I want you to stop that!' The patient looked at me in disbelief for a moment. Then she started laughing out loud. At the end of the session, she said: 'I'm curious if this will stop now!' As she was leaving, she looked back to the persecutor's chair and said: 'And you stay here now!' In the next therapy session, the patient spontaneously expressed: 'I didn't think that yelling at a chair would be so effective!' From this point on, the patient questioned her delusion of persecution.*

The therapist and the patient *represented* the delusion scene with the persecutor externally in the therapy room and *interacted* with the persecutor in the as-if mode of play. Thus, the patient's tools of mentalizing were liberated from working in emergency mode as mechanisms of dreamwork. This stopped the delusional production and promoted insight into the illness.

**Central idea**

The auxiliary world method stabilizes the inner systemic process of self-development (see Sect. 9.4) and, thus, stops the disintegration of self-development.

When using the auxiliary world method, the therapist completes the following steps:

1. The therapist *represents* the patient's self-image in the delusional reality with a second chair next to the patient. She gives it a personally appropriate name or calls it his "dream ego" (see Sect. 9.8.1).
2. She *switches to* the *doppelganger dialogue* and represents (see Sects. 9.8.4 and 9.8.5) the patient's interaction partners involved in the delusion scene with empty chairs and hand puppets as inner object images externally in the therapy room (see Fig. 2.9 in Sect. 2.8): 'These are the two demons whose voices you heard. I'll place these two chairs to represent these demons." Or: "Ah, there were *three* police cars. I represent them here with these three chairs. The three police cars drove up behind you and chased you!" The persons or figures who do good to the patient in his delusion reality should *look at* his 'persecutor' or the 'voices' shoulder to shoulder together with him.
3. In the as-if mode of play, the therapist and the patient collaborate to recreate the recalled interactions in the patient's delusion scene and even develop them further beyond reality through rehearsal. For example, the *patient* tells the therapist what the voice he hears says to him. *The therapist* lets change the patient to the chair of his 'dream ego'. She then represents the 'voice' with a chair opposite him. She steps behind the chair of the 'voice' and repeats as an auxiliary ego: "The voice says to you: I know the company where you work. The story about your boyfriend is also a wild one." The therapist waits for the patient's reaction. Again she steps next to the patient and asks: "What are you thinking and feeling right now? Please, tell that to the man?"
4. The therapist then works with the patient to develop the interaction sequences in the delusion scene into a meaningful story. Action and reaction in the delusion scene should interlock like the hooks of a zipper. In this way, the patient shapes the reality and causality in the delusion scene *with self-determination*. In doing this, the patient needs time to mentalize. Then, he shall become "the creator of his own life" (Moreno, 1970, p. 78).

5. The patient can and should correct the therapist's statements continually. She then takes what was said and immediately integrates it into the delusional co-production.
6. The therapist lets the patient also switch to the role of his interaction partner *for a short while* if necessary. But he is only supposed to *show* how his dead grandmother or the "persecutor" *would* react to his actions. He should *not* clarify the relationship with the conflict partner in a psychodramatic dialogue with repeated role reversal (see Sect. 9.12).
7. Often a delusional figure *endangers the patient's life* or *violates his dignity*. In such a case, the therapist supports him by acting as a doppelganger, similar to his approach in the therapy of persons diagnosed with a masochistic personality disorder (Sects. 4.8 and 8.5). She consciously notices the emotions triggered *in her* in the external presence of the "persecutor" as a chair and allows herself to experience the feeling in the as-if mode of play. Then as the patient's doppelganger, the therapist actively opposes the "persecutor" or the "voice" by *interacting* psychosomatically on the patient's behalf. She speaks clearly with the "conflict partner". She yells at the "voice" when necessary (see case example 95 in Sect. 9.8.8) and angrily tells it to stop its destructive behavior. In doing so, she justifies her request appropriately: "You are Ms. H.'s grandparents. But you are already dead! You can't want your granddaughter to join you in the world of the dead! She will die for sure! As a grandparent, you must want your granddaughter to live!" Or: "I'm outraged. You are Mrs. D.'s boss! How dare you watch Mrs. D. on the toilet! It is violating! As the boss, you surely want Mrs. D. to do her job well. Then please stop bothering Mrs. D. at work too!"

**Recommendation**

If necessary, the therapist grabs *the chair* for the persecutor or the voice and moves it 3 or 4 meters away by the window. Or she even takes him out of the room. In doing so, she explains her actions to the patient: "I can't think when I feel threatened. The secret service man is too close for me. That's why I'm putting the chair for him over there!" She sits down on her own chair again and feels her emotions: "Yes, that's better!"

**Central idea**

As a doppelganger, the therapist *stabilizes* the patient's internal process of self-development through vicarious acting *and mentalizing in the as-if mode of play* (see Fig. 9.2 in Sect. 9.8.4). Thus, she supports the patient's inner process of self-development.

8. In the case of patients with *delusions of grandeur* (ICD: F25.0), the therapist uses empty chairs to place one or more supporting *fictional 'helpers'* beside them. For example, "Jesus" needs "several disciples" who support him. A patient who is "preparing to be a prophet" needs an "angel" to tell him whether he "should make his religious announcements *now* or wait."
9. The therapist can try to conclude a contract with the patient's conflict partner in his delusion scene *on his behalf*, for example, the "voice". Romme and Escher (1997, p. 73, p. 75 ff.) have found that patients can also do this *on their own*: "It has helped others who have experienced something similar to you. Ask the

voices not to bother you until after 8 p.m. Tell the voices you first need to focus on your work in your company!"

10. In the auxiliary world method, the therapist and the patient try to rewrite what happened in the delusion scene in the as-if mode of play into a coping story (see Sect. 9.8.4).
11. Together, the therapist and the patient try to integrate the logical consequence following the delusional reality into everyday reality.

**Case example 96 (Krüger, 2013a, 2013b, 2013c, p. 184 f.)**

*The 35-year-old, attractive, intelligent Ms. G. had been suffering from a chronic delusional disorder (F22.0) for three years. She kept hearing the voices of her neighbors in her apartment. The "neighbors" complained she was too loud or snoring at night. She had already moved four times in the last three years because of "intense sound absorption" in her apartments. The patient was friendly and overadjusted in everyday life. However, in intimate relationships, she could not maintain this attitude in the long term and often reacted uncontrollably and angrily. That irritated her. The therapist represented the angry inner ego state, similar to working with a patient with a borderline organization (see* Sect. 4.9*), with an empty chair next to her: "On the one hand, you are the kind, needy Renate. The other chair next to you represents what you call the 'disgusting Renate'."*

*In the 28th therapy session, the patient reported that she was doing well. She no longer heard the "neighbors" speak, even without medication. For the first time, she had been open with her boyfriend about her tendency to over-adapt and even found new, less perfect solutions with him. The therapist was pleased with her progress. Ms. G.: "I also use earplugs now because Robert snores very loudly. Therefore, I hear no more voices. It's not even possible."*

*The therapist was startled. He noticed that the intelligent patient was still mixing her delusional reality with her everyday reality. As a metacognitive doppelganger, he immediately modified the therapeutic relationship into a transmodal encounter. He pointed to the empty chair of her dream ego next to her: "Now you put earplugs in your ears at night." He set up two additional empty chairs three meters away from the patient for "the female neighbor" and "the male neighbor": "You can no longer hear the two neighbors because of your earplugs. But what do they say about that? They want to complain to you that you are too loud! The neighbors will surely think that these earplugs are mean." Ms. G.: "No, they don't complain directly to me. They only gossip about me!" The therapist turned the two chairs for the "neighbors" around such that they looked at each other: "So they talk to each other. They're an old married couple. They're bored and always pay attention to what's happening in the house." Ms. G.: "No, they're my age. But they are successful, intelligent, and good-looking. They don't have any problems!" Ms. G. added: "Ever since I was in secondary school, I've often felt inferior to people who have a good education, have their lives under control, and everything is fine with them." The direct psychodramatic encounter with the "neighboring couple" in the as-if mode of play on the room stage, allowed the patient to spontaneously integrate a problem from her everyday life in her delusion scene. At the end of the session, Ms. G. said: "Today you hit a weak spot in me!" (continued below).*

**Central idea**

People with psychosis experience the voices they hear or their persecutor as *external reality*. But, they *cannot see them and interact with them*. Therefore, they don't know *who with whom, how, and why*. Moreno (1939, p. 2) has already recognized the significance of psychosomatic acting in the therapy of psychoses: The therapist asks the patient to "throw himself back into the hallucinatory experience when it is still most vivid in his mind. He is not asked to describe it: he must act it out."

The following reasons explain the therapeutic effect of the auxiliary world method:

1. The joint *construction* of the delusion scene creates the patient's inner self-image and inner object image in the delusion and answers the question: Who with whom? The conflict partners can be represented *only* with chairs and hand puppets. The auxiliary world method helps the patient *to encounter* their conflict partner *psychosomatically* in the delusion scene in the as-if mode of play. The joint psychosomatic *interaction* of the therapist and the patient creates chronological interaction sequences in the delusionary world and answers the question: How? The joint *rehearsal* in the delusion scene answers the question: Why? The joint *action* stabilizes the inner systemic process of self-development in the delusion scene. The joint mentalizing in the delusion scene frees the tools of mentalizing from their function as mechanisms of dream work and, thus, stops or reduces the current delusional production (see Sects. 9.4 and 9.8).
2. In contrast to the purely verbal doppelganger dialogue, the therapist and the patient enter the delusional scene *psychosomatically*. Thus, the patient experiences his doppelganger as *physically* present beside her in the delusion scene. This *psychosomatically* eliminates the patient's existential loneliness in his delusional reality (see case examples 88 and 90 in Sects. 9.8.1 and 9.8.2).
3. The patient represents her conflict partner in the as-if mode of play with a chair opposite her and gives him a name. Representing and naming the conflict partner is an act of self-empowerment. It gives the patient a sense of self-efficacy.
4. The patient *directly interacts* with her "persecutors" in the as-if mode of play. The chronological order of the *interaction sequences* in the delusion scene constellates the *reality* contained in the delusion scene.
5. The therapist and the patient work together to create *cause and effect* in the delusion scene through rehearsing. They attempt to *rewrite* the traumatizing delusional experiences into individual coping stories, activating the patient's self-healing system (see Sects. 5.13 and 5.14).
6. The patient's *internal systemic process of self-development* starts anew (see Sect. 9.4). Through their joint action, the patient and the therapist integrate the *free-floating elements* of delusion production into a new psychosomatic resonance pattern that is separate from the patient's everyday reality. A psychosomatic resonance pattern interconnects five different memory centers of the brain, namely sensorimotor interaction patterns, physical sensations, affect, linguistic

concepts, and thoughts. The new holistic psychosomatic resonance pattern integrates the high-energy affect which had triggered the decompensation into psychosis.
7. The high-energy conflict image of the delusional scene contained in the psychosomatic resonance pattern links itself with the patient's current everyday conflict after it has been *fully mentalized*. For example, the patient in case example 96 (see above and below) spontaneously understood her feeling of inferiority in relation to the 'voices' of her neighbors as a symbolic image of the inferiority she feels in her everyday life when comparing herself to people who are well-educated and have no problems. Her spontaneous integration was an indication that she had adequate ego strength to complete this integration with biographical conflicts without negative side effects (see Sect. 9.6).
8. The joint development of delusion stabilizes the process of self-development thereby improving the patient's ego strength. The vicious circle between being delusional and being traumatized by the fear of going insane is broken. The patient is, therefore, better able to cope with some conflicts in her everyday life *even without discussing them in therapy*.
9. Over time, the patient learns to *autonomously* reduce or stop her current delusion production by interacting in her delusion scene. In doing this, she integrates the as-if mode of play into her delusional thinking and thus becomes the "creator of her own life" (Moreno, 1970, p. 77).

**Case example 96 (1st continuation)**

*In the 35th therapy session, Ms. G. returned exhausted from a 14-day vacation. She said, feeling disappointed: "I was on holiday with my boyfriend in Tenerife. All hell broke loose in two days. The voices were back. I thought I would have to admit myself to a Spanish hospital. I had forgotten my pills. I haven't used them here at home for a long time. But I panicked on the island. On the fourth night, I heard the neighbors talking again. The neighbor said to his wife: 'I know the company where she works. It's a wild story with her boyfriend too!' At first, I was shocked and scared. But then I thought: 'It can't be that someone from my company is here!' I got angry. I consciously thought of a lie and thought: 'And I'm sure you were with me at the kindergarten in Celle!' I kept repeating this sentence to myself. And then the neighbor really said to his wife: 'And you know, I used to go to the kindergarten in Celle with her!' Then I deliberately added something crazy and thought intensively: 'Yes! And my mother was on vacation with your mother in Turkey last year too!' Then I heard the neighbor's voice again, who said: 'And by the way, my mother was on vacation with her mother in Turkey last year!' Then I realized: 'I have control over what happens.' That was very relieving!".*

*The therapist: "And then the neighbor was quiet." The patient: "Yes, I didn't hear the neighbors from then on." Ms. G. did not take any psychotropic drugs in the last two years of her therapy. She didn't have any psychotic symptoms, even three years after the end of treatment.*

During therapy, the patient developed a permanent insight into her illness and spontaneously integrated her delusional conflict with an important life conflict. She, therefore, became angry at the voices when they bothered her again. She *internally represented* the delusion scene between herself and the 'voices', *interacted* with the voices, and tried to influence them through *mental rehearsing*. Internally, she suggested to her "neighbors" what they should think and say. Her "neighbors" reacted to her inner actions like puppets. The patient realized that she could control the 'voices' *through her own actions*. She developed ego control over her internal object image—the 'neighbor's voices'—in the delusion scene. Her representing, interacting, and rehearsing liberated her tools of mentalizing from their function as mechanisms of dreamwork in emergency mode. Thus, she stopped her current delusional production.

10. Patients with psychosis are often not aware of their new ability to stop or reduce their delusion production. This is because they *don't* detach their experience from the concrete situation and view it from a meta-perspective. They act in the as-if mode of play, but cannot yet detach the self-healing technique from the delusion scene. Therefore, the therapist must help them to internally represent their healing experience as a 'self-healing technique' *in the as-if mode of thinking*. In doing so, the therapist looks *at the two chairs* representing the "dream ego" and the "voice" in the delusion scene (see Sect. 9.8.1) and asks the patient: "Remember your experience with your voice! Try to use this experience as a self-help technique in other situations as well!" The therapist encourages the patient to include this self-help technique in their crisis plan.

***Case example 94 (continued from* Sect. 9.8.6)**

*In the 7th therapy session, the therapist recommended a 20-year-old student, Mr. C., to directly ask his "voices" to behave differently. He told him how the patient in case example 96 (see above) had done this. In the next therapy session, Mr. C. reported spontaneously: "What you suggested didn't work! I heard my friend's voice. So I thought of a certain sentence that I wanted him to say. I suggested this sentence: 'What I am saying here has no purpose; it makes no sense!' There was a voice that said what I said. But it wasn't my friend's voice!" The therapist: "And how did it continue?" Mr. C.: "Then the voices were gone for four to five days. That was positive. But it wasn't my friend's voice that said what I wanted!' Therapist: 'I don't think you can always dictate everything exactly to your voices. They have their own right to exist. However, I am pleased that you addressed your friend's voice directly. You achieved what you wanted! You found a way to make a voice you hear disappear for four days!" Mr. C. is still dissatisfied: "But the voice came back after five days!".*

*In this situation, the therapist uses the doppelganger dialogue to have the patient describe the exact situation in which the voice spoke to him again: Mr. C. went to a party in the evening. It was a farewell party for the man he used to buy drugs from when he was a hash addict. This man has now gone abroad as a soldier in the federal armed forces. When the patient arrived at the drug dealer's house, he heard a girl's voice. He knew her voice from earlier "psychotic fantasies." Mr. C.: "I was shocked to hear a voice again after five days. Then I thought with all my might: 'Get out, get out!' Then the voice said: 'Oh, yes, yes!' Then I got angry. I thought: 'I can think whatever I want in my head, nobody cares!' So I said to the voice: 'Speak more clearly!'" Therapist: "And then the voice asked you: 'Why should I speak more clearly!'" Mr. C.: "No, then the voice was gone!" Therapist: "You have now made one of your voices disappear for the second time!".*

*Therapist: "Maybe it's not a good idea for you to go to your former drug dealer's party as a clean hash addict! That stresses you internally." Mr. C.: "Actually, I didn't want to go there. But a friend took me. He also has cannabis-induced psychosis. Unlike me, however, he has not taken any medication for five years. He has only been sitting at the computer and playing for five years. He hasn't worked in five years!' Therapist: 'Well, maybe your way is better after all. At least you've got your high school diploma!".*

**Central idea**

The patient's *self-determined* representation and interaction with his object image in the delusion scene is therapeutically a leap in quality that reduces or stops the current delusion production (see Sect. 9.8). Therefore, even small actions dealing with delusional figures have a tremendous therapeutic effect (see case example 101 in Sect. 9.12).

**Recommendation**

The therapist can stop *only the current* delusional production with the help of the doppelganger dialogue and the auxiliary world technique. Therefore, the disappearance of voices happens differently in each patient over days, weeks, or months (see case example 94 in Sects. 9.8.6 and 9.8.8, and 96 in Sect. 9.8.8). Moreno already said that the frequency of therapy sessions should depend on the extent of the current delusional production. In the acute stage, the frequency should be higher (Moreno, 1945a, p. 5 f.) (see Sect. 9.11).

***Case example 97***

*A young patient, Ms. H., had regularly heard the voice of a monster and rapist during the night. During the doppelganger dialogue, the therapist placed an empty chair for this perpetrator in the therapy room opposite the patient. The patient and therapist looked at this "man" in the chair. Then, the therapist spoke directly to Ms. H.'s "persecutor" and loudly demanded that the monster respects the patient's right to integrity and her dignity as a human being. He called him a "rapist". Two sessions later, Ms. H. said: "It was important that I realized that I could talk about him here and that nothing happened! Because the rapist threatened to kill me if I told anyone else about him."*

The auxiliary world technique *also helps the therapist*. The therapist transforms her own natural resistance against the patient's current delusion production into therapeutically fruitful interventions when using the auxiliary world method. In doing so, she resolves her natural disintegration-related countertransference (see Sect. 2.10) and finds her way back to her inner spontaneity in the therapeutic relationship.

### 9.8.9 Application of the Auxiliary World Method to Delusions of Grandeur

The doppelganger dialogue is also the primary psychotherapy intervention in patients with delusions of grandeur. Patients with delusions of grandeur (see case example 86 in Sect. 9.7) fail by definition to assert their own perception of reality in the external world. They end up in a vicious circle. The feeling of failure reactivates old traumas in them. As a result, they have to compensate for their feelings of failure again with delusions of grandeur. In the doppelganger dialogue, the therapist and the patient construct the delusion scene externally in the therapy room and interact with the interaction partners in the scene. In doing so, they paradoxically *try to convert* the patient's delusions of grandeur into reality (see case examples 83 in Sect. 9.5 and 86 in Sect. 9.7). For this purpose, the therapist places fictional helpers on the patient's side. They help him to enforce his ideas of grandeur. The therapist represents them with chairs, hand puppets, or real auxiliary therapists in the therapy room.

***Case example 98***
*The 22-year-old Mr. I. smashed furniture in the hospital ward during his inpatient psychiatric treatment. During supervision, his therapist asked about the possibilities of psychodramatic intervention in such a situation. The supervisor let the therapist enact her patient's role, and he took on the 'therapist' role. As a 'therapist' in conversation with the 'patient', he summoned a 'ward staff member' with some psychodrama experience: 'Nurse Birgit, could you please come here? You have some experience with meditation. Mr. I. here is enlightened. I would like you to have him as your teacher for half an hour every day and talk to him about his enlightenment experiences." The therapist turns to the "patient": "I also have a request of you: Your enlightened spirits have commissioned you to make a mark in the world. These spirits will surely contact you again. If they get in touch, please connect with Nurse Birgit to discuss how you can best carry out the spirits' mission here on the ward. By the way, I would also like to speak to your spirits! There are three of them, right." The therapist places three chairs across from the patient and, as a doppelganger, addresses the "spirits" as fictional helpers: "You want Mr. I. to make a mark in this world. You want people to reflect on themselves and be less destructive. I ask you to stop Mr. I's mission for the time being as he is currently overwhelmed by this endeavor. He's here for treatment in a psychiatric hospital! He smashed the furniture in the ward on your behalf. As a result, as an enlightened person, he must stay here longer in the psychiatric clinic. His medication has also increased. As spirits, you can't want that! I think you are asking too much of Mr. I. As Mr. I.'s doctor, I urgently ask you to let Mr. I. calm down! He needs to recover!" The supervisor then explains this method to the supervision group.*

The fictional helpers enter the patient's delusion scene, interact with him and try to support him in the as-if mode of play in realizing his delusions of grandeur in everyday life. For example, "Hitler" needs his "aides," Goering and Goebbels. Similarly, "Jesus" is dependent on his "disciples". It often takes the therapist a day or two to think of a creative way to appropriately use the auxiliary world technique with this particular patient experiencing delusions of grandeur.

The fictional helpers should *interactively* support the "summoned" in gaining appropriate external recognition and position in the world or at least create suitable conditions for success (see case examples 83 in Sect. 9.5, 86 in Sect. 9.7, and 91 in Sect. 9.8.3). Of course, the fictional helpers *also* fail in this project. If they didn't fail, it wouldn't be a delusion. However, the patient is not lonely and does not fail alone; he fails *together with the therapist* as his doppelganger. Thus the patient learns that his feelings of failure and being overwhelmed could be justified and appropriate in this situation. He is comforted and witnessed in his suffering. As a result, his old traumas are not *as strongly* triggered. He doesn't have to continue compensating for them with his delusion of grandeur. The repeated interruption in the delusional production makes the patient autonomously aware of his illness over time (see case examples 83 in Sect. 9.5 and 86 in Sect. 9.7).

The auxiliary world technique breaks the vicious circle of negative transference and disintegration-related countertransference between the therapist and the patient. The patient feels taken seriously because of the *collaborative, serious effort* to realize his delusions, *even if their effort fails to produce tangible results*. It is precisely the paradoxical, absolutely authentic seriousness of the joint effort to convert the delusion into a reality that helps the patient notice that his *inner* construction of reality doesn't match his *external* reality.

## 9.9 Transforming a Depersonalization Process into a Creative Process of Self-direction

**Central idea**

In the case of depersonalization, there is a split between the patient's acting ego and observing ego (Wurmser, 1998, p. 425f.) (see Sect. 5.10.2). In therapy, the therapist represents the patient's split-off 'acting-ego' *externally* with a second chair in the therapy room and lets the patient *interact* and *rehearse* a dialogue between his two ego states using role reversal. Thus, the patient carries out his splitting *as a psychodramatic process* in the as-if mode of play. He resolves the defense through splitting and *integrates* his experience of mental decompensation with a triggering everyday conflict.

***Case example 82 (continued, see Sect. 9.3)* (Krüger, 2001a, *p. 263 ff., modified)***

*A 54-year-old patient, Mr. B., had repeatedly suffered from psychotic decompensation since he became a young adult. He has been participating in outpatient group therapy for patients with psychosis for twelve years now. In today's group session, he turns to the therapist right at the beginning and complains: "It's happening again. I'm not here anymore!" The group members and the therapist are shocked. After a brief group discussion, the therapist addresses the patient: "You are Mr. B., sitting there and feeling that you are no longer there." The therapist takes a second chair and places it in the other corner of the room, representing the patient's acting ego: "You lost yourself? Your lost Bernd is sitting in that chair back there." The therapist stands next to the patient as a doppelganger and addresses the missing Bernd's empty chair (the acting ego) in the other corner of the room: "What is this? You just took off!" Then he addresses the patient directly: "Could you swap roles and respond to me as Bernd, who has disappeared?" Mr. B. sits in the second chair of "Bernd" (in the role of his acting ego) and spontaneously recommends to the 'patient' in the first chair (of his observing ego): "You must remember how it was a year ago when you got sick! You took breaks at work. That did you good!" The therapist lets Mr. B. switch back to his first role of his observing ego. Mr. B. suddenly talks about his current conflicts at work without any confusion: "I have to make payments that would otherwise be forfeited. I have five urgent files on the table. Earlier I used to take breaks in between and tidy up in peace. Or I would do some photocopying. I can't do that anymore!" The play suddenly turns into a group discussion. Some participants urge Mr. B. to resolve the conflict differently: "Can't you tell your manager that? You are severely disabled!" The group wants Mr. B. to be different from what he is. He should assert himself when speaking to his boss! Mr. B. replies, "My boss knows it is impossible."*

*At this point, the therapist intervenes in a disorder-specific manner in the group discussion. He reinterprets the patient's depersonalization process radically positively and evaluates it as appropriate self-protective behavior: "I don't think it's good for you if you openly resolve the conflict with the boss. You are someone who, like everyone else in this group, is easily overwhelmed by conflicts. Otherwise, you would not experience psychosis. You are more sensitive than others. This is a common characteristic in people with psychosis. Therefore I like your solution better! If you can't withstand the demands of your job anymore, just split off your feelings and block them! It's not the best solution, but it's a solution!" The therapist steps up next to the patient and speaks to him in the role of his observing ego: "Mr. B., allow me to throw Bernd (the acting ego) out along with his feeling of being overwhelmed! He'll only cause you problems!" The therapist, acting as the patient's doppelganger, turns to the imaginary Bernd (his acting ego) in the other corner of the room: "Sit down and shut up! I'll close the door now, then you're gone and can't disturb me anymore. I can't stand your feelings of being overwhelmed! I have to work!" The therapist holds two imaginary door handles and locks the "door" between the patient and the missing Bernd (the acting ego). Mr. B. laughs uncertainly: "No, you can't do that!" Some group members protest indignantly: "That's impossible!' The grotesque solution causes astonishment and laughter in the group. However, the therapist defends his approach: "But what if Mr. B. can't stand the conflict!" A lively group discussion follows. Two participants share similar situations of feeling overwhelmed at work.*

*In the further group sessions, Mr. B. clearly describes his boss as a "workaholic" for the first time after twelve years of participation in the group: "He had a heart attack five years ago. And now he's saying—and he really said that—that one is serious about their work only if they eventually have a heart attack. There is no praise or recognition! He doesn't understand if you tell him something about stress or psychosis!" The therapist advises the patient: "So your boss knows everything, but he doesn't understand anything! Mr. B., please be careful! Don't get into a conflict with your boss. You can't withstand it! Just do your work, one step at a time, as well as possible."*

*A week later, in the group session, Mr. B spontaneously reported: "Last time's role play was good for me. However, the workload hasn't decreased. Out of six people, only three of us are currently on duty. A colleague who is ten years junior can not cope with the stress either. But I can organize my work better again. I also met my boss on Tuesday. He rode the elevator with me to grab a bite. He asked me how I was doing. I said: 'There's a lot to do!' Then he said: 'You'll manage it!' That's how he always reacts! I could have strangled him when he said that!" The therapist: "Be careful! Don't get into a conflict with your boss! You can't withstand the stress of a conflict." Finally, the therapist asked him about his emotional numbness. Mr. B says: "It went away after the last session. I can feel again." Unlike before, the patient only decompensated into a psychotic episode three years later. He felt better again after one day with the help of a similar therapeutic procedure.*

In this case example, the therapist worked *explicitly metacognitively* (see Sects. 2.4 and 2.14). He had the patient resolve the *defensive* split between his acting ego and his observing ego by reconstructing the *process* of splitting in the as-if mode of play and working out its *positive function* in the holistic process of the patient's self-regulation. It turned out that the patient's masochistic defense through identification with the aggressor and his massive feeling of failure had led to the disintegration of his inner process of self-development. His inner representation of the conflict thus became the mechanism of the dream work 'Inner thoughts are perceived as outer reality' (see Sect. 9.3). Representing the split *psychodramatically* and interacting and rehearsing in the dysfunctional process of his self-development stopped his current delusional production and transformed his external perception of "I'm not here anymore" back into a metaphor. The dysfunctional perception "I'm not here anymore" turned out to be a *symbolic expression of* his feeling of being overwhelmed at work: "It's *as if* I'm not here anymore!".

## 9.10 Healing Psychotic Disintegration of Self Through Psychodramatic Play with Hand Puppets

Some patients with psychosis, experience a disintegration of the internal process of self-development and their psychosomatic resonance patterns *without* delusional production (ICD-10 F23.8). They have sufficient ego strength to prevent their tools of mentalizing from turning into mechanisms of dream work. But, they dissociate and split off their psychosomatic ego (sensorimotor interaction patterns, physical sensations, and affect) from their cognitive ego (linguistic concepts and thoughts) (see Sect. 2.7). Patients who split off their cognitive ego tend to become depressed (see case example 99 below). Patients who split off their psychosomatic ego tend to become rather manic (see case example 100 below). The patients experience metacognitive confusion between internal self-images or object images, ego states, emotions, interaction patterns, and internal symbols. The spatial and temporal organization in conflict processing is lost. People can experience psychoses *without delusions* in the case of post-traumatic stress disorder (F43.1), emotionally unstable personality disorder (F60.3), or dissociative disorder (F44.-).

Non-delusional psychotic patients evoke feelings of chaos and helplessness in the therapist. The therapist himself feels the confusion that the patient *would* feel if she *could* internally admit and label her feelings. In such a case, the therapist and the patient orient themselves together and grasp the patient's *current feelings* and internal images in the *current* situation. They *name* and *represent* the feelings with stones on the table stage or with chairs and hand puppets. First, they play them out *individually* and then let them interact *with each other*. Together, the patient and the therapist try to shape these interaction sequences into a holistic story with the process qualities of space, time, and logic using mental rehearsing with role reversal (see Fig. 2.5 in Sect. 2.3, Plassmann, 1999).

***Case example 99***

*The 48-year-old, Ms. J., was experiencing chronic psychosis and retired early. She had been traumatized several times during her childhood, including being an unwanted child. At the beginning of each new phase of the illness, she developed paranoid delusions of grandeur (F25.0). Subsequently, she became severely depressed (F25.1). One day Ms. J. comes to the therapy session severely depressed. She reports: "I've only been at home for a fortnight. I just sit there and do nothing!" The patient finds it difficult to talk about herself and her feelings. The therapist feels a tenacious heaviness in the encounter. In coordination with Ms. J, he represents her feelings in the current situation with hand puppets and enacts the roles to some extent: the slightly worn-out hand puppet of a girl is sitting in the armchair as 'the depressive girl'. She wants to read a book but can't concentrate. She has a sack filled with "emptiness." The therapist introduces a fictitious, helpful doppelganger into the patient's play. It is a hand puppet of a little boy. The 'little boy' wants to play with the 'depressive girl' girl. However, the patient reacts with displeasure. She finds the little boy to be "annoying". The therapist lets him go away: "Okay, I can come back tomorrow and ask you to play with me!".*

*In the next session, the patient reports emotionally: "I haven't been depressed in the last week. I felt the fragility of my soul. That was very nice!" The therapist asks her: 'Buy yourself a hand puppet that looks like the 'depressive girl' here and put it on the table at home in plain sight!' The patient protests: "That is unreasonable! The feeling that arises in me is far too intense!" In the following session, the patient does not speak; she refuses. Finally, when asked, she says: "I'm angry. You don't take my feelings seriously." The therapist does not allow himself to be irritated: "You are not doing well. I'm trying to understand you." He chooses a hand puppet of a magician to represent himself and puts it on the table: "That's me as a therapist." He lets the "therapist" engage in a monologue: "I know, I still have to orientate myself; it's not that easy! I think I still have to learn. I hope Ms. J. will help me with this!" The therapist takes another puppet and turns to the patient: "That's you as the angry one." He also lets the 'angry one' engage in a monologue. In doing this, he integrates Ms. J's earlier communications: "I feel like I'm in school here, dumb and stupid!" Ms. J. nods in confirmation.*

*In the following session, the patient says, "I haven't been scared for the last week. I no longer feel inferior; instead, I feel alone!" The therapist takes a different hand puppet 'for the lonely one'. This puppet is "a four-year-old child. The mother has gone away". Once again, the therapist invites a helpful doppelganger, a penguin hand puppet. The penguin wants to play with the lonely child. However, Ms. J. rejects the penguin again: "I want to be alone!" The therapist introduces another helpful doppelganger into the play, a "prince". Ms. J. turns him away too. However, rejecting the fictional helpers stabilizes the patient's self. She spontaneously talks about her work and plans at the Red Cross. The therapist takes the puppet of a princess: "I am the lively one. I want to experience the world!" The "lively one" wonders about "the girl who is alone". Ms. J. protests: "But I also want to be able to hibernate sometimes. Being alone is not bad! I feel safe when I am alone!".*

*In the following session, Ms. J. says: "I had a good week! I have now experienced 40% of my feelings instead of 10%." The therapist has the patient symbolize her current feelings with stones on the table: "the lively one who is sometimes even happy", "the anxious one who is afraid of everything new", the "depressive one", the "angry one," and "the lonely one". The therapist and the patient concretize these affective states as hand puppets and let them interact: the anxious and the lively ones talk to each other about the sad one* etc. *It reveals that "the anxious one" represents the patient's healthy adult thinking and mediates between the other affective states. Ms. J.: "The lively one is much too bold. But I don't want to just sit there like the depressed one either!" The therapist plays the anxious hand puppet's role, says goodbye to the cheerful one, and turns to the sad one. Both sit there quietly for a long time. Ms. J. keeps crying a little during the "play". She is very touched. In the debriefing, she shares: "I have experienced a variety of emotional states in the last few weeks. At first, I was afraid to accept my mixed feelings. I didn't want to feel any of them." The therapist symbolizes the "fear" and the "mixed feelings" with small stones. He playfully places them next to the corresponding hand puppets, the "fear" next to the "anxious one," and the "mixed feelings" next to the "depressive one".*

*In a joint review of the patient's experiences over the past few weeks, the patient and the therapist determined that the more time the "depressive" patient took, the lighter her feelings became. But the less time she had, the darker the feelings. Therapist: "I know it's hard for you to grasp your feelings. But our joint work has helped me to understand you better." Two weeks later, Ms. J. says: "Working with hand puppets was quite exhausting. But it also helped me feel relieved! I realized that I have feelings! I haven't felt too overwhelmed in the last few weeks. I've been more true to myself than I used to be."*

The freely floating fragments of the patient's self thus develop relationships with one another, thereby strengthening the patient's sense of coherence.

In such a mentalization-oriented approach, the therapist, *as a doppelganger*, *verbalizes* the patient's *current feelings*, *names* them, and *represents* them externally with hand puppets on the table. The patient and therapist then have the hand puppets interact with each other. In this way, every emotion has a right to exist with its unique identity in the interaction system. The self-fragments, which previously existed side by side without being connected, develop relationships with each other and with associated affect by naming, representing, interacting, and rehearsing with role reversal in the as-if mode of play. The patient creates cause and effect in a holistic story. In this way, puppetry stops the disintegration of the inner process of self-development. The internal systemic process of self-development becomes coherent. The new *relationships between* the different self-fragments coordinate the patient's inner conflict processing in the further course of therapy.

***Case example 100* (Krüger, 1997, *p. 44 f., slightly modified)***
*A 40-year-old female patient, Ms. K., repeatedly decompensated psychotically. Her individual psychotherapy involved the use of symbolic images and metaphors such as the 13-year-old boy "Peter", "Sleeping Beauty", the "Buddha Child," and the "Black Fairy". The patient repeatedly associated these figures with her bodily sensations. For instance, when she felt her spleen, she would say that "Sleeping Beauty had contacted her again." One day, Ms. K. happily surprised the therapist with the message: "The 13-year-old boy 'Peter' and the 'Buddha Child' have now integrated. I'm very happy." The therapist was pleased but unsure. He sensed that the "integration" she was referring to might just be a cognitive construction.*

*The therapist did not want to take away the patient's joy and confront her with his doubts. But he didn't want to pretend that he shared her opinion either. So he went transmodally into the patient's thought process in the equivalence mode. He asked her to "show and enact" the "path of integration" between her inner characters. He let her choose a puppet for each of her internal characters and produce a puppetry between them (continued below).*

*Puppetry* in the therapy of patients with psychosis follows Straub's (1972) model of *therapeutic hand puppet play* developed in the therapy of children and the treatment of patients with obsessive–compulsive disorders. The patient selects a variety of hand puppets that interest her from a box. She plays with them individually at first. In this process, the therapist interviews each puppet. The patient and therapist then *verbally* connect the actions of each puppet into a logical story. The therapist makes sure that the story has a happy ending and thus becomes a coping story. The patient and therapist then enact the story together using hand puppets. The patient begins. When the therapist has learned enough about the actions and intentions of a puppet chosen and played out by the patient, he exchanges the puppet with the patient. He exaggerates the puppet's emotional expression in the play by about twenty percent when re-enacting. By reversing roles, the patient remains the author and director in the interaction space of her mental processes. In the reenactment of the story, the characters relate to each other and develop their own identities. The play should end as planned.

***Case example 100 (continued)***
*Ms. K.'s hand puppet show was lively and unobtrusive. Her inner figures related to each other in the play and developed their own identities. The therapist actively*

*participated in the interacting and rehearsing with role reversal between the characters. Later he felt that he now better understood the patient's internal self-regulation. He was, therefore, surprised that Ms. K. suddenly said, deeply shaken, in the debriefing of the play: "I'm shocked at how fragmented my soul is." She later said that she had read that the principle of "integration" was healing in the therapy of psychoses. The effort of representing, interacting, and rehearsing with role reversal between her self-fragments in the as-if mode of play allowed the patient to experience her soul's 'fragmentation'. Her autonomous attempt at "integration" was just an associative cognitive construction.*

*Over the next six months, the patient worked through her inner identity conflicts in her everyday life with hand puppets. Then, one day, she surprised the therapist with the message: "I've made my decision: I'll give up trying to integrate everything." The therapist felt deeply touched. Ms. K. had recognized the true meaning of the word "integration". Six months later, the patient ended her therapy and no longer took any medication. She had not decompensated into psychosis again, even after five more years. She led an active, social life in her family and her workplace.*

**Central idea**

Integration is the last step of mentalizing in conflict. Integration of the delusion with personal everyday conflicts requires successful naming, representing, interacting, and rehearsing in the delusion scene (see Sect. 2.2).

## 9.11 Moreno and Casson's Theoretical and Practical Insights

Moreno first described his disorder-specific psychodrama therapy for people with psychosis in 1939 and 1945. Many of his theoretical explanations are still valid. They only need to be translated into today's customary language: By acting playfully, the patient shall bodily and mentally experience the relationship images that are "outside spontaneous controls" in psychosis (Moreno, 1939, p. 5) (i.e., cannot be thought of in the as-if mode—ed. by the author). As early as 1945, Moreno spoke of an "imaginary reality" (Moreno, 1945a, p. 3 f.) created by the auxiliary world technique when the auto-tele (the relationship to oneself, ed. by the author) has dissolved: "In this imaginary reality on the psychodramatic stage, the patient finds a concrete setting in which all his hallucinatory and delusionary thoughts, feelings, and roles are valid ... On the therapeutic stage ... she finds a new 'reality' that was tailored just for her." By "being normal and 'as if' psychotic, at the same time, she develops spontaneous controls (the ability to consciously expand and thereby also control the delusional experience in the as-if mode of play, ed. by the author). The outside event becomes a part of herself" (Moreno, 1939, p. 13 f.). With this approach, the patient controls the process of her delusion: "She has found a tie to her existence." "Through the *performance of insanity,* she could return to herself and become the center of events" (Moreno, 1939, p. 25). Enacting the delusion produces "a higher frequency and a wider range of associations when compared to the course of her illness." It enables the patient "to take action and activates her core conflicts physically and mentally. She thus senses all possible solutions more clearly and, of her own free will, seeks a new path that will lead her out of her impotent and perverse struggles [...]. Psychodrama embraces the mind and the body [...] and brings them to a new synthesis" (Moreno, 1939, p. 28 f.).

Moreno gained four important experiences in his practical approach to the psychotherapy of people with psychosis:

1. The patients should *act out* their delusions during therapy and *not just report* them. They should develop their *delusional scene* further and try to rewrite it as a coping story through interacting and rehearsing with the help of the therapist in the as-if mode of play. (see Sects. 9.5 and 9.8.8): "From the point of view of a fully integrated personality, the tele formations (the relational pictures, ed. by the author) existing *during the psychotic phase* have to be brought back into the common reality. [...] In psychodrama, production is creation in its complete sense" (Moreno, 1939, p. 5ff.).
2. The external representing of and interacting in the auxiliary world is the basis for the patient's processing of his delusional conflict. It is necessary for the patients "as an anchor if their experiences are not to be permanently reduced to the level of false signals and symbols" (Moreno, 1945a, p. 4). According to Moreno (1945a, p. 6), patients do not require a *continuity* of "reality" in their psychodramatic auxiliary world created for them appropriately. "It appears to be sufficient if they are placed within this imaginary world at certain crucial times, to establish certain *points of coordination*" of the delusion to a corresponding reality.
3. The more acute the delusional disorder, the shorter must be the *time between* therapy sessions in which the auxiliary world technique is used (Moreno, 1945a, p. 5 f.). "The pauses between one psychodramatic session and the next must remain flexible and carefully coordinated with the patient's inner activities. In psychodramatic work, patients can just as easily be undertreated as overtreated."
4. The therapist must not be satisfied with the spontaneous remission of his patient's delusion. In Moreno's experience, people with psychosis try to remain free from symptoms by anxious adjustment. However, as long as "unintegrated elements persist in some manner near the individual or are scattered [...] outside of the patient's *spontaneous controls*, similar occurrences can always trigger the patient and upset his balance" (Moreno, 1939, pp. 5 f.). Therefore, the therapist should go transmodally into past delusional experiences and work through them with the patient *even if he is not experiencing psychosis at the moment.*

In his first essay on therapy for psychosis in 1939, Moreno called his method "psychodramatic shock therapy". With "psychodramatic shock therapy," the patient can "gradually integrate the psychotic contents and gain control of the roles she played during the psychotic decompensation" (Moreno, 1939, p. 3). The therapeutic shocks, "which follow one another, prevent the patient from ridding herself of her psychosis prematurely. We artificially prolong the experience, thereby keeping the psychosis alive in her."

**Central idea**

Patients experiencing psychosis can split off unprocessed psychotic content or suppress it with medication, similar to how traumatized people deal with their flashbacks. But then the high-energetic psychotic images continue to smolder beneath the surface like the embers in a fire that has not been fully extinguished and are actualized by suitable triggers. That is why, when people with psychosis decompensate *again*, they produce the same delusions over and over. Similar to flashbacks in trauma therapy, the delusional content must be processed into a coping story so that it can *no longer* be triggered.

Over time, individual delusions are burned into memory like chronic nightmares (Spoormaker, 2008). If a patient once believed that he was "a chip" during psychosis, then he is also convinced of it in his next psychotic decompensation. Therefore, it is crucial that patients who *decompensate into psychosis for the first time,* gain ego control over their psychotic processes as quickly as possible in the as-if mode of play. Then the subsequent disorders that arise from the trauma of "going mad" and possible traumatizing psychiatric treatments do not have to be compensated for in therapy.

Casson (2004) has shown in a research paper that psychodrama is more successful and financially affordable for people with psychosis than conventional inpatient or drug treatment. He used a special type of psychodrama, called *drama therapy.* From 1996 to 2000, he treated forty-two psychotic patients in group and individual therapy. In doing so, he also communicated transmodally with his patients. He used hand puppets, masks, drums, dollhouses, tangram stones, buttons, ribbons, perfumes, make-up, babushka dolls, and animal figures to further develop the delusion content. He worked on a four-level glass table and used role-playing games.

Casson described his method in detail in two case examples from the individual setting: The therapy of a 40-year-old woman with psychosis comprised 156 sessions (Casson, 2004, p. 126 ff.), and that of a 34-year-old man only 44 sessions (Casson, 2004, p. 182 ff.). Both experienced severe psychosis and were symptom-free at the end of their therapy. Casson (2004, p. 139 f., 143, 190) also described how he dealt with the patients' severely destructive impulses and problems in the therapeutic relationship. According to Casson, the therapist and patient must go *through the heart of their delusion* together to succeed. Casson (2004, p. 187) experienced that auditory hallucinations often express feelings that the patient *cannot directly experience in the current situation.* People with psychosis have mostly had traumatic experiences. They would now have to learn to change themselves and their attitude toward their voices. They should try to interact with their own voices and guide them so that they are less threatening. According to Casson, patients can understand themselves better through this method, thereby reducing their serious relationship problems.

## 9.12 Group Psychotherapy for People with Psychosis

Psychodramatic group therapy for people with psychosis is usually oriented to *social psychiatry*. Patients should learn to *live with their psychosis* in the group. They must take enough medication to improve their psychological well-being. Inpatient stays should become unnecessary or shorter. Social and professional integration is encouraged. The relationship between the group members and the therapist is based on the traditional psychiatrical framework (see Sect. 9.2). The psychotic symptoms are viewed as a *deficit* and not understood as a paralogical expression of personality (see Sect. 9.4).

A disorder-specific approach according to the therapy model described in Sect. 9.8 with transmodal relationship design is *possible in the group* only in exceptional cases. In doing this, the therapist should proceed with tiny steps, according to the motto: "Less is more." Simply *representing* the delusion (see Sects. 9.8.4 and 9.8.8) can stop the current delusion production.

***Case example 101* (Matthias Ewald, 1997, *only orally communicated*)**
*In a therapy group for people with psychosis at a day clinic, the therapist noticed that a patient was withdrawing. It was apparent that he was hearing voices again. The therapist addressed the patient. The patient confirmed the assumption that he had just heard voices. The therapist then had the patient line up all the voices in the room in front of him. There were five of them. His fellow group members took over the roles of the voices. Each of the auxiliary egos was assigned a typical sentence as a "voice". In their role as voices, the fellow members repeated their respective sentences to the patient. The therapist saw the patient's suffering and expressed compassion. This seemingly simple technique of representing and interacting with 'voices' resulted in the prompt disappearance of the protagonist's auditory hallucinations. His medication did not need to be increased. The patient did not decompensate again until six months later when he heard voices in the group again. The therapist wanted to proceed therapeutically in the same way as before. This time, however, the group members were unwilling to take on the role of the voices in embodying the patient's hallucinations in the group room. Therefore, the patient's medication was increased.*

In this crisis intervention, the therapist let the group members *represent* the object images in the patient's delusion externally in the therapy room and *interact* with the patient as his 'voices'. This process liberated his tools of mentalizing from the maelstrom of disintegration of the inner systemic process of self-development and their emergency mode as mechanisms of dream work (see Sects. 9.3 and 9.6). This transformation of mentalization stabilized his process of self-development and stopped the disintegration of his internal self-development and current delusion production. Perhaps in the patient's second crisis, the psychotherapeutic work *with empty chairs* in individual therapy (see Sect. 9.8.8) would have been just as helpful as the voices played out by other group members.

**Recommendation**

In the group therapy of people experiencing psychosis or hearing voices, *the therapist himself* should not apply the doppelganger dialogue and enter the delusion transmodally because it confuses *the other group members* in their social-psychiatric learning goal of understanding their delusional experience *as an illness*.

The group members may become afraid of losing touch with reality and distance themselves from the protagonist's delusional reality: "That's very unlikely after all." Such feedback destroys the stabilization of the patient's inner process of self-development through transmodal therapy and *often intensifies* the protagonist's psychotic symptoms (see case example 84 in Sect. 9.5). Therefore, some therapists (Bender & Stadler, 2012, p. 85) proposed including only those patients with psychosis in the group "who are able to work in groups, form a psychotherapeutic working alliance, and are willing to get involved with the method of psychodrama". However, these *selection criteria* exclude many patients with psychosis from group therapy.

**Central idea**

In his sanatorium in Beacon, Moreno worked with patients with psychosis *only in individual settings* (Straub, 2010, p. 28). He certainly knew that the *transmodal relationship formation* in group therapy was difficult to sustain. In group psychotherapy *with patients experiencing psychosis*, psychodrama therapists should not try to do what Moreno himself wasn't able to do. They should not overwhelm *the group members or themselves*.

Some therapists simplify Psychodrama in group therapy and use it as a *pedagogical role play* (Arbeitskreis Pedagogical Role Play eV, APR, 1989). In doing so, they forego the central psychodrama techniques of doubling, mirroring, role reversal, and scene changes. But, they do *not* go transmodally into the patient's delusion. Instead, the group participants work on *current* conflicts with *protagonist-centered* plays without reversing roles. For example, they review their behavior in dealing with their superiors at work, with work colleagues, or with flatmates in their residential group and try to improve it.

The *social-psychiatry oriented psychodramatic group therapy* does *not* change the core *metacognitive* disorder of patients with psychosis. However, it promotes communication between group members and enhances their ability to play and their role flexibility. The therapist can, for example, proceed in a *topic-centered* manner. He can place a rope on the floor as a *"lifeline"* and ask the patients to "place symbols for the important events in their lives" along the rope. The beginning of the rope represents the patient's birth, and the end represents their current age. In this way, patients indicate the good times in their lives as well as the phases of illness. In another group session, they can each develop their *personal emergency plan* (see Sect. 9.8.6). They write down the plan, put it in their wallet, and try to use it when needed. In the *"doctor's visit" exercise* (Moreno, 1945a, p. 9), the therapist asks a patient to play the role of her own doctor. The patient should inform the therapist about the course of her illness *from the role of the doctor*. She describes her current condition from a meta-perspective and, as a "professional", makes recommendations for her own therapy. The group participants share and empathize with the others during the *topic-centered group work*. They recognize themselves in the other as in a mirror and, in doing so, learn to understand themselves and others better.

*Improv games* are also helpful in group therapy. The therapist lets the group participants formulate a common group theme and translate this into a symbolic image. The participants then enact the theme with distributed roles as a group play. For example, the statement "I am listless in my free time" is converted into the symbolic image of "the family is sitting at the breakfast table on Sunday morning and thinking about what they could do". The therapist encourages the group members to find a role in this picture and act it out: "Who will play the father? Who will play the mother? Who would like to play one of the children?" The participants can enjoy the listlessness in the symbol play. Or they develop unconventional wishes. Taking *on the roles of other people* in improv games makes it easier for the patients to establish relationships with their fellow patients, to set themselves apart, or to argue, *all while being in the safety of these fictitious roles.*

*The therapist* is generally more active in the group therapy of patients with psychosis than in the treatment of people suffering from neurosis. He structures the group sessions more firmly. He also evaluates imperfect solutions as solutions. Patients with psychosis are more clumsy in group work than those with neurosis. However, group therapy still has therapeutic effects. In a scientific study, Bender et al. (1991) demonstrated that patients with psychosis in psychodramatic group psychotherapy achieved significantly better therapeutic results than patients who only visited leisure clubs for mentally ill people.

**Recommendation**

Resolving a relational conflict with an important attachment figure using psychodramatic dialogue with role reversal is *contraindicated* in group therapy. This is because an open conflict with an important attachment figure may actualize the patient's self and trigger an inner pathologic introject or old trauma experiences (see case example 31 in Sect. 4.14). Clarifying the relationship can thus lead to psychotic decompensation. *A spontaneously occurring open* conflict *with a close reference person in everyday life* is often an indication of the beginning of a new psychotic decompensation in the case of patients with psychosis.

Garde et al. (1987) have developed a unique psychodrama format for *work in an acute psychiatric ward* called the *"fairytale drama"*. Siebel (1998, verbal communication) used this group method successfully for fifteen years in the acute psychiatric ward of the Medical University of Lübeck. She described the steps of the procedure as follows: A "fairy tale group" takes place on the ward once a week. All patients *and therapists* on the ward take part. They come up with a fairytale together. A therapist begins. Another therapist goes from one group member to the next with a tape recorder and records what is said. In this way, the group develops *a continuous* story. *Everyone* contributes a part to the story. The group takes a short break when the story is finished and recorded on tape. Two or three group members and two therapists summarize the story as "dramatic advisors". They determine which roles appear in the fairy tale. Then the group gets back together. The "dramatic advisors" narrate the story again in summary. They name the roles and ask the group members to choose one of the roles for the fairy tale play. The patients and therapists then act out the fairy tale *together* from start to finish. Ute Siebel said that as a ward doctor, "she once played Gretel, a highly psychotic patient played Hansel, and the ward nurse played the wolf". As Hansel, the patient protected her, "Gretel", the ward doctor, from the "big bad wolf", the ward nurse.

Inpatient fairytale drama can help expand, structure, and coordinate the inner images of relationships between the patients and therapists on a ward. In the fairytale play, the participants experience each other differently. New *shared* inner relationships emerge in which good triumphs over evil. The development of mutually complex inner relationships impacts everyday life in the acute care unit. Thus, it can be assumed that a fairy tale drama group reduces drug treatment costs in an acute psychiatric ward.

**Conclusion**

Interested psychotherapists should each treat at least one or two patients experiencing psychosis in long-term therapy. This allows them to practice and stabilize *their own ability* to reverse logic. They get to know the heart of psychosis therapy, which is the development of the self, and absorb this knowledge into their intuition. The systemic process of self-development is *also* the basis *for* the therapy of other mental disorders.

## References


Aaltonen, J., Seikkula, J., & Lehtinen, K. (2011). The comprehensive open-dialogue approach in Western Lapland: I. The incidence of non-affective psychosis and prodromal states. *Psychosis, 3*(3), 179–191. https://doi.org/10.1080/17522439.2011.601750. Routledge.

Arbeitskreis Pädagogisches Rollenspiel e. V. (APR) (Ed.) (1989). *Spielen und Anwendung – Rollenspiel Arbeitsbuch Nr. 1*, Textsammlung aus den „Materialien zur Praxis des Rollenspiels" Nr. 1–4 (2nd ed.).

Auchter, T. (1995). Über das Auftauen eingefrorener Lebensprozesse. *Forum Psychoanal*, Vol. 11, 62–83.

Balint, M. (1970). *Therapeutische Aspekte der Regression.* Klett-Cotta.

Bender, W., & Stadler, C. (2012). *Psychodrama-Therapie. Grundlagen, Methodik und Anwendungsgebiete.* Schattauer.

Bender, W., Braunisch, N., & Kunkel, G. (1991). Psychodrama mit Psychose-Patienten. In M. Vorwerg, & T. Alberg (Eds.), *Psychodrama.* Karl F. Haag.

Benedetti, G. (1983). *Todeslandschaften der Seele. Psychopathologie, Psychodynamik und Psychotherapie der Schizophrenie.* Vandenhoeck & Ruprecht.

Bleuler, M. (1983). *Lehrbuch der Psychiatrie.* Springer.

Böker, H. (1992). Concepts of mental illness: An ethnopsychiatric study of the mental hospital's inpatient and outpatients of the Kathmandu Valley. *Contributions to Nepalese Studies, 19*, 27–50.

Casson, J. (2004). *Drama, psychotherapy, and psychosis. Dramatherapy and psychodrama with people who hear voices.* Brunner-Routledge.

Ciompi, L. (2019). *Ciompi reflektiert. Wissenschaftliches, Persönliches und Weltanschauliches aus der Altersperspektive.* Vandenhoeck & Ruprecht.

Ciompi, L., Harding, C. M., & Lethinen, K. (2010). Deep concern. *Schizophrenia Bulletin, 36*, 437–439.

Diener, G. (1971). *Heilung eines „Wahnsinns" durch „psychische Kur".* Athenäum.

Dürckheim, K. G. (1976). *Vom doppelten Ursprung des Menschen* (3rd ed.). Herder.

Fonagy, P., Gergeley, G., Jurist, E. L., & Target, M. (2004). *Affektregulierung, Mentalisierung und die Entwicklung des Selbst.* Klett-Cotta.

Freud, S. (1966). Die Traumarbeit. Vorlesungen zur Einführung in die Psychoanalyse. *Gesammelte Werke Band XI*, 4th ed., S. Fischer.
Freud, S. (1975). *Psychologie des Unbewussten.* Studienausgabe Bd. 3. Fischer-Verlag.
Frith, C. D. (1992). *The cognitive neuropsychology of schizophrenia.* Lawrence Erlbaum Associates.
Garde, T., Erdmann, R., Sander, H., & Drees, A. (1987). Märchendrama – Eine psychotherapeutische Stationsgruppenmethode für Ich-gestörte Patienten. *Psychiatrische Praxis, 14,* 137–141.
Goldman-Rakic, P. S. (1994). Working memory dysfunction in schizophrenia. *Journal of Neuropsychiatry Clinical Neuroscience, 6,* 348–357.
Grube, M. (2018). Psychodynamische Aspekte stationärer Mutter-Kind-Behandlungen bei Frauen mit postpartalen Psychosen. In: N. Nowack (Ed.), *Psychodynamische Psychosen-Psychotherapie und sozialpsychiatrische Behandlung von Psychosen* (pp. 157–176). Psychosozial-Verlag.
Hartwich, P. (2018). Die Fragmentierung des Selbst im Spiegel. Ein Beitrag zur Neuropsychodynamik der Schizophrenie. In N. Nowack (Ed.), *Psychodynamische Psychosen-Psychotherapie und sozialpsychiatrische Behandlung von Psychosen* (pp. 177–212). Psychosozial-Verlag.
Krüger, R. T. (1974). Zur gegenwärtigen und künftigen Bedeutung der Leistungsförderung bei psychiatrisch betreuten Patienten und psychiatrischen Institutionen. *Der Nervenarzt, 45*, 16–21.
Krüger, R. T. (1978). Die Mechanismen der Traumarbeit und ihre Beziehung zu den heilenden Vorgängen im Psychodrama. *Gruppenpsychotherapie Und Gruppendynamik, 13*(2), 172–208.
Krüger, R. T. (1997). *Kreative Interaktion. Tiefenpsychologische Theorie und Methoden des klassischen Psychodramas.* Vandenhoeck & Ruprecht.
Krüger, R. T. (2001a). Psychodrama in der Behandlung von psychotisch erkrankten Menschen – Praxis und Theorie. *Gruppenpsychotherapie und Gruppendynamik, 17*, 254–273.
Krüger, R. T. (2001b). »Das Lachen in die Psychiatrie bringen!?« – Entwicklung von Raum und Zeit in der Psychotherapie von psychotisch erkrankten Menschen. In G. Kruse & S. Gunkel (Eds.), *Psychotherapie in der Zeit – Zeit in der Psychotherapie* (pp. 49–73). Hannoversche Ärzte-Verlags-Union.
Krüger, R. T. (2013a). Wo das Wünschen noch geholfen hat. Die Arbeit mit dem Bewältigungsmärchen. *Zeitschrift für Psychodrama und Soziometrie, 12*(1), 103–112.
Krüger, R. T. (2013b). Die therapeutischen Funktionen und Indikationen des Doppelns. *Zeitschrift für Psychodrama und Soziometrie, 12*(2), 217–232. https://doi.org/10.1007/s11620-013-0196-7
Krüger, R. T. (2013c). Warum es wichtig ist, spielen zu lernen. Die zeitgemäße Anwendung der störungsspezifischen Psychotherapie von psychotisch erkrankten Menschen nach Moreno. In G. Ittzés (Ed.), *Cura mentis – salus populi. Mentálhigiéné a társadalom szolgálatában. Festschrift für Teodóra Tomcsányi zum 70. Geburtstag* (pp. 173–188). Semmelweis Egyetem, Egészségügyi Közszolgálati Kar, Mentálhigiéné Intézet.
Lincoln, T., & Heibach, E. (2017). *Psychosen.* Hogrefe.
Mentzos, S. (1992). *Psychose und Konflikt. Zur Theorie und Praxis der analytischen Psychotherapie psychotischer Störungen.* Vandenhoeck & Ruprecht.
Mentzos, S. (2011). *Lehrbuch der Psychodynamik. Die Funktion der Dysfunktionalität psychischer Störungen* (5th ed.). Vandenhoeck & Ruprecht.
Moreno, J. L. (1939). Psychodramatic shock therapy. A sociometric approach to the problem of mental disorders. *Sociometry, 2*(1), 1–30.
Moreno, J. L. (1945). *Psychodramatic treatment of psychoses.* Beacon House.
Moreno, J. L. (1959). *Gruppenpsychotherapie und Psychodrama. Einleitung in die Theorie und Praxis.* Thieme.
Moreno, J. L. (1970). *Das Stegreiftheater* (2nd ed.). Beacon, N. Y.: Beacon House. Original work published 1923, Potsdam, Berlin: Gustav Kiepenheuer.
Moreno, J. L., Moreno, Z. T. (1975a). *Psychodrama, Volume II. Foundations of psychotherapy*(second edition). Beacon House.
Neraal, T. (2018a). Familiendynamik und psychoanalytische Familientherapie bei Psychosen. In N. Nowack (Ed.), *Psychodynamische Psychosen-Psychotherapie und sozialpsychiatrische Behandlung von Psychosen* (pp. 29–46). Psychosozial-Verlag.

Neraal, T. (2018b). Die psychotische Krise als Chance zur Neuorientierung. Familientherapie als intrapsychische, interpersonelle und soziale Integration. In N. Nowack (Ed.), *Psychodynamische Psychosen-Psychotherapie und sozialpsychiatrische Behandlung von Psychosen* (pp. 229–246). Psychosozial-Verlag.

Nowack, N., Tonn, B., Kluttig, T. & Hoffmann, K. (2018). Geschichte der 'ISPS-Germany' von der Gründung 1975 bis heute. In Nicolas Nowack (ed.): *Psychodynamische Psychosen-Psychotherapie und sozialpsychiatrische Behandlung von Psychosen*. Psychosozial-Verlag, 329–360.

Plassmann, R. (1999). Körperpsychologie und Deutungstechnik – Die Praxis der Prozessdeutung. In W. Kämmerer (Ed.), *Körpersymptom und Psychotherapie. Der Umgang mit dem Symptom: Zur Spannung zwischen krankem Körper und Person*. VAS.

Plassmann, R. (2019). *Psychotherapie der Emotionen. Die Bedeutung für die Entstehung und Behandlung von Krankheiten*. Psychosozial-Verlag.

Putzke, M. (2018). Institutionelle Abwehr in der Psychiatrie. In N. Nowack (Ed.), *Psychodynamische Psychosen-Psychotherapie und sozialpsychiatrische Behandlung von Psychosen* (pp.299–308). Psychosozial-Verlag.

Red, H. (2018). Aus der „Dokumentation zur Psychotherapie der Schizophrenie" zusammengetragen von Norman Elrod. Die Züricher Jahre 1948–1956. In N. Nowack (Ed.), *Psychodynamische Psychosen-Psychotherapie und sozialpsychiatrische Behandlung von Psychosen* (pp. 329–360). Psychosozial-Verlag.

Romme, M., & Escher, A. (1997). *Stimmenhören akzeptieren*. Psychiatrie-Verlag.

Schindler, R. (1996). Moreno durchbricht einen depressiven Stupor. In B. Erlacher-Farkas, & C. Jorda (Eds.), *Monodrama. Heilende Begegnung. Vom Psychodrama zur Einzeltherapie* (pp. 7–10). Springer.

Schneider, F., et al. (2007). Neural correlates of working memory dysfunction in first-episode schizophrenia patients: An fMRi multicenter study. *Schizophrenia Research, 89*, 198–210.

Schwarz, F. (2018). Analytische Psychosen-Psychotherapie – Indikation, Durchführung und Zeitverlauf. In: N. Nowack (Ed.), Psychodynamische Psychosen-Psychotherapie und sozialpsychiatrische Behandlung von Psychosen (pp. 107–126). Psychosozial-Verlag.

Sechehaye, M. A. (1956). Die Übertragung in der Réalisation symbolique. *Psyche – Zeitschrift für Psychoanalyse und ihre Anwendung, 10*, 482–496.

Spoormaker, V. (2008). A cognitive model of recurrent nightmares. *International Journal of Dream Research, 1*(1), 15–22.

Straub, H. (1972). Theoretische Anmerkungen zur psychodramatischen Behandlung von Phobien, Zwangsneurosen und anderen psychischen Störungen. In H. Petzold (Ed.), Angewandtes Psychodrama in Therapie, Pädagogik, Theater und Wirtschaft (pp.177–194). Junfermann.

Straub, H. (2010). »Seit fünfzig Jahren arbeite ich mit dieser spannenden Methode.« In D. Ensel, G. Stiegler (Eds.), »Ein Stück im Himmel«. Psychodramatikerinnen begegnen sich (pp. 25–42). *Zeitschrift für Psychodrama und Soziometrie* 9 (Suppl. 2).

Winnicott, D. W. (1985). Vom Spiel zur Kreativität (3rd ed.). Stuttgart: Klett Cotta. (Original work published 1971: »Playing and reality«, London: Tavistock).

Wurmser, L. (1998). *Das Rätsel des Masochismus. Psychoanalytische Untersuchungen von Gewissenszwang und Leidenssucht* (2nd ed.). Springer.

Zubin, J., & Spring, B. (1977). Vulnerability; a new view of Schizophrenia. *Journal of Abnormal Psychology, 86*, 103–126.

# Chapter 10
# Addiction Disorders

## 10.1 Psychotherapy for Addiction Disorders

Psychotherapy for persons with addiction disorders has developed only recently. The World Health Organization recognized alcoholism as a disease only in 1952; in Germany, it was recognized as a disease only in 1968. In the 1970s, the training of mental health professionals in therapy for addiction disorders was limited to the treatment of *symptom-related consequences*. I myself learned *what's special* about psychotherapy from persons with addictions (Krüger, 1988) in a social psychiatric counseling center from 1974 to 1976 and from 1977 onward in a group for persons with addictions in my practice as a psychiatrist and psychotherapist.

Many psychotherapists *do not treat* patients with addiction problems. In a seminar on therapy for addiction disorders, the participants supported this stance with the following reasons: "I have no affinity for it." "I have no trust." "I have no success." "It's so difficult to understand." "I don't treat them because I don't have any options of working with inpatient facilities." "These drug addicts have misled me so often. I hate them." "I can't compete with the alcohol." Only one participant contradicted these resigned statements: "They fascinate me; working with them is challenging. I like challenges."

**Central idea**

Persons with addiction often unsettle the therapist (see Sect. 10.7) through their oscillation between addictive thinking and healthy adult thinking. The problem is: the therapist must take the patient's statements seriously, knowing that the opposite could also be true.

I sat in a group of 10–18 persons with addictions each Thursday for thirty-three years in my practice. They laughed a lot and taught me the art of failing. It helped me develop humility toward truth, life, and human dignity.

***Case example 102***

*An alcohol-dependent lieutenant in the German Armed Forces, Mr. A., came to me every week for six months in the polyclinic for depth-psychological individual*



R. T. Krüger, *Disorder-Specific Psychodrama Therapy in Theory and Practice*, Psychodrama in Counselling, Coaching and Education 4,
https://doi.org/10.1007/978-981-99-7508-2_10

*psychotherapy. One year after the end of therapy, I accidentally ran into him again while visiting an addiction clinic. He laughed and told me: "Back then, during my treatment, I always stopped drinking two days before a therapy session. After visiting you, I would drink again."*

***Case example 103***
*A patient addicted to clomethiazole was in individual therapy with me for half a year. I helped her work through her conflicts with her mother and other attachment figures psychodramatically. I experienced a lot myself, but the patient felt much less. In each session, I would ask her how many clomethiazole capsules she had taken in the past week. When it was 'only' 3–4 a day, I was happy about the 'progress' she was making in therapy. However, I was disappointed when it was again 6–8 capsules a day. We ended therapy without any significant improvement in the symptoms. The patient later underwent withdrawal treatment.*

Some of the typical problems in the psychotherapy of persons with addiction are as follows: (1) The patients are likely to experience repeated relapse. They *want* to be abstinent, but they can't do it. (2) In psychotherapy, relapses result in repeated crises and nullify progress. This disruption discourages not only the therapists *but also* the patients. (3) The patients suffer from the consequences of their addiction, but they do not give adequate importance to their addiction in its developmental stages. (4) The patients lie to *themselves and others.* Their defense through denial helps them to continue taking addictive drugs *despite* the negative consequences. (5) They seduce the therapist, *through their self-deception,* into overlooking their addiction problem in treatment or understanding it as *only a result* of psychological problems or conflicts.

**Central idea**

Initially, persons with addiction start using addictive drugs because of their problems. However, the cause and effect are reversed *in the addiction stage.* They *have problems because they use addictive substances.*

***Case example 104* (Krüger, 2004b, p. 165, *modified)***
*A new group member, Mr. C., told the group about his alcohol dependence and marital problems. At the end of the session, he asked, "I drink because of the problems in my marriage. What can I do about it?" The therapist wanted to continue talking to the patient about his marital problems. However, an experienced group member answered his question spontaneously: "Solve your marital problems, and you won't have to drink anymore!" The therapist was amazed. He suddenly realized: "That is exactly it. As long as the patient drinks, he will not be able to solve his marital problems."*

At the beginning of an addiction seminar, *eleven* participants suspected an addiction problem in 17 of their psychotherapy patients and clients. At the end of the seminar, they estimated that 62 patients were addicted, four times more than initially assumed.

**Central idea**

Many psychotherapists think they *don't want to* work with persons with addiction in psychotherapy. However, if they look closely at a seminar, they will see that they *also* treat people with addictions. But because they didn't think so, they have not worked with them in a disorder-specific manner so far, thereby reducing the success of the therapy.

## 10.2 The Definition of Addiction and Dependence

**Important definition**

In 1957, the World Health Organization defined 'addiction' as 'a condition of periodic or chronic intoxication caused by repeated use of a natural or synthetic drug'. The following criteria must exist *simultaneously* to define addiction: (1) an *uncontrollable desire* to procure and consume the drug, (2) a tendency to *increase the dose* (increased tolerance), (3) the psychological and mostly also physical *dependence on the effects* of the drug, and (4) its harmfulness for individuals and the community.

This WHO definition of addiction also applies to *non-substance-related* addiction disorders (see Sect. 10.10) if we replace the word 'drug' with the specific type of addictive behavior, such as playing video games or watching pornography. In 1968, the WHO replaced the term 'drug addiction' with 'drug dependence'. However, the word 'dependent' is vague when *talking to patients*. It minimizes the *existential* threat experienced by persons with addiction due to the loss of human dignity and the risk of death (Gallus, 2017,verbal communication). For example, if a patient takes half a sleeping pill to sleep at night for several years, he is *'dependent'* on its effects *but not 'addicted'* to it as he *didn't increase* the dose in all these years. He has not yet suffered *any harm* from taking the tablets. That is why I use the word 'addicted' in this book when describing the subjective experience of those affected. I use the word 'dependent' where the *medical term* 'addiction disorder' is intended.

**Central idea**

The *four* WHO criteria mentioned above *must all be met* to define addiction or dependence. They are crucial for the diagnosis and self-knowledge of dependent patients. Therapists should not change or weaken these criteria.

For example, Kern (2013, p. 24), in an effort to develop *an understanding of addiction based on role theory*, defined addiction far *too generally*: "In certain situations, it is impossible for a person suffering from addiction to react in adequate role configurations, even if this behavior is detrimental to their health and social integrity." This definition doesn't include specifics of *dependency*. Even people with depression, neurosis, or psychosis *without* comorbid substance abuse cannot react 'in adequate role configurations in certain situations', even if this is detrimental to their health.

There are addiction disorders *with* substance abuse and addiction disorders *without* substance abuse. The diagnosis of 'mental and behavioral disorders' *with substance abuse* (ICD-10 F10, F19) refers to the abuse of alcohol (F10.-), opioids, cannabinoids

(F12.-), sedatives or hypnotics (F13.-), cocaine, stimulants, hallucinogens, tobacco, volatile solvents, *or* multiple substance use (F19.-). This can lead to *acute intoxication* (with alcohol F10.0), *harmful abuse* (F10.1), a *dependency syndrome* (F10.2), a withdrawal syndrome (F10.3), a withdrawal syndrome with delirium (F10 0.4), a psychotic disorder (F10.5), an amnesic syndrome (F10.6), a 'residual state and a delayed psychotic disorder' (F10.7), and *other* mental and behavioral disorders (F10.8). According to the ICD, in the case of a 'residual disorder', patients suffer from "changes in cognition, affect, personality or behavior beyond the period [...] during which a direct substance-related effect might reasonably be assumed to be operating". Dependency disorders *without substance abuse* and behavioral addictions (see Sect. 10.11) include, for example, eating disorders (F50.-), abnormal habits, and impulse control disorders (F63.-) such as pathological gambling (F63.0), pathological arson (F63.1), pathological stealing (F63.2), sex addiction, and porn addiction or internet gaming addiction.

The ICD-10 defines the *'harmful use' of addictive substances* as the "consumption of psychotropic substances that cause damage to one's health, for example, liver damage or depression". In this sense, patients with problem drinking, relief drinking, or occasional drinking practice *harmful alcohol use* and are *alcoholics.* But they do not suffer from dependency syndrome because *harmful use* doesn't include the WHO criterion of the "uncontrollable desire to procure and consume the addictive substance". Alcoholics Anonymous (AA) refer to this 'uncontrollable desire' as a 'loss of control'. There is no addiction without a *loss of control.*

**Important definition**

A patient with a loss of control has suffered harm from substance use and thus made a *conscious decision* to drink less or nothing at all. However, he cannot stick to this resolution *he has made himself*. We can diagnose this as 'loss of control' if *one* of the following criteria is met: (1) *Contrary to his previous intentions,* the person, consumes addictive substances again. (2) He consumes *more* than he intended. (3) He *shortens* the abstinence phase planned by himself.

Unlike persons with addiction, patients with *'harmful use'* of alcohol can still control their addictive substance use (see Fig. 10.2 in Sect. 10.5). They reduce consumption if necessary or even stop it altogether. The psychotherapeutic treatment of depression, borderline syndrome, or a trauma-related disorder can still be successful *in this stage* of harmful use. But, the therapist should seriously discuss the harmful use of an addictive substance with her patient because psychotherapy is significantly less effective if the patient drinks 'two glasses,' i.e., 0.4 L of wine every evening during treatment. Or if he drinks a liter of beer or consumes hashish *every day*.

**Recommendation**

In such a case, the therapist negotiates a contract with the patient. The patient should completely stop his drug consumption or at least reduce it significantly. For example, he should *decide* 'only to drink *in the company of others* and that too only one glass at most'. The *process of contract negotiations* and the degree of compliance helps the therapist recognize the extent of the patient's dependence and improve the chances of success in therapy.

If the patient makes a specific resolution and *does not stick to it*, he is usually already addicted. As a result, his ability to deal with conflict and participate in psychotherapy is impaired because he will likely slide into addictive thinking and behavior again (see Sect. 10.5).

There are two types of *dependent use of addictive substances*: chronic drinking and excessive drinking in the case of alcohol abuse. In *both cases*, the person concerned suffers from substance abuse and continues drinking anyway. He cannot control the amount of addictive substance he consumes. According to the ICD, he "has a strong desire to ingest the substance, difficulty controlling its consumption, and is persistent in using addictive substances *despite harmful consequences*". Most of the time, those affected drank *differently* than others, excessively, more frequently, hastily, or with memory lapses, even before the onset of alcohol dependence.

With *chronic level drinking*, the body's *physiological* processes have adjusted to the continuous supply of alcohol such that withdrawal symptoms such as hand tremors, palpitations, and sweating occur after twelve hours of abstinence at the latest. Alcohol consumption is *less noticeable* to chronic drinkers than healthy people who have drunk *the same amount* of alcohol because their body has gotten used to a certain alcohol level in the blood. For example, level drunkards can often still balance themselves while walking, despite a 2.5 per mil alcohol level in their blood, if they are clinically examined for suspected drunkenness on the road. Despite their constant excessive consumption of alcohol, they are often able to work for a long time. Level drunkards drink alcohol continuously throughout the day. They usually do this for years without attracting attention to their alcohol consumption.

However, *excessive drinking* only lasts for 3–14 days as it *quickly leads* to significant physical, familial, and social problems. The patient becomes helpless in a drunken stupor and, at some point, is admitted to a clinic.

An addiction disorder traumatizes the soul with the compulsion to consume addictive substances *against all reason* (Krüger, 2004a, 2004b, p. 166). The person concerned is trapped by the loss of control: (1) He tries to drink in a controlled manner but fails every time. (2) But because of his addiction, he cannot flee from alcohol either. (3) He is permanently exposed to an unmanageable stressful situation due to the physical, mental, and social damage: He loses his driving license. His wife separates from him. His employer writes a warning. He is drowning in debt. He suffers from liver damage. (4) He has to increase his drug use over time as his *physical* tolerance to the addictive substance increases. (5) His *secondary* feelings of failure, shame, fear, and guilt hinder the desired effect of the addictive substance. Therefore, the patient has to increase the amount of alcohol to create the desired psychological effect.

A "*chronic addiction disorder*" is characterized by persistent physical and mental damage and familial or social disintegration with dependency on addictive substances.

## 10.3 Epidemiological Data and Treatment Statistics

The medical significance of addiction disorders and their impact on society is highly *underestimated*.

**Central idea**

According to a study by the Institute for Therapy Research in Munich (Kraus et al., 2014, p. 9), the number of persons with alcohol addiction in Germany was 1.65 million in 2012. Another 1.69 million people drank a whole lot. About 7.4 million consumed more alcohol than the maximum quantity recommended by experts. About 4.17 million people were addicted to tobacco. 229,000 were addicted to cannabis. About 1.74 million were dependent on pain relievers, sleeping pills, or sedatives.

Persons with addiction often suffer from a *comorbid mental disorder*. According to a review (more than 53 studies) by Simpson and Miller (2002) (quoted from Schäfer & Reddemann, 2005), 27–67% of women and 9–29% of men with addictions were sexually abused in childhood. In addition, 33% of women and 24–33% of men were physically abused in childhood. There is a close correlation (Schmidt, 2000; Harrison et al., 1990, cited from Schäfer & Reddemann, 2005) between the severity of addiction, early onset of addiction, willingness to consume hard drugs, and the severity of childhood traumatization. Traumatized persons with addiction cause more problems in therapy than those *without* trauma (Schäfer, 2005). They drop out of treatment more often. They relapse more often. They have more trouble in the therapeutic relationship and trigger feelings of insecurity in their therapists more often than others.

**Central idea**

Up to 80% of all persons with alcohol addiction and 75.6% with opiate addiction also have a personality disorder diagnosis (Schneider et al., 2009, pp. 182, 191). In addition, 20–73% suffer from affective disorders, mainly from depression (Hiller, 2014, p. 2).

"According to various studies, 40% of all women and 60% of all men with a borderline personality disorder (BPD) diagnosis meet the criteria for alcohol or drug abuse" (Dulit et al., 1990, quoted from Hintermeier, 2013, p. 105). Many patients with schizophrenia have an addiction problem.

**Central idea**

"Every year, around 70,000 people in Germany die as a result of their alcohol consumption [...], of which 15% [...] die by suicide" (Hiller, 2014, p. 3).

Only about 10% of persons with addiction in Germany receive help *within one year*. In 2000, for example, only 1.7% of those affected were treated in specialist clinics and 7% in specialist counseling centers (Wienberg & Driessen, 2001, quoted from Waldheim-Auer, 2013, p. 205). Around 1–2% of those affected go to self-help groups. According to the 2011 annual statistics of professional addiction aid (Steppan et al., 2013, p. 217), 39.5% of patients remained in *outpatient* therapy for up to three months and a total of 62.5% for up to six months. Only 17% of treated persons with alcohol dependence have been in therapy for more than a year.

**Central idea**

In 2013, the Diakonisches Werk Schaumburg-Lippe e. V. counseling center for addiction disorders (Peter Gallus, written information from February 27, 2014) saw 67.6% of the clients and their caregivers for *less than ten* counseling sessions. In addition, 26.4% of the clients had only one contact, and 12.5% came for treatment more than 50 times.

*Inpatient treatment* for alcoholism lasts 1–2 weeks for withdrawal treatments and an average of twelve weeks for medical rehabilitation measures (Steppan et al., 2013, p. 217). When using illegal drugs, those affected stay in the clinic for an average of six months (Steppan et al., 2013, p. 217). "About 70% of persons with alcohol addiction contact the doctor at least once a year, *without* their addiction being discovered or addressed. [...] Around 24% are admitted annually to internal or surgical wards. [...] About 1% go to a specialist clinic" (Hiller, 2014, p. 18). *Outpatient medical rehabilitation* treatments include up to 120 sessions in eighteen months.

**Recommendation**

The duration of outpatient counseling or treatment for persons with addiction is usually *relatively short*. Therefore, psychotherapists and psychiatrists should offer *disorder-specific* advice and treatment to those affected *right from the start*.

The first three months of outpatient addiction therapy provide *information* about addiction disorders and *motivate* people to abstain (see Sect. 10.6.1). Treatment often begins when the person is still consuming addictive substances. According to the psychotherapy guidelines, health insurance companies in Germany pay for psychotherapy *even if* the person concerned does not abstain until the first ten hours of therapy. However, the abstinence must then be recorded with a medical certificate.

The abstinence rates of persons with alcohol dependence are 9.6% in the male and 14.9% in the female population (Waniczek, 2003, p. 22). After inpatient treatment, *around a third* of alcoholics drink alcohol again within the *first six months*, *half* within the *first year*, and even more after four to five years (Körkel, 2001, p. 523, quoted from Waldheim-Auer, 2013, p. 196). The test results deviate strongly to the positive in individual studies. For example, in a catamnestic study for outpatient, abstinence-oriented psychodramatic treatment in their addiction counseling center, Waldheim-Auer (2013, p. 196) reported that 73% of the patients were still abstinent *after one year* or were abstinent after a one-time, brief relapse (see Sect. 10.6.5). After five years, 52% of those treated were still abstinent. In a study by Waniczek et al. (2005, p. 13), 72.9% of 70 patients with addiction who *had participated* in the catamnestic examination had not relapsed again after psychodramatic group treatment.

## 10.4 Diagnosis and Addiction-Specific Symptoms

**Exercise 26**

What is at the *core of the suffering* of persons with addiction? As a reader, first of all, please answer this question *yourself*!

The therapists of an advanced training seminar for addiction therapy responded to the above question as follows: inner emptiness, relationship problems, shame, powerlessness, feelings of worthlessness, loneliness, aimlessness, and joylessness. Only one therapist mentioned the problem of addiction: "Being trapped in something, stuck in a straitjacket, having no free will".

**Central idea**

*Being addicted* is at the core of the suffering of persons with addiction. *Any other* explanation does *not* get to the heart of the addiction disorder. Persons with addiction can only remain abstinent in the long term if they admit to being addicted (see Sects. 10.5 and 10.6). Thus, their internal self-image is split into a 'healthy adult thinking ego' and an 'addicted ego'. "I am Alfred" should become "I am Alfred, I am an alcoholic".

The therapist should take *every indication* of a possible addiction problem seriously and clarify the diagnosis primarily. The therapist freely asks direct questions to the patient: "Are you drinking too much?" Or: "Are you an addict?" There are three different ways in which patients are likely to *react* to this question:

1. The patient convincingly *denies* the addiction problem.
2. The patient *evades* the question. In such a case, the therapist *works with him* to determine which addiction-specific symptoms are *present and which are not yet present*. This helps him to decide whether he should see himself as an alcoholic or an addict or not.
3. The patient more or less *confirms* their addiction problem.

**Central idea**

The *therapist* also has to decide *for herself* whether she wants to see the patient as an addict. Because if she depends on the patient's self-assessment, she may behave *co-dependently* and join him in minimizing his core problem.

The therapist makes her decision based on the addiction symptoms of the person concerned (see below and Fig. 10.1 below). She can also use psychodramatic self-supervision if the diagnosis is unclear (see Sect. 2.9). For this purpose, she engages in a *fictional* psychodramatic dialogue with the patient *in his absence*. She expresses her anger, confusion, and helplessness to the 'patient'. In the case of a person with addiction, *her negative affect* is unresolved in the first twelve steps of self-supervision (see Sect. 2.9). She, therefore, continues the self-supervision with steps 13–17 (see Sect. 2.9). She places a second empty chair next to the 'patient's' chair to represent his addictive thinking, feeling, and behavior (see Sect. 10.5) and then explains this intervention to 'the patient': "I think you have an alcohol problem. I'll place this second chair next to you to represent the same." The diagnosis of "a person with addiction" is probable if (1) The two-chair technique resolves the therapist's negative affect and inner tension, and if, (2) after *changing into the role* of the patient, the therapist feels touched by the truth of "the alcohol problem". As a 'patient', she sometimes even feels relieved that her real suffering is addressed.

**Central idea**

Persons with addiction suffer from *metacognitive confusion* between their *healthy* adult thinking and *addictive* thinking and feeling (see Sect. 10.5). They switch unconsciously between these two contrary ego states. The *unconscious switch* is an expression of a *disturbance in the metacognitive processes* of conflict resolution. It wreaks havoc on the patient's *cognition*. An addicted patient acts out being addicted in equivalence mode. He explains his drinking with external causes: "I must drink because the external situation is the way it is." But, the decision of being addicted integrates the as-if mode of thinking in equivalence mode (see Sect. 2.6). The patient shouldn't explain his addiction with external causes but by internal causes: "I am addicted. Therefore, I am drinking." Thus, his identity as an alcoholic becomes an inner representation. Over time, the patient gains control of his ego over his addictive thinking.

Therefore, the therapist and the patient look for symptoms to help the patient admit to *being addicted*.

In a report to the World Health Organization (WHO), Jellinek developed a questionnaire (see Fig. 10.1) for patients and their therapists to determine whether one is "in all probability an alcoholic". Today there are also other scientifically well-proven questionnaires. But I prefer Jellinek's 30 questions because they describe the most important *symptoms of an addiction disorder* from an experiential perspective and not the observer's position. These questions help the patients to understand the therapist when they ask about their addiction symptoms. In counseling or therapy, Jellinek's questionnaire (see Fig. 10.1 in Sect.10.4) helps record the patient's addiction problem qualitatively and quantitatively. During the therapeutic conversation, the therapist writes down which of the patient's answers directly or indirectly *positively* confirm each of Jellinek's questions. If necessary, she reads out her list of positively answered questions to the patient at the end of the conversation. She also gives the patient the questionnaire (see Fig. 10.1). The patient should fill it out peacefully at home. Most of the symptoms mentioned in Jellinek's questionnaire are *also* present *in other addiction disorders*, such as pill addiction, gambling addiction, sex addiction, and other behavioral addictions (see case examples 124 in Sect. 10.10.3, 127 in Sect. 10.10.4 and 129 in Sect. 10.10.5).

**Central idea**

Jellinek's addiction symptoms especially grasp the patient's problems *resulting from* their substance abuse. The *more addiction symptoms* the patient has to confirm, the greater his motivation to abstain. This is because the patient would reduce or even eliminate his problems and symptoms just by abstinence.

The therapist should know the meaning of every Jellinek question *and explain* it to the patient if necessary:

1. *Memory lapses* resulting from substance abuse tend to unsettle persons with addiction. The patient does *not remember* whether he behaved abnormally or violently the day before. Instead, he observes the reactions of his relationship partner and deduces from their behavior whether something has happened or not. In this case, some appropriate diagnostic questions are: "Do you remember how you got to bed last night?" "Do you remember what you said to the others?"
2. A person is *drinking secretly* only if he *knows* that his drinking behavior is not normal. Those who are *not addicts* do *not* hide the fact that they drink beer or wine! Some insightful questions to ask are: "Do you often go to the basement

**Are you an alcoholic?**

The Stages of Alcoholism.
According to a report by the World Health Organization (WHO) by Prof. E. M. Jellinek

| Yes | No | **Preliminary Stage** |
|---|---|---|
| ☐ | ☐ | 1. Do you suffer from memory lapses after heavy drinking? |
| ☐ | ☐ | 2. Do you drink secretly? |
| ☐ | ☐ | 3. Do you often think about alcohol? |
| ☐ | ☐ | 4. Do you drink the first few glasses in a hurry? |
| ☐ | ☐ | 5. Do you feel guilty about your drinking? |
| ☐ | ☐ | 6. Do you avoid references to alcohol in conversations? |
| | | **Critical Phase** |
| ☐ | ☐ | 7. Do you have an irresistible urge to continue drinking after the first few glasses? |
| ☐ | ☐ | 8. Do you make excuses as to justify your drinking? |
| ☐ | ☐ | 9. Do you show particularly aggressive behavior towards the environment? |
| ☐ | ☐ | 10. Do you tend to feel remorse and constant guilt about drinking? |
| ☐ | ☐ | 11. Do you try to be totally abstinent every now and then? |
| ☐ | ☐ | 12. Have you tried a drinking system, e.g. not drinking before a certain time? |
| ☐ | ☐ | 13. Have you changed jobs frequently? |
| ☐ | ☐ | 14. Do you organize your work and life around alcohol? |
| ☐ | ☐ | 15. Have you noticed a loss of interest in things other than alcohol? |
| ☐ | ☐ | 16. Do you show conspicuous self-pity? |
| ☐ | ☐ | 17. Have there been any changes in your family life? |
| ☐ | ☐ | 18. Do you tend to stock up on alcohol? |
| ☐ | ☐ | 19. Are you neglecting your diet? |
| ☐ | ☐ | 20. Have you been admitted to a hospital for alcohol abuse? |
| ☐ | ☐ | 21. Do you drink in the morning regularly? |
| | | **Chronic Phase** |
| ☐ | ☐ | 22. Have you ever been drinking for days at a time? |
| ☐ | ☐ | 23. Do you notice a moral degradation in yourself? |
| ☐ | ☐ | 24. Has your thinking ability been adversely affected? |
| ☐ | ☐ | 25. Do you drink with people who are way below your standard? |
| ☐ | ☐ | 26. Do you occasionally drink technical alcohol products (hair tonic or methylated spirits)? |
| ☐ | ☐ | 27. Has your alcohol tolerance decreased? |
| ☐ | ☐ | 28. Do you experience morning tremors? |
| ☐ | ☐ | 29. Has drinking become a compulsion? |
| ☐ | ☐ | 30. Have you ever experienced alcohol delirium? |

If honest self-assessment requires you to answer ìyesî to more than five questions, it is likely that you are an alcoholic.

**Fig. 10.1** E. M. Jellinek's 30 questions (Alcoholics Anonymous): "Are you an alcoholic?"

or the garage to get something or do handicrafts?" "Do you often go to your allotment garden *alone*?" "Has your divorced wife or boyfriend talked to you about your excessive drinking?" "Has your employer issued a warning to you because of your drinking?"

3. *Frequent thinking about alcohol*: A patient with dependent drinking occupies himself a lot with planning his consumption, the procurement worries, the concealment, and guilt. Frequent thinking about alcohol during periods of abstinence indicates a risk of relapse into substance abuse. It can progress to *'dry drinking'*.

**Important definition**

According to Alcoholics Anonymous, 'dry drinking' is a *mental state* in which a person with addiction experiences *addictive thinking and feeling*; however, they have *not yet consumed* addictive substances again.

Indications of 'dry drinking' include (1) An abstinent person with alcohol addiction tells his self-help group, *with gleaming eyes*, about his experiences under the influence of alcohol. (2) In doing this, he remembers his feelings of grandiosity, freedom, and apparent meaningfulness and enjoys them. (3) His interpretation of his fights and suffering *as an intense life* are *unbalanced*. (4) Even now, he enjoys the memory of the mental 'kick' or the physical and mental borderline experiences he had under the influence of his addictive substance. If the patient engages in *addictive thinking and feeling* again in a group session, the group members or the therapist must point this out. It can help the patient not to relapse again.

4. Persons with alcohol addiction *often gulp the first few glasses down.*

**Central idea**

Alcoholics drink alcohol because of its *effects* and not 'because they like it'. Therefore, they find as many reasons for their alcohol use as needed not to be ashamed of *themselves and their relationship partners.*

Alcoholics drink 'because of marital problems', 'because of stress', 'out of frustration', 'because I was depressed', 'because the wine tasted good', 'because I couldn't say no', 'because I wanted to', or 'because I was feeling good'. When one reason to drink fails, they find another. If there is *no* reason, they create a reason. For example, he can hurt his wife emotionally. She then reacts emotionally and devalues him. This altercation gives the patient *the excuse* to go to the pub. He rants to his 'friends' about 'women' and drinks. He 'can't do anything else'.

**Central idea**

With many addicts, relapses occur *not because of a problem* but from a state of well-being. However, those affected *themselves* do not want to know this and *also* "lie" *to others*. Their self-deception is an expression of their addictive thinking.

5. Persons with addiction repeatedly resolve to reduce or end their addictive substance use because of private, social, or physical harm. However, they often fail to stick to this resolution. *As a result*, they develop *feelings of guilt*, shame, and self-esteem problems, leading to depression. Failure to achieve one's good

intentions is a defeat to oneself. They play football as if they want to win but shoot the ball only *into their own goalpost*.

**Central idea**

Feelings of guilt arising from substance abuse are *justified* because the patient *himself* destroys his dignity as a person. Therefore, the therapist should *not* interpret an addict's feelings of guilt about their substance abuse *as neurotic* or justify them with the patient's difficult childhood experiences. An alcohol-dependent patient with trauma who had been dry for eight years said in the group: "I am an alcoholic. But I mustn't see myself as an alcoholic. Because if I were *sick*, then I couldn't help it! Then I would have an excuse to drink."

Alcohol abuse gives persons with alcohol addiction something positive. Over time, however, the dependency traumatizes the soul (Krüger, 2004b, p. 163; Stadler, 2013, pp. 85, 86). The person affected is, as it were, trapped. He *cannot* live *with* the alcohol but also *not without* it.

***Case example 105***
*An otherwise responsible, empathetic doctor, Ms. D., used to 'drink herself away' from alcohol in her clinic in the evenings. Then, as a single mother, she drove home to her 15-year-old son late at night, drunk. He was always waiting for her. Finally, she came into therapy 'because of depression'.*

***Case example 106***
*A 40-year-old senior civil servant had been hospitalized for very high liver values four times in the past five years. Most recently, he had a Gamma GT of 1400. His liver values dropped drastically every time he reduced his alcohol consumption. The intelligent man, however, lied to himself and others. He trivialized his alcohol problem and told the therapist in a naive and honest way: "I drink two or three beers in the evening or a bottle of wine with my wife. The doctor told me to be careful with alcohol. So far, however, no doctor has told me not to drink anymore!"*

6. Persons with addiction *avoid conversations and situations which remind them of their 'alcohol problem'*. They repeatedly fade out their addiction problem from their perception. They want to be taken seriously by their reference persons *despite their drug consumption* and 'lying'. If they succeed in deceiving their reference persons, they take it as a sign that their problem is *not yet severe*. The therapist, therefore, asks, for example: "Do you switch to another channel while watching TV in the evening when the topic of alcohol comes up in a program?".

**Exercise 27**
Why *can* addicts *not* learn to *control* their drug abuse?

7. The *irresistible craving to keep drinking* indicates the fundamental criterion for addiction—'loss of control'. In persons with addiction, the *desired effect* does not occur after one beer or two. After a period of abstinence, many dependent people hope to return to their drinking habits from *before the addiction*. But this is an

illusion because they have now developed an addiction memory (see Sect. 10.5). They drink in a controlled manner *for a while* because they want to prove *to themselves and others* that they are *not addicted*. But, if they are dependent, they lose control in any case, at the latest, after six months.

**Central idea**

Addicts long for the *effects* of the addictive substance. It is, therefore, unsatisfactory for them to only drink a glass or two of beer. The *conscious consumption* of the addictive substance (see Sect. 10.6.5) overrides their *existential decision* to live abstinently. It triggers their addictive patterns of thought, feeling, and behavior stored in their *addiction* memory (see Sect. 10.5) and the associated mechanisms of self-deception. The patient longingly remembers the *emotional intensity* of his addiction experience. Everyday life cannot offer this intensity so easily.

## Exercise 28

Why do persons with addiction trivialize and lie so much? Are they weak in character, or what is the reason?

8. *Making excuses*: Persons with addiction make excuses to justify the consumption of their addictive substance *to themselves and others*. One may drink *because of a particular problem* in the beginning. But persons with addiction drink *because they are addicted*. The drug increasingly becomes "the only thing the person has a significant emotional relationship with" (Groterath, 1993, p. 258). The other "possibilities of today appear banal and stale" (Stimmer, 1993, p. 276). The affected person has to be abstinent *for a few months* so that he can perceive his world and problems as a healthy adult again, realistically and differentiated. As a result, small experiences would gain meaning again.

***Case example 107***

*A 35-year-old man, Mr. F., comes to the group for persons with addiction for the first time. He reports his problems and subliminally presents himself as a victim. Suddenly an experienced participant yells at him: "Stop lying! I can't take it!" The therapist is shocked and thinks: 'He'll never return to the group!' But the experienced participant continues to yell: "And do you know why I can't take it? I used to always lie to myself! Now I don't want that anymore!" The therapist is impressed. He could never have confronted the new patient so authentically because of his excuses.*

**Central idea**

The 'lying' in persons with addiction is not a sign of weakness. It is a symptom of addiction disorder. It is caused by the *unconscious* defense through denial. This develops because the patient would admit to himself the true extent of his addiction problem if he told the truth about his substance abuse to his therapist or his reference persons. This admission would increase his guilt and shame and reduce the *desired effects* of the addictive substance. He'd have to *drink even more* to numb his guilty feelings.

Therefore, the therapist represents the patient's addiction problem with a second chair *next to him* (see Sect. 10.6). She symbolizes the patient's 'lying' with a stone or a building block on the chair for his 'alcohol problem': "You trivialize your problem and make excuses. It is an indication of your addiction. People who can drink normally make *no excuses.*" The *second chair* helps the patient and therapist perceive his 'lying as an expression of his 'addictive thinking' and *not* a part of himself.

9. *Aggressive behavior* in persons with addiction often indicates their *addictive thinking* in the equivalence mode (see Sects. 2.6 and 10.5). He does not distinguish between his inner representation of outer reality and the outer reality itself. When he feels angry, he thinks that his wife, who is sitting across from him, is making him angry. When he feels guilty, he believes that *his partner* is accusing him. His thinking in equivalence mode leads to disturbances in nearly all relationships.

10. & 16. *Inner contrition and guilt* are an expression of the patient's *healthy* everyday thinking. They occur when persons with addictions *re-experience damage* through their substance abuse. Although a*ppropriate feelings of guilt* in the sense of real justified guilt are healthy for those affected, *exaggerated self-pity* indicates addictive thinking and easily results in relapse. The patient increasingly becomes self-destructive, as he consumes himself, as a 'suffering drunkard', with his self-reproaches: "Everything is lost anyway", or "I am a mess". This makes it easier for him to drink *again* or to *continue* drinking.

**Exercise 29**

Is the treatment prognosis more favorable if the patient has already taken breaks from drinking *or* has never been abstinent in the last few years?

11. *Drinking breaks* are periods of *complete abstinence* lasting for a few days, weeks, or months. *Many* people do not drink alcohol for a few days after an excess. However, they do not think long about their alcohol consumption. They have no guilt about their substance use and drink again when they feel like it.

**Central idea**

But, persons with addiction take *complete* drinking breaks because they *experience* a loss of control over their alcohol consumption despite some harm.

They want to prove to themselves and others that they are not addicted. In doing so, it is noticeable that persons with addiction mostly fail to *stick to their original resolution.* They decide not to drink anything for six months but start consuming again after three months. A plan for one year-long abstinence turns into a maximum of six months of abstinence.

12. *Establish a drinking system*: Many with alcohol addiction plan to start drinking at a precise time as it helps them reduce negative consequences. For example, they drink 'only in the evening' because they

don't want to attract attention at work during the day. However, the 'evening' often starts at 5 p.m. On the weekend, they drink not only in the evening but *also throughout the day*. Some people have heard that many *real* alcoholics have the compulsion to drink alcohol as soon as they wake up in the morning. That is why they *consciously* drink 'in the morning *only after* 11 o'clock'. Many of those affected *consciously* plan their leisure activities, so they can drink a *lot* of alcohol in the company of others *without attracting any attention*.

13, 14, & 17. Severe addiction tends to result in *changes in the workplace, family life, and lifestyle*. The decline in performance at work due to substance abuse is almost always greater than what persons with addiction believe. *Even* alcoholics have a hangover in the morning after drinking at night. They find it difficult to concentrate and hide their alcohol consumption. A patient with a *high* position always ensured that workplace meetings were scheduled only in the afternoon. He was afraid of attracting attention 'because of his alcohol breath'.

15. *Loss of interest*: Persons with alcoholic dependency syndrome are more preoccupied with their substance abuse than they think, and others notice. They think about how to get the addictive substance. They look forward to finally being able to drink properly in the evening or on the weekend. They struggle with physical and psychological consequential damage. Persons with alcohol dependency syndrome are continuously stressed because of their familial and social conflicts and their battle against addiction. The stress robs them of the energy to be interested in their family, friends, and hobbies. In the end, they experience everything as empty and meaningless. The meaninglessness is often a reason to drink again.

**Central idea**

Persons with addictions are not 'lazy' but often 'more diligent' than healthy people. For example, after being laid off by their employer, they usually find a new job faster than others. However, their employers often exploit them because of their needs and feelings of guilt. After a while, they are exhausted, drink more, and get laid off again. It is not true that persons with alcohol addiction have 'no will'. It takes a lot of strength to fall into the patterns of substance abuse repeatedly and then start all over again and repair the damage.

18, 20. & 21. The more *dependent* an addict is mentally and physically on the consumption of addictive substances, the more he ensures that he always has a *supply of alcohol* in the house. Because of their *physical* dependence, chronic drinkers experience *withdrawal symptoms* after 6–12 h of abstinence. As a result, they often have to 'refill' at four or five in the morning. Maybe they'll vomit the first sip. But even then, they still get enough alcohol in the body that *the second sip* 'stays in'. Many alcohol addicts prevent withdrawal symptoms. They hide full bottles of alcohol in cupboards, the basement, the garage, or the garden shed so their caregivers cannot access them. Severe withdrawal symptoms or delirium with sweating, palpitations, tremors, and hallucinations lead to *hospitalization*. Hospital admissions also occur due to liver damage, suicidality, or accidents. *In the hospital,* it is often the first time the patient is asked about their alcohol problem by the doctor.

19. *Neglect of diet*: A bottle of wine has around 800 cal, and three liters of beer are equivalent to six sandwiches in terms of nutritional value. The lack of hunger, the general stress syndrome, the lack of pleasure, adverse developments in private life, and the narrowing of thinking through the consumption of addictive substances often lead those affected to neglect their diet. For example, they consume too little protein. Over time, this leads to liver damage or damage to the nerves from polyneuropathy.

**Central idea**

Regular consumption of *70 g of 100% alcohol daily* leads to liver cirrhosis in men after 20 years. For women, *50 g of pure alcohol daily* is sufficient to cause similar damage. It amounts to 0.6 L of wine or 1.4 L of beer a day for men and 0.45 L of wine or 1 L of beer for women.

22. Chronic drinkers (see 18, 20, & 21) drink more or less continuously throughout the day and night as they are also *physically dependent*. They need to maintain a certain level of alcohol in the blood to avoid withdrawal symptoms. Those who *drink excessively* can 'binge' for a maximum of one to two weeks and then stop because their body can no longer keep up with the drinking. They become helpless. Excessive drinking leads to *social and private consequential damage* much quicker than chronic drinking. *Physical* damage generally occurs later in the event of excessive drinking because of the necessary drinking breaks. So-called quarter drinkers do not really exist. On closer examination, it becomes apparent that they are almost always persons with addiction who drink excessively. Their so-called quarters are sometimes seven weeks and at other times sixteen weeks long.

23, 24, 25, & 26. *Moral degradation, intellectual capacity*: In the chronic phase of alcoholism, those affected experience a decreased ability to concentrate, think, and remember. However, these symptoms often can recede with abstinence. For example, a chronic drinker with suspected incipient dementia may be able to think entirely as per his age after six months *if he is abstinent*. However, *in the long term*, chronic heavy alcohol consumption leads to metabolic disorders and consequential neurological damage in the brain. All the more so if the patient has inadequately nourished himself. Brain damage due to chronic alcohol abuse is called

Korsakoff Syndrome. Some patients *even drink technical products that contain alcohol*, such as methylated spirits. Many *drink at the snack bar or the kiosk* because the 'friends' there don't ask unpleasant questions. Women are more likely to drink alone. Over time, chronic self-deception and the failure of one's resolutions are traumatic for the soul. Patients generally become more indifferent and unable to love themselves and others. Their ethical values and attitudes change. Their goals in life are primarily limited to drinking and procuring the addictive substance.

27, 28, 29, & 30. Persons with *chronic alcohol addiction* can tolerate increasingly *lesser* amounts of alcohol over the years due to the consequential physical damage. Therefore, sometimes it appears as if they can now control the amount they drink. But the real reason is that their metabolism slows down because of liver damage. As a result, the alcohol now stays in the blood for a prolonged duration. Therefore, they can maintain the required alcohol level *longer* with *lesser* alcohol. Trembling of the hands and nausea in the morning are predictors of alcohol withdrawal. They indicate *physical* dependency. Other predictors of withdrawal include insomnia, general vegetative restlessness, racing heart, and vomiting. Alcohol consumption can then alleviate the withdrawal symptoms. But *drinking becomes a compulsion.*

**Exercise 30**

Practice answering Jellinek's 30 questions (see Fig. 10.1 above) for the patient in case example 108. In your opinion, which of the questions should be answered with a yes for the patient? You will find the answer to this question after the case example.

***Case example 108***

*Ms. G. is a 51-year-old, single, slightly overweight nurse. She comes to psychotherapy "because of a burnout". In the initial interview, she says: She was facing "many problems" at her job. She was "always ready to step in and help others". As a result, she would often feel overwhelmed. She could no longer sleep adequately "because of many unfortunate life events". "That's why she often drank two or three glasses of wine in the evening." Ms. G. was in a crisis when her only good friend broke off their relationship. She would experience nausea and vomiting at night. Her family doctor admitted her to a hospital, which led to the discovery of "extremely high liver values". Ms. G. then went to a psychosomatic clinic. The therapist there invited her to take part in behavioral mindfulness training.*

*The patient has been on sick leave for four months. At 51, she is living at home with her parents for a few weeks, 300 km away from her previous workplace. She wants to look for a new job here. She takes "five milligrams of zolpidem to sleep in the evening". But she still doesn't sleep well. She wishes: "I need psychotherapeutic support with rehabilitation for sleep disorders so that I can stop the zolpidem." Ms. G.*

*seems anxious and agitated. However, outwardly she appears loud and self-confident. With understanding and humor, the therapist tries to relate as many of her symptoms as possible to her substance use. Additional symptoms of addiction disorder start to appear with every passing session. The patient finally reports consuming "a bottle of wine a day and up to two tablets of zolpidem". The therapist: "That is a whole lot in total." Ms. G.: "But I still can't sleep well." Therapist: "Then the zolpidem won't help you sleep at all! Don't take it anymore!" Ms. G. complains: "My family doctor berated me for drinking too much alcohol. I expected more help from him!".*

*Ms. G. had "not consumed a drop of alcohol" for nine weeks since the beginning of her stay in the psychosomatic clinic. She is proud that she has "already lost 13 kg". The therapist explains: "A bottle of wine has 800 cal. If you skip the wine and drink water or tea, you will lose weight! You are doing well! In the next therapy session, I would like to continue working with you on whether you should see yourself as an alcoholic or not." The therapist gives her the Jellinek's questionnaire used by Alcoholics Anonymous: "Please fill it out and bring it back for the next session!" A week later, the patient's father calls the therapist and tells him that the patient had "gone to an addiction clinic". Three weeks later, the therapist received an interim report from the clinic, which shows that the patient drank up to two bottles of wine a day at home until recently. In addition, she took two zolpidem 10 mg sleeping pills at noon and two in the evening. The therapist evaluates the patient's stay in the hospital as a positive result of his outpatient therapy because the treatment increased the patient's level of suffering from her substance abuse.*

*The patient returns to the therapist after eight weeks of inpatient addiction therapy. She would like to continue outpatient therapy. She now sees herself as an alcoholic and has 'capitulated'. After her stay in the clinic, Ms. G. is well-informed about alcoholism. She seems euphoric. She spontaneously reports that she had a massive relapse before her stay in the clinic. She had taken wine and sleeping pills at home. But then, she had swallowed even more tablets in a drunken stupor. She slipped, broke her nose, and suffered a concussion when she went to the bathroom. She came to the hospital and, from there, went to the addiction clinic. The therapist assessed this dramatic course of events as a massive loss of control: "Maybe your crash will help you to let go of the alcohol and the zolpidem!"*

Ms. G. originally went to the psychotherapist "because of burnout". However, you will notice: The patient would have to answer Jellinek's questions 2, 3, 5, 6, 8, 9, 12, 14, 15, 16, 17, 19, 20, and 28 (see Fig. 10.1 in Sect. 10.4) with a 'Yes'. Even if she answers 'only' 5 of these 14 questions with a 'Yes', she would have to consider herself 'probably addicted'.

## 10.5 Psychodynamics of Addiction Development

**Exercise 31**

Why is *immediate* treatment of a second mental illness generally contraindicated in patients with addiction disorders?

Patients with addiction disorders start to consume addictive substances because of internal tension, sleep disorders, self-esteem problems, anxiety, relationship difficulties, or inhibitions. These difficulties can be symptoms of a trauma-related disorder, personality disorder, or other emotional problems.

**Central idea**

Patients with addiction disorder resort to consuming addictive substances as their first step *because they have problems*. But, the before and after are reversed over time: (1) Patients with addiction get into trouble *because they consume addictive substances*. (2) The patient's addiction *prevents them* from solving their original problems.

Many patients with addiction disorders come to therapy because of their addiction problems. The therapist then empathizes with their *suffering* from dependence. But she often overlooks that substance abuse *gives those afflicted also something positive*. Many people with addiction disorders feel a positive effect *when they start drinking alcohol during the day,* even with dependency syndrome. Their inner inhibitions and tensions get resolved. They temporarily exceed their individual limits. *Subjectively*, they sometimes experience a kick and develop incredible stamina or new skills. They *believe* they suddenly understand things and can get to the heart of the issue. The change in consciousness caused by the addictive substance and the play with the limits of life could sometimes convey the feeling of a creative flow.

***Case example 109***

*Participants in a group for people with addiction disorders talk about their experiences in their "wet time": "Waking up in a taxi in London with no pants, no money, and no passport." "Always being the last to leave when partying." "I have been hospitalized twenty times in the past two years. Once I had a cardiac arrest in the ambulance." Mr. H. asks the therapist provocatively: "Mr. Krüger, do you know what we're talking about?" The therapist replies meekly: "Well, I also have been completely drunk twice." The group roared with laughter (continued below).*

Addictive substances have a mind-altering effect. They are psychotropic. The *effects are different* with different addictive substances. But the *dependence* on addictive substances always develops *in a similar way*. It progresses as follows (see Fig. 10.2 see below):

1. At first, the patient drinks inconspicuously. There is still *no harm* from drinking. He is, therefore, not addicted.
2. *Stage of harmful use*: (1) The patient suffers psychological, social, or physical damage as a result of using addictive substances. (2) But he continues with his substance use anyway because he does not want to do without the *subjectively positive effect* of the addictive substance. (3) To do this, he has to dissociate from and deny his self-doubt and feelings of shame. Increasingly, he justifies his substance abuse to himself and others with an *addictive logic*. The addictive logic overrides his self-doubt and shame and contradicts his *healthy everyday thinking*. (4) Over time, the patient *alternates* internally between his *healthy everyday logic* and his contrary *addictive logic* (see Fig. 10.2 see below). When he wants to drink, he *identifies* with his excuses: "You don't treat yourself to

anything else." However, self-doubt, feelings of inferiority, and shame surface when he is sober or clean. The patient develops an *addicted identity* in addition to their *everyday identity*. It is "as if they were different persons whose identities can be assumed with a slight change of consciousness" (Shengold, 1989, p. 146).

**Important definition**

Neuropsychologically, the "addicted identity" is a special psychosomatic resonance pattern (see Sect. 2.7) in the neural *connections between* the *memory centers* of behavior patterns, physical sensations, emotions, linguistic terms, and thoughts. The psychosomatic resonance pattern is triggered by associated emotions, thoughts, or behavior patterns. The psychosomatic resonance pattern of the "addicted identity" is also called "addiction memory" (Schwehm, 2004, p. 141; Waldheim-Auer, 2013, p. 196).

We develop many such psychosomatic resonance patterns in the course of our life. They develop through training or habituation and are updated when necessary. In addition, they help us avoid having to relearn specific recurring actions *repeatedly*, for example, driving a car. Ciompi (1999, p. 215) refers to these neural interconnections as "thought, feeling, and action tracks".

3. *Dependent substance use*: The patient suffers *further* social and psychological damage. He can *no longer* or only temporarily control the amount of his substance use. He drinks consistently and even increases the amount of his addictive substance. The logic of his addicted identity overrides his healthy everyday thinking repeatedly. The failure to control the amount of alcohol *traumatizes* his soul over the course of two to ten years (Krüger, 2004b, p. 166) and impairs his healthy everyday thinking. Ultimately, it creates a *metacognitive confusion* between the patient's healthy adult thinking and his contrary addicted identity (see Fig. 10.2).

**Important definition**

Addictive thinking is a *dysfunctional metacognitive process* (see Sec. 4.2). It is the general principle that gives rise to different dysfunctional cognitions of *addictive* thinking. The addictive thinking controls the patient's mentalization process (see Sect. 2. 2) such that he evaluates his substance abuse *positively* and ignores the negative consequences of consumption.

When applying addictive thinking, addicts act *in the equivalence mode* (see Sect. 2. 6). They do not differentiate between their *inner addicted reality construction* of the outer reality and the *outer reality itself*. They imagine the world the way they need it to be. For example, they ignore the personal negative consequences of their substance abuse. They quickly find a convenient excuse to logically justify their substance use to themselves and others: "I would say that I am allowed to have a glass!" They project their *internal* assumptions onto the *external* reality. Their grandiose or masochistic addictive fantasies determine *their actions in the external world*. They are the hero Django *or* the one always afflicted by the world's misfortune.

***Case example 109 (1st continuation)***

*A 58-year-old patient, Mr. H., told the group: "That was very easy for me. One day I thought, 'I'm an alcoholic; that's why I don't drink.' Another day I thought, 'I'm*

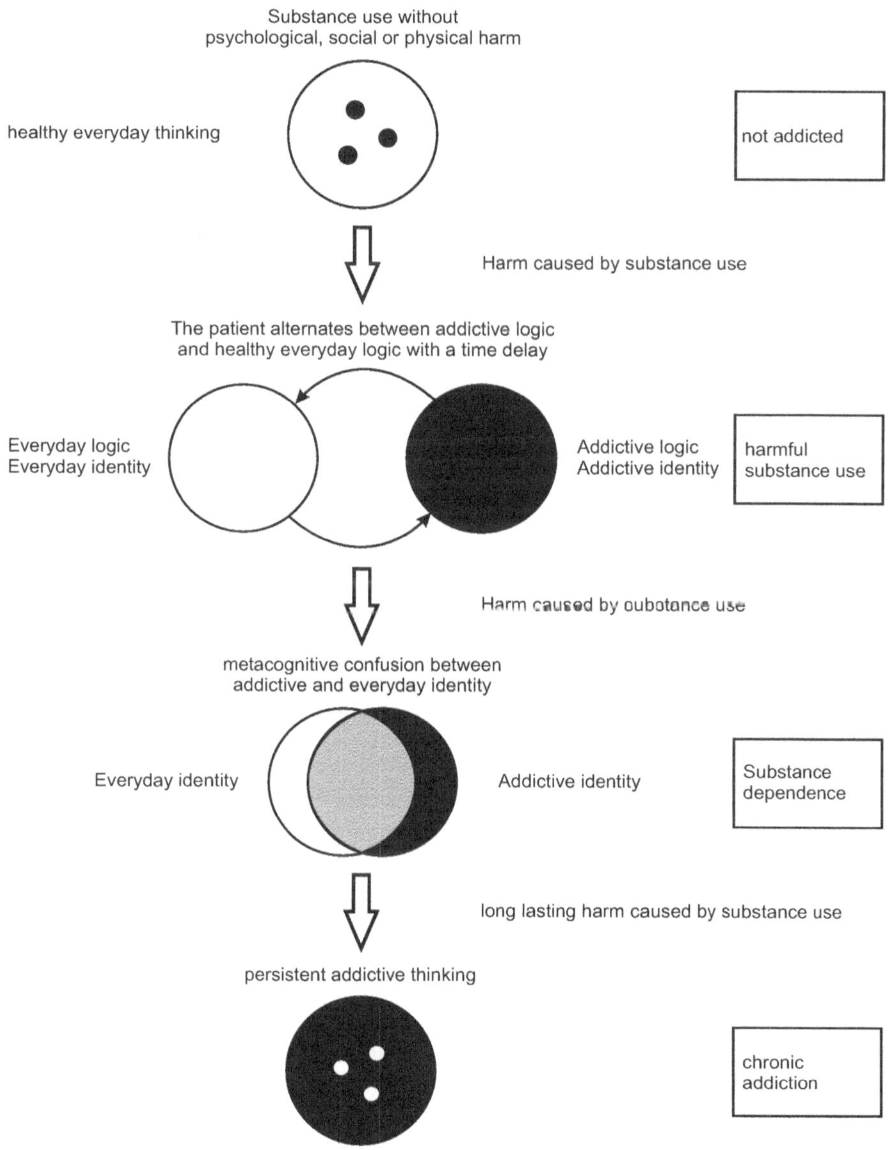


**Fig. 10.2** The development of the metacognitive disorder in people with addiction disorders

*an alcoholic. Ninety percent of alcoholics drink.' Then I went out and drank." In another context, Mr. H. once said: "If alcoholism were a question of intelligence, most of us wouldn't be here!" The therapist looked around the group and noticed: Mr. H. was right (continued in Sect.* 10.6.4*).*

4. *Chronic addiction disorder* (see Fig. 10.2 see above): The patient suffers from persistent physical and mental damage and often from family or social disintegration. He has *given up trying to control* his substance use. Instead, he drinks according to his addicted identity's desire. His addictive thinking *permanently* dominates his healthy everyday thinking and destroys the goals, values, and norms of his healthy everyday identity. As a result, he experiences a "change in character", as Alcoholics Anonymous call it.

## 10.6 The Nine Phases of Addiction Therapy

At the beginning of my work as a psychiatrist, I felt helpless and powerless when working with patients with addiction disorders. As a therapist, I had to learn to *surrender* and endure my ignorance and uncertainty to treat them (see Sect. 10.6.4). Initially, I consciously argued: "I cannot treat people with addiction because *I'm not* addicted. Persons with addiction are the *professionals*!" My *surrender* then opened up a *new* opportunity for me in addiction therapy. I listened to people with addictions and learned from them. I was fascinated time and again. Some wise afflicted persons dealt with the inconsistencies of their self-regulation with humor. There was a lot of laughter in the group discussions. Today I know: They had control *over alternating* between their healthy everyday logic (see Sect. 10.5) and addictive logic (Krüger, 1988, 2004b, p. 170 ff.).

**Exercise 32**
Why is *only cognitive*-behavioral therapy for addiction disorders inadequate?

People with addiction suffer from a *metacognitive disorder* in their mentalization (see Sects. 2.8 and 10.5). Their self-development is usually blocked by a rigid defense pattern even before developing an addiction disorder. But, in the state of dependence, their self-development is further impaired through feelings of guilt and shame because of the consequences of addiction. This results in *metacognitive confusion.* The therapist and the patient can no longer differentiate if the defense through grandiosity or masochistic self-censorship is the *result of or reason* for addiction. Therefore, *in disorder-specific psychotherapy*, the therapist must explicitly address the metacognitive confusion. Therefore, the method described here also differs from a purely *social psychiatric treatment.* Psychiatrists often treat 'only' the symptoms caused by the disruption in the metacognitive processes and appeal to reason.

**Central idea**

In therapy, the patient should not only learn to live abstinent without his addictive substance but also develop an *awareness of his metacognitive confusion.* This confusion results from the unconscious splitting between everyday thinking and addictive thinking and the protection of this splitting through denial.

**Important definition**

The method described here implements *metacognitive* therapeutic interventions from *schema therapy* and interactive psychoanalytic interventions from *depth-psychological psychotherapy.*

Unlike *cognitive-behavioral* therapy, it is not enough to replace unfavorable thoughts with more favorable ones in psychotherapy for people with addiction (see Sect. 2.14). For example, in the case of addictive pressure, it does not help to think about *positive experiences without* addictive substances. Because patients with addiction *cognitively* know how they *should* behave in the event of a risk of relapse. But when they wish to drink again, they shift, *without even realizing it*, from their healthy everyday thinking to the psychosomatic resonance pattern of their addicted thinking. They act in equivalence mode and think about the world in a way that suits their addictive thinking. Therefore, they believe it is *logical and normal* to consume their addictive substance when tempted to consume it again. An affected person once said: "If I wanted to drink, nobody could have dissuaded me!" For this reason, behavior therapy requires an approach aimed at the dysfunctional *metacognitive process* of self-regulation, as in schema therapy.

The method described here also implements *interactive psychoanalytic interventions*. The therapist *does not work with regression*, transference, and resistance to compensate for childhood deficits and trauma. Instead, the therapy process focuses on *depth-psychological work* on the rigid defense through denial (see Sect. 2.4.2) and splitting *in the present* (see Sect. 2.4.1). The patient should learn *to notice his alternation* between his two contrary ego states—healthy adult thinking and addictive thinking (see Sect. 10.5)—and bring it under the control of his ego. One can do so by naming, representing, and *playing* out the contrast between the two contrary ego states *in the as-if mode* (see Sect. 2.6).

**Exercise 33**

Why is it essential for people with addiction to be *completely* abstinent?

**Recommendation**

The therapist should pay close attention to *any indication* of substance abuse in her patients and immediately look for addiction-specific symptoms (see Sect. 10.4). This process *also applies to* patients with trauma-related disorders, depression, borderline syndrome, or anxiety disorders. In doing so, the therapist asks openly: "How do you deal with alcohol?" Or: "Do you take any drugs?"

**Central idea**

Nothing is more vital than abstinence for people with addiction because thirty to ninety percent of their physical, mental, and social problems are reduced *simply by* letting go of their substance and abstaining. The stress of conflict in the other areas also reduces *as abstinence liberates* the patient from feelings of guilt, shame, self-devaluation, self-accusation, and excessive adaptive behavior (see case example 110 in Sects. 10.6.2 and 10.9). For this reason, the therapist first treats the addiction disorder and only then addresses *the remaining problems*.

Two-thirds of patients with addiction are in counseling or treatment *only for one to ten sessions* (see Sect. 10.3). Therefore, it is vital to address the core issue of addiction using a disorder-specific approach *in the first ten sessions* when *counseling* people with addiction. Disorder-specific *psychotherapy* for patients with addiction lasts at least two years. It comprises the following sequential steps (see Fig. 10.3):

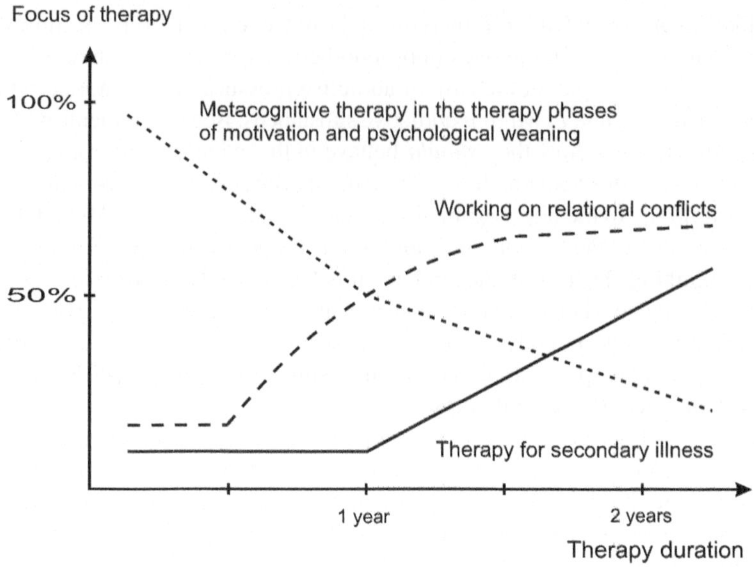


**Fig. 10.3** The main focus of treatment in the course of therapy for people with addiction

1. The development of awareness of the addiction diagnosis and the *motivation* for disorder-specific psychotherapy with the two-chair technique.
2. The *decision* to abstain.
3. Participation in an addiction therapy group or a self-help group alongside individual therapy.
4. Discovering the personal rock bottom and the surrender.
5. Disorder-specific addiction therapy for *psychological weaning*.
6. Relapse prevention.
7. Integration of the inner change in the current relationships.
8. The co-treatment of a possible second illness, a trauma-related disorder, an anxiety disorder, or a personality disorder. This should only begin after 6–12 months of abstinence.
9. Post-traumatic maturation (see Sect. 10.6.4). The patient mourns the lost years of personal development. He develops a transpersonal conscience, humility in life, compassion, wisdom, creativity, and humor.

### *10.6.1 Awareness of Addiction, Level of Suffering, and Motivation*

**Central idea**

At the beginning of psychotherapy, the patient should *decide* whether he wants to see himself as an addict. Without the decision to identify oneself as an addict, there is no need to abstain.

> The metacognitive confusion remains. The addictive *thinking* is then not decoupled from the *consumption* of the addictive substance.

The patient mostly comes into treatment with the *secondary motivation* to work on the problems arising from their addiction. He must transform it into a *primary motivation* to work directly *on his addiction*. Through her therapeutic interventions, the therapist tries to *expand* the patient's direct *suffering from their addiction* (see below). In doing so, she takes the following steps:

1. The therapist engages in a psychodramatic conversation with the patient, as with patients without addiction. For this purpose, she sets up two additional chairs in the therapy room for the problem *spontaneously defined* by the patient from his everyday life (see Fig. 2.9 in Sect. 2.8). For example, in the case of a marital conflict, she places an empty chair next to him for his inner self-representation and another chair opposite him to represent his wife.
2. For every problem the patient mentions in the first interview, the therapist invites him to place a stone or a colorful building block *on the empty chair of his self-representation* in everyday life. For example, he places a stone each for his marital conflict, sleep disturbances, depression, morning tremors, job loss, and loneliness.
3. The therapist openly *addresses* the patient's suspected addiction problem in a suitable situation and states it as follows: "Do you drink alcohol regularly? How much is that every day?" "Do you consider yourself to be an alcoholic?" The question "Do you have an addiction problem?" should also be asked when the patient is *in an addiction clinic* because the answer is the basis for the first step in therapy, the *awareness* of addiction disorder.
4. When the patient responds to these questions, the therapist *almost immediately* sets up an additional third empty chair next to the patient (see Figs. 10.4 and 10.5): "This chair represents your alcoholism", "... your alcohol consumption", "... your addictive thinking". The therapist chooses the name that the patient can identify with personally. Setting up the third chair for the "addiction" focuses the conversation on the subject of dependency.
5. The therapist tries to engage the patient in the subject of 'addiction'. As she sets up the second chair, she explains to the patient *why* she is addressing his dependency: "I know you often think as healthy adults. The chair you are sitting in stands for your healthy adult thinking. But the empty chair that I placed next to you stands for you as Karl, the one who drinks. We must talk about your alcohol consumption. It is important because if you have an alcohol problem, we have to proceed *differently* in therapy. Otherwise, the psychotherapeutic treatment of your depression will not succeed."
6. The therapist asks him to pick up each problem, represented on the chair for his self-representation *in the symptom scene* with a building block. She checks with the patient whether this problem is *associated with his substance use or the 'normal' everyday conflicts*. If applicable, the patient places the symbol on the chair of his 'addicted ego'.

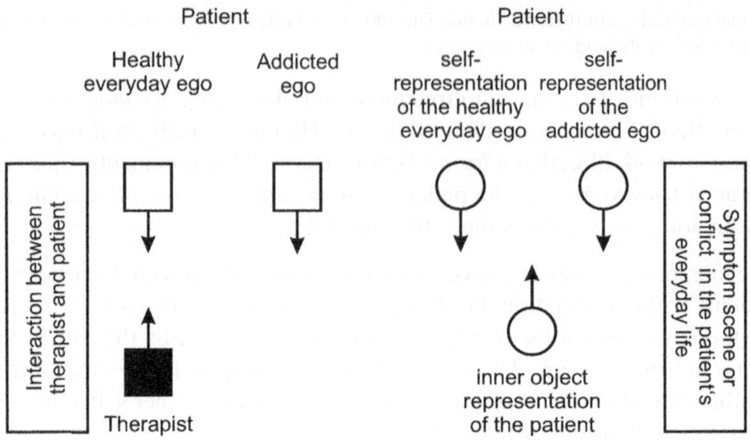


**Fig. 10.4** The resolution of the metacognitive confusion in people with addiction using the two-chair technique

7. Many people with alcohol addiction *downplay* their substance use in response to questions about their addiction. Or they hesitate and add to the "yes": "Well, maybe …", "Actually yes, but …", "Yes, I think so …" Any addition beyond a simple "yes" is an indication that the patient has *not yet clearly acknowledged* that he is an addict.

**Central idea**

The therapist pays attention to *her feelings* triggered *by the patient's response.* If she *remains doubtful and suspicious*, it is an indication that the patient has not acknowledged his addiction. The therapist then often vicariously senses the uncertainty that the patient does not allow *himself* to feel in metacognitive confusion and delegates it to the therapist through defense through projective identification (see Sect. 2.4.4).

8. However, many patients with addiction also *spontaneously confirm* that they have an alcohol problem. In such a case, the therapist, as a metacognitive doppelganger (see Sect. 4.8), playfully switches to *identification with the patient's addictive thinking* and asks him, a little indignantly, how he came to this conclusion: "Why do you believe that? How do you know that you are an alcoholic?" The patient should justify his statement *himself.* The therapist then works with the patient to determine which of his symptoms indicate an addiction and which do not (see Sect. 10.4). Again, the patient symbolizes his addiction symptoms with colorful building blocks and places them on the chair for his "addicted ego": "Your secret drinking, loss of interest, and your excuses are certainly indications of addiction." However, the patient places the stones for his feelings of guilt, inferiority, or shame on the table directly in front of him because they are part of his *healthy adult thinking.*
9. Sometimes the patient denies having an addiction problem *despite clear indications.* In such a case, the therapist takes the chair for his addiction problem and

puts it far away in the corner of the room: "Okay, I'll put your alcohol problem far away from you!" This therapeutic intervention translates the patient's trivialization of his problem into action *in the as-if mode of play*, paradoxically bringing it to the patient's awareness even more.

10. During the conversation, as an implicit doppelganger (see Sect. 2.5), the therapist *points with her* hand to the chair for the patient's *"addicted ego"* whenever he thinks *as an addict*. She points to the chair of his *self-representation in the symptom scene* when he narrates an episode from his *everyday life*. Or she points to the chair he is sitting on when she wants to highlight that the patient is speaking as his *healthy everyday ego*. In this way, she links *the patient's self-regulation* with his three *externally represented* ego states (see Fig. 10.4 in Sect. 10.6.1). Thus, the patient learns to differentiate the three ego states *also internally*.
11. The therapist and the patient work together to develop individual concrete *memories* of his substance abuse *into complete stories*. The therapist points her hand to the chair for the patient's self-representation in his everyday life (see Fig. 2.9 in Sect. 2.8) and lets him describe his thoughts, feelings, and behaviors associated with his *substance abuse in its chronological sequence*, from beginning to end, with all its consequences.

**Central idea**

*As a metacognitive doppelganger*, the therapist actively helps the patient develop these narratives: (1) Together with the patient, she *chronologically* goes through the patient's self-regulation and the events related to his substance use, like in a film script, and adds missing set pieces. (2) She makes the patient aware of the contradictions between his addictive thinking and the real events. (3) She verbally marks the patient's existing addiction symptoms as such (see Sect. 10.4).

Completing the addiction stories heightens the patient's *suffering* in his addiction and improves his *insight* into the addiction disease. In doing this, the therapist makes *statements as a doppelganger* marking indications of addictive thinking, feeling, and acting: "You wanted to be able to sleep! So you opened the best bottle of wine. What did you think and feel before you drank? What happened next? What did you feel when you had the first glass? Ah, yes, you didn't even sit on the sofa. You stopped and immediately poured yourself a second glass. So you gulped the first glass down. The good *taste* of the wine didn't matter as you were concerned about *the effect* of drinking! Yes, you sat on the sofa. What did you think and feel there? You were indifferent to everything. So you got yourself a second bottle of wine. Yes, you went to bed. You slept well. I believe you. If you drink alcohol to get a good night's sleep, you fall asleep faster. But then you surely woke up after five hours and continued to have a night of *disturbed* sleep. People with addiction have told me about this experience. They said their sleep is much more restful *without alcohol*, even if one wakes up more often." Or: "You are an intelligent man. But despite your liver damage, you wanted to drink yourself away." Patient: "Yes, I always did that with a guilty conscience, but in the end, I didn't care." The therapist points to the chair for addictive thinking: "If you have already canceled appointments to drink in the evening, you have probably used *excuses in front of yourself and others*. For example, you might have said you had a stomach ache. Then it must have been easier for you to drink." Or: "If you drank *more than one bottle of wine a day*, you probably bought the bottles from different stores. Otherwise, the cashier at the supermarket checkout counter would have noticed that you had a drinking problem." Or: "If you took two zolpidem tablets every night, you probably went to *different* doctors to get them." Patient: "Yes, my family doctor and my neurologist." Therapist: "But they didn't know that you already got some sleeping pills from the other doctor." Patient: "Yes, I didn't say that." Therapist: "By the way, this is also understood as *secret* drug abuse!" Or: Therapist: "You felt like Django, the greatest. You knew everything better than the others and were having fun. But then you blacked out and no longer remember how you got home. You wonder whether something bad may have happened there. How are you now?" If necessary, the therapist also addresses abnormalities in the patient's appearance and informs him professionally: "You can no longer think so well. Your ability to concentrate has decreased. If you let go of the addictive substance, however, your mental abilities will probably be fully back in six months!".

12. The therapist lets the patient *switch* from the chair of his healthy everyday thinking to the chair of his addictive thinking *externally,* at least once, and also *enact the addictive ego psychosomatically* in the as-if mode of play.

**Central idea**

The therapist, as a metacognitive doppelganger (see Sect. 4.8), enters the patient's addictive thinking *internally* and, *together with him,* verbally works out *the positive function* of his addictive thinking in his holistic process of self-regulation. The patient thus feels understood and doesn't need to lie and downplay his suffering.

As a metacognitive doppelganger, the therapist exaggerates the positive function of his addictive thinking slightly paradoxically: "Then you are Django! You have the situation under control!" In doing this, the therapist practices the therapeutic attitude: "The patient's soul does nothing for free." Together with the patient, she looks for the advantage of thinking and acting addictively for him. The patient's eyes often light up as they verbalize the thinking and feeling in their addicted ego state. Eventually, someone realizes the positive meaning of drug consumption for the patient. Together with the patient, the therapist thus supplements the psychosomatic resonance pattern of the patient's addictive thinking with associated sensorimotor interaction patterns, physical sensations, emotions, linguistic concepts, and thoughts (see Sect. 2.7) until the patient *himself*, all of a sudden, senses the absurdity of his addictive thinking and thinks as a healthy adult about the consequences of his addictive actions. The therapist marks such a shift in thinking by letting the patient switch back to the chair of the healthy adult thinking externally.

13. When the patient shifts back to the chair of his healthy everyday thinking, he leaves his "identity as an addict" *externally on the other chair*. The *outer* distance also gives him an *inner* distance to his addictive thinking. Often

it is only through the *external* change of roles that he perceives the difference between his addictive thinking and his healthy everyday thinking *also psychosomatically*.

**Exercise 34**
You cannot understand the effect of the two-chair technique only by reading. Therefore, I suggest you rehearse it by acting psychosomatically in a role-play with a colleague. First, enact the initial conversation with a patient with addiction *without a second chair* for his addictive thinking. Then repeat the role play, but this time place a second chair for the "alcohol problem" or the "addicted ego" next to the "patient". You will notice: *Without* the second chair, when *in the role of the patient*, you experience the "therapist" as a persecutor and you shut down internally. *With* the second chair, when i*n the role of the therapist*, you will notice that the second chair for the "addicted ego" of the patient reduces the pressure of conflict in the therapeutic relationship and resolves your defense-related metacognitive countertransference (see Sects. 2.10 and 4.8) toward the patient's addictive thinking. You psychosomatically act as a metacognitive doppelganger for both, healthy adult thinking *and also* addictive thinking.

The patient psychosomatically perceives his addiction problem as a second ego *separated from himself* through external representation. He *actively relates* to his addicted identity from the observer position in the as-if mode of play. (1) The two-chair technique systematically resolves the patient's defense through denial. (2) By naming, representing, and enacting *the addictive thinking and feeling* in the as-if mode of play, the patient completes his psychosomatic resonance pattern (see Sect. 2. 7) of his addictive thinking. He learns *to think* addictively *in the as-if mode* and gains ego control of his addictive thinking. 3. Thus, the patient notices his addictive thinking sooner. His addictive thinking becomes more seldom and shorter and he sometimes must laugh about it himself. He can then freely choose whether he wants to continue thinking, feeling, *and acting* in an addictive manner or act in a new way and remain abstinent. According to Moreno, the patient becomes *spontaneous* and direct in dealing with his addiction conflict (1974, p. 13) (see Sect. 2.14).

The two-chair technique *also helps the therapist*. Many therapists develop a defense-related metacognitive countertransference toward patients with addiction in the therapeutic relationship as a reaction to their own *negative feelings*: (1) They internalize their negative emotional reaction: "I am a bad or incompetent therapist." (2) Or they try to convict the patient as the persecutor of his misdeeds, as it were. (3) Or they react to *their own* emotional reaction by refusing a relationship and sending the patient to another therapist.

**Central idea**

The two-chair technique, however, resolves the therapist's countertransference. As a reaction to the patient's opposing ego states, symbolized by two chairs, *she also* develops two contradicting psychosomatic resonance patterns *within herself*. On the one hand, she empathizes with the patient suffering from the addiction but thinks *as a healthy adult*. On the other hand, switching back and forth as a metacognitive doppelganger, she empathizes with *the patient's addictive thinking* and, together with him, paradoxically works out its *positive function* in his holistic self-regulation.

**Exercise 35**
Why should the therapist make statements in addiction therapy and rather not ask questions?

Patients with an addiction disorder act out their metacognitive confusion *in the equivalence mode* (see Sect. 2.6). The patient imagines the external world in alignment with his inner addictive thinking needs. He thinks in black-and-white patterns. Usually, he misunderstands the therapist's questions, for example, "Could it be that you sometimes drink more than three liters of beer?" *as a statement*: "I know you are lying". But, in the case of a *concrete* statement such as: "Sometimes you probably drink five or six glasses of beer. And one glass then contains a liter of beer", the patient *must directly disagree or agree* with the statement: "Yes, sometimes I drink four or five, but I try to stick to three." The therapist becomes a *witness to the patient's truth* through her open and honest language. The patient no longer needs to hide the truth (see Sect. 10.7).

Patients who are *not addicted* answer the therapist's question about an addiction problem authentically and confidently in the negative. Other patients may 'just' be *habitual drinkers.* They abuse their addictive substance (ICD-10: F10.1) but are *not yet dependent* (ICD-10: F10.2). But, the therapist explicitly marks "only" *harmful use of addictive substances* as the "first stage of addiction". In such a case, she asks the patient to be consistent with himself: "You say *you can still control* the amount of alcohol. Then I want you to really do that! As someone who is not addicted, that should actually be easy for you!" The patient then should make a *contract with himself* about his substance use in everyday life. In doing so, the patient *himself* determines how he wants to limit his drug consumption in the future. He should keep this resolution for at least a year. *For example,* he can decide: "I will no longer drink *alone*, but only when I have company. And I will drink a *maximum* of one glass of beer or wine." Over the next few weeks, the therapist discusses with the patient his experiences with his resolution. If the patient does *not* stick to his plan, he is probably addicted after all. In such a case, the therapist works with him to record his addiction symptoms using Jellinek's questionnaire (see Fig. 10.1 in Sect. 10.4). On the other hand, if the patient keeps his promise, the therapist is happy: "I don't wish anyone to be alcoholic!"

Alcohol-dependent patients need at least six months of therapy before they can therapeutically use the concept of *two opposing identities in their soul.* If a patient immediately answers the question, "Are you an alcoholic?" with a "Yes", then they will need six months to fill the term "alcoholic" with their *own experiences* and understand *its true meaning*. Other patients may respond hesitantly: "Yes, maybe. But I don't think it's that bad for me yet." They will need six months of therapy to internally understand their addiction-specific symptoms (see Sect. 10.4) as an expression of addiction disorder. The decision to identify as an addict helps those affected accept the *existence of two identities* in their soul, their everyday ego, and their addicted ego: "I am Karl. I'm an alcoholic." The patient can now attribute many of his problems and weaknesses *to his addiction*. He no longer perceives his addiction as a character weakness. Alcoholics Anonymous says, "It's not a shame to be sick, but it's a shame *not to do anything about* it."

The patient is almost always thinking in an addictive manner in *the chronic dependence stage* (see Fig. 10.2 in Sect. 10.5). Therefore, the therapist does not place a chair for his addicted ego but one *for his "healthy everyday thinking"* externally next to him: "Well, you are alcoholic, and you drink. So I will call the chair you are currently sitting in the chair for the *alcoholic* Karl. But I am placing a second chair next to you for the other part, which engages in healthy adult thinking. I am putting two stones on this chair. One symbolizes your fear of dying. You said your liver wouldn't last much longer. The second stone represents your insight that you need therapy. You came to me for treatment."

**Central idea**

A chronically dependent patient feels that the therapist also perceives him as a person *with 'healthy adult thinking'* through the *external* symbolization of his healthy everyday thinking with a second chair next to him. For the first time in a long time, he feels he is being taken seriously again. This feeling reduces the pressure of conflict in the therapeutic relationship. In addition, it improves the patient's motivation to accept help, at least from low-threshold social psychiatric services.

### *10.6.2 The Decision to Abstain*

The necessity of abstinence has been an ongoing controversial discussion. In Germany, health insurance companies pay for long-term psychotherapy for persons with addiction *only if* the individual chooses abstinence after the first ten sessions. Catamnestic examinations of persons with alcohol addiction show "that 2–10% had developed a more or less *inconspicuous alcohol consumption* after successful therapy [...]" (Hiller, 2014, p. 9). Alcoholics Anonymous contradicts this statement and says: "As an addict, anyone who learns to drink in a controlled manner in therapy was probably just a *habitual* drinker and *not addicted*." For the last 40 years, I have read a new scientific study about every ten years, which aims to prove that alcohol-dependent patients *can* learn to drink in a *controlled* manner. That would be a paradigm shift in addiction therapy. But I remain skeptical. Persons with alcohol addiction can reduce the amount they drink for six months, *even without therapy*, if they want to *prove to themselves or others* that they are *not* addicted. But finally, they plunge back into their addictive substance abuse. Such soft therapies also do *not* use the narcissistic wound caused by the loss of personal dignity and the fear of death in a therapeutically positive way as an impetus for inner change and maturation (see Sect. 10.7).

**Central idea**

I find it problematic to override the basic healing principle of abstinence in addiction therapy helpful for 92–98% of those affected *in favor of only 2–10%* of those with addiction.

**Central idea**

The metacognitive psychodramatic psychotherapy for persons with addiction aims that those affected decide *for themselves* if they identify as addicts and want to abstain. This decision is the prerequisite for *not immediately acting addictively* when thinking addictively.

The therapist helps the patient *to decide* to be abstinent by the following means:

1. During the first three months of therapy, the therapist asks the patient to abstain for "at least a period of self-awareness". She predicts that his addiction *symptoms* will likely improve significantly due to abstinence. *The patient* notices that his symptoms decrease by at least 30% within 3–14 days and often even by 80–90% in the long term. Also 'migraines', 'stomach pains', or 'depression' decrease without alcohol consumption. The 'sleep disturbances' reduce over time *without sleeping pills.* Suppose a patient with addiction is drinking *in a controlled manner temporarily*, then the therapist tries to motivate him to abstain *completely:* "After what you say, you only drink one glass of wine in the evening. You bravely fight against your addiction. But you drink *because of the effects* of alcohol. If you drink only one glass of wine now, you will not achieve the effects you crave! But that one glass of wine prevents you from being proud that you can do *without your addictive substance.*"
2. The patients should decide *for themselves when* they want to stop using addictive substances. Because if they violate their own decision, then they are *guilty of themselves.* This guilt increases their awareness of their addiction. Therefore, at the beginning of therapy, if the patient wants to postpone the decision to abstain for a few more weeks, he should do so.
3. The decision to abstain from alcohol should not be combined with quitting smoking cigarettes *immediately* because nicotine addiction does not lead to a loss of dignity like alcohol addiction. Nicotine abstinence often spontaneously follows alcohol abstinence after five to eight years.
4. *Psychotropic medication* such as sleeping pills, antidepressants, or herbal medications should be gradually discontinued in psychotherapy for patients with addictive substance abuse, if possible. This is because they keep the patient *psychologically dependent* on the medications. The patient then believes that *the medications* are alleviating their symptoms. Instead, the patient should *experience* that the depression disappears with abstinence, *even without* antidepressants. This holds true in 80–90% of cases. The experience of abstaining *without* chemical aids improves the patient's self-confidence and motivation to stay abstinent. He learns to trust himself and his body. The self-healing powers of the soul reappear.

**Case example 110**

*A 40-year-old businessman, Mr. K., participated in a psychoanalytic psychotherapy group for three years to seek help with his panic attacks. His anxiety symptoms had not gone away by the end of this therapy. Therefore, the patient continued to come for an individual therapy conversation every four weeks after group therapy. One day, Mr. K. informed the therapist that he was "probably drinking too much alcohol". The therapist initially suspected that the patient was masochistically devaluing himself. He paradoxically said to him: "Come to the addiction group in my office for four sessions on Thursdays. That will help you assess whether you are an alcoholic." The therapist was amazed in the group. The patient reported to the group members about the true extent of his substance abuse. Mr. K. drank excessively, but he took the sedative Lorazepam to avoid attracting attention during the day. After eight months of participation in the group, Mr. K. saw himself as an "alcoholic". Another six months later, one day, he went into his bathroom with a hammer and smashed the remaining Lorazepam tablets he had always carried with him for safety. He threw the powder in the toilet and flushed it down. It felt like "the end of the world" to him. But his panic attacks disappeared forever without any additional therapy for the anxiety disorder. The panic attacks had obviously been an expression of a latent fear that he was heading toward a personal disaster through alcohol and pill abuse. Before taking part in the addiction group, the patient unconsciously preferred to have panic attacks rather than confront the real justified fear of failing in his professional and personal life through addictive consumption (continued in* Sect. 10.9*).*

**Central idea**

People with addictions cannot imagine a life without addictive substances. At the beginning of their abstinence, they often feel as if they are crossing a bridge that is not yet built, but with every step, they are adding a new stone to the bridge. However, if they are abstinent in everyday life, they will find new solutions to cope with everyday situations *all by themselves*. They have no other choice.

5. The therapist recommends that those affected adhere to the *24-h rule* of Alcoholics Anonymous: "We only live in today and for today. *Today* is the only day that matters. So we decide to stay sober *today*—and not drink for the *present* 24 h." Experienced dry alcoholics add to this rule: "Sometimes, when the addiction pressure is high, I shorten the 24 h to just one hour and say: Not now!" An hour is quite long. The individual *will do* something distracting during that hour. He will think of something else. It is helpful if he thinks about *his inner low point* through the consumption of addictive substances (see Sect. 10.6.4). This may put him at a distance from his addictive thinking.
6. The therapist recommends physical withdrawal to the patient if necessary. In the case of *outpatient withdrawal*, the patient should meet the therapist for 20 min *every day* for the first three days of abstinence. In these discussions, the therapist checks whether the patient is experiencing withdrawal symptoms and whether *inpatient admission* may still be required. She provides assistance and information: "With alcohol withdrawal, the restlessness and tremors are worst on the second day; however, it gets better from the third day." With tablet withdrawal, the withdrawal symptoms last a few days longer. The therapist reminds the patient of the Alcoholics Anonymous 24-h rule: "Always think about this one day. It

doesn't matter what you do. You are just not allowed to consume alcohol. Otherwise, the duration of your withdrawal symptoms will be longer." As a doctor, the therapist can prescribe 25 tablets of clomethiazole to the patient for withdrawal if necessary. Contraindications include a history of epileptic seizures or impending delirium. The prerequisite is that the patient has a *caregiver* at home who will give him the tablets. The doctor discusses the dosage *with the caregiver*: The 25 tablets should be spread over four days. The caregiver gives the patient two tablets at 6 p.m. and three at 10 p.m. on the first day. She gives him 2–2–2–3–4 tablets through the second day, two in the morning and three in the evening on the third day, and two in the evening on the fourth day. The caregiver must personally promise the doctor that the drug administration will not be increased or extended under any circumstances. Intense vegetative restlessness, confusion, or even hallucinations indicate the beginning of delirium. In such a case, the therapist will refer the patient to a clinic for inpatient withdrawal.

### 10.6.3 Participation in a Self-help Group

The therapist can recommend that the patient attend a self-help group *parallel to the individual therapy* sessions: "Participate in at least four group sessions. If you don't like the group, switch to another group and try participating there!" The therapist discusses the patient's group experiences in the following individual sessions because patients with addiction tend to be impatient or prematurely devalue the group process according to the black-and-white pattern.

By *participating* in a self-help group, the patient testifies to himself and others once a week that he sees himself as an "alcoholic". In Alcoholics Anonymous, members usually begin with an introduction and acknowledgment of their addiction: "I'm Karl, and I'm an alcoholic." In doing so, they are once again implicitly confirming to themselves and others that they are aware of the conflict between their healthy everyday ego and addicted ego (see Sect. 10.5). The weekly group participation is a way of realizing the inner *conflict between* the two egos and *once again* learning to alternate between them *consciously* in the as-if mode of thinking. This process is stabilizing for persons with addiction as they practice abstinence. Around 1–2% of people with alcohol addiction in Western industrialized countries join a self-help group.

In their self-help group, persons with addiction can *learn to accept* their feeling of failure together with others who experience similar distress: "It's not a shame to be sick, but it's a shame to not do anything about it!" They learn through experience that you can also live well *with abstinence*. This realization reduces their shame and feelings of guilt. It encourages them to be more committed to themselves in their social environment. In most self-help groups, there are some who are abstinent and have *matured post-traumatically* in their personality by confronting their 'weaknesses' and by surrendering to alcohol. They have become wise, creative, humorous, and empathetic to a certain extent. They support their self-help group as long as they do not narcissistically abuse other group members and do not relapse. They enable the participants to develop in the group. The two founders of Alcoholics Anonymous (AA) were believed to be such special people. The AA self-help group concept they developed is brilliant. It describes the self-healing of persons with alcoholic addiction in twelve steps (see Sect. 10.7) and sets out three life rules for them (see Sect. 10.6). The participants in the self-help groups try to orient themselves toward this process of self-healing. Alcoholics Anonymous supposes that about a million people meet in AA support groups *each week* worldwide. In 1988, Alcoholics Anonymous had approximately 1.5 million members in 118 countries worldwide (Edwards, 1986, p. 215). But there are also many other self-help groups or groups called "circle of friends". Some have church sponsors. In Germany, for example, we have the groups of Blue Cross or the Caritas.

Participation in the group always adds emotional depth to the *word* "alcoholic" for those with addiction. They refresh their knowledge of the *existential level* of their problem. They remember the loss of their dignity as human beings and their own threat of death. The newcomers are likely to lie and talk their way out. They feel guilty and afraid. They show the 'old' group members through their behavior and stories, similar to the psychodramatic mirror technique, how they used to be when they were still consuming addictive substances. The encounter with their suffering protects the 'old' members from possible relapses. They feel: "I don't want to go there again!" On the other hand, the experienced group members are also role models for the 'newcomers'. They uncover the contradiction between everyday thinking and addictive thinking among newcomers with a profound sense of humor. They express their compassion through their own stories and *sharings* (see case example 107 in Sect. 10.4). Even if abstinent, they are *also affected* by the addiction disorder and thus *listen differently* to those *without* addiction. Based *on their own experiences,* they can intuitively grasp what the others in the group want to tell them about their addiction problem.

### *10.6.4 Working Out the Personal Rock Bottom and the Surrender*

**Exercise 36**

Why is it essential for the patient to acknowledge being addicted?

**Central idea**

The therapist has to accept *her own feelings* of helplessness and powerlessness when working with patients with addiction and use them for therapeutic benefit (see Sect. 10.6.1). She *shouldn't* hold on to her grandiose helper ideal and try *to protect* the patient from *every* possibility of harm. She has to surrender her grandiose demand on herself to become more important to the patient than their addictive substance. *The therapist's* humility toward the addictive substance is the prerequisite for *the patient himself* to become humble before the truth of his addiction and to surrender.

People with addictions usually *permanently* abstain only when their *existence* is threatened, i.e., when *they have lost* their dignity through substance abuse or feel threatened with death. The existential *experience* helps them experience human dignity or recognize the value of life for the first time. People with addictions have mostly experienced many *external* rock bottoms: the threat of death, embarrassment from caregivers, loss of employment, a road accident under the influence of alcohol, suicidal fantasies, or separation from the family. Every low point is an *opportunity* to surrender (Krüger, 1988, p. 72).

**Important definition**

*An inner rock bottom* is defined as a personal experience that triggers the patient's surrender. It can, therefore, always only be determined in retrospect. Surrender and capitulation is an emotional paradigm shift in the patient, a creative leap in his conflict management. The individual lets himself be affected *emotionally* by his suffering and failure. This impact gives him a chance to leave the level of well-being and gain access to the *transpersonal level of salvation*. This paradigm shift manifests itself in apparently small things, such as the realization: "I am addicted."

**Central idea**

The transpersonal level of salvation is a healing principle that *supplements and sometimes replaces* narrowly defined depth psychological and behavioral approaches. The loss of one's own dignity or the threat of death injures people in their *pathological narcissism*. It opens the way to *healthy, basal narcissism*, to 'living instead of doing' and accepting one's vulnerability. The individual is part of the whole. Healthy, basal narcissism is at the core of motivation for abstinence. Humans experience this healing principle in connection with *transpersonal experiences* also in nature, religion, art, and love. Such experiences are often associated with an inner change of identity. A transpersonal experience puts the norms and values of well-being into perspective and supplements it with a level of salvation resulting in the development of a *transpersonal* conscience.

**Recommendation**

Persons with addiction can gain access to the transpersonal level of salvation if they let themselves be deeply affected by the *loss of their own dignity* as human beings and the *threat of death* through their substance use. The therapist should, therefore, primarily work out all the events in the patient's life in which *he lost* his dignity or his life *was threatened* and mark those experiences as such.

A dependence disorder is indeed a disorder. However, by surrendering, the patient assumes *full* responsibility for his addictive behavior and the resulting consequences on the transpersonal level. Sometimes the patient reaches rock bottom when his five-year-old son naively says to him at the dinner table: "Dad, you stink!" Alcoholics Anonymous (1980, p. 3) describes the *surrender* with the sentence: "We admit that we are powerless over alcohol—that our lives had become unmanageable." It cannot go on as before. For years, persons with addiction have split off, pushed away, and numbed their suffering, the quiet inner voice of their conscience, and their feelings of guilt. The existential experience of loss of dignity and the threat of death now overrides their defense through denial and rationalization.

**Important definition**

According to Alcoholics Anonymous, a person with addiction *surrenders* when he *accepts* the defeat in the struggle with alcohol, unconditionally confesses that he is an addict, and *therefore* lives abstinently.

Karlfried Graf Dürckheim (1982, p. 88 f.) has described the quality of the inner change through surrender in a parable: "Avoiding or combating suffering is natural. But when it exists, the point is to accept and transform it so that we can gain something that lies beyond suffering. [...] One must accept defeat [...] and not pretend nothing has happened. One must overcome the resistance within, a kind of humility toward the powers stronger than us [...]. Two Japanese knights fought each other with a spear. During the fight, one knocked the other off his horse, and his spear rolled away. The victor dismounted, but instead of killing his victim, he spread his legs and commanded him to crawl under it—what humiliation! The vanquished did so without hesitation; then the victor picked up the spear of his defeated opponent, gave it back, helped him up, and said: 'You are the real victor because I don't know if I could have done that!'

**Exercise 37**

What is post-traumatic growth in addicts?

Surrender is the endpoint of an *internal process* of self-development. By surrendering, patients give up their identity of being a hero in controlling their addiction or their identity of being a loser because of their addiction. They humbly recognize the existence of the *two identities* within (see Sect. 10.6.1) (Krüger, 2004b): "I am Karl. I'm an alcoholic."

***Case example 111***

*After participating in an addiction group for nine weeks, a 50-year-old patient, Ms. M., told the others: "I now know I am an alcoholic. That's really why I'm drinking now!" Afterward, the patient drank excessively for eight weeks. But then she had to be admitted to a clinic. This dramatic ending was undoubtedly less damaging to her body organs than if she had continued to drink chronically for years. The patient only reached her inner rock bottom through absolutely uncontrolled drinking. The excessive drinking threatened her life. Only through this existential experience did she surrender and choose abstinence.*

In self-help groups, *abstinent addicts* sometimes say to a group member who is still drinking: "We cannot help you. You are not ready yet! You first have to fall on your face to make the jump." In other words, the patient has not yet let his suffering *affect* him internally and thus cannot surrender. On the other hand, those who are abstinent have *not always* capitulated.

***Case example 112***

*A 38-year-old entrepreneur, Ms. N., stopped drinking alcohol on the advice of her therapist. But she avoided identifying as an alcoholic. After two years of abstinence, the patient began to drink heavily again. She then joined a group of addicts. Only then did she admit that she was an alcoholic. A year later, she told the group, "I didn't surrender until I realized I couldn't stop drinking. I have noticed that my problem is taken seriously here in the group. After the first group meeting, I immediately did two things differently: I booked my own room for the vacation trip with my parents and sister. I have always stayed in a room with my sister in the past. And I told my friend that I would no longer look after her dog while she goes on vacation." Surrendering had liberated the patient from her general old attitude of adaptation. In her relationships, she now lived according to the motto: "Once the reputation is ruined, you live completely unabashedly." The patient suddenly could differentiate and assert herself on her own in her everyday conflicts. She succeeded in doing this without discussing her everyday conflicts in therapy.*

**Central idea**

People with addiction learn to accept their "weaknesses" by surrendering. They reconcile with themselves. They become humble before the truth of addiction. In accepting the truth, they become more courageous *in all walks of life*. They potentially develop empathy, humor, creativity, and wisdom. If necessary, they also break the unwritten rules of the family or the community (see case example 112 above). Because the *first rule of life* in Alcoholics Anonymous applies to them: "First things first." Nothing is more important than staying sober or abstinent. Everything else is *secondary*. Because those who use substances *again*, sooner or later, will not be able to meet their obligations, plans, and values. They are always the loser in conflicts.

***Case example 109 (2nd continuation, see Sect.* 10.5*)***

*Mr. H. was an important member of his addiction group. He was diagnosed with borderline personality disorder. He thus caused severe relationship conflicts in his social environment even when sober. But he often stabilized himself in crises with the insight: "Other people always try to achieve something special or great in their lives. I do not need that because I am a dry alcoholic. Only 10% of alcoholics manage to stay sober in the long term. So when I, as an alcoholic, lead a completely normal life, I've already achieved something special. I don't have to do something to be special."*

In the end, it remains a mystery why one person with an addiction will succeed in surrendering and *not another*. The therapist or the group can create conditions that increase the chances for this creative leap to occur. However, the surrender happens *autonomously*. As those with addiction themselves say, "Ultimately, it is grace or fortune". It is a gift for the patient and also a gift for the therapist.

The work on the inner rock bottom and the surrender are also crucial in the psychotherapy of *abstinent addicts*. The patient should actively remember his personal low point, his surrender in a crisis, and his humbleness before the truth of addiction. The remembering brings the healing powers of his surrender back to life in him.

***Case example 113***

*An alcoholic patient with narcissistic personality disorder had built homes for mentally ill persons for twelve years after choosing abstinence and had become wealthy. He had already achieved incredible things through his abstinence. Nevertheless, over the past few years, he has developed moderate depression. In the initial interview, the therapist learned that his abstinence had become an issue for him. She, therefore, confronted him: "You have unachievably high expectations of yourself. You are missing out on the "satisfying abstinence" of Alcoholics Anonymous. As a dry alcoholic, you are something special without having to perform grandiosely. Therefore, you don't need to do anything special anymore." At first, the patient took note of this interpretation only ungraciously. But the new self-image eased his depression immediately.*

Alcoholics Anonymous tries *to facilitate* the way from the inner personal low point to surrender and keep it open with their 'twelve steps' (Krüger, 2004b, p. 184 f.). In doing so, they use the collective image of 'God' handed down in our society. They interpret the healing path as establishing and forming relationships with 'God—as we understood Him'. In this context, I understand the term 'God' as the *natural self-healing system* present in every human being (see Sect. 5.13). Alcoholics Anonymous deal with 'God' in *six of its twelve steps.* Step 2 of Alcoholics Anonymous reads: "We came to believe that a power greater than ourselves could restore us to sanity." Step 3: "We made a decision to turn our will and our lives over to the care of God as we understood Him [...]." Step 5: "We openly admitted to God, ourselves, and to another human being our wrongs." Step 6: "We were entirely ready to have God remove all these defects of character." Step 7: "We humbly asked Him to remove our shortcomings from us [...]." Step 11: "We sought through prayer and contemplation to improve our conscious contact with God as we understood Him. We only asked Him to discover His will for us and to give us the power to carry that out."

The Alcoholics Anonymous Twelve Steps are an ingenious self-healing concept. They activate the *natural* self-healing powers of persons with alcohol addiction and allow them a progressive healing path. In the first step, the patient should project their *inner* self-healing system outwardly onto the symbol "God". Next, he should imagine the healing powers in the clothing of this symbol as coming *from outside* and visualize them as a resource *on the object level.* Then, in steps 3, 5, 6, and 7, the patient establishes a good relationship with the *external* self-healing system "God". Finally, he integrates the prerequisites, demands, and values of the *natural* self-healing of humans (see Sect. 5.13) into his own self *without noticing it.*

**Central idea**

In step 11, Alcoholics Anonymous humbly turn the self-healing powers, initially *projected outwardly onto "God"*, into *their own inner self-healing powers.* This is because they ask "God" for the ability and permission to carry out his "will" on *their own* responsibility. Alcoholics Anonymous is thus potentially going on a path that Moreno (Leutz, 1974, p. 71 ff.) has already described. Moreno recommended further development of the image of God from the He-God via the You-God to the I-God. With the term "I-God," he meant one's inner transcendence.

### *10.6.5 Relapse Prevention and the Therapeutic Approach to Relapses*

Many persons with addiction try to live abstinently but experience frequent relapses. That is *part of* a dependency disease. Therefore, the question isn't *whether* a patient will relapse but *how* he and his therapist *will deal with a relapse.*

**Important definition**

A renewed use of addictive substances is called a "relapse" (1) if the person concerned had *previously decided* to view himself as an addict, alcohol-dependent, medication-dependent, or drug-dependent, *and* (2) if he, therefore, *wanted to try to* abstain *permanently*.

In groups for persons with addiction, there is always a dispute about whether *unintentional* alcohol consumption can be assessed as a relapse. For example, sometimes, an acquaintance *secretly* pours schnapps into the patient's apple spritzer, and the patient takes a sip.

**Exercise 38**
Why is it dangerous to drink non-alcoholic beer?

**Central idea**

The decisive criterion for relapse is that the patient *consciously* consumes alcohol after deciding to abstain. If he knows that the praline he is eating contains alcohol, he will relapse. If he *doesn't* know that, he *won't* relapse. He will relapse if he notices the alcohol in his spiked apple spritzer with the first *accidental* sip *and consciously takes a second sip*. Similarly, if he *consciously* takes a second spoonful of the alcoholic dessert, he has relapsed.

The *physical* effect of such a small amount of alcohol is naturally minimal. However, the problem is that a person with alcoholism relinquishes his humility before the truth of addiction and switches to his "addictive thinking" again by *consciously* consuming alcohol.

**Important definition**

The patient activates a *pre-abuse syndrome* with addictive thinking or dry drinking: (1) He fixates on drinking fantasies without thinking about the *negative consequences* of his drinking. (2) The closer he gets to the first sip of alcohol, the more he thinks in the equivalence mode (see Sect. 2.6). He perceives the world such that there is no other way but to drink. (3) He no longer thinks of the impact of his addictive actions on himself and his caregivers.

In the pre-abuse syndrome, the patient overrides his *inner* capitulation. Surrender means humbly admitting: "We accept to be powerless over alcohol".

**Central idea**

In the case of persons with addiction, the success of abstinence is *not a matter of willpower but a decision*. This decision also has a transpersonal level. It's about the fear of losing human dignity and one's own life.

*After a relapse*, the therapist works with the patient to specially identify the loss of human dignity and the possible threat of death in their life history. For example, she *actively searches for* instances of suicidal ideation or events such as drunk driving: "So you are already at risk *to die* due to your alcohol abuse!" Or she uses psychodramatic responding to confront the patient with the existential threat posed by his addictive substance consumption (see Sect. 10.7): "You believe you cannot be abstinent. That makes me sad. I'm scared for you. Well, not everyone can do it. But *with alcohol*, you will most likely die in ten years. You will become a helpless and dependent person in a few years. You might also kill yourself. Do you ever think of suicide?—Your life is at stake here! You were abstinent for a year three years ago. You noticed that you were not depressed then. You were also in contact with your wife and children again. I would like you to *give yourself a chance to live*. You're going to die *anyway* at some point. But *with alcohol*, you lose your life even *earlier* and also your dignity as a human!"

In learning to abstain permanently, persons with alcohol addiction *often* relapse *one last time* after their first decision to admit being an alcoholic and stop drinking (Waldheim-Auer, 2013, p. 199). A *one-time* relapse can paradoxically *solidify* the decision to abstain because the patient learns he will *never* reach the goal of 'being stable' in himself. He learns humility. He understands the truth about what it means to be addicted.

**Exercise 39**
What is a dangerous relapse?

**Central idea**

A relapse with 'just' a glass of beer is more dangerous than a *quick* fall into addictive drinking. Because '*one glass of beer*' doesn't force the patient to humbly admit the truth of his addiction. Instead, it seduces alcohol-dependent patients to think addictively again and to crave a sense of well-being: "Maybe I can control my alcohol consumption after all." After a fortnight, however, the second and third beers follow. At least six months after a relapse, persons with alcohol addiction drink as much as they did before their abstinence phase. Therefore, it is generally advantageous for persons with addiction if their relapse has immediately led to a loss of control or an existential threat.

The following rules will help avoid or process *a relapse* into substance abuse:

1. The patient decides to admit to being an alcoholic again.
2. He gives up the fight with alcohol (see Sect. 10.6.2). As a result, the many ifs and buts disappear.

**Central idea**

It's just a matter of 'leaving the first glass standing'.

3. The patient tries to adhere to the Alcoholics Anonymous *24-h rule*. *Every day, he* decides *anew not* to drink anything on *this one day* and he tries *not* to think about future days. He lives according to the motto: "I live today".

***Case example 114***
*A new participant, Mr. R., complains in the group: "I can't imagine not being allowed to drink my whole life. I can never do that!" An experienced member replies: "But you don't even have to imagine that! Maybe you'll get hit by a car tomorrow. Then you would have tormented yourself with the question in vain! But you can go 24 h without alcohol. That's possible. Just live the 24 h! You can decide anew every morning how you want to live today. Alcoholics Anonymous recommends this 24-h rule. At times I would be surprised by the number of days I spent being sober consistently." Another experienced member adds: "Sometimes 24 h were too long for me. I felt an inner pressure to drink and believed that it had to happen immediately. I then shortened*

*this rule to only an hour: 'Not this hour!' Sometimes I still need this rule. However, my feeling usually changes after one hour!"*

4. Anything that will help the patient stay dry is considered good. Conflict resolution in everyday life may seem absurd or neurotic (see case examples 108, 110, and 113 in Sects. 10.4 and 10.6.9). The patient and the therapist become humble.
5. Persons with addiction have relatively high demands on 'happiness'. Or they love the 'kick' in their life. They are often dissatisfied with their achievements (see case example 113 in Sect. 10.6.4).

**Central idea**

Persons with addictions fear relapse if they are abstinent. Therapists share this fear. In such a situation, cognitive-behavioral therapists recommend that the patient distract himself with pleasurable things and think about the *improvements* in his life that are an outcome of his abstinence. But experience suggests otherwise. It doesn't help to humbly admit the truth of addiction. Because it only addresses the level of well-being. It is more effective for persons with addiction to look back on their inner *personal rock bottom* (see Sect. 10.6.4). The patient should visualize his actions, physical sensations, affect, and thinking from this catastrophic situation. In doing so, he gains access to the internal *psychosomatic resonance pattern of his low point*. This often helps him, to remember the truth of his addiction and to remain abstinent.

6. It is helpful for persons with addiction to *chalk up an emergency plan* for themselves. The patient notes the following: (1) "When I think about drinking, I will name my feeling and thinking as addictive thinking or dry drinking." (2) "When I think about drinking, I will visualize my actions, thoughts, *and feelings from the worst situation* I have experienced due to my substance abuse." For this purpose, the person concerned writes down his experience of the worst situation in minute details *as a story*. (3) "I will always carry the written emergency plan with me and read it if necessary." When reading the story, the patient remembers his suicidal fantasies, helplessness, senselessness, shame, and the loss of his dignity. He senses the existential distress from back then again and realizes: "I don't want to experience that again!" (4) I humbly accept that I am an addict. Humility does not mean submissiveness. Humility should "only" relate to the experience that intellect alone is not enough to remain abstinent.

**Central idea**

Whenever the patient believes that he has *achieved the goal* of abstinence, it is a sign of great danger because he thinks he has good control over his addiction now. But he has to learn to understand his *uncertainty as progress*. In doing this, his personality can mature post-traumatically due to his addiction disorder (see Sect. 10.6.4).

**Exercise 40**

What triggers relapse in persons with addiction?

7. Many therapists assume that relapse especially occurs when persons with addiction mentally *feel bad*. However, relapses often occur completely unexpectedly, even if the person *feels good* (Waldheim-Auer, 2013, p. 196). Those affected are

no longer humble before the truth of their addiction. They forget their distress and think: "Maybe I can control the drug consumption now that I am feeling fine again." Or: "Now I am stable!" Sometimes even a thought such as "Now I would normally have a beer, but I don't do that anymore!" attracts addictive thinking and feeling like a magnet.

8. At the end of the therapy, the patient should be able to recognize, both physically and emotionally, if and when he engages in addictive thinking *without using* addictive substances. Alcoholics Anonymous refers to addictive thinking as "dry drinking" (see Sect. 10.4).
9. Medications have not been proven successful in *preventing relapse* because it impedes *psychological* weaning and their surrender before the existential truth of addiction. The patient then remains in the "I am not allowed to drink" stage, according to Alcoholics Anonymous. He doesn't reach the stage where he can humbly say, "I don't want to drink" or "I don't need to drink".
10. The patient should openly inform *at least one* person who is a close relative (but not his life partner) that he sees himself as an addict or alcoholic. This coming out strengthens his self-regulation. He humbly accepts his identity conflict between a healthy adult ego and an addictive ego. The fact that someone else knows about his condition may protect him from being seduced into drinking by ignorant people again. However, the patient *should not inform his employer* about his addiction problem. There is a risk that the employer will find his abstinence admirable *at the beginning*. But in the *event of a conflict* between them, he would perceive the patient as "an alcoholic" and mentally ill.
11. The patient should avoid anything that *specifically* triggers his addictive thinking and memory and threatens his humility before the truth of his addiction.

**Central idea**

For example, it is *not advisable* to keep returning to your old drinking buddies or work in a pub or bar. Even the apparent harmless consumption of *non-alcoholic* beer is problematic as it serves to feel the familiar taste of beer and to *disguise* the need for abstinence. In my 30 years of work with persons with addiction, I have not seen an alcoholic who drank *alcohol-free* beer during his abstinence and then did *not* relapse. Surrendering to the struggle with the addictive substance requires a *certain humility*.

***Case example 115***

*A man with alcohol addiction repeatedly reported to the group proudly: "There have been two bottles of wine in a basket next to my sofa in my living room for many years now. I've never touched them in the last ten years!" The patient was proud of his supposed willpower in the fight against alcohol. But unlike other group participants, he would relapse recurrently. Indeed, he would not empty the bottles from the basket. But instead, he purchased other bottles and emptied them.*

### 10.6.6 The First Two Years of Disorder-Specific Psychotherapy

The first year of psychotherapy for persons with addiction consists of the phase of promoting insight into the illness and developing motivation (see Sect. 10.6.1), the decision to abstain (see Sect. 10.6.2), defining the personal rock bottom (see Sect. 10.6.4), and working on the topic of relapse prevention (see Sect. 10.6.5). If and when necessary, the therapist and the patient return to one of these therapy phases.

If the patient has been abstinent for some time, his metacognitive confusion resolves. He *no longer traumatizes himself* through addictive acting. Thus, he perceives his internal and external conflicts more clearly, thereby increasing his suffering in the conflicts. He is thus forced to approach these conflicts *newly*. One patient described this in retrospect with the words: "I had to make up for twenty years of development." At first, the patient's family and friends often treat him with suspicion as he had repeatedly disappointed and lied to them during the phase of substance abuse. The residual mistrust frustrates the patient. In such a case, the therapist recommends patience: "Your wife must first learn to trust you again. Because you often did not keep your promises in the past."

In the first two years of abstinence, patients gradually develop new ego strength and a renewed sense of self-worth as self-traumatization through substance abuse stops. Their improved self-esteem often leads to *new conflicts* in the family and social relationships. Indeed, many spouses are happy when the patient *no longer* lets himself be done with everything. But some struggle with a relationship on an equal footing. Others were perhaps also *co-dependent* (see Sect. 10.11 and case example 130 in Sect. 11.7). They had denied that they suffered from their partner's addictive disorder and pushed aside their exhaustion and anger. But they notice their anger *now when* the patient starts to feel better. Therefore, the therapist interprets the emergence of *new* conflicts during abstinence in a radically positive way: "In the past, you were always the loser because you were drunk. Nobody took you seriously. That is changing now." *After two years of abstinence*, there is another high point in marital separations.

The therapist uses the technique of psychodramatic conversation (see Sect. 2.8) and the seven steps of psychodramatic dialogue with role reversal (see Sect. 8.4.2) in individual therapy for processing the *relationship conflicts* in the patient's everyday life. But in doing so, she places a *second chair* next to the protagonist for his "addicted ego" (see Sect. 10.6.1). In this way, she integrates the work on the *intrapsychic addiction conflict* into the *interpersonal relationship clarification,* thereby preventing the patient from distorting the reality of the relationship conflict in the play.

***Case example 116* (Krüger, 2004b, p. 176 f., *Modified*)**

*In the supervision group, a therapist reported on a 35-year-old woman who had been addicted to heroin for a long time and had just relapsed again. It had made her "helpless". After a period of abstinence, the patient started consuming hashish again. Soon she was also drinking alcohol regularly again. The supervisee enacted a therapy session. She stepped into the role of the patient during role reversal and resignedly said: "I know, I will soon start with the heroin too." The patient attributed her relapse to a conflict in her relationship with her father. She complained: "My father never saw me: I simply had to function." This conflict with her father had flared up again at her brother's funeral. The supervisee had let the patient enact this conflict psychodramatically in group therapy "to reduce the addiction craving".*

*A participant in the supervision group suggested a different therapeutic approach and tried it out together with the supervisee. The therapist took on the role of her patient. The second therapist also responded to the "patient's" request. However, he used the two-chair technique in the psychodramatic exploration of the relationship with the "father". He placed a chair next to the "patient" for her "addicted ego". In playing the role of the patient, the supervisee experienced that when she enacted the role of the father in role reversal, she perceived herself much more realistically when looking at her two egos. On the one hand, she saw herself as a woman with healthy adult thinking. The chair for her "addicted ego" helped her recognize that her father's reservations are related to her as an addict and not her as a person. This helped her to "better understand her father's reservations." In the role of the patient, on the chair of her "healthy everyday ego", she felt less devalued by the representation of her "addicted ego" next to her.*

**Exercise 41**

Let *one of your patients with addiction* conduct a psychodramatic dialogue with a relative. As shown in Fig. 10.4 in Sect. 10.6.1, you represent his "addictive thinking" *with a second chair* next to him. You will notice: The second chair changes the patient's self-perception and external perception in the conflict. By reversing roles, the patient understands the reasons for his conflict partner's thoughts and feelings more clearly. The presence of the second chair for the "addicted ego" also allows *you, as a therapist*, to see your patient through different eyes.

In the therapy of persons with addiction, the therapist must often proceed in small steps when working with the psychodramatic dialogue (see case example 19 in Sect. 4.6) and mentalize on the patient's behalf. For example, if the patient enacts the role of his conflict partner *by reversing roles*, the therapist takes on *his* role and verbalizes what *she* feels and thinks *in his role* as his *doppelganger*. In doing this, she also integrates facts known to her from her interaction with the patient *before* the play (see Sect. 8.4.2).

In case of *repeated relapses*, the therapist can use the *self-regulation circle* technique (Krüger, 2010a) to resolve the patient's defense through denial and rationalization (see Sect. 2.4.2 and 2.4.3). This technique records the patient's *self-regulation* as he moves from a good state to relapse and out of his relapse back to a good state.

***Case example 117***

*A 45-year-old teacher, Ms. I., claimed that she suffered repeated relapses "because of her depression". The therapist asked her to draw a large circle on an A3 size paper and then write down how she went from being in a good mental state to relapse and from relapse to a good state, in a clockwise manner. The patient wrote down what she had thought, felt, and done, what followed, how she had reacted to it, etc., step by step along the timeline. At the end of her self-regulation circle, it became clear that Ms. I's crises and relapses always began with her cleaning her house from the basement to the attic for two to three days. As a result, she would end up feeling completely exhausted. She would then grab a beer in the evening "to do something good for herself". However, she would continue to drink the following morning. As a result, she became depressed. The therapist: "You always clean your house thoroughly before you have a drink. Maybe you do this as a preventive measure. If your daughter finds you drunk in the next few days, she cannot allege that you neglect your apartment as an alcoholic." The therapist recommended that the patient refrains from excessively cleaning the house in the future. Ms. I. followed this recommendation. She did not relapse again until the end of therapy a year later and didn't become depressive. Ms. I's depression was a consequence of drinking and not the cause. Cleaning up had been part of her addictive thinking.*

The patient can also write down their *addiction history* from when they started using substances to this point in time. The addiction history should answer the following questions: (1) When did I first notice that I was drinking *differently* than others? (2) When did *someone else* say to me for the first time: "You drink too much?" (3) What was *my best experience* under the influence of an addictive substance? (4) What was *my worst experience* while drinking? (5) Has my life been endangered even once due to the effects of the addictive substance? (6) Have I ever been *a helpless person*? (7) What did I experience at *my personal rock bottom* (see Sect. 10.6.4)? What happened then? (8) What made me *surrender* in the fight against alcohol so that I became abstinent? (see Sect. 10.6.2) (9) How have my thoughts, feelings, and behavior *changed positively* due to abstinence? (10) The patient should illustrate the positive changes through three small anecdotes.

In each of the following therapy sessions, the therapist dedicates 10–20 min to discussing the patient's progress in writing their addiction history. Afterward, the patient adds the missing parts in writing. In the end, *both* agree that the story has *come to an end*. The addiction history integrates many negative and seemingly senseless experiences into a whole. It relates these experiences with the patient's recognition that they are an alcoholic. It creates new meaningfulness in the absurd and the chaos of experiences. The patient can read the history again if necessary when they have a crisis again. Writing down one's addiction history helps the patient to think and process their addiction experiences from the equivalence mode in the as-if mode.

**Central idea**

In the first year of therapy, the therapist repeatedly uses the two-chair technique to address the patient's *metacognitive disorder*. The patient should also use it on his own, in the therapy room and at home, if necessary. As a result, the patient gradually learns to act out his *addicted thinking* and feeling in the as-if mode *only in his imagination, without acting* addicted simultaneously (see Sect. 10.6.5). He then notices it in less and less time when he is back on the wrong path and thinks and feels addicted in his everyday life. This is a prerequisite for him to stop his addictive thinking *of his own will*.

Benzinger (2013, p. 18) describes this development in a case example:

**Case example 118**
*"A patient in her late 40s [...] came back for addiction therapy after having relapsed massively for months with up to two bottles of wine a day." The therapist used the image of the two opposing identities—the everyday ego and the addicted ego—in her individual and group therapy and represented them with two chairs. In group therapy, two group members assumed the roles of the patient's two opposing identities.*

*At the end of the therapy, the patient said that she had "found a new solution to protect herself against relapses: 'Whenever this pressure arises, I remember the image of the two identities. I then sit on the sofa in the living room and symbolize both sides with two objects on the table. In doing so, I have both sides in view and can intervene if the addicted side becomes dominant. Sometimes I even talk to both sides.' Ms. A. was proud that she could regain self-control and master the situation with the help of this method."*

Benzinger (2013, p. 19) developed *a three-chair technique* based on this experience. In his therapeutic approach, he represents a "third position" with *a third chair behind* the two chairs that symbolize the patient's everyday ego and the addicted ego (Benzinger, 2014, oral communication). He then lets the patient change *between these three chairs* in the therapy session and helps him work out the *three* different identities. I understand this "third position" as the observer- or meta-position to the two contrary ego states of the patient with addiction. However, I recommend that dependent patients *first* dissolve their defense through splitting using the *two-chair technique* described *before*. The patient has to fill each of the terms "everyday ego" and "addicted ego" *with their personal experiences* into a holistic psychosomatic resonance pattern, discern the contrast between them in the *as-if mode of play* and gain ego control over his change into addictive thinking. The *external* process of role change between the two chairs paves the way for the *internal* role change the patient has to go through repeatedly to *remain* abstinent: (1) The patient recognizes that he has the desire to drink and *names* it "addictive thinking". (2) In this way, he links his desire to drink with the term 'addiction' in his memory centers. (3) Thus, he can more easily *think* of his desire to drink *in the as-if mode* with all the negative consequences in the end. (4) Then his negative psychosomatic resonance patterns autonomously connect with the terms 'low point' and 'surrender'. In this way, he gains an inner distance from his addictive thinking. If necessary, the patient should access his emergency plan and *emotionally remember his inner rock bottom.*

### *10.6.7 The Co-treatment of a Comorbid Psychological Illness*

At least 30% of patients with addiction suffer from trauma-related disorders and up to 80% from personality disorders (see Sect. 10.3). Some therapists recommend *early* co-treatment for a comorbid condition (Stadler, 2013, p. 82). In Hintermeier's experience (2013, p. 112 f.), patients with addiction and a diagnosis of borderline personality disorder require a holding therapeutic relationship to be developed before the actual addiction therapy can begin: "It is only after a stabilization phase (sometimes years) [...] that one can work on developing alternatives to the consumption of addictive substances or other dependent behaviors."

**Exercise 42**
Should the therapist treat a comorbid psychological illness from the start in the case of persons with addiction?

There are some problems in the *early* co-treatment of a comorbid psychological illness in a *substance-related* addiction disorder:

1. The therapist may overlook the fact that some of the patient's symptoms are caused or exacerbated *by substance abuse.* For example, depression is often the result of substance abuse and not the cause (see case examples 110 in Sects. 10.6.2 and 10.9, and 117 in Sect. 10.6.6).
2. The actualization of childhood deficit experiences or traumatic experiences can make the patient unstable and cause him to regress pathologically (Waldheim-Auer, 1993, p. 205).
3. The co-treatment of a comorbid condition can strengthen the patient's belief that he drinks *because* he had a terrible childhood and was traumatized. But by no means every person with childhood trauma is addicted. In mentalization-oriented, disorder-specific addiction therapy, the patient should recognize that, in the meantime, he is *having problems because he is drinking* and must do something about his addiction.

**Central idea**

A one-sided, depth-psychological *genetic explanation* for the addiction and the early co-treatment of a comorbid condition can reduce the patient's appropriate feelings of guilt and shame about his addiction. However, the patient needs the guilt to move away from the level of well-being and to develop humility before the truth of his addiction in the encounter with death or the loss of dignity (see Sect. 10.6.4). A depth-psychological explanation concerning childhood experiences may reduce the probability to surrender before the addictive substance. The patient may not develop humility before addiction. The therapist doesn't use the *impact of transpersonal therapeutic factors.* However, these have proven to be very effective in addiction therapy. For example, they are the basis of the work of Alcoholics Anonymous.

4. Patients with addiction traumatize their souls with substance abuse (see Sect. 10.5). Substance abuse reduces the ego strength needed to process genetic conflicts with therapeutic help.
5. The *direct psychotropic effect* of the addictive substance on the working memory structures of the brain also reduces the patient's ability to process conflicts during therapy. *The therapeutic effect of co-treating* the comorbid condition is thereby reduced.

**Central idea**

Many patients develop a transpersonal conscience as a result of their abstinence (see Sect. 8.8.4). In this way, they learn humility before truth and life. They learn to *accept themselves* with their weaknesses as they are. Thus, they *spontaneously* become more courageous in dealing with their conflicts *without talking about their conflicts in therapy*. This development happens even *without* the co-treatment of trauma or deficit experiences in childhood (see case examples 110 in Sects. 10.6.2 and 10.9, and 118, 119 in Sect. 10.6.6, and 121 in Sect. 10.8).

***Case example 119***

*A 55-year-old teacher, Mr. L., participated in a group for persons with addiction. Participants took into account the experience of Alcoholics Anonymous. Mr. L reported in this group: "Before I came here, I went to a psychotherapy group for patients with addiction for a year. We always tried to solve our problems, so we no longer had to drink. But that didn't work. Only when I did the reverse in this group and quit drinking first I could address my problems. As a result, I have developed a different attitude toward myself. I always used to bother myself with my compulsions and tried to overcome them by drinking alcohol. Now I can accept myself as a loner. I am what I am. I am kind to myself. It is important for me to think about my inner rock bottom time and again. Back then, I would wander around the main train station at night. I was empty and unstable inside. I wanted to throw myself in front of the train. Nothing worse can happen to me!"*

Alcoholics Anonymous promotes the change to a transpersonal conscience in their "Three Rules of Life". They make recommendations that appear to have been developed for behavioral *mindfulness training* for people with personality disorders. *The first rule* of life for persons with addiction is: "'First things first.' This means that the alcohol problem always comes first. [...] *The second rule* of life is: 'Hurry with less speed' [...]. Many of us often act on the wrong principle—'either all or nothing'—and therefore take on too much. Often we achieve nothing by doing this. [...] *The third rule* of life is: 'Live and let live' [...]. Especially we, who have longed in vain for a little understanding during our drinking time, should use as much of it as possible for other people and their problems. [...] We can never be patient enough. [...] It is important for us that we live together trouble-free and in harmony with our environment. Because every argument and any excitement can plunge us into the danger of drinking again" (Translated from Alcoholics Anonymous in German language, edition 1980).

## 10.7 The Therapeutic Relationship and the Psychodramatic Responding

Patients with addiction disorders involve the therapist in their metacognitive confusion through projective identification (see Sect. 2.4.4) and their acting out in equivalence mode. Sooner or later, *the therapist* unknowingly internalizes the split-off emotions on the patient's behalf. As a result, she feels latently insecure, confused, or helpless. She often reacts to this with *defense-related metacognitive countertransference*. Indications for this countertransference are: (1) The therapist acts *co-dependently* and colludes with the patient in minimizing or *denying* his addiction problem. (2) The therapist wants to convict the patient. She devalues the patient, claims the authority to express, and becomes, as it were, a persecutor. (3) Or she privatizes her feelings, feels incapable, and *refuses to establish a relationship with the patient*.

***Case example 120***
*In a social psychiatric counseling center, 20–40 people with alcohol addiction met weekly in a kind of self-help group. They drank coffee and smoked so much that the whole room was fogged. They had heated discussions with each other. One day one of the members, Mr. P., relapsed. The doctor and the group leader paid him a visit at home together. The group leader himself had an alcohol addiction but was abstinent. As they entered Mr. P.'s neglected room, they saw he was in poor health. The doctor was disappointed with the patient's relapse and gave up on the patient internally: "Not everyone manages to stay dry." The group leader, however, greeted his 'wet' colleague warmly. He put his hand on his shoulder and, as a competent specialist, confronted him empathically about the trivialization of his addiction: "Ralph, it's good! It's good that you drank again! Thus, once again you know that you are an alcoholic!" The doctor was amazed and fascinated by the coherent logic of this argument.*

The therapist can prevent countertransference or dissolve it by reversing the process of projective identification together with the patient (see Sect. 2.4.4) and addressing the patient's *metacognitive confusion* in therapy: (1) She justifies *her own feelings* of insecurity and helplessness. (2) She links her negative feelings to the patient's acting out through denial and splitting. (3) She sets up a *second* chair next to the patient for his "addicted ego".

The *two-chair technique* (see Sect. 10.6.1) helps the therapist take the patient seriously in what he says, thinks, and feels, and *yet to know* that perhaps the opposite could also be *the truth*. She develops empathy for *each of the two externally visible* contrary ego states and accompanies him, as a metacognitive doppelganger, in each of the respective ego states.

**Central idea**

With this approach, the therapist *consciously does not* bother about the contradiction in the patient's two metacognitive processes (see Fig. 10.2 in Sect. 10.5). This contradiction is part of his illness. The therapist playfully tries *not knowing* the patient's truth, not knowing it *always*, and not knowing it *all at once*. In doing so, she delegates the responsibility of searching for the truth to the patient. With the use of the two-chair technique, the patient *himself* experiences feelings of contradiction, confusion, or helplessness and develops awareness of his addictive thinking. He may even sense the absurd in his contradicting thoughts and develop a sense of humor.

In addiction therapy, the therapeutic relationship always has the latent character of an *existential encounter* (Krüger, 2000, p. 72 ff.). The therapist recognizes the human suffering in the patient sitting across from her. It is what it is. There is no right and wrong. There is only the truth. Together, the patient and the therapist explore the truth of his soul actively and playfully. However absurd it may be, it should be made clear. The therapist remains curious about all of this. She follows her intuition. She is more likely to make statements and ask fewer questions. When she asks something, she explains to the patient the rationale behind her question. She also explains why she recommends something or expects something specific from him.

The therapist cannot induce abstinence and capitulation in the patient; she can only create favorable conditions that encourage abstinence and surrender. She humbly surrenders to her aspiration to be more powerful than the addictive substance. This helps her to resolve mutual idealization and possible narcissistic collusion with the patient. She knows that she cannot heal every person with an addiction. The less structured patients with addiction are (see Sect. 3.3), the heavier the drug use, and the more chronic the addiction, the greater the pressure of conflict in the therapeutic relationship. The therapist sometimes feels at the mercy of the patient's suffering and her helplessness. In such a case, the therapist can technically intervene in two different ways:

1. She focuses her attention on the *transpersonal quality* of the patient's suffering. Without abstinence, the patient would *further* lose his dignity as a human being, fail in life, and perhaps even die. The therapist, therefore, speaks plainly, as with patients with suicidal tendencies (see Sect. 8.8), and calls things by their proper name. Even if their behavior sometimes seems provocative or aggressive to others from the outside. Through a direct injury, she tries to open *the way to* the patient's primary, healthy narcissism. That hurts sometimes. However, in doing so, the therapist takes the patient seriously and gives him a chance. The alternative is indifference and breaking up the relationship. The therapist tries to be *persistent and empathetic* in the right place.
2. The therapist can also *respond psychodramatically* to the patient when their own therapeutic ability to act is *blocked* (see Sect. 4.13). She names her *three general therapeutic tasks* and, if necessary, represents them with three chairs (see Fig. 10.5 see below). (1) The chair on which the therapist sits represents the ego state of the 'encountering human'. This ego state is the starting point in therapy. As an 'encountering human', she suffers along with the patient and sometimes feels powerless, helpless, overwhelmed, or sad as a reaction to his actions. (2) The therapist represents her ego state as a 'competent expert therapist' with *a second chair* to her right. As an expert, she asks the patient diagnostic questions, shares her expert knowledge, and designs his therapy plan with him. (3) She can also set up a third chair to her left for her ego state as a 'grandiose therapist'. In this role, she would help the patient *in any case*. If necessary, she even tries to expand the limits of human capacity heroically (see Fig. 10.5). In normal conversation with her patient, the therapist internally switches back and forth between these three ego states. In *psychodramatic responding*, she realizes this *inner* change *also externally* in the as-if mode of play and sits down on the appropriate chair.

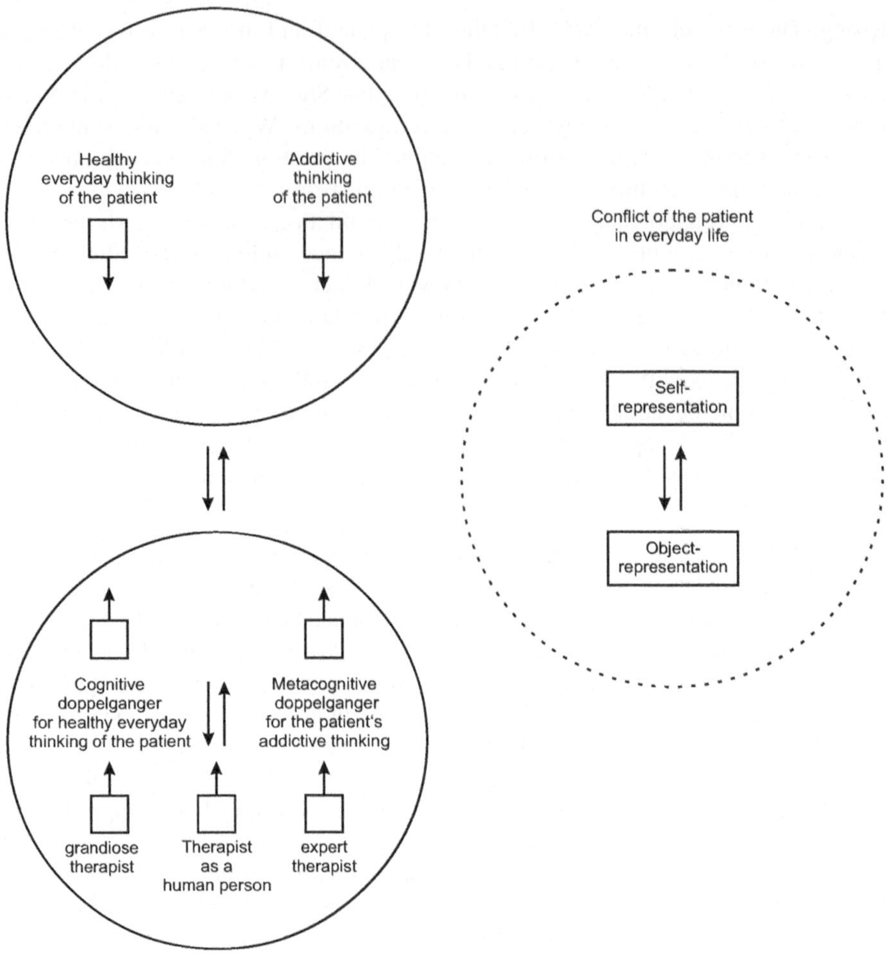


**Fig. 10.5** The therapist's three changing patient-related ego states in addiction therapy

**Exercise 43**

You cannot understand the technique of psychodramatic responding only by reading. Experience it through psychosomatic acting in therapy with a patient with alcohol addiction (see case example 19 in Sect. 4.13). As *a beginner* in this method, represent 'only' your thinking and feeling like an 'expert therapist' with a second chair next to you. In the encounter with the patient, switch from your chair of the 'encountering human' to the second chair of the 'expert therapist' and back again, *depending on your current patient-related task*. Name the role from which you are speaking at the moment: "As *the encountering human*, I want to tell you: ..." Speak out loud *and tell the patient* what you think and feel toward him as a human *or* as an expert.

If you have some experience with it, you can also place the chair for the 'grandiose therapist' next to you (see Sect. 4.13). In the case of a *negative transference of the patient*, you can also set up *a fourth chair* for his transference figure a little further away (see Fig. 4.4 in Sect. 4.13). This makes it easier for you and the patient to differentiate the real conflict from the transference conflict in the therapeutic relationship (see Sect. 2.7). You can practice the method of psychodramatic responding in a role play with a colleague before using it on patients (see Exercise 12 in Sect. 4.13).

Psychodramatically trained therapists can also conduct *psychodramatic dialogues with role reversal between their three* patient-related ego states and openly verbalize *their conflicts between* their patient-related tasks to the patient: For example, the therapist sits on the chair of the 'grandiose therapist' and speaks up *to the patient*: "As a grandiose therapist, I say: We'll get through this together. I have a lot of experience. Actually, it's straightforward! Always leave the first glass standing!" The therapist then switches to the chair of the 'expert therapist' and laughs at the grandiose therapist: "As an expert, I say: I think you're crazy. You are overdoing it again. That is precisely the problem with persons with alcohol addiction. They *can't* leave the first glass standing!" The therapist switches back to the grandiose therapist's chair again: "As a grandiose therapist, I say: But I want to help Mr. S.!" Finally, the therapist sits on the chair of the 'encountering human' and turns to the 'grandiose therapist': "As a human, I say: You want to expand the limits of human capacity *again*! But I know you. You will start as a tiger and then end up as a bedside rug. You know very well that it is not that easy. I think we should be honest with Mr. S. Then, at least, he will know what he is deciding for or against!".

If a patient with addiction *relapses*, the therapist can employ the technique of psychodramatic response to use her feelings of disappointment and helplessness *therapeutically* and confront the patient with truths about his illness and treatment in the as-if mode of play *without devaluing him personally*. In doing so, she sits on the chair of the human who 'encounters as a human being' and says to the patient: "As a human, I say: I am at a loss. I don't know what to do either." But then she moves to the chair of the 'expert therapist' next to her. She looks at the chair of the 'encountering human' and speaks out aloud in the presence of the patient: "In this chair, I am the expert, and I say: But Helga, you know that persons with addiction often relapse! That is part of the disease. Not everyone can cope with life without alcohol. Maybe Mr. S. is one of those who *can't* cope. In Germany, 70,000 people die every year from alcohol addiction!" The therapist then switches back to the chair of the 'encountering human', turns to the chair of the expert therapist', and protests: "As a human, I notice that I am feeling sad! I don't want Mr. S. to die! I do not want that! I have put so much effort into helping him! And please don't talk so negatively about him in his presence. That is hurtful. Then maybe he'll give up completely!"

The therapist is *helping herself* with the psychodramatic responding. She dissolves *her inner blockage* caused by the patient's actions by externally representing her three patient-related ego states. She visualizes her *other two* patterns of thinking, feeling, and acting newly as a real *possibility* by *representing* them *externally* with chairs in the as-if mode of play. She can then switch to another of the three chairs on the outside and act out her thoughts and feelings in that role authentically and truthfully, *separately from the other*.

**Central idea**

When the therapist's ability to act is blocked internally, the *inner* role change between her three therapeutic tasks is also blocked. As a result, she *herself* experiences metacognitive confusion and thinks in the equivalence mode. The *external* role change between the three chairs then *liberates* the therapist from this internal blockage. It introduces the as-if mode of play into the therapist's thinking in the equivalence mode. This strengthens her spontaneity in the therapeutic relationship.

But, the therapist's *psychodramatic responding* also relaxes the patient's rigid defenses as the therapist does *not oppose* the patient's defense. Instead, she uses the strength of his defense like in judo. In the as-if mode of play, she *first justifies his expectations* and takes on the task *he requested*. If the patient wants a quick solution, she reacts as the 'grandiose therapist': "Yes, of course, we'll try that!" The therapist then supplements this first desired truth with the *second opposite truth*. For example, she moves to the chair of the "encountering human" and says: "The problem is: Whenever I wanted that, I usually started as a tiger and ended up as a bedside rug." The therapist does *not resolve her inner contradiction* in psychodramatic responding. The contradiction between her answers remains *externally visible* in the form of the three chairs *next to each other*. Therefore the therapist's conflicting truths *do not* cancel each other out, even *in the patient's perception*. The patient integrates the therapist's *three different truths* in his internal object image *side by side* (see Sect. 4.13). As a result, he internally perceives the 'yes-but' of the therapist's statements as an 'as well as'. His thinking in equivalence mode is resolved.

## 10.8 Group Therapy

Psychodrama therapists often work with persons with addiction in groups in *inpatient* settings. In *outpatient* settings, group therapy *usually* takes place only as part of the medical rehabilitation of *addiction counseling centers*. Psychotherapists in private practice rarely offer group therapy for persons with addiction. Some important psychodrama techniques have proven to be successful *across schools* in the context of group therapy for persons with addiction. These include the psychodramatic role play, the social atom, and the experiments with new solutions for problems that have already been identified or anticipated (Waniczek, 2003, p. 59). Weiner (1965, pp. 27 and 164 f.) emphasized that psychodrama when compared to some other methods promotes spontaneity and creativity in persons with addiction along with integrating the emotions of those affected: "Psychodrama offers life to people with addiction [...]. It ensures immediate timely help in terms of specific problems and situations. It not only tries to change human behavior, but also helps promote self-regulation, understand the current reality, and improve communication skills."

In the psychodrama therapy of persons with addiction, the therapist is *tempted to act out* her feelings of helplessness as compensation and to overwhelm the patient as a persecutor, so to speak, with a multiplicity of psychodramatic techniques. But the therapist can avoid acting out her defense-related metacognitive countertransference *if she* applies the disorder-specific methods described above (see Sects. 10.6.1–10.6.6) in group therapy and focuses her attention on the patient's *metacognitive disorder*. Patients with addiction disorders *otherwise* show "little willingness to play and a high potential for fear and resistance" in groups (Waldheim-Auer, 1993, p. 197).

**Recommendation**

Elements of symbolic wish fulfillment and the enactment of early desires with alternative experiences are contraindicated in group therapy for persons with addiction. This is because regression-inducing methods destabilize patients with addiction disorders. "In the case of persons with alcohol addiction, regressions are used only restrictedly and can only be justified with simultaneous ego support to prevent the protagonist from unprotected relapse" (Waldheim-Auer, 1993, p. 205).

***Case example 121***

*35 years ago, I conducted a fortnightly group for persons with addiction in a clinic. One patient, Ms. Q, strangely attracted the group's aggression. I worked with her to resolve a workplace conflict using a protagonist-centered play. In the play, the trained pediatric nurse lovingly cares for a premature infant. My experienced co-therapist and I believed that Ms. Q. would have experienced something precious through her intense emotional involvement. In the following group meeting two weeks later, Ms. Q. was absent from the group. I checked her ward and heard that she had decompensated after the psychodramatic play. She was still in a state of dissociation and believed that she would act in a movie. The patient's defense system had collapsed due to the fulfillment of her longing in the regressive psychodramatic play. The inappropriate aggression of the group members had paradoxically stabilized the patient previously.*

In group therapy, persons with addiction tempt the therapist to take on the alpha position in the group (see Sect. 2.11), to feel wise, and to teach the patient. However, it is therapeutically more effective to consciously take the beta position of yes-but: "Yes, I am the expert therapist, but I am as powerless as you are in comparison with your addictive substance." The therapist can *externally* represent her task-related ego states in the group room with two chairs for her *inner* conflicts (see Sect. 10.7), one for her as the 'encountering human' and another for her as the 'expert therapist'. If necessary, she switches back and forth between these two chairs and, in doing so, indicates the ego state she is speaking from *at the moment*.

**Central idea**

Sitting *on the chair of the encountering human*, the therapist humbly acts out the powerlessness in the face of the addictive substance with the patient. She recognizes that the group participants who have been *abstinent for a long time* are the 'professionals' in addiction therapy. She may even leave the group leadership to one of these group members at times. With this inner attitude, the therapist acknowledges the 'first rule' of Alcoholics Anonymous: "First things first."

**Recommendation**

In the group, the therapist evaluates everything that helps patients with addiction to stay dry *positively*. This *also applies if* the patients' solutions appear strange or neurotic initially.

**Case example 122**

*A therapist in the supervision group reported on the protagonist-centered play of one alcohol-dependent, abstinent patient. She psychodramatically demonstrated how she had directed the play: The 'patient' wanted to pay for fuel for her car at a gas station. She went into the shop at the gas station. In doing so, she saw beer bottles and liquor bottles on the shelf to her left. She panicked. She quickened her pace, paid quickly, and hurried back to her car. She immediately drove to her mother. Because she didn't want "to get any stupid ideas". After the play, the therapist and all group members were concerned about the patient and discussed with her how she could get through the coming weekend without relapse. The group was depressed.*

*A participant in the supervision group suggested an alternative approach. He enacted what he meant. In this play, the supervisee took on the role of her patient. She went to the gas station while in the role of the patient and was startled when she looked at the 'alcohol' and then fled 'to the mother'. In the debriefing, the second 'therapist' strengthened the 'patient' in her problem-solving skills, unlike in the original version: "Wonderful! You noticed what it's all about now. As a patient, nothing is more important for you than staying dry! You have found two helpful solutions for yourself in this critical situation! When you saw the alcohol bottles on the shelves of the gas station, you dashed to the checkout counter and back to your car instead of walking normally. The second solution was: You did not go home but went to your mother's instead. You needed someone to talk to so that you could distract yourself." The second 'therapist' now turned to the other 'patients' in the 'therapy group'. The roles of 'group participants' were played by the other supervisees. "What solutions did you find when you noticed that you were thinking about drinking?" In the alternative play, the participants in the supervision group, playing the roles of group patients, cheerfully and spontaneously produced fantasies about how they, as 'patients with addiction disorder', could help themselves if they feel afraid of relapsing.*

*The second 'therapist' modified the approach and appreciated the patient's solutions radically positively. Such an approach has an ego-strengthening effect because this patient actually didn't need any help to remain abstinent. Instead, she needed validation of her problem-solving skills. Indeed, as someone with thoughts about drinking, the patient had entered the omega position in her therapy group (see* Sect. 2.11*). But the alternative solution-oriented approach would have put her in the alpha position in the group because she followed the first rule of Alcoholics Anonymous despite having thoughts of drinking and was a role model for the other group participants.*

**Recommendation**

During the *enactment of addiction stories,* the therapist should use trauma therapy elements (see Sects. 5.10.6 and 5.10.7). For example, she lets the patient tell their addiction story from the *observation room.* At the same time, a doppelganger and several auxiliaries re-enact his story in the *action room on the stage* using the playback method. The meta-position to one's own addicted acting strengthens the patient's cognition.

In doing so, the therapist stands with the patient in the narration and observation room. As a metacognitive doppelganger, she supports the patient in telling their addiction story: "I would like to work with you on your worst experience with the use of addictive substances. If you want to abstain, you need an important reason."

## 10.9 Pill Addiction and Drug Addiction

The number of people addicted to pain relievers, sleeping pills, or tranquilizers is roughly the same as those addicted to alcohol, about 1.74 million.

***Case example 110 (continuation of* Sect. 10.6.2*)***
*Mr. K, who suffered from panic attacks, was addicted to drinking only small amounts of alcohol during the day. During the day, however, he took Lorazepam, a sedative. Thus, he was inconspicuous and could work. He then drank 'properly' in the evening. In therapy, he acknowledged that he was addicted to alcohol and pills. After that, he was abstinent. Nevertheless, "just to be on the safe side", he still carried a supply of the sedatives in a small jar without taking any of them. One day the patient crushed his pills with a hammer, threw them in the toilet, and flushed them down. It was only after this ritual that his panic attacks disappeared. The patient had taken the final decisive step in his surrender.*

The disorder-specific treatment of persons with drug addiction follows the basic principles of the therapy model described in Sect. 10.6. In Jellinek's 30 questions symptom list (see Fig. 10.1 in Sect. 10.4), questions 1–18, 20, 22–26, and 28–30 also apply to persons with drug addiction. You have to replace the word 'drink' with 'pill intake' or 'drug consumption' in the questionnaire. The seven therapeutic steps derived from the theoretical concept of metacognitive confusion (see Sect. 10.6) remain the same. In the case of pill addiction, physical withdrawal lasts 7–14 days. Those affected consume their addictive substance more covertly than persons with alcohol addiction. It is easier for them to hide their substance abuse. They become less conspicuous on the outside. About 13–29% of persons with alcohol addiction (Hiller, 2014, p. 2), therefore, combine their alcohol consumption with sedatives or sleeping pills, such as Lorazepam, Bromazanil, Zolpidem, or Flunitrazepam. They are more likely to take pills during the day and only drink "properly" in the evening after work. Obtaining pills is more difficult than obtaining alcohol. Germany requires a prescription for most sedatives, pain relievers, and sleeping pills. Those affected need to find a doctor's office where healthcare professionals *don't look closely* at repeat prescriptions. Or they visit *several* doctors with specific complaints. However, they do *not* tell them that they have already received the same tablets from another doctor. Many with drug addiction *themselves* work in the medical field.

In addiction therapy groups, a combination of persons with alcohol addiction and pill addiction is possible because metacognitive confusion exists *in all* persons with dependence (see Sect. 10.5). However, rivalries can easily arise between those affected by *different* substances *in one* therapy group. The subgroups of persons with addiction differ in their explanations for their substance use, age, social status, values, and prejudices. For example, some with pill addiction do not want to be placed on the same level as those with 'alcohol addiction'. In such a situation, the therapist should repeatedly use the two-chair technique to emphasize the *common* theme of dependency and metacognitive confusion and encourage mutual listening.

In *persons with cannabis addiction*, the addiction usually begins between the ages of 12 and 18. Therefore, in contrast to persons with alcohol addiction, those with cannabis addiction are usually *less developed in their personalities*. They are more likely to have no professional training and *less life experience*. For example, they also have less experience with long-term partnerships. About 30% of persons with *drug addiction* suffer from post-traumatic stress disorder (Stadler, 2013, p. 81 f.), twice as much as those with alcohol addiction. Because of their *structural deficits*, patients with drug addiction have to develop their tools of mentalization and inner images and have to learn to play *more than* those with alcohol dependency. Self-stabilization techniques from trauma therapy are helpful, for example, the technique of the safe place (Sect. 5.10.5). The average duration of *inpatient* treatment for opiate addiction is half a year, twice as long as for alcohol addiction. According to the 2011 annual statistics of professional addiction aid (Steppan, Künzel & Pfeiffer-Gerschel, 2013, p. 217), *outpatient* treatment lasts *longer* than two years for 12% of the population with drug addiction. In the case of alcohol addiction, 'only' 5.3% have been in therapy for *more* than two years.

**Recommendation**

The process model of *metacognitive addiction therapy* described in Sect. 10.6 is helpful for *all* addiction disorders, including behavioral dependencies that are *not substance-related* (see Sect. 10.10). The patient's *metacognitive disorder* is the focus of therapeutic work. Addiction leads *all people with dependence* to feelings of shame and guilt, secrecy, ego-splitting, and metacognitive confusion (see Sect. 10.5).

The metacognitively oriented work with the two-chair technique (see Sect. 10.6.1) can also help to stop a threatening *pathological regression* (Hintermeier, 2013, p. 112).

***Case example 123***

*A patient who had been addicted to heroin since her youth, substituted with methadone, was repeatedly traumatized. She was initially treated with trauma therapy. But the memories of her experiences of abuse during the time of her multiple drug use unsettled her to such an extent that "her desire to use heroin increased again." As a reaction, the therapist 'had her set up the two role clusters—'heroin-addicted ego' and 'wanting to be independent ego'—with intermediary objects.' The patient and the therapist concretized the patient's two contrary ways of thinking, feeling, and acting with representational symbols. The patient experienced this assignment as a "mirror of her inner turmoil". This procedure helped the patient to accept herself more: "She implicitly understood that there were alternative courses of action to consumption." In the next few months, the substituted patient no longer expressed any desire for additional consumption and changed her external appearance. She no longer wanted to be reminded of her "junkie times" (continued in* Sect. 10.11.2*).*

## 10.10 Non-substance-Related Addictions

### *10.10.1 Psychodynamic and Therapy*

Non-substance-related addictions are behavioral addictions. The patients are dependent on their emotional ecstasy and the 'kick' they achieve, for example, from online games, porn films, or playing on slot machines. There are entire industries that make huge profits from potentially addictive offerings.

Patients who suffer from non-substance-related addictions should be treated with disorder-specific addiction therapy as early as the first third of therapy. They will progress in psychotherapy only when they give up their addictive action.

**Recommendation**

In the case of *non-substance-related* dependence, addictive behavior is *more strongly* determined by the patient's psychodynamics than substance-related dependence. The therapist, therefore, also works out the personal *positive function* of addictive behavior in the holistic process of these patients' self-regulation. Their addictive behavior *gives them a good feeling* though it ends in self-harm. The patient's soul does nothing for free.

Patients with non-substance-related dependence get into a trance-like state with the help of an object or partial objects. They latently fulfill a personal longing through their addictive behavior. They think in the equivalence mode and turn their inner wishful fantasy into outer perception. For example, the patient with sex addiction in case example 127 (see Sect. 10.10.4) told the therapist: "Sure, I know that sex workers play a pretend role during sex, but I ignore that." The patient was playing a self-hypnotic game in acting out his behavioral dependence. After the end of this 'game', the self-hypnosis broke down again due to the onset of reality. The feeling of inadequacy became even stronger: "Afterward, I always had a guilty conscience and felt stupid."

**Central idea**

*Cognitive*-behavioral therapy is not sufficient for *non-substance-related* addiction disorders. A metacognitive approach such as that implemented in schema therapy is required. In using it, the therapist should focus on the metacognitive confusion between healthy adult thinking and the metacognitive ego state of addictive thinking.

In patients with non-substance-related addiction, as in those with alcohol dependence, the therapist works on the patient's *metacognitive disorder*. However, she supplements the procedures described in Sects. 10.6.1–10.6.6 with the following steps:

1. The therapist sets up two chairs in the room for the patient, one for his 'everyday ego' and one for his 'addicted ego'.
2. Together with him, the therapist attributes suitable thoughts, feelings, and experiences to his *two contrary ego states* and represents them on the respective chair with stones or wooden blocks.

3. The therapist works with the patient using the technique of the *ideal addiction scene* to work out the *positive function* of his addictive behavior in his holistic process of self-regulation (see Sect. 10.10.2).
4. The therapist clarifies with the patient whether he should see himself as an addict. To do this, she uses Jellinek's list of symptoms for persons with addiction disorder (see Sect. 10.4).
5. She recommends that the patient *try to live abstinent for a while 'for self-awareness'*. However, *the patient* should decide for *himself* when and how long he wants to be abstinent. His psychological and social symptoms of illness will often decrease in just a few weeks of abstinence (see case examples 124 in Sect. 10.10.3, and 127 in Sect. 10.10.4, and 129 in Sect. 10.10.5) because, *with abstinence*, the patient stops his repeated self-traumatization (see Sect. 10.5).
6. *After the beginning of his abstinence*, the therapist *actively* asks the patient *for signs of improvement* in his self-esteem and ability to deal with conflict, as well as his performance and enjoyment skills.
7. In the context of the patient's attempt to abstain for improved 'self-awareness', the therapist paradoxically asks the patient to *give up* his abstinence *again* after 8–12 weeks "*on an experimental basis for self-awareness*": "If you are unsure whether you are addicted, start behaving like an addict again! Soon you will realize that you are feeling bad again. But then you will know better *why* you are letting go of your addiction."
8. Sometimes an abstinent patient feels mentally worse again after a temporary improvement, *apparently for no reason*. This is then often due to a hidden relapse. The therapist expresses this assumption openly to the patient.
9. Even patients with a non-substance-related addiction have to decide whether they want to see themselves as addicts and *therefore* want to try to be abstinent. They should record their personal rock bottom and work out an *emergency plan*. Their feelings of guilt and shame are the prerequisite for developing a transpersonal conscience (see Sect. 10.6.4) and for the success of the therapeutically salutary capitulation, *regardless of difficult childhood experiences*.

### 10.10.2 The Ideal Addiction Scene and the Positive Function of Addictive Behavior in Self-regulation

The therapist captures *the positive function of addictive action in the patient's self-regulation* using the *technique of the ideal addiction scene*. In doing this, she takes the following steps together with the patient:

1. The therapist sets up two chairs next to the patient for the symptom scene in his everyday life (see Sect. 2.8).
2. She points to the chair of his self-representation in everyday life and reconstructs with him his thinking, feeling, and behavior during his *last addictive action in a chronological sequence* from beginning to end with all consequences. As a metacognitive doppelganger (see Sect. 4.8), she helps the patient to fill gaps in

the *temporal* sequence and the psychosomatic resonance pattern (see Sect. 2.7) of his addicted thinking, acting, and feeling.

3. Together with the patient, the therapist looks for an action sequence in his addiction scene that *deviates* from the actions *of other people* in the situation. For example, for a woman with an eating disorder, this may be how she *hastily* stuffs food into herself while standing at the refrigerator. In a man with a slot machine addiction, it is noticeable *how* the patient operates *five* slot machines *at the same time*.
4. The therapist lets the patient *switch to the chair of his addictive acting in everyday life* and asks him about his *ideal addiction scene* for the conspicuous situation: "What are you *truly* longing for when you act addictively? If what you are longing for *were to be* fulfilled, what *should* it be then? And, if your wish came true, how would you feel?" *By definition, addictive* action occurs in equivalence mode. The patient feels an ecstatic pull or kick. But he has never thought about what he is *truly* looking for in his addictive behavior. The patient's soul does nothing for free. Therefore, the therapist lets the patient explore his *actual longing* in the conspicuous action sequence in his addiction scene in the as-if mode of play. In doing so, the therapist helps him as a metacognitive doppelganger. In the *ideal addiction scene*, under the guise of fantasy, "the spirits of the unseen come to life" (von Kamphoevener, 1975, p. 27).
5. As a metacognitive doppelganger (see Sect. 2.5), the therapist does *not* ask any *questions*. She only makes statements while standing shoulder to shoulder with the patient. She fantasizes with him about what *should* happen when his real longing is fulfilled (see case examples 125 in Sect. 10.10.3, and 127 and 128 in Sect. 10.10.4).
6. The therapist and the patient summarize the positive meaning of his addiction in a *symbolic sentence*. For example, the patient in case example 127 (see Sect. 10.10.4) found the sentence: "My wish will come true!" Another patient with sex addiction longed to be "totally accepted." In the case of a patient with anorexia, the sentence could be: "I'm sure! I can control my greed *better* than anyone else!" The therapist then explains the *positive function* of this thinking in the holistic process of self-regulation to the patient: "Yes, greed used to be one of the seven deadly sins."
7. The therapist lets the patient switch back to the chair of healthy adult thinking.
8. The therapist and the patient look to *amplify* the individually positive sense of the patient's addictive behavior in fairy tales, myths, or social contexts. Desires are human. The patient in case example 127 (see Sect. 10.10.4) recognized himself in the sentence Julius Caesar wrote about himself 2000 years ago after he conquered Gaul: "I came, I saw, I won!".

**Central idea**

The patient and therapist think through the patient's addictive longing *in fantasy* to the point of *true fulfillment of the longing*. They joyfully *imagine* this fulfillment together, shoulder to shoulder. In doing so, they *separate* the patient's addicted fantasy from reality in the as-if mode of play. At some point, the patient will slip back into his healthy adult thinking and become sad. He realizes that his *actual* longing will not be fulfilled. The therapist then lets him switch back to the chair for healthy adult thinking. In this way, the patient becomes more aware of their *addictive* acting *in the equivalence mode*. As a result, it is more difficult for him to *behave addictively* in his everyday life and to find further satisfaction in it.

9. After working with the technique of the ideal addiction scene, at some point, the patient asks himself why *his true longing* is so important to him personally. The therapist waits until the patient *spontaneously* recognizes a connection between his ideal addiction scene and his deficit experiences or traumatic events from his childhood and integrates them. His addictive behavior has often served as a substitute for fulfilling childhood needs.
10. The therapist gives meaning to such a spontaneous understanding of the patient: She places an additional empty chair next to him in the therapy room for his "inner abandoned child" or for his "inner traumatized child" (see Sect. 4.7). However, she then turns her attention to the patient's *conflicts in everyday life* and the therapeutic relationship.

**Recommendation**

Like people with a personality disorder, those with an addiction disorder usually suffer from a structural metacognitive disorder. Their treatment involves the risk of *pathological regression*. The patient acts out his intrapsychic conflict *in current relationships* through projective identification, denial, and rationalization. Therefore, the therapist *initially* centers the therapeutic work on treating the disturbance in the *current therapeutic relationship* and the conflicts *in the* patient's *current everyday life*. She initially does *not* let the patient re-enact childhood memories *psychodramatically*.

11. The therapist encourages the patient to share their *actual childhood desires* hidden in their addictive behavior with at least one close person in *their current life*. They can be a good friend, for example. In this way, the patient learns to *accept himself* with his childlike desire and is, nevertheless, confronted with the limitations of life.

### *10.10.3 Gambling Addiction and Eating Disorders*

Gambling is a big business for providers. In 2015, they made a profit of 12.7 billion euros in Germany alone. The state earns money through taxes levied on these vast profits. Persons with gambling addiction pay for these profits with suffering and economic ruin. The therapist works with patients with gambling addiction (ICD F63.0) explicitly metacognitively (see Sect. 2.14).

***Case example 124***

*Mr. S., a patient with an addiction to slot machines (F63.0), was facing financial and family ruin after his company became aware of his gambling addiction. The therapist treated him similarly to alcohol-dependent patients with the method described in* Sect. 10.6. *Mr. S. learned to define himself as an addict after using Jellinek's symptom questionnaire. His metacognitive confusion was resolved with the help of the two-chair technique* (see Sect. 10.6.1). *The relatively well-structured patient was abstinent from the third month of therapy. His therapy consisted of only twenty-five sessions in one year and a half. He ended the therapy after two years of abstinence without relapse.*

In addition to working on metacognitive confusion, patients with a gambling addiction and *severe structural disturbances* should also understand the positive function of their addictive behavior in the holistic process of their self-regulation (see Sect. 4.8).

***Case example 125 (*****Sailer, 2000, p. 199 f.*****)***
*A therapist invited a student with obsessive–compulsive symptoms and a slot machine addiction (F42.1, F63.0) to conduct a psychodramatic dialogue with his slot machine using role reversal. The therapist doubled him in the play and, together with him, grasped his latent true longing. Acting addictively in the as-if mode of play, the patient became aware of his 'self-restraint and his concentration on the mini-world of the machine': His mini-world was 'pleasant where nobody makes demands on him. The discs rotate, he can intervene by pressing a button, but he doesn't have to. That's the way it works.' Nobody decided for him. He wished that the machine should be there for him, accept him and validate him, 'without having to perform for it [...]. With time, it became increasingly clear to him that his urge to play slot machines was always strongest when his desire for closeness, affection, and acceptance was within reach.' This wish occurred, for example, when a desirable girl approached him. This realization 'triggered further development. His compelling need to visit the slot machine parlor gradually subsided as he became aware of the substitute function of the slot machine game and this [...] gave way to an acceptance of his existing needs and desires.' In the successful group therapy, the patient worked psychodramatically on primarily coping with his problems in the present and not on the conflicts in his childhood.*

This metacognitive method can also be used in the treatment of *eating disorders* (F50.-) and other addictions, for example, work addiction. These patients also experience metacognitive confusion. Their feelings of guilt and shame lead them to keep their addictions a secret from others and themselves. They use excuses. The secrecy and shame lead to an ego-split. The therapist, therefore, uses the two-chair technique to resolve their metacognitive confusion.

***Case example 123 (continued from* Sect. 10.9*) (*****Hintermeier, 2013, p. 113 f.*****)***
*A patient had undergone methadone substitution therapy for heroin addiction and stopped using heroin due to the disorder-specific work with the two-chair technique. The therapist now applied the two-chair technique a second time to treat the patient's eating disorder and obesity: "After ending prostitution and with methadone substitution, she [...] had become addicted to eating again." One day the patient repeated 'the wish to reduce her excess weight'. The therapist had her enact the 'two souls in her breast' which now also concerned her eating/being. She represented the soul that 'always wants to get fatter' with the 'need for protection' [...] and the 'fear of being desired as a woman'. In addition, she represented the soul, which 'wants to*

*become thinner', with the 'desire to feel physically better' [...], and 'concern for her physical health'. The therapist experienced the patient's addictive eating ego state as still very 'heavy' at this point. Nevertheless, an initial definition of the problem regarding her binge eating had been established internally." The therapist reports: "I didn't believe it was possible. But a few months later, Sophie told me that she had started to eat less and to do sports."*

In the case of an eating disorder, the therapist and the patient go through the following steps together: (1) The therapist names the abnormal eating behavior and represents it with a second chair next to the patient. (2) The patient fills out Jellinek's questionnaire (see Fig. 10.1 in Sect. 10.4). This helps him decide whether or not he wants to consider himself an addict. A patient suffering from binge eating answered 20 questions with "Yes" (Marén Möhring 2023, verbal communication). (3) The therapist and the patient give the 'addicted self' a personal name, for example, 'my eating ego' or my 'devouring ego'. (4) They symbolize the patient's symptoms and assign them to "healthy adult thinking" *or* to the "devouring ego". (5) Together, they work out the patient's ideal addiction scene (see Sect. 10.10.2): "If your real longing were to be fulfilled by eating, what would happen?" The therapist helps the patient as a metacognitive doppelganger. In the as-if mode of play, the patient sits on the chair for his "devouring ego" with a pack of chips in his hand and says, for example: "I feel nice and warm. I become very calm. I am no longer sad. I am self-sufficient. My mother can't take anything away from me. It annoys me when others criticize me. Others are much more disturbed than I am." (6) The therapist invites the patient to engage in a psychodramatic dialogue through role reversal with a burger from the fridge: The 'burger' is afraid of being crushed by the patient's teeth. The patient feels powerful in his own role. He is self-sufficient. In this way, the therapist and the patient individually work out the *positive function* of the patient's eating in the holistic process of his self-regulation. (7) The patient also describes the personal emotional low point that he experienced through his eating. In doing so, the therapist marks his experience of loss of dignity and shame. (8) The patient attempts to abstain. (9) He makes an emergency plan for when he has addictive thoughts again. Therein, he describes his low point through his addiction. (10) He reads the contingency plan again when needed, and, thus, internally updates his emotional experience of loss of dignity at his lowest point. The primary goal of therapy is not that the patient *stops eating* too much. He should *learn to psychosomatically notice when* he switches from his "healthy adult thinking" back to his 'devouring ego'. Eating in the equivalence mode should become eating *in the as-if mode of thinking*. Thus, the patient gains ego control over his "devouring ego".

In my experience, patients with *anorexia nervosa* (ICD: F50.0) and/or *bulimia nervosa* (ICD: F50.2) should be treated metacognitively similarly to *patients with personality disorders* (see Chap. 4) because their adaptation to the demands of an inner self-injurious authority is at the core of their dysfunctional self-regulation (see Sect. 4.7). Self-injurious, masochistic thinking, and acting are mostly the result of childhood trauma. The therapist symbolizes the patient's 'self-injurious thinking' with an empty chair: "I have the impression that you are having self-injurious thoughts. I am placing this chair across from you to represent your inner voice, which devalues you. This is your inner soul killer. He says to you: 'You are greedy!' 'You are fat!'" The therapist places a red, grinning devil puppet on the chair: "That is the blind inner soul killer that devalues you!" The therapist places yet another chair next to the patient for her self-protection through adaptation': "You obey this blind soul killer just as the princess obeyed the mountain troll in Hans Christian Andersen's fairy tale 'Der Reisekamerad'. Your anticipatory obedience and heroic abstaining from eating protect you from further devaluations by the soul-killer." The therapist points to the chair on which the patient is currently sitting: "But you also have your healthy adult thinking in you. In thinking as a healthy adult, you know that you will break down physically if you continue on this path." Patient: "But if I were to eat more, it would take me all day to eat. I wouldn't be able to do anything else!" The therapist points to the chair of the patient's self-representation in her symptom scene in her everyday life (see Fig. 2.9 in Sect. 2.8): "Can you show me how you sit at your table in your room and why it takes two to three hours to drink a glass of vegetable puree? I would like to know how you feel and think while doing so." The patient switches to the chair of her self-representation in her symptom scene. As soon as she takes a sip of the vegetable puree, the 'evil mountain troll' comes alive in her head and says: "You are greedy! You are not fulfilling your promise to me. You wanted to be different from the others and now you aren't!" The patient promptly obeys her 'blind inner soul killer' by interrupting her meal. She waits until her self-injurious thinking becomes silent. Only one hour later, she can think as a healthy adult again: "Now I'll take the next sip!" She drinks a second sip of the vegetable puree.

### *10.10.4 Sex and Porn Addiction*

Sex and porn addiction have not yet been included in the ICD-10 as independent diagnoses. So far, they have been recorded under the diagnoses "increased sexual desire" (F52.7) or "impulse control disorders" (F63.-). In these patients, too, the development of addiction leads to ego-splitting and metacognitive confusion.

**Question 44**
Why is cognitive-behavioral therapy not enough for sex addiction?

***Case example 126* (Krüger, 2004b, p. 171 f., *modified*)**
*A 24-year-old student, Mr. T., comes for a psychiatric consultation in acute psychosis. He reports: Two days ago, he was sitting in the lecture hall and daydreaming. A female fellow student spoke to him: "Zero one nine zero, zero one nine zero..." That's how the sex hotline phone numbers start. Usually, the colleague's provocation would have been fun. However, Mr. T. had spent thousands of euros by calling numbers starting with 0190. He had also secretly sought out sex workers time and again. As a result, he was now in debt. Nobody knew about it. He kept a low profile and appeared like a righteous young man. For example, he went to college and had a girlfriend for*

*four years, a lovely young girl. Mr. T. assumed that his fellow student had discovered his secret. He panicked. He drove home to his girlfriend as quickly as possible and confessed everything to her. The commitment to his sex acts collapsed the wall between his two contradicting inner worlds. He decompensated psychotically.*

*During therapy, Mr. T. defined his actions in the secret world as "sex addiction". He found an ingenious solution for how he wanted to deal with his sexual desires in the future. He decided only to do things in the sexual area that, if in doubt, he could also tell his girlfriend and those close to him. In doing so, he transferred his conscience to the outside world. This safety measure protected him from relapsing and possibly decompensating again. After six months, Mr. T. stopped taking his medication. At the end of one year of treatment, he was mentally stable and mastering his life. He did not psychotically decompensate again in the next twenty years.*

The topics of sex or porn addiction quickly trigger aversive reactions in humans because those affected suppress the human element in their sexual objects and treat them narcissistically and functionally through *their addictive actions*.

**Central idea**

In cases of sex addiction on the part of a patient, the therapist easily reacts with character-related metacognitive countertransference (see Sect. 2.10) and acts out healthy everyday thinking *on behalf* of the patient. In such a case, however, the therapist can resolve her countertransference by using the two-chair technique to explicitly address the patient's metacognitive confusion in therapy (see Sect. 10.6.1).

The therapist represents the addictive thinking and acting of the patient with a second chair next to the patient. She and the patient together name it as the patient's 'ego who watches porn' or his 'ego who goes to sex workers'.

***Case example 127***

*The 29-year-old, Mr. U., sought psychotherapeutic treatment for his depressive mood and relationship problems. Outwardly, the young man looked like an ideal son-in-law. But he was filled with shame when he shared that he had started going to sex workers six months after starting his relationship with his girlfriend. Three months ago, he had confessed his sexual actions to his girlfriend. He had since ceased his sexual relations with sex workers. But, the following indications suggested that Mr. U. had a sex addiction. He suffered from an invincible desire: "I have often resolved not to go to sex workers. I wanted to stop and be strong-willed. But I realized that I couldn't do that." He increased the number of his visits. In doing so, he harmed himself and others: "When I was on that path again, I devalued my girlfriend afterward. For example, I told her that her pelvis was too wide. I was distant from her. I doubted whether she was the right woman for me."*

*In the 6th therapy session, Mr. U. complained: "I feel terrible. I am so insecure. I don't know who I am at the moment." The therapist set up two chairs to represent his two identities* (see Sect. 10.6.1), *one for his 'everyday ego' and one for 'his formerly lived sex world'. Therapist: "As long as the two worlds knew nothing about each other, did you feel stronger?" Mr. U.: "Yes. I still have such fantasies. I look at women on the street and imagine how they would look undressed." Therapist: "Please sit here in the chair for your addicted ego and role-play what you long for when you meet a woman on the street." The therapist set up a chair for 'the desired woman' and asked: "What if your actual longing were to be fulfilled?" Mr. U.: "Then I become the be-all and end-all for this woman. She's fallen for me!" Mr. U. imagined his wishful fantasy: "The woman is undressing. She wants me. We have sex." Therapist: "What happens next?" Mr. U. was completely amazed: "That's it! There is nothing more! I get dressed and go. My ego is strengthened." In the debriefing, Mr. U. referred to himself as a 'hunter' in his sex world.*

*In the 8th session, Mr. U. reported: "I broke up with my girlfriend yesterday!" At the end of the session, he casually recalls: "I have been browsing porn on the internet for 2–3 h every day for a week now. Afterward, I was annoyed with my girlfriend again. If we have sex with each other, that's not enough for me!" So the patient had first relapsed and only then broke up with his girlfriend! The therapist pointed out this chronological sequence to the patient: "So despite your resolution to be abstinent, you have relapsed. As a result, you broke up with your girlfriend."*

*In the 9th session, Mr. U. had been abstinent for a week again. He wanted to "talk about his sex addiction". The therapist let him describe his relapse again and paradoxically work on the positive function of his addictive behavior in the holistic process of his self-regulation. Mr. U.: "When I look at the porn sites, I can't get away from it. I then look for newcomers, for beautiful pictures. I read the descriptions and wonder if it might be worth going there." Therapist: "You need a harem with 40–80 women." Mr. U.: "Yes, at least. Otherwise it would be boring." The therapist asked the patient to sit on the chair for his 'sex world': "You have always changed sex workers?" Indeed, Mr. U. had visited around 45 sex workers in the last few years. He met only two of them a second time when he "didn't find anyone better". The therapist: "The greater the number of women, the better it was for you?" Mr. U.: "Yes, always something new. That gives me a thrill. I know that they only enact the sex acts, but then I ignore that." Therapist: "You conquer women. They fall for you. You have the power to determine everything. It's like Julius Caesar. After his war in Gaul, he said: 'I came, I saw, I won.' Every time you meet a new woman, you conquer more land. And you ignore the reality of these women!" Mr. U.: "Now when I walk into the street where the camper van of a woman I know is parked, the area disgusts me!" Therapist: "I think you have little fantasy in everyday life and are not very spontaneous!" Mr. U.: "Yes, that's right. I always plan everything very precisely. Nothing should disturb my plan." Therapist: "Maybe it would be better for you if you also tried to do something crazy in your everyday life!".*

*In the 10th session, the patient and the therapist deliberated together whether Mr. U. should consider himself as 'addicted' based on Jellinek's questions for persons with alcohol addiction (see* Fig. 10.1 in Sect. 10.4*). They agreed that the patient would have to answer 'yes' to the following questions: Question 2: His addictive behaviors were secret. 3: He thought about it often. 5: He felt guilty about his addictive behavior. 6: He avoided talking about it. 7: He repeatedly failed to keep his decision not to see sex workers again because of his irresistible desires. So he lost control of himself. 8: He used excuses: "Life is boring." "My girlfriend's pelvis is too wide." 9: He was aggressive toward his girlfriend and others. 11: He consciously took breaks in* *his addictive actions. 15: He suffered from a loss of interest and stopped playing sports, for example. 16: He had excessive self-pity. So Mr. U. had to answer ten such questions with "Yes". Five would have been enough to suspect an addiction disorder.*

*At the 12th session, the patient had been abstinent for three weeks. Mr. U.: "I have started playing sports again. They were all happy to see me again." Therapist: "You are more aware of your neediness during abstinence." Mr. U.: "I am much more open now. People come up to me at work. I enjoy meeting other people. Earlier, I used to be more alone. After the last therapy session, I was pretty sad for three days. I longed for spring. Yesterday was a wonderful day. I saw the sun and the little flowers that are blooming everywhere." Therapist: "Your thinking is no longer restricted. You perceive the world in a more differentiated manner again because you have fewer feelings of shame and guilt." This clarification was followed by a conversation about the beginning of his sex addiction. Mr. U. lied to his partner for the first time when she wanted to move in with him: "If I had moved in with Ulrike, I would have had to deliver power and control to her. I didn't want that." The therapist recommended that Mr. U. set up two symbols at home, one for his neediness and a second for his identity as a conqueror: "Look at these more often and think about your two opposing sides!"*

In patients with structural disorders (see Sect. 4.4), the symptoms that are independent of the addiction are intensified by sex addiction. Watching pornographic films can also become a pathological sex addiction.

***Case example 128***

*Mr. V. had decompensated into a severe depressive episode with suicidality (F32.2) and was treated as an inpatient in a psychiatric clinic for a long time. He decompensated when his gay partner discovered that he was watching porn. Mr. V. was "immensely ashamed" and retreated from all social contacts. In the 20th therapy session of individual outpatient therapy, the therapist wanted to clarify whether Mr. V. was addicted. He asked him to fill out Jellinek's questionnaire. The patient answered the following ten questions with "Yes": 2, 3, 5, 6, 7, 10, 11, 14, 16, and 20 (see* Fig. 10.1 in Sect. 10.4*).*

*Mr. V felt excluded from people in everyday life. He found himself "extremely ugly": "When I see myself in the shop window, I think: 'Oh God, who is that! A meatball!'" The therapist paradoxically worked with the patient on the positive function of his addictive behavior in the holistic process of his self-regulation (see* Sect. 10.10.1*). He asked the patient to switch from the chair of his healthy everyday thinking to that of the 'porn viewer' and to describe his experiences during his addictive acting. Mr. V.: "I step out of my body and become a voyeur. I watch as two dominant, well-built guys get down to business. It goes off without tenderness. Afterward, they just part again. The men are not sensitive, no bitches. They are by no means an image of me. They mustn't remind me of myself!" Watching porn served a compensatory function for the patient. The positive function of his self-regulation was: Mr. V. could stop the strong guys in the computer of his own volition. But he could also let them continue their sex acts of his own free will. If he didn't like the actors, he changed them and watched other films. So he himself determined what* *happened. He felt free, powerful, and empowered: "Nobody tells me: 'You are not wanted here' or determines what I should do!"*

*During the one-year-long weaning phase, the therapist worked with the patient to determine the difference between his state of being in abstinent times and in times of acting out addictive behavior. For example, after eight weeks of abstinence, Mr. V. reported: "I had a week's vacation. I wasn't doing so well. But I'm going back to work tomorrow. That's strange: I'm looking forward to working. I want to power through. And I haven't seen any porn! When the idea came up, I simply denied it on my own." The abstinence dissolved the patient's depressive inhibition. Two weeks later, he said: "For the first time, I asked my boss something openly in a team meeting." The therapist immediately connected the patient's abstinence and his positive change: "This time, you did not take sick leave before the team meeting like the last two times. Presumably, that was also because you haven't seen porn for ten weeks now. As a result, you have less self-doubt. You devalue yourself less. You no longer think about killing yourself. Your improved self-esteem has now helped you approach your boss directly and ask him for information."*

*Two weeks later, at the beginning of the session, Mr. V reported a relapse: "I saw another porno. I was free and didn't know what to do. I was at home and thought, 'You used to watch porn when you were free. But you don't do that anymore!' An hour later, I did it." This story shows the grotesque nature of addictive thinking. The patient had thought addictively in the equivalence mode (see* Sect. 10.6.1*) and did not perceive a cognitive negation as negation at all. He just felt the addictive emotion contained in his addictive thinking. But the addictive emotion resulted in his addictive action. Mr. V. told: He had already started to think addictively from the day before his relapse. He had blamed his partner for no reason. He had also masochistically imagined a catastrophic scenario in the long-term conflict with a difficult colleague: "In the end, I was convinced that she put me down in front of our boss. I already knew what negative things my boss would say to me when I returned to work."*

*The therapist asked Mr. V. to sit on the chair of his 'addicted ego': "Please feel into yourself and talk to yourself about what you thought negatively about your partner yesterday!" Mr. V. exasperated on the chair for the 'addicted ego': "Why doesn't Volker notice that I've seen porn? Why is he still being loving and nice to me?! If he's so nice, he doesn't offer me any space to attack! Why does the idiot allow something like that to be done to him!" The therapist asked the patient to switch back to the chair of his everyday self and said: "Apparently, part of your addictive thinking is that internally you are looking for a fight with your partner." Mr. V.: "When I was fine at work last week, I was proud of myself. The fog in me had lifted. I noticed that I was technically up to date. I didn't feel insecure at all. The bitchy employee had no chance. On the other hand, I think: 'If I'm such a fool, no one wants me!'" Therapist: "So you relapsed when you were doing particularly well! You will likely be fine after a period of abstinence. I suggest you allow yourself to be well for a while! Enjoy it for a few hours or days! I don't think you are used to being well. You are like a first grader in school who learns to write. You just are learning to be ok!" Mr. V.: "I find this chair work to be fascinating. I would never have thought I could make my disdain for my partner come to life in the other chair the same way as in real life. And that I believe that I don't have a chance at work! You have to tell me how to work with the chairs one day!"*

## 10.10.5 Internet Gaming Disorder

Internet gaming addiction or computer game addiction has been recently recognized as an addiction disorder. It was included in the current version of the Diagnostic and Statistical Manual of Mental Disorders (DSM-5) as Internet Gaming Disorder (IGD). About 8.4% of males and 2.6% of female adolescents and adults between the ages of 12 and 25 years suffer from internet gaming addiction (Wartberg et al., 2017, p. 419f.). If they answer five of the following twenty questions with 'yes', those affected are addicted to online games:

Internet gaming addiction is a terrifying example of how commercial providers deliberately exploit people's weaknesses and further damage them to make a profit.

***Case example 129***

*The 27-year-old Mr. W. was a carpenter by profession. As a child, he grew up in a broken family. The family broke up, among other things, because of his mother's alcoholic addiction. Mr. W. is intelligent. However, he had massive neurotic learning difficulties in school. Now he lives partly on welfare with his wife and two children. He came to therapy because of recurrent depressive episodes, painkiller addiction, and chronic recurrent relational conflicts with borderline personality disorder (F33.1, F55.2, F60.31). After a year of therapy, the patient, who was now painkiller-free, raised his relationship problems again: "The relationship is very shaky at the moment. My wife thinks my level of aggression is just as high as it was before I started my therapy."*

*The therapist remembered that Mr. W. had once said that he used to play video games on the computer for up to 5–6 h a day. He had often argued about it with his wife. The therapist asked Mr. W. how he dealt with the computer in his current life. Using the two-chair technique, it turned out that the patient was addicted to internet games (ICD-10: F63.-). The therapist was astonished and shocked at what the patient reported about internet gaming during his treatment: Mr. W. played online games for 2–3 h at night. The game was about planting a bomb. Others have to defuse the bomb 'before it goes off'. There are 15 points for killing a person. If a player plants the bomb themselves, they get the most points. If a player defuses it, they get lesser points. Mr. W.: "People now want to index the game after the rampage in Winnenden." There are ten different ranks in the game. One needs 5000 points to move one rank higher: "Everyone tries to reach the top rank. I'm aiming for fifth place." If you play the game once, you get 500 points. Getting another 500 points 'is very tricky'. Mr. W. had only managed this once so far. The player's score is shown online under the player's name and is visible to everyone else: "Everyone can see another person's name and then think: Oh, that's pretty good!" There is a world ranking list in which players are listed in the order of their game points. Mr. D. was at number 1243 in the world rankings. He said: "A friend of mine has 185,000 points." The names of all players currently online are listed in one place on the Internet: "Sometimes a name is online in the morning as well as in the evening. Then it moves up in the world rankings." To be able to go online, every player has to buy a gold chip for the game console for 40 euros per month. Mr. W. had received the first 'gold card' from Microsoft "without paying anything for it". When a player has paid for his playing card, a card in gold can be seen on the Internet next to his name. If you don't have the money, this display changes from gold to silver: "Everyone can see that you haven't paid." The competitors and fellow players are called 'friends'. When Mr. W. made his first attempt at abstinence as part of his internet addiction, he saw on the internet: "Eight friends have already deleted me."*

*During his first attempt at abstinence during therapy, Mr. W. noticed: "At first, I felt empty and was fidgety. I needed to play somehow. But that feeling has disappeared since yesterday. Now it's nice to play with my little son." Mr. W. adored his two-year-old son: "He is brilliant. I would do anything for him!" Contrary to this sentiment, Mr. W. had rejected his little son while acting addictively: "Indeed, I could turn off the game console if my son wanted to play with me. But then I think about the game all the time. I deliberate on how I might be able to solve the current problem. If a solution occurs to me, I go to the PC in between and check whether the solution works. My son then comes after me immediately and insists on playing along with me! I would have to turn to him. But in reality, I am angry with him. But now I don't go to the PC anymore. And my son also plays alone more often! He notices that I am not so fidgety anymore and that I am not constantly looking for video game solutions!"*

*Due to his addictive thinking and acting, Mr. W. had lost interest in other things and withdrew socially: "I hate having fixed appointments. That's why I don't meet friends anymore. When I had to take my game console for repairs in December, there was a three-week break." Therapist: "Did you do something different then?" Mr. W.: "I was more sociable. I felt more human and cared for my family. I was doing much better. I was pleased that the game console broke. That's a real compulsion!" Therapist: "That sounds like an addiction. You didn't stop playing, even though it would have ruined your relationship with your son and wife!" Mr. W. agreed: "Four weeks ago, I promised my wife I would not buy a new gold card for the game console. I kept my promises. I felt liberated afterward. That was nice. Now I don't need to worry about how to get the money for the gold card. Otherwise, I would keep obsessing over it in my head. I notice that when I play on the PC, I can't stop."*

**Exercise 54**

Before reading on, please try to determine which of the 20 questions about Internet gaming addiction (see Fig. 10.6) did Mr. W. have to answer with "Yes".

You will notice that the patient had the following addiction symptoms: Question 1: The patient played at night. So he played secretly in front of his wife. 2: He thought about playing a lot, even when he was busy with other things. 3: He felt guilty about treating his son and wife like he did. 4: He avoided talking about his computer games

**Are you addicted to internet gaming?**

Based on the World Health Organizationís (WHO) report by Prof. E. M. Jellinek, modified for Internet Gaming Disorder by Reinhard T. Kr¸ ger

| Yes | No | | **Preliminary Stage** |
|---|---|---|---|
| ☐ | ☐ | 1. | Do you play games on the internet secretly so that others wonít know? |
| ☐ | ☐ | 2. | Do you often think about gaming? |
| ☐ | ☐ | 3. | Do you feel guilty about your gaming? |
| ☐ | ☐ | 4. | Do you avoid references to internet gaming in conversations? |
| | | | **Critical Phase** |
| ☐ | ☐ | 5. | After playing for the first time, do you have an irresistible urge to continue playing? |
| ☐ | ☐ | 6. | Do you make excuses to justify playing internet games? |
| ☐ | ☐ | 7. | Do you show particularly aggressive behavior towards the environment? |
| ☐ | ☐ | 8. | Do you consciously try to abstain from playing internet games for a while? |
| ☐ | ☐ | 9. | Have you set up a specific gaming system, e.g. not to play before or after certain times? |
| ☐ | ☐ | 10. | Have you changed jobs frequently ? |
| ☐ | ☐ | 11. | Are you organizing your work and life around gaming? |
| ☐ | ☐ | 12. | Have you noticed a loss of interest in things other than gaming? |
| ☐ | ☐ | 13. | Do you show conspicuous self-pity? |
| ☐ | ☐ | 14. | Have there been any changes in your family life? |
| ☐ | ☐ | 15. | Are you neglecting your diet? |
| ☐ | ☐ | 16. | Have you been admitted to a hospital as a result of gaming? |
| | | | **Chronic Phase** |
| ☐ | ☐ | 17. | Have you ever played for days in a row? |
| ☐ | ☐ | 18. | Do you see a moral degradation in yourself? |
| ☐ | ☐ | 19. | Has your ability to concentrate and learn been adversely affected? |
| ☐ | ☐ | 20. | Has gaming become a compulsion? |

If honest self-assessment requires you to answer "yes" to more than five questions, it is likely that you are addicted to internet gaming.

**Fig. 10.6** 20 questions "Are you addicted to internet games?" based on the World Health Organization's (WHO) Report by Prof. E. M. Jellinek, modified for IGD by Reinhard T. Krüger

in conversations. For example, he hadn't talked about it in therapy either. 5: He made up his mind to only play until 10 p.m., but would then think: "Oh, just one more game!" and continued playing. He couldn't control his addictions. 6: He used excuses to allow himself to gamble. 7: He displayed aggressive behavior toward those around him. 8: He had already taken breaks from playing and had deliberately abstained from playing for two days. 9: He seriously considered installing parental controls on his PC to prevent him from playing at certain times. 12: He realized that he had lost interest in other things. When the game console was in the repair shop, he began to enjoy family life and friendships again.

The patient should therefore have answered "yes" to ten questions about Internet gaming disorder. But even five questions answered with "yes" are sufficient to indicate that a person is "most likely" suffering from an addiction.

## 10.11 Co-dependency and Secondary Traumatization of Caregivers

Co-dependency is not the same as a *dependent personality disorder* (F60.7). The therapy of a patient with dependent personality disorder follows the method described in Chap. 4.

**Important definition**

A *co-dependent person* allows herself to be drawn *concordantly* into the actions of her addicted relative, for example, into the thoughts, feelings, and actions of her addicted husband. She takes on the role assigned by the husband and adopts his explanations for his addictive behavior out of fear of punishment or shame in the social world. *Just like the husband* does, she tries to hide his addiction. The co-dependent wife uses excuses to explain why her husband didn't go to work on Monday or why he didn't keep an appointment. She justifies his behavior even in front of their children. Her co-dependency makes it easier for the addicted husband to trivialize his drug consumption to himself and other people in line according to the motto: "It's not that bad."

A co-dependent patient seduces the therapist into participating in *her* defense system. For example, the patient only talks *about* how she can *help her alcoholic husband even better*. When the therapist goes into this problem, she blindly adjusts to the patient's expectations. The therapist then acts co-dependently toward the co-dependent patient.

**Central idea**

A co-dependent patient must *also* surrender. She has to give up trying to help *her addicted husband* and humbly accept defeat. The following sentence also applies to *co-dependent* patients: "Alcohol is mightier than me!"

The therapist therapeutically resolves a patient's co-dependency through the following steps: (1) She uses the concept of metacognitive confusion to explain alcohol addiction to the co-dependent patient. She asks her to read more about addiction disorders on Wikipedia. (2) She asks her to fill out Jellinek's questionnaire *on behalf of* her addicted husband. (3) The co-dependent patient should decide *whether she herself wants to see her husband as an alcoholic or not.* In doing so, she mustn't adapt to her husband's decision. (4) As a caregiver, the patient no longer assumes the concealment and excuses of her partner with addiction. Instead, she *actively and openly* talks to selected friends and relatives about *her own* difficulties with her addicted husband. This liberates her from her co-dependency. (5) She may also attend a self-help group for caregivers.

***Case example 130***
*The 40-year-old Ms. X. went to the therapist and asked how she could help her husband: "He drinks too much. I believe that he is addicted to alcohol." Therapist: "I recommend you go to a self-help group for caregivers of addicts! But, tell your husband that you are doing this. Your husband won't take it well. It will bother him if you decide to regard him as a person with addiction!" The patient then visited a group of Blue Cross members on her own. After six weeks, her husband promised that he would stop drinking if she stopped going to the group. The patient accepted his offer and stopped going to the group. Her husband, however, started drinking again after only four weeks.*

Alcohol has a disinhibiting effect. Some patients with addiction are sometimes violent under the influence of alcohol. But *socially inconspicuous* alcohol addicts also harm their relatives. They are not emotionally available, and they lie and trivialize their conflicts and torment their caregivers with their constant oscillation between their healthy everyday thinking and addictive thinking. The inconsistency drives the caregivers crazy. The caregiver may even be *secondarily traumatized*. Relatives of persons with addictions often develop exhaustion syndrome, depression, or post-traumatic stress disorder.

In such a case, the therapist lets the *co-dependent patient* clarify the relationship in a fictitious psychodramatic dialogue with a role reversal with her addicted relative (see Sect. 8.4.2). But she sets up two chairs *for the ego-split of the co-dependent patient*, one for "Clare who sympathizes with her husband or even loves him" and another for "Clare who hates her husband". During the interaction with her "husband", the patient is supposed to switch to the chair of the "loving Clare" during the argument with her "husband" when she feels sympathy for her husband. But she sits down on the chair of the "hating Clare" when she is angry with her husband.

The therapist also lets the co-dependent patient conduct a psychodramatic dialogue with role reversal between *her own two egos*, between the one who hates her husband and the one who loves her husband. In this way, the patient can discover what she needs to make the relationship with her addicted partner bearable for herself *in a specific life situation*. Her hating and compassionate ego states should grant each other a right to exist because they can give each other something important: The "hating Clare" can protect the "loving Clare" from being overwhelmed and help her to create sufficient distance from her addicted husband. The "loving Clare" can get the "hating Clare" to help her addicted husband *appropriately*. In this way, unlike her addicted husband, the patient remains *true* to her ideal human values *without* betraying herself. In the therapy of co-dependent patients, the therapist focuses her work primarily on the *current conflicts* of those affected (see case example 49 in Sect. 5.12 and Sect. 5.15).

The therapist proceeds similarly in the case of secondarily traumatized daughters or sons of dependent parents. She lets the son clarify the relationship with his addicted "father" through a psychodramatic dialogue with role reversal (see case example 49 in Sect. 5.12). But the son should also represent *his* struggle between his "loving ego" and "hating ego" with chairs and process the conflict between his two egos with the help of the role reversal. In doing so, he always seeks a *situationally appropriate* compromise between his two opposing egos.

Some therapists have a secondarily traumatized patient set up two chairs *for the addicted father* in a psychodramatic dialogue with their addicted father. One chair should represent the "good father", and the second chair the "addicted father". In the case of *a co-dependent patient*, however, the therapist should treat the *co-dependent patient's metacognitive confusion* and *not his father's addiction*. The two-chair technique must be used *for the secondarily traumatized son or daughter*.

## References


Alkoholiker, A. (1980). Zwölf Schritte und Zwölf Traditionen. 2. *überarb. Aufl.(nach der 17. amerikanischen Auflage von 1978).* Ohne Ort.

Benzinger, H. (2013). Zum Verständnis von Abhängigkeiten aus psychodramatischer Sicht. *Zeitschrift für Psychodrama und Soziometrie, 11*(Suppl. 1), 5–22. https://doi.org/10.1007/s11620-012-0159-4

Dulit, R. A., Fyer, M. R., Haas, G. L., Sullivan, T., et al. (1990). Substance use in borderline personality disorder. *American Journal of Psychiatry, 147*(8), 1002–1007.

Dürckheim, K. G. (1982). *Der Weg, die Wahrheit, das Leben. Erfahrungen auf dem Weg der Selbstfindung. Gespräche über das Sein mit Alphonse Goettman.* Scherz.

Edwards, G. (1986). *Arbeit mit Alkoholkranken. Ein praktischer Leitfaden für die helfenden Berufe.* Beltz.

Groterath, A. (1993). Und wenn sie nun doch nicht krank sind? Psychodrama als Probe für das Leben im Centro de Solidarietà. *Psychodrama, 6*(2), 249–269.

Harrison, P. A., Edwall, G. E., Hoffman, N. G., & Worthen, M. D. (1990). Correlates of sexual abuse among boys in treatment for chemical dependency. *Journal of Adolescent Chemical Dependency, 1*, 53–67.

Hiller, W. (2014). Klinische Psychologie-Mainz.de/downloads/materialien/alc.pdf, 25 February 2014.

Hintermeier, S. (2013). Borderline und Abhängigkeit. Einen theoriegestützter Erfahrungsbericht über psychodramatische Einzeltherapie mit Borderline-PatientInnen mit komorbiden Abhängigkeitserkrankungen. *Zeitschrift für Psychodrama und Soziometrie, 11*(Suppl. 1), 103–116.

Kern, S. (2013). Zur Ätiologie der Sucht. Wer sich in ein Labyrinth begibt, sollte den Ariadnefaden nicht vergessen! *Zeitschrift für Psychodrama und Soziometrie, 11*(Suppl. 1), 23–46.

Körkel, J. (2001). Rückfall und Rückfallprävention von Alkoholabhängigkeit. In F. Tretter & A. Müller (Eds.), *Psychologische Therapie der Sucht* (pp. 519–547). Hogrefe.

Kraus, L., Piontek, D., Pabst, A., & Gomes de Matos, E. (2014). Kurzbericht Epidemiologischer Suchtsurvey 2012. Tabellenband: Trends substanzbezogener Störungen nach Geschlecht und Alter: Prävalenz und Hochrechnung 1997–2012. Online: https://ift.de/?id=429, 14 June 2023.

Krüger, R. T. (2000). Begegnung als Rahmen psychodramatischen Denkens und Handelns. *Psychodrama, 10*, 65–90. https://doi.org/10.1007/978-3-531-92044-3_4

Krüger, R. T. (2004a). Schöpferisch sein – wieder schöpferisch werden. Kreativität als Ressource des Menschen und als Mittel der Heilung in der Psychotherapie. In S. Gunkel, G. Kruse (Eds.), *Salutogenese und Resilienz – Gesundheitsförderung, nicht nur, aber auch durch Psychotherapie?* (pp. 257–249). Hannoversche Ärzte-Verlags-Union.

Krüger, R. T. (2004b). Zwei Seelen in der Brust haben – Theorie und Praxis der störungsspezifischen Psychodramatherapie mit suchtkranken Menschen. *Zeitschrift für Psychodrama und Soziometrie, 3*(2), 161–194. https://doi.org/10.1007/s11620-004-0017-0

Krüger, R. T. (2010a). Der Selbststeuerungskreis. In Wiederholungskonflikten vom Objekt des Geschehens zum Subjekt des eigenen Handelns werden. *Zeitschrift für Psychodrama und Soziometrie, 9*(1), 149–160.

Krüger, R. T. (1988). Der Weg der Heilung in der Psychotherapie mit Alkoholkranken. *Gruppenpsychotherapie und Gruppendynamik, 24*, 66–81.

Leutz, G. A. (1974). *Das klassische Psychodrama nach J. L. Moreno*. Springer.

Moreno, J. L. (1974). *Die Grundlagen der Soziometrie. Wege zur Neuordnung der Gesellschaft* (3rd ed.). Westdeutscher Verlag.

Sailer, R. (2000). Der mächtige Kleine – ein Nein-Sager bekommt Lebensraum. *Psychodrama, 10*(1/2), 195–106.

Schäfer, I. (2005). Traumatisierungen bei SuchtpatientInnen. Kölner Kolloquium zu Suchtfragen, 28.10.2005.80.92.48.160/addiction.de/fileadmin/user_upload/pdf/documents/Schaefer_Trau-maundSucht.pdf, 15 April 14

Schäfer, I., & Reddemann, L. (2005). Traumatisierung und Sucht – eine Literaturübersicht. *Zeitschrift für Psychotraumatologie und Psychologische Medizin, 3*(3), 9–18.

Schmidt, S. A. (2000). *Prävalenz sexuellen Kindesmissbrauchs bei Opiatabhängigen – Themenbezogene Grundlagen, Konzept, Durchführung und Ergebnisse eines Kontrollgruppenvergleichs*. VWB-Verlag für Wissenschaft und Bildung.

Schneider, U., Schmidt-Ott, G., & Haltenhoff, H. (2009). Persönlichkeitsstörungen bei Sucht- und Abhängigkeitserkrankungen. In H. Haltenhoff, G. Schmid-Ott, & U. Schneider (Eds.), *Persönlichkeitsstörungen im therapeutischen Alltag* (pp. 180–200). Pabst Science Publisher.

Schwehm, H. (2004). Wirkfaktoren des Psychodramas bei der Behandlung Abhängiger. *Zeitschrift für Psychodrama und Soziometrie, 3*(2), 133–159.

Shengold, L. (1989). *Soul murder. The effects of childhood abuse and deprivation*. Yale University of Press.

Simpson, T. L., & Miller, W. R. (2002). Concomitance between childhood sexual and physical abuse and substance use problems: A review. *Clinical Psychology Review, 22*, 27–77.

Stadler, C. (2013). Posttraumatische Belastungsstörung und Suchterkrankung. Doppeldiagnose, Komorbidität und Behandlungsimplikationen. *Zeitschrift für Psychodrama und Soziometrie, 11*(Suppl. 1), 73–90. https://doi.org/10.1007/s11620-012-0169-2

Steppan, M., Künzel, J., & Pfeiffer-Gerschel, T. (2013). Jahresstatistik 2011 der professionellen Suchtkrankenhilfe. In Deutsche Hauptstelle für Suchttherapiefragen e. V. (Ed.), *Jahrbuch Sucht 2013* (pp.197–226). Pabst Science Publishers.

Stimmer, F. (1993). Real-irreal-ideal-normal: Wirklichkeits- und Wunschbilder bei Suchtkranken. *Psychodrama, 6*(2), 275–278.

von Kamphoevener, E. S. (1975). *An den Nachtfeuern der Karawan-Serail. Märchen und Geschichten alttürkischer Nomaden*. Rowohlt.

Waldheim-Auer, B. (1993). Die Chancen des Psychodramas bei Alkoholabhängigen. Ein Therapeutischer Ansatz. *Psychodrama, 6*(2), 193–207.

Waldheim-Auer, B. (2013). Leben mit Konsum und Rückfällen. *Zeitschrift für Psychodrama und Soziometrie, 11*(Suppl. 1), 195–207. https://doi.org/10.1007/s11620-012-0176-3

Waniczek, S. (2003). *Eine Evaluationsstudie zur Wirksamkeit der Psychodramatherapie in der ambulanten Gruppentherapie von Abhängigen am Beispiel der Psychosozialen Beratungs- und Behandlungsstelle Sigmaringen*. Dissertation: Universität Klagenfurt. Unveröffentlichtes Manuskript. Summary. https://silo.tips/download/evaluation-von-psychodramatherapie-bei-abhngigen-waniczek-2003a-icd-10-f10-12-17, 13 June 2023.

Waniczek, S., Harter, K. E., & Wieser, M. (2005). Evaluation von Psychodramatherapie bei Abhängigkeitsstörungen. *Psychotherapie Forum, 13*, 12–16. https://doi.org/10.1007/s00729-005-0073-6

Wartberg, L., Kriston, L., & Thomasius, R. (2017). The prevalence and psychosocial correlates of internet gaming disorder. Analysis in a nationally representative sample of 12-to 25-year-olds. *Deutsches Ärzteblatt International, 114*, 419–424. https://doi.org/10.3238/arztebl.2017.0419
Weiner, H. B. (1965). Treating the alcoholic with psychodrama. *Group Psychotherapy, 18*, 27–49.
Wienberg, G., & Driessen, M. (Eds.) (2001). Zit. nach Körkel, J. (2002). Kontrolliertes Trinken: eine Übersicht. *Suchttherapie, 3*(6), 87–96.

# Chapter 11
# Pathological Deviant Behavior

## 11.1 Peculiarities in the Treatment of Persons with Pathological Deviant Behavior

Similar to people with addiction (see Sect. 10.5), patients with pathological deviant behavior suffer from a metacognitive confusion between healthy adult thinking and a deviant dysfunctional ego. In this case, it is the "stealing self," the "gambling self," or similar.

***Case example 130***
*Ms. B suffered from alcohol addiction. She had become abstinent with the help of a therapy group for people with addiction. Four months later, she reported to the group with shame: "I want to tell you something. But I would like this information to stay in the group!" In response, the group participants renewed their promise of confidentiality and assured that they wouldn't share information with anyone outside the group. Ms. B. said: "I have recently started stealing from department stores." She reported on seven such events: "As a manager in the public sector, I cannot afford it at all! I see this as a displacement of my addiction." The group discussion made it clear that "stealing" gave Ms. B a "kick". It was about playing with the boundaries. Ms. B. felt driven to do something crazy so that she could feel: "It worked!" She further added: "I thought I must address this openly here. Perhaps then I'll be able to stop doing that." In sharing this, the patient "openly admitted her mistakes" to the group (5th step of Alcoholics Anonymous). Five years later, she reported that she stopped stealing (ICD10: F63.2) soon after this group session. In addition, she continued to abstain from alcohol and stabilized herself mentally.*

People with pathological deviant behavior often suffer from a personality disorder or trauma-related disorder. However, their deviant behavior causes *additional secondary symptoms*, similar to Jellinek's list of addiction symptoms (see Fig. 10.1 in Sect. 10.4 and case example 108 in Sect. 10.4). Patients carry out their symptomatic behavior secretly (2nd question in Jellinek's questionnaire). They think about



R. T. Krüger, *Disorder-Specific Psychodrama Therapy in Theory and Practice*, Psychodrama in Counselling, Coaching and Education 4,
https://doi.org/10.1007/978-981-99-7508-2_11

their symptom behavior consistently (3rd question), feel guilty about their deviant behavior (5th question), avoid talking about it (6th question), use excuses to justify their behavior (8th question), and try to be completely abstinent from time to time (11th question). The patient in case example 116 (see Sect. 10.6.6) repeatedly drove to his vacation spot on his own to indulge in his acts of fetishism for days in a row (22nd question). The following symptoms can additionally appear: The patient behaves aggressively toward his environment (9th question). He has a system for when to act on his impulses and when not (12th question). His pathological deviant behavior became a compulsion for him (29th question).

## 11.2 Case Example of a Patient with Fetishistic Disorder

***Case example 131 (*Krüger & Lutz-Dreher, 2002, p. 231 ff., *Modified)***
*31-year-old Mr. A. had been married for five years and had a daughter. He was seeking treatment because, after being haunted by it for a long time, his "problem was exposed" four weeks ago. His wife had discovered lingerie in the packages he had ordered. She felt jealous at first, thinking he had a mistress. Then she feared that he might sexually abuse his own daughter. She confronted him. Eventually, she believed him that he wore the lingerie himself. With his consent, she arranged an appointment with a psychotherapist for him.*

*In the initial interview, Mr. A. reported a 'liking for lingerie'. He described his rituals of fetishism. He usually retired to a room alone. He would secretly wear women's clothes and imagine being a 17-year-old girl. As a girl, he is standing in front of an attractive middle-aged woman with a voluptuous form. The woman sternly orders him, the "girl", to wear the ugly clothes of an old woman. As a girl, he had to obey this demand. Following the orders would arouse Mr. A sexually, and he would masturbate. After such rituals, he suffered from feelings of guilt and shame.*

*Mr. A. was usually anxious, inhibited, and insecure in social contexts. He always tried to meet the expectations of his superiors, colleagues, and his wife. He tried to gain recognition through extra work to stabilize his frail self-esteem. In doing this, he would overwhelm himself. He was often exhausted. He suffered from stomach pains whenever he was under tremendous pressure at work.*

*His therapy lasted only 24 sessions (see* Sects. 11.3 *to* 11.6*). In a follow-up examination two years after the end of therapy, Mr. A. reported that he had not practiced his fetishistic acts for more than two years. He hadn't ordered any more lingerie. The disorder-specific therapy of his fetishism resolved his low self-esteem, inhibitions, and longstanding depressive symptoms (see* Sect. 11.5*). He was able to assert himself well in all his relationships. He drew clear boundaries at work, represented his point of view more convincingly, and thus gained recognition. He no longer allowed his colleagues to put all the work on him. He no longer felt overwhelmed: "I work a lot. But I enjoy that." He was also better able to assert himself toward his superior and dared to ask for a higher salary: "I outdo her. A few weeks ago, she asked if I could imagine being a manager. I want to do that,* *but not yet." Mr. A. built a new house with his wife and moved out of his in-laws' house. They fought an awful lot over there. The patient openly asked his wife about her sexual fantasies, which embarrassed her. Now, the couple enjoyed being sexually intimate more often: "My sexual idiosyncrasies have taken a back seat. These sexual feelings do surface now and then. But it helps that my wife is proactive again." At the end of the treatment, the patient said: "In therapy, it was important for me to recognize the causes. It helped that we examined the connection I made to my childhood experiences" (continuation in* Sects. 11.4 *to* 11.6*).*

## 11.3 The Psychodynamics of Patients with Pathologically Deviant Behavior

Some depth psychology-oriented therapists *immediately* try to grasp and treat the "conflicts behind the symptom" in a patient with deviant behavior. They suspect that the deviant behavior disappears when the depressive symptoms are treated therapeutically.

**Central idea**

*In the beginning*, the deviant behavior helped the patients reduce inner tensions and deal with self-esteem issues resulting from childhood deprivation or trauma. Later, however, the cause and effect are reversed. The shame and guilt resulting from the deviant behavior lead *secondarily* to depression and self-esteem disorders. The therapist should, therefore, first treat the symptom of the deviant behavior in a disorder-specific manner. The patient's depression dissolves *on its own* when he stops his deviant behavior.

The patients in case examples 131 (see Sects. 11.2 and 11.4 to 11.6) and 132 (see Sects. 11.6 and 11.7), for example, developed depressive symptoms *as a result* of their acts of fetishism. Understandably, they hid their symptoms from the outside world. Thus they ended up developing the defense mechanism of splitting. They alternated between two contrary ego states—the 'everyday logic' and the contrary 'disguise logic' (see Fig. 10.2 in Sect. 10.5). Over time, *identity confusion* arose. After all, they justified their actions to themselves with excuses and believed they were bisexual. The patient in case example 131 seriously considered sex reassignment surgery.

Sigmund Freud (1975, p. 384) interpreted acts of fetishism as substitute acts *caused by castration anxiety*: the little boy would discover that his mother does not have a penis like himself. That would trigger castration anxiety in him. The boy is afraid of losing his penis and therefore has to deny that his mother does not have a penis. He, thus, shifts his interest to the 'mother's' breasts as a substitute for a penis.

**Central idea**

Freud confused cause and effect in his interpretation of the psychodynamics of fetishism. The castration anxiety is *a consequence of fetishism and not its cause*. The boy initially *identifies* as a child when wearing women's clothes in a kind of role-play with his mother. By wearing women's underwear in the as-if mode (see Sect. 2.6), he creates the intimacy he longs for but is missing in his relationship with his mother (see case examples 131 and 132 in Sects. 11.2 and 11.4 to 11.7). But the reaction from the social environment shames him. Therefore, he begins to enact his role plays secretly. Only the concealment of the enactment gives rise to pathological defense through splitting and identity confusion.

Freud (1975, p. 224 ff.) used the example of his grandson, who was just under two years old, to describe the ability of children to process conflicts *in the as-if mode of play* (see Sect. 2.6). His grandson's mother regularly went out of the house during the day and only returned after a while. The little boy obviously didn't like that his mother separated from him *of her own will.* In response, he invented the following game: He let a spool of thread roll under a cupboard and sadly commented, "Oh". Then he pulled the thread out again and greeted the reappearance of the spool with a joyful "Aah!" Freud recognized that his little grandson was *actively* staging the separation from his mother, which had happened to him painfully *passively* at first, in a play of symbols (see Fig. 2.11 in Sect. 2.14). In doing so, the little boy controlled the painful separation *with his own will* and determined when his "mother" disappeared and when she returned to him. He developed "the aspect of the creator" (Moreno, 1970, p. 78) of his destiny by *symbolically* representing the passively suffered separation by playing with the thread spool. *In his fantasy*, he became the director in his interaction with his "mother". In doing so, he got rid of the *blocks in his fantasy* caused by the passively suffered separation.

In childhood, acts of fetishism are initially a creative solution to conflict processing. However, in adulthood, they are accompanied by shame and guilt due to the *sexualization* of latent desires for intimacy. The acts of fetishism then become self-injurious acts. Indeed, as the creator of the "game", the patient establishes closeness to his "mother"; however, after masturbating, he once again becomes the little boy who acted out a "forbidden" desire for intimacy. His shame intensifies his feelings of loneliness and worthlessness.

## 11.4 The Disorder-Specific Therapy of Pathological Deviant Behavior

A *criminal thief* has different psychodynamics than a patient who suffers from "*pathological stealing*" (F63.2) (see case example 114 (see Sect. 10.6.4). A thief exactly *plans* his criminal acts before executing them *in the as-if mode of thinking.* He strives for *real external gain* from objects, wealth, or power. Pathological stealing, however, primarily serves *internal gain.* The patient builds up a pleasurable tension before his act of theft and works it off, feeling a kick, through stealing. He thinks self-hypnotically *in equivalence mode* (see Sect. 2.6): He looks for the proper *external framework*, for example, a department store, in which he can act out his *inner fantasies* of power or potency in a kind of role-play. Thinking in the equivalence mode is the basis for pathological deviant behavior in pathological stealing (F63.2), pathological arson (F63.1), acts of fetishism (F65.0, F65.1), and also in deviant sexual behaviors (F65.2-F65.8) such as sadomasochistic practices.

**Central idea**

Pathological deviant behavior is the manifestation of a *metacognitive disorder*. A purely cognitive behavioral therapy approach is, therefore, not sufficient. Instead, the metacognitive disorder must be treated with *metacognitive therapy*. In the *disorder-specific therapy* of deviant behavior proposed here, the therapist makes the patient's metacognitive confusion the subject of therapeutic communication.

The patient acts out his pathological deviant behavior in the equivalence mode. In doing this, he precipitates himself into a hypnoid state seeking a 'kick', and believes that he has to act in a deviant manner to reach that state. In metacognitive therapy: (1) The patient separates the psychosomatic resonance pattern (see Sect. 2. 7) of his pathological deviant behavior from his healthy adult thinking. (2) He thinks through his deviant behavior as a holistic story with all consequences. (3) Internally, he *consciously alternates* between his healthy adult thinking and his psychosomatic resonance pattern of pathological deviant behavior in the as-if mode of thinking. He thus gains control of the ego over his metacognitive confusion. He mustn't become a new person. He shall only *truly feel and think* in acting in a deviant manner, and *not deceive himself* in the equivalence mode. Therefore, he must be able to remember the procedure of his deviant behavior *psychosomatically* with all consequences.

Patients with *pathological stealing* are more likely to act out grandiose desires, whereas those *with fetishism* are more likely to act masochistically. Nevertheless, the sequential *steps of metacognitive therapy* are the same. I describe them using the example of the treatment of fetishism (see case examples 131 in Sects. 11.2 to 11.6, and 132 in Sects. 11.6 and 11.7):

1. Patients with deviant behavior often justify their behavior with excuses. However, the therapist refers to this deviant behavior as "self-injurious".
2. The therapist represents the patient's two ego states involved in his metacognitive confusion in the therapy room. To do this, she sets up an additional chair *next* to the patient for his "disguise ego".
3. She explicitly interprets the deviant behavior in the second chair as "*unconscious role play*".
4. As a metacognitive doppelganger (see Sect. 4.8), the therapist asks the patient to verbally describe his own feeling, thinking, and acting in the course of a *typical fetishism ritual* or theft action from the chair of the everyday ego.
5. The therapist *represents* the person the patient interacts with in his ritual scene with an extra chair opposite the "disguise ego" in the therapy room.
6. She has the patient *shift* from the chair of his everyday ego to the chair of his "disguise ego" and *also psychosomatically* experience his disguising in the as-if mode of play.
7. The therapist lets the patient act out the interaction in his most stimulating theft scene or his most stimulating fetishism scene beyond reality *in a psychodramatic dialogue* with role reversal.

8. *In a role reversal*, the patient determines the *conflict partner's* thoughts and feelings in the fetishism scene and the motivations behind their actions. In doing this, he determines the conflict partner's specific behavior *that is arousing for him*.
9. The therapist and the patient look for a connection between this special interaction pattern and the patient's traumatic childhood experiences.
10. The therapist recommends that the patient refrains from performing his acts of fetishism for at least two months "to experience himself" and live abstinently (see case example 116 in Sect. 10.6.6). The patient should have a tangible experience of his feelings without his symptom action.
11. The therapist offers the patient the opportunity to give up his abstinence on a trial basis: "Your depression has disappeared after you stopped playing dress-up as a woman. If you miss something, *try* dressing up as a woman *again*. If you feel worse, you can stop disguising yourself again." The *conscious deviant action* helps to complete the psychosomatic resonance pattern and the holistic story of deviant behavior with all consequences, if necessary.
12. The patient chalks up an emergency plan for himself. This plan includes thinking, feeling, and acting during his personal low point and his most humiliating experience resulting from his deviant behavior.
13. The therapy phases of relapse prevention and integration *of the inner change in the current relationships* follow (see Sects. 10.6.5 to 10.6.6). Finally, if necessary, the therapist also treats the patient's underlying condition (see Sect. 10.6.7), for example, his narcissistic personality disorder (see case example 132 in Sect. 11.6 and 11.7).

***Case example 131 (1st continuation)***

*In the initial therapy sessions, Mr. A. seriously considered whether his dressing up as a "girl" meant that he "unconsciously" wanted a gender change. In the fourth therapy session, the therapist placed a second chair next to him. He pointed to the chair with his hand and said, "When you put on women's clothes, you are actually role-playing. You are creative!" The patient reacted skeptically: "Actually, I don't see it as creative. I always think I shouldn't do that and feel guilty." Nevertheless, the patient was relieved by the reinterpretation of his fetishistic behavior as role-playing.*

*In the fifth session, the therapist asked Mr. A. to freely associate a fairy tale image for further diagnosis (*Krüger, 1992, p. 230 ff.*): "Tell me the name of a fairy tale. When you think of this fairy tale, which person or figure do you see in front of you? - Please describe the current situation of this fairy tale figure! What is the person doing at the moment?" The technique of fairy tale association naturally tends to bring to mind content and images with high energy. Therefore, the associated image is usually a symbol for a patient's central conflict. For example, Mr. A. spontaneously named the fairy tale "Little Red Riding Hood": "Little Red Riding Hood goes through the forest to see her grandmother. She is wearing red shoes." The therapist: "Do you know why you thought of Little Red Riding Hood, who is on her way to see her grandmother?" Mr. A. spontaneously drew parallels between the seven-year-old Little Red Riding*

*Hood and his childhood dress-up games. Between the ages of five and nine, he and his older sister found discarded clothes that belonged to his grandmother and mother in the attic. At that time, he often dressed up with his sister and engaged in role-playing games. They would enjoy dressing up: "Back then, I was just as naive and innocent as the Little Red Riding Hood."*

*In the seventh session, the therapist asked the patient to tell him the exact sequence of a fetishism ritual. The therapist pointed his hand at the chair on which the patient was sitting across from him: "This is you as a grown man who comes home stressed out from work!" He placed a second chair for the "girl" next to the patient. He asked Mr. A. to move to the "girl's" chair. The therapist questioned the patient in the girl's role and, as a doppelganger, helped him verbalize his experience in this role. Mr. A. as the "girl": "I always imagine an attractive elderly lady with heavy makeup sitting across from me. She is the girl's mother. She is 45–50 years old, and the girl is 17 years old. Unlike the mother, the girl is unattractive, a wallflower. She behaves submissively. The mother orders the girl to wear an older woman's clothes that would make the girl look ugly and inconspicuous."*

*In the debriefing, Mr. A. noted with relief, looking at the chair next to him: "That's good! I was afraid that my urge to play dress-up as a woman was a sign that I unconsciously wanted a sex change. But," he pointed to the "girl's" chair next to him and then to himself as "man", "if I want, I can always go back to this chair and become a man again!" (Continued in Sect.* 11.5 *and* 11.6*).*

With the help of the two-chair technique, the therapist resolved the patient's identity confusion between him as the man and him as the "girl". After three years of therapy, another patient with fetishism, 50-year-old Mr. C. (case example 132 in Sects. 11.6 and 11.7), described his identity confusion with very similar words: "I used to think of dressing up as part of my personality. I thought that maybe I was bisexual and couldn't be any different. I told my wife that too. But now, after two years of abstinence, I don't believe that anymore. My wife no longer believes that either. It would insult my wife if I were to dress up again."

**Central idea**

The two-chair technique is the basis of metacognitive therapy for people with pathological deviant behavior. Using the two-chair technique, the patient perceives the second chair for his "*disguise ego*" as spatially separated *from the meta-position*. It liberates his healthy everyday self from the metacognitive confusion with his "disguise ego". In addition, the psychodramatic role change between the two identities allows the patient to experience the contrary logic of his two opposing identities, psychosomatically and mentally separate from each other.

## 11.5 Developing Deviant Behavior into a Holistic Story

**Central idea**

The patient thinks in the equivalence mode when engaging in pathological deviant behaviors (see Sect. 2.6). He realizes his *inner* fantasy in his *external* action. However, the *external* reality does *not* adapt to the imagination. As a result, the patient's *inner* fantasy remains fragmented. The patient continuously needs the scenic stimulus of *real external objects* to activate his fantasies.

The therapist understands the patient's deviant behavior as an *unfinished* story. She let the patient think through the course of his deviant behavior *in the as-if mode of play* (see Sect. 11.4). The patient consistently shapes the reality, the logic, and the meaning (see Fig. 2.5 in Sect. 2.3) in the scene of his pathological behavior with the help of the therapist as a metacognitive doppelganger. In doing this, he completes the narration of his deviant behavior with its consequences. He learns to think of his symptomatic behavior in the as-if mode. It liberates him from the need to *act out* his deviant behavior in equivalence mode *using objects in the external world*. He can detach it from the *external* objects, such as the paraphernalia of disguise as a woman, and *only fantasize* about the disguise scene. The *external* shame-inducing situations fall away.

***Case example 131 (2nd continuation)***

*The therapist and Mr. A. understood the patient's fetishistic behavior as "role-playing" and resolved his metacognitive confusion with the two-chair technique. In the sixth therapy session, Mr. A said: While masturbating, "I no longer have the urge to put on women's clothes. Instead, I only fantasize about dressing up."*

*In the eighth therapy position, the therapist said to the patient: "I would like to understand what goes on in you when you wear women's clothes. What was it like the last time you did that?" The patient and the therapist set up the scene of his inner imagination with chairs in the therapy room. It consists of one chair for the patient as an adult man, a second chair next to him representing him as the submissive "girl", and the third chair opposite for the "mother". Mr. A. changes to the role of the "girl". On a table between his "disguise ego" and his "mother" lay "women's clothes". The patient: "The mother orders me to wear these clothes". The therapist gives the "mother" a voice: "Put these clothes on!" Mr. A. defends himself as the "girl": "But I don't want to wear them!" As the "girl", however, the patient finally gives in: "The girl is sulking a little now". The patient finds it difficult to act like he is sulking: "I can't do that!" The therapist lets the patient change into the role of "mother". As an auxiliary ego, he takes on the girl's role and plays her according to the patient's instructions. In the role of "mother", the patient commands with great delight and authority: "You must wear these clothes now! Otherwise, you can't get out of here!" The therapist stands up, stands next to the patient, and asks the "Mother" curiously: "What do you want to achieve by ordering the girl to wear these women's clothes?" "Mother": "I always want the girl with me. I want the girl to accompany me when I meet my friends for coffee." The therapist: "Just look at the girl! Do you see that the girl enjoys pretending as if she obeys you?" The patient as "mother": "Oh that's not good at all!" In the debriefing, the patient describes the "mother's" behavior towards the girl as "sadistic". The therapist: "Yes, she is dominating! But the 'mother' is afraid that the 'girl' might leave her!"*

*When sharing his history at the beginning of therapy, Mr. A. said he was the youngest of three children. He'd always been a good boy. There was always work at home. His father had been a craftsman and also managed a small farm. His mother had little time and was always busy: "That's why my mother locked me in a crib when I was two and three years old. She would leave me screaming in there." Mr. A. was a "model student" in his first two years at school. But, he usually got the short end of the stick in the scuffles. That's why he learned judo. He wanted to be able to defend himself better. As a teenager, he was shy and inhibited, especially around girls. He moved out of his parent's house at 21 because he "no longer wanted to be a child". His mother was very disappointed at the time and broke down mentally.*

*After enacting the fetishism scene, the therapist drew the patient's attention to the connection between his "dressing up" and his childhood experiences: "Mr. A., when you moved out of home, your mother was disappointed and broke down. In your fetishism scene, the mother also wants the girl not to leave her. The girl should therefore dress ugly." The patient: "Yes, the way you say it makes it clearer to me now." The therapist: "Mr. A., are you also submissive in other relationships?" Mr. A.: "Yes, if my supervisor arrives with additional work shortly before the end of work hours, then I always stay back and complete it. But I don't want to do that at all. I then act like the girl." At the end of the session, the patient said: "It is quite incredible to role-play in the disguising scene and go further beyond reality." Three weeks later, the patient reported with astonishment: "I now am much better at managing different areas of my life. I can draw much better boundaries in relationships."*

## 11.6 Fetishistic Acts as Masochistic Behavior

***Case example 131 (3rd continuation, see Sects. 11.2, 11.4 and 11.5)***
*In the 21st session, the therapist lets Mr. A. visualize his fantasy contained in the acts of fetishism one more time with chairs in the therapy room: "Imagine the interaction between the daughter and the mother again. Do you notice that you always determine what you play when you dress up and that you are the director of the process?" The patient is amazed: "Then I'm holding the strings in my hand!" Therapist: "That's right!" Mr. A.: "Yes, I have always enjoyed being able to control my imagination when in the role of the girl!" The therapist: "When was the first time you experienced someone ordering you, like the mother in your dress-up game, and you felt very ashamed in the end?" Mr. A.: "As a child. We had little money. So I had to put on my sister's discarded red boots. At first, only at home, I wasn't ashamed of that. But then I also had to wear them outside. The other children laughed at me. That's when I realized that I was wearing girls' shoes!" The patient also had to wear his older sister's clothes as a child. His mother would insist even though Mr. A. protested as a boy. Finally, she threatened that his father would punish him if he didn't obey.*

*The therapist and the patient together represent the patient's childhood conflict system with different chairs in the therapy room. They set up a chair for the patient himself as a boy, another for his older sister, one for his mother, one for his father, and a little further away, some chairs for the children who laughed at him. When looking at the family system, the patient spontaneously says: "At that time, my mother held the strings in her hand." The therapist: "That's true. But, as an adult, you are now harming yourself, just like your mother used to, by playing dress-up. You don't even need your mother for harming yourself anymore!"*

**Central idea**

Patients with fetishism act masochistically. Mr. A. was unaware that he repeatedly re-enacted his childhood trauma through his acts of fetishism. In doing this, as a director, he initiated the events and carried them out *of his own will.* Disguised as a girl, he obeyed the 'elder woman', similarly as he obeyed his mother in childhood, but defied her secretly and, thus, became sexually aroused. Afterward, however, he felt embarrassed in the presence of his attachment figures, just as he did in the presence of his classmates when he was a little boy. Masochism is "a cry for empathy" (Rohde-Dachser, 1976, oral communication).

The disorder-specific method described in case example 131 (see Sect. 11.2 to 11.6) was also the basis for the therapy of the patient in the following case example:

***Case example 132***
*50-year-old Mr. C. sought psychotherapy because of chronic depression (F34.1 and F65.1). His acts of fetishism were so closely interwoven with his sense of identity that he subjectively did not understand them as symptoms of illness. In the 7th session, the therapist placed a second chair next to the patient for his "disguise ego" and asked him: "What does a dress-up game include for you so that everything feels emotionally right for you?" Mr. C. described the scene: Wearing white tights and a white bra, he sat down with it in front of a mirror and moved erotically. The reflection in the mirror aroused him sexually, and he used it for masturbation. The therapist asked curiously: "Can you also see your head in the mirror?" Mr. C. was amazed and irritated: "I don't know!" The therapist: "Then please try it out at home!" In the following therapy session, the patient said: "No, of course, I can't see my face! Otherwise, I wouldn't see a woman in the mirror!' The therapist asked the patient to switch to the chair of his 'disguise ego' and enact the scene with the 'woman in white' in a psychodramatic dialogue. During the role reversal, Mr. C. felt only emptiness in the role of the 'woman in white' (continued in* Sect. 11.7*).*

The patient's fetishism scene was also consistent with his childhood experiences with his mother. She was the epitome of beauty. His father admired her and fulfilled all her wishes. He shielded her from all conflict. Once, as a boy, Mr. C. had been in a Boy Scout camp. His mother visited him there. She was wearing all white. Then all the boys ran up to him and adored her for her beauty. But, when Mr. C. approached his mother to greet her, she refused to hug him. As a boy, Mr. C. *couldn't reach his mother*. The therapist: "You couldn't get a foot in the door with your parents!" The patient: "I was always nice as a child. But my intentions never counted!" Like Mr. A. (see case example 131 in Sects. 11.2 and 11.4 to 11.6), Mr. C. had been playing dress-up with his mother's clothes since *the age of seven*. In this way, he felt close to his unavailable mother. Symbolically, he self-injuriously re-enacted his childhood trauma through his acts of fetishism.

The patients in case examples 131 and 132 (see Sects. 11.2 and 11.4 to 11.7) had varied their acts of fetishism over the years. In Mr. A.'s symptomatic actions, for example, the "little girl" sometimes faced a strict 50-year-old aunt. She tied her hair in a bun like a teacher. Or the "girl was younger than 17" and met a 45-year-old "strict stepmother". Or the patient played a "younger, disobedient sister" who had to obey a "strict, older sister" in his fetishism ritual.

## 11.7 Importance of Abstinence from Deviant Behavior for Inner Mental Transformation

Like people with substance addiction, some patients with *pathological deviant behavior* become *dependent* on their symptom behavior (see Sects. 10.2 and 11.3). 50-year-old Mr. C. (see case example 132 in Sect. 11.6 and below) practiced his acts of fetishism from the age of seven for *forty-three long years*. His treatment lasted five years because of his chronic symptoms and his narcissistic deficit experiences in childhood. Before treatment, the patient firmly believed that he was bisexual. He had also convinced his wife of the same. Nevertheless, their marriage always had conflicts because of his "secrecy". During an argument, his emotionally dynamic wife insulted him: "You are selfish!" "You are not social." "Don't be so rude!" "You are hysterical!" His wife's devaluations hurted the patient. But they also served as a justification to himself for his retreat into acts of fetishism. In the "disguise world", *he* was the director of the events. Nobody criticized him. He could, as it were, make the puppets dance: "I'll recover then." Mr. C. lived together with his wife and children. But he had no friends.

***Case example 132 (continued)***
*In this case, too, the therapist first treated the patient's metacognitive confusion with the help of the two-chair technique. Unlike the patient in case example 131 (see Sects.* 11.2 *and* 11.4 *to* 11.6*), who was twenty years younger, Mr. C. did not spontaneously stop his fetishism rituals. Therefore, after a year, the therapist recommended: "Please, try not to dress up in women's clothing for six months! Do it to experience how you feel without dressing up!" His attempt at abstinence changed Mr. C.'s life decisively. After only a week, he reported that "Two days ago, I packed all my women's clothing in a suitcase and took them to the loft. But now I am aggressive towards all sorts of people." After nine days of abstinence, he said in astonishment: "I am no longer so afraid and have no guilty conscience. I didn't even know I was capable of feeling this way! However, I am also missing something. Earlier, I always had something to do. But if my wife drives away now, I will miss her! I am not so offended anymore. I take more interest in people and am more lively!" After sixteen days of abstinence, Mr. C. felt: "I am happier and more alert. I often have a smile on my face. Work was often excruciating for me in the past, but now it doesn't bother me so much. I also sleep more with my wife. I have more fun now. I think I took a lot away from my life by dressing up. Earlier, I used to think that dressing up gave me a lot! That was the purpose of my life. Withdrawing and disguising were like a port. It had something pleasant, something protective, something calm. But I don't start it anymore. I'm going out of the house more now. Everything is more interesting!*

*I'm even better at tennis now." After eight weeks of abstinence, Mr. C. said: "I feel more now. I feel the pressure at work and then the exhaustion. As a manager, I have become more aggressive towards my people. I am less conflict-averse and clearer. I recently said to an apprentice: 'Your mere presence is not enough for me, you have to do something!' My colleagues have already noticed the change in me. I used to be scared of being looked at by people. I was deliberately generous to them because I thought: 'If I am nice to them, they will not judge me later when they discover my dressing up.' I am no longer afraid!"*

*The patient had invested a lot of time and energy in planning and hiding his fetishistic acts, inventing explanations, and pushing away feelings of shame and guilt. After ceasing his acts of fetishism, he felt truly free for the first time in his life. He developed new interests. He learned to face conflicts in his everyday life and take more space in his relationships. Sometimes the patient found his life exhausting. The therapist then offered: "If you want, try dressing up again! Then you will discover whether it increases your positive attitude towards life, as you used to believe. Or whether it will get worse again. You can then stop doing it again!" However, Mr. C. did not want to lose the "new life energy". He was continuously "abstinent" during the last four years of psychotherapy. However, his improved self-esteem led to massive conflicts in his relationship with his wife. His wife had been codependent. After her husband started being abstinent, she also started psychotherapy. At the end of the treatment, Mr. C. and his wife developed a lively relationship and dealt with conflicts as equals. The patient bought his dream car and also made friends with men.*

## References

Freud, S. (1975). *Psychologie des Unbewussten.* Studienausgabe Bd. 3. Frankfurt a. M.: Fischer-Verlag.

Krüger, R. T. (1992). Der Märchen-Assoziationstest. *Psychodrama, 5*(2), 229–238.

Krüger, R. T., & Lutz-Dreher, D. (2002). Zur störungsspezifischen psychodramatischen Behandlung von Fetischismus und Masochismus. Kreativität als Ressource in der Psychotherapie. *Zeitschrift für Psychodrama und Soziometrie, 1*(2), 231–252.

Moreno, J. L. (1970). Das Stegreiftheater (2nd ed.). Beacon, N. Y.: Beacon House. Original work published 1923, Potsdam, Berlin: Gustav Kiepenheuer.

# Bibliography


Klüwer, R. (1983). Agieren und Mitagieren. *Psyche – Zeitschrift für Psychoanalyse und ihre Anwendung, 37*, 828–840.

Krüger, R. T. (2002). Psychodrama als Aktionsmethode in der Traumatherapie und ihre Begründung mit der Rollentheorie und der Kreativitätstheorie. *Zeitschrift für Psychodrama und Soziometrie, 1*(2), 117–146. https://doi.org/10.1007/s11620-002-0016-y

Rogers, C. R. (2009). *Eine Theorie der Psychotherapie*. Ernst Reinhardt.

Sturm, I. (2009). »Elisabeth« – Drehbuch für die Präsentation einer Kasuistik. Zur Anerkennung des Psychodramas in der Schweiz. *Zeitschrift für Psychodrama und Soziometrie, 8*(1), 120–140.

Ziem-Kossatz, H. (2013). 20-Minuten-Psychodrama in der allgemeinmedizinischen Sprechstunde. Das Doppeln in der psychotherapeutischen Beratung. *Zeitschrift für Psychodrama und Soziometrie, 12*(2), 263–267. https://doi.org/10.1007/s11620-013-0199-4




R. T. Krüger, *Disorder-Specific Psychodrama Therapy in Theory and Practice*, Psychodrama in Counselling, Coaching and Education 4,
https://doi.org/10.1007/978-981-99-7508-2

# Author Index


**A**
Aaltonen, Jukka, 396
Allen, Jon G., 13
Ameln, Falko von, 12
Amrein, Luzia, 414, 421
Andersen, Hans Christian, 519
Arntz, Arnoud, 94, 132–135, 160, 351
Auchter, Thomas, 405

**B**
Baim, Clark, 250, 255–257
Bakhit, Christiane, 247
Balint, Michael, 43, 377, 391
Bannister, Anne, 250, 254
Bateman, Anthony W., 13
Bekoff, Marc, 50
Bender, Wolfram, 398, 449, 450
Benedetti, Gaetano, 386, 388, 425
Benzinger, Hans, 500, 501
Beuys, Joseph, 391
Blanck, Gertrude, 50
Blanck, Rubin, 50
Blatner, Adam, 69, 343
Bleckwedel, Jan, 94
Bleuler, Manfred, 386, 388
Bode, Sabine, 342
Böker, Heinz, 396
Bonhoeffer, Dietrich, 203
Brockmann, Josef, 13, 43
Buer, Ferdinand, 12, 76
Burbridge, Jennifer, 209
Burge, Michael, 202, 227, 250
Burmeister, Jörg, 215, 226, 250, 257, 258

**C**
Caesar, Julius, 521
Caro, Tim, 50
Casson, John, 447
Cattanach, Ann, 94
Chesner, Anna, 94
Ciompi, Luc, 8, 11, 15, 48, 49, 386, 393, 394, 474
Csáky-Pallavicini, Krisztina, 163, 239, 242, 329
Czigány, László, 62, 108

**D**
Damasio, António, 45, 50
Daniel, Sue, 64
Dayton, Tian, 215, 250
Dieckmann, Hans, 66, 233
Diener, Gottfried, 403
Domes, Martin, 80
Drees, Alfred, 450
Drews, Robert, 320
Driessen, Martin, 460
Dührssen, Annemarie, 31, 36, 371
Dulit, R.A., 460
Dürckheim, Karlfried Graf, 3, 157, 203, 375, 378, 394, 491

**E**
Edwards, Griffith, 489
Eleftery, Dean, 398
Elrod, Norman, 386
Escher, Sandra, 432
Ewald, Matthias, 448




R. T. Krüger, *Disorder-Specific Psychodrama Therapy in Theory and Practice*, Psychodrama in Counselling, Coaching and Education 4,
https://doi.org/10.1007/978-981-99-7508-2

**F**
Ferenczi, Sándor, 22, 317
Fonagy, Peter, 12, 13, 43, 44, 46, 51, 392
Fooken, Insa, 203
Frede, Ursula, 346
Freud, Anna, 29, 317, 318
Freud, Sigmund, 25, 33, 390, 391, 395, 396, 535
Frith, Chris, 395
Fuhr, Ulla, 127, 228, 366

**G**
Gallus, Peter, 457, 461
Gandhi, Mahatma, 60, 339
Garde, Timm, 450
Gast, Ursula, 187
Genderen, Hannie van, 132–135, 351
Gendlin, Eugene T., 363
Gergeley, György, 392
Gerstenberg, Wolfgang, 398
Giesen-Bloo, Josephine, 123
Ginn, Ildri, 254
Goethe, Johann Wolfgang von, 403, 404
Goldmann, Elaine E., 34
Grande, Tilman, 102
Grawe, Klaus, 81
Greenson, Ralph R., 26
Grimmer, Karl, 164, 206, 271, 280, 291, 292
Grimm, Jacob, 275
Grimm, Wilhelm, 275
Groterath, Angelika, 467
Grube, Michael, 395
Gunkel, Stefan, 111, 184, 185

**H**
Habel, Ute, 395
Hahnemann, Samuel, 19
Harrision, Patricia, 460
Harter, Klaus Ernst, 77, 461
Hartmann, Ernest, 238
Hartwich, Peter, 388, 389, 395, 426
Heibach, Eva, 387, 425
Heigl-Evers, Annelise, 69, 71, 81, 172, 245, 247, 275
Heigl, Franz, 172, 245, 247, 275
Hiller, Wolfgang, 460, 461, 485, 511
Hillmann, James, 169
Hintermeier, Sonja, 460, 501, 512, 517
Hirsch, Mathias, 183, 234
Hitler, Adolf, 397
Hochreiter, Karoline, 86
Holmes, Paul, 12
Hudgins, Mary K., 87, 226, 249
Hüther, Gerald, 187

**J**
Janssen, Paul, 102
Jellinek, Elvin Morton, 463
Jennings, Sue, 94
Jurist, Elliot L., 392

**K**
Kämmerer, Wolfgang, 130
Kamphovener, Marie Luise von, 19, 515
Karp, Marcia, 209, 215, 221, 222, 224, 227, 250, 252
Kast, Verena, 349
Kellermann, Peter, 12, 69, 164, 203, 206, 208, 215, 221, 226, 227, 249–252
Kernberg, Otto F., 118, 119
Kern, Sabine, 457
Kirsch, Holger, 13, 43
Klein, Ulf, 94
Klosko, Janet S., 112, 160
Klüwer, Rolf, 66
Kollenbaum, Carmen, 303
König, Karl, 26, 245
König, Oliver, 69
Körkel. Joachim, 461
Krakow, Barry, 239, 242
Kraus, Ludwig, 460
Kriz, Christoph, 2, 10, 101
Künzel, Jutta, 512

**L**
Lauterbach, Matthias, 94
Lesemann, Klaus, 227
Leutz, Grete, 11, 12, 16, 77, 79, 86, 159, 209, 227, 290, 291, 493
Lewin, Kurt, 184
Liebel-Frazer, Ingeborg, 94
Lincoln, Tania, 387, 425
Llosa, Mario Vargas, 238
Lorenzer, Alfred, 15

**M**
Mahler, Gustav, 3
Marineau, René F., 15, 46
Markowitsch, Hans, 224
Marlok, Zsuzsa, 62, 108
Martos, Tomás, 62, 108
Mathias, Ulrike, 86

Meldrum, Brenda, 94
Mentzos, Stavros, 102, 111–113, 117, 183, 190, 210, 268, 269, 271, 289, 295, 309, 369, 388, 393, 394, 419
Miller, William R., 460
Mitchell, Steve, 94
Mitscherlich, Alexander, 25
Mitscherlich, Margarete, 25
Möhring, Marén, 518
Moreno, Jacob Levy, 1, 3, 7, 11, 12, 16, 19, 23, 28, 40, 42, 44, 46, 49–51, 65, 73, 74, 76, 86, 88, 89, 144, 206, 280, 288, 289, 320, 321, 339, 371, 386, 395–401, 406, 423, 431, 434, 435, 445, 446, 449, 483, 493, 536
Moreno, Zerka, 16, 76
Morgenstern, Christian, 25, 120
Morschitzky, Hans, 269

N
Neraal, Terje, 387, 394
Nowack, Nicolas, 387, 399

O
Oberbracht, Claudia, 102
Ott, Jürgen, 172, 245, 247

P
Parin, Paul, 35, 132, 310
Pellegrini, Anthony D., 51
Pellis, Sergio M., 50
Pennebaker, James, 62
Pesso, Albert, 94, 281
Petzold, Hilarion, 86, 94
Pfeiffer-Gerschel, Tim, 512
Plassmann, Reinhard, 17, 23, 363, 395, 401, 442
Pörtner, Paul, 209
Powell, Andrew, 21, 152
Prometheus, 47, 144
Pruckner, Hildegard, 131, 226
Putnam, Frank W., 115, 186
Putzke, Michael, 389

R
Radebold, Hartmut, 203
Reddemann, Luise, 181, 186, 187, 191, 202, 208, 221, 239, 242, 460
Red, Hans, 387, 389, 404, 427
Reimer, Christian, 372
Richter, Horst E., 275
Ringel, Erwin, 372
Rogers, Carl, 310
Rohde-Dachser, Christa, 120, 135, 347, 542
Roine, Eva, 209, 227, 250, 253
Romme, Marius, 432
Rost, Christine, 205
Rothfeld, Alfred, 430
Roth, Gerhard, 48
Rudolf, Gerd, 42, 102, 113, 119, 121, 131
Rüger, Ulrich, 172, 245, 247
Runge, Gudrun, 413

S
Sabelli, Hector, 10
Sáfrán, Zsófia, 163, 239, 240, 242
Sattelberger, Ruth, 138
Schacht, Michael, 7, 10, 42–45, 86, 92, 268, 365
Schäfer, Ingo, 460
Scharnhorst, Ursula, 127
Schattenhofer, Karl, 69
Schiepek, Günter, 50, 90
Schiller, Friedrich, 12
Schindler, Raoul, 70, 73, 75, 85, 399
Schmidt, Henning, 460
Schneider, Frank, 395, 460
Schrenker, Leonhard, 281
Schulte-Herbrüggen, Olaf, 188
Schulte-Markwort, Michael, 11
Schützenberger-Ancelin, Anne, 16
Schwarz, Frank, 404
Schwehm, Helmut, 88, 89, 474
Séchehaye, Marguerite, 386, 404
Seidel, Ulrich, 12
Seikkula, Jaakko, 396
Selman, Robert L., 42
Shengold, Leonhard, 474
Siebel, Ute, 450
Siirala, Martii, 386
Simpson, Tracy L., 460
Smith, Ruth S., 11
Socrates, 78, 84
Spoormaker, Victor, 447
Spring, Bonnie, 393
Stadler, Christian, 398, 449, 501, 512
Stangier, Klaus, 286
Stasch, Michael, 102
Stelzig, Menfred, 86
Steppan, Martin, 461, 512
Stickgold, Robert, 391
Stimmer, Franz, 467

Straub, Heike, 1, 76, 290, 304–306, 396, 444, 449
Streek, Ulrich, 516
Sturm, Ingrid, 17

T
Tarda, Gabi, 246
Target, Mary, 392
Thomae, Helmut, 30
Thunberg, Greta, 394
Török, Gábor, 62, 108

V
van der Hart, Onno, 209
van der Kolk, Bessel A., 45, 186, 187, 207, 209, 215, 231
van Genderen, Hannie, 94, 160
Vygotsky, Lew, 44

W
Waldheim-Auer, Bettina, 77, 460, 461, 474, 495, 496, 502, 509
Wamsley, Erin, 391
Waniczek, Sabine, 77, 461, 508
Wartberg, Lutz, 524
Watkins, Helen, 115
Watkins, John G., 115
Weiner, Hannah B., 508
Weishaar, Majorie E., 112, 160
Wells, Adrian, 114
Werner, Emmy E., 11
Wicher, Monika, 92
Wienberg, Günther, 460
Wieser, Michael, 77, 461
Wilber, Ken, 347
Wilkinson, Richard, 263, 264
Winnicott, Donald, 51, 405
Wittchen, Hans-Ulrich, 188
Wolf, Hans Ulrich, 184
Wurmser, Léon, 88, 187, 198, 216, 439

Y
Yablonsky, Lewis, 40, 371
Yalom, Irvin, 380
Young, Jeffrey E., 112, 160

Z
Ziehm-Kossatz, Heidrun, 316
Zilch-Purucker, Birgit, 139
Zubin, Joseph, 393

# Subject Index


**A**

Abandoned child
  ego state, 134
Abstinence
  alcohol addiction, 461, 477, 485
  attitude, 424
  decision, 478, 494, 503
Abuse
  narcissistical, 129
  physical, 186, 191, 245, 255, 277
  sexual, 186, 253–255, 257, 306
Act out, 119, 120, 141
Acute stress reaction, 265
Adaptation, 51
  defense, 35, 268, 271–273, 278, 279, 310, 492
Addiction disorders
  abstinence, 461, 477, 489, 490, 503
  addiction memory, 467
  chronic dependence, 485
  co-dependence, 498, 527
  cognitive behavioral therapy, 476
  definition, 457–459
  depression, 460, 499, 522, 524
  diagnose, 456–458, 462
  dry drinking, 465
  emergency plan, 496, 501, 514
  excessive drinking, 459, 470
  existential experience, 487
  explicit metacognitive therapy, 474, 476
  gambling, 516
  group therapy, 77, 508, 511
  harmful use, 458, 473
  ideal addiction scene, 514
  internet gaming, 525
  level drinking, 459, 470
  loss of control, definition, 458, 466
  medication, 497
  metacognitive confusion, 463, 474, 476
  non-substance related, 513
  personality disorder, 460
  post-traumatic growth, 488, 491, 496
  pre-abuse syndrome, 494
  psychodramatic responding, 507
  psychodynamic, 168, 473, 474, 513
  psychosomatic resonance circuit, 482
  relapse, 465
  rock bottom, 378, 490, 496, 503
  secondary trauma, 459, 471, 474, 502
  self-help group, 488, 528
  self-regulation circle, 499
  sex addiction, 521
  steps of therapy, 477, 498
  surrender, 491, 492
  therapeutic relationship, 462
  trauma disorder, 186, 460
  treatment, 88
  two chair technique, 468, 482, 483, 485, 498, 504
  weaning phase, 523
  withdrawal, 487, 488
Addictive ego state, 459, 486
Adolescent, 340
Adult ego state, 280
Affect
  psychosomatic resonance circuit, 21, 23, 25, 40, 48, 49, 54, 58, 115, 146, 155, 166, 190, 201, 205, 208, 209, 227, 266, 278, 289, 300, 311, 315, 322, 325, 326, 406, 423, 435
  psychosomatic resonance pattern, 23, 34
  psychsomatic resonance circuit, 482




R. T. Krüger, *Disorder-Specific Psychodrama Therapy in Theory and Practice*, Psychodrama in Counselling, Coaching and Education 4,
https://doi.org/10.1007/978-981-99-7508-2

Agoraphobia, 269, 275
Alcoholics Anonymous, 378, 458, 465, 476, 485, 488
  24-hour rule, 487, 495
  rules of life, 492, 503
  satisfying abstinence, 492
  twelfe steps, 239, 493
All-identity, 44
Alpha position, 71, 73, 85
  definition, 70
  fighting omega position, 71
  of therapist, 85
Amplification
  definition, 38, 315
  practice, 38, 274, 327, 377, 515
  practise, 158
Anorexia nervosa, 394
  metacognitive therapy, 518
Antisocial, 202
Anxiety disorder
  addiction, 486
  chair work, 278–280
  cognitive therapy, 292
  countertransference, 287
  crisis intervention, 287
  defense, 268, 271
  diagnose, 267, 268
  frequency, 269
  generalized, 269
  metacognitive therapy, 272, 273, 276, 279, 289, 292
  negative transference, 272
  psychodynamic, 265, 272, 273
  self-protective behavior, 274, 276
  steps of therapy, 272, 279
  structural disorder, 287
  trauma, 203, 279
As-if mode of play, 12, 65, 82
  definition, 44
  obsessive-compulsive disorder, 299
  personality disorder, 125, 126, 143, 146
  psychosis, 445
  self-development, 289
  trauma disorder, 201
As-if mode of thinking, 44, 51
  definition, 44
  personality disorder, 144
Attunement and agreement process, 40, 69, 78, 102, 130
Authoritarian system
  religious, 132
Auto-tele, 395, 396
  psychosis, 445
Auxiliary ego, 11, 78, 79
  contraindication, 337
  definition, 1
  de-rolling, 79
  group therapy, 257
  puppetry, 444
  therapist as, 124, 137, 280, 324, 336, 345, 351, 397, 401, 431
  trauma processing, 223, 231
Auxiliary reality, 395
Auxiliary world method, 43, 397, 398, 404, 445, 446
  definition, 430
  doppelganger, 432
  indication, 446
  practicing, 432
  steps, 431
  theory, 434
  therapeutic effect, 431, 437

**B**

Bacteriophobia, 290
Basic human fears, 3, 203
Beacon, 1, 386, 396, 397, 449
Behavior addiction
  abstinence, 543
  fetishism, 543
  psychodynamic, 535
  steps of therapy, 537
Behavioral psychodrama, 304, 305
Behavioral therapy, 2, 76, 255, 290
  addicition, 490
  anxiety disorder, 289
  cognitive, 4, 292
  metacognitive, 4
  role play, 290
  third wave, 4
  trauma disorder, 181
Beta position, 75, 81, 84, 85
  definition, 70
  of therapist, 85
Bipolar affective disorder, 369, 395
Bomb attack, 250
Borderline personality disorder, 47, 134, 141
  addiction, 524
  countertransference, 117, 151
  definition, 117
  diagnose, 120, 415
  ego states, 21, 62, 118, 119, 134
  equivalence mode, 150
  psychodynamic, 111, 117–120, 149, 153

psychotic episode, 177
symptoms, 111
therapeutic relationship, 120, 150
trauma disorder, 186
treatment, 111, 122, 127, 141, 150, 167, 175, 177, 433
Bulimia, 185, 208
metacognitive therapy, 518
Bullying, 113, 141
Burnout
therapist, 249

C
Cannabis addiction, 512
Capitulation mentally, 377
*see* surrender, 494
Caritas, 489
Catharsis, 11
crying, 364
integrative, 217, 224, 251, 257, 320, 364
laughing, 152, 339, 397, 431, 440, 476, 504
Causality-organization, 321
Chair work, 3, 62, 89
anxiety disorder, 278–280, 287
effects, 148, 193
personality disorder, 136, 138
practicing, 279
theory, 144
Chaos theory, 365
Character trait, 112
definition, 116
ego state, 114
treatment, 116, 144
Child
abandoned, 119, 120, 132, 133, 516
angry, 119, 276
ego state, 156, 280
healthy, 219, 305
hospital trauma, 206
inner, definition, 133
traumatized, 119, 130, 133, 156, 175, 189, 193, 196, 197, 200, 201, 234, 236, 244, 274, 279, 298, 516
unwanted, 114
Childhood development, 43–45, 51, 393
Children therapy, 28, 51, 305
coping story, 406
ego strength, 406
trauma disorder, 254
Child traumatized
personality disorder, 133
Christian Bible, 330
Circular questioning, 53
Climate crisis, 9, 394
Coaching, 76, 104–107
Co-dependence
definition, 498, 527
treatment, 527
Cognition
strengthen, 362
Cognitive behavioral therapy, 54, 160, 255, 537
addiction, 476, 496, 513, 519
psychosis, 387, 425, 426
Cognitive therapy, 87
personality disorder, 148
psychodrama, 87, 88, 90, 92, 148
Coherence, sense of, 443
Communication training, 174
Compassion, 246, 424
Complexity, 7
conflict processing, 10, 149
inner structures, 10, 49
Compulsive actions, 295, 301
Condensation, 43
Conflict
actual, 102
neurotic, 103
Conflict processing
aspects, 9
as perpetrator, 256
creative process, 17, 101
qualities, 102, 106, 107
Conscience
absolute, 375, 377
childlike, 375, 394
community, 375, 394, 520
transpersonal, 158, 394, 478, 490
Constellation work, 138, 139, 144, 160, 161
cognitive, 148
metacognitive, 148
practicing, 148, 160
Control of ego
psychosis, 446
spontaneity, 445
Cooperation, 9, 59, 60, 62
role reversal, 9, 330
therapist and patient, 18
Coping fairy tale, 204, 387
group therapy, 242
personality disorder, 164
practicing, 236, 240, 241, 245, 348
Coping story, 540
Counceling

plan, 154
Counseling, 62, 104, 106–108
addiction, 463
a family, 53
a team, 53
diagnose, 106
plan, 104, 191
practicing, 53
Countertransference
addiction, 483, 504, 520
anxiety disorder, 272, 287
character-related, 120, 147
definition, 66
depressive disorder, 328
disintegration-related, 388, 389, 437
masochism, 349, 354
metacognitive, 483, 504
personality disorder, 140, 142, 161
psychosis, 389, 407, 439
resolving, 61, 64, 69, 147, 171
trauma disorder, 181, 191, 193, 224, 226, 243, 245
Couple therapy, 334
mutual neurotic allergy, 234, 333
negative transference, 234, 333
psychodramatic dialogue, 234
separation, 234
Creative ego
definition, 50
development, 273
Creative human, 1, 3, 13, 49, 60, 81, 82, 102
definition, 2
neurophysiology, 49
Creative leap, 490
Creative process, 10
conflict processing, 17
of play, 16
phases, 7, 8
Creator
aspect in his own life, 47, 89, 93, 123, 189, 205, 431, 536
Crisis intervention, 126, 172, 287
personality disorder, 113, 126, 170
psychosis, 413, 415, 427, 449
rampage, 252
suicide fantasy, 373–376, 379, 381
trauma disorder, 172, 194, 196, 199–201
Cultural atom, 140, 148, 160

**D**

Death
encounter, 203
fear of, 346
Debriefing
child therapy, 254
psychotic disorder, 397, 398
trauma disorder, 214
Defense
adaptation, 273
definition, 7, 19, 65, 112, 332
denial, 198, 268, 271
positive function in self-regulation, 143
resolving, 319
rigid, 62
splitting, 198, 396
through grandiosity, 116, 142, 271, 273, 355
Defense mechanism
definition, 19, 20
eight central, 17
psychosomatic resonance pattern, 278
Defense system, 271, 358
anxiety disorder, 268, 271
definition, 154, 156
personality disorder, 154
Delusion
depth psychological meaning, 392
grandeur, 412, 432, 438, 442
Jesus, 393
persecution, 431, 432
Delusional scene
definition, 416
Denial
addiction disorder, 467, 483, 516
defense, 88, 119, 131, 149, 270, 272
definition, 24, 120, 131
dissolving, 25, 26, 211, 311, 327
trauma disorder, 187, 191
Dependence
definition, 457, 459
Depersonalization, 186, 187, 191, 392, 439
Depressive disorder, 47
addiction, 460, 486, 499, 522, 524
diagnose, 313
group therapy, 337
medication, 370
neurotic development, 317, 319
pathological deviant behavior, 534
psychodynamic, 309, 310, 314, 317, 318
self-development, 310
severe, 167, 175, 312, 442
structural conflict, 311–313, 368
symptoms, 309
trauma disorder, 203, 252

Depth psychological therapy, 2, 65, 272, 273, 296, 302, 358, 477, 490, 502
addiction, 476
pathological deviant behavior, 535
psychosis, 424
Derealization, 186, 187, 222
De-rolling, 79
Desensitization, 289, 290
Detachment conflict, 286
Diagnose, 61, 63, 102
psychodramatic, 52
structural, 102
Dignity human, 490
Directing style, 65, 77
abstinent, 81, 424
directive, 74, 331, 424
individual-focused, 84
system-focused, 81, 84
Director
alpha position, 72, 73, 75, 81
beta position, 72, 75
directive style, 73, 75
omega position, 73
role of, 88
sociodynamic function, 72
Displacement, 42
Dissociating
as perpetrator, 256
defense, 221, 439, 440
definition, 88, 184, 186–188, 198, 210, 224, 231, 250
dissolving, 199, 210, 229
group therapy, 231, 439
neurophysiology, 207
psychodynamic, 187
psychosomatic resonance circuit, 188
treatment, 78, 88, 221, 224, 229, 439
Dissociative disorder, 186, 187, 252
Dizziness, 165
Doll, 133, 155
Doppelganger, 124, 215
addiction, 482, 499
borderline personality disorder, 128, 151
definition, 23, 400, 432
depressive disorder, 315, 323, 324
effect, 330
fictitious, 158, 162, 206, 257, 316
implicit, 2, 18, 39–41, 49, 129, 141, 146, 190, 195, 196, 220, 222, 243, 245, 362, 376, 388, 480
indication, 126, 127, 257, 359
interacting, 39, 197, 206, 432
masochism, 351
metacognitive, 197, 299, 350, 400, 480, 504, 515, 540
obessive-compulsive disorder, 300
personality disorder, 126, 138, 145, 351
practicing, 23, 91, 127, 197, 199, 222, 223, 229, 282, 286, 322, 324, 328, 339, 359, 364, 379, 397, 432, 438, 440, 442, 443
suicide fantasy, 362
surplus reality, 206
theory, 438
trauma disorder, 214, 218, 220, 222, 230, 239, 246, 247, 257
Doppelganger dialogue, 43
Benedetti, 425
definition, 400, 401
delusion of grandeur, 438
effects, 403
indication, 415, 421
Moreno, 399
practicing, 400, 401, 404, 417
steps, 416, 418–420
theory, 403, 423, 424
therapeutic effect, 412, 422
Double bind, 119, 151
definition, 120
Doubling, 313
central psychodrama technique, 16
contraindication, 126
practicing, 23, 79
suggestive, 292, 338
the auxiliary ego, 78
verbal, 23, 79, 315, 361
Dream interpretation, 362, 367
Dream mechanisms
psychodrama techniques, 4
Dream mode
definition, 43
of mentalizing, 42, 43
Dream work, 238, 391
compression, 390
exchanging subject and object, 390
mechanism, 42, 390
mechanisms, 17
psychosis, 390, 405
shifting the focus of attention, 390
Drug addiction, 512
Dysthymia, 226

**E**

Eating disorder, 185

ideal addiction scene, 518
metacognitive doppelganger, 518
metacognitive therapy, 517
psychodynamic, 394
rock bottom, 518
steps of therapy, 518
Ecological, 45
Ego
definition, 50
in the service of, 43
Ego confusion, 267, 278, 279
trauma disorder, 210
Ego control
definition, 46, 47, 152, 424
over a defense, 143
psychosis, 396, 403, 404, 423, 424, 436, 445
Ego split, 198, 236
Ego state
addictive, 474, 504, 523
categories, 161
chair work, 116
definition, 114, 115
different forms, 131
dominant dysfunctional, 154
hand puppet, 145
metacognitive, 114, 116, 124
needy, dependent, 118, 149, 150
of therapist, 161, 166
pseudo-autonomous, authoritarian, 118, 119, 149–151, 153
representing, 106, 115, 131, 136, 142, 144
role change, 169
role reversal, 280
Ego strength
psychosis, 406
Ego-strength, 304, 306, 362
definition, 53
Electroconvulsive therapy, 389
Emancipation, 342
Emergency plan
addiction, 496
psychosis, 428
Empathy, 63, 229, 236, 256, 287, 326
therapist, 245
Encounter, 63
existential, 245, 246, 362, 421, 429, 504
last, 343
on an equal footing, 418
psychotic disorder, 401
therapeutic relationship, 161
with death, 375
Encounter-Focused Therapy, 63, 124, 146, 171, 174, 176, 412
psychosis, 421
psychotic disorder, 401
Enemy image, 27
Energy of conflict, 9, 10, 15, 49, 80
psychosis, 395
Equivalence mode
addiction, 463, 474, 483, 484, 500, 513, 516, 523
borderline personality disorder, 119, 150
definition, 43
flashback, 202
masochism, 352
obsessive-compulsive disorder, 295
of mentalizing, 42–44
pathological deviant behavior, 536, 537
personality disorder, 126, 139, 143, 144, 166, 170
pre-suicidal syndrome, 372, 379
psychosis, 392, 403, 405, 418, 423
structural disorder, 123
trauma disorder, 181, 210
Evolution, 7, 8, 19, 50, 90, 393
Exam nerves, 287, 290
Existential experience, 204
addiction, 487, 489, 490
psychotic disorder, 395
Existential psychotherapy, 375, 380

**F**

Face to face, 199
psychosis, 400
Fairy tale, 274
Fairy tale association, 38, 538
Fairytale drama, 450
Fairy tale play, 35, 75, 392, 450
Family dynamic, 394
Family secret, 234, 342
Family therapy, 53
psychosis, 394
Fantasy space, 216, 361
inner, 362
Fantasy story, 305
Fear
confrontation, 291
exaggerated, 267
human, 245, 422
object related, 268
pathological, 267
real justified, 264–266, 270

Fetishism
behavior addiction, 543
masochism, 542
psychodynamic, 535, 542
treatment, 534
Flashback
consequences, 181, 188, 197, 200, 208
definition, 186, 187, 210, 221, 222, 250
psychodynamic, 187, 351
treatment, 189, 201, 224–226
trigger, 182, 196, 210, 255
Focusing, 363
Focus of therapy, 53, 130, 131, 291
Folie á deux, 420
Free will, 47

G
Gambling addiction, 516
metacognitive confusion, 516
Gamma position, 73
definition, 70
Gestalt closure, 15, 45
God, 493
I-God, 493
You-God, 493
Grief work, 252, 343–345
Group
alpha position, 70, 73, 81
beta position, 70, 81
gamma position, 70, 73
omega position, 70, 73
resistance, 73, 75, 81
role of director, 72
self-help, 460, 488, 504
self-organization, 70, 72, 73, 76, 81, 339
sociodynamic functions, 70, 71
systemic view, 81
Group dynamic, 72, 73, 75, 76, 81, 85
training group, 75
Group therapy
addiction, 501, 508, 509, 511
children, 254
coping fairy tale, 242
definition, 1
directing style, 450
effects, 338
fairytale drama, 450
focus of therapy, 80
group resistance, 74
hospital setting, 55, 77
improv game, 450
personality disorder, 139, 148, 172
psychosis, 439, 448–450
relationship conflict, 67, 70, 72
rules, 81, 117
therapeutic effects, 250
topic-centered, 449
trauma disorder, 199, 231
Guilt justified, 466

H
Hand puppets, 3
anxiety disorder, 279
child therapy, 255
indication, 255
masochism, 351, 352, 354
obsessive-compulsive disorder, 297, 299
personality disorder, 116, 139, 145, 147, 153, 175
psychosis, 442–444
puppetry, 444
trauma disorder, 182, 200
Healing
conditions, 429
Healthy adult thinking, 124
anxiety disorder, 274
borderline personality disorder, 118
compulsive actions, 299
definition, 132, 133, 158
developing, 103, 156, 159
practicing, 146
spontaneous, 132
trauma disorder, 199
Heart phobia, 269, 292
Helper syndrom, 25
Here and now, 82
Heroin addiction
metacognitive therapy, 512
Homelessness, 105, 389
Homosexuality, 341
identity, 341
Human dignitiy, 494
Human dignity, 371, 408, 422, 457, 489
Hyperarousal, 186

I
ICD-10, 101, 106
Ideal addiction scene, 514
Idealization, 20
Identification with the aggressor
definition, 29, 317, 318, 321
masochism, 135
resolving, 30, 321
Identification with the system

defense, 310
definition, 36
resolving, 367
Identity, 37
addicted, 474, 484
change, 490
conflict, 112, 203, 367, 394
confusion, 539
sense of, 112
social, 3
systemic, 3
transpersonal, 3
Illness insight
psychosis, 424, 435
Imagery Rehearsal Therapy, 239, 242
Impromptu theater, 450
Impromptu theatre, 1, 35, 46
Individual therapy, 5, 250, 254
indication, 76, 77, 305
practice, 336
psychodrama, 76, 77
psychosis, 430
trauma, 228
Initiatory therapy, 3
Inner child, 280, 284
Insomnia, 224
Integrate, 163, 257
addiction, 516
definition, 14, 445
memory fragments, 207, 208
personality disorder, 155
practicing, 233
psychosis, 423, 433–435
theory, 49
tool of mentalizing, 14
trauma disorder, 207
with images from childhood, 163
with images of childhood, 290, 332
Interact
definition, 14
tool of mentalizing, 14, 209, 434
Internet gaming disorder, 128, 136
diagnose, 524, 525
Jellinek's questions, 524
metacognitive therapy, 524
Interpretation, 34
confrontational, 136
Interrelationship circuit
psychodramatic play and mentalizing, 18, 77
Interview technique
definition, 24
practicing, 24
psychodrama technique, 325
Introject
pathological, 235, 236
Introjection
defense, 319
definition, 22, 317
resolving, 23, 24, 59, 91, 307, 325
Intrusion, 186
Intuition
definition, 15, 18, 155
holistic process, 13
led psychodrama, 39, 81, 336
of patient, 47
of therapist, 322, 429
secret of, 15
Involuntary admission, 378, 382, 401, 413, 414, 428

J
Jellinek's questions, 168, 463, 465, 466, 468, 472
gambling addiction, 516
pathological deviant behavior, 533
sex addiction, 521, 522
Jesus attitude, 40
Justice
intersubjective, 330
legal, 330

L
Learning disorder, 137
Linguistic concept, 21, 23, 25, 27, 34, 40, 48, 49, 54, 58, 115, 146, 155, 166, 201, 205, 208, 214, 251, 266, 278, 289, 300, 311, 315, 322, 325, 326, 406, 423, 441, 482
Loneliness, 203, 422, 434
Long term therapy
plan, 154
Love madness, 421

M
Mania, 369, 395, 441
Marital seperation, 498
Masochism
behavior addiction, 536
countertransference, 365
defense system, 295
definition, 135, 347
diagnose, 349
ego states, 367

pathological deviant behavior, 537, 542
psychodynamic, 135, 231, 347, 355, 381, 518, 523
psychotic disorder, 432
symptoms, 348, 358
therapeutic relationship, 113, 350
trauma disorder, 189, 222, 231
treatment, 124, 129, 140, 146, 170, 280, 281, 299, 300, 314, 350, 354, 356, 359, 363–366, 377, 523
Medication
addiction, 486, 497
Memory
addiction, 474
autobiographical, 224
false, 222
procedural, 224
Mentalization
definition, 12
oriented psychodrama therapy, 2, 3, 5, 76, 80
Mentalization-based treatment, 13, 83
Mentalizing
ability to play, 51
deficits, 77, 103, 121, 153, 362
definition, 12, 13, 102, 121
development of modes, 42
disintegration, 103, 312
evolution, 8
functions, 17
intuition led, 15
levels of disturbance, 102
modes, 42, 403
on behalf, 103, 126, 145, 230, 322, 360, 416, 419, 432, 442, 499
process, 15, 101
psychotic disorder, 390
represent, 430
tools, 4, 19, 20, 42, 319, 390, 401, 422, 436
Metacognition
definition, 33
Metacognitive confusion, 114
addiction disorder, 463, 474, 476, 480, 520
behavior addiction, 537
eating disorder, 517
gambling disorder, 516
pathological deviant behavior, 535
personality disorder, 147
psychotic disorder, 390, 409, 441
sex addiction, 513, 519
Metacognitive countertransference
addiction, 509
definition, 520
Metacognitive doppelganger
addiction, 481–483, 504, 514
borderline personality disorder, 151
definition, 401, 409, 423
deviant pathological behavior, 540
eating disorder, 518
masochism, 350
psychosis, 400, 401, 405, 409, 413, 418
psychotic disorder, 403
trauma disorder, 246
Metacognitive process, 3, 17, 18, 61, 87
personality disorder, 154
psychodrama techniques, 160
tools of mentalizing, 160
Metacognitive therapy, 4
addiction, 476, 486, 512, 513
anorexia nervosa, 518
anxiety disorder, 273, 276, 279, 287, 289
constellation work, 148
definition, 4, 114, 350, 387
depressive disorder, 313
dissociating, 196
explicit, 4, 103, 114, 124, 148, 272
implicit, 4, 87, 114
masochism, 350, 352
obsessive-compulsive disorder, 296, 298
pathological deviant behavior, 533, 537
personality disorder, 114, 125, 147, 148
practicing, 33, 131, 138
psychodrama techniques, 94
psychotic disorder, 387, 398, 405, 421, 424, 426
splitting, 441
theory, 4
trauma disorder, 190, 192, 210, 212, 365, 367
two chair technique, 539
Metacognitive tools, 13, 18
Metacognitve doppelganger
psychosis, 401
Metaperspective mode, 33, 45
Migraine, 203
Mindfullness
training, 503
Mindfulness, 234
Mirroring
central psychodrama technique, 16, 32, 322
idication, 32
in role reversal, 316, 320

practicing, 32, 71, 327
psychodramatic conversation, 54
self-help group, 489
trauma processing, 250
Monodrama, 1, 76, 77, 123, 139
psychotic disorder, 449
trauma disorder, 228
Mutism, 394

**N**
Narcissism
healthy, 490, 505
pathological, 490
social development, 263
Narcissistic abuse, 47, 195
Narcissistic personality disorder
dominant defense, 156
hidden, dependent grandiosity, 116
open grandiosity, 116
psychodynamic, 116
sex addiction, 520
treatment, 128, 136, 142, 226, 492
Narrative, 238
addiction, 500
develop, 251
psychosis, 444
*see* story, 481
trauma, 187
Narrative mode
of mentalizing, 45
Neurophysiology
psychosis, 395
Neurotic
conflict, 103, 334
definition, 19, 319
New beginning, 365, 377, 378
Nicotin addiction, 486
Nightmare, 186, 222, 224, 242
rewrite, 242

**O**
Obesity, 517
Object representation, 45, 55, 131
definition, 22, 52
development, 59, 122, 136, 325, 330, 342
Obsessive-compulsive disorder, 290
countertransference, 296
definition, 295
hand puppets, 297, 304
metacognitive therapy, 302
psychodynamic, 22, 295, 301
role play, 304
self-injurious thinking, 296
self-protective behaviour, 299
steps of therapy, 298, 302
Obsessive thoughts
steps of therapy, 302
Omega position, 71, 73
definition, 70
fighting alpha position, 71, 72, 75
Online therapy, 61
Operationalized psychodynamic diagnostic, 18, 42, 102
Opiate addiction, 512
Organizational consultation, 1

**P**
Pain syndrome, 63, 314
Panic attack
chair work, 278
definition, 268
psychodynamic, 268, 270–272, 487
secondary fear, 269, 274
therapy, 268, 272, 274, 275, 278, 279, 291, 292, 486
trauma disorder, 216
Parents good, 162, 206, 280, 281, 287, 291
Pathological arson, 536
Pathological deviant behavior
diagnose, 533
emergency plan, 538
equivalence mode, 537
two chair technique, 539
Pathological introject, 30, 119, 136, 183, 354, 365
Pathological regression, 275
Pathological stealing, 533
psychodynamic, 536
Peace work, 60
Perpetrator
conflict processing, 256
Personality disorder
addiction, 460, 501, 503
anxious avoidant, 140
clinical patterns, 111
countertransference, 142
defense mechanisms, 154
definition, 111, 112, 130
dependent, 267, 527
depressive, 349
diagnose, 123, 162
dominant defense pattern, 140
group therapy, 139, 148

hand puppets, 139
metacognitive therapy, 125
psychodynamic, 112, 114, 120, 140, 161
treatment, 113, 114, 123
Pesso therapy, 281
Phobia, 268, 269
treatment, 289, 290
Play
ability, 51, 122, 392
free, 51
mentalizing, 51
symbolic, 28, 51, 301, 406
theory, 17, 18, 44, 46, 50, 51, 57
Playback, 214, 221, 228, 252, 510
Political prisoner, 210
Porn addiction, 47
metacognitive therapy, 519–522
Post-traumatic growth, 203
addiction, 485, 488, 496
definition, 491
Pre-abuse syndrome
addiction, 494
Pre-suicidal syndrome, 360, 379, 381
definition, 372
Problem awareness, 272, 278, 279
Process qualities, 17, 395, 442
Projection
definition, 24, 26, 59, 318
resolving, 27, 29, 59, 91, 164, 304, 307, 325, 326, 328, 331
Projective identification, 365
addiction, 480, 503
countertransference, 66
definition, 35, 38, 166, 245
masochism, 349
psychodynamic, 37
resolving, 37, 38, 246
therapeutic relationship, 141
Projective personalization method, 116, 158
practicing, 302, 303
Prostitution, 519, 520
Protagonist
choosing, 67, 70, 71
indication, 338
sociometric selection, 73
Psychoanalysis, 4, 17, 42, 51, 76, 172, 399, 477
defense mechanisms, 20
intersubjective therapy, 172
psychotic disorder, 425
trauma disorder, 181
Psychodrama
classical, 3
cognitive therapy, 87, 88
definition, 12, 76
format group therapy, 76
holistic systematic theory, 83
metacognitive therapy, 114, 131, 148
role-focused, 86, 87
rules, 79
unique selling point, 4, 18, 86
Psychodrama techniques
dream mechanisms, 4
effects, 64, 82
eight central, 16, 17
indication, 18, 76, 81
metacognitive effect, 4
theory, 4, 16–18
tools of mentalization, 4
Psychodramatic conversation, 52
effects, 32, 53
indications, 55, 272, 311, 315, 327, 479
practicing, 52, 53
Psychodramatic dialogue, 163
addiction, 498, 528
childhood scene, 162
effect, 233, 234, 330
ego states, 201, 280
personality disorder, 35, 124, 125, 164
seven steps, 82, 107, 322
short form, 326
with inner child, 156
with the symptom, 148
Psychodramatic responding, 161, 166, 354, 355, 369
addiction, 494, 505, 507
effect, 174, 508
indication, 166
practicing, 166–169
trauma disorder, 246
Psychodramatic spiral, 34
Psychopathology, 389
Psychosomatic resonance circuit, 9, 23, 49, 57, 146, 149, 166, 266, 273, 311, 315, 327, 337, 362, 435, 482
addiction, 474, 515
borderline personality disorder, 151
definition, 48, 50
dissociating, 184
ego state, 115, 154
pathological deviant behavior, 537
psychosis, 406, 418, 423
role change, 27
soliloquy, 289
trauma disorder, 200, 201

Psychosomatic symptoms, 34, 165, 181, 186, 235, 268, 269, 354, 359, 377
Psychotic disorder
  acute episode, 520
  acute psychosis, 407, 412–414
  affective, 394
  chronic, 407, 410
  cognitive behavioral therapy, 387
  control of ego, 446
  coping story, 433, 446, 447
  costs of treatment, 386
  countertransference, 388, 407, 409, 416, 442
  crisis intervention, 413, 414, 448
  defense through splitting, 396
  definition, 385
  delusional scene, 416
  delusion of grandeur, 438
  delusion of persecution, 430, 431, 437
  depth psychologic treatment, 404
  diagnose, 415
  drug abuse, 394, 427, 437
  ego strength, 435
  emergency plan, 449
  everyday ego, 409
  fairytale drama, 450
  family dynamic, 394
  follow-up study, 386
  group therapy, 439, 449
  hand puppets, 442–444
  hear voices, 436, 447, 448
  history of treatment, 386
  hospital admission, 414
  illness insight, 387, 398, 402, 404, 418, 420, 423–426, 431, 435, 439
  integrate, 434, 435
  medication, 388, 399, 426, 427
  mentalizing, 390
  metacognitive confusion, 390, 409
  metacognitive therapy, 21, 398, 405, 410, 426
  neurophysiology, 395
  prognosis, 386
  psychodynamic, 185, 390, 393–395, 422, 425, 438, 439
  psychodynamic therapy, 405
  psychotic episode, 177
  role reversal, 397, 450
  schizophrenia, 396
  social development, 386
  steps of therapy, 410
  symptoms, 388
  therapeutic relationship, 409, 412
  therapy plan, 424, 427, 429, 446
  transmodal relationship, 401, 403, 404, 413, 423, 444, 447
  traumatizing experience, 185, 393, 395, 422
  vulnerability, 393
Psychotropic drugs, 123, 252
PTSD
  causes, 185
  definition, 183
  psychodynamic, 183
  refugee, 246
  symptoms, 185
  traffic accident, 257
  trauma processing, 216
  war, 188


**R**


Rampage, 252
Rape, 184, 216, 222, 224, 238, 247, 252, 253, 306
  psychodynamic, 253
Rationalization
  definition, 31, 32
  ideological, 36
  resolving, 32, 54
Reality construction, 43, 44
Reflective mode
  of mentalizing, 44, 45
Refugee
  trauma processing, 246
Regression, 20, 509
  addiction, 509
  pathological, 175, 218, 228, 232, 240, 502, 509, 512, 516
Rehearse
  definition, 14
  psychosis, 436
  tool of mentalizing, 14, 29, 436
Relapse
  addiction, 496
  definition, 493
Relationship
  mutual neurotic allergy, 334
  systemically fair, 323, 330
Relationship trauma, 111, 196, 234
  definition, 183
  psychodynamic, 192
  symptoms, 192, 202
Religion, 490
Represent
  an ego state, 278

definition, 14
delusional scene, 405
externally, 124, 272, 278, 279
internally, 278
psychotic disorder, 430
tool of mentalizing, 14
Repression
definition, 33
resolving, 34, 35
Resilience, 185
Resistance, 69, 429
definition, 65
group therapy, 65
resolving, 66
Resources, 81, 204, 219, 247, 291, 315, 330, 362
activation, 82
Retraumatization, 134, 182, 187, 203, 250
Reversal into the opposite
dream work, 391
Ritual, 238
therapeutic, 252
Rock bottom, 492
addiction, 490, 496
Role
definition, 86
focused therapy, 87
psychosomatic, 45
result of mentalizing, 86
systemic, 356, 357
training, 88
Role change, 291
between ego states, 22
central psychodrama technique, 27, 29
definition, 27
practicing, 22, 290
Role cluster, 89
Role confusion, 86
Role deficit, 86
Role development, 42, 44
Role feedback
central psychodrama technique, 23
definition, 23
focal, 322, 326
practicing, 23, 79, 81, 326
Role flexibility, 86
Role level
according to Schacht, 42
psychodramatic, 43
psychosomatic, 43
sociodramatic, 44, 45
Role pathology, 87
Role play, 1
behavioral therapy, 290, 304
central psychodrama technique, 16, 25–27, 29, 44, 51
child therapy, 254
definition, 27
practicing, 1, 290
psychosis, 397, 399, 449
training, 16
Role repertoire, 86
Role reversal, 103
ability, 122, 123
central psychodrama technique, 1, 16, 45
contraindication, 226, 227, 450
cooperation, 9
definition, 45
effects, 30, 59, 62, 92, 233, 326, 330, 339
ego states, 280
history, 288, 289, 320
internal, 31, 45, 48, 58
practicing, 126
psychodramatic self-supervision, 56
psychosis, 397, 449
puppetry, 444
systemic view, 2
theory of development, 59
with the fear, 291
with the perpetrator, 339
with the symptom, 148
Role theory, 86, 87, 92
problems, 86, 325

S
Sadomasochism, 537
Safe place, 224, 228, 230, 231
definition, 202, 206, 216
effects, 247
indication, 125
practicing, 214, 216, 217, 219, 220, 244, 258
Safe vault technique, 198, 201
Scene
childhood, 226, 228, 333
Scene change, 16
central psychodrama technique, 34, 35
definition, 34
practicing, 34, 35
Scene construction, 16, 43
central psychodrama technique, 20
indication, 18
practicing, 78, 79, 335

psychotic disorder, 405, 434
Schema therapy, 3, 4, 132–135
addiction, 476, 513
definition, 160
Schizophrenia, 396
Secondary traumatization, 234, 236, 247, 249
addiction, 528
psychodynamic, 236
therapy, 236
Self
definition, 134, 280, 310, 330, 390
development, 390
parts, 90
sense of, 359, 365, 381
Self-actualization
definition, 310
improve, 328, 330, 331
masochism, 349, 355
Self-authorship, 363
Self-development, 90
addiction, 493
addiction disorder, 476
definition, 2
depressive disorder, 310
masochism, 347
process, 102, 103
psychodramatic self-supervision, 59
psychosis, 434
represent with chairs, 52
structural disorder, 121
theory, 2
trauma disorder, 190, 232, 233
Self-effective, 18, 310, 434
Self-empathy, 221, 241, 256, 280, 287, 291, 324, 365
Self-empowerment, 434
Self-harming behaviour, 135
Self-healing system, 238, 305, 434
activate, 238, 242
addiction, 489, 490, 493
development, 239
Self-injurious thinking, 61, 62
definition, 135, 161
ego state, 124, 135, 161, 296, 299, 301, 350
*see* masochism, 349
treatment, 141, 159, 283, 352, 518
Self-organization, 7, 121
definition, 59
group, 70, 80, 81
of group, 85
Self-protective behavior
anxiety disorder, 272–274, 276, 278, 279
borderline personality disorder, 114, 119
definition, 131, 132
ego states, 278
ego states of, 131
therapy, 278
through adaptation, 131, 296, 519
through grandiosity, 131
through self-stabilization, 131
Self-reflection, 64
Self-regulating circle
addiction, 499
perpetrator, 256
practicing, 193, 195
Self-regulation
addiction disorder, 481
sense of, 360, 362
Self-representation, 55
definition, 22, 52
development, 59, 136, 325, 330
splitting, 236
Self-stabilization
definition, 181, 202
distancing technique, 201
positive counter-image, 243
techniques, 132, 202, 205, 207, 219, 239, 258, 346
transpersonal, 203
Self-supervision, psychodramatic, 60–62, 64, 107, 149, 350, 355
addiction, 462
effects, 58, 60, 63, 233
group resistance, 74
indication, 60, 66, 175, 193
personality disorder, 124, 162, 165
resistance, 60
steps 1-12, 56, 326
steps 13-17, 61, 150
Sensorimotor interaction pattern, 21, 23, 25, 34, 40, 48, 49, 54, 58, 115, 146, 155, 166, 184, 190, 201, 205, 207, 208, 210, 214, 227, 253, 266, 278, 289, 315, 322, 325, 326, 406, 423, 441, 482
Separation conflict, 286, 340, 342
Sex addiction
equivalence mode, 513
metacognitive therapy, 519–521
Sex offender
psychodynamic, 255
Sexual abuse, 208

Sharing, 16, 214, 250, 449
 central psychodramatic technique, 38
 definition, 38
 practicing, 38, 79, 81, 248, 316, 327
 self-help group, 489
Shifting
 dream work, 391
Shoulder to shoulder, 88, 195, 220, 222, 223, 228, 379
 definition, 55
 psychosis, 400, 418, 421
 trauma disorder, 199
Sleep disorder, 216
Social atom, 160
Social phobia, 140, 269, 281, 283, 288
Social psychiatry, 420, 422
 addiction, 485, 504
 psychosis, 386, 388, 389, 399, 448, 449
Sociodrama, 252
Sociodramatic role level, 42, 45
Sociometric method, 1, 67, 75, 85
Socrates attitude, 39, 40, 78
Soliloquy, 23
 practicing, 228, 229, 289
 psychosomatic resonance pattern, 289
Solution-oriented, 82, 195, 335, 339, 361, 362, 365, 379, 391, 440, 450, 496, 510
Somatization, 20
Soul landscape, 199, 313
Space interpretation, 363
Spiritual experience, 45, 204
Splitting
 defense, 118, 177
 definition, 21, 119, 149, 152
 metacognitive therapy, 441
 of society, 27
 psychosis, 408
 resolving, 21, 88, 152, 200, 441
Spontaneity
 control of ego, 445
 definition, 424
 state of, 7, 396
 theory, 19, 399
 therapist, 437
 training, 51
Spontaneous, 3, 51, 60, 62, 63, 82, 321, 483
 definition, 7, 19, 50, 132
 healthy adult thinking, 132
 therapist, 65
Spontaneous man, 102, 309
Stage
 of ego states, 131
 of symptom scene, 131
 of therapeutic relationship, 131
 three stage model, 82
Status nascendi, 7
Stegreiftheater, 47
Stomach pain, 126, 127, 534
Story
 addiction, 481, 500
 coherent, 222
 coping, 399, 402, 410, 433, 434, 444, 446, 447
 holistic, 442, 540
Stress
 acute reaction, 265
 psychosocial, 263
Structural disorder, 128, 131
 addiction, 512, 517, 522
 definition, 121
 development, 121
 diagnose, 53, 103, 122, 123, 126, 312
 treatment, 125, 136, 164, 167, 171, 175
Suicide fantasy
 addiction, 494
 diagnose, 360, 371, 381
 psychodynamic, 186, 377
 therapy, 382
 treatment, 128, 374
Suicide risk
 addiction, 460
 diagnose, 361, 372–374, 381, 415
 psychosis, 415
 therapy, 137, 167, 360, 372, 375, 376, 378–382, 404
 therapy contract, 382
Superego
 externalization, 36
 pathological, 183, 348–350
 sadistic, 22, 146, 295, 323, 365–367, 369, 395
 strict, 289, 303
 treatment, 299, 300, 348
Supervision psychodramatic, 64
Surplus reality, 44, 82, 206, 251, 280, 291, 332, 400
Surrender
 addiction, 476, 488, 489, 494
Symptoms
 definition, 101
 development, 7
Symptom scene, 52, 54
 stage of, 131
Systemic justice, 330
Systemic mode

of mentalizing, 42, 45
Systemic psychodrama, 90, 92
Systemic role, 166, 169, 393
defense, 132
definition, 36, 357
Systemic therapy, 2, 53, 55, 104, 330, 333
of metacognition, 154
Systemic thinking, 32, 60, 80, 327

**T**
Table stage
addiction, 480
coping fairy tale, 240
indication, 362
landscape of soul, 128, 199
personality disorder, 128, 139
practicing, 123, 128, 139, 313, 362, 366
psychosis, 443
suicidal crisis, 361, 376, 380
theory, 33
trauma disorder, 193, 199, 365
trauma processing, 199, 228, 229
Team
counseling, 53
Teleological mode, 42, 43
Tele relation, 69, 395, 396, 446
Terrorist attack, 221
Theater, 46
Theory of mind, 122
Therapeutic community, 1, 386, 396
Therapeutic relationship
abstinence, 424
addiction, 462, 476, 482, 485, 489, 504, 505, 516
borderline personality disorder, 117, 120, 151
child therapy, 254
disturbances, 61, 65
encountering human being, 246
helper attitude, 142
just, 80
masochism, 113, 349, 350
negative therapeutic reaction, 177
obsessive-compulsive disorder, 296
paradigma shift, 142
personality disorder, 112, 113, 131, 141, 145, 148, 166, 174
present moment, 401
psychodramatic responding, 166, 508
psychosis, 388
*shoulder to shoulder*, 222
stage of, 131
suicide fantasy, 378
systemic view, 55
transmodal, 400, 401, 403, 423, 425, 433
trauma disorder, 199, 245, 368
treatment, 69
Therapist
abstinence, 331
auxiliary ego, 137, 280, 335, 431
burnout, 249
character trait, 139
competent expert, 505
directive behavior, 331
encountering as human being, 506
grandiose, 167–170, 172, 505
healer, 169
helper attitude, 142
human being, 166, 168, 169
intuition, 322, 429
mental hygiene, 62, 248, 249
metacognitive confusion, 508
metacognitive ego states, 166
professional competent, 166, 168, 169
secondary traumatization, 234, 248
self-experience, 41, 42, 123, 159
skills, 399, 424, 425, 429
Therapy ending, 177, 335, 368
Therapy plan, 106, 335, 368, 429
Timeline technique, 199, 313, 376, 379
addiction, 499
Tools of mentalizing, 15, 64
Torture victim, 253
Traffic accident, 185, 257
Transference
group therapy, 68
masochism, 354
negative, 66–68, 117, 146, 167, 168, 170, 175–177, 234, 272, 328, 354
of therapist, 63
personality disorder, 175
personality disorders, 113
positive, 65
question, 71
resolving, 67–69, 79, 176
Transmodal, 424
definition, 403
Transpersonal experience, 203, 220
Transpersonal identity, 158, 225, 490
Transpersonal therapy, 2, 3, 158, 203, 204, 217, 220, 225, 235, 248, 256, 257, 490, 494
addiction, 494, 505
Trauma disorder

addiction, 459, 460, 466, 471
countertransference, 181, 224, 243, 248
crisis intervention, 172, 196
defense, 345, 353
diagnose, 181, 193, 196, 201, 244
doppelganger, 222, 246
group therapy, 77
hand puppet, 182, 200
initial consultation, 196, 199
masochism, 222, 225, 347, 353
memory, 187, 207
metacognitive therapy, 190, 192
neurophysiology, 186, 187, 207, 215, 224
obsessive-compulsive disorder, 301
phases of therapy, 191, 250
post-traumatic growth, 225
psychodynamic, 184–188, 192, 208, 231
psychosis, 395, 442
refugee, 246
relationship trauma, 36, 196, 358
secondary traumatization, 234, 236, 247, 358
self-empathy, 201
structural disturbance, 197
symptoms, 185, 186, 192, 345
therapeutic relationship, 181, 196, 220, 243, 245, 369
traumatized child, 156, 196
treatment, 87
two chair technique, 190, 196, 199–201
video technique, 208
war, 203
witness to truth, 188, 190
Trauma memory, 240
Trauma processing
as-if mode of thinking, 205
auxiliary therapists, 213, 214, 221, 222
child therapy, 254
coping fairy tale, 240
distancing technique, 201
doppelganger, 197, 206, 220
four work spaces, 210, 212, 213, 226
group therapy, 77, 199, 206, 215, 231, 249–251, 253
holistic story, 207, 211
interaction room, 223
metacognitive therapy, 210
observation room, 221
rape, 253
retraumatization, 250
role reversal with perpetrator, 227
table stage, 129, 199, 228, 230, 247
Trauma story, 207, 208, 221, 222, 226, 228, 230
Traumatized child, 61
Traumatizing situation, 186, 265
definition, 11, 184
Truth
addiction, 492
complementary, 73, 75, 249, 394
intersubjective, 325
subjective, 234
transpersonal, 60, 225, 376
true second time, 47, 128, 396, 515, 517
witness, 190, 246, 307, 484
Two chair technique, 62, 105, 266
addiction, 462, 468, 482, 483, 498, 504
anxiety disorder, 272
co-dependence, 528
effect, 267
grief reaction, 346
pathological deviant behavior, 537, 539
personality disorder, 145, 147
psychosis, 408, 409
secondary traumatization, 528
theory, 408, 409, 539
trauma disorder, 190, 196, 199

**U**
Universe second, 45

**V**
Video therapy, 41

**W**
Warming up, 11, 45, 78
exercise, 48
rule, 11
War traumatized, 184, 188, 203, 232, 236, 370
Wise woman, 218, 220, 235
Wish fulfillment, 241
Work addiction, 517
Workaholic, 440
World Health Organization, 455, 457, 463
Write down, 34, 57, 116, 163, 238, 240, 281, 283, 302, 327, 500
Writer's cramp, 320

# GPSR Compliance

*The European Union's (EU) General Product Safety Regulation (GPSR) is a set of rules that requires consumer products to be safe and our obligations to ensure this.*

*If you have any concerns about our products, you can contact us on ProductSafety@springernature.com*

In case Publisher is established outside the EU, the EU authorized representative is:

Springer Nature Customer Service Center GmbH
Europaplatz 3
69115 Heidelberg, Germany

The manufacturer's authorised representative in the EU is Springer Nature Customer Service Centre GmbH, Europaplatz 3, 69115 Heidelberg, Germany. If you have any concerns regarding our products, please contact ProductSafety@springernature.com

Printed and bound by CPI Group (UK) Ltd, Croydon, CR0 4YY

30/09/2026

02225296-0019